STUDIES IN THE VARIETY
OF RABBINIC CULTURES

Photograph by Alan S. Orling

JPS דור דור
SCHOLAR ודורשיו
OF DISTINCTION
SERIES

GERSON D. COHEN

STUDIES IN THE VARIETY OF RABBINIC CULTURES

The Jewish Publication Society
Philadelphia • New York 5751—1991

Library of Congress Cataloging-in-Publication Data
Cohen, Gerson D. (Gerson David), 1924–
    Studies in the variety of rabbinic cultures/Gerson D. Cohen. — 1st ed.
        p. cm. — (JPS scholar of distinction series)
    Includes bibliographical references and index.
    ISBN 0-8276-0383-5
    1. Judaism—History. 2. Jews—Historiography. 3. Bible. O.T.—
Criticism, interpretation, etc., Jewish. 4. Rabbinical literature—
History and criticism. I. Title. II. Series.
BM45.C59   1991
296'.9—dc20   *90—20704*
                                                            CIP

Designed by Adrianne Onderdonk Dudden

עֲשֵׂה לְךָ רַב וּקְנֵה לְךָ חָבֵר וֶהֱוֵי דָן אֶת־כָּל־הָאָדָם לְכַף זְכוּת

Pirke Aboth 1.6

For some ten years now, a small but devoted band of men and women has gathered once a month, at eight in the evening, to study with Gerson Cohen. For each of the ten regular participants, those gatherings have been a great adventure and a source of strength and delight. The publication of this volume of Dr. Cohen's essays is funded by them as a token of their gratitude, respect, and affection for their teacher.

Ḥanukkah 5751

Contents

Foreword

Sixty years ago, during the week of October 19 to 26, 1930 and in the midst of the great depression, The Jewish Theological Seminary of America dedicated its new campus of three buildings at the corner of 122nd Street and Broadway in a panoply of ceremony. One of those buildings was the Jacob H. Schiff Memorial Library, with its majestic, two-story reading room. Two generations of Seminary-trained rabbis and scholars were to imbibe their knowledge of Judaism in that room, to the recurring rumble of the Broadway subway. As one entered that sanctum, one's eye immediately fell upon an imposing marble relief at the other end, hiding two opposing stairways leading to the door of the rare book and manuscript room at the top—a *bimah*-like structure with a recessed holy ark at the center. Two large, seven-branched candelabrums on either side of the center added to the overall synagogue effect of the design.

At the top, where the stairways met, the solid marble banister was designed with eight low-relief columns that bore an inscription—like many a synagogue *bimah*—that alluded to the spirit of the space. Probably designed by Alexander Marx, the Seminary's renowned librarian and Professor of Jewish history, and surely approved by the faculty, the inscription unfurled for all to see the institution's collection, its concept of Judaism, and its academic ethos. In a profound way, the rare book and manuscript room was truly the Seminary's Holy of Holies.

On those eight columns was depicted in Hebrew the literary landscape of Jewish cultural expression, the remains of which had been reassembled by the Seminary's great research library. Running from right to left with one genre per column, the inscription reads: Bible, Mishna and

Talmud, law and judgment (*din u-fesak*), aggada and midrash, philosophy and religion (*meḥkar ve-dat*), history, religious and secular poetry,
language (i.e., Hebrew), and literature.

On one level, of course, the text is no more than a catalogue of the
rich collection preserved by the Seminary. But the striking omission of
any reference to Kabbalah, at a time when the Seminary was also compil-
ing the literary vestiges of Jewish mysticism, suggests that we are dealing
with a statement of values and not just contents. Even as the inscription
gloriously froze the anti-mystical bias of the age, it also set forth unequivocally a reconceptualization of Judaism. A century of undogmatic
scholarship had begun to convey the heretofore unimagined dynamism
and creativity of Judaism as a religious civilization. The constricted curriculum of the traditional yeshiva perpetuated a truncated view of
Israel's inner life. To confront the challenge of Jewish life after emancipation called for a fuller and fairer understanding of Jewishness in other
ages. The religious posture of Conservative Judaism, its quest for a truth-
ful piety, rested squarely on the diverse record housed in that rare book
room.

But beyond the conception, there was also an ethos. A new brand of
scholarship was needed to unearth, fathom, and synthesize the fragments of the Jewish experience, a learning as broad as it was deep. Nothing could be properly explained outside its historical context or
disconnected from the vertical and dialectical flow of Jewish creativity.
The sacred texts and religious works of Judaism did not require special
pleading or an exercise of willful ignorance, but only the integrity and
empathy of a competent expositor. The inscription bespoke a commitment to master all the branches of Jewish literature, while respecting the
centrality of its biblical and rabbinic trunk (columns 1 to 4). It reaffirmed the validity of an integrated mode of critical study—the
Seminary's trademark since the days of Solomon Schechter and the intellectual basis of its religious vision.

In the decades that followed, no one came to personify this long-
forgotten inscription more than Gerson D. Cohen, the Seminary's fifth
chancellor and its Jacob H. Schiff Distinguished Service Professor of
Jewish History. His scholarly achievement, a part of which has now been
collected in this precious book, symbolized the maturation of the Seminary. Through him the institution evinced its capacity to transplant the
wissenschaft-ethos to these shores and to train American scholars worthy of the mantle of their European mentors. That spirit would not
wither in a climate slightly too comfortable for its self-denying rigors.

At the same time, the linkage of the inscription to Dr. Cohen is also
quite concrete. His chair bears the name of the incomparable benefactor
after whom the old library building was named, and his brilliant critical
edition of Abraham ibn Daud's *Sefer Ha-Qabbalah* in 1967 owes its

inception to the sage counsel of Professor Marx, who was both his teacher and friend. No less poignant is the fact that Dr. Cohen succeeded him after his death in the important post of Seminary Librarian.

The essays of this collection glisten with the traits of Seminary scholarship as indeed, I believe, does much of the work of that small but gifted cohort of Seminary students to which Dr. Cohen belongs. There is the never-ending quest to be conversant with the totality of the Jewish experience. These essays run the gamut from the Bible to Buber, from the literature of ancient Israel to the legacy of German Jewry in the modern era. They are informed by the conviction that to be a good specialist you have to be a well-read generalist, for Jewish creativity bristles with intertextuality. The individual specimens were rarely hermetically sealed off from one another for long, and the process of interpenetration never ceased.

The same fluid versatility is evident within the individual essays. Indeed, their kinetic energy is enormous, as Dr. Cohen roams backward and forward in time to extract the full historical meaning of his text. His essays are often structured in concentric circles, reaching out to ever larger and more remote bodies of material to effect a bracing new synthesis. In consequence, it is not easy to pinpoint his special field of study. With his extraordinary linguistic skills, he can as readily revert from a medieval text to the corpus of rabbinic literature as from a rabbinic text back to the biblical canon or forward into the expanse of medieval Jewish literature.

Let it be said then that Dr. Cohen is a student of rabbinic culture in all its permutations. The seamless web of his research is testimony to the underlying unity of a culture with a deeply exegetical manner of thinking that is constantly reworking the same vast sacred canon of biblical and rabbinic literature. Whatever the outside influences, and no one is more attentive to their manifold presence than Dr. Cohen, they were gradually assimilated and recast in terms of the language, values, and praxis of rabbinic culture. That culture is the pivot on which so much of Jewish history turns, both before and after the emancipation, and Jewish scholarship must be anchored in its mastery. Therefore, among the subjects taught by Dr. Cohen in his early years on the Seminary faculty, in addition to Jewish history, was Talmud. And what did he not teach during his many summers as a professor-in-residence at one of the Seminary's Ramah camps!

Yet, undeniably, the permutation of rabbinic culture for which Dr. Cohen's oeuvre displays a special affinity is that which had been wrought on the Iberian peninsula, and his command of Arabic gave him the tool to cultivate his preference. The cultural symbiosis effected by the Jewish courtier class of Andalus was not to be censored in terms of "the standards of Troyes, Mainz, and Cracow."

Rather, we submit, they lived in a unified milieu which, however unique and out of tune with the major themes known to us from other communities and periods of Jewish history, was integrated and endowed with an inner harmony. The hymns and the prayers, the *geulahs* and the *ahabahs*, were composed in the same idiom and the same style as the idyls and the paeans, the eulogies and the barbs. . . . Why assume that, in enjoying this world, a religious man had to forget the source of his pleasures and his pains, of his conquests and his defeats? Who is to decide that love of wine and song, or even of women and young boys, is secular by nature and alien to the spirit of religion?" (*Sefer ha-Qabbalah*, p. 286)

Methodologically, this was a plea for appreciating the individuality of every age; religiously, it countenanced the validity of pluralism. Still more to the point, Spain offered American Jewry an alternative to eastern Europe, a religious paradigm nourished by cultural openness, intellectual breadth, and religious innovation. Insularity, onesidedness, and compartmentalization were not the only wellsprings for nourishing self-confidence and the will to live.

The rediscovery of the cultural legacy of a Judaism once fertilized by Islam had been one of the great achievements of nineteenth-century wissenschaft. The opening of the Cairo Geniza by Solomon Schechter at the end of the century only served to intensify the interest, and his coming to the Seminary a few years later was to make of the institution one of the world centers for the study of that legacy. From Schechter himself down to Professor Raymond Scheindlin in our own day, the Seminary has been home to an unbroken chain of distinguished scholars who have worked in the Islamic orbit of the Jewish odyssey, though not all have been quite as unabashed about their ideological motivation as Israel Friedlaender in his public addresses prior to the First World War.

What is true of the Spanish Jews of a thousand years ago, is equally true of the American Jews of today (i.e., March 1914). We, too, live in a powerful environment which we cannot, and indeed, dare not disregard. . . . The only solution left to us is that of adaptation, but an adaptation which shall sacrifice nothing that is essential to Judaism, which shall not impoverish Judaism but enrich it, which, as was the case with Jewish culture in Spain, shall take fully into account what the environment demands of us, and shall yet preserve and foster our Jewish distinctiveness and originality. (*Past and Present*, N.Y., 1961, p. 193.)

By the same token, the inscription in the reading room of the old library breathed the spirit of Lucena and Cordova rather than of Volozhin and Slobodka, a world for which the study of rabbinics was central but not exclusive.

The Seminary's kinship with Spain is evident in the attention to language. The literary quality of Schechter's own fluid and lilting English prose set the standard. As once in Andalus, perfection of form was to enhance the power of ideas. Thus, for Dr. Cohen, writing is never a matter of indifference. His style sparkles with a language both lucid and trenchant, rich and vigorous, elegant and graceful. Whatever the complexity of the subject, he never abandons his sense for structure, his aristocratic cadences, his quest for the right word. A dense and exotic culture is to be mediated without jarring neologisms or untranslated Hebrew terms. The search for suitable English equivalents is the burden of the author and not the reader. Forged in an age of transition, the splendor of his scholarly idiom takes aim at the guardians of the academic citadel still dubious about the admission of Jewish studies into the curriculum.

Above all, these essays in the aggregate are a tribute to the power of engaged and empathetic scholarship. Ultimately, the difference between great and pedestrian scholarship is a matter of passion and not technical expertise or analytical acumen. While the latter are surely indispensable, they are still quite insufficient without a touch of wonder and reverence. An adversarial relationship or even one of utter objectivity rarely gets at the truth. No teacher and scholar of Judaica ever espoused the ideal of dispassionate research with greater eloquence than Gerson Cohen, and none ever practiced it with more palpable empathy and love for his subject matter. May his work be an inspiration for generations to come.

Ismar Schorsch
September 1990

Acknowledgments

The essays included in this volume are slightly altered from their originally published form. I am grateful to the following organizations that permitted the republication of these papers that first appeared under their auspices:

The Jewish Theological Seminary of America, for "The Song of Songs and the Jewish Religious Mentality," which was delivered as a Samuel Friedland lecture at a Seminary convocation in Miami Beach, 1962, and "Hannah and Her Seven Sons in Hebrew Literature," from the Seminary's Mordecai M. Kaplan Jubilee volume, pp. 109–122, 1953.

Herzl Press and University Press of America for "Zion in Rabbinic Literature," from *Zion in Jewish Literature*, under the editorship of Abraham S. Halkin, by Herzl Press in 1961, pp. 38–64, and republished by University Press of America in 1988, pp. 38–64.

Random House, for "The Rabbinic Heritage," from *Great Ages and Ideas of the Jewish People*, pp. 173–212, under the editorship of Leo W. Schwarz, 1956.

KTAV Publishing House, for "The Reconstruction of Gaonic History," from Jacob Mann's *Texts and Studies in Jewish History and Literature*, vol. 1, pp. XIII–LXXXVI, 1972.

The American Academy for Jewish Research, for "The Story of the Four Captives," from *Proceedings of the American Academy for Jewish*

Research (*PAAJR*), vol. XXIX, pp. 55–131, 1960/61, and "The Soteriology of R. Abraham Maimuni," from *PAAJR*, vol. XXXV, pp. 75–98, 1967, vol. XXXVI, pp. 33–56, 1968.

Harvard University Press, for "Esau as Symbol in Early Medieval Thought," reprinted by permission of the publishers from *Jewish Medieval and Renaissance Studies*, Alexander Altmann, editor (Philip W. Lown Institute Studies and Texts, IV), Cambridge, Mass.: Harvard University Press, Copyright © 1967 by the President and Fellows of Harvard College.

The Leo Baeck Institute, for "Messianic Postures of Ashkenazim and Sephardim," from *LBI Memorial Lecture No. 9*, pp. 3–42, 1967, and "German Jewry as Mirror of Modernity," from *LBI Year Book*, vol. XX, pp. IX–XXXI, 1975.

This volume would never have been assembled but for Mrs. Shari Friedman, who first collected a number of essays that I had written and suggested where and how they should be republished. Her editorial supervision and advice on a number of subjects helped me considerably, and I am grateful to her. To Mrs. Deborah Shichtman, my secretary, who has struggled with my handwriting and rescued much of what would have otherwise been condemned to oblivion, I give my thanks.

Introduction

The essays included in this volume appeared in various publications in the 1960s and 1970s, that is, before I became chancellor of the Jewish Theological Seminary of America in 1972. Although they do not relate to any one theme or period in Jewish history, they all deal with moments in Jewish history that had an enduring impact on subsequent generations and ages. Since these papers are largely inaccessible because of the wide variety of publications in which they appeared and because of the difficulty in mobilizing them, I believed it would be of service to collect these essays and disseminate them in this form.

The essays included here, though externally unrelated to each other, are united by the overriding subject of the history of ideas. I have long believed that this area has suffered undeserved neglect; I hope that these essays will stimulate other scholars to offer studies in this broad general area.

The Song of Songs has suffered basic neglect in modern scholarship. I include the essay "The Song of Songs and the Modern Jewish Religious Mentality" out of a firm belief that the Song of Songs has had an enormous influence on the Jewish religious perspective. That is all the more true of the second essay, "Zion in Rabbinic Literature." No subject is dearer and more central to the Jewish yearning for the Zion restored that we enjoy today. If there is any implicit point to this second essay, it is that the Zion reborn came into being in consequence of the age-old yearning of Jews for the restoration of a national home.

The story of "Hannah and Her Seven Sons in Hebrew Literature" aims to show the development of a great legend in Jewish literature and how it came to be.

While each of the ages of Jewish history mentioned here had a permanent impact on the Jews and their culture, the Rabbinic or Talmudic age discussed in "The Rabbinic Heritage" made an imprint that was deeper than most others.

Among the themes dominant in the mind of Sephardic Jewry was the marvelous phenomenon of the dissemination of Hebrew culture. This phenomenon is reviewed intensively and analytically in the fifth chapter, "The Reconstruction of Gaonic History."

For centuries, Jewish religious cultural life grew and developed in the areas of Arabic influence in which the Jews were within the orbit of the aggressive and conquering armies of Islam. The Gaonate was the supreme office presiding over Jewish religious life in North Africa and the Near East. Indeed, as far away as Germany—thanks to the development of Jewish settlements such as Andalusian Spain, Provence, and northern Italy—Jewish culture began to flourish. "The Story of the Four Captives" is a study of a legend that has held its grip on the Jews until modern times.

Among the works of culture produced in the Arabic Jewish world, those of Abraham Maimuni stand next to those of his father Moses Maimonides. It is to be hoped that with the study of the religious thought of Abraham Maimuni, as put forth in the seventh chapter, "The Soteriology of R. Abraham Maimuni," further work will be stimulated and extended to the works of the great luminaries and other great teachers.

In Hebrew vocabulary, Rome was referred to as Edom. (In all likelihood, the Hebrew orthography of Edom and Aram was easily confused.) In any event, Edom became the embodiment of Rome and Christendom in the Hebrew vocabulary. Why Esau, whom the Bible identifies as the ancestral father of the Edomites, of all the ancients, should have been accorded so lofty a position in Jewish vocabulary and thought I tried to explain in the chapter "Esau as Symbol in Early Medieval Thought." What I hope emerges from this study is not merely the elucidation of one ancient motif but my conviction that Jewish legends and folklore have been continuously vital components of Jewish tradition and need to be explicated if we are to understand the various strands of that Jewish tradition.

What held Jews together in every age and over the long distances that divided them was the hope for messianic redemption. Despite considerable difference in the messianic speculation and dreams of different Jewish communities, the chapter offered here, "Messianic Postures of Ashkenazim and Sephardim," should show that the messianic dream and occasional activity were not mere formulas repeated by rote.

Of all the Jewish communities that generated Jewish scholarship and thought, none was more productive and challenging than German Jewry. It not only continued the Jewish tradition of scholarship and philosophy but also contributed new realms of original thinking. The tenth chapter of this book, "German Jewry as Mirror of Modernity," seeks to show the importance of the history of Jewish ideas.

STUDIES IN THE VARIETY
OF RABBINIC CULTURES

The Song of Songs and
the Jewish Religious Mentality

I

Sometime around the year 100, the supreme council of rabbis in Jamnia took up the question of the canonicity of certain books of the Bible. Among the legacies of earlier generations was the sanctity of such books as the Song of Songs and Ecclesiastes. According to the reports of one of the earliest of the Tannaim: "Originally, Proverbs, Song of Songs, and Ecclesiastes were suppressed; since they were held to be mere parables and not part of the Holy Writings, [the religious authorities] arose and suppressed them; [and so they remained] until the men of Hezekiah came and interpreted them."[1]

Indeed, some of these verses must have required a good deal of interpretation, for their plain sense did not exactly commend them as Holy Writ. How could the same category of sanctity be applied to the Psalms, Job, Lamentations, and Chronicles—let alone the Pentateuch and the Prophets—as to verses such as these:

> Come, my beloved, let us go forth into the field
> Let us sit among the henna flowers
> Let us get up early to the vineyards
> Let us see whether the vine hath budded
> Whether the vine blossom be opened
> And the pomegranates be in flower;
> There will I give thee my love [Song of Songs 7:2–13].

Need we wonder that despite the belief that these verses were the products of Solomon's pen, some were skeptical of their sanctity? This uneasiness about the book must have continued down to the end of the first century, for even as late as the convocation at Jamnia some still expressed doubts about the true nature of the book. Against these doubts, Rabbi Akiba protested vehemently and cried: "Heaven forbid! No Jew ever questioned the sanctity of the Song of Songs; for all of creation does not compare in worth to the day on which the Song of Songs was given to Israel. Indeed, all Scripture is holy, but the Song of Songs is the holiest of the holy."[2]

Ironically, modern students of Scripture have vindicated the misgivings of Rabbi Akiba's opponents, for they have unanimously dismissed the theory that the Song of Songs was originally a religious work. However, even this "modern" view had adherents in the days of Rabbi Akiba. Indeed, he himself pronounced an anathema against those who crooned the verses of the Song of Songs as erotic jingles.[3] To be sure, modern critics are well aware of the position of Rabbi Akiba, which was accepted by all subsequent schools of traditional Judaism. Modern exegetes, accordingly, respectfully indicate that the Song was included in the canon only because it was believed to be an allegory of the dialogue of love between God and Israel and then turn around and interpret the text quite literally.

Let us, therefore, ask the historical question that needs to be asked. The rabbis of the first and second century, like the intelligent ancients generally, were as sensitive to words and the meaning of poetry as we are. How, then, could they have been duped—or better yet, have deluded themselves and others—into regarding a piece of erotica as genuine religious literature, as the holy of holies! Should not the requirements of elementary common sense give us reason for pause and doubt? Perhaps, after all, the poem was known to them as a religious work; or—granted that modern literary criticism is correct in its appraisal—perhaps, many of its earliest readers felt that the Song, with all its direct and uninhibited expressions of sensual love, best expressed their highest and most profound religious sentiments. Perhaps they seized upon it—regardless of the intentions of its author(s)—as a work of authentic religious expression. If so, why? Why should ancient Jews, who after all were quite modest and socially correct, expose themselves and their most precious book to the kind of "misuse" and misunderstanding that ancients and moderns alike have manifested?

To answer glibly that the work was accepted as an allegory merely evades the basic issue. The problem is, really, why anyone should have thought of treating the work as an allegory in the first place. There must have been works aplenty that were excluded from the canon and that were not reinterpreted. One must, therefore, ask why the scales were tipped in favor of this particular poem that was *a priori* so religiously questionable.

The problem is all the more serious when the Jewish reverence for the Song of Songs is studied against the background of the ancient world. The ancient Israelites and Jews were, of course, sufficiently familiar with idolatrous rites and, above all, with the significant role fertility cults and sacred prostitution played in neighboring cultures. Their religious authorities were horrified by them. This is manifested by the Pentateuchal prohibition not only of sacred prostitution itself, but even of the contribution of a whore's price to the Temple of the Lord; by the repeated prophetic denunciations of anything that remotely hinted at such rites and by the total elimination of the fairer sex from any official role in the Temple; indeed by the prohibition against women even entering the inner courtyard of the Temple. The institution of "sacred marriage" would have been unthinkable to the Hebrew king or priest. Why, then, did a theme such as that of the Song of Songs come to represent a conversation of love between Israel and its God? Note that the very same circles that were insistent on the most scrupulous observance of the prohibition against representing God by any image or likeness not only admitted, but *advocated* the canonization of a work whose idiom makes anthropomorphism a triviality by comparison!

The conclusion is inescapable that the work filled a gap, a void no other work in the Bible could fill. Its very daring vocabulary best expressed, and was, perhaps, the only way of expressing what the Jew felt to be the holiest and loftiest dimension of religion—the bond of love between God and His people. In the final analysis, it is not the canonization of the Song of Songs that needs to be explained but the Jewish conception of the bond of love between God and Israel that made the canonization possible.

II

The explanation, paradoxically enough, is to be sought in the type of religious expression current in the ancient Near Eastern milieu out of which Israelite religion sprang. In the ancient Near East, men spoke of, and to, their gods in terms that were projections of relationships that obtained between humans on earth, most often in terms that reflected—and extended—their relationships with their own rulers. Like the Israelite, the Sumerian, Egyptian, Hittite, Babylonian, and Canaanite of ancient times often addressed his god(s) "by lik'ning spiritual to corporal forms" (Milton), as creator, master, king, source of life, revealer of law, healer of the sick, guardian of the orphan and widow, protector of the righteous, and so on and on. The attributes of the ancient gods expressed the functions their worshippers hoped these kings and deities would fulfill.[4]

Indeed, there are even expressions of intense affection on the part of the worshipper toward his god. However, one metaphor that cannot be found in the literature of any ancient religion outside of Israel is the description of the god as lover or husband of his *people*.[5] This seems odd, for an examination of the myth and rituals of these other religions will reveal a profound paradox about the pagan renunciation and the Israelite adoption of such a metaphor. The ancient peoples had many graphic myths about the lives, struggles, and loves of their gods—myths which ancient teachers like Plato found most objectionable on moral grounds. What is more, the ancient peoples of the Mediterranean world, Semitic as well as Hellenic, regularly celebrated rites of fertility in which carnal union with the gods was enacted in the temple or sacred grove. On the other hand, the religion of Israel alone had no myth, no account of the struggle of God against the forces of chaos, and no sexual ritual. The Lord was master of fertility as he was master of the universe and the fullness thereof. However, the Hebrew God was inscrutable and could not be worshipped by rites that were magical and coercive. Whenever some Israelites did attempt from time to time to introduce rites that smacked of fertility cults, they immediately evoked the wrath and excoriation of those jealous guardians of Israelite faith—the prophets. And yet, after all this, the Hebrew God alone was spoken of as the lover and husband of his people, and only the house of Israel spoke of itself as the bride of the Almighty.

It goes without saying that the source of the metaphor of God as husband of Israel cannot be located in the Canaanite Baalistic rituals in which some, or even many, Israelites may have participated. In the first place, as we have indicated, pagan rituals expressed no such relationship. But even if they had, we would still have to explain how fanatical monotheists, who would have no truck with such rituals or with terms associated with them, could have made peace with such a figure of speech and then proceed to make it central in their thought.

The solution must be sought within Israelite religion itself. A reconsideration of the terms and metaphors employed in this connection suggests that they derive from the very heart of the Jewish religion itself and are actually a midrashic development from the very first prohibition of the Decalogue, "You shall have no other gods beside Me." Absolute fidelity on the part of Israel to one God, come what may, is the sum and substance of the message of the Bible. Now in the life of the ancient Israelite there was only one situation reflecting that kind of absolute relationship, and that was the vow of fidelity of a woman to her husband. Infidelity is a euphemism for adultery, promiscuity, looseness, and prostitution, and it is precisely in these terms that the prophets, from Amos to Ezekiel, represent the hankering after, or the adoption of, the ways of the pagans. The sixteenth chapter of Ezekiel is a religious indictment of the people in terms that even by the canons of ancient tastes must have sounded as quite prurient. And yet its imagery does not seem to have shocked the faithful Jew of Babylon, or of later generations, for it was but a forthright and graphic expression of the theological relationship as the Jew understood it. The promiscuity portrayed by Ezekiel was principally religious infidelity and a violation of the vows of a "religious marriage." The jealousy of God, which the prophet assumes, is properly characteristic of a husband. The very same commandment that forbids the worship of other gods or the making of graven images concludes with a thundering warning: "For I the Lord your God am an impassioned God." The identical root *qana*, impassioned or jealous, is used elsewhere in the Pentateuch, Numbers 15:14, in the technical sense of a husband who is jealous of his wife. In other words, the earliest documents of Israelite religion had already expressed the requirement of religious fidelity in the terms employed for the demands of marital fidelity.

No other ancient people entertained such notions or metaphors of its gods, for no ancient people conceived of itself as having the same intense, personal, and exclusive relationship with its god that Israel did. The God of Israel was not merely the God of earth, of the Land of Promise, and the Lord of the Heavens. He was specifically the God of Israel, the Lord and Master of a particular group, who, in turn, owed Him special marks of duty, the duty of the most intense loyalty, that of a wife to her husband. Ergo, the God of Israel, who would brook no fealty or service to other gods, became the husband of Israel, and the people became His bride.[6]

There can be no more doubt about the antiquity of this conception than there can be of its general acceptance in all circles of ancient Israelite religious leadership. The Bible is replete with more than mere hints of this conception of the relationship between God and Israel. For instance,

> You must not worship any other god, because the Lord, whose name is Impassioned [*qana* = "jealous"], is an impassioned [*qana*] God. You must not make a covenant with the inhabitants of the land, for they will lust [*we-zanu* = "whore"] after their gods and sacrifice to their gods.... And when you take wives from among their daughters for your sons, their daughters will lust [*we-zanu*] after their gods and will cause your sons to lust [*we-hiznu* = "seduce"] after their gods [Exodus 34:14–15].

Or, to quote from a historical work: "And they hearkened not unto their judges, for they went astray [*zanu* = 'whored'] after other gods, and worshipped [Judges 2:17]." The instances we have cited could be multiplied many times, and if we cite one more it is only because of the familiarity it ultimately gained as part of the liturgy of the *Shema'*. In the final section of this recitation from Scripture, the fringes were ordered to be worn on the corners of garments, "so that you do not follow your heart and eyes in your *lustful urge* [Numbers 15:39]." That the lust here is not merely sexual is clear from the following verse: "Thus shall you be reminded *to observe all My commandments* and to be holy to your God."

As there is a positive aspect to the relationship between husband and wife, so, too, there was in the Israelite conception of the relationship between God and His people. It is, therefore, most significant to establish that this positive aspect, namely the loyalty of Israel to its God, was expressed in terms that implied fidelity and love in the very same ancient strata of the Bible that proclaim the negative formulative of jealousy we have been emphasizing. To return again to the Decalogue: "For I the Lord your God am an impassioned God, visiting the guilt of the fathers upon the children, upon the third and fourth generation of those who reject me, but showing kindness to the thousandth generation of those who *love* Me and keep My commandments." Note that already the Decalogue couples, and in a sense thus defines, loyalty to God with love of God and with the faithful observance of His commandments. If one, therefore, wonders what is meant by the moving verses of Deuteronomy, "You must love the Lord your God with all your heart and with all your soul, and with all your might [Deuteronomy 6:5]," one need only look elsewhere in the same book to find the content of this ostensibly platitudinous phrase clearly spelled out: "And now, O Israel, what is it that the Lord your God demands of you? It is to revere the Lord your God, to walk *only* in *His* paths, to love Him, and to serve the Lord your God with all your heart and soul [Deuteronomy 10:12]." And shortly after that: "Love, therefore, the Lord your God and always keep His charge, His laws, His norms, and His commandments [Deuteronomy 11:1]." Clearly, if disloyalty was whoring, obedience and observance of the commandments were the concrete expressions of fidelity; in the language of the metaphorical relationship, of love.

Thus far we have made almost exclusive reference to documents stemming from the legal and priestly circles of ancient Israel. We have done so deliberately, to emphasize that neither the conception of the relationship between God and Israel nor the key terms in which it was later expressed were the exclusive contribution of the prophets. The latter, to be sure, spelled it out, amplified it, and gave it a new intensity. However, they had inherited it from more ancient circles of popular and priestly monotheism.

III

No student of the Bible can fail to be shaken by the pathos and rage of the prophecies of Hosea, who drew much of his imagery and religious insights from his picture of a tragic experience of marital love.[7]

In Hosea's chastisement, the totality of Israel—what the rabbis call *knesset* Israel—is represented by the mother-wife figure, while the individuals of Israel are designated as the children. The mother has been seeking false and foreign lovers, but in the end she will say: "I will go and return to my first husband; for then it was better with me than now [Hosea 2:9]." Here, God is openly and forthrightly—unabashedly anthropomorphically—represented as Israel's husband.

Even if we should grant that Hosea's prophecies were based on his own experience, we must still wonder whether Hosea presumed to construct a religious allegory merely out of his personal frustrations. Is all that we have in the message of Hosea the transference of his own experience to a theological plane? Would it not be more correct to say that Hosea saw a religious message in his own experience or, as is more likely, deliberately enacted a religious allegory, *because* his Israelite mind had been taught from childhood to think of the relationship between God and Israel in terms of marital fidelity, in terms of love! That is indeed the case, and it is significant that Hosea's imagery added nothing to what is already *implied* in the Decalogue. Harlotry meant to him principally religious infidelity, idolatry, worship of strange gods. The greatness of his message thus lies not in the originality of its concepts, but in their direct and poetic formulation. Hosea's poetic power lay not only in his raging passion against the infidelity of Israel, but in his promise of restitution in the same figure of speech:

> And I will *betroth* thee unto Me forever, yea, I will *betroth* thee unto Me in righteousness and in justice, in loyalty and in *love*. And I will *betroth* thee unto Me in faithfulness; and thou shalt know the Lord [Hosea 2:21–22].

This is a promise not of a new relationship, but of a restitution, of repair and restoration to an *original* form.

Nevertheless, in the final analysis, Hosea did contribute something new to the literature and vocabulary of Israel. Hosea made explicit, put into bold relief, a motif that had hitherto been but one among several expressing the relationship between God and Israel. Hosea was the first and for that matter the only one to prophesy daringly: "And it shall come to pass on that day, saith the Lord, that you shall call me 'My husband,' and you shall not call me any longer 'My Baal' [Hosea 2:18]"—a word having the *double-entendre* of mastery and idolatry. No less daring was the *double-entendre* of his vision of the time when Israel would "know the Lord" alone, for in the context of the promise of betrothal the phrase, which to Hosea meant obedience,[8] had distinct overtones of marital union. What had been merely implicit in the speech of the past, Hosea brought out to the full light of day.

Henceforth, this motif was to appear again and again in the speech of the prophets. Jeremiah, the prophet of doom and consolation, took up both aspects of the imagery and gave them renewed poignancy. As modern critics have often noted, Jeremiah was a careful student of the prophecies of Hosea and had been deeply influenced by them. "Thus saith the Lord," he proclaims, "I recall the devotion of your youth, your bridal love, how you followed me through the wilderness, in a land that was not sown [Jeremiah 2:2]." To Jeremiah the idyllic beginnings of Israel's history were the days of the espousals of Israel to its God in a troth of law and love. Accordingly, Israel's turning its back on the covenant is portrayed in similar terms: "Can a maid forget her ornaments, or a bride her attire? Yet My people have forgotten Me days without number [*Ibid.* 2:32]." There is no need to refer to the many instances of the usage in Jeremiah and especially in the prophecies of his disciple, Ezekiel. They are legion and familiar. What it has been our purpose to stress is the direct and continuing chain of the imagery of Israel the wife and God the husband, and in Jeremiah's turn of phrase, of Israel the bride and God the lover. Each of the prophets contributed his own poetic variation on this motif, but the theme itself was a classical one even in ancient times, integral to the Hebrew concept of religion.

The identical theme was taken up by the anonymous prophet of the exilic period commonly referred to as the Second Isaiah. However, in the work of this prophet of hope and consolation, it is the vision of the restitution of the ancient relationship that is graphically portrayed. To the Second Isaiah, Jerusalem is a widow, a picture he may well have appropriated from the author of Lamentations: "How doth the city sit solitary that was full of people! How she is become as a widow [Lamentations 1:1]." In the context of Lamentations, of course, the widowhood of Jerusalem represents despoliation, depopulation, and desolation. But "Isaiah" quickly turned a figure of speech into a symbol: "Fear not," he cries to Zion the desolate,

> for thou shalt not be ashamed. Neither be thou confounded, for thou shalt not be put to shame; for thou shalt forget the shame of thy youth, and the reproach of thy *widowhood* shalt thou remember no more. For thy Maker is thy husband, the Lord of hosts is His name; and the Holy One of Israel is thy redeemer, the God of the whole earth shall He be called. For the Lord hath called thee as a wife forsaken and grieved in spirit; and a wife of youth, can she be rejected? saith thy God. For a small moment have I forsaken thee. But with great compassion will I bring thee back to Me [Isaiah 54:4–7].

This is a very delicate transition from the popular metaphor of a land widowed of her inhabitants to a land whose reunion will be with her Maker as husband. Isaiah carefully refrains from ever stating the metaphor too positively. In this, as in a subsequent passage, he cautiously shifts from one meaning to another:

Thou shalt no more be termed Forsaken. [We would say "divorced"; and once again I must stress that the addressee of his speech is the Land rather than the people.] Neither shall thy land any more be termed desolate; but thou shalt be called, My delight is in her [a term for marital love][9] and My land, Espoused; for the Lord delighteth in thee, and thy land shall be espoused. For as a young man espouseth a virgin, so shall thy sons espouse thee; and as the bridegroom rejoiceth over the bride, so shall thy God rejoice over thee [Isaiah 62:4–5].

Since in the prophecy of Second Isaiah, this is a return, a restoration, we need hardly wonder that later rabbinic exegetes, who fondly searched every word of the Bible for new and undiscovered meaning, would seek to locate in Scripture the exact time of the consecration of this marriage between the bride of Israel and its God. What better occasion could be, and indeed was, selected for this than the theophany at Sinai, when the daughter of Jacob, the house of Israel, was given the Torah as its marriage-ring?[10] What was specifically rabbinic in this interpretation of the narrative in Exodus was the play on words and consequent reading of a metaphor into verses where it was conspicuously absent. But once again, the rabbis were merely amplifying what they had already found in Scripture. To the rabbinic Jew, the Bible was a unit. What was stated in one book could be and should be found elsewhere, even where it is not explicit in the plain sense of the text. Since the theme of an inseparable marital bond between Israel and its God appeared implicitly in the Pentateuch and explicitly in the prophets, the historical beginning for the relationship had to be located.

IV

It is against this background that we are able to understand the pattern of mind that could see in the Song of Songs the very type of expression that would convey positively and fully what was implicitly or but briefly stated in the works of the prophets. Or, to put the matter differently, from the point of view of the Jews of early rabbinic times, without such a work as the Song of Songs the Bible was not quite complete. The prophetic metaphor had been employed either as an admonition against idolatry or as an eschatological vision of the restoration of Israel to its proper relationship with God and to its reunion with its bereaved country. But what of the believing and faithfully observant Jew of rabbinic times? How was he to articulate in the here and now his affirmation of, and his delight in, God's love, his satisfaction in the unique relationship between God and Israel expressed through the Torah and its commandments?

A glance at the book of Psalms is most instructive in this connection, not for what it has but for what it lacks. On the one hand, no other book of the Bible is so continual a paean of love to the Almighty as the book of Psalms. And yet, despite all of its affirmations of submission and devotion, the book of Psalms lacks one quality that the Song of Songs does possess, and that to the rabbinic Jew was all-important: the assurance of the inseverable *marital union* between God and Israel.

The Psalmists speak to and of God as Lord, King, Master, Creator, Father, and so on; they address Him directly and familiarly, but they do not turn to Him as a lover, as the bridegroom of Israel. This omission is probably no accident and has left its mark on subsequent Jewish liturgy. Whatever the reason for this, what is important to stress at this point is that the most challenging figure of speech employed by the prophets was conspicuously missing in the Psalms. Was it indeed impossible to assert somehow what the Jew had come to feel, his yearning and love for his lover, for the One who had designated His name over His people? The Song of Songs filled this gap, and in a way that satisfied religious needs.

Here I will let the ancient students of Scripture speak for themselves: "Why is the work called the Song of Songs? To indicate," the rabbis say, "that the Song is really a collection of songs responding to each other."

> In all other hymns [in the Bible] either the Almighty sings the praises of Israel, or Israel sing the praises of the Almighty. . . . However, only here in the Song of Songs their hymn to God is answered by a hymn to them. Thus, God praises Israel, saying [Song 1:15]: "Behold, thou art fair, my love; behold thou art fair"; and Israel responds with a paean to Him [with the words of the very next verse]: "Behold, Thou art fair, my Beloved, yea, pleasant."[11]

In other words, whereas the other books of the Bible do indeed proclaim the bond of love between Israel and the Lord, only the Song of Songs is a *dialogue* of love, a conversation between man and God that gives religious faith a kind of intensity no other form of expression can.

These then were some of the needs that the Song of Songs filled. As the work of Solomon it was prophetic revelation. As revelation it was the truth. But it was truth in a special sense. It was the most intimate of truths, the type that was vouchsafed only to the true believer. As the ultimate form of theological expression, it was comparable to the one moment in the year when the high-priest entered the royal chamber, as it were, the Holy of Holies, and confronted his God privately on behalf of the house of Israel. It was this moment of supreme religious experience to which Rabbi Akiba compared the effulgence of emotion evoked by the Song of Songs when he said that all the Scriptures are holy, but the Song of Songs—the Holy of Holies.

For an appreciation of the role the Song of Songs played in the canon, it matters not at all who really composed the Song and when. What counted for the Jews who sanctified it was that they believed it to be of Solomon's pen. And this they could readily believe, for the Song was in keeping with a metaphorical usage found and even spelled out, as we have seen, in the Torah and the prophets.

V

It is significant that of all the rabbis who should so vigorously express the importance and unique sanctity of the Song, it should be Rabbi Akiba. It is he who is represented in rabbinic literature as being one of the four types of ancient Jews who indulged in mystical speculation. It is further reported that of the four only Rabbi Akiba emerged as sound in his faith as he had been when he entered.[12] What this report emphasizes is the precipitous height of such an ascent to God—its glories and its dangers. Intense religious passion is risky, for its symbolism can easily be cheapened to the *risqué*. Long after it had been accepted into the canon, the Song of Songs, or at least its interpretation, was accordingly reserved for the elite, for the select few, who had proven their trustworthiness through maturity and their way of life.[13] And even when it was taught publicly, the allegorical interpretation was carefully sifted to avoid open discussion of the mystical states and doctrines the knowledgeable considered to be embedded in it. It was an *allegory* of love, and it was enough for the average man to know that only in the most general terms. To the extent that the Song was interpreted publicly, its verses were represented as being allegories of Jewish history, of the publicly documented contacts between the collectivity of Israel and the divine command. The profoundest secrets of the Song, of its innermost allegory, were restricted to the few, to select individuals, who entered the chambers of mystical knowledge in solitude.[14]

VI

In the final analysis, all that we have really explained up to this point is why the Song of Songs *could* have been admitted into religious Jewish literature. What remains to be explained is why the work was published and allegorized at the time in history that it was.

Scholars are for the most part in accord that while the Song of Songs may contain very ancient strata, the work as we have it now cannot have been completed before the Macedonian conquest of the Near East and rise of Hellenistic culture. In other words, both the work itself and the rabbinic allegory must be considered as aspects of the Jewish culture that emerged as a consequence of the impact, and under the influence, of Hellenism.[15]

In all likelihood, the allegorizing activity took place not long after the Song itself was compiled and both the book (understood quite sensually) as well as the religious interpretation of it reflect two sides of the identical cultural temper. The motif underlying both of these is Love. To the literalist, it is love in a sensual sense, while to the religious exegete it is love in a spiritual, *meta*-physical sense. Now Love-fulfilled, as an *abstraction*, as the highest and therefore the most desirable human experience, was a subject placed in the forefront of the intellectual agenda by the Platonic dialogues. It is from these dialogues, the textbook of the ancient intelligentsia, that the meaning of true love came to be discussed throughout the Hellenistic world. Wherever Greek literature and philosophy went, the problems of Beauty and Love went with them. Literature and artifacts of the early Hellenistic period reflect a considerable increase in the uninhibited concentration on erotic subjects, this interest being expressed in the religious sphere by a growing emphasis on the person of Aphrodite. In the latter half of the fourth century B.C.E., the Greek temple in Knidos displayed for the first time in history a nude Aphrodite, attracting world-wide attention for the daring innovation in the representation of the goddess no less than for the artistic masterpiece of its sculptor, Praxiteles.[16] Hellenistic civilization, it will be recalled, was the soil out of which arose many schools of ethics and thought, each purporting to teach the true, the pure, the noble, the beautiful. For virtually all of these schools Plato's *Phaedrus* and *Symposium* had provided an ultimate goal, an expression of the highest human emotion and state.[17] Indeed, the fixation on, and the definition of, the proper human motives and emotions, are two of the characteristic contributions of Hellenistic thought. Inevitably, Jewish teachers and thinkers, who claimed that their own tradition possessed the sum and substance of all truth, beauty, and goodness, would have to show how their way of life met the needs and demands of the religious spirit. Hence, it is no accident that in this very period many circles in Judaism first reflected deep concern with the intentions of the heart, with purity of thought, with chastity of motives, with love.

Love was thus in the air of Hellenistic civilization, and so were the many programs for the attainment of love. Some of them were quite carnal, the objects of contempt of the philosopher no less than of the rabbi. But other forms were quite the vogue in certain religious-philosophical circles, and to the rabbi these forms were frequently no less repugnant, indeed religiously even more dangerous than the vulgar, carnal type. No rabbi could tolerate the type of "enthusiasm," the spiritual ascent to and the union with the deity, that these forms bespoke. However, if love could not be ignored, it could be channeled, reformulated, and controlled, and this is precisely what the rabbinic allegory of the Song of Songs attempted to achieve.[18]

In the Song itself, the love between male and female is never consummated,[19] and throughout the rabbinic interpretations of the Song, one is aware of a marital relationship between two individual entities that are never united as one flesh. Israel and God are always distinct beings, and never can the twain unite. What binds them in their relationship is the *contract*, but Israel never becomes the mystical body of its deity. The Jewish mystic of ancient times may rise to Heaven and *behold* the glory of the throne, but he will never cease to be an onlooker from the outside, a human whose being and essence can never be altered. The very rapture of the Song became a prophylaxis against the pantheistic enthusiasm and knowledge (*gnosis*) that the Jew must have known from the world about him.[20]

Ultimately then, the Song of Songs bespeaks the great paradox of the biblical metaphor of God as the bridegroom or husband of Israel. On the one hand, the tabu against representation of the deity precluded the attribution to Him of any sexuality; and this was buttressed by the prohibition of any cultic sexual rites. On the other hand, the Bible unquestionably affirmed the masculinity of God and spoke of Him graphically as the husband. Both sides of the paradox were fruitful in producing the unique totality that is rabbinic religion. By denying the sexuality of God, Judaism affirmed His utter transcendence, His absolute freedom from the drives and passions that beset the gods of mythical religions and that made of them but *super*-men. By proclaiming His masculinity, on the other hand, Judaism affirmed His reality and, equally important, His potency. It thus avoided the pitfall of the impersonal deity of the Greek philosophical monotheists, on the one hand, and the mythically anthropomorphic deity of paganism on the other. To go one step further, by denying His sexuality, it eliminated the possibility of a magical and coercive (homeopathic) ritual. By conversely acknowledging His masculinity, it contended that God was a person to whom one could turn with a *supplicatory* ritual. To such a person one could proclaim fealty, submission, and love. However, let it not be forgotten, this love could reach the pitch of ecstasy, but never the stage of mystical *union*. The latter form, the neo-Platonic-Plotinian ecstasy, was but the other (and philosophical) side of the pagan coin of a mythical man-like god. The Hebrew husband-wife metaphor insisted to the last on reaffirming the God of Moses, Hosea, Jeremiah, and the Second Isaiah, who could only be heard or seen, and even then only by the elect.

NOTES

1. *The Fathers According to Rabbi Nathan*, Ch. 1 (Translated by J. Goldin. New Haven, 1955), p. 5.

2. *M.* Yadayyim 3:5, and see S. Lieberman, "Mishnat Shir ha-Shirim" in G. Scholem, *Jewish Gnosticism, Merkabah Mysticism and Talmudic Tradition* (New York, 1960), pp. 118f.

3. *Tosef.* Sanhedrin 12:10 (ed. Zuckermandel), p. 433.
4. See M. Smith, "The Common Theology of the Ancient Near East," *JBL*, LXXI (1952), 135f. and especially 141f. I owe the quotation from Milton, *Paradise Lost*, V, 573 to E. Bevan, *Symbolism and Belief* (Boston, 1938), p. 15; cf. also Bevan's own formulation on p. 30.
5. Smith, *loc. cit.* See also T. Ohm, *Die Liebe zu Gott in den nichtchristlichen Religionen* (Krailling vor Munich, 1950); J. Moffatt, *Love in the New Testament* (London,1930), pp. 9f.
6. For similar, but by no means identical explanations of the origins of the marriage motif and its relationship to the allegory on the Song of Songs, cf. D. Buzy, "L'Allégorie Matrimoniale de Jahve et d'Israël et la Cantique des Cantiques," *Vivre et Penser*, III (1945), 79f.; U. Cassuto, *A Commentary on The Book of Exodus* (in Hebrew) (Jerusalem, 1959), p. 163 (brought to my attention by Prof. J. Goldin); C. Spicq, *Agapé* (Leiden, 1955—*Studia Hellenistica*, No. 10), p. 113 nn. 3–4; E. A. Synan, "The Covenant of Husband and Wife," *The Bridge*, IV (1962), 150. The crucial distinction between "marriage" of the god to the land and a marital relationship between God and the people of Israel is made by A. Roifer in *Tarbiz*, XXXI (1960–61), 140 n. 80.
7. On Hosea's marriage imagery, see H. L. Ginsberg, "Studies in Hosea 1–3," *Yehezkel Kaufman Jubilee Volume* (Jerusalem, 1960), pp. 50f.
8. Cf. Y. Kaufmann, *The Religion of Israel* (Trans. by M. Greenberg. Chicago, 1960), pp. 372 f; idem, *Toledot ha-Emunah ha-Yisraelit*, VI, 113.
9. Cf. Genesis 34:19; Deuteronomy 21:14 etc.
10. See L. Ginzberg, *Legends of the Jews*, VI, 36 n. 200. Cf. also I. Heinemann, *Altjuedische Allegoristik* (Baselau, 1936), p. 31, par. b. For customs in early modern times based on this concept, cf. A. Ben-Ezra in *Hadoar*, 4 Sivan 5721 (1961), 473.
11. Midrash Shir ha-Shirim 1:11 to Song of Songs 1:1.
12. *Tosef.* Ḥagiga 2:3–4 (ed. Lieberman), p. 381.
13. Scholem, *op cit.*, pp. 14f., 36f.
14. Lieberman, *ibid.*, p. 125.
15. See M. Rozelaar, "Shir ha-Shirim 'al Reqa' ha-Shirah ha Erotit ha-Yevanit ha-Hellenistit," *Eshkolot* (Scholia), I (1954), 33f. That allegorical interpretation is one of the hallmarks of Hellenistic literary exegesis is too well known to need belaboring. Whatever distinctions are pertinent between Greek and Jewish allegorization with respect to other Biblical books, in the case of the Song of Songs the Hellenistic features are quite apparent; for in this instance, the allegorical interpretation was doubtless regarded as the true meaning by those persons or circles who read it as Scripture. Cf. Heinemann, *op cit.*, p. 64f. This does not mean to say that many persons did not read the book in its literal sense, or even that strictly religiously oriented groups regarded the literal meaning as false. To them the plain sense of the verses was specious, but could be cited as evidence for "archeological" data. Thus, Heinemann's contention in *The Methods of the Aggadah* (in Hebrew) (Jerusalem, 1949), p. 156, that Eupolemos cited Song 4:4 in its literal meaning is misleading, for Eupolemos did not cite the verse so much as glean historical information it; cf. J. Freudenthal, *Hellenistische Studien*, II (Breslau, 1875), pp. 114 (bot.), 229 lines 21–24. More recently, Professor E. E. Urbach has argued that the allegorical interpretation of the Song cannot be traced to much before the destruction of the Second Temple, and that the mystical interpretation was probably the contribution of R. Akiba. He further points to *M.* Ta'anit 4:8 as clear evidence for an earlier sensual understanding of the Song, presumably even in orthodox circles. Cf. E. E. Urbach, "Rabbinic Exegesis and Origenes' Commentaries on the Song of Songs and Jewish-Christian Polemics" (in Hebrew), *Tarbiz*, XXX (1960–61), 148f. However, neither the citation in the Mishna nor the lateness of the dateable statements of allegorical interpretations are really any proof that the work had not been studied esoterically much earlier. The mere fact that the work was housed in the library of the Dead Sea Sect is sufficient evidence to warrant the conclusion that the work was not regarded as an erotic one long before the destruction of the Temple. Moreover, the exact point of the citation in *M.* Ta'anit, 4:8 is obscure. In all likelihood it is a later gloss that was appended because of the *religious-allegorical* significance associated with the verses; cf. C. Albeck's note in his commentary to *Mishna Seder Moed*, p. 498. However, even if the verse was indeed part of the celebration described in the Mishna—as contended by J. N. Epstein, *Mavo le-Nusaḥ ha-Misha*, II, 686f.—it may have been taken out of an "original"

religious context for this dance. In conclusion, it must be emphasized that no one—not even R. Akiba—ever claimed that many ancient readers did not understand and recite the book in its sensual sense. But that is not really the issue. The question is whether those circles who were responsible for its preservation as a record of revelation did so. We think the logic of the evidence points to a negative answer.

16. For these observations I am indebted to Professor Elias Bickerman, who also referred me to M. H. Chehab, "Les Terres Cuites de Kharayeb," *Bulletin du Musée de Beyrouth*, X (1951–52), XI (1953–54); cf. especially X, 79f., where the frequency of Hellenistic erotic figurines illustrates the new trend in popular religion. Cf. also G.M.A. Richter, *The Sculpture and Sculptors of the Greeks* (Revised ed. New Haven, 1950), pp. 54, 58f., 100f., 260f.; K. Clark, *The Nude* (New York, 1959), pp. 109f.

17. Cf. A. E. Taylor, *Plato, the Man and His Work* (New York, 1956), p. 226; *idem, Platonism and Its Influence* (Boston, 1924), p. 9. On Eros as the object of man's yearning for the good and the beautiful as well as for immortality, cf. W. Jaeger, *Paideia*, II, 189f.; F. M. Cornford, *From Religion to Philosophy* (New York, 1957), pp. 230f.; A. J. Festugière, *Epicurus and His Gods* (Oxford, 1955), pp. 17, 62. On Love as an epithet for the divine (Isis), see S. Lieberman, *Greek in Jewish Palestine* (New York, 1942), p. 140. On the permeation of the "symposial" genre into Jewish literature, cf. M. Stein, *Dat va-Da'at* (Cracow, 1937–38), p. 61; on the influence of Greek doctrines of love on Jewish thought, *ibid.*, pp. 142f.

18. Taylor, *Plato*, p. 209, notes the affinity between the *amor mysticus* of Eros to the allegorical interpretation of the Song of Songs.

19. M. H. Segal, "The Song of Songs," *Vetus Testamentum*, XII (1962) 475, takes Song 4:16 and 5:1 to signify consummation. Whether or not that is the meaning of these verses, the ancient allegorists certainly did not understand them that way. Indeed, the phraseology is sufficiently metaphorical to enable avoidance of any real sexual interpretation.

20. See S. Lieberman, "How Much Greek in Jewish Palestine?" *Biblical and Other Studies* (Edited by A. Altmann. Cambridge, Mass., 1963), pp. 135f.

Zion in Rabbinic Literature

I

In most expositions of Rabbinic theology, Palestine is singularly ignored as one of the central pillars of Jewish religion. At best, the land of Israel is relegated to sections treating Rabbinic eschatology and Jewish messianic aspirations, while the preponderant bulk of the discussion is reserved for analysis of more commonly accepted theological themes: God and His essence, Creation, Revelation, prophecy, conceptions of good and evil, reward and punishment, and the like. There have, of course, been exceptions to this glaring oversight, notably Judah Halevi's *Kitab al-Khazari*, but in the main, Jewish theologians from Saadiah to the present have treated our theme only secondarily.

The reason for this neglect derives from the nature of the stimuli which for the most part evoked systematic Jewish theology. In the main, Jewish theological writing grew out of the need to defend Judaism against competing philosophies and theologies. Consequently, Jewish thinkers confined themselves largely to the discussion of ideas, of theological abstractions, and to the metaphysical grounds for Jewish faith and practice. Stimulated by what were essentially external and foreign challenges, Jewish philosophers also adopted the literary forms of their opponents. Since the latter had inherited their tools from the classics of Greek philosophy, Jews rose to the occasion with the very same tools; abstraction became the rule of the day. Having justified their faith, they doubtless felt that the *realia* of Judaism, its concrete tools and symbols, would fall into place automatically. In modern times, Jewish theologians have adhered to the essentially identical pattern, while Christian students of Judaism have naturally tried to understand the Jewish religion in the same way they treat their own—namely, as a systematic body of ideas. Now, ideas, the philosophers of old maintained, if they are to be of any lasting worth, must transcend the limitations of time and place. If they are true at all, they cannot intrinsically be true only for one people or one country. They must be valid for all persons at all times. Inasmuch as Judaism is a universalist religion, claiming eternal validity for all, Jewish and non-Jewish students of Judaism have treated Judaism as a metaphysical system. Accordingly, what place could Palestine or, for that matter, any particular country have in their system except as a secondary and essentially accidental theme, that is, by virtue of its being the Biblical Holy Land and the messianic land of promise? And so it has been for the most part treated.

However justified this neglect of the Holy Land in systematic theologies, it is unfair to Rabbinic Judaism and misleading to anyone who would understand the Judaism of the Talmud objectively and in its totality. Consider, for example, the fact that while Maimonides conforms to the pattern we have described in his *Guide of the Perplexed*, where in his systematic exposition of Jewish faith the Holy Land enjoys but a tertiary place, in his renowned legal code, *Mishneh Torah*, Palestine and its place in Jewish usage occupies fully one third of the work. It could not be otherwise, for fully one third of the Mishna, and hence of all Jewish law, is inextricably connected with the land of Israel. Of the six divisions of the Misha, Tosefta, and Talmud, nine tenths of the first, fifth, and sixth orders, in addition to not insignificant portions of the remaining three parts, are concerned with the fulfillment of the laws of the Holy Land. In this connection, it cannot be overemphasized that for the evaluation of Jewish ideology on any issue, Jewish law and legal sources are by far the best criteria. We do less than justice to Rabbinic Judaism if we do not stress the inseverable connection it had with the land of Israel not only ideologically, but quite practically and legally. The Rabbis could no more conceive of Judaism without the *land* of Israel than they could have without the *people* of Israel. After all, the entire Bible is a record of that inseverable connection in the divine promise and in the divine injunctions for daily behavior. Jewish mysticism has unfortunately obscured this relationship by its apothegm that God, Torah, and Israel are one. Historically, it would be far more correct to say that in both the religion of the Bible as well as in that of the Rabbis there was an unbreakable covenant between God and the Torah on the one hand, and with the *people* of Israel and the *land* of Israel on the other. It is to an analysis of this nexus that we now proceed.

Of the variety of sources on the Jewish mentality in Talmudic civilization, the form of expression which is most authentically Jewish is the interpretation of Scripture, or *midrash*, which at all times sought to make

Scripture relevant to the Jew in his daily life. Though the midrash often amplifies and expands on the plain intent of Scripture, it also often telescopes in a single statement the Rabbinic attitude to a whole series of questions. One such instance is the sermon of Rabbi Simeon b. Yohai on a verse in the hymn of Habakkuk (Hab. 3:6): "He [i.e., the Almighty] rose and measured the earth. The Holy One, blessed be He, measured [i.e., considered] all generations and found no people fitted to receive the Torah other than the people of Israel; the Holy One, blessed be He, considered all generations and found no generation fitted to receive the Torah as the generation of the wilderness; similarly, He considered all mountains and found none fitted for His presence to dwell on other than the Temple mount; the Holy One, blessed be He, considered all cities and found none worthier of the Temple than Jerusalem; the Holy One, blessed be He, considered all mountains and found no mountain on which the Torah should be given other than on Sinai; the Holy One, blessed be He, considered all lands, and found no land suitable to be given to Israel other than the land of Israel. This is what is meant by the verse 'He rose and measured the earth.'"[1]

Now it is apparent to anyone who reads the verse of Habakkuk in its own context, that, whatever the verse does mean, it did not intend what Rabbi Simeon b. Yohai elicited from it. However, that is relatively unimportant. What is significant is that Rabbi Simeon is expressing an idea about Jewish history and is attaching this conception to the revelation of Scripture. Rabbi Simeon says two things in this passage. First, the great facts of Jewish religious history are not accidental, but are details in a carefully planned and executed divine program. It could not just as well have been any other people that received the Torah, anywhere in the world, who then proceeded to worship Him in any Temple. It was Israel that received the Torah on Sinai according to God's design. It therefore follows that Israel's inheritance of the Land and its obligations therein are equally part of the heavenly design and mandate. If the record of Scripture means anything, Rabbi Simeon says, it means that the nexus between God, Israel, the Torah, and the Land is inseverable. To be sure, no new idea not previously expressed by Scripture is formulated here. The point to remember, however, is that the theme was *emphasized* by the Rabbis and not permitted to remain merely written. The promise of the Land as well as the eternal property of Israel, its eternal sanctity, was a living idea which could not fall into limbo.

It is against the background of this feeling that we can better understand the encomiums on the Holy Land found throughout Rabbinic literature. Scripture had praised it as the land of milk and honey,[2] as Israel's lasting inheritance and resting place,[3] as the land of God.[4] Can we wonder that the Rabbis, who were, in the first place, expositors of Scripture, should continue in the same vein! If we find that the Rabbis called the

Holy Land the land of life, or the land of beauty, the precious, or even the universe itself, nothing more can be gleaned than a passionate love for the land expressed in the classical terms of Scripture.[5] Certainly, they did mean to be taken literally when they said that the Land lacks for naught in the way of fruits.[6] They were simply playing on a verse (Deut. 8:9) out of fondness for Scripture and the country. Little wonder, then, that in Rabbinic Hebrew "*ha-'Ares*," the Land, signifies the Holy Land, while every other country is *hus la-'ares*, outside the Land. Correspondingly, *ha-'Ir*, the city, signifies Jerusalem, which the Rabbis fondly called the very center of the earth.[7]

These are not mere figures of speech. In Rabbinic religion, which had to take account of Jewish communities dispersed throughout all of the known world, Palestine was the umbilical cord of Jewish life. It was *the Land*, the pivot about which all religious life should evolve.

II

However literally such encomiums or sermonic rhetoric were understood, these were in the final analysis but symptomatic of the importance of the Land in the life of the people. The centrality of the Holy Land to Jewish religion derives from the fact that Scripture makes a considerable part of its law and ritual contingent upon possession of the country by the people. All of the agricultural laws of Scripture are, of course, specifically connected with the tilling of the soil of the Holy Land.[8] Moreover, with the Deuteronomic restriction of the sacrificial cult to Jerusalem, the Temple service became confined to one area within the Holy Land. In the area of civil law, the cities of refuge for persons guilty of manslaughter could be established only in Palestine.[9] In short, the Torah itself makes it plain that its law can conceivably be fulfilled in its entirety only in the land of Israel. It is with this area of ritual performance, namely with "the laws contingent upon the Land,"[10] that fully one third of Rabbinic *halakha* is concerned.

The special place of the Land in law endowed the country with legal holiness. "There are ten degrees of sanctity," the Mishna states.[11] "The land of Israel is sanctified above all others in that from it alone may be brought the sheaf of first wheat,[12] the first fruits,[13] and the two loaves.[14] . . . Walled cities [within Palestine] are of even greater sanctity, in that lepers are not permitted to dwell within them. . . . The city within the wall [of Jerusalem] is of greater sanctity than walled cities, since within it one may consume sacrifices of lesser sanctity[15] and the second tithe.[16] . . . The Temple mount is of greater sanctity than the city [as a whole]." Thus this table proceeds to grade the properties of the various parts of the country culminating with the holy of holies, the sanctity of which was such that it was entered only on the Day of Atonement by the high-priest. Palestine and its areas were legally sacred, and he who would live a life of sanctity had to dwell within it.

Under the Rabbinic amplification of Scripture, even the normal structure of the Jewish community could function only in Palestine. Ordination and the prerogatives that went along with it—the imposition of all civil penalties fixed by Scripture and regulation of the Jewish calendar—were reserved for the authorities of Palestine.[17] To be sure, the genius of Rabbinic Judaism lay in its having transcended the limitations of land, Temple, and clergy as prerequisites for personal religious fulfillment. On the other hand, the fixed legal position of the Land made the fulfillment of the Law outside Jerusalem and Palestine possible only to the extent that the obligation was *personal (hobat ha-guf)*[18] rather than *territorial.* Summarizing this point by a Midrash on Moses' plea to God that he be permitted to enter the Land,[19] a Palestinian homilist of the third century remarked: "Why was Moses our teacher so eager to enter the land of Israel? Was he in need of its fruits or of its bounty? Moses, however, pleaded thus with the Almighty: 'The people of Israel have been given many commandments which can only be fulfilled in the Land. Permit me to enter that I too may fulfill them personally.'"[20]

Like the Torah, the Land was God's gift to Israel, and the Jew was quick to associate any other divine favor with the Land. Once the Land had been chosen, the Rabbis declared, prophecy, the supreme gift to Israel's teachers, was confined to those dwelling in the Land. Jonah fled to Tarshish, they said, only because he thought that God's Shekhinah (the Divine Presence) manifested itself solely in the Holy Land.[21] Even the ultimate reward of the resurrection of the dead would be enacted in the Holy Land. Certainly, the dead of the Land would be quickened first. That is why Jacob and Joseph foreswore their descendants to convey their remains to Palestine.[22] How much a part of the Jewish mentality this conception became is illustrated by the innumerable Jews who through the ages went to the Holy Land to spend their last days and die there. Rather than be buried in what some Jews considered foreign soil, R. Meir requested at the time of his death, towards the end of the second century, that his remains be cast into the sea off the Palestinian coast.[23] The medieval pilgrimages and the veneration of soil or relics from the Holy Land were practically what drew their inspiration from the concept of "the Holy Land" which developed within Judaism.

III

Since we have insisted upon the centrality of Palestine in Rabbinic religion, we must also dwell on several widely entertained notions about the Rabbinic attitude to the Jewish state. The Talmud as well as other ancient sources reveal the existence of considerable conflict between the Pharisees and the Jewish rulers during the Second Commonwealth. The acts and policies of John Hyrcanus, Alexander Jannaeus, and Herod and his sons were often at such odds with the doctrines of the Pharisees as to result in open warfare and bloodshed. Furthermore, at the time of the Great Revolt against Rome, Rabban Johanan ben Zakkai, and presumably some of his school, opposed some of the activities of the rebel government so outspokenly that modern scholars have often concluded that the Rabbis were only secondarily concerned with Jewish government; that their chief concern was with undisturbed religious practice and study of Scripture; that they were Torah-centered rather than land-centered.

However, an objective reading of the record, I believe, will indicate that this view is most unfair and represents a projection of modern political ethics on to the Rabbis.[24] True, the Pharisees often rejected the political policies of the Maccabean and Herodian rulers, but they were by no means averse to Jewish self-government. Nor did they wish to remain cloistered in the house of study. During the reign of Alexandra Salome (76–67 B.C.E.) they ousted their Sadducean opponents and took over the administration themselves. Rabban Johanan b. Zakkai may have opposed the revolt against Rome, and even on that question our sources are not unequivocal, but Rabban Johanan was not the only Rabbi in Palestine. During the great war, Pharisees fought alongside Essenes and Sadducees, and no less a Rabbi than Simeon b. Gamaliel was for a time a member of the high council of war.

After the collapse of the revolt against Rome, one of the chief concerns of the Rabbis was to restore some measure of self-government and to accelerate the rehabilitation of the country's economy. The Rabbinic legislation of the period, far from betraying detachment from the mundane problems of government, reveals unceasing concern with the country and its material welfare. The status of the land politically and economically was as much a religious problem to Rabbis as the ritual commandments to be performed in it. This, too, could not be otherwise, for the Bible had not disdained to map out a program for these areas of life in the land. As custodians of the Torah, the Rabbis considered it their solemn duty to carry out its command to Israel to inherit the country and govern it by its law.

It is, accordingly, misleading to point to the absence of political *theory* in early Jewish literature as an indication that the Rabbis were not interested in political *life*. Political theory, like philosophy as a whole, can flourish only where man is obliged to search for himself after the truth or the best forms of behavior. But Judaism precluded such speculation by its postulation of the Revelation as the sum and substance of all truth and as the eternal guide for the good life. Judaism can only interpret, or *apply* the Revelation to the present; it need not, it could not search *de novo*. The law of the just-price, the law of strikes and fair wages, of taxation, monetary damages, transfer and sale of property, to cite but a few examples, along with the machinery for enforcement[25]—these were *political* realities that the Jews fashioned and by which they governed themselves. The Talmudic record of centuries of discussion and legislation in these and parallel areas proves that political life, predicated, to be sure, on the Torah, was one of the primary concerns of the Rabbis and their followers.

IV

The status of the land of Israel was complicated during the Talmudic period by two facts, each of which colored the Biblical picture considerably. First, during the greater portion of the eight centuries comprising the Rabbinic period—i.e., from about 350 B.C.E. to about 450 C.E.— Palestine was an independent Jewish country only for about eighty years, i.e., from about 143 B.C.E. until about 63 B.C.E. It cannot be overemphasized that whatever self-government the Jews did have during the greater portion of this period was, in the last analysis, under leave and sufferance of the governing powers; Persian, Ptolemaic, Seleucid, or Roman. Moreover, throughout these centuries, except for the brief span of eighty years, considerable portions of Palestine were in Gentile or Samaritan hands. Ideally, the Bible defined the boundaries of Palestine as stretching from the mountains of Lebanon to the Isthmus of Suez.[26] In reality, however, the Jews had to reckon with the fact that a whole chunk of central Palestine was not Jewish, and that the extent of actual Jewish territory was considerably less than that included by the Biblical limits. For ritual or administrative matters, therefore, the religious authorities discussed the real Palestine of their own day; Judea, Galillee, and the Transjordan.[27] This territory, which they called the land occupied by the immigrants from the Babylonian exile,[28] was the land granted to the Jews by the Persian government plus what was conquered by the Maccabees. This territory, which the Rabbis regarded as sanctified areas (in contrast with the extended Holy Land described in the Bible, and which they could not rationally regard as Jewish or sanctified)[29] they sought by every means at their disposal to keep in Jewish hands. Above all, they fought to keep and increase the Jewish population in Palestine. Much of the Rabbinic legislation on Palestine, accordingly, has an irridentist flavor, and is aimed at preserving what has been conquered and reclaiming what is not yet possessed.

One of the earliest of the Rabbinic injunctions in line with this tendency comes from the days of the persecutions of Antiochus IV Epiphanes and his son. According to the Bible, only the country west of the Jordan was legally sanctified; all other territory, even the Transjordan, was levitically unclean.[30] Interestingly enough, however, the Rabbis regarded the Biblical classification of countries outside Palestine as unclean only as figurative and date the legal classification of gentile lands as *tame* (unclean) from the second century B.C.E. Henceforth, anyone leaving the Jewish land was automatically defiled and required to undergo ritual purification.[31] Professor Louis Ginzberg, who discussed this injunction in his epoch-making essay, "The Significance of the Halakhah for Jewish History,"[32] has shown that this and a number of other early measures which were couched in the idiom of levitical purity were in reality designed for the social and economic benefit of the country. To forestall easy emigration from the country, Rabbinic law gave the upper hand to either spouse who wished to go to the Holy Land or, conversely, who refused to leave it. "If the husband wishes to go to Palestine," a Tannaitic tradition reads,[33] "but his wife refuses, she may be compelled to go; if she refuses to comply, she may be divorced and forfeits her marriage contract. If she wishes to go, while he refuses, he may be compelled to go; if he refuses, he is compelled to divorce her and pay her marriage contract in full." In line with the policy of having the country stay in Jewish hands, even Sabbath injunctions were somewhat relaxed to enable Jews to close negotiations for the acquisition of territory.[34] The sale of land to Gentiles in Palestine was, of course, absolutely forbidden.[35] In similar fashion they forbade the sale of slaves to anyone outside of Palestine, slave labor being one of the pillars of ancient economy, and fined the purchaser by declaring the slave automatically free.[36] On the other hand, slaves fleeing from abroad to the Holy Land were also to be set free and under no circumstances to be returned home.[37] Emigration from the land even for reasons of economic hardship was declared sinful, except in cases of dire famine, since emigration meant forfeiting the country to others and depleting its population. On this point, they issued a grim warning drawn from Scripture. "R. Simeon b. Yohai said: Elimelech, Mahlon, and Chilion were the outstanding men of their generation, and its recognized leaders. Why [if they were such worthies] were they punished?[38] For they left the land [even in the time of famine]."[39] As a Midrash for the positive side of their view, they drew a lesson from Omri, king of Israel, whom Scripture does not reckon among the pious of antiquity. Why did Omri merit the dignity of kingship? Because, said R. Johanan, he added one principality to the land of Israel, Samaria.[40]

We have no way of knowing how many Jews were deterred by these legal injunctions and sermonic admonitions from carrying out their intentions of leaving the country. But for Palestine as a religious idea in Judaism that is a relatively minor question. The important thing is, and for this there exists very clear evidence, that migration from the country became a religious infraction fraught with guilt.[41] The constant reiteration that he who lives outside of Palestine is an unwilling abettor of idolatry, and that only he who lives in the Holy Land can properly be spoken of as subject to the discipline of God,[42] left its mark. Centuries later, Babylonian authorities might urge Jews not to go to Palestine, the cultural and economic levels of which had sunk to a pitiful state. But, in the first place, they took pains to rationalize their obvious departure from traditional norms; and, secondly, they, too, were powerless to stem the impulses of scholars, who preferred to settle or at least receive their training in the well-spring of Jewish faith.[43]

Underlying all this Rabbinic concern for the national welfare and protection of Palestine as Jewish territory was the absolute refusal of the Jews of Palestine to compromise their national-religious theory with historical facts. Never for a moment did the Rabbis recognize as legitimate the conquest of the country by any foreign power. However passive they had to be in the face of political might, they regarded the Romans as interlopers and their agents as thieves. The Almighty had promised the Land to Abraham and to his seed as their eternal inheritance, and no foreign power or conquest could alter this right. Consequently, it was considered quite legitimate, the Mishna informs us, to evade the taxes of Roman publicans as though they were no better than highway robbers.[44] Obedience to the ruling powers when necessary was one thing; it was another thing for the Rabbis to countenance cooperation with Rome on the part of their colleagues even in the interests of law and order. One does not help one criminal against another.[45] Much of the hostility to the Gentile found in Rabbinic literature can be understood properly only on the background of the humiliation and helplessness to which a politically defeated nation is subject. In the diaspora, Rabbinic authorities could realistically proclaim that the tax-law of the state is binding upon Jews as upon all other inhabitants.[46] However, the Jew of Palestine would not recognize the authority of a Gentile power in the Holy Land. The Rabbinic discussions of whether the mandates of simple ethics and decency apply to Gentiles[47] stem from a community that experienced the indecencies and humiliations of conquering armies and their fiscal agents every day of the week.[48]

V

The Rabbis refused to recognize foreign conquest! However, is not the Bible itself a record of foreign conquest; of seizure of the land of Canaan from its inhabitants by the ancient Israelites! There is evidence that this question was discussed in Rabbinic circles, obviously as a theologico-dogmatic one, but also with considerable attention to the need for a good answer for public morale, or perhaps, for arguments with hecklers or skeptics.[49] "The inhabitants of Africa," an old Rabbinic legend states, "came before Alexander of Macedon to state their case, saying: 'The land of Canaan is rightfully ours, for thus it is written in the Torah of Moses: "the land of Canaan according to the borders thereof [Num. 34:2].'"

Gabiha ben Pasisa, caretaker of the Temple, said to the sages: "Permit me to argue with them. Should I refute them, they will be compelled to admit that the Torah of Israel has refuted them. On the other hand, should they defeat me, you may say that they conquered but a commoner [and not an official spokesman of the Jews]." Having received the permission of the sages, he went forth to debate with them and said: "Have you ever heard of a judgment being only partially valid? If the Torah says 'the land of Canaan,' it also states: 'Cursed be Canaan; a slave of slaves shall he be unto his brethren [Gen. 9:25].'" Needless to add, the legend concludes with a tale of an overwhelming victory for the Jews.[50] Other legends adopted an entirely different talk. The land was rightfully never the property of the Canaanites in the first instance. When Abraham came to the Land of Canaan, Scripture tells us: "They came to the land of Canaan . . . and the Canaanites were then in the land [Gen. 12:5–6]." Why specify that the Canaanites were then in their land? For, the Rabbis say, the land of Israel had been allotted to Shem. At the time that the Holy One, blessed be He, divided the earth among Noah's three sons, Noah enjoined them against entering the boundaries of one another. Now the seven nations of Canaanites came over to Palestine and trespassed into the area; hence, the Holy One, blessed be He, ordered them to be destroyed.[51] In other words, the presence of Israel on the Land was foreordained, and the conquest of the Land by the Israelites was merely a necessary act to obtain what was long since rightfully theirs. A similar apologetic was made famous to all Jews by Rashi in his opening commentary to the book of Genesis, which he quoted from the midrash:[52]

> Rabbi Isaac said: "The Torah should have opened with the verse: 'This month shall be unto you the first of the months [Exod. 12:1],' which is the first commandment given to Israel. What is the reason, then, that it commences with the account of the Creation? Because [of the thought expressed in the text] 'He declared to His people the strength of His works in order that He might give them the heritage of the nations [Ps. 111:6].' For should the peoples of the world say to Israel, 'You are robbers, because you took by force the lands of the seven nations [of Canaan],' Israel may reply to them: 'All the earth belongs to the Holy One, blessed be He; He created it and gave it to whom He pleased. When He willed He gave it to them, and when He willed He took it from them and gave it to us.'"

These apologetics were not in all likelihood meant by their authors to be taken literally. They merely express midrashically the firm conviction that the normal consequences of political conquest do not apply to the Jews, for the land of Israel is theirs. This conviction, however, was charged with the messianic assurance that their claims to the Land would yet be validated by divine intervention and restoration.

VI

If the first great fact of Jewish history in Talmudic times was that Palestine was not all in Jewish hands, the second and equally important fact was that a large percentage of the Jewish people was not in Palestine. To put it briefly, beginning with post-Biblical Judaism the *Galut*, or diaspora, was a fact permanently to be reckoned with in Jewish history. We are no longer dealing with involuntary exile, as in the Bible, but rather with a self-imposed and most often voluntarily accepted migration. Great numbers, perhaps even 1,000,000 Jews, lived in Alexandria and other parts of Egypt; large colonies of Jews were to be found in Rome, Greece, Asia Minor, and Mesopotamia. What is more important, the proportion of Jews outside to those inside Palestine grew ever larger and larger.[53] Wherever they lived, however, and no matter how long they and their descendants had been there, the Jews of the diaspora considered themselves to be, and the Jews of Palestine considered themselves to be, offshoots of the mother country on foreign soil. To be sure, they were accorded rights and fought for them, but were always guaranteed the safety of what they acknowledged to be their national privileges: not to participate in the army, not to have to violate their own holidays, and, above all, to make their pilgrimages and to defray vast sums annually to their mother city Jerusalem in the form of the half-shekel.[54] When opportunities permitted, they intervened on one another's behalf. Nothing, Josephus informs us, could have stopped Cleopatra from overrunning Palestine in the days of Alexander Jannaeus except for the stern warning of her Jewish general that she would thereby incur the enmity of Jews everywhere.[55] When, about thirty years later, the Jews of Asia Minor and Palestine had been robbed of a vast sum of money sent from the diaspora to Jerusalem, the Jews of Rome were instrumental in bringing the offending Roman legate to trial.[56] Josephus informs us that the Jews of Egypt were persuaded by the Jewish leaders of Palestine in 55 and 47 B.C.E. to assist the Romans to conquer the country.[57] It was well known throughout the ancient world that the Jews were one people. Quite apart from political and economic considerations, the Jews looked to Palestine to regulate their annual calendar. The leap year depended on agricultural conditions in Palestine, and the Jews of the diaspora adapted their year to the needs of the mother country. Rabbinic sources preserve the texts of such official epistles sent to Jewish communities throughout the Near and Middle East informing them of the changes in the calendar for a particular year.[58] Thousands of these diaspora Jews flocked annually to the Temple on the occasion of the three festivals and thus preserved their association with the land.[59]

The Jews of Palestine, too, were concerned with the welfare of the *golah*: Jews of Palestine came to Alexandria in the first century to assist the Jews of Egypt in their street fights with the pagans. At about the same time, Jews of Tiberias rushed to the aid of the Jews of Antioch to ward off a pogrom.[60] Most important, however, was the constant interchange of official epistles and the constant stream of religious inquiries from the diaspora to Palestine. From Zion the Torah went forth in the form of books, teachers, and exchanges of letters. If children are any indication of what their parents considered important, perhaps the following story will illustrate the point: When R. Akiba and several of his colleagues came to Rome on an official mission, they recognized the Jewish section by children playing mud-pies and saying: "This one is *terumah*; this one is tithe. This is what the people of the land of Israel do."[61]

The diaspora, as is by now well appreciated, was of crucial importance to the survival of Judaism, for the fate of the people was not determined by the fate of any one community. The destruction of the Temple, the defeat of Bar Kokhba, the continual impoverishment of the land were severe blows, but they were cushioned by the presence of organized Jewish communities elsewhere. Babylonia, for example, rose within Talmudic times to religious hegemony over a considerable portion of the Jewish world, and scholar and layman alike could find political, economic, and religious refuge where conditions were better.

Of equal importance is the second aspect of the diaspora. The latter, even when voluntary, was considered an exile. During the centuries when the diaspora flourished alongside the Jewish community of Palestine it not only learned to adjust to Jewish living beyond the borders of Palestine, but also to maintain the notion of exile. That is to say, by the time Palestine ceased to be the central Jewish community, its centrality had been so impressed upon the Jewish mind that it could not be uprooted. In this sense, the diaspora was the Jewish training ground for religious life after the destruction of the Temple. Long before the year 70 when the Temple went up in flames, the Jews of the diaspora had learned to live their religious life away from the center in Jerusalem without sacrifices and without priesthood. The genius of Pharisaism was in that it had divorced religion from a particular ethnic group and any particular land. The synagogue and the house of study became the local sanctuary to Jews everywhere. But the other side of the coin must not be overlooked. Though the Jews and Judaism were now a part of world civilization at large, they were forever mere outposts of the homeland. That the Jews remained an ethnic group with strong historical ties to the Holy Land down until modern times was owing to the legacy of the idea of *galut* which they had inherited from Temple days. It was the diaspora by its very definition as exile which saved the Holy Land as a living force in Jewish religion. For diaspora implied transiency, a temporary state which would be set aright only by the fulfillment of the messianic promise of return.

From the point of view of later Jewish development, the diaspora and the destruction of the Temple were two of the most crucial phenomena in all of Jewish history. The destruction forced the Jew to live without a Temple, without a government, indeed, even without a land. The diaspora had taught him how to do it.

VII

The destruction of the Temple by the Roman army was a religious catastrophe. Quite apart from its symbolic place as the last stronghold of Jerusalem, as the flag and rallying point of Jewish resistance, its ritual was one of the three pillars of the Jewish universe.[62] "Woe unto us!" cried R. Joshua upon seeing the Temple in ruins, "that this, the place where the iniquities of Israel were atoned for, is laid waste!" The people truly believed that "so long as the Temple service is maintained, the world is a blessing to its inhabitants and the rains come down in season. . . . But when the Temple is not maintained the world is not a blessing to its inhabitants and the rains do not come down in season."[63] Gone with one sweep were the daily sacrifices of morning and evening, the sin offerings, the ritual of the Day of Atonement, and the festival pilgrimages. The footstool of God had been removed and the gates of prayer sealed.[64]

To the simple Jew the first and most natural impulse after the war was over was to withdraw from society and lead an ascetic life of mourning until God should see fit to restore the Jewish people and rebuild the Temple. Until that time man must abstain from all normal pleasures and sit wrapped in sackcloth, covered with ashes, mourning the terrible loss. An incident in Rabbinic literature reflects this sentiment and how the Rabbis reacted to is:

> When the Temple was destroyed, large numbers in Israel became ascetics, binding themselves neither to eat meat nor to drink wine. R. Joshua got into conversation with them and said to them: "My sons, why do you not eat meat?" They replied: "Shall we eat flesh, which used to be brought daily as an offering on the altar now that this altar is in abeyance?. . . Shall we drink wine which used to be poured as a libation on the altar, but now no longer?" He said to them: "If that is so, we should not eat figs or grapes either, because there is no longer an offering of first fruits . . . we should not drink water, because there is no longer any ceremony of the pouring of water." To this they could find no answer; so he said to them: "Not to mourn at all is impossible, because the blow has fallen. To mourn overmuch is also impossible. The Sages, therefore, have ordained thus: A man may stucco his house, but he should leave a little bare in memory of Jerusalem. A man may prepare a full-course banquet, but he should leave out an item or two in memory of

Jerusalem. . . . For so it is said: 'If I forget thee, Oh Jerusalem, let my right hand forget, let my tongue cleave to the roof of my mouth if I remember thee not, if I prefer not Jerusalem above my chief joy (Ps. 137:5–6).'"[65]

Even if, as one modern scholar has suggested,[66] these ascetics were predominantly of the priestly classes or their sympathizers, the problem these Jews faced can be viewed as something of a popular quandary. Not to withdraw from the world in mourning was tantamount to going about one's business in the face of calamity, or filial impiety. Nay, more, it was to give up the hope for traditional Judaism, for the Temple-centered religion of the fathers. On the other hand, to mourn forever, the Rabbis knew clearly, would put an end to Judaism as a vital force. Time, in fact, might heal the wound all too well; the Temple would soon be forgotten, and the Torah might slowly die a natural death. Somehow the Temple would have to be kept alive without paralyzing religious life.

To do this the Rabbis fixed institutions which they called *Zekher le-Hurban*, ceremonials in memory of the destruction. These were simple acts adapted to commemorate the calamity, but also to keep alive the spark of hope that the Temple would soon be rebuilt. The Rabbis advocated a middle course that was geared to overcome the pain of the destruction through channelled expression and, at the same time, to avert the natural adjustment to a world devoid of Temple ritual and priestly sacrament. Indeed, R. Joshua's prescriptions prevail in traditional Jewish circles to this day. The nine days preceding the ninth of Ab, the day of the destruction, were adopted as a prolonged period of mourning culminating in the fast of the ninth of Ab. This, the darkest day of the Jewish year, was ordained as a solemn fast during which the people sat on the earth lamenting the past and pleading for the future.

The Rabbinic instruments to keep the expectation for the Temple alive and the orientation they advocated were eminently successful. Proof of this can be induced from ritual practices of the common people in the post-destruction period. As is well known, the laws of levitical purity were largely connected with the Temple. He who wished to enter the Temple precincts could do so only in a state of levitical cleanness. The scrupulous observance of the laws of purity within Palestine for centuries after the destruction can be explained only on the grounds that the Jews expected the Temple to be rebuilt any day.[67] Further, for two hundred years after the destruction of the Temple, Jews in Palestine preserved and used the ashes of the red heifer to purify those who had been contaminated by contact with the dead,[68] thus testifying to the hope that the priestly rituals of the Temple would soon be restored. It was not idle scribbling on the part of Rabbi Ishmael who, after committing an inadvertent infraction of the Sabbath, made a note of the incident and added: "When the Temple will be rebuilt I shall bring a fat sin offering."[69] God's everlasting covenant assured the Jews that the Land would be restored to its full measure and that the people would once again worship on His sacred mount. In the light of this assurance the Rabbis of the second century discussed and codified those areas of Jewish law which history had made obsolescent. Not only the minutiae of the Temple rituals and architecture were recorded, but the extent of administrative authorities of the high priest, the king, and the Sanhedrin as well. All of them would be renewed in due course, and the people were kept in readiness.

Out of this inseverable attachment to the Temple and its ritual, Judaism was caught in an irresolvable tension between the norms of the past and the demands of religious reality. This is nowhere better illustrated than in the obligations for daily worship.[70] In the course of centuries, there emerged in Judaism a highly individualized form of devotion, in accordance with which each Jew was obliged to pray for himself. In principle, the pattern of prayer in Judaism would appear to be the very antinomy of sacrifice, which cannot be offered without fixed forms and the intermediacy of a priestly caste. But the principle could not be entertained in its pure form. While on the one hand the Rabbis encouraged free and original expression in prayer, they tended increasingly to fix the order and phraseology of the service. There were many historical situations which, from the point of view of the Rabbis, necessitated fixity and uniformity in the service; but underlying them may well be the hankering after a form of worship modelled after the precision of the Temple ritual. Indeed, the prayers were said to be but surrogates for the sacrifices in Jerusalem. Accordingly, the most lyrical of Jewish liturgy—bespeaking in practice liberation from Temple altar and priestly mediation—is simultaneously replete with prayers of supplication for speedy return to Zion and the Temple service. A Jew might pray wherever he happened to be situated, but he was obliged to face in the direction of the Temple.[71]

VIII

On the day that the Temple was destroyed, a popular belief stated, the Messiah was born.[72] Playing on the last verse in Lamentations, and doubtless with an eye at Christians who taunted them that the destruction was clear evidence of the divine rejection of Israel, the Rabbis assured their flocks that divine wrath did not spell rejection.[73] Accordingly just as the people refused to recognize the subjection of Palestine by Gentile rulers, so they refused to accept the finality of the destruction of the Temple. In 114 C.E., scarcely 44 years after the destruction of the Temple, violent pogroms broke out in Egypt and North Africa over the failure of Trajan to authorize the rebuilding of the Temple. Twenty years later, in 133, the masses of Jews of Palestine rose under Bar Kokhba in a desperate effort to restore Jewish independence and the Temple service. On some of the coins which the insurgents minted there is a legend indicating that a priest, Eleazar Hakkohen, was appointed, perhaps as co-chairman of the ruling body of the Jews. After the collapse of the revolt, Jerusalem was closed to the Jews by imperial decree, but Jerome has left us a pathetic description of Jews tearfully bribing the Roman guards to permit them to enter the Holy Land on the ninth of Ab and pray for a few moments at the Temple site.[74] Finally, as late as the fourth century Jews were still appealing to the Emperor Julian to restore Jerusalem as their holy city and to permit the rebuilding of the Temple.

The messianic ideal of return and restoration, born in times of Scripture, now acquired new significance. Every Jew, even the one who dwelt in the Holy Land, now felt himself to be an exile. Three times daily all Jews could now pray with added fervor: "Sound the great shofar for our freedom; raise the standard for the gathering of our exiles, and assemble us from the four corners of the earth. . . . Restore our judges as of old. . . . And to Jerusalem thy city return in mercy and dwell therein as thou hast spoken; rebuild it soon in our days as an everlasting building, and speedily set up therein the throne of David."[75] No grace after meals, no festivity or service was complete without a prayer for the ingathering of the exiles and for the restoration of Zion; "that the priests be restored to their service, the Levites to their song and music, and the people of Israel to their homes."[76]

These prayers were fortified with the assurances of the prophets that God would restore his dispersed seed to their Land; that the dry bones of the nation would yet don flesh once again. The messianic fancy foretold that the borders of the Holy Land would be expanded, far beyond the territory possessed at the height of the Biblical kingdom, to include the ideal borders of the Torah and more.[77] Above all, the Messiah of Israel would be the Messiah for the whole earth ushering in the days foretold by Isaiah and Micah.[78]

Out of this firm faith in the messianic return, a new Jewish hero type was born: Elijah the prophet. Elijah, the Bible tells us, did not die, but was translated to the heavens.[79] Subsequently, the prophet Malachi proclaimed: "Behold I will send you Elijah the prophet before the coming of the great and terrible day of the Lord. And he shall turn the heart of the fathers to the children, and the heart of the children to their fathers."[80] Thus, the Bible assured that Elijah would herald the great day, the day of the Messiah, and that he would also proclaim the new era of peace and harmony on earth. No wonder then if in Rabbinic lore, Elijah became transformed from the fanatical zealot we know from the Bible into the kindly old man known in Jewish folklore—miracle worker and comforter of Israel. He is the symbol of Jewish suffering and Jewish hope; he is the awaited houseguest at every circumcision and at every Passover service. In ancient synagogues, a seat was reserved for him near the ark. Along with the Messiah himself, Elijah becomes the Jewish alter-ego, the symbol for the whole people: exiled and tortured, but alive and hopeful.[81]

At times, the reality of events could try this Jewish faith just a bit too much, and even the staunchest of spirits found himself on the brink of despair.[82] It was the genius of the people that such moments were quickly checked. There is pathetic humor, but also profound faith, reflected in the following incident: "Once when R. Gamliel, R. Joshua, R. Eleazer b. Azaria, and R. Akiba were entering Rome, they heard the din of the city in Puteoli 120 miles away [from Rome]. They began to weep, but R. Akiba broke out into a chuckle. They turned to him: 'Akiba, what makes you so happy when we weep?' He replied: 'What indeed are you crying about?' To this they replied: 'Should we not weep? These Gentiles who worship idols, sacrifice to them, and bow down to images live in security, peace and ease, while the footstool of our God has been consumed by fire and has become a lair for wild beasts!' To this he replied: 'That is just what has made me so jovial. If they that offend God are doing this well, how much better shall fare those that obey Him!' . . . They said to him: 'Akiba, you have consoled us!'"[83] The power of this consolation lay in the fact that the reality of God's promise was infinitely more certain and secure than the ostensible facts of the world with which the Jews came into contact.

The very same R. Akiba is credited with the form of a benediction in the Seder service for Passover that is recited to this day. By means of this statement, the redemption from Egypt became a symbol for the Jewish hope of the future. It summarized not only centuries of hope and patience, but a whole body of Rabbinic law and theology. It illustrated in a word the heart of the Jewish purpose through its centuries of exile. "Blessed art thou, O Lord, our God, king of the universe, who redeemed us and who redeemed our fathers from Egypt, and has brought us to this night to eat thereon unleavened bread and bitter herbs.[84] So, O Lord our God and God of our fathers, bring us to other festivals and holy days that come toward us, in peace, happy in the building of thy city, and joyous in thy (Temple) service. And there may we eat of the paschal offerings and the sacrifices whose blood will come unto the walls of thy altar for acceptance. Then shall we give thanks to thee with a new song for our deliverance and for our redemption. Blessed art Thou, O Lord, the Redeemer of Israel."[85]

NOTES

1. *Wayyikra Rabbah* 13:2 (ed. Mordecai Margulies, pp. 272f.).
2. Ex. 3:8, etc.

3. Dt. 12:9.

4. Josh. 22:19.

5. For references to these and similar terms, cf. J. M. Gutmann, *'Eres Yizrael ba-Midrash u-ba-Talmud* in *Festschrift zum 75 jaehrigen Bestchen des Juedisch-Theologischen Seminars Fraencklscher Stiftung* (2 vols. Breslau, 1929), I, Hebrew section pp. 9f.

6. *Berakot* 36 b.

7. *Tanhuma Qedoshim*, 10.

8. Note the opening formulae in Lev. 19:23; 23:10, 22; 25:2; Dt. 26:1. Rabbinic law extended the applicability of some of these to all countries; cf. *M. Qiddushin* 1:9 and *Talmudim ad loc.*

9. Num 35:9f.; Dt. 4:41f.; 19:1f. Cf. also the law of the expiatory heifer, Dt. 21:1f.

10. *M. Qiddushin* 1:9.

11. *Kelim* 1:6–9.

12. Lev. 23:10f.

13. Dt. 26:2f.

14. Lev. 23:17.

15. E.g., Thanksgiving offerings, peace offerings, the Paschal lamb; cf. *M. Zebahim* 5:6–8.

16. Cf. Dt. 14:22f. and *M. Ma'aser Sheni.*

17. *Sanhedrin* 13b; 11b. An effort to regulate the calendar from abroad following the chaotic state caused by the bar Kokhba revolt was vigorously suppressed; *Berakot* 63a–b.

18. E.g., moral law, sexual law, Sabbath law, *tefillin*, circumcision, dietary laws, etc.

19. Dt. 3:23–28.

20. *Sota* 14a.

21. *Mekhilta de R. Ishmael*, Pisha I, (ed. Horovitz-Rabin, pp. 2–3); *Mo'ed Qatan* 25a.

22. Cf. Louis Ginzberg, *The Legends of the Jews* (7 vols. Philadelphia, 1909–1938), V, 362 n. 345.

23. For a full treatment of this incident, see Gedaliahu Alon, *Studies in Jewish History* (Hebrew) I (Tel-Aviv, 1957), 320–328.

24. For a full treatment of this question, see Gedaliahu Alon, *op. cit.*, pp. 15–47, 219–273. I am much indebted to the insights of these brilliant papers, where the sources are listed and analyzed.

25. These are discussed principally in the third order (*Neziqin*) of the Mishna, Tosefta, and Talmudim.

26. On the limits of Palestine in Biblical sources, see Yehezkel Kaufmann, *Toledot ha-'Emunah ha-Yisraelit* (Tel-Aviv, 1937 et seq.), I, 190f.

27. Cf. *M. Shebi'ith* 6:1, 9:2; *M. Baba Bathra* 3:2; *Tosef. Ketubot* 13 (12):2 (ed. Zuckermandel, p. 275); *Tosef. Sanhedrin* 2:3 (p. 416).

28. *M. Shebi'ith* 6:1.

29. The Samaritan "strip" between Judea and Galilee was considered foreign and, hence, levitically unclean; cf. *Hagiga* 25a.

30. Cf. Josh. 22:19.

31. *Shabbat* 14b.

32. Louis Ginzberg, *On Jewish Law and Lore* (Philadelphia, 1955), pp. 79ff.

33. *Ketubot* 110b; the variant traditions in *Tosef. Ketubot* 13 (12): 2 (p. 275) and *Yer. Ketubot* 13:11, f. 36b do not contradict the essential point. It should be noted that the Babylonian Talmud, *loc. cit.*, and *'Arakhin* 3b, preserves a tradition granting even slaves certain preferential rights in such instances! (The commentators differ on the type of slave and rights referred to.)

34. *Baba Qama* 80b.

35. *'Aboda Zara* 20a (top.)

36. *M. Gittin* 4:6.

37. *Gittin* 45a.

38. Cf. Ruth 1:1–5.

39. *Baba Bathra* 91a.

40. *Sanhedrin* 102b.

41. Cf. the incidents related in *Sifre Deut.* #80 (ed. Louis Finkelstein, p. 146) and *Qiddushin* 31b.

42. *Ketubot* 110b–111a.; '*Aboda Zara* 82 (bot.); *Bereshit Rabba* 46:9 (ed. Theodor-Albeck, p. 466).

43. Cf., *Ketubot* 110b–111a.

44. *M. Nedarim* 3:4; see further, Prof. Ginzberg's essay, referred to in n. 32, pp. 86f.

45. Cf. J. Gutman, "R. Elazar b. R. Shimon in the Roman Government Service of Palestine" (Hebrew), *Zion* XVIII (1953), 1–5.

46. *Nedarim* 28a.

47. Cf. *Yer. Baba Qama* 4:3, 4b; *M. Gittin* 5:8,9.

48. On the attitude of the Jews to the Roman forces in Palestine, see Saul Lieberman, "Jewish Life in *Eretz Yisrael* as Reflected in the Palestinian Talmud," *Israel: Its Role in Civilization* (Edited by Moshe Davis, New York, 1956), pp. 82–91.

49. For a full discussion of the following passages and related texts, see V. Aptowitzer, "Les premiers possesseurs de Canaan," *Revue des Etudes Juives* LXXXII (1926 as well as *Mélanges Offerts à M. Israel Levi*, etc.), 275–286.

50. Scolion to *Megillat Ta'anit*, 25th of Sivan (ed. Hans Lichtenstein, "Die Fastenrolle," *Hebrew Union College Annual*, VIII–IX [1931–1932]), 328f.

51. *Midrash Aggada* (ed. Buber), I, 29.

52. For the translation, which I have changed somewhat, cf. *Pentateuch with Tarqum Onkelos, Haphtaroth . . . and Rashi's Commentary* translated by M. Rosenbaum and A. N. Silbermann, et al. (London, Shapiro Valentine & Co., 1946) 1, 2. For Rashi's source, cf. *Tanhuma* (ed. S. Buber), I, 7 par. 11. On the thought expressed in this Midrash, cf. *Bereshit Rabbah* 1:2 (p. 4 and sources cited there).

53. On the Jewish population during the Talmudic period, cf. Salo W. Baron, *A Social and Religious History of the Jews*, 2 ed., I, 167–171.

54. On Jewish religious privileges in the Roman empire, see Jean Juster, *Les Juifs dans l'Empire Romain* (2 vols. Paris, 1914), I, 354f.

55. Josephus, *Antiquities*, XIII, 13, 2.

56. On this case, in which Cicero served as consul for the offending Flaccus, see Hans Lewy, "Cicero on the Jews in His Speech for the Defense of Flaccus" (Hebrew) *Zion*, VII (1941–42), 109–134.

57. Josephus, *Antiquities*, XIV, 6, 1.

58. *Tosef. Sanhedrin* 2:6 (p. 416); *Midrash Tannaim* (ed. D. Hoffmann), p. 176. Note also the two festal letters preserved in II Macc. 1:1–2:18.

59. Cf. J. Juster, *op. cit*, I, 357.

60. Cf. Gedaliahu Alon, *Toledot ha-Yehudim be-'Eres Yisrael bi-Tequfat ha-Mishna we-ha-Talmud* (2 vols. Tel-Aviv, 1952–1955), I, 225.

61. *Yer. Sanhedrin* 7:19, f. 25d.

62. *Abot* 1:2.

63. *Abot de R. Nathan*, I, 4 (cd. S. Schechter, pp. 19, 21); I owe the translation of these two quotations to Judah Goldin, *The Fathers According to Rabbi Nathan* (Yale Judaica Series, X; New Haven, 1955), pp. 33, 34.

64. For these metaphors, cf. below, n. 83 and *Berakot* 32b.

65. *Tosef. Sota* 15:11 (p. 322); *Baba Bathra* 60b.

66. Adolf Buechler, *Die Priester und der Cultus in Letzten Jahrzehnt des Jerusalemischen Tempels* (Vienna, 1895), p. 22. On the other hand, this ascetic movement persisted right down to the Middle Ages; cf. *Encyclopaedia Hebraica*, I, 167 s.v. "'Abele Siyyon."

67. See the illuminating incident in *Sanhedrin* 5b, and cf. G. Alon, *Toledot*, etc., I, 162f.

68. Cf. G. Alon, *Studies in Jewish History*, I, 326.

69. *Tosef. Shabbat* 1:13 (p. 110).

70. For a penetrating treatment of this subject, see Shalom Spiegel, "On Medieval Hebrew Poetry," *The Jews: Their History Culture and Religion* (ed. Louis Finkelstein, 2 vols. New York, 1949), I, 528ff.

71. *Tosef. Berakot* 3:15–16 (ed. Saul Lieberman, pp. 15–16).

72. Cf. Louis Ginzberg, *Legends of the Jews*, VI, 406 n. 53.

73. *Midrash 'Ekah* (ed. Buber), pp. 59, 161. On the Christian doctrine of rejection of the Jews, cf. A. Lukyn Williams, *Adversus Judaeos* (Cambridge U., 1935).

74. Cited by Emil Schuerer, *Geschichte des Juedischen Volkes im Zeitalter Jesu Christi*, I (1901), 703–704.

75. Benedictions from the daily *Amidah*; cf. S. Baer, *Seder ʿAbodat Israel* (Roedelheim, 1868), pp. 92f; for the early forms of these blessings, see Louis Finkelstein, "The Development of the Amidah," *Jewish Quarterly Review*, New Series, XVI (1925–26), 11f., 154f.

76. From the additional *Amidah* for festivals; cf. S. Baer, *op. cit.*, p. 355.

77. Cf. *Bereshit Rabba* 44:23 (pp. 445f.).

78. Is. 2:1–4; 11:1f.; Micah 4:1–5.

79. II Ki. 2:1–11.

80. Mal. 3:23–24.

81. On Elijah in Rabbinic literature, see M. Friedman, *Seder Eliahu Rabba und Seder Eliahu Zuta* (Vienna, 1902), Hebrew Introduction, pp. 1–44.

82. Note the extremely pessimistic statement of R. Simeon b. Gamliel in *Tosef. Sota* 15:10 (p. 322).

83. *Sifre Deut* # 43 (p. 94).

84. The first sentence of this benediction is ascribed in the Mishna to R. Tarfon.

85. *M. Pesahim* 10:6; on the wording of this blessing, see M. Kasher, *Haggada Shelema* (Jerusalem, 1955), pp. 129, 142f., Text pp. 67, 69. For the translation I have drawn on Nahum N. Glatzer, ed., *The Passover Haggadah* (New York, 1953), pp. 53f.

Hannah and Her Seven Sons in Hebrew Literature

It was neither the familial nor the intellectual attainments of Hannah and her seven sons that gained them renown in popular folklore; rather it was their ingenuous piety and their anonymity. Even in ancient times chroniclers were shaken to the foundations at the "sight" of a mother and her seven sons willingly sacrificing themselves for the public sanctification of the name of God. There were some who saw them as the symbol of the wisdom that triumphs over every kind of suffering and physical pain (as in IV Maccabees). But even more, the memory of this family was held aloft as a symbol of martyrdom for the greater glory of God. In accordance with the words of R. Judah: "It is for Your sake that we are slain all day long, that we are regarded as sheep to be slaughtered [Ps. 44:23]. . . . This refers to a woman and her seven sons."[1] Well over one thousand years after that simple incident, sincere Jews were still pouring out their souls in a similar fashion: "It is over Hannah that my heart is torn. I clothe myself in a sack because of the evil day that she had to face. She was as a candelabrum of seven lamps. I mourn her on the day on which they were seized. As for myself, my spirit falls weeping because of those who fell with the poor woman. They were merciful people who were loyal to the Lord. Because of this I weep and tear my heart."[2] Indeed, it was not the past alone that people saw in the story, but a bitter never-ending present.

The earliest source for the story of Hannah and her seven sons, that in II Maccabees (7:1ff.), is an account of events that took place in the land of Israel during the days of the persecution of Antiochus IV Epiphanes. So quickly, however, did the Christians appropriate Jewish Hellenistic literature, including II Maccabees, that the Jews first learned of Hannah and her seven sons through secondary and tertiary sources, namely, the Talmud, the Midrash, and the Book of Josippon. In addition, during the long process in which Hebrew literature reclaimed this story for itself, a variety of changes were made in the text, each one of which merits attention. Nevertheless, in contrast to the usual practice of historians, we will not concern ourselves in this survey with the oldest extant version of the story except for purposes of comparison; for like the author of the elegy quoted above, and like all those who recited it in premodern times, we are not concerned with the events themselves, but with the literary forms into which these events were cast and with the elaboration of these in sources which continued to live in the hearts of the Jewish people and which resonate even today.

I

According to the events related in II Maccabees, the story of the mother and her seven sons should be dated to the year 167–66 B.C.E., which was the year in which the offensive of Antiochus and his forces against the land of Israel took place. Nevertheless, all the sources in classical rabbinic literature[3] agree that Hannah and her seven sons were seized and executed at the time of the Hadrianic persecutions, known in Hebrew as the *Shemad*. All these rabbinic sources proclaim that the woman and her seven sons were seized by a Roman Caesar; indeed, in Seder Eliahu this person is identified by name: " . . . and the sages say the psalm of Asaf [Ps. 79:1] refers to the fact that Hadrian Caesar came and seized a widow (whose name is Miriam, the daughter of Tanhum) and her seven sons."[4] In medieval times, when the Book of Josippon was still considered a historical document and a reliable witness to the events of the days of the Second Temple, people were cognizant of the Greek date of the story and believed the story as reported in the Talmud and Midrash to be a different event. R. Behayye ben Asher was of the opinion, apparently, that the story cited in the midrashic literature occurred at the time of the destruction of the Temple,[5] but that a second tradition connected the story of the martyrdom of the seven sons with the events surrounding the Ten Martyrs[6] in the time of Hadrian.

Later rabbinic commentators[7] and scholars[8] recognized that the two versions of the story, namely the one in II Maccabees and the one in rabbinic literature, were basically one and the same, except that within the rabbinic tradition the chronological framework of the story had been totally lost and the events ascribed to a date some 300 years later. Most recently, Dr. Joshua Guttman compared the various versions of the story, that is, the ones in II and IV Maccabees and those in the rabbinic literature, and established that the rabbinic version had not merely suffered chronological distortion, but had also been altered in terms of its form and ideology. In the view of Guttman, "The differences in the description of martyrdom (literally, the sanctification of the name of God) in the various sources alert us to changes in the understanding of this basic concept [i.e. martyrdom] in the mind-set prevailing in different circles of the nation." According to Guttman, the purpose of the story in rabbinic sources was "to express the feeling of contempt and disdain that existed in the heart of the author toward paganism, which to him appears to be nothing but the worship of sticks and stones." Guttman finds an excellent example of this attitude in the fact that in the rabbinic version of the story the greatest contempt for idolatry and paganism is put into the mouth of the youngest son; although since the rabbis did not want to attribute to the youngster any desire to argue with his torturers, he responds, like his siblings, only with verses from Scripture. "In II and IV Maccabees," Guttman continues, "the description of the tortures undergone by Eleazar the Elder[9] and by every one of the brothers occupies a major place in the stories. The aim of the writers of these stories was to emphasize the significance of the proud and free posture of the brothers . . . who gave up their lives for their faith in a state of purity and loyalty. . . . In the aggadic sources there is little mention of tortures . . . for to the aggadists it is obvious that when a Jew is compelled to worship an idol he relinquishes his life willingly and does not submit. . . . In II and IV Maccabees the effect of the proud stance of the brothers, at the time of their torture, upon the king and the members of his entourage are mentioned quite frequently. . . . However, in the aggadic sources there is no mention whatsoever of gentiles, whether as part of the king's entourage or as part of the pagan world generally. There is even no mention of the fact that the torturers will be punished. . . . Since it is obvious that the wicked king will be punished . . . there is no need to mention it in any particular way."[10]

These examples should suffice to reflect the penetrating analysis of Guttman,[11] who examined the details of these stories with great thoroughness in order to derive from them the general ideological mind-set reflected in each tradition. Indeed, Guttman was right in his conclusion that "for the aggadic authorities of rabbinic literature, the historical circumstances that had led to martyrdom in the days of the Maccabean period no longer existed, and in their stead were to be found circumstances that derived from the realities of life in the Roman empire in the days of emperor worship. It is in the light of these differing circumstances that the changes in the details of the various versions of the stories must be understood."

However, if we must concede the justice of Guttman's approach to the story, we must take exception to the conclusions he bases on the details of the rabbinic versions. We are certainly not in a position to accept his conclusion that the changes in the aggadic versions offer proof of "changes in the understanding of this basic question [i.e. martyrdom] . . .

in different circles of the nation." Indeed, we are not able to see, as he does, that these changes derive from the pen of the "author" of the rabbinic versions. This perception of the story diverts our attention from the literary type that served as model for this incident; for only by means of a comparison of two examples of the same literary type can we evaluate both the details and the generalities involved here. As we see it, the details of the rabbinic versions must be compared not only with the traditions in II and IV Maccabees but also with the stories of its own period. The comparison of the versions of the rabbinic legend with the versions in the Books of the Maccabees will reflect only a change in the historical background, but the evaluation of the rabbinic background itself can result only from a detailed comparison of the rabbinic story with other stories of the Roman period.

Whoever wishes to compare the traditions and ideas reflected in the pseudepigraphic versions with those found in the rabbinic literature must take into account the fact that II Maccabees (and it goes without saying that this is true also of IV Maccabees) is a product of the literary reworking of the version of Jason of Cyrene, and of the abridgement of that work from which we have inherited the version that is before us.[12] In contrast to this Jasonean version, which appears before us as a thoroughly worked tale, the sources of the rabbinic aggada report the story only as "an incident" from the days of the Hadrianic persecution, and report it without any literary polishing or ideological embellishment.

The story of the mother and her seven sons in the rabbinic aggada purports to tell us of an event that occurred in the days of the persecutions of the second century.[13] But this period and the centuries that followed have also bequeathed to us an enormous Christian martyrological literature that is suffused with both legendary material and historical detail; and it is enough to point to the great researches of Professor Saul Lieberman in the rabbinic literature of this period[14] to demonstrate how much of it can be illuminated by the Christian material. The rabbinic story of the mother and her seven sons is, indeed, a remnant of the Jewish martyrology of the rabbinic period, and it appears to us, accordingly, that it, too, must be interpreted in the light of the period from which it derives. Moreover, it is incumbent upon us to emphasize the importance of the study of the *details* of the story; for as Guttman pointed out, it is only by means of the interpretation of these details that we can evaluate the rabbinic point of view.

II

Our analysis of the rabbinic story of the mother and her seven sons is based in the first instance on the fullest version of that story, which is the

one included in the Franco-German Midrash on Lamentations and in
Seder Eliahu and which transmits in full the details that characterize all
the other versions of this story in the rabbinic aggadic literature.

In the version of Seder Eliahu the story begins with a description of
the seizure of the woman and her sons and of their being brought to trial:
"Hadrian Caesar came and seized a widow (whose name was Miriam bat
Tanhum) along with her seven sons. He said to her: 'What is your status?'
She said: 'I am a widow.' 'Why are these youngsters with you?' She said:
'They are my children.' He then imprisoned each of them separately."
These brief remarks characterize the framework of the story as a whole.
It was customary in Roman trials to begin by ascertaining the name of the
person on trial and his station in society. (This is the meaning of the question, "What is your status?") These questions were posed even when the
facts were well known to the judge. Roman legal procedure demanded
scrupulous adherence to legal detail, and the identification of the person
to be tried was one of the formal aspects of the trial.[15]

On one point, however, the rabbinic versions disagree with each
other. The Franco-German version[16] of the Midrash on Lamentations, as
well as the version in the Seder Eliahu, describes the progress of the trial
on the basis of the assumption that Caesar imprisoned the brothers individually so that none would know what was being done to his companions, an action which coincides with Christian testimonies about the
trials of a number of Christian saints.[17] In the Books of the Maccabees,
however, it is reported that the mother and the brothers stood to the side
and watched the trial, the tortures, and the execution of the verdict in
the case of each and every brother.[18]

Thus in the Franco-German version we read that Caesar "brought the
first of the brothers and said to him: 'Bow down to the idol just as your
brother did,'" and that he behaved in the same way with each of the remaining sons. That is, the order to submit to the worship of the Caesar is
presented in the form of a ruse which gives the impression that the other
brothers (who, it is implied, preceded the one at hand) had already
obeyed this order.[19] In the Books of the Maccabees, as we have noted,
there is no hint whatever of such an attempt at trickery, for the Greeks
sought not only formal compliance on the part of the brothers, but complete submission to the Hellenistic cult. The Roman judges, on the other
hand, only demanded formal submission—that is, a formal acceptance of
the authority of the Caesar and the Roman empire—and they used all
the means available to them to elicit from the mouths of those standing at
judgment a formal denial of their own gods and a formal acceptance of
the supremacy of the gods of Rome. (As we shall see, the use of trickery
has many parallels in the martyrological documents of that age.)

The Sephardic version of the Midrash on Lamentations does not state
that Caesar separated the brothers, either. Moreover, from the words of

the judge it is apparent that each of the brothers knows full well what happened to those who preceded him. We see this in the words of the Caesar to the seventh son: "My son, bow down to the idol, for . . . your brothers had fullness of life and length of years and enjoyed the benefits of this world. However, you are a youngster who has not had years or fullness of life, nor have you ever really enjoyed the opportunities of this world. Bow down to the idol, and I will treat you well." (Even with regard to this issue of "mercy" we find parallels in the Christian literature, where it is reported that judges would plead with the accused to take pity on his own beauty and youth which have "not yet enjoyed the benefits of this world.")[20]

However, what defines the world of the version in the Seder Eliahu is the language of the opening statement which tells us that when Miriam and her sons were taken into captivity, "Caesar took them and placed them within seven *cells*," for here we have the use of a technical Roman juridical term, קרקשן, that clearly reveals the milieu from which the material before us derives.[21] Thus we see that in order to understand the passage before us, we must study it in the light of the non-Jewish and martyrological literature of the period. Consequently we shall not stray far from the truth if we also attempt to evaluate the other details of the story in the light of the parallels to the non-Jewish martyrological literature.

With regard to the basic structure of the story, all of the rabbinic versions are virtually identical: "It happened with Miriam, the daughter of Tanhum, who was taken into captivity along with her seven sons. Caesar took them . . . took the first and said: 'Bow down to the idol,' and the child responded: 'Heaven forbid. I will not bow down to the idol.' He said to him: 'Why not?' He said: 'Because it says in our Torah, "I am the Lord your God."' He immediately removed him and put him to death. He took the second brother and said to him: 'Bow down to the idol,' and the brother said: 'Heaven forbid. My brother did not bow down and I shall not do so.' He said: 'Why not?' He said: 'Because the Torah says: "You shall have no other gods before Me."' At once he decreed death against him and killed him."[22] And so it goes with the next four. In the case of the seventh brother, however, "who was the youngest of them all," the story approaches its climax, for the mercy of the Caesar was aroused on behalf of the youngster, and he suggests a stratagem to the child in order to be able to pass favorable judgment on him. "He said: 'My son, bow down to the idol.' He said to him: 'Heaven forbid.' . . . Caesar said to him, 'Look here, you see that your brothers lie before you executed, and I am going to drop my ring on the ground in front of the idol. Lift it up so that everyone will know that you obeyed me.'" With this command the trial ceases to be a religious one and becomes, in the view of the judge, a matter of civil authority.[23] Although, as we have noted, this kind of tactic is completely lacking in the story as told in the Books of the Maccabees, it has a famous parallel from the Roman period in the reports of the trial of "Lullianus and his brother Pappus, before whom they put water in drinking goblets of colored glass, but they [Lullianus and Pappas] refused to accept it."[24] Just as we read how these two were asked to drink water that *appeared* to be wine,[25] so too we learn about other kinds of tricks employed by Roman judges from the Christian martyrological literature. Some prisoners were asked to offer up incense, even to their Christian god, just so that the bystanders would see them offering up incense![26] "Do not write that you deny your redeemer; write as you choose. But let the people in the audience see that you are writing!"[27] The story of the ring is thus an artistic expression of an experience that was common in second century Roman trials, and it is a logical continuation of the device which is found in two of the sources and to which we referred above (for example, "Bow down to the idol as your brothers did").

It goes without saying that the Romans were not the sole heirs of trickery and deceit. Even of the servants of Antiochus it is told that they begged the aged Eleazar, the priest, to take pity on his life and to show his submission to the authority of the king by eating *kosher* meat, just so the bystanders would be under the impression that he had fulfilled the wishes of the king and had eaten forbidden meat.[28] Still, unlike its minor place in the Books of Maccabees (even in the trial of Eleazar, the priest, the trickery is merely an incidental and unofficial device), trickery occupies a place of great importance in Roman trials and takes its place alongside other parallels between the Jewish and Christian martyrological literature of the Roman rabbinic period, and demonstrates further that it is to this genre of literature that our story should be assigned. In other words, the form of the story was not determined by ideological considerations, but by real situations and real experiences which the rabbinic sages knew first-hand from their own lives.

This same reality will explain the omission of descriptions of torture in the aggadic stories of the rabbis, for again this omission did not result from the tendentious attitudes on the part of the rabbinic transmitters, but rather from the attitude of the Roman empire toward Jews and Christians in the first centuries of the Common Era. Violent death and frightful tortures were decreed against the subjects of Rome in the course of many centuries; however, these tortures were decreed as punishments and not as devices for compelling obedience. As is well known from the correspondence of Pliny with the Emperor Trajan,[29] Roman law considered adherence to Christianity to be a capital crime, and on occasion the punishment for this crime was administered with frightful tortures. Nonetheless, research into the history of Roman law has proven that *in theory* the Romans did not begin to torture Christian captives in order to compel them to religious heresy until the end of the third century.[30] Professor Saul Lieberman has proven that this attitude is reflected even in the capital punishment decreed against Rabbi Haninah ben Taradyon, who was condemned to die by fire and on whose chest wet strings of wool were placed, "so that his soul should not depart from his body quickly." The tortures of R. Haninah were not meant to compel him, but to punish him.[31]

The story of Miriam bat Tanhum and her sons reflects a trial in which the condemned were taken out for execution (apparently by the sword) immediately after judgment was passed against them[32] and hence there is no place for the description of any torture. The rabbis did not, in general, refrain from describing the details of torture, as may be seen in the documents concerning R. Haninah and R. Akiba. Nor would it occur to anyone that these documents reflect an approach to the problem of martyrdom different from those we see in the story of the mother and her sons. In short, we do not find any description of torture in the aggadic story of Miriam because in the second century of the Common Era, that is to say, in the days of the Hadrianic persecutions, martyrs were not put to torture as their predecessors had been in the days of the Maccabees. (And even then torture was decreed only for the leaders of the people, as a warning to those observing the proceedings.) If, on occasion, some judges followed their own desires and did employ severe methods of compulsion,[33] the story of the daughter of Tanhum provides evidence of the more common practice.

We can even catch a glimpse of the historical backgrounds of the various versions of this story in the replies of the brothers to the authorities ranged against them. In the Books of the Maccabees, the sons all deliver short addresses that rationalize their refusal to obey the royal decree and eat meat dedicated to idols, and each at the end of his speech adds that the king himself will be compelled to pay for his wickedness.[34] In the rabbinic aggada, on the other hand, there is no word of explanation or of threat on the part of the sons, except on the part of the youngest of them; every brother stands before Caesar and recites a verse from the Torah that summarizes his reason for refusing to bow down to the idol. The brevity of the style and the method of quoting Scripture do not permit us to arrive at any ideological conclusion, as Guttman does, about the stories in the rabbinic literature. It is certainly impossible to conclude that in the rabbinic legend there is no desire to come to grips with the pagan world—even the authors of II and IV Maccabees did not put any word of polemic with regard to idolatry in the responses of the sons. On the other hand, the rabbis clearly did not refrain from answering the idolaters elsewhere with words of sarcasm and contempt when idolators try to defend their form of worship.[35]

As for the use of Scriptural verses, like the other details of the story

that we have examined, it too is a characteristic mark of the martyrological literature of the Roman period, as both Jewish and Christian
sources testify. When R. Haninah ben Taradyon stood before his judges
and was asked: "Why are you pursuing the Torah?" he replied to them,
"As the Lord my God has commanded me [Deut. 4:5]."[36] And when the
judgment was decreed consigning him and his wife to die and his daughter to sit in a tent of prostitutes, each of them recited a verse from Scripture that justified the judgment against them.[37] In the second century
and later, the fathers of the Christian Church, too, encouraged their disciples to show a strength in the face of the decrees and tortures the
Roman empire forced upon them, and not to engage in any argument
with their judges. It was the obligation of the Christian who was seized
to confess openly that he was a Christian and to respond to questions and
orders by means of verses from the Psalms and the evangelical Book of
Matthew. Cyprian the Christian prepared a small treatise in which he
listed the verses appropriate for quotation at the time of one's arraign-
ment before Roman judges.[38] Eusebius reports that many Christian martyrs walked with joy toward the executioner while quoting the following
two verses from Scripture: "You shall have no other gods beside Me
[Exod. 20:2]" and "Whoever sacrifices to a god other than the Lord alone
shall be proscribed [Exod. 22:19]."[39] It should be noted that in the story
of Miriam bat Tanhum these two verses are recited by two of the sons in
their responses to Caesar! In short, the verses used in the rabbinic
aggada do indeed reflect the attitude of the brothers and of all the Jewish people to idolatry, but no ideological novelty can be derived from this
fact in the rabbinic stories, for the same contempt for idolatry is expressed by the brothers in II and IV Maccabees in very flowery Greek.
This contempt was further emphasized in the rabbinic aggada by putting
into the mouth of the youngest of the brothers the verse, "They have
mouths but cannot speak . . . [Ps. 115:7]." However, the attribution of
this verse to the youngest of the brothers comes only for the sake of the
narrative and for no other purpose.[40] Rabbinic as well as Christian
sources prove that the citation of Scriptural verses was part of the
martyrological rhetoric of that period.

What is most interesting is the fact that the historical background of
the rabbinic stories is revealed not only in the manner in which the
brothers respond to Caesar, but also in the polemical questions the
Caesar addresses to the seventh son: "Is there a God in this world? . . .
Does your God have a mouth? . . . Does your God have eyes? . . . If your
God has all these attributes why doesn't He save you the way He saved
Hananiah, Mishael, and Azariah from Nebuchadnezzar?" The questions
on the part of Caesar and the young man's pointed responses reflect the
vast chasm that divided the Jews from the nations of the world. However,
both the questions and the answers are based on the experiences of the

members of that particular generation. Nowhere do we find Antiochus engaging in religious polemic with the Hasideans of the Holy Land; he did not know Scripture, nor was he interested in Jewish tradition. Caesar, on the other hand, poses his questions in a manner similar to that of the representative of Trajan when he asked Pappus and Lullianus: "if you are indeed of the people of Nananiah, Mishawl, and Azariah, let your God come and rescue you in the same way that He rescued Hananiah, Mishael, and Azariah."[41] The use of this kind of question demonstrates that the sages of the second century were well acquainted with the situation in which Roman judges tried to trick the Jews standing trial by asking them questions derived from the Jewish tradition itself.

An example of the contemptuous and denigrating attitude on the part of the Romans is also found in the story of Miriam bat Tanhum. Upon hearing the judgment pronounced against her youngest son, the mother pleads with Caesar: "By your life, O Caesar, kill me first and kill him next." Caesar responds, "I will not listen to you, for it is written in your own Torah, 'No animal from the herd or from the flock shall be slaughtered on the same day with its young [Lev. 22:28].'" This pseudo-midrash and the questions that were put to the youngest son (and also to Pappus and Lullianus) do not serve merely as literary devices: their true purpose becomes evident in the light of questions of this nature that were put to Christian captives by Roman judges. In the year 304 a Christian captive spoke the following words before a Roman judge: "Those who fulfill His commandments and who show their contempt for tortures for the sake of His name, these are the ones who are true and loyal to the King of Kings." "Of which commandments and of which king do you speak?" the judge asked. "What is eternal life? Who are the seraphim? Sacrifice! Even Moses offered a sacrifice. Obey the command of the Caesar who reigns under the grace of God; for so it is written in your own Scripture: 'The mind of the king is in the Lord's hand [Prov. 21:1].'"

Similarly, Roman judges poked fun at the stories of creation, at the stories of the flood and of Noah's ark, at the story of Jonah, and most especially at the legends of the beginnings of Christianity.[42] On the other hand, rabbinic literature preserved memories of a number of *serious* disputes and conversations between Jews and Romans on the questions of faith and tradition.[43] It follows from all of the above that the questions of Caesar and his words to Miriam are not artistic flourishes, but memories and impressions arising out of the reality experienced by the generation of the Roman persecutions.

The refusal of Caesar to kill the mother before (or at the same time as) her small son, ostensibly on the basis of Scripture [Lev. 22:28],[44] displays nothing more nor less than the contempt that the authorities of Judaism expressed for the feigned legalistic procedure of the Roman empire toward "traitors and rebels" who were imprisoned and sentenced to death because of no other sin than their fulfillment of the command-ments. The Romans, as is well known, boasted a refined legalistic sense and an objective legal discipline, to which the rabbis replied, as it were: "All those laws that you enacted, and that you cited contemptuously from the Torah, you did these for your own purposes." A later tradition recorded these impressions in the midrash "Eyleh Ezkerah," which re-lates how the Ten Martyrs were not put to death until after they had been condemned by the Roman Caesar for the unexpiated sin of the sale of Joseph.[45] A Christian tradition testifies to the very same pseudo-legalism and relates how a Roman judge refused to put a woman to death along with her husband (despite her explicit confession that she was guilty of Christian practice) inasmuch as he had not been given instruc-tion in regard to the execution of women.[46]

Finally, Professor Saul Lieberman pointed to a particular phrase in the legend that also testifies to the period of its composition: In two of the rabbinic sources the mother concludes her words with the promise to her son that he will come into "the bosom of our father, Abraham," one of the stock martyrological phrases that were shared (with some slight variations) by both Jews and Christians executed for their faith in the third century and onward.[47]

All this data compels us to conclude that the details of the story in the midrashic legend reflect different historical circumstances from those reflected in the Books of the Maccabees—but they do not lend them-selves to any ideological exegesis: the purpose and point of view re-flected in II Maccabees are identical with those reflected in the rabbinic story, a fact reflected in the responses of the seventh son to Caesar in both versions:

Midrash on Lamentations
Hananiah, Mishael, and Azariah were worthy men and Nebuchadnezzar was a worthy enough king to have a miracle performed because of him. But you are not worthy, and we have been condemned to suffer death for the sake of heaven. If you don't put us to death, the Almighty has many servants to put us to death, many bears, many wolves, many lions, snakes, and leopards, as well as scorpions who can strike us and put us to death, but ultimately the Holy One, Blessed be He, will.

II Maccabees 7:30–38[48]
What are you waiting for? I will not obey the king's command, but I will obey the command of the Torah that was given to our ancestors by the hand of Moses. But you who have contrived all sorts of evil against the Jews will cer-tainly not escape the hand of God. For we are suffering because of the hands of our own sins and if our living Lord is angry for a little while to rebuke and discipline us, He will be reconciled with His own servants . . . for our broth-ers who are suffering briefly have imbibed a promise of everflowing life

under God's covenant; but you, by the judgment of God, will receive just punishment for your arrogance.

The rabbinic legend adopts the language of Pappus and Lullianus, while in the Books of the Maccabees the child speaks in the language of his period and of his Hellenistic milieu. Both traditions, however, reflect one point of view: the children suffer for their own sins, but the Holy One, Blessed be He, will exact payment from the wicked Caesar. And it must be emphasized here again that even the difference in wording does not reflect any true ideological difference, for the story of the rabbis has come down to us in a popular but, nonetheless, quite original version, while II Maccabees is the product of the reworking and resharpening of an artist as much in command of the art of literary narrative as he was of the Greek language.

In all the versions of the story, apart from that of the Babylonian Talmud, the story is referred to as 'The Story of Miriam bat Tanhum[49] (or Menahem) and Her Seven Sons,' and it may well be that even the name of the heroine was chosen for the purpose of a play on words. Miriam, that is, the bitter one, who will ultimately be consoled (*tanhum*). Such an exegesis is found in the words of the sages:

> Another interpretation: He who sets the childless woman among her household . . . The Holy One, Blessed be He, said: "I set Miriam bat Tanhum barren in order to make her happy, with her sons, in the World to come."[50]

And in all the sources the phrase in Psalm 113:9, "the mother of the child is fortunate," is applied to her. It is possible, therefore, that popular memory preserves the story of a family tragedy which was ascribed to a certain Miriam and her children. Subsequently they attached to this name the story that had been incorporated in the Greek Books of Maccabees, which derived from the Christians in the Holy Land.[51] In any event it should be pointed out that in the Midrash on Lamentations the story about the mother was connected with Lamentations 1:16 ("for these do I weep") not because of any connection between the story and the verse, but because of the apparent connection of the verse with the stories cited in connection with it: It happened with Miriam the daughter of Boethus. . . . It happened with Miriam the daughter of Nakdimon. . . . It happened with Miriam the daughter of Boethus Nahtom (sic!). . . . It happened in the case of Miriam the daughter of Tanhum. In the Midrash on Lamentations it is the name of the mother that was important, not the Scriptural verse.

III

The book of Josippon (ca. 950) restored the story of the mother and her seven sons to its original historical period, that is, the period of Antiochus IV Epiphanes. The author of Josippon derives his facts from the Latin version of II Maccabees and the story appears in his book as it did in its original version, virtually word for word (except for one crucial addition which, as far as I know, has not gained any attention). It was the author of Josippon, however, who popularized the tale under the title of "The Story of Hannah and Her Seven Sons," and it is because of his widespread influence that this version of the mother's name came into common usage and that the story was transformed into a folktale.

Hannah's name appears only in the long version of Josippon and not in its shorter form.[52] In the edition of Mantua (which is the shorter version) the mother is referred to simply as "a woman," as she is in II Maccabees; but in the course of the last 400 years it was the longer reworking of Josippon that became famous and that finally fixed the name of Hannah as that of the heroine. Nevertheless, even as early as the twelfth century the name of Hannah had become symbolic of martyrdom for the glory of God in the books of the Sephardic sages, as is demonstrated in the terse version of Ibn Daud[53] and, above all, in the words of Maimonides in the *Iggeret ha-Shemad Israel* (the *Epistle on the Persecutions*):[54]

> The third class of martyrdom for the sake of God consists of those who are brought under compulsion [in the sin of conversion to a foreign religion]. Be aware that every place where the sages of blessed memory said, "Let him be killed and let him now transgress," if he has been killed, he has already attained the stage of sanctification of the name of God, Blessed be He; and if he was one of ten Jews, he thereby sanctified the name of God publicly, as did Hananiah, Mishael, and Azariah and the Ten Martyrs, and the seven sons of Hannah.

Clearly the name of Hannah was so famous that there was no need to say anything further by way of explanation. It is, however, even more important to indicate that the renown of the name of this mother even entered the Bet ha-Midrash (in the study of Jewish texts) and was responsible for the emendation of various texts. Thus, Israel ben Rabbi Joseph al-Alnaqawa[55] mentions the name of the mother and her seven sons twice in the course of his great work *Menorat Hamaor*, with some minor variations that deserve mention here. From the Midrash on Lamentations he cites the following: "It happened that Hannah, the daughter of Tanhum[!] was captured along with her seven sons. And the Caesar took them. . . ." The second time he cites the story in his work, Alnaqawa cites it according to its *talmudic* source. In our editions of the Talmud (and this is also according to the Munich manuscript), the reading is: "And of them Scripture says: 'It is for Your sake that we are slain all day long, that we are regarded as sheep to be slaughtered (Ps. 44:23); and Judah says this refers to the *woman* and her seven sons to whom the first was brought before *Caesar*. . . .'" But Alnaqawa[56] quotes it in this manner: ". . . Judah says this refers to the incident of *Hannah* and her seven sons whom they brought before *Antiochus of Macedon*. . . ." Thus we find a double emendation in Alnaqawa's quote, for not only is the woman called by her name, but the name of Caesar has been exchanged for that of Antiochus of Macedon. It is self-evident that the only influence one can detect here is that of Josippon, which is responsible for the identification of the woman by the name of Hannah and even for establishing the story in its "correct" historical setting.

Inevitably the question arises: What is the source of the name, Hannah? Why did Josippon, or the source from which he drew, call the mother by that name, a name that has no basis in any of the apocrypha, pseudepigrapha, or rabbinic literature?

Hannah and her seven sons are mentioned in the book of Josippon twice. The first time they are mentioned in their "historical setting," which tells of the persecutions of Antiochus and of the martyrdom of Eleazar, a priest, and Hannah and her seven sons.[57] The second time is in the speech of Amitai, the priest, to his sons, before he was put to death by the sword of Simeon the Tyrant, close to the time of the destruction of the Second Temple.[58] It is here, in this speech of Amitai's, that we are led to the sources of the Josippon. It is best to quote him directly. Amitai complains bitterly about the cruelty of Simeon the Tyrant, who slaughters a father and his sons together, and he says:

> Such wickedness was done earlier in the days of the Hasmonian priests in the wickedness of Antiochus the Wicked who killed seven young men from the children of Israel in front of the mother. . . . This woman was Hannah the Righteous and Pious who sent seven sons before her with joy and gladness of heart. . . . And afterward, she too went to the great light in happiness, and it is of her that the psalmist says: "As a happy mother of children" (Ps. 113:9).[59]

These words demonstrate unequivocally that Josippon or the editor of the long version knew the rabbinic Midrash which cited—*in connection with Miriam bat Tanhum*—the verse: "As a happy mother of children."[60] And if a Midrash of the rabbis influenced the *style* of Josippon, it is not farfetched for us to suppose that it is in the Midrash of the rabbis that we will also find the source for the name of Hannah.

In the Sephardic recension of the Midrash on Lamentations the story of Miriam bat Tanhum concludes with the following words: "After several days, the woman went out of her mind and threw herself to her death from a roof, thereby fulfilling the verse of Jeremiah: 'She who bore seven is forlorn [15:9].' And a voice emerged from heaven and said: 'Happy is the mother of children [Ps. 113:9].'" It is from these two verses that Josippon extrapolated the name of Hannah.

In the prayer of Hannah, the mother of Samuel, the prophet, Hannah says: "While the barren woman bears seven, the mother of many is forlorn [I Sam. 2:5]." Taking this verse, Josippon turned exegete and engaged in a word play which must have gone something like this: It is written in the Book of Jeremiah that "She who bore seven is forlorn," and it is written in I Samuel that "While the barren woman bears seven." Therefore, she who is spoken of in Jeremiah must be the same woman as she who speaks the verse in Samuel. Just as the verse in Samuel was spoken by Hannah the mother of Samuel, so the name of the barren woman in Jeremiah must have been Hannah.

Josippon found some added evidence for his exegesis in the second verse, which is the one used, as we have seen, to conclude the story in the Midrash on Lamentations. In the Book of Psalms we read: "He sets the childless woman among their household, as a happy mother of children (Ps. 113:9)," while in the Book of Samuel, Hannah is quoted as having said: "He raises the poor from the dust/Lifts up the needy from the dunghill/Setting them with nobles/Granting them seats of honor (I Sam. 2:8)." Josippon took the second phrase of Psalm 113:9 as the conclusion of the words of Hannah, and of Hannah he thought it appropriate to say, "As a happy mother of children"; for what was shared by both mothers was that each of them sanctified the name of Heaven through her sons. Josippon revealed the progression of his thinking on this subject in the very words that he put into the mouth of Hannah the mother of seven sons before her death: "And Hannah prayed: 'My heart exults in the Lord; I have triumphed through the Lord, for he wished to be comforted for His people through my sons and that they would be His servants. I gloat over my enemies, for they were unable to reduce a single one of my sons to turn in worship to their acts of folly, which will neither help nor save, for they are all vanity.'"[61] And so this mother continues with her prayer by reciting the verses of Hannah the mother of Samuel and by interpreting them with regard to the deeds of her seven sons, who sanctified the Name of God in the days of the Hasmoneans. The redactor of Josippon, accordingly, knew the legend about Miriam the daughter of Tanhum, but he preferred not to identify the two women, for it was explicitly stated in the rabbinic sources that the incident involving Miriam occurred in the days of the persecution of Hadrian and, moreover, the details in the rabbinic sources were not identical with the details in his major source, namely, II Maccabees.[62]

It is not inappropriate to emphasize that in the shorter recension of Josippon the woman is not called by her name, nor are the words "as a happy mother of children" connected with the words of Amitai, the priest.[63] Nor does the shorter version provide any exegesis of the prayer of Hannah, the mother of Samuel, in the last words of the mother of seven sons. In one manuscript the briefer version of Josippon[64] is connected with the name of Rabbenu Gershom, the Light of the Exile,[65] and it is therefore plausible to conjecture that this briefer version was the one known in France. If our conjecture is correct, it becomes immediately apparent why Joseph b. Rabbi Solomon of Carcassonne never mentions the name of Hannah in his poem for the Sabbath of Hanukkah, "*Odekha Ki Anaftat*"; the Josippon which he had in front of him apparently did not include any reference to the actual name of the mother.[66] On the other hand, those poems that do mention the name of Hannah all come from works of Oriental-Sephardic provenance.

IV

The story of Hannah and her seven sons evoked a particularly strong echo in the hearts of the people, and the Jews sanctified the memory of these martyrs by means of special liturgical poems (*piyyutim*) inserted into the liturgy for the Sabbath of Hanukkah and of the Ninth of Av. Two of these poems, which were composed in the Hebrew language, are based on the Book of Josippon, but the first (#1 in our list) is based on the shorter version of Josippon and the name of Hannah is not known to it, while the second (#2 in this list) is based on the longer version of Josippon and the name of Hannah *is* known here. All the other Hebrew poems are based on rabbinic sources. The following are the poems known to me on Hannah and her seven sons:

1. "I will proclaim You even when You are angry with me," by R. Joseph b. R. Solomon of Carcassonne. Sources: I. Davidson, *Thesaurus of Medieval Hebrew Poetry*, I, 67, no. 1651; IV, 227. Among the photocopies in the Library of the Jewish Theological Seminary of America is one of German origin that contains this poem. In the margin of one of the pages there are two illuminations; the upper one shows Eleazar, the priest, prepared for execution, while the second shows the story of the seven sons. The first son is shown lying on the place of execution, with the extremities of his limbs strewn to the left. Since the mother plays no part in this poem, she is not portrayed in the illustration.

2. "Wretched is the mother of seven," a lamentation in the form of an alphabetical acrostic, (to be sung) to the tune of '*Eshtaḥaveh 'appayim 'arsah*. Sources: *Sefer Allon Bakhuth*.[67] "A collection of laws . . . for the period 'in the straits' [between the seventeenth of Tammuz and the ninth of Av] . . . with the liturgy of the midnight prayer and lamentations . . . and an additional lamentation called

'Qissat Hannah' . . . composed by me for the benefit of the community," by Hayyim Cohen . . . Livorno . . . in 5643. The story of the mother is found in stanzas 1–7. It is based on a rabbinic source (perhaps B. Gittin fol. 57b) where the mother's name is not provided.

3. "She who bore seven is forlorn [Jer. 15:9] and her belly distended." Sources: Davidson, loc. cit., I, 8, no. 1845; IV, 229.

4. "I will give voice to a lamentation and I will shriek and I will not desist day or night." Sources: Davidson, loc. cit. 61, IV, 109, no. 1918; *Sefer Allon Bakhuth.*

5. "My people cried in agonies over Hannah and her seven sons." Source: Davidson, loc. cit., II, 87, no. 1935; IV, 293.

6. "Over Hannah my heart is rent." Source: *Sefer Allon Bakhuth*, fol. 41a–42a. Composed on the basis of the longer version of Josippon.

7. "A dirge over Hannah" (the story of Hannah in Arabic). Source:[68] cf. *Ohel David* of David Sassoon, I, 480, no. 7; 481, no. 547; II, 1034, no. 907.

8. "Seven brothers." A *piyyut* on Miriam bat Naḥum (sic) and her seven sons, in Persian by Joseph Yehudi. Sources: W. Bacher in *ZDMG*, XXXV (1899): 394ff.; JE, VII: 322, col./b.[69] In addition to these *piyyutim*, we must list the popular work of R. Jacob bar Isaac Ashkenazi, *Ts'ena u-R'ena*, which bequeathed to the people at large the traditions of the sages about the Torah and the Five Scrolls, as well as, among others, the story of the mother and her seven sons.[70] The Talmud, the *midrashim*, the *piyyutim*, and popular works like Josippon and *Ts'ena u-R'ena* served to make the story of the mother and her seven sons well known among all sectors of the Jewish people and thus one of the most famous of Jewish legends.[71]

NOTES

1. B.T., Gittin 57b.

2. See below in the list of *piyyutim*, in the text no. 6.

3. The story of the woman and her seven sons appears three times in rabbinic literature:

(A) The most complete version is found in the Franco-German recension of the Midrash on Lamentations and in Seder Eliahu. 1. Midrash on Lamentations 1:16 ("For these things do I weep"). The text that is transmitted in the standard "printed" versions was quoted by two Sephardic scholars, R. Bahya ben Asher (cf. below, n. 5) and R. Israel ben R. Joseph Alnaqawa (cf. below, n. 55). The version of the story in the Midrash on Lamentations (ed. Buber, p. 84) was copied in *Yalkut* Ki Tavo, sec. 938 (Deut. 26:17: "You have affirmed this day"). 2. Seder Eliahu, ch. 28 (ed. R. Meir Ish Shalom, p. 151). The version that is printed in the *Sefer Ha-Ma'asiyot* (ed. Gaster, p. 35) and in *Midrash Hagadol* Ki Tavo (Deut. 28:50: "and the young no mercy") is a later, shorter rendition of the version in the Midrash on Lamentations.

(B) The story is transmitted in an abridged form and in Aramaic in two versions: 1. B.T., Gittin 57b; 2. Midrash on Lamentations *Zuta*, sec. 21 (ed. Buber, p. 69) and in *Yalkut* Lamentations, sec. 1017–19. Although the version in Midrash *Zuta* and in *Yalkut* Lamentations is fuller than the one in the B.T., it is clearly related to it because it proves the similarity of the stories in Midrash *Zuta* (ad loc.) to the story in Gittin ("The story of the 400 children who were imprisoned for shameful uses. . . . Some say that this refers to the woman and her seven sons"). It may be that the Midrash *Zuta* version was expanded on the basis of the Midrash on Lamentations, in which the name of the mother is mentioned ("their mother, Miriam, the daughter of Menahem, said to them"), whereas in the Talmud there is no hint of her name.

(C) The version in Pesikta Rabbati, ch. 43 (ed. R. Meir Ish Shalom, fol. 180b) is different from the versions mentioned above in a number of details (cf. below, n. 62). The fragment in the story of the Ten Martyrs is based upon this version (cf. below, n. 6) and a later version in *Midrash Aseret ha-Dibrot* (*Beit Hamidrash*, ed. Jellineck, p. 70).

4. Seder Eliahu (cf. above, n. 3). Regarding the phrase in brackets, see Ish Shalom's note, p. 151, n. 17.

5. *Kad Hakemah* (Constantinople, 1515), s.v. *evel*,[4] fol. 10d: "Thus, you see that the reason for the destruction of the Second Temple was owing to hatred, not to idolatry, because there were no idolators among them; but they gave their lives to sanctify God's name rather than engage in idolatry. And regarding the interpretation of the woman and her seven sons . . . the destruction of the Temple was already decreed in the wilderness with the incident of the spies."

6. "Since the ten righteous men were executed, seven brothers came to eulogize them, and they wept so, until news of their actions reached Caesar. He sent for them and saw that they were very attractive. He said to the oldest, "Perform an idolatrous act. . . ."" —from the story of the Ten Martyrs and the story of Hannah and Her Seven Sons in *Sefer Tiferet Haim*, ed. S. D. Levinger, *Festschrift* in honor of Haim Zvi Kish (Budapest, 1940), p. 41.

7. Notes of R. Yaakov Emden to B.T., Gittin 57b and the glosses of R. David Luria to the Midrash on Lamentations, loc. cit.

8. See, for instance, Y. L. Zunz, *Ha-Derashot Be-Yisrael*, ed. Hanoch Albeck (Jerusalem, 1947), p. 60 and p. 298, n. 21; S. Lieberman, "The Martyrs of Caesarea," *Annuaire de l'Institut de Philologie et d'histoire Orientales et Slaves*, VII (1939–1944): 430, n. 115; and cf. below n. 10.

9. II Macc. 6:18ff.

10. Joshua Guttman, "The Mother and Her Seven Sons in Legend and in Books II and IV Maccabees," in *The Book of Yohanan Levy* (Jerusalem, 1949), pp. 25ff.

11. Guttman, ad loc., p. 26.

12. II Macc. 2:23.

13. So stated explicitly in Pesikta Rabbati (ed. Ish Shalom): "Our rabbis told a story about Miriam, the daughter of Tanhum, during the time of the persecution." Cf. above, n. 4. In the rabbinic sources the king is referred to as "Caesar." It is obvious that the version in *Midrash Aseret ha-Dibrot* ("The story of a woman who had seven sons who were brought before an official") is a late correction.

14. See "The Martyrs of Caesaria" (cf. above, n. 8), and also S. Lieberman, "Roman Legal Institutions in Early Rabbinics and Acta Martyrum," *JQR NS*, XXXV (1944): 1–58 (henceforth = "Roman Law in Rabbinic Literature"). At this point I would like to express my gratitude to Professor Saul Lieberman, who graciously responded to my inquiries regarding a number of matters and made a number of helpful recommendations.

15. See S. Lieberman, "Roman Law in Rabbinic Literature," p. 24 and n. 153 there. Also Edmond Le Blant, *Les Persécuteurs et les martyrs aux premiers siècles de notre ère* (Paris, 1893), pp. 184ff. (henceforth = Le Blant).

16. Cf. Alexander Marx, in his survey of the Midrash on Lamentations in *O.L.Z.*, V (1902): 293–295.

17. Le Blant, p. 144.

18. II Macc. 7:5, 20–21.

19. Le Blant, p. 144.

20. Le Blant, pp. 41ff.; p. 48, n. 9; p. 103, n. 1; p. 144, and pp. 192ff. Interestingly, even the ancient Syrian Christians took these elements from the Roman milieu to elucidate a story that they took directly from the Apocrypha. See the fragment of the story of Miriam in R. L. Bensley, *The Fourth Book of Maccabees and Kindred Documents in Syriac* (Cambridge, 1895), Syriac section, pp. 104ff.; Eng. trans., pp. XXXVff. On the Christian legends that grew from the incident of the mother and her sons, see the comprehensive survey of E. Bickerman, "Les Maccabées de Malalas," *Byzantion*, XXI (1951), fasc. I, pp. 63–83.

21. For this definition, i.e. "cells," see S. Lieberman, "Roman Law in Rabbinic Literature," p. 19.

22. Based on the printed versions of the Midrash on Lamentations beginning with that of Pesaro of 1519.

23. The sin of contempt for the Roman empire (lèse-majesté) was the most serious of political infractions. See Le Blant, pp. 58ff.

24. Y.T., Shvi'it 4.2 (fol. 35a); Sanhedrin 3.6 (fol. 21b).

25. From Professor Lieberman I learned that this explanation had already been mentioned in the work of R. Solomon Cirilio, " . . . water in drinking goblets of colored glass; red, so that onlooking Jews would think that they had drunk wine in order to deny their faith." Y.T., Shvi'it, Zeraim, with the commentary of R. Solomon Cirilio (Jerusalem, 1935), fol. 55b.

26. Le Blant, pp. 101ff.

27. Ibid. p. 145.

28. II Macc. 6:21.

29. Pliny *Letters* X: 96–97 (Loeb Clas. Lib., II: 400ff.).

30. Le Blant, pp. 203ff., 214.

31. S. Lieberman, "The Martyrs of Caesarea," pp. 429ff.

32. Seder Eliahu says explicitly: "immediately grabbed a sword and decapitated him." In the Midrash on Lamentations it is said in one place, "immediately commanded that he be executed," and in another, "passed sentence and executed him." Both indicate death by the sword (M. Sanhedrin 7:3). Regarding execution by the sword, see Le Blant, pp. 246ff. In Pesiqta Rabbati it is said that they were destroyed by fire (fried; Heb. *tiggen*), but it does not say that this sentence was imposed on them with any specific motive. However, regarding the word "immediate" we have evidence from the martyrological literature (cf. Le Blant, pp. 237ff.). The word "immediately" ("immediately commanded that he be executed") must be understood literally; cf. Lieberman, "The Martyrs of Caesarea."

33. Cf. Lieberman, "The Martyrs of Caesarea," p. 430 and n. 116.

34. See the quote adduced on p. 49, and also II Macc. 7:14–19.

35. See B.T., Avodah Zara 54b–55a.

36. Ibid. 17b, end.

37. Sifre Deut., sec. 307, ed. Finkelstein, p. 346.

38. Le Blant, pp. 110ff.

39. Eusebius *Eccles. Hist.* VIII: x, 10 (Loeb Clas. Lib., II: 285).

40. See also H. Delehaye, *Le Passions des Martyrs et les Genres Littéraires* (Bruxelles, 1921), p. 255.

41. *Meg. Ta'anit*, ed. Lichtenstein, p. 90; *Semakhot* 8:15 (ed. Higger, p. 164).

42. Le Blant, pp. 190ff.

43. Tineius Rufus asked and R. Akiba responded regarding the Sabbath (Sanhedrin 65b; Pesiqta Rabbati, sec. 23 [ed. Ish Shalom, fol. 119b]). Regarding circumcision, Tanhuma Buber, sec. 7, fol. 18a. Regarding "and Esau I hated," Tanhuma Trumah, sec. 3. Regarding disagreements over creation, see, for example, Bereshit Rabbah 1:9 (ed. Theodor-Albeck, p. 8) and Sanhedrin 39a. See also Lieberman, "The Martyrs of Caesarea," p. 421.

44. It is possible that the Caesar "intended" to explain this verse on the basis of the rabbinic understanding that the prohibition against "him and his sons" is practiced regarding women and not men (Sifra Emor, sec. 8, nn. 11ff. [ed. Weiss, fol. 99b]; Hulin 78b).

45. *Beit Hamidrash*, ed. Jellinek, II:64.

46. Le Blant, p. 173.

47. Lieberman, "The Martyrs of Caesarea," pp. 443ff.

48. Based on the translation of Abraham Kahana, *Ha-Sefarim Ha-Hitzonim*, Vol. II, Bk. 1, p. 21.

49. The reading in the printed versions of the Midrash on Lamentations of "Miriam, the daughter of Nahtom" is a scribal error or a printer's error, because all of the other versions, without exception (even the copy of the fragment in the Midrash on Lamentations as recorded in *Yalkut* Shimoni), testify to the reading "Tanhum" or "Menahem."

50. Pesiqta Rabbati, loc. cit. Compare what Rabbi I. Levi wrote in *REJ* 54:139, n. 4.

51. Note also that even the Syriac Church Fathers referred to her as Miriam (see Bensley, above, n. 20).

52. On the edition of the Book of Josippon and its versions, see M. Steinschneider, *Die Geschichtsliteratur der Juden* (Frankfurt a.M., 1905), pp. 28ff. Abraham Kahana's introduction to *The Book of Josippon According to the Printing of Mantua*, ed. David Ginzburg (Berditchev, 1896–1913); and Y. Baer, "The Hebrew Book of Josippon," in *Sefer Dinaburg* (Jerusalem, 1949), pp. 178ff.

53. *Dibrey Malkhay Yisrael Be-Bayit Sheni* (Mantua, 1514): "and by the hand of this Phillipus, Hannah and her seven sons were put to death."

54. *Hemda Genuzah*, sec. 1, ed. Z. H. Edelman (Koenigsberg, 1856), p. 10. This was pointed out to me by Professor Alexander Marx, to whom I am deeply grateful. The reading on Hannah was verified by means of two manuscripts in the library of the Jewish Theological Seminary: Adler 2405 and Enelow 0817.

55. *Menorat Hamaor*, ed. Enelow, 2:337.

56. Ibid. 3:122

57. Josippon (editio Constantinople, 1510, and its progeny), ed. Ginzburg, ch. 19, col. 126ff. (p. 65).

58. Josippon, ibid. ch. 89, col. 488 (p. 246).

59. Josippon (editio Venice, 1544, ch. 89, fol. 136, col. c ff.). On the reading in the Mantua edition, see below, n. 63.

60. Cf. Y. Baer (above, n. 52), p. 148, n. 8.

61. Josippon (editio Venice, 1544, ch. 19, fol. 35b).

62. It has already been pointed out above (n. 3) that the version of the story that appears in the Pesiqta Rabbati differs in a number of details from the other versions of the incident preserved in rabbinic literature. Following a detailed investigation into those differences, I. Levi (*REJ*, 54 [1907]: 138–141) came to the conclusion that the version in the Pesiqta was influenced by the Italian version of Josippon. Furthermore, he concluded that only on the basis of this influence is it possible to explain the differences between the version in the Pesiqta and the other versions in the aggadic literature.

The following are Levi's arguments: (a) In the version in the Midrash on Lamentations nothing is said about the method by which the brothers were executed (cf. above, n. 32), while the Pesiqta Rabbati reads, "Immediately they took him and put him into the frying pan and fried him." This is the exact torture mentioned in II Maccabees. (b) In all the other versions it is told that after the death of her sons Miriam fell from the roof (which may well mean that she committed suicide), while in the Pesiqta Rabbati we read that after the death of the seventh son they "took Miriam and executed her." This is the way it is recorded in II Maccabees. (c) Only in the version in the Pesiqta is the incident of the ring missing. Instead, the youngest son says to Caesar, "I will go and consult with my mother. He went to his mother. He said to her, 'What do you say? Shall I bow to the idol or not?' His mother replied, 'My son, do you wish all your brothers to be accepted into the bosom of Abraham in the world to come?'" Both in the words of the mother and in the hesitation of the son Levi detects an echo of the story in Maccabees and in Josippon. (d) In the version in the Pesiqta the brothers do not quote Scripture. Rather, the eldest says, "I refuse to deny my God," and the remaining brothers speak in a similar manner. Therefore Levi concludes that "it would be superfluous to say that in the apocryphal literature the children do not quote Scripture, and accordingly the stratagem of the king is not discussed." All of the differences that are in the Pesiqta can be explained on the assumption that the Pesiqta was influenced by the Josippon, which, in turn, drew all of its details about the incident exclusively from II Maccabees. But even Levi admits that this conclusion is based upon a second one, i.e., that the origin of the Pesiqta Rabbati is Italian.

Others have already proven that this theory about the place of the redaction of the Pesiqta Rabbati hangs by a thread. Moreover, even if it is correct in the matter of one section, it is not compelling regarding the whole Pesiqta (cf. H. Albeck in his supplement to Y. L. Zunz, *Ha-Derashot be-Yisrael*, pp. 119ff. and in the notes). Or, to put it another way, one cannot draw conclusions from another section about the section that includes the incident of Miriam, the daughter of Tanhum.

Indeed, if one examines the minute details of Levi's theory with respect to our story, without accepting his theory about the origin of the Pesiqta as a whole, it would appear that even here there is little upon which to rely. Neither in Josippon nor in II Maccabees does it say that the mother was executed by the king. It is possible that such was the intended meaning of II Maccabees, but even the author of Josippon was not certain that the mother was executed and therefore contented himself with some general statements: "And it was that after she finished praying and pouring out her heart to God that her life ended; and her soul escaped while she was still speaking, and she fell upon the bodies of her sons, and she was cast into the earth with them." Also, in the version of *Midrash Hagadol* and the *Sefer Ha-Ma'assiyot* (cf. above, n. 3) we see that the king threatens the first son, "Worship idols or I shall torture you," and the text concludes, "At that moment he tortured them in a variety of ways and afterwards executed them and their mother after them." Nor does this version have any other element similar to the version in the Pesiqta Rabbati. From the execution of the mother, and from the torture of the sons no conclusion may be drawn regarding the source of the details in the Pesiqta Rabbati. Moreover, the request of the youngest to the king to consult with his mother does not confirm the influence of Josippon-Maccabees, because this request is absent from those sources. In Josippon-Maccabees it is Antiochus who asks the mother to persuade the child, and she agrees to speak to him. Additionally, the absence of scriptural verses from the sources and their abridged nature do not prove the influence of an outside source, because in the Josippon-Maccabees version each child speaks a few short words. One might say that the Pesiqta Rabbati version is nothing but a summary of the incident taken from different sources. The single similarity between the Pesiqta Rabbati and Josippon is the mention of the frying pan. But this torture is mentioned in the Pesiqta only incidentally, and in Josippon and its sources this is only one of a number of tortures that are mentioned; in the Pesiqta, for instance, nothing is said about the severing of limbs.

On the other hand, the language of the incident in the Pesiqta Rabbati reflects its origin and its antiquity (see above, p. 117, re the phrase "in the bosom of Abraham"). The version cited in the story of the Ten Martyrs (cf. above, n. 6), which is definitely drawn from the Pesiqta, gives the impression of being an abridgement of the aggadic version coupled with other changes, but these changes do not originate with Josippon-Maccabees.

63. In the Mantua printing (ed. Ginzburg, p. 246), the name of Hannah is explicitly mentioned ("and they went and they prepared a place to torture Hannah"), but these words appear to be a later addition because they are missing in Adler 1674 (cf. below, n. 65) and in the body of the incident in that version of Josippon.

64. See ed. Ginzburg, col. 132 (p. 68).

65. Catalogue of Hebrew Manuscripts in the collection of Elkan Nathan Adler (Cambridge, 1921), p. 42, no. 1674.

66. His hypothesis regarding the Sephardic origin of the name Hannah is strengthened by the fact that the homily from Jeremiah 15:9 is missing from Midrash on Lamentations (ed. Buber) and from Seder Eliahu. The words in *Yalkut* Tehilim (sec. 873, near the end of Psalm 113): "Another thing, this is Hannah and her seven sons," are apparently a later addition, since in *Yalkut* Lamentations to which these thoughts point, she is never called by that name. The Meiri, in *Bet Ha-Behirah*, on Gittin (ed. Schlesinger, p. 231), calls her Miriam.

67. The book presents *piyyutim* in Arabic and is clearly directed to Jews of the Orient. I am indebted to R. Hayyim Lieberman, the librarian of the collection of the Rabbi of Lubavitch, who directed my attention to this book and the *piyyutim* included in it and who graciously permitted a copy of the book to remain in my possession for a period of time.

68. This *piyyut*, which is found in the four fasts of the Sephardim, was pointed out to me by Dr. Simeon Bernstein, to whom I am grateful.

69. I am grateful to Dr. Ernst Meinz for drawing my attention to this Persian *piyyut* and the literature discussing it.

70. Cf. *Ts'ena U-R'ena*, "The Destruction of the Temple." I am grateful to Dr. Isaac Rivkind for alerting me to the incorporation of this story in this book.

71. The burial place of Hannah and her sons is mentioned in Jewish literature; see Z. Vilnai, *Masebot Kodesh be-Eretz Yisrael* (Jerusalem, 1951), pp. 242–243.

The Rabbinic Heritage

The Jewish communal framework which developed in Talmudic times was only the most tangible product of historical circumstances and of the peculiar ideology of Judaism. Like other societies, the Talmudic rationalized its communal institutions and hallowed them as part of the sacred system of Jewish belief, and this was, in part at least, because these institutions were indispensable for the communication of the religion to the people at large. Without them, or their equivalent, the survival of Judaism as a vital civilization would have been inconceivable.

However, a mere glance at Christian or Muslim history will indicate that practically identical institutions can develop and yet transmit quite different ideologies. To appreciate the practices and aspirations peculiar to Talmudic society and culture, we must focus our attention on the religious outlook which characterized it and which distinguishes it from other stages of Jewish development before and after.

TORAH: SCRIPTURE AND TRADITION

It will perhaps appear strange that a discussion of Judaism should begin with what is at first blush a second step in the religious process, namely, Scripture. Underlying the sanctity of a book there ought presumably to be a conception of God, a theology, and an explanation of the way in which the Deity makes his will known to mortals, that is, a theory of revelation. Nevertheless, our departure from the accepted canons of theological exposition is, we believe, required in fairness to the idiom and mental processes of the culture we are seeking to understand. It cannot be overemphasized that Talmudic Judaism is not to be comprehended as a logical theological system. For what characterizes the Talmudic culture pattern is precisely its Scriptural and, consequently, nonrational framework. Not only are its basic tenets predicated on the text of the revelation, itself above human reason, but far more significantly, its religious and moral ideology is held together by no more than the sequence of the verses of the Bible. In a word, Rabbinic thought with its complex of values and concepts is essentially a running commentary on Scripture. No more than Scripture can the utterances of different schools of thought be fused into a unified theological system. So the varieties of Talmudic thought cannot be reduced to one cohesive structure of ideas and attitudes.

It is idle to ask: What does *Judaism* have to say about the nature of man, about sin, about the world to come, about God himself? The question is as idle when put to the Rabbinic literature as it is unhistorical when put to its Biblical antecedents. The Bible has incorporated within its canon a number of views of God, a number of conceptions of sin, retribution, love, justice, and so forth. The dogmatic theologian and the religiously committed must somehow try to harmonize contradictions and elicit a unitary point of view. The Rabbis could not avoid either the demand of their own minds or the demand of others for basic consistency. However, the structure of the religious community, with its lack of any formalized hierarchy, prevented the definitive resolution of conflicting views on any but the most crucial questions. For the most part, different teachers expounded different solutions, and as in Scripture itself, they were recorded side by side. All later efforts to reduce Judaism to an integrated system of ideas and values—Maimonides is an excellent case in point—were held in no higher respect than the teachings of Rabbi Eliezer ben Hyrcanus, Rabbi Akiba, Rabbi Ishmael, or hundreds of other commentator-teachers. The only question we can in fairness put to the Rabbinic sources is this: What did each of the Rabbis make of one or a number of statements in Scripture? What do their eclectic theologies and commentaries have in common?

It is this common denominator that justifies us in beginning our analysis of Talmudic religion with its conception of Scripture. For not only does the Torah serve as the foundation of Talmudic ritual and values, but whatever conceptions the Rabbis had about God, revelation, human nature, Israel, and even about Scripture were formally derived from Scripture itself. To be sure, Scripture was not the only source of Talmudic insight and ideology; some of the basic features of Talmudic Judaism are quite new to the Bible. Ultimately the real source and stimulus for a vital orientation to life had to be the environment and the novel challenges which each day produced. However, to achieve a serious hearing and to attain a measure of validity an idea had to be attached to a verse. Occasionally this might involve tearing a phrase out of context, emending the holy text, or, *mirabile dictu,* interpreting a Hebrew word as though it were synonymous with a similar-sounding Greek one! The net effect was the same: the interpretation had been "derived" from Scripture.

Every school of Talmudic thought engaged in reinterpretation of Scriptural verses to suit immediate needs, for all Jews of Talmudic culture agreed on the postulate that the Torah was the first and final revelation of God's will and command. Accordingly, it was eternally relevant and everlastingly binding, and it was the source of all truth and wisdom. "Not only with you do I make this covenant and this oath," Moses proclaimed, "but with him that standeth here with us this day before the Lord our God, and also with him that is not here with us this day." No one should be misled by the ostensible parochialism of Scripture, which often plainly addresses itself to a community with a primitive economy, and so seems totally inadequate to the complexity of the Greco-Roman world. "Scripture speaks in details of its own milieu," the Rabbis explained, but the details merely illustrated principles that were everlasting. Earlier we pointed out that the Talmud is very much alive to Orthodox Jews even in our atomic-technological century. That is because "the Sages [of the Talmud] speak in terms of their own present," while their law and its principles go on forever. The medieval Jew made of the Talmud exactly what his Talmudic ancestor had made of Scripture. Hence Solomon ibn Gabirol, Abraham ibn Daud, Maimonides, or Gersonides could discuss the merits of Platonic and Aristotelian ideas in the light of the words of Moses, Amos, and Isaiah and in the idiom of the Talmud.

The doctrine of an eternally valid Scripture, relevant to the problems of all generations and societies of man, is undoubtedly the most enduring and pervasive legacy of Talmudic civilization to Western society. What the Jewish philosophers and lawyers did to their heritage was amply duplicated by Christian and Muslim, who subjected the New Testament and the Koran to the same legalistic and philosophic tailoring. For centuries, to cite one outstanding example, the Christian Church, which forbade usury among Christians, provided for an uninterrupted source of capital loans by reinterpreting the Deuteronomic law so as to make it apply to Christian creditors, but not to Jews lending money to Christians. Beginning with the Crusades, the Schoolmen argued against this traditional dichotomy and against any form of usury by appealing to other Biblical texts which might prove that Christians and Jews were not "strangers" in the Scriptural sense. When in the sixteenth century Calvin undermined the age-old restrictions against usury and thus smoothed the progress of capitalism, he could do so only by reinterpreting the Biblical verses and "proving" that they were no longer applicable. The history of European economy is thus intimately bound up with the history of the interpretation of two verses in Deuteronomy that were set down in writing in Palestine seven centuries before the Christian era.

In the United States, the Puritan ethic, the American Revolution, and the war over slavery were often grounded in the exegesis of Scripture, for Scripture contained God's revelation and guide for the construction of a just and equitable polity. Throughout the world, in thousands of churches and synagogues, countless sermons are preached on social, political, and economic issues, the solution to which is "indicated" by the verses of Scripture. The sermon is the literary form in which the Bible is applied to contemporary issues. Only the sermon, or in Rabbinic parlance, *midrash* (literally, ferreting out, hence, interpretation), has made of the Bible a living book rather than a literary classic read merely for pleasure or edification. The Rabbis made the Bible the cornerstone of Jewish life, and Christianity transmitted their method to every portion of the world that came under its influence.

In Talmudic antiquity, as in the Middle Ages, the legalistic power of the Bible was a fact of daily experience, making itself felt in all those areas of life that were subject to social control and legislation. That Jewish law, like its Christian and Muslim counterparts, was authoritarian, at least in theory, was owing to its Scriptural origin, and Scripture was all-embracing. The contrast with modern canons of behavior and belief is instructive. Even the normally devout and genuinely religious person in democratic society is outraged by prelates who issue religious pronouncements on styles of clothing or who attempt to censor frank and impartial discussion of sex, science, or political legislation. We appeal to our democratic faith and the right to learn the truth and judge according to our *reason*. Modern man regards these things as beyond the purview of religious ritual, and brooks no interference with his privacy.

The Midrashic schools of Talmudic civilization could conceive of relatively few domains which are "private" concerns. One of the most instructive documents for the history of Judeo-Christian civilization is the nineteenth chapter of Leviticus, which is generally known only for part of one verse, that proclaiming the law of brotherly love. Too often the context of this verse is overlooked, and the Hebraic point of view accordingly mutilated. The very chapter that proclaims the lofty ethical ideals of social life insists in the same breath and tone: "Thou shalt not let thy cattle gender with a diverse kind; thou shalt not sow thy field with two kinds of seed; neither shall there come upon thee a garment of two kinds of stuff mingled together." Though Pauline Christianity abrogated much of the Jewish ritual law, in principle it agreed with the Talmudic exegete who stated that "the laws of purity and impurity, of menstruation and of [sacrificial] bird offerings are the essentials of the Torah." The mother and daughter religions differed with regard to which parts of the Bible remained binding and which could be codified, and as to how the details of Scripture were to be interpreted for practical application. But both religions agreed on the postulate of a Scripturally governed life.

The only way that the revelation could be kept relevant to new problems was to interpret the written word so as to make it apply to the activities of the peasant and the businessman, the housewife and the servant, the schoolboy and the scholar. It is this interpretive body of literature that Judaism calls its legal Midrash, or Oral Law. The primary function of Midrash was to make the Torah a living legal document, so that every act of life might be performed in accordance with the divine command. Though the Torah obviously did not spell out the correct behavior for every situation, surely the Revealer must have foreseen every possible contingency and made room for it in His Law. God undoubtedly worded His revelation in such a way as to provide the key to its everlasting application and fulfillment. The Word must, accordingly, be studied and thoroughly examined for hints of the right direction to follow, and a loophole sought where its plain sense has to be relinquished. The kind of Midrash the Jew took most seriously was the Halakhic or legal exegesis, for it gave him the answer to the one question he considered most pertinent to his life: What does God command me to *do*, how would He have me *act* in the face of this or that situation?

From Scripture the Jew inferred, too, that it was not his function to distinguish between important and unimportant commandments. Had not God put the ethical and the ritual together to indicate their equal importance? "Be heedful," his rabbi taught him, "of a light precept as of a weighty one, for thou knowest not the reward of each precept." Another authority put it even more plainly: "If one says 'This law does not seem right,' he has no share in the world to come." Not that the reason for ritual and civil laws was not sought or discussed. As we shall see, a whole body of Midrashic literature deals with the rationale of Jewish life, the whys and wherefores of the Torah. But in the last analysis, the reason was secondary to the performance. Following Rabban Johanan ben Zakkai, who summed up the Biblical laws of purity, the observing Jew felt he must perform the whole Torah: "Neither do the dead impurify, nor do the ashes of the red heifer purify. This is my decree, such is my ordinance; ye may not transgress it!"

The Torah was searched over and over for the detailed ways in which the Jew might fulfill Scripture. The Decalogue forbade work on the Sabbath. What was "work" and what was not? Midrash was the technique by which rest and work were completely defined. From a single command prohibiting cooking a kid in its mother's milk, a whole corpus of dietary laws was derived forbidding the consumption of meat and dairy products together. Scripture, to cite a renowned example of the Midrashic technique, had promulgated the law of retaliation, "eye for eye, tooth for tooth, hand for hand, foot for foot." This, the Pharisees declared, in flat contradiction of the plain sense of Scripture (and of their Sadducean opponents), signifies the requirement that a physical injury inflicted by one man on another must be compensated for in funds. "Why?" the Talmudic authorities asked. "Does the Torah not say *eye for eye?*" The Talmudic reply is a precious specimen of the Scriptural lesson as it was taught in the ancient Jewish schoolhouse. "You might think that where a man put out his fellow's eye, the offender's eye should be put out, or where he cut off his arm, the offender's arm should be cut off, or again where he broke his leg, the offender's leg should be broken. Scripture, therefore, has stated: *He that smiteth any man, and he that smiteth a beast mortally shall make it good.* [Scripture used the word ("smiteth") in both cases to teach us that] just as in the case of smiting a beast compensation is to be paid, so also in the case of smiting a man compensation is to be paid." Verse by verse the teachers proceeded until the hundreds of Biblical commandments had multiplied into thousands.

The first source of law was the text as confronted by the needs and realities of life itself, and mediating between the two was the scrupulous explication of Scripture. At times, the Midrashic method was of itself inadequate, for the scholars could find no means of connecting their own wishes with the provisions of Scripture. At this point they resorted to innovation, provided, of course, they could avoid open contradiction of the Torah. The *takkanah,* or legislated ordinance, if it gained the acceptance of the community of scholars, took on the authority of law and was enforced. In spirit it was intimately bound up with the Midrashic orientation, for its purpose was always to preserve the spirit of the Law as the Rabbis understood it. In the realm of economic life, Hillel the Elder came to the rescue of the small entrepreneur and farmer by the institution of *prosbul,* which enabled creditors to collect their loans even after the seventh year of remission. By guaranteeing repayment, he ensured the uninterrupted flow of credit from the moneyed classes to the poor. Much more significant than the institution itself—which was avowedly borrowed from the Hellenistic courts of his day—is the way in which Hillel rationalized it. To allow the Biblical law of the remission of debts to continue undisturbed, he stated, would risk the violation of the Deuteronomic command, "Thou shalt surely open thy hand unto thy poor and needy brother." In every generation of the Talmudic and post-Talmudic community, new features were added to Jewish life by legislation that plainly had to be fabricated by mortals.

Innovation for the sake of the spirit of the Law brings us face to face with the Rabbinic definition of the spirit of Judaism. No matter how concerned the Rabbis were with ritual performance, the choice of alternatives compelled them to formulate some kind of abstract principle by which the followers of the Torah should be guided. It is here that the Prophetic and Hagiographic books played a crucial role in the definition of Judaism. The spirit of the cult and its ritual was clearly undefinable, except in relative and conjecturable terms. So God had ordained, and so it was to be done. But what had God intended by the injunctions and precepts which He had revealed? To the Rabbinic mind Micah had stated in a nutshell what the prophets had been declaring from the days of Abraham and Moses to the close of the Biblical age: "It hath been told thee, O man, what is good, and what the Lord doth require of thee: only to do justly, and to have mercy, and to walk humbly with thy God." Where Micah and other prophets had protested against Israelite cultism, later Judaism explained, it had only been to deny the automatic efficacy of ritual. Ritual could achieve nothing of itself. The personal *intention* behind it was the crucial factor. The Torah and its rituals were a discipline reminding one at every step of the imperative for justice and humility of behavior, which lead in turn to deeds of mercy and loving-kindness.

Hospitality to wayfarers, visiting the sick, dowering the needy bride, bestowing charity anonymously, attending the dead to the grave and comforting their mourners, and the making of peace between man and his fellow—these became the supreme and symbolic virtues of daily life. Hence social legislation was fashioned along the emotional lines enunciated by the prophetic school. The latter were regarded as the first interpreters of the Torah, and those who claimed their mantle followed in what they regarded as the prophetic footsteps. The cold and impersonal commands of the Pentateuch were charged with the emotional pitch of prophetism, of dedicated worship and loving service. The multiplicity of Talmudic charity laws and institutions, the honor accorded to the communal charity officials, and the incessant concern with the poor and indigent in civil law are one of the glorious chapters in every Jewish code from the Mishna to the *Shulhan Arukh*. Amos' feeling for mankind was codified and incorporated into the sacred ritual.

If law was the heart and body of Judaism, the second type of Midrash, Aggada, or homiletical interpretation, was its lifeblood and marrow. Here, too, the Talmudic doctors clung to the pattern cut out for them by Scripture.

The Torah is not only a law book, it is much more. Considerable portions of the Bible are purely informative; history begins with the first day of creation and ends with the rebuilding of the walls of Jerusalem under Nehemiah. Other portions contain lyrical poetry, liturgical selections, theological reflection, and pure wisdom literature. To what purpose all of this? The conclusion easily imposed itself on the mind of the Jew that the Bible was not only a code of behavior but a guide to the totality of life. In it one would find the clue and the key to every form of authentic wisdom and to every genuine insight. Its historical record of ancient generations—from Adam to Ezra—was not only sacred history, but, above all, a parable of all human activity, a model from which all men could profit. The Rabbis declared that prophecies relevant only to their immediate audience were not recorded; only those revelations which were essential for all generations were committed to writing. To the historical portions of the Bible their reaction was the same. God would not have troubled later generations of Israel with a record of mere trivialities. Every detail of Scripture was in reality an archetype, a carefully selected and worded bit of information from which to learn.

Every phrase, verse, and story, every proverb, poem, and prayer—in short, the entire Bible from Genesis to Chronicles—was studied, analyzed, and interpreted. Where the plain sense of Scripture seemed obscure, the exegetes elucidated the text and translated it into their own idiom. Where the Bible had omitted details in a story, they speculated on what probably happened. How did Adam react when he experienced the first nightfall in the Garden of Eden? What did Cain say to his brother Abel just before killing him? What motives lay behind the building of the Tower of Babel? In connection with this kind of speculation we cannot do better than refer the reader to Professor Louis Ginzberg's monumental seven-volume work, *The Legends of the Jews,* where a modern master of Rabbinics has assembled all of the material and transcribed it in the form of a running narrative parallel to the Biblical story. To the Talmudic Jew, ancient history became current events, and the challenges of the day were met under the inspiration of Scriptural antiquity. The feuds between Jacob and Esau, Joseph and his brothers, Moses and Pharaoh, became eternal struggles symbolizing the conflicts of Jews (and for that matter, of all men) throughout history. Thomas Mann's *Joseph and His Brothers* is one of hundreds of literary efforts which drew quite consciously on this genre of Midrashic technique.

Nothing in the homiletical form of interpretation makes the intentions and methods of the Rabbis so plain as does their allegorical treatment of the Song of Songs. A blunt and impassioned compilation of love ditties, the work was incorporated into the Biblical canon only because it was read as a dialogue of love between God and the community of Israel. "Thy two breasts are like two fawns," sings the lover. "Thy two breasts," the Rabbi explained, "are Moses and Aaron." To the ancient, there was nothing strange in this manner of reading, for Greeks and Romans regularly employed the same technique in their own classical poetry and mythology. To the Jew, the text and its Midrash infused a feminine quality of love and warmth into a life of rigor and unending duty. In Aggadic Midrash the imagination ranged freely, releasing the emotion of the devout, and so converting law to love and ritual to caress. The Bible was no longer only the guide and master of the Jew; it was his intimate companion, his alter ego.

Aggada, or the homiletical exposition of Scripture, supplied the Jewish idiom expressive of the phenomena of life and history. Its clichés and catchwords became the vehicles for the communication of values, ideals, and emotional response. While the Greek philosopher had built a logical structure whereby the universe was systematically rationalized, the Jew thought and spoke in terms saturated in value concepts, terms that had moral and emotional overtones, that conveyed the Hebraic evaluation of every fact as either right or wrong. The sun, moon, and stars, the elements and animal life—these were not mere natural phenomena. They were manifestations of God's love or God's justice depending on how human society experienced them.

Through Aggada the Talmudic Jew engaged in theological speculation. Though open discussion of the essence of God was discouraged officially, the learned Hellenistic milieu, with its mystical outpourings and theological debates on the nature and essence of the deity, inevitably penetrated the Rabbinic academy. The visions of Isaiah, Ezekiel, and Daniel, even the impersonal account of the creation in Genesis, provided fertile ground for Jewish conjecture about God and His being. But above all, theological expression roamed freely when it came to the subject of God's relation to man in general and to Israel in particular. To the Jew, naturally enough, the two most engaging subjects for consideration were the Torah, the supreme gift of God, and God's selection of the Jews as His chosen people. The virtues of the Torah, of its precepts, and of its loyal followers were inculcated on every occasion, thus providing the rationale for a militant faith undaunted by subjection, persecution, or even defeat.

The two forms of Midrash, Halakha and Aggada, grew side by side. Often a sermon or scholarly discourse was at the same time a skillfully woven tapestry of legal and homiletical exposition, providing the regimen and its motive together. However, there was a fundamental difference between the Halakha and Aggada in the demand they made on the individual Jew. Law—civil, ritual, and domestic—was normative, binding, and absolute. To be sure, there were differences of opinion and practice with regard to questions of the Law, but the essential point was that a person could be held socially accountable for his behavior, and his peculiarities had better not be idiosyncrasies. On the other hand, the homily was subjective and hence essentially without binding force. The only restraints or limits upon Aggada were the dogmatic presuppositions bound up with the acceptance of the Torah as the revelation. Although Aggadic statements were expressed in terms of traditional value concepts, the latter were by no means codified forms. The ultimate difference between the two classes of interpretation appeared in the net result of the exegesis. A legal statement in Scripture could in theory have only one possible meaning; in other words, the Law had to be logically derived from the formulation of the precept in Scripture. Legal contradictions had to be harmonized. In contrast, Aggada proceeded, verse by verse, providing no necessary connection between the homily expounded in one verse and the interpretation given to the next. Further still, the very same verse lent itself to any number of Aggadic interpretations and rationalizations even by the same commentator. Homilies varied with their authors or with the same author's moods and insights. What need to harmonize incompatible emotions and reactions, when Scripture itself accorded them an equal hearing?

Rabbinic Judaism, though it has survived to become the oldest organized religion of Western civilization, never could formulate a systematic theology. Individuals like Maimonides, Albo, and Crescas might attempt to formulate creeds, but in the absence of an organized and fully disciplined hierarchy their ideas had no official sanction, and each Jew could accept or reject which of them he pleased. Characteristically the medieval Talmudist regarded the philosopher as an Aggadist, a homiletician whose insights could inspire but not ordain.

Not that Talmudic Judaism had no dogmas, but these, significantly enough, were often stated negatively. So we find in the Mishna: "The following have no share in the world to come. He who denies resurrection, he who denies the divine origin of the Torah, and the Epicurean." Translated into contemporary terms, the statement excludes from the community of Israel whoever denies divine retribution, the sanctity of Scripture and its oral exegesis, and Divine Providence. Actually, these principles of faith all follow from the one assumption that the Torah is God's revelation to Israel. If the Torah and its application in daily life were not ordained by God, the Rabbinic schoolhouse had no meaning. Assume that it makes little difference to God how we act, or that he will not justify the righteous and condemn the wicked, and the perseverance in a Jewish way of life against the current of the whole pagan world is nothing but a masochistic comedy. But how these dogmas were to be translated into a positive creed was left to the individual Jew to decide.

But Rabbinic dogma can also be stated in positive form. From the axiom that the Torah was divine revelation, it followed that the historical accounts it contained were statements of fact. Whatever the significance of these accounts for the future, they were, in the first instance, a record of events which really took place. With one notable exception—the story of Job (which some rabbis considered only a parable)—no fact of Scripture could be questioned or contradicted. Thus the chosenness of Israel was as much a fact of the Bible as the assertion that God rested on the seventh day of creation. Every Jew was certain that God would redeem His people just as the Bible promises. Every believer was as certain of these articles of faith as he was that the Law had to be fulfilled. Beyond these obvious deductions the meaning of faith was the subject of considerable diversity of opinion. Aggadic Midrash never ceased to change so long as the Bible remained the acknowledged source of human guidance.

If the conception of an eternally valid Scripture is the most important of Rabbinic legacies to civilization, there is another Talmudic postulate bound up with it, and hardly less important. God revealed the Torah to *all* of Israel and holds every man and woman individually responsible for its fulfillment. Providence and individual retribution were the logical corollaries of personalized faith. The prophetic assertion that God held each person accountable for his deeds in the moral realm was extended in Talmudic civilization to the cultic-ritual domain as well. For the external, visible Temple cult, Talmudic Judaism increasingly substituted an internalized conscience at least as strong in its grip as that of visible ceremonial. This conscience dictated a ceremonial of its own, often quite colorful and performed in congress with other Jews. But given its internalized character, responsibility rested with the individual, who of course was also subject to social pressure. True, autonomous Jewish society had disciplinary means at its disposal, such as fines, flogging, and excommunication. But its real achievement was the inculcation of a strong sense of guilt in the sinner, and it was this, not physical coercion, in any case poorly developed, that held Jewish society together in a firmly knit unit. Daily prayer and individual proficiency in the Book were but the most obvious elements in the personalization of religious obligation and responsibility. The most far-reaching result of the new conception of faith was an active universalism, directed to converting the pagan to the chosen way of life.

What made the Jew an alien in every community he inhabited was not so much his ethnic attachment—the Jew was not unique in this respect—but his militant insistence on his foreign habits and values. Not only did he behave in Rome as the Jerusalemites do, but he made no bones about concealing his contempt for the misguided, if not downright sinful, civilization of the majority. Whoever takes offense at stubborn and militant sects, like Jehovah's Witnesses, need but read the Book of Esther to appreciate Haman's reaction to Mordecai. It made little difference to the Gentile that the Jewish rejection of Greco-Roman civilization was not intended as a deliberate affront; that it was the only course open to adherents of a jealous monotheism and a levitical code that made a priest of every believer. So much the worse for their superstition, the pagan replied; look at Jewish behavior objectively, and you will find that it bespeaks a deep contempt for the whole human race. The Jew's answer was his actions. The worth of a human being, he declared, depends not on his birth but on what he does. The Torah and its salvation were given to all who would but enter the covenant of Abraham. Thus Talmudic culture broke down forever the ethnic barriers to membership within the Jewish group. Conversion to the faith, submission to the yoke of the Torah—these were the keys to chosenness. For the first time in history a people nullified its ethnic status and reconstituted itself as a church.

It is a widely circulated belief that Judaism does not encourage conversion or missionary activity among the Gentiles. How false this notion is about Talmudic culture may be seen from the early Christian documents, which frankly confess that their easiest access to Gentiles was in the synagogue where the latter came to hear the Jewish sermon. The Talmudic literature records with pride the activities of some of the more distinguished proselytes, a number of whom were of pagan royalty. Simultaneously with its intense ritual separatism, Talmudic civilization proclaimed and fostered a new universalism, without which Christianity and Islam could never have spread as they did. So widespread and recognized did Jewish missionary activity become that Christianity, at the very moment of its break with the Jewish people, proclaimed itself the new and the true *Israel*.

Along with the Talmudic conception of Scripture, the Jewish view of individual religious responsibility altered the course of Western civilization. Jewish-Christian hostility dates back in large measure to the first two centuries, when the two religions openly and heatedly competed for the conquest and salvation of human souls and, in fact, claimed the same name.

Membership in the Torah made of one a fully accepted Jew; indeed, it obligated the convert to *ethnic* Jewish duties and responsibilities. However, so obsessed was the Jewish expounder of the Torah with spreading its message that full conversion was not required of those who wished to observe its law and yet balked at full identification with the Jewish people. "The pious of the nations of the world" and "fearers of the Lord" were two of the religious categories used to designate Gentiles who unofficially accepted more or less of Judaism. All of them had to renounce idolatry—note the negative formulation—blasphemy, murder, theft, and sexual promiscuity and had to agree to live a strictly moral life in civil transactions. Others adopted one or more of the more commonly known Jewish practices: some renounced pork, others rested on the Sabbath, while women, in particular, were known to light the Sabbath candles in their homes. Though obviously not as deserving as converts, these Gentile fellow travelers were the elect of the nations and were assured of a share in the world to come.

The life of the Torah, besides prescribing rules of conduct and attitudes to the problems of life, made of the Jews a people of the Book in two fundamental senses. The holy Book, or any fragment of it, became a sacred object to the Jews. Before the Torah, Jews are commanded to rise; a scroll that is unusable may not be cast away, but has to be buried or stored. The skins, the ink, the script, and of course the spelling of the scrolls were ritually regulated; the omission of one letter was sufficient to disqualify an entire scroll for synagogal use. Fragments of the Torah, such as those contained in *tefillin* (phylacteries) and *mezuzot* (doorpost mementos), were sacred and must not be desecrated. The language of Scripture became the sacred tongue, and though Talmudic universalism necessarily recognized the validity of study and prayer in any language—Philo most certainly prayed and studied Scripture in Greek— Hebrew occupied a special place in the scale of Jewish values. To be sure, Hebrew was also a vehicle of ethnic identification and preservation. But every ethnic aspect of Jewish life capable of religious association was sanctified.

The physical veneration of the Book was, of course, but the more tangible expression of the awe in which the revelation was held. Profounder worship lay in the study of the contents and meaning of the Torah. Such study became the most honored ritual and profession in Talmudic civilization. It was more than a mere quip when one Palestinian teacher paraphrased a verse in the Bible saying: "Would that the children of Israel leave Me [i.e., God] and pursue my Torah." In the hierarchy of values, Rabbi Akiba and his school argued, study takes precedence over performance, for study is the key to fulfillment. In Rabbinic parlance, wasting time was waste of study time, for every available moment must be dedicated to memorizing and understanding. On this subject the homilists harped without end. The study of the Torah was the Jewish calling, and its followers were assured of the perpetual companionship of the Divine Presence. The renowned little tractate in the Mishna known as The Ethics of the Fathers is really not a treatise on ethics at all, but essentially an exhortation to the acquisition of Torah. "An illiterate does not fear sin," Hillel the Elder said. This statement by one of the fathers of Talmudic Judaism cryptically sums up a whole complex of Jewish values and the Jewish man's vocation on earth. Righteousness, the Talmudic Jew contends, does not consist in spontaneous goodness alone, but in a life disciplined in the heavy harness of the Torah. In one form or another, Talmudic homilists maintained that greater merit accrued to one who fulfilled the Torah out of a sense of duty than to one who did it out of personal choice. Learning in the precept and wisdom of the Torah was the path to performance and consequent acceptance into the kingdom of Heaven.

What we have been describing is, from the historical point of view, the theory expounded by the scribes, elders, and Pharisees in their struggle for authority over Jewish society in the Second Commonwealth. The effect of their teaching was the establishment of a new Jewish aristocracy replacing the traditional priestly and noble classes. Nobility of birth, wealth, or social station was categorically denied as justification of authority. "A learned bastard," the Rabbis said, "takes precedence over an ignorant high priest." This sounds the familiar note of an aggressive class, yes, a subversive one, that is patently advocating the reform, if not the overthrow, of an accepted social framework. To us, the Pharisaic program foreshadows one of the basic features of modern democratic theory.

The new noble was the teacher, together with the man of promise, his disciple. Like all nobility, the Talmudic sages produced their own genealogy, which resembled in some ways the pedigree of the Greek philosopher. Of what import was it whose son you were? What mattered was whose disciple you had been, and how intimate your association with him. Tacitus' complaint that Jewish proselytism broke up stable Roman families was equally applicable to established Jewish homes in Palestine. If what counted was not life, but a life of Torah, one's physical parents were hardly as important as one's spiritual masters. The Mishnaic law is more revelatory here than whole tracts of exhortation. It declares: "[He who seeks] his father's lost property and that of his teacher, his teacher's has first place, for his father did but bring him into this world, but his master that taught him wisdom brings him into the world to come. . . . If his father and his teacher each bore a burden, he must first relieve his teacher and then relieve his father. . . . If his father and his teacher were kidnaped, he must first ransom his teacher, and then ransom his father!" The course of initiation into the Torah, therefore, meant the conscious adoption of a new father, who was heeded and imitated so as to learn the good life. Knowledge of the Book in itself was manifestly useless, for the Law was often applied in a way far different from the ostensible meaning of the injunction. "Exile thyself to a center of Torah" was the Rabbinic advice to the aspiring student. Only in that way could he become a link in the chain of tradition.

The singular concern of Jews with the education of their children—the modern, secularized hope for a son who will turn out a lawyer, a doctor, a professor—dates back to the cultural revolution which Talmudic civilization produced. In oft-quoted passages, Josephus proudly boasts of the proverbial learning of Jewish children in the Torah and, significantly enough, engages in invidious comparison with the adult populations of the Gentile culture he knew well: "Above all we pride ourselves on the education of our children, and regard as the most essential task in life the observance of our laws and of the pious practices, based thereon, which we have inherited." Reflecting on the significance of universal education among Jews, he says:

> Indeed, most men, so far from living in accordance with their own laws, hardly know what they are. Only when they have done wrong do they learn from others that they have transgressed the law. Even those of them who hold the highest and most important offices admit their ignorance; for they employ professional legal experts as assessors and leave them in charge of the administration of affairs. But, should anyone of our nation be questioned about the laws, he would repeat them all more readily than his own name. The result, then, of our thorough grounding in the laws from the first dawn of intelligence is that we have them, as it were, engraven on our souls. A transgressor is a rarity; evasion of punishment by excuses an impossibility.

Had he lived in a less hostile atmosphere, or written in his native tongue, Josephus would no doubt have desisted from such wishful thinking. Nevertheless, it remains true that in comparison with the average Gentile, the lay Jew was lawyer, philosopher, and priest all in one.

Success and achievement have never been an ideal breeding ground for the human virtues of humility, warmth, and kindliness. Scholars on occasion all too easily identified the honor of the Torah with its human bearers, a step that was made all the easier in view of the oral nature of the Talmudic tradition. To counterbalance this natural tendency, the sin of pride and the virtue of humility as a *legal* duty were emphasized constantly. Arrogant Pharisaism was a contradiction in terms. Ideally, the Torah could be fulfilled only in consonance with the three virtues enunciated by Micah. That not all men lived up to the ideal is not a reflection on the society or its faith, but simply proof that men are mortal. We should not indulge in such a truism if it were not for the one-sided picture of Pharisaism presented by New Testament writers and exegetes. Tendentiousness, too, is a human attribute, but regrettably the Gospels have been taken to be objective truth even by historians who should know better.

THE NEW HERO TYPE

A hero, according to the Shorter Oxford English Dictionary, is "a man who exhibits extraordinary bravery, firmness, or greatness of soul, in connection with any pursuit, work or enterprise; a man admired and venerated for his achievements and noble qualities." The hero symbolizes those ideals and values which the members of his society would like to emulate in their own struggles for success and immortality. From the anthropological point of view, the facts of his life—indeed, whether he ever existed at all—hardly matter. The crucial thing is not the real events of his life, but the legends told of him. For these legends are the uncensored transcription of impulses and aspirations that are often repressed in normal converse. A hero, of course, implies a villain, the archetype of all that the society holds mean and contemptible. A seed of low caste, deceitful and arrogant, he represents the eternal foe of the hero (and of his people), whom he constantly seeks to undermine.

And now to the hero and villain types of Talmudic civilization. In the first instance, the most suitable archetypes for Talmudic civilization were the figures of the Biblical narrative from Adam to Esther. Throughout Talmudic times a new genre of pseudepigraphic literature circulated in Jewish society purporting to contain the secrets of heaven and of history, which had been committed to writing by the great figures of antiquity. The very names of these works—generally called apocalyptic because of their form and subject matter—Adam and Eve, Enoch, The Testaments of the Twelve Patriarchs, The Assumption of Moses, Baruch, (Pseudo-) Ezra—reveal the deep awe with which the Talmudic Jew regarded his Biblical ancestor. The heros here achieved and set down in writing what every Jew in the Greco-Roman world keenly pined for: a direct revelation from the heavenly court on the ultimate justification of the righteous in the end of history. Talmudic legend elaborated on the lives of the Biblical actors and made them participants in the contemporary Jewish struggles with Greco-Roman civilization. Abraham became a saint, Isaac a martyr, Jacob a scholar; needless to say, all three were devout ritualists. Conversely, Esau was none other than Rome the wicked, Balaam was the anti-Jewish propagandist, Jeroboam was the apostate and renegade.

But heroes are forever being born, if we but have the eyes to recognize them. Hillel the Elder came to Palestine at the age of forty, an obscure scion of the house of David—note his pedigree—studied forty years, and ministered to his people for another forty. Like Moses, who did not gain universal recognition until the age of eighty, he lived to the age of a hundred and twenty. So great was his passion for Torah, but so dire his poverty, that when he could not pay the entrance fee to the lecture in the academy, he eavesdropped through a hole in the roof. On this occasion he was so rapt in attention to the lecture that he completely failed to notice that he was caught in a snowstorm and his life imperiled. Later, on a Passover Eve, when the elders of Judea were, to a man, stumped by a ritual problem on which the observance of the festival depended, only Hillel could solve the problem and save the day. For this one feat he was appointed prince of the Sanhedrin. His character and temperament were no less heroic. No one could exhaust his patience, nothing could shake his humility or cool his natural warmth. Even the most negligible of his disciples was worthy of being a prophet, had he but lived in Biblical times.

Like Hillel, Rabban Johanan ben Zakkai—who in defiance of all chronology is called his youngest disciple—lived six score years, the last two of which he spent as president of the Sanhedrin. Like Hillel's, the poverty of Rabbis Joshua, Akiba, Judah, and others was matched by the profundity of their learning. Rabbi Eliezer ben Hyrcanus, the disciple of Rabban Johanan, remained totally illiterate until the age of twenty-two, when he renounced his share in his father's millions and ate dung from the street in order to sit at the feet of the wise. Every schoolboy knew the love story of Rachel, the heiress to a fortune, who married Akiba, an ignorant shepherd, and starved that he might begin to study the alphabet at the age of forty. Not only did he rise to become the dean of Jewish scholars, but he continued to teach until he died a martyr's death with the *Shema* ("Hear O Israel") on his lips.

Nor were the women neglected. The sufferings of Akiba's wife were proverbial even in her own day. Rabbi Joshua's mother, while she bore the future scholar in her womb, visited the academy in order that the atmosphere might seep into her unborn son. Beruria, the wife of Rabbi Meir, distinguished herself by her Rabbinical acumen and profound religiosity. Rabbi Ishmael's mother insisted on the privilege of washing her son's feet, in order to share in the merit of Torah.

The descendants of the very people that first produced mature historical writing—the Books of Joshua to Kings, Chronicles, Ezra, Nehemiah, Esther, and Maccabees—now abandoned historiography as a creative outlet. The historical books that were not canonized—to say nothing of the books of the renegade Josephus—fell by the wayside and became the property of the Christian Church. The fragments of history which have been preserved in the Rabbinic library are only those directly connected with Scripture and the Oral Law. History as a chain of human events ceased to exist, for only Torah was of lasting import, and it had already taken account of whatever history was of significance. Indeed, what use was history to a people whose political existence had been torn to shreds and whose only hope lay in the promises of the Torah?

Torah now took on an added meaning. Not only did it signify the Pentateuch, the Oral Law, and the Prophets. The Midrash of every generation, legal and homiletical; theology, mysticism, liturgy, ethics, and folktale—all were part of the vast tapestry of Torah, which to the Jew became the mirror of the good life and the reflection of God's will.

THEOLOGICAL IDIOM

It has often been remarked with amazement that a culture so theocratically oriented as the Talmudic should have so *relatively* little to say of its God, and virtually nothing of a dogmatic nature beyond what is explicit in Scripture. God is the creator of heaven and earth, the revealer of the Torah, the judge of mankind, who will one day quicken the dead and restore Israel. How God does these things or why, many a Jew tried to state, but in the end he had to admit that one guess was as good as another.

There was a commonly accepted idiom, however, and it is on this basis that we shall try to formulate a few generalizations about the Talmudic conception of God. Underlying the vocabulary of theological commentary were certain implicit assumptions. We can only formulate these assumptions in a general way, for it is impossible to be precise about a subject concerning which precision and finality were shunned.

Prayers of supplication in Jewish liturgy begin with the rubric, "Our father, our king." There is nothing in these words to convey any distinctly Talmudic conception of God. Indeed, one may comb the Jewish liturgy of Talmudic origin only to find a paraphrase of Biblical verses put together to form a magnificat or a supplication. With the possible exception of the affirmation of resurrection—which the Rabbis "traced" to Scripture—Rabbinic liturgy remained remarkably free of Midrash. The relatively few references to angels are of a later vintage. However, the supplicatory rubric and many like it were on the lips of every Jew, and in unofficial moments Jews spelled out more fully what the words conveyed to them.

If the God of Scripture generally appears to be the stern King and meticulous administrator of justice, the God of Talmudic culture is also the warm and protecting Father, whose chief concern is over the welfare of His children. Present in the writings of prophets and psalmists, the idea is much older than Talmudic culture; yet the frequency with which it is now expressed indicates a distinct shift in emphasis. Wherever we turn in the Talmudic world, we feel that a new intimacy has been achieved between man and God. In keeping with the new religious duties and responsibilities of the individual, God is now near to every man, not only in isolated lyrical moments, but always, everywhere. To Him the Jew may weep about his household problems quite as freely and as fervently as in his supplications for the restoration of His people. God himself, the Rabbis assure the people, is not above weeping at the plight of His children in their exile and their sorrow. God, too, smiles with unconcealed pleasure as He witnesses a debate between two scholars over a technical point of the Law. In other words, God is the head of the heavenly and human families—of the angels and the hosts of heaven, of mankind and the physical world. As the Father, He has all the qualities of a human parent, only infinitely magnified. As Father, He plans, orders, achieves, comforts, chastises, and heeds those who will but call.

God, of course, is no less the King, no less the exacting judge and master. But the God of the Decalogue, the Prophets, Job, and the lyrical psalmist is now felt as a single, if complex, force, present and the same in every variety of circumstance. After the Second Destruction, there arises a new sensitivity in religious and moral matters. It is the outcome of the reforms of Ezra, the wars with Antiochus, and the preaching of Pharisees, Essenes, and visionaries. It takes the form of an unquenchable thirst for God.

The divine-human encounter in its new complexity is signalized in Talmudic idiom by means of two concepts, or moods, if one likes, that conveyed the antipodal manifestations of the Father-King in the universe: God's loving mercy (*rahamim*) and his exacting justice (*din*). As instances of His mercy one might reckon the bounties of nature, His revelations, and His salvation in time of need. His justice, on the other hand, is manifested in such phenomena as war, exile, pestilence, and destruction. Normal and abnormal phenomena, the banal and the miraculous, all reveal God as forever intervening in the order of nature. The universe is an implement in the moral order of things, serving God's purpose to reward the righteous and punish the wicked. Casting a shadow upon these dialectical categories was the eternal question of Job—the problem of the suffering saint and the happy villain. It is the Biblical caveat against any easy solution which would reduce God or his universe to the dimensions of human reason. As we shall see, Talmudic Judaism had an answer to Job's question, but it was an answer that it wisely refrained from applying to the visible world.

How does one approach the omniscient and omnipotent Almighty, the ineffable Holy One blessed be He? His very name (YHWH) was tabu to all but the high priest, who uttered it only on the Day of Atonement. So awesome was his name, so wary was the Jew of taking it in vain, that even "God" (*Elohim*) was not employed in conversation, nor even the euphemistic "Lord" (*Adonai*). How then could one speak to the utterly transcendent creator? By prayer, the Jew replied, by deeds of loving-kindness, by study and fulfillment of the Torah; in short, by bringing oneself fully under the yoke of the kingship of heaven. Obedience to His will moves God to cause His presence to dwell among men. Man can breach the gulf between earth and heaven or widen it. Sin and defection cause God to withdraw, in other words, to leave man at the mercy of the cold and cruel world.

The average Jew of Talmudic times was little concerned over the belief in God. Over and above a perfunctory note of condemnation for a renegade like Elisha ben Abuya, who left the fold despondent and shouting, "There is neither Judge nor justice," one senses in the Talmudic account of him a deep feeling of pity and horror for a man who has lost all hope and has sunk to the last depth of despair. Open denial of God, or atheism, was a rare phenomenon in the ancient world; even the Cynics and Epicureans did not deny the existence of gods. Much more demanding than the philosophic question of belief was the religious question of man's relationship to God, his service to Him, and trust in Him.

The chief source of the Jew's knowledge of God and of the way to serve him was the revelation and its Midrash. To the King, Master, and Father one comes with awe, reverence, fear, loyalty, and love. Here again the Talmudic hero type illustrates in a nutshell what tomes of theory can only adumbrate. The heroine of II Maccabees who urged her seven children to go to their death rather than submit to idolatry became the theme of many an ancient sermon. In the words of the Psalmist, she was "a joyful mother of children." Rabbi Akiba is portrayed as smiling at the moment of his unendurable tortures, virtually thanking his executioners for having enabled him to fulfill the commandment, "Thou shalt love the Lord thy God with all thy heart, and with all thy soul, and with all thy might." The martyr is but the supreme witness to God's call and command.

Martyrdom is an extreme form of the type of experience that a Jew should properly be undergoing at every moment of his conscious life. Every act, no matter how trivial or neutral, must be oriented toward God. Personal cleanliness, eating and sleeping, business, amusement, and marriage are all acts that can be elevated to the service of the Almighty; for each, indeed, there is an appropriate blessing, which rules out the possibility of a purely human area of experience. The Jew was truly a priest forever ministering at the altar of God. Prayer became the surrogate of sacrifice not only in the sense that it was now the vehicle for supplication to God, but in the sense that it made of each Jew a sacerdotal officer, who must ever stand on duty. In one sense, however, Rabbinic prayer was the very opposite of sacrifice; or, to put it in another way, Talmudic prayer followed in the tradition of Hosea rather than of Leviticus. Prayer was supplicatory and emotional, varying from day to day and from one person to another. Such an approach to God bespeaks the personal and individual character of the religious experience enshrined in Rabbinic Judaism. The placing of religious life in the hands of the individual was but a logical consequence of belief in a universal God. The Torah and its God are no longer the property of the Jewish people alone. Whoever accepts the kingship of God and orients his *life* accordingly has entered the fold of the elect.

"Honor thy father and thy mother, that thy days may be long upon the land which the Lord thy God giveth thee." The injunction is hyperbole, for even a fool can see that experience does not bear out the promise. To what avail Torah, to what purpose renunciation, if Rome fiddles while Judea goes up in flames! God's reply to Job failed to satisfy even the most committed Scripturalists, and could not go unamplified. Above all, it contradicted the endlessly repeated assurances of the Torah,

Prophets, and Psalmists that God would reward each according to his due. The problem of theodicy could not be left to God alone. History, and in particular Jewish history, made this impossible.

The initial premise of Talmudic as of all subsequent monotheistic thought is that God rewards justly. To deny retribution is to deny divine justice. And to the Rabbis the denial of God's justice is the essence of atheism. The Talmudic solution of this problem served to introduce "other-worldly" religion to Western civilization. "That thy days may be long," God had said, but obviously he could not have meant a span of seventy, or even a hundred twenty, years. Length of days could only signify life in a world where ephemerality will reign no longer, where decay, suffering, and death are unknown. Happily, Talmudic culture had inherited the lofty prophetic visions of "the end of the days," when "the wolf shall dwell with the lamb, and the leopard shall lie down with the kid"; when people "shall beat their swords into ploughshares and their spears into pruning-hooks"; when, in short, "they shall sit every man under his vine and under his figtree, and none shall make them afraid." What the prophets had foreseen for mankind corporately, the Talmudic exegete now understood to apply to the individual: not only for men in the future, but for men here and now; all would be reborn new human beings to enjoy "the world to come." The resurrection of the dead, the requital of the righteous and the wicked, each according to his just deserts—this is the sum of the divine assurance.

Israel and the righteous of the Gentiles, all "will have a share in the world to come." This Rabbinic affirmation became a dogma, practically the only one that had no patent foundation in Scripture. Yet so fundamental was it to the individualistic moral orientation of the overwhelming majority of Jews that to deny it, to refuse to affirm it in the daily liturgy, meant automatic exclusion from the religious community. But here, too, no official interpretation or amplification of the dogma was forthcoming. Theories abounded about the world to come, about the state of the human frame and soul in the interval between death and the resurrection, but all of them remained theories. It remained for God to disclose the full truth at His appointed time.

A promise of reward in the future, if it is to be convincing, requires an answer to the obvious question, "Why later? Why not here and now?" What is the explanation of this ephemeral stage of life, with its woes and frustrations? That Talmudic Judaism had no definitive answer to this question perfectly illustrates what we have said concerning its undefinitive theology. One preacher might explain that the suffering of the righteous in this world was a test of their devotion to God. Another might with equal plausibility explain that God was settling the small accounts here and now, requiting the sins of the righteous and the virtues of the wicked in this world, so as to be free for categorical rewards in the world to come. Still another might say that the pure of heart were suffering to expiate the sins of their generation. Too many answers are no answer at all; so Job's question remained.

The unwillingness to theologize went along with an unwillingness to psychologize in credal terms. Only a system which claims to comprehend God can claim to understand man. Judaism has entertained pessimistic psychologies—"Man is basically evil and sinful"—and optimistic ones—"Man is inherently good." Ultimately no theory could be measured except by one criterion: Did it or did it not imply full acceptance of the law of the Torah and trust in God's command?

THE ELECTION OF ISRAEL

Modern apologists of Judaism often betray an uncomfortable feeling when confronted with the Scriptural and Talmudic statements about God's relation to the children of Israel. Particularly in recent years, traditionalist Jews have sought refuge in the view that the election of Israel, while it implies a special responsibility, does not imply that Israel is superior to other peoples. Yet the fact is that there is only one possible justification for the missionary activity of the Rabbis and for their eagerness to expose new souls to the burden of ritual and Torah. It is the firm conviction that the Jewish people by virtue of its Torah is superior in its faith, morality, and ultimate destiny. There was nothing racial about this belief. Modern theories of racism were as foreign even to the most ethnically oriented of the Rabbis as were modern conceptions of democracy to the most liberal among them. They sought to convert Greeks, Syrians, and Romans into Jews, because they *knew* that they were God's people, that theirs was the only true way of life. To be sure, they felt themselves far more responsible and accountable as Jews for their actions than did Gentiles, but then, as now, *noblesse oblige* meant special rights and privileges. No one, Jew, Christian, or Muslim, could fail to assume that his was the one true religion. Wedded to this conviction, the Talmudic Jew carried all over the world what Scripture had told his ancestors on their own soil.

Reading Scripture, the Jew could see perfectly clearly that the story of creation culminated in Abraham; that the lives of the patriarchs led to the Exodus, and the Exodus to the revelation at Sinai. And bound by the logic of Scripture, he believed that Israel and the Torah were God's chosen possessions. In his relations with God and his fellow men, whether Jew or Gentile, the Jew found himself governed by a regimen of life that at once gave him a key to every situation. His *amixia*, or refusal to break bread or intermarry with Gentiles, was essentially no more invidious in intent than his refusal to copulate with his wife during her menstrual period. All nations had ancestral laws and tabus; those of the Jews were merely more embracing. Not that the Jew of Talmudic culture always acted out of impersonal consideration for the Law. But whatever his motives on occasion, the Jew knew that he was fated to carry out the Law, no matter what the price.

The concern of the Talmudic Jew with Scripture and God's justice inspired the attempt to rationalize God's choice of Israel as the keeper of the Torah. By his own criteria, it was clear that whichever people God had chosen to receive the Torah would as a matter of course have become the elect, the cream of mankind. Why did it have to be Israel? At first blush Scripture proffered no satisfactory answer. "Because the Lord loved you, and because He would keep the oath which He swore unto your fathers"—was not this merely begging the question? No, the exegetes replied; the verse thus cited itself proves that God chose Israel because of the merit of their fathers, because of the piety of Abraham, the devotion of Isaac, and the righteousness of Jacob. By their actions, these men earned the oath and covenant of God for their seed unto all eternity. Were it not for this protecting merit, Israel would long since have been destroyed because of its sins. It is not that the Jews as a people are intrinsically worthy of election; they live by the grace of their fathers. Far more important than this attempt to explain history is the concept of theodicy reflected in the idea of corporate reward and punishment, which so profoundly influenced the Jew's view of the vicissitudes of his people.

The concept of corporate retribution is the one inculcated by Scripture. "I the Lord thy God am a jealous God, visiting the iniquity of the fathers upon the children, and upon the third and upon the fourth generation of them that hate me, and showing mercy unto the thousandth generation of them that love me and keep my commandments." Affirm as he would Ezekiel's doctrine of individual responsibility, the Jew knew that in life the innocent often suffer along with the guilty. The Decalogue passage just cited proclaims a corporate responsibility vertically; in practice, Talmudic Jews applied it horizontally. Allegorically they explained the destruction of the Second Temple as being due to the hatred that existed between two prominent Jews. Let each Jew, then, mind his ways, lest he bring calamity on the whole community. Let no Jew beam with success; his pleasant lot may well be only a reward to his father or righteous neighbor. Can this idea be brought into line with the idea of individual justice? No, but Scripture proclaims both, and God alone knows how and when each principle comes into play.

Yet this rationalization of the election of Israel was not entirely satisfactory. After all, it left the Gentiles out in the cold. At least the Torah might be offered to them! Once again, Aggada stepped into the breach. The nations had been offered the Torah, but they turned it down to a man. Esau (i.e., Rome) would not stand for "Thou shalt not murder"; Ammon for "Thou shalt not commit adultery"; Ishmael (the Beduin) refused to accept "Thou shalt not steal"—and so on. Only Israel willingly proclaimed, "All the words which the Lord hath spoken will we do."

To some extent, this concern with God's motive for the election stemmed from the obsessive concern of the Jew with justice and fair play, in other words, with the translation of the civil law of the Torah to the ethnic sphere. But over and above the religious motive, the realities of life, even the life of Jews themselves, called for an apologetic. Dispersed and under frequent attack from various quarters, the Jews could only stand up to the forces arrayed against them by means of an equally vigorous morale. A fine chosen nation it is, they heard said openly, that was abandoned with its Temple to the Roman legions. The tenacity of the Jew was bizarre enough; but his proselytizing zeal was utterly ridiculous. To offset all this the Jew and his teachers concentrated on the one comfort left them: the promise of the future to God's elect. Their sufferings had a purpose and would be recompensed, if they but continued in the path chosen for them. The solidarity born of their religion gained momentum from each attack from without. So the gulf widened between Jew and Gentile, to be spanned only when the forces of modern democracy broke the ghetto walls and dissolved Jewish ethnic existence.

Nothing is more difficult even for the best-intentioned student than a detached view of Jewish-Gentile relations, not even those of two thousand years ago. We have already seen that present-day accounts of the riots of Alexandria, for example, or the disturbances in Judea, are charged with the suppressed tensions of the twentieth century and have the character of diatribes or apologetics. Here, too, we venture to set forth the hypotheses and assumptions of our ancestors without evaluating them morally.

To the Jew, Scripture made it plain that all Jews were "brothers," all Gentiles "aliens" or "strangers." The dichotomy at once excluded the Gentile from participation in all communal cultic observances and put him beyond the protection of those civil rights in which ethnic or religious elements played a role. In Talmudic society, certainly under the system of Rabbinic authority, a Gentile could not normally give testimony in a Jewish court; a Jew might licitly lend him money on interest and demand repayment of a loan even after the Sabbatical year. On the other hand, Talmudic community leaders ordered that charity be dispensed to Gentiles alongside Jews; that Gentile dead be buried by Jews; and that normal courtesies by accorded them "for the sake of peace." It is thus clear that for all the ritual separation between Jews and the rest of the world, and despite deep-seated antagonism between the peoples of Torah and idolatry, Jews and Gentiles lived side by side harmoniously and peacefully for centuries. Outbreaks of violence were the exception.

It is when we examine the evidence of friction and antagonism that modern sensitivities lead to the temptation to take sides. Essentially the antagonism stemmed from two independent situations, each of which had religious roots. In the Greco-Roman Diaspora Jews demanded—and often received—full protection and equality of rights with the Gentile citizenry. To the Jew a guarantee of rights signified the opportunity to partake in communal activities, yet without having to compromise his own principles. Jews, for example, refused to appear in court on a Sabbath or a festival. In contributing to civic functions, they often stipulated that no Jewish funds be utilized for civic pagan rites. On the other hand, Jews diverted large sums of money annually to the Temple in Jerusalem, a practice to which local Gentile entrepreneurs were extremely sensitive. Add to this the uninhibited remarks which Jews sometimes made about pagan rites and beliefs, and you sense the raw material for a pogrom.

In Palestinian Talmudic society the issue was further complicated by the refusal of the Jews to recognize the legitimacy of alien conquest. Since the Gentile population of Palestine was almost always sympathetic to the foreign conquerors, the Scriptural spark was fanned to a flame. Wherever the Torah had spoken of brothers, many an exegete argued, only Jews were meant. Corporate conceptions of justice and responsibility battened on the political-religious realities and reflected solidarity in the face of a common opponent. (Incidentally, the contrast with Babylonian society is most telling. Living in an autonomous community under the protection and good will of the state, the principle that the civil law of the state applies to Jews was upheld as Jewish law.)

Why then the modern misunderstanding of the true significance of Jewish-Gentile relations in Talmudic civilization? In part, the Rabbis of the Talmud were at fault. Interpreting the Torah in the light of the actual situations they encountered, they simply formulated without qualification their response to a problem. (Unfriendly historians have regrettably ignored qualifications even when they were offered.) From the time Talmudic law became canonized, the Jew was left with an undated legacy which later often embarrassed him. That it did not embarrass him too much may be set down to Christian-Jewish relations beginning with the fourth century. However holy the new Roman Empire claimed to be, the Jew felt that it was nothing but Roman through and through. Jews and Christians each contended that the other group was "the stranger" of Scripture, and each group behaved accordingly. The tensions of the Talmudic age were transferred to Europe and preserved for centuries.

One other source for the self-conscious assertion of the election must be mentioned, for here strangely enough the Jews were the cause of their own embarrassment. The effectiveness of Jewish missionary activity, it is well known, immeasurably facilitated Christian preaching of the

Gospel to the Gentiles. What is often glossed over is the claim of the Christian preachers to represent the true Israel, their contention that the new sect was the rightful heir to God's revelation to the Patriarchs, Moses, and the Prophets. The Talmudic community, beginning with the second century, often found itself forced to defend its claim to the title of Israel. One of the deep sources of tension between Judaism and Christianity—one that never appeared in Jewish-Muslim relations—was the debate of two pretenders to the same title. For reasons of prudence, the Christian Church later chose not to emphasize the question of the Israelite name; but the claim to succession is one which the Church never has given up. The Jew, in turn, all the more aggressively affirmed his lineage and his election against all pretenders. Jacob was again at war with Esau over the primal birthright.

The Jew never suffered a moment's doubt within himself as to who the rightful heir was. He might argue with his neighbor as to why God chose Israel of all nations as keepers of the Torah. But on one point he and his fellow Jews were adamant. God elected Israel for one purpose above all others: to fulfill the Torah and bring its truth to the world. Whatever glorified the Torah was good; whatever discredited it, evil. Israel's mission was to sanctify God's name through the length and breadth of the earth. The most venial of sins was unatonable if it reflected on the Torah: ill manners, shabby dress, legal connivance would undermine a decade of missionary activity. The slightest act of virtue, on the other hand, if it caused a Gentile to say, "Blessed be the God of the Jews who could command such behavior," earned everlasting merit.

The greatest achievement of Talmudic culture on the ethnic level was just this kind of solidarity. The Jews forever kept an eye on the effect of their activity on the world. It is one of the paradoxes of history that few of them could see that if the Jews did not conquer, their Torah did, and thereby brought the civilized peoples under the yoke of the God of Israel.

THE HOLY LAND

Most expositions of Talmudic religion relegate the Holy Land and its place in Talmudic Judaism to a parenthesis in the section on eschatology or retribution, and thence proceed to elaborate on the various theories of the messianic age expounded in ancient Palestine. The chief reason for this misplaced emphasis lies in the effort to treat Rabbinic Judaism as a systematic theology, that is, as a body of abstractions and metaphysical principles. It is argued that a land can only play a contingent role in a religion, that like a ritual or concrete symbol, it is merely the "accidental" embodiment of faith and its imperatives. The theory behind the symbol is infinitely more significant; it is by the theory that the ritual or sacred symbol stands or falls.

However justified such reasoning may be for theology, it is not only totally misleading when it comes to the study of the Talmudic mind, but it also misses the essential factor in nonsystematic religion. Recent anthropological and psychological studies have demonstrated that ancient autochthonous religions were originally a body of rituals and sacred symbols around which the theory (myth or theology) grew later out of a need for rationalization. Religions did not operate as we should like to believe our own religions operate, namely, theology coming first and ritual following as mere symbol. In its treatment of the relative importance of the two types of exegesis, legal and homiletical, Rabbinic Judaism offers an excellent instance of the real order of things. As a general rule, the Halakha came first and the Aggada came afterwards to validate or rationalize it.

In the complex of Jewish rites, symbols, and values, the land of Israel occupies a primary position because of two factors. First and foremost, it is the land of promise designated at the time of the covenant between God and Abraham and is repeatedly reaffirmed throughout Biblical times as the gift of God to Abraham's seed. Nothing is more central in the people's saga. It is always there: in the forty-year sojourn in the desert or in the generations of conquest from Joshua to David. But this factor alone, however important for the early history of Israel, might not have weathered the passage of time, if it were not for the second and more characteristically Pentateuchal-Talmudic feature of the country. Palestine has ever been one of the pivotal foundations of whole blocs of Jewish law and ritual which cannot be fulfilled beyond the borders of its sacred soil. Because of the cultic sanctity of the land, the Jew of Talmudic civilization, no matter where he happened to live, could no more conceive of Judaism without the land of Israel than he could have conceived of it without the people of Israel.

The central importance of the Holy Land in Jewish religion lies in the fact that Talmudic society took with the utmost literalness those sections of Scriptural law which are introduced with the phrase, "And it shall be, when thou art come in unto the land which the Lord thy God giveth thee." All of the agricultural laws and sacrificial laws, as well as considerable portions of the levitical holiness code and parts of the purely civil law became inextricably connected with Palestine in general and Jerusalem in particular. To fulfill the Torah in its entirety, therefore, required dwelling on the holy soil. In the Rabbinic interpretation of Scripture, even the machinery of the Jewish community structure could function fully only in Palestine: ordination and the powers of the Sanhedrin were the exclusive prerogative of the Holy Land. Consequently, the communal functions that required the vote of ordained scholars could be exercised only in the mother country: civil and capital punishment, regulation of the Jewish calendar, and adoption of universally binding legislation (*takkanot*). The genius of Talmudic Judaism in having transcended the limitations of ethnic group, land, and even priestly intermediacy applied only to the rituals that fell within the jurisdiction of the individual: prayer, the Sabbath and festival rest, dietary laws, and marital relations. The sizable bulk of the Law which Scripture had explicitly associated with the land—fully one third of the Halakha—the Rabbis not only did not attempt to abolish, but actually strengthened and amplified.

Since we have asserted the centrality of Palestine to Talmudic religion, we must deal with a widespread misconception of the Rabbinic attitude to the mother country and the Jewish state. The Talmud, as well as other ancient sources, reveals the existence of considerable conflict between the Pharisees and the Jewish rulers of the Second Commonwealth. Alexander Jannaeus and the house of Herod were often at such odds with the Pharisees and their adherents that not only open hostility but occasional bloodshed resulted. At the time of the great revolt against Rome, Rabban Johanan ben Zakkai, and presumably some of his school, went to the length, it would appear, of utterly rejecting the political campaign, so great was their opposition to the activities of the zealots. Modern scholars conclude that the chief concern of these men was with undisturbed religious practice and the study of Scripture, not with the fight for political independence. In other words, the religious leadership of Talmudic civilization was Torah-centered rather than land-centered.

This antinomy between land and Law is actually nothing but a projection of modern theological universalism onto the Rabbis. But to them the dichotomy would have appeared utterly ridiculous. It is true enough that the Pharisees often went to great lengths in their opposition to the political policies of some Maccabean and Herodian rulers and of political zealots. However, their opposition to particular Jewish governments did not mean opposition to all Jewish government. What they wanted was to control the government themselves; for as keepers of the Torah they regarded their policies as the only ones in consonance with the teachings of Scripture. For example, during the reign of Queen Salome (76–67 B.C.E.), the Pharisaic party ousted the Sadducees from control and took over the administration with a vigorous hand. During the great revolt against Rome, Pharisees and Rabbis fought alongside Essenes and Sadducees, and some of them actually directed military operations. After the collapse of the rebellion, as we have seen, the Rabbis did not in any way shy away from political control. Nor was Rabbinic legislation after the Destruction confined to the cultic sanctity of the country. Since civil law was as much a part of the Torah as sacrificial law, they sought to regulate every aspect of life: labor-employer relationships, prices, real estate equity, market contracts, and so on. As custodians of their people, they even raised purely material enactments on behalf of the general welfare into religious principles. Whatever had to do with Jewish society had to do at the same time with the sacred society and the Holy Land.

Thus, to discourage the mass flight from the country during adverse circumstances, the Pharisaic leaders decreed that anyone leaving the Holy Land automatically incurred ritual defilement. Later Rabbinic law permitted a woman to refuse to follow her husband out of the country, while enabling either spouse to oblige the other to migrate to it from abroad. To prevent ruinous economic competition from foreign markets, they similarly subjected certain imported products to an automatic state of defilement. Sale of Jewish property in Palestine to Gentiles was absolutely forbidden, but it was allowable to purchase land from Gentiles, even if this meant the temporary violation of the more peripheral Sabbath injunctions.

The underlying motif of all Rabbinic discussion of the Holy Land is the intransigent refusal of the Jew to accept the political reality of the world in which he lived. For the greater part of the Talmudic age, Palestine was a vassal territory to one of the Mediterranean empires. For most of the centuries of subjection, Palestine was a servant of Rome, even when its immediate administrators happened to be Jews. But never for a moment did the religious leadership or the Jewish masses recognize as legitimate the conquest of the country by a foreign power. However passive they were obliged to be in the face of political might, most Jews regarded the Romans as interlopers and their agents as common thieves. Publicans in Rabbinic literature, no less than in the New Testament, are equated with the scum of the earth. Obedience to the ruling powers when necessary was one thing, and the majority of the Rabbis counselled against fanatical and hopeless rebellion, but it was quite another to cooperate actively with the conquerors, even in the interests of law and order. To hand over a Jewish thief to the Romans, as one Rabbi did, was to side with one criminal against another.

The Romans, of course, had come to Palestine on serious business, and their actions said as much. Little remained for the average Jew but to hate his enemy with an intensity that was commensurate only with his impotence. Much of the Talmudic hostility to the Gentile can be understood properly only against the background of Jewish political helplessness. More than on any other subject, the Rabbinic homily on the Holy Land betrays a sense of urgency that stems from a fear of despair. Hoping to keep the people in the land, they pleaded for superhuman patience and infinite trust in God's judgment and promise of restoration. As for the bleak present, God's Presence, they preached, rests only on the land of Israel, and only if the land remains in Jewish hands. Great rewards were in store for those who braved the adverse conditions of Roman rule.

The dead of the Holy Land would be resurrected before all others; indeed, the Jew who lies in the consecrated earth can reckon himself buried under the altar of the Lord. God is driven to tears at the sight of His children in exile and at the desolation of the country.

For each of these statements the Talmudist could supply one or more proof-texts from Scripture. But he could not alter the course of history. The Holy Land progressively dwindled in wealth and population and became increasingly a theoretical reality, a symbol of the brilliant past and of a glorious future. That it nevertheless remained a pillar of Jewish life in Palestine and abroad testifies to the deep attachment Scripture and its exegetes had successfully inculcated. The Torah that bound the Jews into a people declared only Zion home and all else exile. Though the Diaspora proved, it could never admit, that the Holy Land and Temple were expendable. Every Jew bore in his heart a sense of guilt at his inability to turn the injunction into a reality.

It was not only by divine decree and Rabbinical exhortation that Zion remained a reality in the life of the Jew. Nothing demonstrates so well the profound emotional grip of the country as the practices of the Jews in the Diaspora. So long as the Temple stood, Jews from all the world sent their annual tax of the half-shekel to the Temple, in addition to voluntary contributions for sacrifices and other Temple needs. The Flavian emperors of Rome knew what they were about when they converted this tax to the coffers of Jupiter Capitolinus; a sacred offering was now being poured into the hated pocket of an idol of the despots of the world. Daily prayer, from early Talmudic times to the present day, has been oriented toward Jerusalem, a practice which has left its mark even on the popular vocabulary: Palestine was spoken of by Babylonian Jews as "the West" or simply as "over there," while European and African Jews designated it as "the East." The pilgrimage—venerated in the Middle Ages by both Christians and Muslims—owes its high religious rank to the honor accorded it by the Jews of Talmudic culture. Even the efforts of Babylonian religious leaders to discourage emigration to Palestine, efforts that stemmed from the fact that Babylonian community life and religious organization had far surpassed that of Palestine by the end of the third century, testify to the normal impulses of the people and the direction of their loyalties.

Even those Jews who frankly preferred to await the return of the Messiah knew that in many ways Palestine governed their lives. The annual calendar was regulated chiefly according to agricultural and husbandry conditions in Palestine. Festal letters and other directives went forth regularly from the mother country along with teachers, preachers, and books. Even children played "Holy Land," as a group of Rabbis learned when they saw youngsters in Rome designating mud pies as "priestly offerings" and "levitical tithes." Judah Halevi, Moses Nachmanides, and Obadiah Bertinoro, like many another pilgrim of a later day, merely carried out in their own lives ideals and dreams on which they had been suckled from earliest infancy. On one level, modern Zionism is a translation of this yearning into a concrete program for reclamation of a land the Jew had always claimed—with Gentile concurrence—to be his own.

We have noted that social and political realities oriented Talmudic culture in two directions: the idealized past of Biblical times and the even more glorious future pictured by the prophets. What the individual hoped would be the divine reward for his present suffering and frustration, the nation awaited as recompense for painful fidelity to its ancestral God and Torah. "Renew our days as of old," the author of Lamentations cried, despite the obvious truth that the garden of man had probably been no greener in pristine times than it was in Exilic or post-Exilic days. In one sense, however, the hope for renewal was justified: the Jew had formerly lived on his own soil, under his own kings, and his own law. All the woes and travails of Talmudic civilization were traced to the curse of subjection and dispersion. Accordingly, all the hopes and dreams for happiness were telescoped into the catchword of "Return." Resurrection, righteousness, peace and plenty for Israel and all mankind— indeed, would not all men be the same?—were forecast for the day of the Return.

"For the vision is yet for the appointed time, and it declareth of the end and doth not lie; though it tarry, wait for it, because it will surely come; it will not delay." These words from Habakkuk expressed the Jewish hope that the end of history had already been decreed and sealed. Practically every prophet from Moses to Daniel had reassured the people on this score. There was nothing to do but to wait and to behave so as to be assured of a share in the final reward. Once again, we must clearly distinguish between dogma and personal speculation. The books of Daniel and of other apocalyptists abound with theories as to the exact date of the messianic End. That people took these religious mathematicians seriously is evident from the Rabbinic excoriation of "calculators of the end." Then as now well-meaning but deluded people managed to convince themselves and others that they were partners to the heavenly secret. No less a man than Rabbi Akiba ben Joseph declared that he could discern the messianic herald in Simeon bar Kokhba. The retort of one of his colleagues has become a classic *bon mot* on the subject: "Grass will have sprouted from your cheeks, Akiba ben Joseph, but the Davidic Messiah will not yet have arrived."

Akiba's hopes and his colleague's retort reflect the two attitudes that pervaded the Jewish community—impatient expectancy and resilient sobriety. So imminent was the sounding of the trumpet of freedom in the minds of the people, that throughout Talmudic times and afterward the Jews were the preeminent prey of messianic pretenders. The faintest rumor of the divine messenger's appearance caused whole communities to pack their belongings and take to the nearest highway on their way to Jerusalem. As each pretender failed to produce the expected sign, that is, met with an inglorious end, the people slowly recovered from their shock and girded themselves for the next chance. How close at hand the event was thought to be may be gleaned from the ritual practices of the Jews of Palestine in Talmudic times. The levitical laws of purity, whose fulfillment was a prerequisite to entering the sacred precincts of the Temple, were accorded careful observance for centuries after the Destruction. The laws of sacrifices and Temple protocol were carefully rehearsed in the Palestinian academy in readiness for the resumption of the normal state of affairs.

More than any other single factor, this preoccupation with the Return kept the Jews an ethnic group with a unified vision of their political role. More than anything else, too, it kept in being the tension born of a universalist and personalized religion that was yet centralized by a land and a Temple site. Even the increased fixity of Jewish liturgy after the Destruction was probably due largely to a profound nostalgia for the Temple service with its rigid protocol and precise regulation. That the Jew failed to resolve this tension until the nineteenth century, when Reform and political Zionism took a hand and separated ethnicism and universalism into separate programs of action, shows how strong were the roots of Talmudic Judaism in all subsequent stages of Jewish history. Judaism continued to profess its hope for the salvation of all society and for the restoration of God's chosen people. It proudly boasted that it was at home everywhere, and proved it, yet never ceased to bemoan its alienation and exile on foreign soil. Modern intellectual Jewish history begins with the renunciation of one or the other half of the messianic ideal. Classical Reform Judaism, secular Jewish democrats, and Jewish socialists adopted the universalist creed and gave up the ethnic aspiration for return to the homeland. The vision of the prophets might well find fulfillment in Vienna, Berlin, or Moscow. What need, therefore, of a Mount Zion? On the other hand, Zionism despaired of a divine salvation or of a Gentile change of attitude, and so took matters into its own hands with the adoption of a humanized program for the traditional restoration.

In Scripture, the Messiah, or anointed one, is a designation used for the high priest and more commonly for a legitimate king. The anonymous prophet popularly called the Second Isaiah refers to Cyrus king of Persia as God's messiah because the exiles of Judea looked to him for the restoration of the Temple. It is clear, therefore, that by the middle of the sixth century B.C.E. the term "messiah" had taken on the added meaning of divine messenger and human savior, a meaning that in ensuing centuries was practically to displace its original sense. Who would be the Messiah and how would his coming be announced? These were questions that aroused the interest of every Jew.

In the usual way, answers were elicited from a combination of relevant verses in Scripture. "Behold," said the prophet Malachi, "I will send you Elijah the prophet before the coming of the great and terrible day of the Lord." The fanatical and implacable prophet of Gilead was to return from his heavenly home and usher in the new era. Little wonder that in Rabbinic society the personality of Elijah underwent a major metamorphosis. Pastor, counselor, and comforter to the Jewish people, he miraculously appears in order to admonish, encourage, and pronounce that the long-awaited day of the Lord will yet arrive. It is he who soothes the faithful and bids them wait patiently for the awful events that God has announced. He will soon make his appearance to all men, proclaiming the new era. Then the great day will have begun.

The day of the Lord, Amos had long since made clear, would be one "of darkness, not of light," and Malachi says much the same thing. It was a simple matter to associate these hints with the fuller treatment of Ezekiel of the battle with Gog and Magog, of that final but most terrible conflict between the human forces of good and evil. The forces of the Lord would, according to God's plan, suffer a temporary setback, but only to tempt the hordes of Gog and Magog still further. Great faith would be required, for the initial setbacks must not deter one from playing his role. The prophets had announced that as a first step in the restoration, God would repair the breach between Judah and Israel and make them again into one people. And to this end God would bring back the remnants of the lost ten tribes of the North and align them in one array with the seed of Judah. Talmudic folklore foresaw that at the head of the rejuvenated people of Israel would stand the king of the lost ten tribes, the Messiah of the seed of Joseph, who would himself perish on the field of battle. But the people would again rally under "the shoot of the stock of Jesse," the Messiah of the seed of David, who would deal the enemy a crushing and final defeat. Then would the visions of all the prophets, of Isaiah, Micah, Jeremiah, Daniel, and the others, come to pass: resurrection, peace, prosperity, and universal acknowledgment of the kingship of God.

Is this combination of Biblical fragments the official Rabbinic dogma on the subject of the Messiah? Yes, but only in the sense that no believer would question the words of the prophets, although a Talmudic exegete could declare that these words referred not to the future, but had already been fulfilled. As late as the twelfth century we find a Spanish Jew defending the more common Talmudic opinion that the prophetic promises will yet come to pass. Obviously, the gates of interpretation and speculation, perhaps even of doubt, had not been completely closed. Above all, the theories of apocalyptists and of exegetical computers as to the time of the messianic era, no matter how wide an audience they had gained, could never assume credal finality. "The secret things," the Jews had to admit, "belong unto the Lord our God." Time and again they would hear the clatter of hooves of the Messiah's cavalry, but no bones rose again.

There is a serious objection to this eschatology. The prophetic pronouncements on the Messiah and the Day of the Lord would seem to reduce the role of the individual to insignificance. He is at best but one of the "extras" in a drama, the end of which has long been preordained. If the savior of Israel will come in any case, if the first stage will bring defeat in its wake and will be inevitably followed by victory, what need can there be for personal exertion or sacrifice? Obviously God would make good his promise in His own good time. Did not the Rabbis discourage the people from attempting to hasten the end? The fruit would ripen only in due season; to rush matters would bring on disaster.

The objection is of course a commonplace. If the march of events is ineluctable, if nothing can arrest the arrival of the Davidic Messiah or the classless state—why praise or condemn individuals for their behavior? Judaism had no official answer to the question, nor could it have in an area not covered by the prophets. Yet the preachments against the temptation to leave things to the preordained march of history show that the difficulty was keenly sensed. The various solutions all agreed that the Messiah's date of arrival depended on man. One theory that gained considerable popularity in Rabbinic circles stated that the Messiah had long been due, and that it was only the imperfection of Israel that delayed his coming. Others felt that the time had not yet come, for God would not delay the fulfillment of His promise once the time arrived. But Israel's moral responsibility was undeniable, for God would surely have shortened the ordeal if the people had but given evidence of their worthiness. A third school wisely placed no limits on the period of waiting. The Messiah would not come until a perfect generation appeared. But theory or no theory, the individual was assigned a role of immeasurable importance in this drama of human fulfillment and national restoration. God had created the Messiah; everyone to a man was responsible for making him a reality on earth.

THE LEGACY OF TALMUDIC CIVILIZATION

The complex of institutions and values that were born of Talmudic culture passed on into the Middle Ages virtually intact, unaccompanied by any awareness that an age of eight centuries was drawing to a close. True, the rich community life of Palestine felt the impact of the financial collapse of the Roman Empire and, later, of Persian and Byzantine invasion. The Christianization of the Mediterranean world brought in its wake an incessant harassment of Jewish community activity, a progressive curtailment of its autonomous powers, and outright pogroms and confiscation of property. Many Jews and even whole Jewish communities suffered appallingly. But the culture itself remained intact owing to the strong roots it had struck in the Babylonian community. There Talmudic life continued well into the eleventh century and even beyond it, preserving the ethnic-religious independence of the people at the same time that it acted as a Jewish center to which other communities could look for counsel and instruction, and so bolster their sense of unity and continuity. In the ensuing centuries new Jewish communities spring up throughout Southern and Western Europe, and while their growth is generally veiled in darkness, they all come to maturity with the assumption of a community structure patterned after the Talmudic prototype. The importance of the Babylonian, Palestinian, and Italian communities in this regard is immeasurable. Everywhere the Talmudic law became the constitution of Jewish organization. Above all, the stability of the Babylonian community enabled it to establish the hegemony of its law over Jewish Palestine itself and over the whole of the Jewish world.

Medieval Judaism thus became synonymous with the law of the Babylonian Talmud. The permanent legacy of the Palestinian center was now refracted through the window of an Exilic center that had first grappled with the problem of autonomy under the law of the Palestinian Mishna. What the Bible had meant for Talmudic civilization, the Talmud now meant for medieval Jewish life. The Talmud and the Midrash became the new Scripture by which Jews everywhere were to regulate their daily lives, civil, domestic, and religious, until the beginning of the emancipation in the eighteenth and nineteenth centuries. Whatever the differences between the various Jewish communities during the twelve centuries from the downfall of the Roman Empire and rise of Islam to the emergence of the modern democratic nation-state; whatever the barriers between them, barriers that were geographic, linguistic, and even cultural, the law of the Talmud and the vocabulary of its faith were the unitive forces that made all differences seem ephemeral and contingent.

Modern students of Judaism often deplore the relative neglect of Scripture by the traditional Jew of medieval and even of modern society. The neglect is relative, yet it is true that Jewish attention shifted from Scripture to Rabbinic text and commentary. Still, for the traditional Jew, the charge leaves out of account a fundamental consideration. Actually, the Jew continued to read Scripture unremittingly throughout the Middle Ages. But to understand the true meaning of Scripture he had to know the Talmud, which held the clue to its treasures. In the same way the Church of Rome stressed the importance of patristic and canonical literature for the understanding of Scripture. Of what value is a treasure without the keys to the vault in which it is lodged? Jews and Christians alike began to study Scripture afresh, and independently of accepted presuppositions, only after the collapse of the exegetical culture that Talmudic civilization had inaugurated.

Of far more influence on world history than the Talmudic legacy to succeeding generations of Jews was the Talmudic impact on European and Near Eastern civilization. The growth and development of Talmudic culture in Palestine and Babylonia took place within imperial frameworks that tolerated, and in some ways even abetted, the emergence of a Jewish community structure in which the Jew fashioned his own way of life and insulated himself against the Gentile cultural milieu. The Christian and Muslim states of medieval Europe, Asia, and Africa followed the Roman precedent with respect to the Jew, even as the Romans and Hellenistic monarchs followed the Persian precedents. Jewish life thus continued to flourish within a self-imposed and tolerated ghetto, which afforded infinitely greater protection against cultural assimilation than a thousand sermons or edicts of toleration.

Over and above the framework of autonomy, and despite the more vocal hostility between Jew and Gentile in the medieval world, Talmudic culture had a far more suitable climate in which to flourish in the medieval world than it ever had in the Hellenistic-Roman world. And this climate was of Talmudic making. Jew, Christian, and Muslim might vilify each other's faith openly and unceasingly, but underneath their condemnations and disputations they moved in a common universe of discourse. All three faiths based their claim to truth and knowledge on a revealed book, which in turn became the subject of exegesis and interpretation and was thus made applicable to changing human experience. All three religions provided their flocks with a regimen of life from cradle to grave which was based on the premise that no differences existed between the secular and the sacred. The new churches, like the mother faith, came with a program of individual salvation that cut across ethnic barriers and created new international alignments. Church, prayer, and the promise of other-worldly retribution—these all stemmed from Talmudic universalism. Debate between the religions, whenever it took place, was not about fundamentals but details. Jews and Gentiles, whatever the hatred between them, understood each other extremely well. The Jewish missionaries may have lost to their competitors of the two younger monotheisms the world which they had set about to conquer. But in a profounder sense, they had won: they had called the rules by which the game was to be played. The God of Israel and his moral values became the law of the nations.

Finally, Talmudic culture bequeathed its messianic vision and zeal not only to Christianity and Islam, but to secular modern civilization as well. The cults of nationalism, democracy, socialism, fascism, and communism have all at one time or another appropriated the fervor and soteric claim of the monotheisms against which they revolted. Their byword, each in the name of its own god, reads like an age-old verse originally associated with the advent of the Messiah of the seed of David. "On that day the Lord shall be one and his name one." Each has announced that it alone can bring to pass the prophecy of Zechariah—the prophecy that is the aim and substance of Talmudic civilization.

The Reconstruction of Gaonic History[*]

Introduction to Jacob Mann's *Texts and Studies*

THE INTELLECTUAL ANCESTRY OF MANN'S SCHOLARSHIP: 1. RAPOPORT

Scientific study of Gaonic history (ca. 650–ca. 1200),[1] the area of Jewish scholarship to which Jacob Mann made monumental contributions, began almost dramatically in the years 1829–1832 with the publication of a series of biographies of great medieval Jewish figures by Solomon Judah Loeb Rapoport of Lwów (Lemberg) in the Hebrew periodical *Bikkurray ha-'Ittim*.[2] These brief monographs, accompanied by extensive notes and supplemented by appendices that occupied far more space than the texts of the papers, spelled out all the available information on Saadiah Gaon, Nathan ben Yehiel of Rome, Hai Gaon, Hananel ben Hushiel, and Nissim ben Jacob ibn Shahin, authorities whose names were well known to every student of rabbinics but whose activities and historical settings were in many respects a mystery. The essays gained immediate acclaim and have since been universally regarded as cornerstones of modern Jewish scholarship that rank with the works of Nahman Krochmal, Leopold Zunz, and Samuel David Luzzatto.

---

[*]This essay is a study of modern historiography, not a study in the history of the Gaonic period or even a survey of modern scholarship on Gaonic culture. Accordingly, it has been written on the assumption that the reader is familiar with the basic outlines of the history of the period but, on the other hand, without reference to many significant works of scholarship on the literature and culture of the period. For the most concise and up-to-date treatment of the Geonim, see *Encyclopaedia Hebraica*, X, 131–140, where a synchronized table of the Geonim is given. An earlier, somewhat less complete, table is provided in the *Jewish Encyclopedia*, V, 571. For a chronological table of the exilarchs, see Goode, p. 169.

By focusing on key figures whose literary works and communal activities left permanent imprints on Jewish literature and thought, by providing, wherever possible, explicit chronological and geographical data that defined the historical contexts within which these men had functioned, by attempting to conclude the temporal and spatial settings wherever clear data were not available, and by subjecting every datum to thorough critical scrutiny, Rapoport opened a new avenue of research into the intellectual and religious history of the Jews.[3] What was especially dazzling was Rapoport's uncanny skill in assembling relevant and complementary details from the most isolated sources and in arranging them in a logical and contextual framework.

The present-day reader who has been nurtured on sophisticated historical thinking and writing is likely to be repelled by the dry and fragmentary character of these essays, made up largely of bibliographical and lexicographical items strung together with verbs and peppered with an occasional adjective. They can by no stretch of the imagination be classified as biographical or historical studies. The footnotes are a further stumbling block of a special kind. Often minor tracts in their own right, they contain vast amounts of substantive information along with documentation and extended critical and polemical discussions. It was principally in his notes, and notes to notes, that Rapoport's writing occasionally burst with vitality, for the location of a datum and the weighing of its credibility challenged his fancy most. The net result was a staggering array of data with almost no connective thread, a vast number of trees with no forest in sight.

But in all fairness to him, Rapoport made no claim to writing history. He construed his papers as sources of information *for* historians, who would not otherwise be likely to come upon the information that he had rescued from oblivion. He was content to provide the bones of historical research and to leave the supplying of flesh and soul to the professional writers of history. He intuitively sensed the distinction between antiquarian, a role in which he displayed himself to be a consummate practitioner, and historian, which he never attempted to become. If he cannot, then, be held accountable for the tendency of others to identify the two, and to attach greater worth to the work of the former, it is nevertheless important to emphasize that his work did set the tone and the style which many of the best trained students of Judaica subsequently sought to emulate. Since this approach to much of the Jewish past and especially to Gaonic studies can hardly be an accident, for it remained the dominant one until relatively recently, its particular attraction for Rapoport and his disciples merits explanation.

Rapoport himself was quite aware of the immediate stimuli and models determining the designs he gave to his research. In the introduction to one of his essays, he indicated that he hoped to write for the benefit of historians (namely, Markus Jost) the biographies of men mentioned in the *Arukh* of R. Nathan ben Yehiel (ca. 1025–1106) and that he had been goaded to this undertaking by a remark on the unreliability of chronological data in Jewish sources in Pierre Bayle's *Dictionnaire historique et critique* (1697, 1702).[4] Nathan ben Yehiel and Pierre Bayle were his acknowledged sources of inspiration and, we would add, his models. Rapoport was transported by critical dictionaries, and he was most at home when dealing with a single datum—a name, a date, a technical term. Lexicons, like the *Arukh* of Nathan ben Yehiel and of Solomon ibn Parhon (1160)—to the edition of which he supplied an introduction[5]—and biographical-chronological registers, such as Abraham Zacuto's *Yuḥasin* and Yehiel Heilprin's *Seder ha-Dorot*, were his favorites and his conceptual models. In short, his creative mind was primarily oriented to dictionary entries, and his greatest work, *'Erekh Millin* (Prague, 1852), was a compilation of critical entries, alphabetically arranged, of Talmudic terms. From Zacuto and from Bayle he was inspired to think of history in terms of persons described as lexicographical entries. From Bayle he got humanistic confirmation of a method that had long been in vogue in critical rabbinic works of verifying each statement by a bibliographical reference and of evaluating *in extenso* previous statements on the subject in footnotes that often turned out to be miniature essays. He thus deliberately wrote in the style of an *encyclopédiste*, and the thought of a note to a note on a note did not faze him at all.

Now this style of scholarly writing was but half a step removed from the kind of textual-legal-philological *novellae* which characterized much of the later rabbinic literature in which Rapoport had been schooled and at which he had even tried his hand in his younger days.[6] In his new essays of critical scholarship, the ideology of the Haskalah was advanced by writing that was humanistic in form but simultaneously close enough to rabbinic antecedents to allay any sense of radical break with the conceptual framework in which he had been reared. Whatever distinctions there were between the traditional and new approaches to scholarship had been considerably blurred shortly before Rapoport began his researches by developments within certain Lithuanian rabbinic circles. In a paper read before the American Academy for Jewish Research in December 1969, Professor Chaim Zalman Dimitrovsky cogently argued that the new critical spirit of the *maskilim* of Galicia had largely been inspired by the bibliographical and historical-geographical researches of Abraham (d. 1808), the son of the Gaon R. Elijah of Vilna, whose *Rav Pe'alim* (Warsaw 1894, 1896)[7] was fundamentally an alphabetical dictionary of midrashic literature to which Rapoport's *'Erekh Millin* bore a striking resemblance in form and method. The affinities between rabbinic critical research and the style of the *encyclopédistes* explain not only the attraction of this style of study and writing to one who began as a writer of *ḥiddushim,* but also why so many of his readers and disciples should confuse this genre with mature historiography. Jacob Mann, as we shall see, never quite overcame the methodological base dignified by the pioneer in his field, and he wrote his best work largely under the spell of its canon.[8]

Rapoport would doubtless have insisted, as Mann later did, that the inchoate state of the field and the disjointed nature of the available materials precluded any more systematic form of genuine scholarship. Anything beyond episodic notes could yield little more than fanciful theories spun from webs of conjecture and imagination. But in reality this hardly need have been the case. Had Rapoport, or more precisely those who have defended his type of scholarship over genuine historiography, been willing to concede that no scholarship can hope to be definitive and that the evident tentativeness of any historiography in no way disqualifies its relative merit, Gaonica would not have remained the esoteric preserve of a few antiquarians. Not the dearth of material has inhibited many Jewish scholars from formulating their findings in mature historical terms but rather a basic lack of historical orientation shaped by disciplined training in asking historical questions. A generation after Rapoport's biographies, Graetz still did not have very much new material with which to work; however, his picture of the Gaonic age was not only a lot more readable but, the grimaces of his detractors to the contrary notwithstanding, a lot more instructive and stimulating to further research and profounder understanding than Rapoport's *tours de force.* Rapoport did have materials at his disposal that lent themselves to historical narrative. But Rapoport simply did not think in those terms. That he himself was not concerned "that every individual investigation should reach outward toward a larger orientation of historical knowledge; [that] every local inquiry should relate itself to a general pattern of development," to quote John Higham's apt characterization of genuine historiography,[9] may be dismissed as a personal idiosyncrasy. That it became the dominant tone of much subsequent research in this field can only be attributed to a culturally rooted inhibition and the dominating influence of precedent.

But in the final analysis Rapoport did point to the road that any further historical research would have to take if it was to illuminate the obscurities of the Jewish past. Not only names of men would have to be treated as historical phenomena but all *realia,* even rabbinic and communal titles, would have to be defined and placed in historical context! Rapoport even tried his hand at indicating some of the partisan ideological tendencies of the principal Geonim, like Sherira and Hai; and while some of his unorthodox remarks aroused the fury of other scholars more inhibited by traditional orientations to ancient luminaries,[10] Rapoport had posed problems that have remained on the agenda of scholarly investigation. Not the least of his contributions was to alert students of the new field of Jewish history as to how little was really known about major blocs of time of earlier centuries, despite the authority that the men of those ages held in the traditional scheme of things. Rapoport had blazed a small trail, but his image would be felt even long after major discoveries had totally antiquated his pioneering studies.

THE INTELLECTUAL ANCESTRY OF MANN'S SCHOLARSHIP: 2. THE REVIVAL OF KARAITICA

That whole chapters of Jewish history could be recovered from hitherto unknown works became increasingly apparent in the decades following the publication of Rapoport's celebrated biographies. In 1836, the Karaite press in Yevpatoriya issued the great Karaite code of Judah Hadassi (ca. 1150),[11] *Eshkol ha-Kofer,* which contained (in sections 97–98) a brief account of Jewish sectaries—Abu Isa of Isfahan, Yudghan, Isma'il al-Ukbari, Abu Umran al-Tiflisi, and Mishawayh of Baalbek—who were otherwise totally unknown. Further confirmation of this report came not long after from a totally unexpected source, an account of philosophic and sectarian schools in the first centuries of Islam by Hadassi's contemporary, the Muslim historian of religions, Abu-'l-Fath Muhammad Shahrastani.[12] These accounts revealed more than mere names and doctrines, so that the dynamic character of medieval Jewish society in the Gaonic age had now begun to become apparent, albeit hazily and quite fragmentarily.

However, the second major turning point in modern Gaonic studies came in 1860—the very year in which the volume on the Gaonic age in Heinrich Graetz's monumental *Geschichte* appeared—with the publication by Simhah Pinsker of *Lickute Kadmoniot* (Vienna, 1860).[13] The work—in two volumes, one a chronologically arranged directory of Karaite authorities, and another, an appendix consisting of medieval texts—was a treasure trove of information derived principally from manuscripts by and about Karaites from the origins of their schism until the middle of the fourteenth century.

Scholarly interest in the history of Jewish sects, and indeed in Jewish dissidence in ancient and medieval times, had been growing in the wake of the Reform movement in Germany and of the *Haskalah* in Galicia. Isaac Markus Jost had recently issued an abridged recast of his comprehensive history of the Jews, but with a significant addition to the title that bespoke the shifting orientation to the Jewish past: *Geschichte des Judenthums und seiner Sekten* (1857–59).[14] Simultaneously, Abraham Geiger published his epoch-making study on the history of the text of the Bible, *Urschrift und Uebersetzungen der Bibel in ihrer Abhaengigkeit von der innern Entwicklung des Judentums* (1857), which was explicitly described by its author as a study preliminary to his intended history of Karaism. Geiger contended that Karaism preserved dogmatic and legal traditions of ancient Sadducean and Samaritan origin, and that a fuller understanding of Karaism would shed considerable light on the origins and development of rabbinic Judaism.[15] Seven years later he sharpened his formulation with a definitive conclusion that has since been associated with his name: "The Karaites—to state it briefly—are the spiritual and corporeal descendants of the Sadducees."[16] A somewhat different brand of Jewish reformers in Brody, led by Abraham Krochmal and Joshua Heschel Schorr, had been loudly and testily debunking hallowed notions of the history of rabbinic usage and literature thereby heightening interest in materials that undermined the fanciful notions that in premodern times normative Judaism had not suffered from internal dissension and doctrinal dissidence.[17] But Pinsker's publication was a veritable bombshell, for it was based not on astute analysis and clever inference but on a mass of new documentary evidence that could not be dismissed.

Although Pinsker did not attempt to synthesize the mountain of materials that he had collected into a systematic exposition, he did indicate briefly the radically new orientation to Karaism that he felt the materials had proved to be valid. The myth perpetrated by Abraham ibn Daud in 1161 that Karaism had always been a minor and sterile sect with little to its credit in the way of creative thought, literature, and scholarship now had to be discarded *in toto*. The formidable mass of information that Pinsker had marshalled demonstrated a rich and continuous tradition of Karaite learning and productivity that was given expression in several literary genres. A dispassionate reading of the evidence compelled one to the conclusion that the Karaites justifiably boasted a long line of creative scholars and poets of vast erudition and of no mean literary skill. It was no less evident that the Karaites had not been merely a foul nuisance of little real consequence in medieval times, but that they had posed a formidable intellectual challenge to the spokesmen of Rabbinism in the Gaonic age. Indeed, much of the Rabbanite literature of the Gaonic period could now be seen to have been a deliberate effort at response to the Karaite challenge.

Pinsker's personal scholarly interests lay principally in the area of linguistics, and the major emphasis of his research was on the development of Karaite studies in the Hebrew language as well as in the closely related areas of Karaite exegesis and poetry. However, the intimate connection between these Karaite pursuits and their doctrinal controversies with Rabbinism compelled him to include hitherto unknown materials that illuminated the Karaite positions on fundamental religious issues and in particular on their arch opponent in the Rabbanite camp, Saadiah ben

Joseph al-Fayyumi. Henceforth, no one could study the history of the
Gaonic age, and especially the rapidly growing library of Saadyana,
without a thorough study of Karaite literature. Karaitica, in short, had at
once become a subject of direct interest to the student of medieval Jewish history, and an indispensable area to the student of the Geonim.

Pinsker was keenly aware that the form of his work did not do justice
to the significance of the material he had presented. Structurally and
stylistically it was not much of an improvement on Rapoport's method.
The model of Zacuto's register of scholars, of which the unabridged version had been published only three years before Pinsker's work, still exercised a dominating influence. Pinsker contented himself with
composing a directory of Karaite scholars in chronological order and
with providing whatever information he had gathered on the authority
he was treating under his name. While some entries were manageably
small and lucid, others turned into extended essays with copious quotations from the writer's works, and these passages were generously
weighted with Rapoportian footnotes and references. The task of explaining the rise of Karaism Pinsker left to others, contenting himself
with the suggestion made twenty years earlier by Rapoport[18] that
Karaism and other sectarian revolts that had troubled Islam in the eighth
century, and with Geiger's refinement of the medieval Jewish view that
Karaism represented a revival of Sadduceean practices that had long lain
dormant. While a real historical account could thus not be gained from
Pinsker, his work had lifted the curtain that had hitherto obscured a
whole area of Jewish history. For all its structural shortcomings and despite the sharp objections of several scholars to a number of his conclusions on the debt of Rabbanite literature to Karaite inspiration,[19] the
work remains to this day a primary and indispensable tool of research for
anyone working in the field of Gaonica, let alone in Karaitica.

Pinsker's publication evoked scholarly responses almost instantane-
ously.[20] Even before the work had appeared in print Jost and Graetz had
been permitted to consult page proofs of parts of the work and to incor-
porate information they gleaned from them into their respective histories.[21] (In the revised edition of his volume on the period, Graetz drew
on it heavily.) In the course of the following decade two histories of
Karaism, one in German by Julius Fuerst and another in Hebrew by
Abraham Baer Gottlober, provided a genuine narrative framework for
the story of the sect. While these two works are justifiably ignored today
as hopelessly antiquated,[22] they both signalized a principle that has
stood the test of time, to wit the profound interrelationship between
Rabbanite culture and Karaism and the indispensability of a full understanding of the latter for a critical evaluation of the normative tradition
of the Rabbanite communities in countries where Karaites had succeeded in making inroads. Henceforth, any student of Gaonic history

would have to consider the possibility that any particular phenomenon he was studying was in some way affected by the presence of a sectarian challenge, even if the Rabbanite leaders of the community did not so much as hint at such considerations. The soundness of this principle became increasingly evident after the discovery of the great horde of manuscripts in the Cairo Geniza. Consequently, virtually every one of the great students of Gaonic history and culture in the last nine decades— A. A. Harkavy, Samuel Poznanski, Louis Ginzberg, B. M. Lewin, Jacob Mann, Moses Zucker, S. D. Goitein—has simultaneously contributed to our knowledge and understanding of Karaite literature and communal activity. It was thus no accident that the second volume of Jacob Mann's *Texts and Studies* should have been totally dedicated to Karaitica, to appropriate the apt subtitle of the book which Mann gave it. Mann saw full well that Gaonica and Karaitica had become two branches of the identical subject.

THE REDISCOVERY OF GAONIC HISTORY: 1860–1897

As was indicated earlier, Graetz's volume of *Geschichte der Juden vom Abschluss des Talmud (500) bis zum Aufbluehen der juedisch-spanischnen Cultur* appeared almost simultaneously with Pinsker's work, thus providing the scholarly public with an updated historical framework with which to study the period. Graetz, to be sure, had neither created his framework *ex nihilo*, nor did his account provide any radically new insight into the major developments of Jewish history in the centuries of Gaonic supremacy. Detailed chronological data and the categories with which to label the division of periods were part of accepted Jewish vocabulary, having been established by the *Seder Tannaim va-Amoraim* (ca. 850) and the renowned Epistle of R. Sherira Gaon (986) from which they were appropriated by Abraham ibn Daud (1161), Manahem ha-Meiri (1299–1300), Abraham Zacuto (1504), and the later Jewish chroniclers.[23] Furthermore, the histories of Basnage and Jost, while drab and superficial in their treatments of Babylonian Jewry, had provided accounts of the Babylonian academies—of their exilarchs and their occasional conflicts with the Geonim—and of the Karaites and their doctrines, within the context of Jewish and general history. Basnage had already been able to exploit some of the new information uncovered by Jacob Trigland and other seventeenth-century Christian scholars who had studied the Karaites and their literature;[24] and while some of Basnage's critical theories bordered on the fantastic,[25] he blazed a trail of sorts by insisting on the inclusion of later Karaite developments on the agenda of Jewish historiography. Jost, accordingly, treated not only the Karaites to the extent that his information warranted, but in the revised version of his *Geschichte* incorporated the information on other dissidents revealed by Hadassi and Shahrastani. It was *prima facie* not overly taxing for Graetz to revise and amplify these accounts of the Geonim and the sects by incorporating the results of recent research in Germany and Galicia and, in addition, the new data he had had the opportunity to glean from the samples of Pinsker's work that had been made available to him.

But Graetz sought not merely to update his history by amplification and refinement of earlier models. Above all he felt it vital to make his account of the Geonim a demonstrably organic part of the totality of Jewish history, and to show that that segment of the history, while displaying a special vitality appropriate to the singular conditions governing its course, bespoke nevertheless a logical continuity with the mainstream of Jewish history, as Graetz construed it. Accordingly, the Gaonic period was introduced with a caption designating it as "the fourth epoch of the first [i.e., Talmudic] period." In other words, the period was not just one more chapter in his book or even in the history of the Jews itself. It was intimately connected with the epochs that preceded it—the Saboraic period had been labeled as the third epoch of the first period—and it represented the culmination of a distinguishable stage in Jewish history.[26] Graetz took deliberate pains to dispel any doubts on this score. The introduction to volume V bristled with passion in an affirmation that Jewish history after the destruction of the Second Temple was neither "ein blosses Conglomerat von zufaelligen Ereignissen" nor the dry record of books and their authors, but the history of a cohesive group that retained its national character and responded to events as a self-conscious corporate body. Accordingly, Graetz felt driven by the need to infuse life and breath into fossilized and skeletal records that had been committed to writing in Gaonic times and preserved in all their dessication down to his own day. It was his sad lot often to be understood and appreciated, at least in scholarly circles, better by enemies like Treitschke than by "Genossen" whose Jewish anomie had blinded them to the orignality of his undertaking and the brilliance with which he gave *legitimate* structure and context to ostensibly disjointed data.[27] It was, in the final analysis, Heinrich Graetz who rediscovered Jewish history in the Gaonic age and who articulated the guidelines by which it should be recorded.

Graetz recognized the necessity of accounting for the emergence of a new stage in Jewish history in terms of the major changes that had engulfed the whole of the Near East in the middle of the seventh century. In Graetz's view the emergence of the exilarchate and Gaonate as governmentally recognized institutions that wielded power over the Jewish community effectively could only be understood as consequences of the Muslim conquests of the Persian empire and of Muslim concessions to a cooperative minority. In support of this contention he noted that the

Muslims had similarly appointed cooperative Christians to the dignity of Catholicos, who exercised functions parallel to those of the Geonim. Although Graetz did not pursue in depth the metamorphosis wrought in Jewish life as a consequence of the new complex of institutions and culture that the Muslims introduced, his insights made it evident that one of the primary challenges facing the Jewish historian was to explain Jewish history by delineating those forces that radically affected the life and destiny of vast areas and then to correlate developments within the Jewish community with the appropriate currents in general history. Thus, Graetz even adopted Rapoport's suggestion that the very term "Gaon" was not a native Hebrew one but a loan-word from Arabic or Persian. This was not the only instance of a view that subsequent evidence made obsolete. But the plausibility and tenability of specific explanations are not the only criteria guiding the genuine historian. Graetz made each of his statements part of a larger effort to create a coherent picture of Jewish history.

From the Apocalypse of R. Simeon b. Yohai, Graetz concluded that the Jews had welcomed the Muslim conquerors as liberators from Persian as well as Byzantine oppression. The point was part of Graetz's insistence that the Jews were not merely passive and helpless objects whom the winds of history tossed about as they would. However limited their effective role in shaping the course of general history, the Jews had participated in it and, what was to Graetz of infinitely greater consequence, reacted to it and reoriented their inner life in response to the new atmosphere they encountered. He dwelt on conflicts of the exilarchate and the Gaonate and described them in terms that made eminent sense to an age that was enjoying some great historical writing on the medieval conflicts of papacy and temporal powers. Finally, the responsa and homiletical literature were exploited for echoes of social change and partisan ideologies, which, in turn, reflected the fullness of the autonomous Jewish communal experience in this new "epoch." Jewish historiography had finally gained a forest, the trees of which could be studied individually, but also as part of a greater whole and of a continuum that had antecedents and consequences. The forest that Graetz fashioned has been greatly expanded in consequence of modern discoveries and innumerable spots within it illuminated. But for the internal world of Babylonian Jewry his account has not yet been displaced. Next to his encompassing and coherent history of the Gaonic period, the accounts of Dubnow and Jawitz are pale achievements. Graetz remains the most lucid and penetrating introduction to Gaonic *history.* Much of subsequent scholarship in this area, has been commentary, vital and enriching, but commentary nonetheless that in many respects has to this day not displaced the original text. Paradoxically, Graetz's account is also the best introduction to the researches of Rapoport, for it is in the light of Graetz's framework that the method, findings and problems taken up in Rapoport's monographs stand out in their originality and brilliance.

Nothing quite as original and as enterprising as Graetz's history of the Gaonic period was undertaken again for almost a whole generation. It was only in 1887 that two volumes appeared almost simultaneously that made genuinely new contributions; indeed, the second left an enduring imprint on all subsequent Gaonic studies.

The fourth volume of Isaac Hirsch Weiss's monumental history of Jewish tradition, *Dor Dor ve-Dorshav,* traced the history of Jewish learning and religious doctrine from the age of the Saboraim until the close of the Gaonic period. In addition to detailed analyses of the legal and doctrinal pronouncements of the heads of the Babylonian academies, the volume devoted one of its five parts to Karaism and another to the spread of rabbinic learning to Europe. Although twenty-seven years younger than Graetz's history, and although it dealt with aspects of Gaonic culture and thought far more extensively and intensively than the latter, the work is today hopelessly outdated; the subjects studied by Weiss have been radically enriched by the enormous amount of material that has since come to light from repositories of Hebrew medieval materials as well as by the extensive and fundamental research on the intellectual history of medieval Islam and of the Jews who were influenced by it. Our very assumptions about the intellectual and religious stimuli underlying the work of Saadiah, Sherira, and Hai, and of the rabbinic academies that rose on the periphery of the Gaonic world, are so different from those that Weiss could possibly have had that we sense at once the intellectual chasm separating our age from that of Weiss and, in consequence, of the divide between his questions about the Gaonic world and ours. Not only was much of Saadiah's work as yet unavailable, but even the treatment of Saadiah's philosophic treatise, *Kitab al-Amanat w'al-I'taqadat* (Heb., *Ha-Emunot ve-ha-De'ot*), makes not so much as a passing reference to Kalam and its role in Saadiah's approach to religion.[28] Reliable data on the intellectual and theological views of sectarians and dissidents would only become available long after Weiss's work had been completed.

And yet the work is still rewarding. In focusing his sights on ideas and in assembling the materials of legal and theological import in accordance with the succession of Geonim, Weiss justified independently, for the realm of ideas and social thought, the claim made by Graetz about Jewish history generally. Weiss opened his volume by articulating his conviction that the only permanent feature of history is change, in ideas and beliefs no less than in men, events, and institutions. Since he had relatively little ready material with which to work, Weiss combed the available responsa literature and the medieval codes, *novellae* and chronicles for remains of Gaonic data. What emerged was the first reasoned account in the annals of Jewish scholarship of the development of rabbinic learning and creativity, a veritable intellectual history. The endless chain of names and dates in the medieval lists of rabbis now took on a dynamic intellectual character and, thanks to Weiss' cultivated sense of history, many views in the halakhic literature a firm *Sitz im Leben.*

This volume of Weiss' work has never gained the appreciation it deserves. While he has been read and studied far more carefully than Graetz in certain scholarly quarters, his readers, judging from the way he is mentioned is subsequent literature, frequently examined him with an eye to writing their own *novellae* in rebuttal of specific points. Since Weiss had even less of an antecedent literature than Graetz on which to pattern much of his work, he was in some respects pioneering into totally unchartered areas. It was not hard for reviewers to detect slips or gross misstatements on almost every page. While citation from rabbinic sources was an old skill in Jewish circles of learning, an appreciation of the tasks and methods of intellectual history was not. It took intellectually trained eyes like those of Solomon Schechter and Louis Ginzberg, which were as sensitive as anyone's to Weiss' shortcomings, to appreciate the magnitude of Weiss' achievement.[29] Very few have risen to the challenge of treating rabbinic learning as the material of intellectual history, and those that have, have not displaced Weiss' work. Alongside the more encompassing work of Graetz, Weiss' intellectual survey made subsequent research on the Geonim and their opponents infinitely easier, for it provided a total framework in which a multitude of details could be inserted, corrected, or interpreted.

The second momentous volume to appear in 1887 was a collection of Gaonic responsa assembled by Abraham Eliyahu (Albert Yakovlevich) Harkavy from four manuscripts in the Imperial Public Library of St. Petersburg. While several collections of Gaonic responsa had long been available in print—six new ones had been published since the beginning of the nineteenth century[30]—the new collection of *Teshubot ha-Geonim* (*Harkavy*, as the volume came to be known) was quite novel in a number of significant respects. Quite apart from the not insignificant fact that the texts in this collection were often fuller and more accurate than versions of the same responsa published in earlier collections, Harkavy's compilation teemed with hitherto unknown historical *realia*, which the editors or copyists of earlier collections had either altered or omitted. Original and official names, titles of senders and recipients, as well as the names of places to which the responsa were sent, were preserved in this collection, which thus provided a mound of new data on a Jewish society in Gaonic times. Men who had formerly been mere names, among them Elhanan ben Shemaryah of Fostat and Nissim ben Jacob ibn Shahin of Qairawan, suddenly took shape as genuine historical figures thanks to their correspondence with the presidents of the Babylonian academies. The official formula of the appointment of judges by the office of the exilarch and Saadiah's corroboration of a decision handed down by the court of David ben Zakkai,[31] the exilarch with whom he was to lock horns, were merely two gems among the hundreds of scraps of new information that shed new light on the Gaonic world. The Arabic base of Gaonic society became far more apparent than it had been hitherto from the queries and replies that Harkavy transmitted in their Arabic originals along with Hebrew translations of his own. Harkavy further enriched this collection with penetrating explanatory notes that elucidated the linguistic and historical setting from which these collections had emerged.

Although Harkavy himself may at the time not have been quite aware of the fact, his publication actually inaugurated a new stage in Gaonic studies, for, as we know today, the original source of the manuscripts owned by the Imperial Public Library was the Cairo Geniza,[32] which was soon to become the wellspring for all new research in the field. More immediately, however, Harkavy's edition of responsa accentuated the need, long appreciated in traditional rabbinic circles, for systematic classification and annotation of the ever mounting number of Gaonic responsa. Many of the texts of these replies had been published in truncated form and without any indication of halakhic context or author. Such basic information on the historical setting of a responsum was vital not only to the historian but even to the pure halakhist in his evaluation of the interpretations that had become part of the implications of any given law. Indeed, David Luria and Israel Moses Hazzan, two traditional scholars of the nineteenth century, each of whom had developed a critical approach to classical sources, independently compiled such critical notes to the collection of Gaonic responsa published in Salonica in 1802 under the title *Sha'arey Teshuva*.[33] On the basis of information embedded in medieval works they identified wherever they could the authors of the responsa and the specific legal context to which an obscure decision had to be assigned. The works of both Weiss and Harkavy make it further evident how vital it was to bring together and classify the whole corpus of free floating material, so that it would be consulted critically and fruitfully by the historian of ideas and institutions.

The annotated guide to Gaonic responsa by Joel Mueller, *Mafteah li-Teshuvot ha-Geonim* (1891), a painstaking description of the whole of the Gaonic responsa literature that Mueller could track down and a major effort at filling a lacuna in scholarly tools, has today only limited value. Eight decades of scholarly work have so augmented the literature of Gaonic responsa and judicial decisions that any use of Mueller's guide can only be the first step in assembling the data.[34] Nevertheless, the enduring importance of the work cannot be gainsaid, even in the face of the additional limitation that Mueller's index was designed to answer the needs of scholars whose approach to history was still largely biographical and bibliographical. In consequence, anyone wishing to study the institutions of Gaonic society will hardly find Mueller's work a facile guide. Mueller considered it his task to provide a detailed description of each of the published collections of Gaonic responsa and a brief reference to each of the responsa and legal decisions of each Gaon. The latter he classified under the name of the issuing Gaon, subdividing the sections with brief digests of each reply and decision according to the arrangement of materials in Maimonides' *Mishneh Torah.* Anyone concerned not so much with the spiritual biography of a Gaon as with social life would have to go through each section and prepare his own index. Nevertheless, Mueller did inaugurate the age of tools for medieval literature, and since it has never been superseded it remains indispensable.

Major advances in the rediscovery of the Gaonic world seemed destined to come in pairs, for toward the end of 1891, the year in which Mueller's guide appeared, Harkavy issued a new and truly exciting volume, the fifth in his renowned series of *Studien und Mittheilungen aus der kaiserlichen oeffentlichen Bibliothek zu St. Petersburg.* With an eye for dramatic effect, Harkavy scheduled the work, entitled *Zikhron ha-Gaon R. Saadiah al-Fayyumi u-Sefarav,* to appear on the occasion of the putative millennium of Saadiah Gaon's birth, so as to do honor to the supreme genius of the Babylonian Geonim and simultaneously to alert the scholarly world to the electrifying riches still being secreted in medieval manuscripts. The volume contained fragments of two works by Saadiah: the first his poetic dictionary entitled *Sefer ha-Egron* (Compendium)[35] and the second the Gaon's *apologia pro vita sua* entitled *Sefer ha-Galuy* (Disclosure).[36] Portions of Saadiah's lexicographical manual, it is true, had been published and discussed during the twenty years preceding the publication of this volume, but the real character and, more important, the historic significance of this composition of Saadiah's youth only now became apparent. In the first place, it clearly established Saadiah as a trailblazer in the revival of medieval Hebrew poetry,[37] a favorite subject in scholarly circles of the nineteenth century,[38] for the work was, at least formally, designed as a handbook for composers of Hebrew verse. However, the introductions to Saadiah's two editions of his book made it plain that the Gaon's concern for good Hebrew usage was stimulated, on the one hand, by widespread lack of competence in the language and, on the other hand, by at least one Arabic work on the same theme for versifiers in Arabic. Thus, the seeds of the renaissance in this area, as in others in which Hebrew productivity in Arabic society attained new heights, were now manifestly seen to have been sown by Saadiah. Moreover, his composition was clearly no mere philological exercise but a conscious response to the challenge presented by the inroads of Muslim culture into the Jewish community. Finally, Harkavy made no secret of the contemporary consolatory overtones which he considered this fragment to bear, for it put a strong damper on Pinsker's thesis that it was the Karaite challenge rather than native Rabbanite vitality that had generated the revival of Hebrew creativity in medieval Jewish society. The evidence of indigenous energies for response even to the foreign Muslim challange was a matter of no mean importance to a philologist-bibliographer, who, while ensconced in St. Petersburg, shared the agonies and yearnings of the apostles of national-cultural revival in Vilna and Odessa.[39]

However, it was for the second half of the volume that Harkavy reserved his stunning contribution. That a work entitled *Sefer ha-Galuy* had contained biographical material about Saadiah and probably something about the controversies in which he had become embroiled had long been a matter of common knowledge. But beyond that, the work and its author remained a mystery. In 1872 Geiger published a fragment from a Karaite work, which recounted in considerable detail the furious broadsides of Saadiah's opponents at the time of the Gaon's battle with the exilarch David ben Zakkai and other members of the Jewish establishment of Baghdad.[40] While some of the statements in this fragment bordered on the downright obscene and evidently were to be explained by the intensity of the imbroglio, some of the details could not be so summarily dismissed. Clearly, it would have been nice to have a fuller explanation and at least to hear Saadiah's side of the story. The *Sefer ha-Galuy*, of which Harkavy had managed to retrieve several sizable fragments, now turned out to be an autobiographical *apologia* generated by the very dispute which the fragment published by Geiger had described. It illuminated much of Saadiah's stormy history both before as well as after his rise to the presidency of Sura and shed considerable light on the Gaon's personality and his self-image. Several other fragments composed by Saddiah and Aaron ben Meir of Palestine, which Harkavy added as appendices, shed unexpected light on the controversy over the calendar that had thrown Near Eastern Jewry into a turmoil in 921. Cultural and institutional history was now enriched by a new dimension, the personal and the partisan, thus giving the dynamics of history which Graetz had intuited a quality of reality that could ultimately be gained only from material reflecting the mundane drives and conflicts of real people. The stuff of genuine biography had finally begun to come to light.

Our survey of the slow but sure progress made in the course of six decades of research on the Gaonic world should make it evident that the revelations yielded by the opening of the Geniza some five years after Harkavy's publication on Saadiah, while they unquestionably revolutionized the subject, were not made in a vacuum. The broad outlines, into which the new and often electrifying scraps of information retrieved from the cache of Cairo could be fitted, had long been drawn and seemed almost to be awaiting the riches which Schechter's expedition made accessible. Alas, there is another side to the story, which must in all candor be recorded. Harkavy, for all his keen sensitivity to the dramatic import of his findings, and despite his brilliant grasp of historical problems, persisted in the monographic tradition that Rapoport had introduced. He composed scintillating notes and appendices to the Hebrew translation of Graetz's *History*, but no synthesis of his own. Nor was he insensitive to the challenge which the enormous bulk of materials he had studied beckoned him to face. In his publication of the Saadyanic fragments he promised that a future volume of the *Studien und Mittheilungen* would synthesize the materials through a biography of Saadiah.[41] But disciplines seem to engender inhibitions into their very tradition, and it was, therefore, hardly an accident that while he continued to produce works of major scholarly significance for well over a decade longer, he never got around to completing his original synthesis. Accordingly, although volume VIII of the *Studien und Mittheilungen* appeared in 1903, volumes VI and VII of that series never did. I belabor this point somewhat, for it seems to me vital for anyone wishing to understand the tradition that Jacob Mann inherited when he came to Gaonic studies. Harkavy's failure to complete a synthesis of his own was particularly regrettable, for he was a master Rabbinist and Arabist and appreciated the complex influences to which Jewish life in the Gaonic age had been subjected. He also had models aplenty on which to draw had he wished. Quite apart from the works of Geiger, Graetz, and Weiss, Jewish scholars like Salomon Munk, Ignace Goldziher, and David Kaufmann had effectively demonstrated how the history of Judaism could be enriched by a synthesis of Jewish and Arabic materials, and Harkavy was in a position to do that in ways that no other scholar was. However, such is the power of styles of thinking and of work that what had been effectively achieved in other areas of scholarship could not be readily applied to the world of the Gaonic yeshiva and to the religious leadership of the Jewish community. Narrative historiography was left to other, less expert, hands, and the results have often merely served to sustain the ego of specialists who could not, or would not, face up to the task and challenge of rewriting Jewish history.

One interesting effort at historical synthesis was made in the closing years of the century and was published almost simultaneously with the announcement of Schechter's first finds in the Geniza in 1897. Yitzhak (Isaak) Halevy's *Dorot Harischonim*[42] is all but ignored today by critical historians. Although Halevy's trenchancy as a critic of other historians is regularly conceded, his own constructions were hardly more plausible than those he so competently tore down. What is more, Halevy's undisguised religious orthodoxy and his uncontrolled vituperation against the leading critical scholars of his day predetermined many of his historical judgments and alienated even those predisposed to give him a fair hearing. However, a willingness to overlook his stylistic quirks and to give the work a dispassionate reading can be very rewarding. Halevy was an acute student of classical rabbinic texts and endowed with consummate control of rabbinic literature. He had an uncanny talent for detecting the loopholes in theories spun by the scholars of his day, and he insisted on exposing them before they became part of the accepted baggage of the scholarly tradition. The third volume of his work is a structured intellectual history of the Gaonic age with many keen insights into the chronology and religious developments of the period. His analysis of Gaonic texts is always valuable, for he was meticulous in interpreting these traditions in terms of their proper rabbinic context, which he was often able to delineate far better than others.

FIRST FRUITS OF GENIZA RESEARCH

Fragments from the Cairo Geniza had begun to appear in a steady stream in the learned journals just at about the time that Solomon Schechter was gaining his first direct experience of the fabulous riches that had been hidden for centuries in the repository of the Cairo synagogue. New "Egyptian Fragments" published by Elkan Adler, Adolf Neubauer, Israel Abrahams, and others in scholarly journals signalized the beginning of a new stage in Jewish study of the Middle Ages, and the development was accorded recognition by the novel entry of "Geniza (Cairo) MSS" in the table of contents of volume X of *The Jewish Quarterly Review*.[43] While Schechter's own first publications of Geniza material consisted of fragments of lost classical texts—notably Ben Sira and specimens of the old Palestinian liturgy[44]—he kept his eagle eye open for manuscripts that would shed new light on Jewish history, and the results were as startling as they were rewarding.

Neither the title nor the size of Schechter's contribution to *The Jewish Quarterly Review* of July 1899 (volume XI) gave any indication of the unsettling impact that one Geniza fragment could have on Jewish historiography. "Geniza Specimens. A letter of Chushiel," an eight-page paper accompanied by two photographic facsimiles, launched Jewish historians on a hunt which has never been concluded to the satisfaction of all scholars.[45] A badly mutilated epistle, much of which remained frustratingly opaque, from Hushiel ben Elhanan of Qairawan to Shemaryah ben Elhanan of Cairo plainly discredited Abraham ibn Daud's story of the four captives as a romantic fantasy. Through all its obscurities the letter shed sufficient new light on the status of Jewish learning in North Africa at the turn of the millennium to require a total revision of the old conception of the way in which Jewish learning spread to the far corners of the Mediterranean littoral. Hushiel's letter confirmed what Harkavy's collection of responsa had already made evident, to wit, that by the year 1000 fully developed and quite literate Jewish communities dotted the whole length of the North African Muslim domain. Above all, the letter raised the possibility that a thorough examination of the Geniza would open up totally unanticipated vistas of Jewish history.

Schechter himself seemed to take special delight in confirming this suspicion by planting periodic bombshells in *The Jewish Quarterly Review.* Two years after his publication of Hushiel's letter he issued the text of "The Oldest Collection of Bible Difficulties, by a Jew," which he aptly described as "one of the most puzzling" "of all the riddles the Geniza offers."[46] Several months later, he initiated a series entitled "Saadyana,"[47] which not only retrieved new materials from Saadiah Gaon's stormy career, but even more significantly shed totally new light on the history of the Palestinian academy in its last days on native soil in the eleventh century. Thus, not only individuals were beginning to emerge from oblivion but whole communities, not the least significant of which was the one in the Holy Land itself.

New documents were seeing the light of day with dazzling speed. In 1903 Harkavy again threw a cornucopia of riches into the hopper as volume II of *Lickute Kadmoniot.* Consisting of fragments of the codes of Anan, Benjamin Nahwendi, and Daniel al-Qumisi, the collection uncovered the legal foundations of Karaism to the understanding of which Pinsker had provided the basic tools some four decades earlier. Schechter himself subsequently filled in some of the gaps in Anan's Book of Laws by issuing part II of his *Documents of Jewish Sectaries* in 1910.[48] The dizzying potpourri of material that had become available over and beyond what had been accumulated before the opening of the Geniza beckoned for organization and interpretation.

Hayyim Yehiel Bornstein, the first to attempt to assemble and explain all the available materials on one theme, was one of those human gems of pristine Eastern Europe, who, for lack of a university post or record of activity in public affairs, remained for long relatively unknown even to some professional historians.[49] The loss, in this instance, was particularly regrettable, for Bornstein, although but an autodidact, who from 1889 earned his livelihood as secretary of the renowned synagogue on Tlomackie Street, in Warsaw, succeeded in solving several difficult problems in the history of Judaism which students long after him have tried to solve from scratch and with far less satisfying results. A consummate Hebraist and Talmudist, his favorite areas of study were mathematics, astronomy, and chronology, particularly as they were reflected in Hebrew literature and classical Jewish institutions, and from time to time he contributed small papers on various subjects to Hebrew and Polish periodicals. In 1904, however, he contributed a full-sized monograph in

Hebrew to the Nahum Sokolow jubilee volume, "The Dispute of Saadiah Gaon and Ben Meir over the Calendation of the Years 4862–4684, a Chapter in the History of the System of Jewish Intercalation." While well over a third of this study was taken up by annotated texts relevant to the controversy, the body of the work and the appendices represented a major effort—and it remains one of the most penetrating ever undertaken in this field—to focus on a single issue exercising the authorities of the Gaonic world and to explain it historically. In the course of his exposition, Bornstein surveyed the history of the different systems of calendation employed in the medieval Jewish communities of Palestine and Babylonia, the history of the Palestinian academy as far as it was known at the time, and the history of the relations between the rabbinic authorities of Babylonia and the Holy Land in the centuries preceding the controversy. Thus, materials on a dispute about an abstruse ritual astronomical issue had provided a gifted scholar with the opening by which to give a coherent picture of significant aspects of life in communities under Gaonic control.[50]

For all the novelty and brillance of its approach to Gaonic history, Bornstein's study was actually symptomatic of a new trend toward thematic studies of aspects of Gaonic culture. If scholarly publications in this field in the first decade of the twentieth century are any index, a growing need was sensed for classification and systematization of the ever increasing bulk of materials diffused in widely scattered scientific publications and medieval texts, and even manuscripts of whose contents some scholars had become considerably aware.

This incipient shift in emphasis was markedly reflected in the studies of a younger protégé of Bornstein and his circle, Samuel Poznanski.[51] After completing his formal training in Berlin, he returned in 1896 to Warsaw, where he became co-rabbi in the very synagogue in which Bornstein was employed and where he rapidly gained a reputation as one of the foremost authorities in the history of medieval exegesis. His mastery of Judeo-Arabic as well as of rabbinic literature enabled him, as it had Harkavy, to write articles and books in several languages on a wide variety of subjects, among them the burgeoning field of Gaonica and Karaitica. (He was, understandably enough, one of Schechter's first choices for the professorship of biblical exegesis and medieval Jewish history in the newly reorganized Jewish Theological Seminary when Schechter was recruiting scholars for his faculty.)[52] Several years before the appearance of Bornstein's study, he issued the first of a series of bio-bibliographical studies on personalities of the Gaonic age whose names kept on cropping up in the newly growing literature but about whom relatively little of a reliable and specific character was known or, at least, readily accessible even to scholars. His exhaustive studies of Anan, Jacob ben Ephraim, Ephraim ben Shemaryah, and Dosa ben Saadiah were thus basically Rapoportian in design, but thanks to Poznanski's lucidity, thoroughness, and good judgment, eminently more readable and digestible.[53]

Poznanski's capacity to combine clarity with exhaustiveness, critical judgment with linguistic versatility, and modern techniques with an immense classical rabbinic apparatus reflected the influence of German training on his Polish-Jewish foundations. And it was doubtless his exposure to the West European atmosphere, in which the grand compilations of Zunz and Steinschneider were acknowledged as the supreme achievements of Jewish scholarship, that made him turn to the more ambitious projects of bibliography-prosopography that gained him a place of eminence in the history of Gaonic scholarship. As one who knew virtually every nook and cranny of the Gaonic literature that was coming to light, he appreciated the frustrating difficulties that even specialists were experiencing in encountering obscure names about whom information was available only after laborious searches through far-flung sources. Accordingly, he focused on three problems and produced works that have remained staples in Gaonic research to this day. In *The Karaite Literary Opponents of Saadiah Gaon* he arranged by century the name of every author known to have issued anti-Saadyanic polemics along with documented summaries of the contents of their works.[54] While ostensibly merely an exercise in bibliography, Poznanski's guide demonstrated conclusively the immense impact of Saadiah's thought and activity on medieval literature and simultaneously provided a framework within which all subsequent research on this area could be conducted. Saadiah, it was now apparent and demonstrable, had evoked an echo that was sustained for centuries after his death. What is more, the ever growing body of information on the Karaites was now given a systematizing tool that would further pave the way for genuine historical research. The second monograph, *Anshay Qairuan*,[55] appropriately published in the jubilee volume in honor of Abraham Harkavy, gave an alphabetical list of every Jew known to have functioned, albeit temporarily, in the renowned North African community, along with fully documented studies of every entry. Although clearly inspired by Henri Gross's *Gallia Judaica*, it was a pioneering effort of major importance that still awaits imitators. Finally, in a study that appeared on the very eve of the First World War, Pozanski extended the horizon of Gaonic studies by his *Die Babylonische Geonim im nachgaonaeischen Zeitlater* in which he gave a chronologically arranged prosopography of all those bearing the title Gaon—and for that matter of Nasi—after the eclipse of the Gaonate and exilarchate in the eleventh century.[56] While Poznanski's findings, impressive as they were, could not displace the age-old scheme which placed the end of the Gaonic age at the death of Hai, Samuel b. Hofni, and Hezekiah the Exilarch, they did serve as a major corrective to the impression that an age in Jewish history came to an end as suddenly and as definitively as Ibn Daud had represented. The academies and the Babylonian institutions of communal organization, it was now apparent, lingered on for centuries after the cessation of their effective power and influence over Jewish communities in the Near East and North Africa. Indeed, the activities and difficulties of Maimonides in Egypt now began to take on new significance in the light of the efforts of vestigial Babylonian institutions to retain the loyalties of Jewish communities that had long since outgrown their need of these historic centers. Poznanski's study was the first probe into a dark age of Jewish history, and along with his earlier compilations helped free Jewish scholars for the task of analysis rather than the task of training to become merely walking computers of Gaonic fragments.

There was, to be sure, one area of study in which a solid framework for critical scholarship and synthesis had long been in the making, and that was in the area of Gaonic halakhic literature. In this area of scholarly research, discussion reflected the highest degree of sophistication and historical sensitivity, for it was part of a considerable body of higher criticism that developed in the course of the nineteenth century in the study of classical rabbinic literature. Some of the most astute Jewish critical minds—among them Zvi Hirsch Chajes, Nahman Krochmal, S. J. L. Rapoport, Joshua Heschel Schorr, Zvi Menahem Pineles, Markus Friedmann (known in Hebrew as Meir Ish-Shalom), Isaac Hirsch Weiss, Jacob Bruell, Nehemias Bruell, Solomon Buber, Zechariah Fraenkel, David Hoffman—had produced an impressive array of books and articles on source analysis of rabbinic texts and on the formation and compilation of classical rabbinic literature. Their discussions, while often heated, were governed by the canons of scientific philology and by a historical orientation that went far beyond the mere collection of data. Introductions to the Mishna, Tannaitic and homiletical midrashim, and the Babylonian and Palestinian Talmudim were buttressed by penetrating researches into the character of the Tosefta, the methodology of the Babylonian Talmud and the process by which it achieved its final form, the development of rabbinic law and homily, and finally into the history of rabbinic linguistic usage.[57] It was relatively easy, and certainly logical, to extend the techniques and scholarly results of this area of study to the halakhic and homiletical compilations of Gaonic times. Gaonic and medieval rabbinic literature were, after all, outgrowths of, and commentaries on, Tannaitic and Amoraic literature. No one engaged in serious study of the classical literature could avoid coming to grips with the medieval commentaries, *novellae*, and codes and the information they gave of the growth and process of transmission of the earlier layers of rabbinic tradition. Accordingly, the appearance of new Gaonic legal works, and of compilations that drew on them, almost immediately evoked scholarly statements on the history of the codes and on the relationship of these tracts to the known body of literature.

In this area, too, it was Rapoport who had set the ball rolling by one of his long communications in volume VI of *Kerem Chemed* (1841), where he set forth his theories on the relationship of the *Halakhot Gedolot* to other early codes.[58] Some forty years later, Israel Meir Freimann prefaced the second volume of his edition of *Sefer ve-Hizhir*—a legal-homiletic compilation in Hebrew similar in character to the Aramaic disquisitions of R. Aḥai known as *She'eltot*—with a survey of all the known Gaonic codes; and in 1886 Solomon Joachim (Sheneor Zalman Hayyim) Halberstamm provided a further analysis in the light of the data that had become available in the codes edited by Hayyim M. Horowitz and Aryeh Loeb Schlossberg.[59] At about the same time, Jacob Reifmann published a critical introduction to the *She'eltot* that analyzed the work linguistically, legally and structurally.[60] These studies, needless to say, were quickly absorbed and utilized by Weiss, Mueller, and Harkavy, and, finally, by Abraham Epstein (1902) in his incisive analysis of the two recensions of the *Halakhot Gedolot*.[61] In this phase of Gaonic research Jewish scholars were clearly at home, and their discussions, even when conjectural or displaying confessing puzzlement, bespoke a maturity and fundamental assurance about the basic character and history of the legal tradition and of the literature transmitting it. Even treatises that did not conform to literary stereotypes, such as the handbook on liturgical usage known as *Seder Rab Amram Gaon*, the Arabic handbook by Saadiah to the laws of inheritance and the same Gaon's versified list of the 613 commandments, could quickly be classified and studied in context.[62] One key element in this discussion was still lacking, and that was a critical analysis of the role of these works in the socio-historical context of Gaonic culture; that is to say, a reasoned historical explanation of the new genres of literature adopted by the Geonim for the dissemination of their norms for Jewish life, in the light of the social, political, and intellectual conditions of their times.

Clearly any such appraisal could be advanced with some cogency only after the resolution of the problems posed by a body of medieval historiography that had been considerably augmented by recent publications and that provided the indispensable chronological framework for any historical discussion. Apart from the considerable chronological information in these medieval works, this historiography furnished accounts or hints of focal incidents and, most important, periodized histories of the two Babylonian academies and their relationship to each other as well as to the exilarchs. The trouble was that these medieval works were often in hopeless disagreement, not only on details, but with respect to such fundamental questions as the dating of the Gaonic period, the relative authority of each of the academies, and the actual place of the exilarchate in the hierarchy of Jewish society. The two fullest accounts, those of Sherira Gaon and Abraham ibn Daud, flatly contradicted each other on the place of the presidency of the first three "generations" of Geonim. The briefer account by Nathan the Babylonian, while invaluable for the light it shed on the academies, the exilarchs, and the lay leadership of the community, took a far different view of things than both Sherira and Abraham ibn Daud. And the historical survey of rabbinic succession by Menahem ben Solomon Meiri of Perpignan on occasion differed with all of them in details as well as basic understanding.[63]

Once again the task of systematization and evaluation was undertaken by an amateur who had gained considerable distinction in consequence of his researches in the history of rabbinic literature and folklore. Abraham Epstein of Staro Konstantinov had been a relative latecomer to serious scholarship, having spent the first three and a half decades of his life amassing a fortune in business and agriculture. Nevertheless, he had always been addicted to books and was an example of the new type of Hebrew critical scholar: from adolescent days he had published typical *maskilic* tidbits in the Hebrew press. Finally, after moving to Vienna at the age of thirty-six, he progressively withdrew from business and dedicated himself to disciplined research. His articles and books were chaste treasure troves of information about a host of subjects in midrashic and medieval literature, and included studies on the history of Gaonic codes and medieval exegesis, an edition of the different recensions of the Eldad ha-Dani story, and a potpourri on midrashic and folkloristic traditions entitled *Mi-Qadmoniot ha-Yehudim.*[64] By 1909 he had become a revered member of the scholarly circle of East European Hebraists and, accordingly, contributed a paper to the Harkavy jubilee volume on Gaonic historiography that, like Poznanski's, was to make literary history.[65]

Epstein isolated two strands of historical writing which he traced respectively to the two Babylonian academies, the historical views of Pumbeditha being represented in the *Epsitle of Sherira,* and those of Sura in the *Seder Tannaiam va-Amoraim,*[66] the account of Nathan the Babylonian, the lost Introduction to the Talmud of Samuel ibn Nagrela and the History of Tradition by Abraham ibn Daud. These two traditions differed not only in their details and in their evaluations of the relative places of the academies, but in their periodization of Jewish history as well; for while Sherira dated the beginnings of the Saboraic and Gaonic ages in 500 C.E. and 589 C.E. respectively, the Sura school dated the beginning of the Gaonic age well after the rise of Islam, and thus made the age of the Saboraim of much longer duration. Epstein made it very clear that in matters of detail the Pumbeditha tradition was to be accorded far greater credence than the one emanating from Sura, since the hectic history of the latter academy had caused its records to become a shambles. Epstein further utilized this classification to evaluate Ibn Daud's picture of history and all those sources that had relied on it. In short, the student of Gaonic history was now offered clear criteria with which to weigh the information he derived from medieval historians. It was a brilliant effort, and one which still bears a vital message, in spite of the fact that most of Epstein's evaluations and explanations, notably the supposed Suran conception of history, must be totally discarded. But however untenable Epstein's theories may be, he left no room for doubt that any use of medieval historiography can properly be made only after consideration of the source of the report and the relative amount of credence that ought to be accorded it in the face of opposing information. Thus, Nathan the Babylonian may have been oriented to a higher regard for Sura and the exilarchs than Sherira was, but his account bore marks of authenticity that made of it a most illuminating source.

The last point was driven home with singular skill by a master of rabbinics who recognized that the time had come for a fresh and encompassing synthesis of the Gaonic sources and modern research. In the first of his two volumes entitled *Geonica* (1909), Louis Ginzberg undertook to examine the Gaonate as a historical institution and to elucidate the salient features of its history. The particular merit of Ginzberg's study lay in its singular focus on Gaonic history and culture; for Ginzberg dwelt on those aspects of the Gaonate that characterized it as a historical institution and that distinguished it from parallel communal institutions in other times and areas of Jewish history. Taking a cue from Graetz, Ginzberg emphasized the Arabic soil on which the Gaonate became the institution that it did, and from there he proceeded to describe the political overtones of Gaonic pretensions to power, the social stratification of the Gaonic class, the clashes of the Gaonate with other communal agencies, the intra-Gaonic struggles for power and money, and, finally, the decline of the Gaonate as an institution of central control over the Jewish communities of the Arabic world. In this analysis the account of Nathan the Babylonian—on the original language of which Ginzberg indulged in a polemic with Israel Friedlander that was as unfortunate stylistically as it was substantively[67]—was exploited judiciously and profitably. The first section of Ginzberg's book was thus a pioneering effort at a sociological understanding of the Gaonate and of the academic personnel of Babylonia, and it remains to this day the best treatment of this aspect of Gaonic history.

If, on the one hand, the Geonim were a self-sustaining Jewish oligarchy who were jealous of their power, they were, on the other hand, united and fired by a conception of Jewish living that determined the form and content of the literature they and their disciples produced. Gaonic culture was fundamentally halakhic, and it was an effort at the standardization and dissemination of uniform halakhic practice that underlay all of their literature. Everything else, the homilies, historiography, and hortatory letters, was subservient to this fundamental ideal. Accordingly, Ginzberg then proceeded to analyze the relationship of the various halakhic works and responsa collections one to the other. While his work, therefore, treated many of the scholarly questions on the agenda of scientific discussion, it provided a unique, grand, and unifying conception of an age of Jewish culture that was creative in terms of its own ideals and criteria. To be sure, Ginzberg had not encompassed all of Gaonic culture. He did not pay much attention to the sectarian and skeptical forces in the Jewish community and to the role that philosophy played in Gaonic expression; and, it must be noted, even in his day there was enough to say something of importance on the subject. Clearly, Ginzberg's exclusive focus on the halakhic character of Gaonic creativity derived in no small measure from a lifelong polemic that he had maintained with Jews and Christians in which he had argued for the centrality of Halakhah in Judaism and for the intellectual respectability and religious validity of exegetical legalistic religion. The master of the Jewish legend was also the relentless exponent of a Judaism that was fundamentally halakhic.[68] But whatever the motives that may have oriented the design of his work, the fact is that his conception of the Gaonate and its culture did get to the heart of the matter. In Gaonic society, all non-halakhic forms of expression were maidservants of Halakhah, and even the sects were organized groups of counter-halakhic systems. The fights between Geonim, and between Geonim and exilarchs, were fundamentally on who should be the effective exponent of the halakhic system. The controversies between the Palestinian and Babylonian authorities were again over issues that were fundamentally halakhic. To fail to emphasize this is to miss the boat completely on the character of a culture that spanned centuries as well as continents. Ginzberg understood that if history is the reasoned account of the past, the primary duty of the historian should be to recapture and mirror the values held and articulated by the spokesmen of the age, and this Ginzberg achieved admirably.

Ginzberg's basic approach underlay the exposition of Simon Eppenstein, who extended his researches to other aspects of the Gaonic world. Eppenstein's studies, which had actually begun to appear in the *Monatsschrift fuer Geschichte und Wissenschaft des Judentums* before the publication of Ginzberg's work, were issued collectively in 1913 as *Beitraege zur Geschichte und Literatur in geonaeischen Zeitalter.* The most unfortunate aspect of the work was the word *Beitraege* in the title, for the word belied the systematic and penetrating exposition, and probably contributed to the neglect of the book by non-specialists in Gaonic history. Eppenstein's "contributions" attempted to see the halakhic culture of the Gaonate as an integral aspect of Mediterranean culture in the

heyday of Muslim power. While treating a number of the subjects that
Ginzberg had, and very much in the same spirit, he also tried to show the
influence of the temper of the age on halakhic literature. He further
gave a prominent place in his book to the Palestinian academies in
Gaonic times and to the rise of new major centers of Jewish life in the
West. It was impossible, Eppenstein also emphasized, fully to understand the Gaonic world without taking into account the Jewish communities of Cairo, Qairawan, and Cordova. The rabbinates of these
communities, and of the Holy Land, were vital links in the cultural complex of the Gaonic world, and their history was a key to the understanding of Gaonic activity and ultimate decline.

SPECIALIZATION AND PROFESSIONALISM: GAONIC STUDIES SINCE WORLD WAR I

By 1914 the Gaonic period had come into its own as a recognized and
developed area of research that was increasingly cultivated by scholars
with special areas of expertise. While many dark spots still required clarification, a broad general consensus on the history and cultural character
of the Gaonic age had crystallized, thus transforming what had been a
dark age of Jewish history into a meaningful link in the chain of Jewish
tradition and communal history. While literally thousands upon thousands of manuscript pages awaited examination, transcription, and interpretation, the task of the scholar now lay in tracking down information in
specific areas of inquiry. And though scholars eagerly joined in the
search for new illuminating data and published innumerable articles,
monographs, and editions of texts, there were to be relatively few electrifying discoveries.

Israel Davidson's publication of Geniza fragments containing a sizable portion of Saadiah's polemic against Hiwi al-Balkhi was symptomatic
of the next stage of Gaonic research as a whole. Some years before the
outbreak of the war, Samuel Poznanski had issued another of his masterly
papers in which he assembled all the medieval references upon which he
could lay his hands to the doctrines of the infamous Hiwi whom Saadiah
was reported to have refuted in writing.[69] What emerged was a picture of
an astute blasphemer, who subjected Scripture to a searching examination in order to prove its contemptible infantilism and rank immorality.
Clearly, Hiwi was no mere heretic of the Karaite sort but apparently a
Jewish version of Iranian critics of Judaism and Christianity, some of
whose doctrines had become common knowledge to students of medieval Persian texts. Poznanski had even been able to reconstruct the bare
outlines of the literary structure of Hiwi's attack in the form of questions
against Scripture. In response to Solomon Schechter's urging, Davidson
examined some of the fragments of Hebrew verse in the Geniza and soon

came upon a fragment of an authentic copy of Saadiah's counterattack. To be sure, the find was not only exciting but also represented a substantive contribution to a significant problem.[70] But in the final analysis Davidson had only provided a more solid foundation and had broadened the scope of facts that had already been largely established. It was an instance of genuine scientific progress, but hardly a stunning breakthrough into unanticipated spheres.

Most of the work in Gaonica during the last six decades has been of that nature. By 1940, the year of Jacob Mann's death, the appearance and dimensions of Gaonica were qualitatively different from what they had been around 1914, but the changes had come about through methodical, painstaking research and synthesis by specialists and professionals. Indeed, if the work of Poznanski, Ginzberg, and Eppenstein heralded anything, it was the passing of the age of the amateur bibliophile as torchbearer in this field of scholarship. The yield of the Geniza, and of course of the scholarship that had preceded its discovery, had converted the Gaonic age from an unexplored wilderness into a jigsaw puzzle for which the missing pieces, the general character of which could now often be surmised, had to be located and into which they had to be fitted. Every new scrap of information now had to be coordinated with the received body of knowledge, and the latter refined and reinterpreted in the light of the former.

One further example from the field of rabbinics, an area that has been immeasurably enriched in consequence of Geniza research and the application of scientific techniques, will serve as a characteristic illustration. In 1856, Judah Rosenberg had published the text of a commentary on the order of Tohorot, which, on the authority of Rapoport, he ascribed to Hai Gaon.[71] In the course of the following five decades scholars expressed their assent to, or rejection of, this ascription without the matter ever being conclusively resolved. In 1915, J. N. Epstein, who was later to become the first professor of Talmud at the Hebrew University in Jerusalem, published a full-length analysis of this Gaonic commentary on the Mishna, and, on the basis of careful examination of the manuscripts containing all or parts of the work, concluded that the author of the work must have been Saadiah Gaon. Six years later he issued the first installment of a new edition of the text with the promise of a new Hebrew introduction. The latter finally appeared in 1945, enriched by new manuscript data, but Epstein now ascribed the work to Simeon Qayyara, the author of *Halakhot Gedolot*.[72] Epstein's evidence and line of reasoning were pregnant with implications of considerable importance for any reconstruction of the cultural atmosphere of the Geonim. They were the consequence of a combination of a consummate mastery of all rabbinic literature, a philological expertise in Semitic and classical languages, and a painstaking hunt for relevant manuscript materials during a period of thirty years. His conclusions were, accordingly, not the yield of lucky discoveries but of a disciplined and well-defined quest.

To a greater or lesser extent this was true of all the great contributions to Gaonic research in the post–World War I period. While a number of versatile men contributed to the advance of several subspecialties in the field of Gaonica, their researches were now addressed to students and colleagues with defined areas of interest and, in ever growing measure, training as well. Thus, men like Simha Assaf, J. N. Epstein, Louis Ginzberg, and Benjamin M. Lewin, and more recently Mordecai Margalioth, Shraga Abramson, and Moses Zucker, specialized in the editing and interpretation of rabbinic texts—codes, homilies, responsa, commentaries. Lewin established a new journal, *Ginze Kedem*, to serve specifically as "a Geonitic Periodical" and dedicated the last twenty years of his life to the assembling and systematization of Gaonic responsa and commentaries on the Babylonian Talmud in an encyclopedic work entitled *Otzar ha-Geonim*. Others like Israel Davidson, Heinrich Brody, M. Zulay, A. M. Habermann, and Shalom Spiegel concentrated on retrieving the corpus of Hebrew poetry and liturgy composed in Palestine and Babylonia in the age before the bards of Ibn Shaprut's court had begun to twitter. Here again, thrilling discoveries, while occasionally the consequence of sheer good fortune, were usually the end product of disciplined research that was forever being refined and improved. Following the example set by the pioneering spirits in several fields in the Weimar Republic,[73] a German-Jewish bibliophile, philanthropist, and Zionist, Zalman Schocken, established an institute for research on medieval Hebrew poetry, which issued "reports"[74] that mediated information in an area that quickly developed into a profession in its own right.[75] All areas of Gaonic study were enormously enriched by the ever growing number of competent Arabists whose researches into law, linguistics, philosophy, and prosody, in Karaite as well as Rabbanite literature, gave a new orientation to the cultural atmosphere in which Gaonic culture came to flower.

These new tools, techniques, and contributions to knowledge inevitably had a major effect on the understanding of the history of the period. But even in the area of historical "facts," narrowly defined, the major progress that was made thanks to the researches of Jacob Mann, Simha Assaf, and Shelomo Dov Goitein were not so much the product of chance as of endless search and patience. There was also a further form of specialization that contributed to the understanding of the history of the period. Professional historians, whose principal interest lay in synthesis and historical exposition, rather than in the location and decipherment of raw materials, brought the refined techniques of modern historical scholarship to bear on the subject. While, as in many another field requiring special philological apparatus, philologists and historians have often belittled each other's work, the two groups have not only coexisted but have in reality stimulated and enriched each other. Accordingly, there has been a steady concurrent progress on two levels of historical research—in the retrieval and interpretation of factual raw materials, and, on the other hand, in the organization, evaluation, and synthesis of the data into accounts that have sought to explain the dynamics of Jewish society and the course of its development in the Gaonic age.

MANN'S CONTRIBUTION TO THE STUDY OF GAONIC HISTORY

In this new age of professional and highly specialized research, Mann stands out as the one who contributed most to the fund of data on the history of the Jews in the Gaonic period.[76] Indeed, the implication of the last sentence may be somewhat misleading, for Mann's interests and writing spanned many more areas than the one normally understood by "history." His voluminous studies on ancient homiletics and liturgical usage, while intimately connected with Geniza studies, were basically textual-exegetical and reflected competence in many more areas of research than the one with which his name is most widely associated. Moreover, his interest in the Karaites stimulated by his fresh discoveries in the Geniza materials, but apparently also nourished by his own East European roots, prompted him to search out materials on Karaite history in Eastern Europe down to the early modern period. Mann, in short, was an insatiable investigator of manuscripts for data shedding new light on areas of Jewish history that he felt had been lamentably neglected and the rediscovery of which, he hoped, would stimulate a fuller and more judicious portrayal of the Jewish past. A hunter who was determined to confine his quest to new game, and who was, accordingly, limited to what the ravages of time had not eliminated, Mann designed his research in accordance with canons of historical research that were, at the time he began his work, only beginning to captivate the thinking of Jewish historians and that, accordingly, merit precise formulation.

Underlying all of Mann's researches was the spirit of social history, often called *Kulturgeschichte*, that had stimulated new orientations in historical writing in Europe and the United States and that had shaped the celebrated works of Gustav Freytag, Jacob Burckhardt, Frederic William Maitland, and John B. McMaster.[77] The quest for records reflecting life as it had actually been lived, rather than for official records of political and ecclesiastical developments, had also found expression in Jewish studies in the works of Moritz Guedemann and Israel Abrahams. The related emphasis on the economic and legal realities of past ages generated the novel efforts of research of Joseph Jacobs, Georg Caro, Simon Dubnow, Ignacy Schipper, Arthur Ruppin, and others. Mann brought an appropriate parallel approach to Gaonic society. From his very first publications in the area of Gaonica, Mann indicated that he hoped to uncover the *realia* of Jewish life in all their diversity and complexity, and without preconceived canons of judgment that would predetermine his selectivity. *Nihil Judaicum sibi alienum putavit*, and the details of Karaite community organization were as significant and worthy of study as the codes and official pronouncements of Geonim and their courts. Mann, to be sure, was somewhat less than fair in his blanket characterization of earlier Jewish historiography on the Gaonic age "as a collection of biographies of the prominent spiritual and communal leaders."[78] Clearly, far more than that had been achieved even by Isaac Hirsch Weiss, let alone by Bornstein, Ginzberg, and Eppenstein. However, it was true that for all their diversity Gaonic studies, to the extent that they did go beyond biography, chronology, and textual analysis, had concentrated almost exclusively on the official institutions of Jewish society and on the people that represented or opposed them. Mann was quite right in his complaint that precious little attention had been paid to "the internal life of the Jews: their relations to the authorities and to their non-Jewish neighbours, their economic position, their communal organization, and their standard of culture and morality."

Mann, accordingly, began his efforts to fill this lacuna in a series of papers entitled "The Responsa of the Babylonian Geonim as a Source of Jewish History" in which he set forth the realities of Jewish life reflected in the responsa literature, supplemented to some extent by modern researches and by whatever material from the Geniza had become available to him. Mann himself was fully aware of the limitations inherent in the very design of his papers. Responsa are, after all, a very incomplete mirror of life and, by their very nature, a distorted one, for the responsum is necessarily evoked by an abnormal situation. However, the large number of responsa from a period stretching over several centuries did enable him to extrapolate at least from the questions and superscriptions attached to them considerable information on (1) the location of sizable Jewish communities that had turned regularly to the Geonim as well as the nature of their relationship to the Babylonian rabbinate; (2) the political status of the Jews under Muslim domination and the relations between the Jews and local Muslim officialdom; (3) the economic life of the Jews, i.e., their occupational pursuits; (4) the structure and effectiveness of local Jewish communal institutions, especially the local Jewish courts. Despite the limitations of the study, inherent in the self-imposed restrictions on the sources used and in the character of these sources themselves, the results were illuminating and enriching. Indeed, for sheer comprehensiveness the study remained the best, until the first installment of Goitein's study on the Jews in Mediterranean society half a century later superseded it in quality no less than in quantity. In fact, Mann's study is still rewarding, particularly as an introductory orientation to Gaonic society, provided also, of course, that it is read or studied with a clear notion of a further limitation, namely Mann's very style of exposition.

It is important to face up to the shortcomings no less than to the virtues in Mann's method of exposition, if we are to appreciate his true importance in the progress of Jewish historiography with regard to the Gaonic age. Even in his papers on the Gaonic responsa Mann already betrayed some of the forbidding expository techniques that were to become one of the outstanding features of his writing. When he had completed his papers on "The Responsa of the Babylonian Geonim," Mann was given access to Geniza fragments of historical interest by the University Library at Cambridge, by the Bodleian, and by the British Museum. The materials which Mann came across proved to be so pregnant with historical significance that he interrupted the sequence of chapters and published in two installments appendices containing texts and other information that he had managed to glean and evaluate. For anyone seeking an introduction to the social history of the Jews in the Gaonic age the results were as disastrous as they were indubitably enriching, for the material was fragmentary, Rapoportian in style in the extreme, and, what is more, had little connection with the sources which Mann had described as the focus of his research. To be sure, the materials he had unearthed were chock-full of historical information, but they did not fit into the neat running exposition that Mann had promised to give. But Mann evidently could not overcome the desire to share with the learned the results of his finds, particularly since what he did turn up were hard facts, and it was the fact that he adored most. Accordingly, anyone really wishing to read Mann's papers on the responsa of the Babylonian Geonim intelligibly had best read installments 1, 4, and 5 (*J. Q. R.*, N.S., VII, 457–490, X, 121–151, 309–365) before proceeding to read the appendices published as installments 2, 3, and 6 (*J. Q. R.*, N.S. VIII, 339–366, IX, 139–179, XI, 433–471). In mid-course, then, Mann underwent a change of heart, for he decided to forego the pursuit of social history in favor of historical facts of whatever nature on the Gaonic age. The result some years later was a monumental and epoch-making contribution to Gaonic history which is in many ways a quasi-primary source, *The Jews in Egypt and in Palestine Under the Fatimid Caliphs*.

Mann, to be sure, would never have conceded that even his two-volume publication was anything but social history, for what he assembled were raw materials on the actual communal life of the Jews in Egypt and Palestine, on the actual interrelationships of the Jewish communities, and on the relations between the Jews and their Muslim overlords. They were and remain a veritable gold-mine of historical information on every aspect of Jewish life in the Near East. It was the exposition that made his works forbidding even to the most trained non-specialist. Where was the specialist who could conjure up some kind of coherent picture from the endless string of facts held together by the thinnest of narrative threads? What emerged to the naked eye was a warehouse of information in which no two items resembled one another or necessarily had any internal connection with one another. But Mann was content to leave synthesis in depth to others and to toil himself in the salt-mines of raw historical data and to classify the materials he had found in such a way that subsequent students could utilize his findings fruitfully. Accordingly, he introduced each chapter with a compact summary of the overall political and chronological framework into which the data would be placed and then proceeded to expose the new information he had gleaned from the Geniza materials. Mann assumed that readers would come to his work with full awareness of what had already been learned of the Gaonic period in the publications that had preceded his, and that his work would be read, the proper verb is really "used," as a source of additional and corrective information. But in the end, Mann's work was to historiography what *novellae* were to Talmudic commentary. In going through his massive expositions one cannot help feeling that hovering over the work was the spirit of his family ancestor Solomon Judah Loeb Rapoport and of the Talmudic novellists in whose method and literature he had gained his earliest training.[79]

All this adds up to the simple conclusion that Mann, in fairness to him, ought not to be classified or evaluated as a historian. Historiography was not what he set out to write. A master antiquarian, like Rapoport he sought merely to make precise data available to the historian and to delineate the basic guidelines for the utilization of his materials. Accordingly, one will find only one chapter in the first volume of Mann's *Jews in Egypt* that in any way approaches a historical essay, and that is the last one on "Communal Organization." In this section Mann extrapolated the data from the documents he had previously utilized in order to construct a skeletal picture of autonomous Jewish communal officialdom and institutions. Here Mann showed the historical value of titles and honorific expressions for anyone seeking to recapture the hierarchy of local Jewish officials in the Gaonic age. He further attempted to give a reasoned explanation of the high sounding phrases and titles that were employed and of the powers inherent in the offices to which they referred.

For all its technical-antiquarian orientation, Mann's work is of abiding value for a far wider audience than the small coterie of Gaonic specialists, but in a way that was probably remotest from Mann's intentions. If Mann's work is studied, not in the sequence of chapters and volumes in which it was published, but in the sequence of steps by which Mann wrote, the work emerges as a rare pedagogical gem in the techniques of advanced historical research. To anyone reading attentively, it becomes apparent that each section of volume I of *The Jews of Egypt* is a brief *commentary* on the texts that Mann published in volume II of that work. It was the individual text that was the subject of Mann's focus. Accordingly, if one reads Mann's work by beginning with the single text in volume II and then proceeds to Mann's introductory and extrapolatory material in volume I he will find that he has been brought into the antiquarian's laboratory and permitted to follow the master at work in every step of his research. By reading Mann as he wrote, we encounter not only the raw materials of history but exemplary demonstrations of how the documents are to be correlated with received bodies of information and exploited for the broadening and deepening of our historical perspective. Without any special pleading or subtle pontification Mann's texts and companion-studies illustrate better than a thousand lectures or handbooks on historical method; 1) how tailored and, accordingly, unrepresentative of historical realities works of history frequently are in their concentration on certain types of events and personalities to the exclusion of others; 2) how complex and multifaceted Jewish life in the Middle Ages really was, not only in the now well-accepted sense that Jews played games, wrote poetry, and engaged in all kinds of activities other than those represented by the codes and responsa, but from the perspective of the social forces that shaped Jewish communal life, often without the awareness of the participants themselves; 3) how truly human and responsive to social, economic, and political pressures the Geonim and other Jewish communal leaders were in actual life; 4) how pregnant with fruitful information even seemingly insignificant materials, such as trivial marriage contracts, book-lists, and rent receipts, can be once they are properly weighed and interpreted. Mann's work, to be sure, will be intelligible only to the advanced student, but by no means to the Gaonologist alone.

From whatever perspective Mann's work is approached, whether as a source of information on various specific areas of Jewish history or as a model in the interpretation of documentary raw materials, Mann's two subsequent volumes, *Texts and Studies in Jewish History and Literature*, will quickly be seen to be a sequel to his earlier papers and volumes. In the later volumes, Mann facilitated the study of the texts and commentary by placing both groups of materials in close proximity to each other thus eliminating the need for the complicated code of cross-references he had had to devise in his work on *The Jews in Egypt and Palestine*. Each chapter in *Texts and Studies* thus lends itself to study as a discrete unit. However, the two later volumes were not merely a collection of highly informative studies with new texts on many aspects of Jewish history. By the very nature of their diversified contents Mann's later volumes proclaimed a methodological message that has since become a byword to all students of Jewish history in the Near East and Mediterranean littoral in the Middle Ages. The Geniza documents, deriving from a geographical expanse stretching from Spain to Kurdistan, and over a period of time spanning some four centuries, demonstrated graphically the underlying cultural unity of the Jews living under Muslim domination, their sporadic but nonetheless significant connections with Jews living under Christian rule, and the vast influence exercised by the Geonim and the Karaites for many centuries and throughout many lands. Polyhistor that he was, Mann was able to demonstrate through halakhic, poetic, and exegitical texts, as well as through simple letters, the varieties of sources that any historian seeking to give a representative picture of Jewish history in the Middle Ages would have to exploit. In his studies Mann thus overcame the ever growing splintering of study that specialization had stimulated. His studies also laid the groundwork for the several historical syntheses that have appeared in the last three decades and, above all, for the qualitative advance in the social history of the period represented by the more recent work of Shelomo Dov Goitein.

Given the vast number of documents that Mann assembled, transcribed, and interpreted, and considering the plethora of subjects that he discussed, any characterization of the historical themes which he covered in his two major studies of the Gaonic world would amount to a forced and distorted delimitation of his work. However, there can be no doubt that there were several general guidelines that determined his selection of materials and that, accordingly, yield certain broad themes that structured his volumes. His earlier study on *The Jews in Egypt and Palestine* uncovered the strong network of institutions that had developed in Palestine quite independently of, and often in open competition with, those of the Babylonian community. What emerged, too, was the existence of several different Jewish communities in Egypt, Palestino-centric Rabbanites and Babylono-centric Rabbanites, as well as a vigorous Karaite group, and finally an indigenous Jewish officialdom that often had diverse and conflicting interests. The soil on which Maimonides and the dynasty of his descendants struck roots was thus shown to be one with a long history of mature Jewish activity. The consequence of Mann's researches was that it was no longer possible to speak without some qualification of a Gaonic age dominated exclusively by the Babylonian Gaonate. While the importance of the Babylonian Gaonate could still not be gainsaid, the atmosphere in which it exercised its influence was now seen to be far more complex than later ages had ever dreamed. What also became clear was why Maimonides and his descendants succeeded in establishing a base for their activities in Egypt rather than in any other country of the Near East. It was precisely the political history of Egypt and of the Jewish community within it that made this particular development possible, with such rich and enduring effects on all subsequent Jewish history and culture.

Mann's *Texts and Studies*, while touching briefly on some of these themes, filled in the picture with developments in Babylonia and above all in other parts of the Diaspora. *Texts and Studies* illuminated the period of Babylonian decline by retrieving letters from the period when the attachments of Jewish communities to the Babylonian center were beginning to weaken for reasons quite beyond the control of anyone involved. The foci of Jewish communal activity were beginning to shift to the Jewish communities of the West, and nothing that Sherira or Hai could have done would have averted the ultimate outcome. But the texts that Mann published and explained, like those from a somewhat later period published by Assaf,[80] showed how active and tenacious the Babylonian academic heads were in their leadership. Ibn Daud's thesis that Jewish learning had moved westward, advanced in his graphic tale of the four captives, remained valid, to be sure, but as a consequence of the new material the picture was a far more credible and intelligible one than the simplistic sermon implied by his story. In short, *Texts and Studies* provided new materials on the circumstances under which the sun of Baghdad had begun to set and that of Cairo, Qairawan, and Cordova had begun to emerge.

The second volume of *Texts and Studies*, with its subtitle *Karaitica*, had a clearly integrated theme. Ostensibly, its contents, too, were determined by the manuscripts which Mann happened to turn up in the course of his researches. However, a closer examination will reveal that the volume, while built on the principles of Mann's earlier works, was further inspired by the conviction that Jewish historiography had done itself and the Karaites a gross injustice in dismissing later Karaite history as so inconsequential as to require no intensive treatment. The posture of most Jewish historians with regard to this corner of Jewish history was nothing more than a latter-day continuation of the flippant judgments that Abraham ibn Daud had passed on all of Karaite activity. Pinsker, to be sure, had shown for earlier periods how unfair this partisan judgment was, and subsequent research by others had demonstrated how disastrous it was for our understanding of the activity of Rabbanite leadership. However, modern Jewish historians still treated later Karaite affairs very much as Otto of Freising had done with respect to Jewish history after the destruction of the Second Temple.[81] Mann's research on the Jews of Egypt and Palestine had proved to him how integral and influential a part of the Jewish community had been in the Middle Ages. Moreover, that Karaites had continued to be consciously creative and responsive to changing conditions even in late medieval and early modern times was apparent even from the unanalytical history of the Jews of the Ottoman Empire that Rosanes had begun to publish in Hebrew in 1930. The time had come, Mann properly felt, to accord the Karaites the same respect that Jewish historians were demanding for their area of interest and to study the Karaites by the same scholarly canons that were applied to all recognized fields of historical research. His plea has not yielded the fruits that Mann had hoped it would, since for various reasons the later history of Karaism, like many another aspect of Jewish history, still awaits its chronicler-analyst. However, Mann's textual and analytical studies provided much of the stimulus for the new studies of early Karaite history that did begin to appear shortly after his death, and which will be discussed presently.

Although in keeping with Mann's own emphases we have stressed his concentration on social history and the realities of life reflected in the most mundane as well as official documents, at least a passing reference must be made to his significant contributions to the more traditional aspects of Jewish study illuminated by the documents of the Geniza. Mann's researches into Jewish life in Palestine in the Gaonic age and into communities in Egypt adhering to Palestinian ritual usage helped him uncover the traces of old Palestinian liturgy and liturgical practices that had in the course of time given way to the levelling pressures of the Babylonian Gaonate and to the pressures for the standardization of practice fostered by Maimonides and his descendants. Schechter (1898) had much earlier published fragments of the old Palestinian liturgy, but Mann now (1925, 1927) extended these researches to many more areas of liturgical practice. He also embarked on a vast research project, only half of which he lived to complete (1940; the second having been edited from Mann's notes and complemented by independent research on the part of his colleague, Professor Isaiah Sonne [1966]), on the evidence in midrashic literature and medieval Hebrew payyetanic remains for the prophetic portions read and sermons preached in the triennial cycle followed by Palestinian communities. Mann's interest in historical realities thus led him to make original and substantive contributions to the history of synagogal practice that have become standard works of reference. Coupled with his other studies these works of scholarship made him one of the most versatile, not to mention one of the most prolific, of all scholars in the field of Gaonica.

THE GAONIC AGE IN RECENT JEWISH HISTORIOGRAPHY

In the final analysis, the style and method of Mann's exposition made his monumental contribution much more akin to philology and textual scholarship than to historical synthesis. The need for new comprehensive interpretations of the vast amount of materials that had come to light in this field, as in so many others in Jewish history, was reflected in several efforts at rewriting Jewish history in the interbellum period. All of the standard histories—of Zeeb Jawitz, Simon Dubnow, Salo Baron, Marx and Margolis—now gave accounts of the history of the period that reflected the new knowledge and, of course, the particular interest of the historian. Jawitz construed the history of the period very much in the biographical-spiritual terms to which Mann had taken such outspoken objection. In an account that never went very much below the surface of events Dubnow emphasized the geographic areas of concentration, the communal structure, and the institutional controls that shaped the life of the Jewish population or provoked the disaffection and defection of certain elements within it. Marx and Margolis presented a cut-and-dried narrative that adhered largely to the chronological frameworks first set forth by Sherira and Ibn Daud, but which was considerably amplified by factual elements extrapolated from the new discoveries.

Only Salo Baron's brief analysis in his first edition of *A Social and Religious History of the Jews* gave a fresh treatment that reflected not only digestion of all the primary and secondary materials that had become available but an understanding of the dynamics of Gaonic and sectarian history in terms of the social forces, external as well as inner ones, shaping the destiny of the Jewish community. A few years later, in a survey of the institutional and structural history of *The Jewish Community*, Baron gave a separate analysis of the communal structure of Jewish life in Gaonic times in a chapter that summarized their situation under the heading "Protected Community." While Baron's treatments were necessarily brief, they were professional in their penetration and lucidity of exposition, and they had the added merit of being copiously annotated so that the interested student could pursue the subject further and, most important, intelligently. The encyclopedic second edition of Baron's *Social and Religious History* has more recently recapitulated and amplified all of the material covered in his two earlier works and has further synthesized the religious and literary developments of the Gaonic age, again with full documentation. While Baron's presentation of Gaonic history and culture is the most comprehensive and up-to-date of all scholarly treatments, it is not an area of special concern or of concentrated account in his work, even to the extent that it was in the histories of Graetz, Dubnow, or Jawitz. In Baron's treatment each of the components of Gaonic history, culture, and institutions is discussed in conjunction with the contemporary generic phenomena that obtained in other communities. Thus, the political situation of the Jews under Muslim rule is described in the same section dealing with Jewish political status under Christendom, while homiletics, poetic compositions, linguistic studies, and philosophy, to cite only a few of the many topics covered by Baron, are each treated in separate sections that also present parallel developments elsewhere. Hence, while Baron is scrupulous in delineating the *Sitz im Leben* of each phenomenon, and with reference to cultural activities makes clear how they were outgrowths of, and responses to, the milieu in which they emerged, his treatment is thematic rather than chronological and thus presupposes a considerable degree of orientation to the historical setting. In short, while no historical analysis of the Gaonic age approaches that of Baron for comprehensiveness and consistency of depth—not to speak of bibliographical reference—it cannot fill the need for an introduction to the period or survey of its history.

The distressing fact is that no such work has been composed that in any way begins to reflect in depth the present state of the field. While surveys of the Biblical period or of the literature of the Dead Sea Sect continue to pour forth with a rapidity that is overwhelming, and while virtually every other major area of Jewish history has evoked some kind of serious synthesis, the Gaonic age seems to repel historians or inhibit them from composing systematic summaries. Accordingly, while some excellent historical studies on particular aspects of the Gaonic age have been published since the First World War, only one work of general introduction to the period and its Rabbanite culture, comparable in design to Louis Ginzberg's *Geonica*, has appeared.

Simhah Assaf's *Tequfat ha-Geonim ve-Sifrutah*, compiled by Mordecai Margalioth from Assaf's lecture notes and articles, was an attempt to fill this need with an updated synthesis of the vast corpus of Gaonic literature that had become available. Comprehensive in its treatment of the major aspects of Gaonic history and culture, at least as these are defined by traditional Jewish categories, the work is lucid throughout, and indeed often makes for pleasurable reading. The volume is divided into three fairly equal sections, entitled "The Gaonic Period," "Gaonic Literature," and "Studies in Gaonic Literature," of which only the first two parts are germane to our discussion. While virtually every significant feature of Rabbanite society and Gaonic literature is described and explained—and where the issues are controversial they are evaluated by the author in the light of his own researches—the work, for all its genuine learning is manifestly Rabbanite in its concerns and orientation and rather superficial in its exposition of the historical background of institutional and intellectual developments. Neither Assaf nor Margalioth, both of whom were superb textual editors, had had much formal training in historical method, and they were not oriented towards asking the kinds of questions that historians generally pose today. Among other things, then, the work is a fairly good index of the persistent gap dividing experts in rabbinic texts and students of Jewish social and intellectual history. Accordingly, while the work is a superb "primer"—obviously for the mature student, who not only reads Hebrew with ease but who also has achieved a considerable grounding in rabbinics—anyone seeking a rounded orientation to the period will have to supplement this introduction with other material.

Shelomo Dov Goitein's work on *Jews and Arabs: Their Contacts*

Through the Ages, while a popular work not meant for the scholar, can serve as a useful introductory companion to Assaf. While in style of writing and organization, the work is not one of Goitein's best performances, even the potboiler of a master can be instructive and stimulating, and in sheer versatility and control of all aspects of Judeo-Arabic culture Goitein is the supreme master of the age. To be sure, Goitein's volume, as its title makes plain, is not confined to the Gaonic age, and in fact devotes relatively little space specifically to this area. However, what pages it does dedicate to the Geonim clarify their place in the larger context of Judeo-Arabic history and provide an illuminating perspective from which to view the various components of Jewish society and culture in the Gaonic period. Goitein's volume also clarifies the role that Arabic political institutions, economic patterns, language, poetry, and philosophy played in shaping Jewish expression in lands under Muslim rule, and thus provides a healthy counterpoise to the largely halakhic orientation that underlies Assaf's survey. For more penetrating and documented analyses, the student will have to repair to the works of Baron, to other great studies by Goitein himself (to be discussed further on), and especially to some of the fine monographic studies of recent years.

Despite the disproportionate amount of concentration on textual, philological, and bibliographical matters in Gaonic studies, significant contributions to historiography, i.e., to historical understanding and interpretation, have been made in the last half-century, and some of them have become and are likely to remain cornerstones of study in Gaonica. These are best treated in terms of the problems they have sought to solve or clarify, rather than in the chronological order of publication.

From a strictly traditional Jewish point of view, the Gaonic age is the one in which the Babylonian construction of rabbinic Judaism, as articulated in the Babylonian Talmud and its offshoots, gained supremacy over most Jewish communities of the world and successfully displaced or suppressed much Palestinian usage and literature even in the Holy Land itself. For centuries, this development had been taken for granted by Jews as a natural or logical consequence of the course of Jewish religious history, or was rationalized by the claim that the Babylonian Talmud was more lucid than the Palestinian or superior to it in other ways. The justice of these claims was, of course, evident only to those who had actually prejudged the issue or had decided that the outcome of history is always the right one. On one point, in particular, there appeared to be no room for disagreement, and that was that the Babylonian Talmud embodied the legal-religious expression of a living community that enjoyed an unbroken continuity far beyond the date of its compilation, while the Palestinian Talmud was the deposit of a community that had ceased to function effectively and creatively.

Modern Geniza research has required the discarding of many of these notions by revealing the evidence of continuing vigor and creativity of the Palestinian community even in the Gaonic age and the continued cultivation of an indigenous Palestinian religious-halakhic tradition that at least in part succeeded in resisting the Babylonian incursion. In the Hebrew and English introductions to his *Commentary on the Palestinian Talmud*, Louis Ginzberg documented the persisting vitality of the Palestinian schools and their traditions not only in the mother country but in those communities that were its cultural tributaries as well. Moreover, he showed that the Babylonian Geonim went to great lengths to suppress Palestinian forms that were at variance with their own but never quite succeeded in displacing these traditions and gaining an unchallenged mastery of the whole Jewish world. The relative triumphs of the Babylonian Talmud and of the Gaonate were not self-explanatory phenomena but consequences of demographic and political configurations of the Arab empire and of the Jewish communities within it. As was the case with so much else in the history of culture, the face of the Jewish world took on a particular hue as a consequence of circumstances that may or may not have been providential, but that were certainly as capable of rational explanation as many a political development.

The Babylonian authorities, of course, even if they were aware of the social processes advancing their cause, did not sit idly and wait for things to take their "natural" course. Instead, they conducted a vigorous and sometimes bitter campaign to gain the fealty and adherence of all Jewish communities within their reach. The effort probably had its roots in late Talmudic times but it was sharply articulated and pursued by the court of Yehudai Gaon, whose brief term at the helm of the academy of Sura in the second half of the eighth century must be reckoned as one of the most influential of all periods in the four hundred years of Gaonic activity. Among the documents articulating the Babylonian view most poignantly are the polemical tracts of Pirqoi ben Baboi, of which fragments preserved in the Geniza were published by several scholars and the significance of which was most thoroughly discussed by Louis Ginzberg in a collection of *Geniza Studies*.[82] More recently, in connection with his publication of a new fragment of this collection, Shalom Spiegel provided a penetrating summary of Babylonian rabbinic ideology and the immediate targets at which it was directed. Spiegel's is not only a model study of the historical value of seemingly trivial liturgical controversies but is the best introduction to date of Gaonic political theory, a subject that has long been neglected except in connection with the later controversy between Saadiah and Ben Meir. Thanks to Spiegel's treatment we are now able to see clearly how deep were the roots of the claims for the authority of the Babylonian rabbinate and how keenly the later Geonim felt about challenges to their mastery that came from new settlements in the West. Moreover, thanks to the analyses of Ginzberg and Spiegel, the

codes and exhortations of the Babylonian Geonim have taken on a significance for the social and intellectual historian that goes far beyond their
textual importance.

To students of Gaonic history the generation of Yehudai's presidency
was further renowned as the age of the Karaite schism under the leadership of Anan ben David. The revelation in the nineteenth century of the
existence of several other pre-Karaite sects stimulated several scholarly
efforts to explain the sudden rash of doctrinal breaks with rabbinism and
even of armed insurrection against the Muslim government. Rapoport
has long since suggested that there was some connection between the
emergence of Jewish heterodox groups and the outbreak of Muslim heresies and political splinter groups.[83] On one point, however, virtually all
scholars seemed to be in accord, and that was in accepting the picture,
apparently originally painted by David al-Muqammis, and transmitted
by Qirqisani, Shahrastani, and Judah Hadassi, of an intimate historic connection between Karaism and the earlier Jewish sects of the Muslim East.
On the other hand, none of these theories had been able to posit a convincing explanation of the singular characteristics of the Jewish sectarian
groups in terms of specific Muslim manifestations.

A major contribution in this direction was made by Israel
Friedlaender in the early part of this century in a series of papers in
which he demonstrated the chronological, geographic, linguistic, and
doctrinal affinities between Muslim Shiite beliefs and Jewish sectarian
behavior and messianology in the eighth century.[84] Friedlaender's analysis elucidated the Persian anti-Omayyad character of Muslim as well as
Jewish defections, and thus provided a socio-political *Sitz im Leben* to
the bizarre characteristics of these fringe movements. Confining his argument largely to the Isaunians and Yudghanites, Friedlaender judiciously ignored the lumping together of all Jewish sects, which earlier
scholars had done in the wake of the medieval accounts. (Parenthetically,
it should be noted that his sound judgment has recently been upheld by
two independent studies of the Maghariya sect by Norman Golb and
Harry Austryn Wolfson, each of whom, out of quite different considerations, traced the home of this sect to pre-Muslim Alexandria.)[85] Friedlaender also vigorously argued for the lack of any connection between the sectarian revolts in Persia in the eighth century and
the Ananite schism against Gaonic-Talmudic authority in the heartland
of the Jewish settlement of Babylonia. In Anan and Karaism,
Friedlaender saw a highly intellectual anti-Talmudic system of law and
exegesis that had emerged out of purely internal Jewish considerations.
On the other hand, he offered no new explanation of the genesis and
growth of Karaism, so that the basic explanation of the medievals, refined and reformulated by Geiger, of the persistence of a subterranean

Sadduceean halakhah that has re-surfaced under the leadership of Anan, continued to dominate the intellectual scene.[86]

Even on the assumption that Geiger's thesis on the origins of Karaite practice was basically sound—and that, too, did not go unchallenged[87]—the basic problem remained of providing an explanation for the anti-Rabbanism of Anan and the Karaites and for its eruption when and where it did. What was lacking, in other words, was not so much an explanation of the sources of Karaite usage as of the historic phenomenon of Karaism in the context of the Babylonian Jewish community. On this problem, little substantive progress had been made. Simon Dubnow, in his multivolume history of the Jewish people issued shortly after the First World War, adhered to the nineteenth-century liberal understanding of Karaism as a revolt against the constricting rigidity of Talmudic discipline, which had reduced the life of the average Jew to an authoritarian formalism devoid of genuine religious experience. On the other hand, Dubnow felt that, however healthy its basic motivations, Karaism vitiated its primary goals by substituting one rigorism for another and, worst of all, by cutting itself off from the national mainstream of the Jewish people.[88] Dubnow's view was in its details a piecing together of conclusions of nineteenth-century scholarship but, *au fond*, a judgment drawn from his own partisan understanding of the one dissident movement that he had studied intensively, namely Hasidism. Like his study of the latter, so his understanding of Karaism was a theory that struck responsive chords in secularist-nationalist circles that detested rabbinism but simultaneously favored mass Jewish expression.[89] His analysis, however, had one fruitful effect, and that was that it stimulated one of the most astute and versatile historians of the twentieth century to subject Karaite sources to a fresh and penetrating analysis.

Raphael Mahler's *Kara'imer* appeared in Yiddish in 1947 at a time when the Jewish scholarly world as a whole was even less disposed than it had generally been to give a sympathetic hearing to a Marxist analysis of Jewish society. The time had passed for students of Judaism to entertain the stock clichés of rabbinic authoritarianism, oppressiveness, insensitivity to mass Jewish needs and aspirations, and the smug propagation of passive acceptance of subjection and exploitation in the Diaspora. Mahler made no effort to disguise his partisan approach to the historic problem of Jewish sectarianism. He saw Gaonic culture as a tissue of doctrines and institutions deliberately calculated to feed the interests of the Jewish "establishment," and made his feeling plain that these interests were diametrically opposed to mass aspirations for messianic liberation from the whole fabric of machinery that kept the people at large socially, economically, and politically immobile. But Mahler could not be summarily dismissed, for he was by no means a Marxist hack but an acute student of Jewish history who consulted primary sources at first hand and interpreted them with a freshness and originality that were challenging. Mahler further made it clear that he was not really forging new methodological paths but merely applying to a significant Jewish historical phenomenon the same type of analysis—albeit with admittedly far different premises—that scholars like Weber, Troeltsch, and others had been employing for well over a generation in the study of Christian sects and of religiously structured societies elsewhere.

It was the substantive challenge in his work that compelled serious scholars to take notice of the work and to register their reasoned, and unquestionably justified, negative reactions. Reviewers took pains to point out that many of Mahler's fresh explanations of texts and institutions of early Karaism were simplistic and often in downright contravention of materials that Mahler himself had cited in other contexts. Worst of all, his dogmatic socio-economic approach to historical problems had simply blinded him to the possibility that a schism of major proportions could have emerged out of purely, or even primarily, doctrinal considerations, about which people not nurtured on Marx, Weber, or Borochov could have felt keenly enough to warrant their tearing apart the fabric of their community.[90] Mahler's thesis has, accordingly, been well-nigh unanimously rejected in scholarly circles. However, Mahler's work has had a genuinely seminal role in recent Jewish historiography that has justified its forever being recalled as a significant milestone in the modern study of the Gaonic age. For whatever the shortcomings of his work, and despite the widespread rejection of his interpretation, Mahler did succeed in putting the subject on a new level. He had established that Karaism was a social phenomenon that had displayed remarkable vitality and appeal over several continents and for several centuries. If Mahler's answers could be rejected, the questions he had asked could not be dismissed.

The two most distinguished Jewish historians of the age apparently did take Mahler's challenge seriously, and while they themselves could not free themselves to engage in fresh research in this area, they did encourage two of their most gifted students to do so. It can hardly be an accident that two efforts at social analysis of different aspects of early Karaism appeared in works that had their origins in seminars conducted by Professor Yitzhak Baer at the Hebrew University in Jerusalem and Professor Salo W. Baron at Columbia University in New York. Both of these ranking historians of the generation had been engaged in fresh examinations of vast areas of the Jewish past and had been stimulating their students to do the same, particularly with respect to the connections between social currents and religious ideologies. The spotlight directed by Mahler on the field of Karaism evidently elicited their assent that the materials warranted fresh examination.

In his brief analysis of early Karaite legal codes, Hayyim Hillel Ben

Sasson of Jerusalem rightly noted, as other reviewers already had, that Mahler's conclusions relied heavily on Karaite polemical materials for support. However, a phenomenological study of the *legal* writings of Anan and the other early fathers of Karaism, materials that Mahler largely ignored as inconsequential, yielded a considerably different picture from the one that Mahler had elicited from the querulous and plaintive materials on which he had drawn. Mahler had cited only those legal provisions of the early stages of the sect that lent themselves to his construction, but he had not subjected the total body of halakhic writings of the trailblazers of the schism to a searching analysis for the social picture that they might yield. Furthermore, Ben Sasson protested against Mahler's adherence to the medieval Rabbanite schematology that reduced all the stages in the development of Karaism to a single and monolithic break and all Karaite ideology as the unfolding of a drive that remained basically the same. Ben Sasson, accordingly, studied the halakhah of the first two great legislators of proto-Karaism, Anan and Benjamin al-Nahwendi, who, in keeping with the testimony of the early Karaites themselves, had to be classified as pre-Karaite leaders. From this examination, Ben Sasson could detect no traces of messianic, democratic, or socialist tendencies in the legislation or exegesis of these men. Nor was there any liberalizing rationalism permeating their decisions. Ben Sasson concluded that Anan had merely sought to organize into a separate but cohesive community the opponents of rabbinic practice and to give systematized formulation to usages that had been followed by unorganized dissidents long before that time.[91] Benjamin al-Nahwendi, on the other hand, while no more of a rationalist or messianologist than Anan, was far more concerned with the property rights of the new dissidents and with the prestige of the pillars of the young community. If anything, then, Benjamin's law was more akin to the spirit of rabbinic social decision than removed from it but, interestingly, far less inhibited in rendering far-reaching decisions that protected the interests of the elders of the community! So much, then, for the interests of the masses in proto-Karaism!

Before turning to the second examination of the social motivations in early Karaism, mention must be made of an entirely new avenue of approach to the origins of Karaism opened by a specialist in the history of Jewish exegesis. Moses Zucker is primarily a textual scholar who has exploited his combined expertise in rabbinic and Arabic legal-exegetical literature to restore from the remains of the Geniza the lost halakhic works of Saadiah and his circle and to interpret them in the light of classical Jewish as well as Muslim exegetical principles. Since this material is saturated with anti-Karaite polemic, Zucker (1955–58) has sought to understand the mentality and vocabulary of the Geonim and their schismatic opponents by invoking the rich, but hitherto untapped, legacy of the early Muslim legists. Although Zucker is still in the process of publishing his illuminating findings, the material he has already made available to the public has shed some fundamentally new light on the culture of the Geonim and their opponents. In the first place, he has recovered fragments containing Saadiah's evaluation of Karaite halakhah and has also garnered considerable data in support of the Gaon's contention that much of Anan's legislation was inspired by Muslim practice. Friedlaender's contention that Karaism must be studied as a phenomenon sociologically and culturally quite different from other pre-Karaite sects may, accordingly, have to be revised. Simiarly, the theory advanced by Revel that Anan's halakhah was in large measure a revival of Philonic law, and the somewhat different argument advanced by Ben Sasson that Anan had merely institutionalized and formalized dissident practices that had long been in vogue on the periphery of the Gaonic community, were demonstrated by Zucker to be without substantive foundation. Paradoxically, Benjamin al-Nahwendi, on the other hand, actually narrowed the gap between Rabbinism and proto-Karaism by invoking novel Muslim methods of exegesis. In one respect, then, Zucker upheld Ben Sasson's contention that social motivations were not the driving force in Benjamin's legislation. On the other hand, Zucker has accepted, albeit in revised form, Mahler's assessment of Karaism as an attempt to give expression to traditional and widespread messianic hopes. This, to be sure, was not true of the proto-Karaitic stages identified with the names of Anan and Benjamin al-Nahwendi but of the third, and first genuinely Karaitic, stage of development when the movement matured under the leadership of Daniel al-Qumisi.[92] In other words, while sharply limiting the extent of his endorsement of Mahler's thesis, Zucker did second the latter's claim that the Karaite materials had much relevant information for the social historian.

All of the various syntheses and surveys discussed here had one feature in common with respect to their treatment of Karaism, and that was their concentration on the origins and earliest stages of Karaite development. However, the materials that Mann had assembled from later periods revealed not only the presence of Karaites in all the communities that the Geniza materials illuminated but their possession of means and influence. Mann's volume of *Karaitica* extended the findings of Poznanski on the Karaite settlement in Palestine and demonstrated that in the tenth and eleventh centuries the Karaites in the Holy Land had generated a community of scholars as well as of merchants who were collectively proud, creative, and influential far beyond the immediate sphere of their activity. While taking account of some of these materials, Mahler was quite avowedly more concerned with the origins of the movement and the extent to which it continued to represent a response to, and protest against, Rabbanite faith and institutions. At no point did he, or for that matter any other historian, attempt to treat the Karaites as Mann had pleaded they should be, to wit, as a discrete historical group that merited study as a social unit in its own right.

It was this task that was undertaken in what may properly be considered the second response to Mahler in a work by Zvi Ankori (1954), a student of Salo Baron and later successor to him at Columbia. Ostensibly the development of a doctoral thesis on the Karaites of Byzantium from the latter part of the tenth through the middle of the twelfth centuries, Ankori's work went far beyond the mere collection of materials and the placing of them in a historical context. By studying Karaite literary works as responses to social conditions, Ankori succeeded in recapturing the moods and concerns of a sectarian community that reacted to the special challanges posed by its new Byzantine surroundings in ways very much akin to those in which orthodox Jewish communities reinterpreted the legacies they had inherited from earlier generations. Thus, Ankori began with the premise that the Karaites of Byzantium were a minority whose survival and vitality—no less marvelous than that of the Jews as a whole—had to be explained in the light of the answers given by the leaders of the group themselves, augmented, to be sure, by further data and critical evaluation. The picture that emerged was not a startling one, for Byzantine Karaism was not an aggressive missionary movement that arose—as the earlier stages of Karaism had in Palestine and Babylonia—as a protest against rabbinic government, but rather an offshoot and transplantation of Palestinian Karaism to Diaspora soil. In their new Byzantine home, the Karaites were essentially a petty-bourgeois society largely on the defensive. Torn between their loyalties to an ideology that posited the Holy Land as the central force in faith and religious usage, and the need to make of their religion a viable system in a Diasporic setting that was politically and culturally totally different from the Judeo-Arabic atmosphere of Palestine, the Karaites of Byzantium painfully but steadily forged a vocabulary and coherent value system that would express their basic loyalties as well as their contemporary needs. Byzantine Karaism was now portrayed as a *Byzantine* Jewish phenomenon that, very much like Rabbanite Jewish communities throughout history, forged its own response to the challenges that beset it and bequeathed a legacy of its own to later stages of Karaism in the Ottoman Empire and Eastern Europe. While Ankori, somewhat like Mahler, understood the history of the pre-Karaite sects and of early Karaism as a history of Jewish messianic expressions fired by a protest against Rabbanite Diaspora-rooted Judaism—although it must be emphasized that Ankori eschewed Mahler's emphasis on economic exploitation of the Jewish masses—he judiciously insisted on studying Karaism in its various stages as a discrete cultural complex that was not merely a protest but also a response to the problems of life facing any cohesive community of men.

Sects or dissident movements have frequently engaged the attention of historians, for in one way they lend themselves to study and interpretation far more readily than the body of society as a whole. Fired by special aims and concerns, the pronouncements and activities of a counter-culture are often dynamic and betray some guiding principles other than the accident of birth and the interest of self-perpetuation. It is perhaps the absence of discernible movement and dynamism in the literary remains of much of the Gaonic period that has inhibited many historians from undertaking similar analyses of many stages and aspects of the rabbinic mainstream. To the trained historian, the difficulties of exploiting the *Halakhot Gedolot* or the *She'eltot* as materials of social history are enormous. The responsa, on the other hand, particularly those of any one Gaon, are often so fragmentary in their aggregate as to yield no coherent composite picture of society. Only where there is evidence of some change or tension, as in the case of the polemics issuing from the academy of Yehudai Gaon, have historians occasionally attempted to discern the social conditions surrounding them. Thus, Hayyim Tyckocinski (1929) assembled all the materials on Gaonic special legislation (*taqqanot*), which by its very nature was social and economic, and summarized briefly the purposes and significance of the new institutions. However, the connection of these institutions with the periods in which they were adopted and their historic *Sitz im Leben* were not fully explained. The task would have required special study of each problem in the light of Jewish and Arabic sources of which there were too few to warrant the initiation of such a scholarly venture. The kind of meticulous spadework that will have to be done to recapture the social background of Gaonic halakah becomes evident from the illuminating studies recently begun by Mordecai Friedman on marriage documents in the Geniza. Earlier (1923) Tyckocinski had also assembled all of the known documents on the Bustanai story and classified them according to the partisan interests that the various recensions reflected. He thereby provided a complete survey of one ongoing battle between exilarchs and their opponents on the issue of the legitimacy of the former. While Tyckocinski provided a fine analysis of the background of the story and of its repercussions in later Gaonic society, the value of his study was predominantly textual rather than socio-historical. What these and other studies, such as that by Felix Lazarus on the pleas of contending Jewish factions to the Muslim authorities on the choice of an exilarch, provided was merely fleeting glimpses into tensions and contentions that must obviously have been perennial affairs in the life of the Jewish community of Babylonia. But how insufficient was the data with which to construct a sustained historical account and rounded picture of the background of the events will become evident from the summary of all the known materials on the exilarchate by Alexander D. Goode, compiled some thirty years ago. Goode's list of exilarchs and their dates is indispensable to anyone studying the field, and the types of issues with which they became involved is adumbrated from his collection of all the published data. But exilarchs, after all, were princes or quasi-kings, and doubtless had political interests that would make fascinating studies for the historian, were there information available. From the standpoint of the internal history of Babylonian Jewry during the first two and half centuries of life under Muslim rule, relatively little has been added to our knowledge since 1910 when Louis Ginzberg presented his characterizations of the social and political orientations of the Gaonate and exilarchate.

The situation takes a veritably dramatic turn for the better with the age of Saadiah. In the case of no other Gaon are we so well informed about the man as a person "with his faults and virtues, his passions and convictions, his sufferings and rejoicings, his victories and defeats,"[93] and this knowledge is particularly valuable, for the data about the man are often connected with events that became key issues in the Jewish community. Thus the relative amplitude of material about Saadiah not only furnishes us with rarely duplicated material about the life, work, and personality of a major Jewish figure, but it also provides us with a window through which to see whole cross-sections of Jewish life and activity in Palestine as well as Babylonia in the days when the Babylonian Gaonate was beginning to decline and to express itself more feverishly than ever. That Saadiah was an inviting vantage point from which to view a period of the Gaonate in depth was seen half a century ago by his biographer Henry Malter. Despite the fact that considerable and significant data on the life and times of Saadiah have come to light since Malter's work appeared, and thus have rendered his work somewhat antiquated,[94] its comprehensiveness and lucidity make it an enduring mine of information and an indispensable work for students of every aspect of Gaonic society and culture, including Biblical exegesis, Hebrew philology, Jewish philosophy, halakhah, Karaism, and so on endlessly.

The literature by and about Saadiah, if enormous when Malter came to the subject, has now grown to mountainous proportions, and with good cause. For it is becoming increasingly clear that Saadiah articulated and provided the basic direction for the synthesis of Jewish and Arabic cultures that achieved towering heights of creativity in the "Golden Age" of Spanish Hebrew literature. Indeed, now that recent research has also established his crucial influence on Ashkenazic pietism,[95] his importance extends far beyond the limits of his age and of the Muslim empires. Yet the fact remains that the medieval leader who exercised an influence second only to that of Maimonides proved to be a nearly calamitous fiasco as a communal leader, at least from the standpoint of those who had pinned many hopes on him and had supported him. Fortunately, the communal debacle that erupted as a consequence of his activities and the efforts to heal the breaches have become increasingly clear thanks to the data on the role of the Jewish banking houses of Baghdad unearthed by Walter Fischel and subsequently reevaluated by Mann (1935). But perhaps the most trenchant and perspicacious attempt to see Saadiah's whole career in the light of his times, and his multifaceted work as an integrated effort to respond to the challenge of his day, was made by Salo Baron in a study of Saadiah as communal figure. Baron construed Saadiah's whole life and work in terms of the driving ambitions of a political-theological leader whose activites were both symptoms and consequences of the conditions surrounding the Jews of Babylonia in the first half of the tenth century. The attempt to construe a rich and variegated life that stretched over decades and over several different areas of the Near East, in terms of one or two aims, is, to be sure, one that will be questioned by many. But whatever the conclusion, it remains the merit of Baron's essay that it showed how literary materials can be and must be correlated to social and political conditions, and how the Jewish culture of any period must be understood as a function of communal aims and orientations. There can be little doubt that Baron, like his contemporary Yitzhak Baer, opened up the eyes of many a student to the possibilities of studying medieval rabbinic materials as genuinely historical data. The influence of his approach is evident in the work by Ankori discussed earlier.

The abundance of material available to the potential historian continues with ever mounting bulk for the period after Saadiah's generation. It is at this point that the chapters on the Babylonian Gaonate in Mann's *Texts and Studies* provide a solid foundation for the historian to attempt a rounded synthesis of the type that scholars have attempted for Saadiah and his age. For the period of Gaonic decline, especially for the seven decades of the combined presidency of Sherira and Hai, there is a mine of material, Jewish as well as Muslim, waiting to be elucidated in terms of the activities of the Geonim in the context of the society of their day. And this abundance of material continues far beyond the traditional date assigned to the end of the Gaonate. The valuable collection of letters from the generation of Samuel ben 'Ali, published by Assaf,[96] overflows with information that lends itself to historical analysis far beyond the cursory one accorded it by its editor.

Happily, the task has been made all the more capable of achievement, and accordingly all the more pressing, in the light of the vast advances made in recent years in the study of the history and culture of Jewish society on the periphery of the Gaonic center. Thus, the introductory essay to volume II of *Sefer ha-Yishuv*, compiled under the editorship of Simha Assaf and L. E. Mayer, provides a comprehensive review of the history and culture of the Jews of Palestine from the Muslim conquest (637) until the invasion of the country by the armies of the First Crusade

(1098). This essay deserves particular attention, for it brings together information on Jewish cultural life long the private domain of specialists in esoteric textual disciplines, and integrates it with all the political, economic, and topographical information available in 1944 in a story that is as lucid as it is authoritative.

However, a truly new chapter in the study of the transition from the Gaonic age to the rise of culturally autarchic Jewish societies in Egypt, North Africa, and the Maghreb (including Arabic Spain) has been opened up in the last fifteen years by Shelomo Dov Goitein.[97] A scholar who is thoroughly at home in Jewish as well as Arabic civilizations, Goitein turned relatively late in life to a fresh study of the Geniza for the possible light it might shed on Jewish social life in the Middle Ages. Goitein was convinced that students of the Geniza had largely neglected materials, particularly those in Arabic, that did not reveal on initial perusal manifest connection with the world of the academies or other known phenomena of Jewish history. Since Judeo-Arabic documents were as accessible to him as those written in Hebrew, and since he was familiar with virtually every nuance of Arabic and Jewish culture of the Judeo-Arabic world from Yemen to Spain, he began to restudy the Geniza piece by piece for "historical" data. The results have not only been revolutionary for our understanding of Jewish life from the tenth to the thirteenth centuries in Spain, North Africa, and Egypt, but they have made the study of the Geniza and of the Jews of the Mediterranean world subjects of interest to historians who would otherwise have had no concern with the Geonim, the Jews of Qairawan, Tahert, Sijilmasa, and the like, or with the structure of Jewish society. What distinguishes Goitein's work from that of virtually all his predecessors is his capacity to combine pedantic exactitude in his pursuit of the minutest textual and philological detail with a keen eye for the relationship of the detail to the broader canvas of history; in Goitein's work "every local inquiry . . . [does] relate itself to a general pattern of development."[98]

To the student of medieval history generally, Goitein has immortalized himself by rediscovering the information on the trade routes that extended from Spain to India from the eighth to the thirteenth centuries and by his thereby rendering the *coup de grâce* to the myth that Europe and Byzantium were largely cut off from direct and active intercourse with the Orient and the Arabic domains. Goitein made no claim that the Jews were the most active participants in this international and transcontinental trade, but he did insist on the importance of the Geniza as the only surviving repository of archival data on this trade and of Jewish society as a representative mirror of society generally. Treating every aspect of economic life in the area that he studied, he has constructed a detailed picture of the mail routes, the rates of exchange of precious metals, the nature of the slave, employee, and entrepreneur classes, the commodities imported and manufactured, the nature of business associations, the details of sea and overland travel, the methods of trade and granting of credit—in short, of the realities that enveloped the lives of millions of people of all faiths and nationalities in one of the aspects of history that had been largely unknown to Arabists, European historians, and indeed even students of the Geniza. Little wonder then that Goitein's first volume on Mediterranean society has been hailed as a landmark in modern scholarship that alone would have sufficed to gain him the eternal gratitude and esteem of medievalists.

However, at the very same time that Goitein was revealing the progress of his findings and preparing his larger synthesis, he kept pouring forth new texts with analyses and historical interpretations of neglected Geniza materials that illuminated new corners of the inner life of the Jews during the period in question. Many of these studies were sensational—revealing intimate details about the life of Judah ha-Levi, Nissim ibn Shahin, Moses Maimonides, and Abraham Maimuni as well as other prominent Jewish men of affairs who were either mere names or celebrities about whom all too little was known. Goitein has a keen flair for the dramatic, and he fortunately cannot resist the temptation to explain the full significance of a document he has deciphered. On the subject of Jewish schools and educational practices as illuminated by the Geniza he managed to gather approximately 180 new documents and to add to them the forty that were known, and to compile a small volume giving an inventory of data on formal education during the Gaonic age and the centuries immediately following it.[99] All of this material is intrinsically interesting and, given the fine surveys of Jewish society in the Arabic west now available, easily correlated to the general picture of medieval Jewish history.

However, there is an overall significance to Goitein's papers that must be given special attention. On the one hand, Goitein has demonstrated how intimately bound up with Arabic society and culture the Jews of the Gaonic and post-Gaonic ages were on every level of their experience—political, economic, educational, social, doctrinal. On the other hand, he has insisted, and cogently, on the integrity of Jewish culture and on the need for understanding it on its own terms. In a word, Goitein's research exemplifies the principle that Jewish historiography must be predicated on an understanding of the Jewish community as an integral part of the society in the midst of which it existed but, simultaneously, as a discrete phenomenon with its own dynamics and its independent concerns.

Goitein's findings provide an atmosphere in which the fine histories of the Jews in Spain, North Africa, and Egypt by Hirschberg and Ashtor (Strauss) can be read and understood. He has placed the poetic activity of the Golden Age of Spain and elsewhere, illuminated for us most recently by Schirmann, Zulay, Mirsky, Fleischer, Levine, and Pagis, in a new framework. Above all, he has trained students to pursue the task of unearthing the data of the social and legal life of the Jews of Judeo-Arabic society.[100] It is thanks to his inspiration that a tentative inventory of historical materials in the Geniza and a bibliography of materials published on the basis of Geniza manuscripts was drawn up by his student Shaul Shaked. The world generated by the Palestinian and Babylonian academies and the expansion of Islam is becoming ever clearer. What remains to be done, over and beyond the expansion and refinement of knowledge in these areas, is to recapture the world of the Babylonian Geonim themselves in all its diversity and complexity. After all, it was they whom Jewish historians had set out to discover originally, and it was they who molded the Judaism that has become the mainstream since their time.

NOTES

1. For pre-modern surveys of Gaonic history, from which modern scholarship appropriated the basic framework for the historical study of the period, cf. below, to n. 21. On the periodization of rabbinic history, and specifically of the Gaonic period, cf. Cohen in *Ibn Daud*, pp. 178ff.

2. These papers have all been assembled in Rapoport (1913). For the most recent study of Rapoport's work and its relationship to nineteenth-century scholarship, cf. Isaac Barzilay, *Shlomo Yehudah Rapoport [Shir] (1790–1867) and His Contemporaries* (s.1., 1967). Cf. also G. Kressel, *Cyclopedia of Modern Hebrew Literature* [in Hebrew] 2 vols. Merhavia, 1965), II, 874f.

3. This is not to gainsay the importance of Zunz's trailblazing essay on Rashi, which was published seven years before the first of Rapoport's essays and which doubtless influenced the latter in designing his research. However, Zunz himself acknowledged the qualitative advance represented by Rapoport's studies; cf. S. Bernfeld, *Toledot Shir* (Berlin, 1899), pp. 21, 32; Harkavy (1891), p. 2.

4. Rapoport (1913), I, vf. On the thrust of Rapoport's Introduction, cf. Barzilay, pp. 80f. On Rapoport's discovery of Bayle, cf. the apocryphal story in Bernfeld, p. 8.—On Bayle's style, see the fine introductory essay by Richard H. Popkin in his translation of Pierre Bayle, *Historical and Critical Dictionary, Selections* (Indianapolis, 1965), especially pp. xiii, xlif.

5. Barzilay, pp. 46, 199f.

6. Bernfeld, p. 7; Barzilay, p. 197 *sub* 1815.

7. Although the work was printed long after the author's death, it probably circulated in manuscript along with several other of his works. One of these, the introduction to an edition of *Aggadat Bereshit*, was plagiarized in an edition that was published two years after that of R. Abraham himself; see S. Buber, *Yeri'ot Shelomoh* (Warsaw, 1896), p. 5, note to *Rav pe'alim*, p. 6. In a private conversation Professor Dimitrovsky observed that the idea underlying Rapoport's first piece of critical research, his essay on the independent Jews of Arabia and Ethiopia (cf. Barzilay, p. 198 *sub* 1823), may well have been inspired by R. Abraham's *Gevulot Erets*, a fragment of which was published in Vilna, 1801 (and which I have not been able to examine). I am grateful to Professor Dimitrovsky for his assistance and discussion of this matter with me.

8. Cf. below, n. 79.

9. John Higham *et al.*, *History, the Development of Historical Studies in the United States* (Englewood, N. J., 1965), p. 6.

10. Cf. Weiss, IV, 20; Harkavy (1887), pp. ixf., xvif. For a sharp critique of Rapoport's introductory essay to Cassel, see J. H. Schorr, *Hechalutz*, VIII (1869), 138f.

11. Cf. Ankori (1959), p. 28 nn. 4–6; *idem* (1961).

12. See *Encyclopaedia of Islam*, IV, 263, s.v. Shahrastani.

13. On Pinsker, cf. Kressel, II, 620f.

14. Jost, II, 294f. See also below, n. 20.—On Jost, cf. Salo W. Baron, *History and Jewish Historians* (Philadelphia, 1964), pp. 240f.; Kressel, II, 69f.—Josts's new orientation to Jewish history as a mainstream with tributary sects was, to be sure, an echo of the intellectual orientation of German Protestant historiography to the history of Christianity. On the other hand, there was considerable indigenous Jewish stimulus for this new perspective in the form of renewed interest in, and sympathy for, Karaism on the part of Jewish *maskilim;* cf. Reuben Fahn, "Maskilay Yisrael ve-Ḥakhmay Miqra," *Ha-Tequfah*, XII (1922), 200f.

15. See the index to the 1928 edition of Geiger's *Urschrift*, s.v. Karaiten, and the index to the Hebrew translation, *ha-Miqra ve-Tirgumav*, s.v. Qara'im.

16. Geiger (1864), ch. 17; for the quotation, see 1910 edition, p. 227, English trans., p. 262.—For a full and documented discussion of Geiger's view of Karaism, cf. S. Poznanski, "Geschichte der Sekten und der Halacha," *Abraham Geiger, Leben und Lebenswerk* by Ludwig Geiger et al. (Berlin, 1910), pp. 358f., 380f.

17. Cf. Kressel, II, 797, 896 for brief summaries and bibliography.

18. Rapoport, in *Kerem Chemed*, (1841), 204; Pinsker, pp. 11f.

19. For a summary of these reactions, cf. Fahn, *Ha-Tequfah*, XIII (1922), 261f. Further material, buttressed with a measure of fresh orthodox vituperation, in Abraham Korman, *Zeramin ve-Khitot ba-Yahadut* (Tel Aviv, 1966), pp. 249f.

20. Cf. Schorr's acid review in *Hechalutz*, VI (1861), 56f., and Jost's rapturous praise and notes based on Pinsker in the "Zusaetze und Berichtigungen," pp. 3f., printed separately and appended to some copies of his *Geschichte*, III (1959), following p. 424. (The mistaken entry in Josts's index, s.v. Karaim, "C 426," was apparently a consequence of the decision [of the printer?], taken after the index had already been set in type to give these *Zusaetze* a new pagination.)

21. Cf. Pinsker, p. vi, note.

22. Fuerst's work elicited some scathing reviews almost from the moment of its publication. For Steinschneider's devastating critique, cf. Baron, *History and Jewish Historians*, pp. 300, 460 n. 45. For Harkavy's negative reactions to Fuerst's scholarship generally, cf. Harkavy (1891), pp. 6 n. 6, 7 n. 1 and *Jewish Encyclopedia*, VII, 446–end.

23. For the literature, cf. M. Steinschneider, *Die Geschichtsliteratur der Juden* (Frankfurt a.M., 1905), which should now be supplemented by M. M. Kasher and J. B. Mandelbaum, *Sarei ha-Elef* (New York, 1959).

24. Cf. Poznanski in *Hastings Encyclopedia of Religion and Ethics*, VII, 670; Fahn, *Ha-Tequfah*, XII (1922), 197f.

25. Cf. Jacques Basnage, *L' Histoire et la Réligion des Juifs*, I (Rotterdam, 1707), Book II, chs. 8–9, pp. 433f. In ch. 9, pp. 458f., Basnage propounded his own theory of their origin in the reign of Ptolemy Philadelphus and his association of Karaism with the school of Shammai and "les Docteurs de la Loi" of the New Testament.

26. Graetz was apparently forever toying with new schemes of periodization, for the one given at the end of the Introduction of volume V differed in some ways from the one he had formulated seven years earlier in the Introduction to volume IV and retained in the captions to the sections of volume V! Graetz evidently felt no embarrassment with this inner contradiction, for it only served to emphasize his conviction of the warp and woof binding the events of Jewish history.

27. Graetz's history of the Gaonic period is as good an example as any of his nationalist conception of Jewish history, a subject which will be treated in the introduction to a forthcoming new translation of his essay *Die Konstruktion der juedischen Geschichte* by my colleague Professor Ismar Schorsch. See also the essay by Samuel Ettinger in Zvi Graetz, *Darkhay ha-Historia ha-Yehudit* (Jerusalem, 1965); Michael Meyer, "Great Debate on Antisemitism, Jewish Reaction to New Hostility in Germany 1879–1881," *Leo Baeck Institute Year Book*, XI (1966), 137f., and especially pp. 154f.—That Graetz was sensitive to scholarly Jewish disdain for the motivations underlying his approach is manifested by the

Vorwort to the first edition of volume V (1860), where he took special pains to emphasize the independence of his account from that of Jost. (This Foreword was omitted in later editions.) For Graetz's view on the place of the Gaonic age in the mainstream of Jewish history, see his preface to volume IV of the *Geschichte*, and above all his remarks in *Die Konstruktion der juedischen Geschichte* (Berlin, 1936; Buecherei des Schocken Verlags, 59), pp. 49f.; Heb. trans. *Darkhay ha-Historia*, pp. 77f.

28. In fairness to Weiss, it should be indicated that medieval philosophy was not his field, and he had no way of differing with the rather meager regard which Salomon Munk had expressed for Saadiah's work as a treatise in philosophy. While Munk had dwelt at length on the influence of Kalam on the Karaites, he made no reference, as far as I can determine, to its place in Saadiah's thinking; cf. S. Munk, *Mélanges de philosophie juive et arabe* (Paris, 1859), pp, 472f. David Kaufmann, *Geschichte der Attributenlehre* (Gotha, 1877), ch. I, while subjecting Saadiah's thought to a much more detailed analysis, and while invoking some parallels from Muslim thought, did not give much more *historical* analysis than Munk. His main concern in this area was evidently to combat the notion that Saadiah's polemic was anti-Christian.

29. Cf. Solomon Schechter, *Studies in Judaism, First Series* (Philadelphia, 1896, 1911 etc.), pp. 182f. for a lively appreciation of Weiss' *History of Tradition*, where a few remarks are made about Weiss' treatment of Gaonic culture and especially Karaism. For an appreciation of Weiss and his work, cf. Louis Ginzberg, *Students, Scholars and Saints* (Philadelphia, 1928), pp. 217. Cf. also Kressel, I, 668f.

30. Cf. Mueller (1891), pp. 4f. Harkavy's collection is described there, pp. 34f.

31. Harkavy (1887), p. 80 no. 180; p. 276 no. 585. Harkavy had earlier summarized these two pieces in *MGWJ*, XXXI (1882), 167f.

32. Kahle (1959), pp. 5f.; Goitein (1967), p. 25.

33. Mueller (1891), pp. 19f.; Kasher and Mandelbaum, p. 246 no. 4.

34. Cf. Ginzberg (1909), I, 187f. for a critique of Mueller's work.

35. The work has now been edited afresh with an exhaustive introduction and with a bibliography of Saadyana by Allony; see Saadiah (1969).

36. For this translation, cf. S. M. Stern, "A New Fragment from the 'Sepher ha-Galuy' of R. Saadyah Gaon" [in Hebrew], *Melilah*, V (1955), 134f.

37. This appraisal, first articulated by Abraham ibn Ezra, was reaffirmed by Harkavy (1891), pp. 1, 22. It has again been reasserted in a penetrating study of Saadiah's poetic style by M. Zulay (1964), especially pp. 19f.

38. For a survey of nineteenth-century scholarship in Hebrew poetry, cf. the Introduction of J. Schirmann to I. Davidson, *Thesaurus of Mediaeval Hebrew Poetry* (4 vols. New York, Ktav Publishing House, 1970), I, xivf.

39. On Harkavy, cf. Zvi Harkavy in S. K. Mirsky, ed., *Personalities and Figures in Jewish Studies in Eastern Europe* [in Hebrew] (New York, 1959), pp. 116f.; B. Z. Dinur, *Benay Dori* (Tel Aviv, s.a.), pp. 13f.; Kressel, I, 629f. 3.

40. A. Geiger, "Abhandlungen . . . III. David ben Sakkai gegen Saadias," *Juedische Zeitschrift fuer Wissenschaft und Leben*, X (1872), 172–178. Geiger's transcription was preceded by a very brief introduction, and his notes confined to Hebrew translations of Arabic phrases and words.

41. Harkavy (1891), pp. 31 n. 2, 142, 147, 148.

42. On Halevy (Rabinowitz), cf. Kressel, II, 819f.

43. For early statements reflecting the excitement over the new hoard of manuscripts, see E. N. Adler, "An Eleventh Century Introduction to the Hebrew Bible," *JQR*, IX (1897), 669f., and the immortal account of Solomon Schechter, "A Hoard of Hebrew Manuscripts," *Studies in Judaism, Second Series* (Philadelphia, 1908), pp. 1f.—There is now a considerable literature on the Geniza and its history. Clear and reliable accounts are given by Norman Golb, "Sixty Years of Genizah Research," *Judaism*, VI (1957), 3f., and by Goitein (1967), pp. 1f. While the account of Leo Deuel, *Testaments of Time* (Pelican Books, 1970), pp. 371f., is not quite as accurate as it is attractive in style, it places the discovery of the Geniza in the context of other modern quests for repositories of ancient archives. The discovery of the Geniza is thus seen to be an aspect of the same search that has enriched modern knowledge in other areas, notably in the field of papyrology, which is the closest non-Jewish analogue to Genizology.—On rabbinic traditions underlying the institution of

the Geniza, cf. *Encyclopedia Talmudit*, VI, 232f.—For modern publications of Geniza materials, see Shaked.

44. For a detailed bibliography of Schechter's publications, cf. Adolph S. Oko, *Solomon Schechter, A Bibliography* (Cambridge, 1938). For materials referred to in the text, see p. 32f.

45. For a survey of scholarly opinions, cf. G. D. Cohen, "The Story of the Four Captives," *PAAJR*, XXIX (1960–61), 70f.

46. For the latest and most convincing solution to the riddle, cf. Flesicher (1967).

47. Schechter (1903).

48. For further fragments, cf. Mann (1919) and J. N. Epstein (1935–36).

49. Cf. Kressel, I, 194f. Sternberg's cavalier dismissal of Bornstein in the introduction to Solomon Gandz, *Studies in Hebrew Astronomy and Mathematics* (New York, Ktav Publishing House, 1970), pp. ixf., derives apparently more from partisan prejudgment than from considered examination of the materials.

50. For further discussion and bibliography, cf. Malter, pp. 69f., 410f.; Baron, *SRH*, V, 30f., 304 n. 34f.; M. M. Kasher, *Torah Shelemah*, XIII (1949), 122f.

51. Cf. Kressel, II, 576f.

52. The story of the negotiation, as well as of Schechter's hopes to get Poznanski to contribute a volume on Cairo to the Jewish Publication Society community series, is clearly spelled out in a delightful volume edited by Abraham Yaari, *Solomon Schechter's Letters to Samuel Poznanski* [in Hebrew] (Jerusalem, 1943).

53. For a full bibliography, see *Livre d'Hommage à la Mémoire du Dr. Samuel Poznanski* (Warsaw, 1927), pp. xxixf.

54. Besides the work of Gross, there were other models that doubtless shaped his conception of the needs of modern scholarship, notably the works of E. Renan and A. Neubauer, "Les Rabbins Français au Commencement du Quatorzième Siècle," and "Les Ecrivains Juifs Français du XIVe Siecle," which appeared in the *Histoire Littéraire de la France*, XXVII (1877), 431f., XXXI (1893), 351f.

55. In 1903, beginning with the issue of Friday, January 3, the Hebrew daily *Hazefirah* issued in installments Poznanski's study of the Jewish community of Fez and its literati. Despite the fact that the articles were remarkably scientific and replete even with bibliographical references, they were of necessity somewhat oriented to popular consumption and, accordingly, and only two of the eight installments were devoted to Gaonic times. Although highly readable and informative, they were more in the nature of a synopsis of the materials available on the cultural history of the city than a study of the community, or of any of its aspects, in depth. For a full listing, see the Poznanski bibliography (cf. above, n. 53), p. xxxi, no. 65.

56. The material on the later exilarchs was supplemented by Mann (1927) in a paper appropriately published in the aforementioned *Livre d'Hommage*.

57. The history of modern rabbinic scholarship, particularly on the literature and religion of the period of the Second Temple and the Talmudic age, and the relationship of this scholarship to the ideological currents of the last 150 years is a challenging study that would shed considerable light on modern Jewish intellectual history.

58. Cf. Barzilay, pp. 97f., 199 *sub* 1841, Mikhtav 14.

59. See *Halakhot Pesuqot'ow Hilkhot Re'u*, edited by Aryeh Loeb Schlossberg, with an introductory letter from S. Z. H. Halberstamm (Versailles, 1886). For updated summaries of the whole problem, cf. Assaf (1955), chs. 5–6; Samuel Morrell, *Mehqar 'al Sefer Hilkhot Re'u* (Doctoral diss., Jewish Theological Seminary of America, 1966).

60. Jacob Reifmann, "Biqqoret Sefer She'eltot de-Rav Aḥai Gaon," *Beth Talmud*, III (1882–83), 26–29, 52–59, 71–79, 108–117, 144–148.

61. Epstein, *Mi-Qadmoniot*, pp. 378f.

62. Full bibliographical information on these works in Kasher and Mandelbaum.

63. See above, n. 23.

64. See Epstein's autobiography in *Kitvay R. Abraham Epstein*, I, 14f.; cf. also Kressel, I, 136f.

65. Epstein, "Meqorot," *Mi-Qadmoniot*, pp. 410f.

66. For a penetrating critique of Epstein's theory on *Seder Tannaim va-Amoraim*, cf. M. Auerbach, "Die juedische Geschichtschreibung im Mittelalter," *Jeschurun*, XV (1928),

196f. These criticisms were later adopted by K. Kahan in the introduction to his edition of *Seder Tannaim weAmoraim* (Frankfurt a.M., 1935), pp. xivf. For further analysis of Epstein's theory, cf. Cohen in *Ibn Daud*, pp. 177f.

67. Cf. Friedlaender (1905). On Nathan's account, cf. Baron (1943), pp. 25f.

68. Cf. Louis Ginzberg, *Eine unbekannte juedische Sekte* (New York, 1922), pp. vf.; *idem, Students, Scholars and Saints*, pp. 88f., 109f.; *idem, On Jewish Law and Lore* (Philadelphia, 1955), p. 78. See also the delightful biography by Eli Ginzberg, *Keeper of the Law: Louis Ginzberg* (Philadelphia, 1966), especially pp. 145f.

69. Cf. *Livre d'Hommage ... Poznanski*, p. xxxiii, no. 120.

70. For the latest discussion, see Judah Rosenthal, *Hiwi al-Balkhi* (Philadelphia, 1949). On the Iranian background, cf. Jacob Neusner, "A Zoroastrian Critique of Judaism," *JAOS*, LXXXIII (1963), 283f.—A curious incident that occurred after the publication of Davidson's edition has long been the subject of scholarly gossip and merits clearing up, if only because it involved two of the leading figures in Jewish scholarship in the first half of the twentieth century. Although Davidson's edition appeared after the outbreak of the war, the author managed to send a copy to Poznanski, who, in a postcard dated July 18, 1915, duly acknowledged receipt of the volume and further stated his intention of writing a full review for the *JQR*. This review never arrived. Instead, several months later Poznanski began issuing a new edition with commentary in *Hazefirah*. Poznanski made it quite evident that he had not discovered new fragments or even had an opportunity to examine afresh the fragments that Davidson had discovered; he was simply appropriating Davidson's text and writing his own commentary as well as supplying his own conjectural emendations. The installments were issued in 1916 collectively as a separate volume with title pages in Hebrew and Polish, neither of which made any reference to Davidson's edition. To be sure, in his introduction, Poznanski took note of Davidson's volume and stated that since he felt the whole work merited becoming available to a Hebrew-reading audience, and since he differed with Davidson on a number of points, he was issuing the work anew. Poznanski must soon have gotten wind of Davidson's chagrin over the affair, for the former's was not a review or a genuinely new edition. In any event, in a letter to Davidson dated September 29, 1919, which it may be noted was only a few days before Yom Kippur of that year, Poznanski wrote among other things: [I retain Poznanski's wording and spelling for the most part without the usual "sic," for this would have had to be added several times.—GDC] "I send you my recension of your Saadiahs polemic and yet some small matters. My two books on the Geonim of Baghdad and the introduction to Elieser of Beagency that are issued on the beginning of the war you probably received. During the war I could only little work. The circumstances do not forward the scientific work, and my health is also not quite well. [new paragraph] That I did not place your name of [sic!] the title page of my hebrew edition of Saadiah Polemic there was no bad intention. I speak of your merits concerning this publication with the greatest approbation in my preface." Davidson accepted Poznanski's new overture, and they remained fast friends. Poznanski was instrumental in helping members of Davidson's family get out of Russia, while Davidson not only continued to send Poznanski materials but also contributed an article to the Poznanski memorial volume.—The information for this note is based on the Poznanski-Davidson file in the Library of the Jewish Theological Seminary of America, which was graciously brought to my attention by the Librarian, Dr. Menahem Schmelzer.

71. Judah Rosenberg, *Qobes Ma'asay Yeday Geonim Qadmonim* (Berlin, 1856), part I.

72. J. N. Epstein (1915, 1921, 1945).

73. On the role of "institutes" which were established outside the formal academic structures of the Weimar Republic, and in which, incidentally, Jews figured especially prominently, cf. Peter Gay, *Weimar Culture* (New York, 1968), pp. 30f.

74. See bibliography, s.v. Schocken Studies.

75. See Schirmann (cf. above, n. 38), pp. xxivf.

76. On Mann, cf. Kressel, II, 378; the prefatory papers in Mann-Sonne (1966); Goitein in Mann (1920–1922, reprint); bibliography by Raphael Mahler, *YIVO Bletter*, XVI (1940), 178f., XVII (1941), 92, Shaked, pp. 316f.

77. Cf. H. E. Barnes, *A History of Historical Writing* (2 ed., New York, 1963), pp. 310f. and the bibliography on p. 329.

78. Mann, "Responsa," *JQR*, NS, VII (1916–17), 459.

79. Mann's emotional and methodological ties to Rapoport have been stressed by Reichert and Sonne in their papers in Mann-Sonne (1966).

80. Cf. below, n. 96.

81. Otto of Freising, *Chronica sive Historia de Duabus Civitatibus*, edited by A. Hofmeister and W. Lammers (Darmstadt, 1961), p. 374 (= end of Prolegomenon to Bk.V).

82. Ginzberg (1928–1929), II, 504f.

83. *Kerem Chemed*, V (1841), 204; Pinsker (1860), pp. 11, 13.

84. Friedlaender (1910–1913). Especially in the last installment of this study, Friedlaender attempted to show the re-emergence of some of the medieval sectarian-messianic notions among Jewish messianic pretenders of the late Middle Ages, most notably Sabbethai Zevi and Jacob Frank.

85. Norman Golb, "Who Were the Magariya?" *JAOS*, LXXX (1960), 347f.; Harry Austryn Wolfson, "The Preexistent Angel of the Magharians and al-Nahwandi," *JQR*, NS, LI (1960–61), 89f. While Wolfson refused to posit any direct link between the earlier sect and al-Nahwendi, Golb conjectured that the doctrines of the Magharya made their way to al-Nahwendi through books.

86. Harkavy, *Jewish Encyclopedia*, I, 553; cf. also Poznanski (1917–18), who rejected Friedlaender's radical distinction between Karaism and the other sects.

87. Cf. Revel (1913). On the other hand, it should be noted that the connection between Karaism and the legal-linguistic-ideological data in the Dead Sea Scrolls has been forcefully argued by Wieder (1962). For earlier theories on the connections between the Karaites and the Dead Sea Scrolls, cf. H. H. Rowley, *The Zadokite Fragments and the Dead Sea Scrolls* (Oxford, 1952).

88. Dubnow (1926), sections 61–61; *idem, Nationalism and History* (Philadelphia, 1958), pp. 295f.; *idem, Toledot ha-Hasidut* (Tel-Aviv, 1944), p. 2. See also next note.

89. Cf. Raphael Mahler, "Ha-Kittot ha-Datiyot ve-ha-Zeramim ha-Tarbutiyyim be-Divray Yemay Yisrael le-Shittat Dubnow," *Simon Dubnow in Memoriam*, edited by Simon Rawidowicz (London, 1954), pp. 89f., and especially pp. 100f.

90. See the reviews by A. S. Halkin, *Jewish Social Studies*, XI (1949), 79f.; Leon Nemoy, *JQR*, NS, XL (1949–50), 307f. A fine specimen of over-reaction is the review in *Kirjath Sepher*, XXVI (1949–50), 121f.

91. The same view of Anan's activity is advanced by Wieder, p. 256.

92. Zucker (1959), pp. 143f., 159f.

93. Malter (1921), p. 10.

94. For the latest summary of the biographical data, cf. Marx (1944).

95. Cf. Joseph Dan, *The Esoteric Theology of Ashkenazi Hasidism* [in Hebrew] (Jerusalem, 1968), pp. 22f.; Gershom Scholem, *Major Trends in Jewish Mysticism* (3 ed. New York, 1961), pp. 86f.

96. Assaf (1929–30). Cf. also Ben-Jacob (1965), ch. 2.

97. See the (already incomplete) bibliography in Shaked, pp. 289f.

98. See above, n. 9.

99. Goitein (1962).

100. See bibliography, s.v. Golb and Friedman.

The Story of the Four Captives[*]

I

The seventh and final section of Abraham ibn Daud's chronicle, *Sefer ha-Qabbalah*,[1] opens with the following story, the renowned tale of "The Four Captives."

TRANSLATION[2]

"Prior to that[3] it was brought about by the Lord[4] that the income of the academies[5] which used to come from Spain, the land of the Maghreb, Ifrīqiya, Egypt, and the Holy Land was discontinued. The following were the circumstances that brought this about.

"The commander of a fleet, whose name was Ibn Rumāḥiṣ,[6] left Cordova, having been sent by the Muslim king of Spain, 'Abd ar-Raḥmān an-Nāṣir.[7] This commander of a mighty fleet set out to capture the ships

[*]In addition to those whose specific help has been acknowledged in the notes, I wish to express my gratitude to Professor Saul Lieberman and to Professor H. Z. Dimitrovsky for their critical advice. I am especially indebted to Professor Abraham S. Halkin, who contributed unsparingly of his time and learning at every stage of the writing of this paper.

The following abbreviations have been used: Baron, *SRH* = S. W. Baron, *A Social and Religious History of the Jews* (8 vols. and Index. New York and Philadelphia, 1952–60); *EI* = *Encyclopedia of Islam; HUCA* = *Hebrew Union College Annual; JE* = *Jewish Encyclopedia; JQR(NS)* = *Jewish Quarterly Review (New Series); MGWJ* = *Monatsschrift fuer Geschichte und Wissenschaft des Judentums; MJC* = *Medieval Jewish Chronicles and Chronological Notes* (2 vols. Edited by A. Neubauer, Oxford, 1887–95); *MS(S)* = *Manuscript(s); PAAJR* = *Proceedings of the American Academy for Jewish Research; SHQ* = *Sefer ha-Qabbalah* by Abraham ibn Daud. Biblical and classical Rabbinic works have been referred to by standard abbreviations.

of the Christians and the towns that were close to the coast. They sailed as far as the coast of Palestine and swung about to the Greek sea and the islands therein. [Here] they encountered a ship carrying four great scholars, who were travelling from the city of Bari to a city called Sefastīn,[8] and who were on their way to a Kallah convention.[9] Ibn Rumāḥiṣ captured the ship and took the sages prisoner. One of them was R. Ḥushiel, the father of Rabbenu Ḥananel; another was R. Moses, the father of R. Ḥanokh, who was taken prisoner with his wife and his son, R. Ḥanokh (who at the time was but a young lad); the third was R. Shemariah b. R. Elḥanan. As for the fourth, I do not know his name. The commander wanted to violate R. Moses' wife, inasmuch as she was exceedingly beautiful. Thereupon, she cried out in Hebrew to her husband R. Moses and asked him whether or not those who drown in the sea will be quickened at the time of the resurrection of the dead.[10] He replied unto her: 'The Lord said: I will bring them back from Bashan; I will bring them back from the depths of the sea.'[11] Having heard his reply, she cast herself into the sea and drowned.[12]

"These sages did not tell a soul about themselves or their wisdom. The commander sold R. Shemariah in Alexandria of Egypt;[13] [R. Shemariah] proceeded to Fostat[14] where he became head [of the academy]. Then he sold R. Ḥushiel on the coast of Ifrīqiya. From there the latter proceeded to the city of Qairawan, which at that time was the mightiest of all Muslim cities in the land of the Maghreb, where he became the head [of the academy] and where he begot his son Rabbenu Ḥananel.

"Then the commander arrived at Cordova where he sold R. Moses along with R. Ḥanokh. He[15] was redeemed by the people[16] of Cordova, who were under the impression that he was a man of no education. Now there was in Cordova a synagogue that was called the College Synagogue,[17] where a judge[18] by the name of R. Nathan the Pious, who was a man of distinction,[19] used to preside.[20] However, the people of Spain were not thoroughly versed in the words of our Rabbis, of blessed memory. Nevertheless, with the little knowledge they did possess, they conducted a school[21] and interpreted [the traditions] more or less [accurately].[22] [Once] R. Nathan explained [the law requiring] 'immersion [of the finger] for each sprinkling,' which is found in the tractate Yoma,[23] but he was unable to explain it correctly. Thereupon, R. Moses, who was seated in the corner like an attendant, arose before R. Nathan and said to him: 'Rabbi, this would result in an excess of immersions!'[24] When he and the students heard his words, they marvelled to each other and asked him to explain the law to them. This he did quite properly. Then each of them asked him all the difficulties which they had, and he replied to them out of the abundance of his wisdom.

"Outside the College there were litigants who were not permitted to enter until the students had completed their lesson.[25] On that day, R. Nathan the judge walked out,[26] and the litigants went after him. However, he said to them: 'I shall no longer be judge. This man who is garbed in rags and is a stranger[27] is my master,[28] and I shall be his disciple from this day on. You ought to appoint him judge of the community of Cordova.' And that is exactly what they did.

"The community then assigned him a large stipend and honored him with costly garments and a carriage. [At that point] the commander wished to retract his sale. However, the king would not permit him to do so, for he was delighted by the fact that the Jews of his domain no longer had need of the people of Babylonia.[29]

"The report [of all this] spread throughout all of Spain and the Maghreb, and students came to study under him. Moreover, all questions which had formerly been addressed to the academies were now directed to him. This affair occurred in the days of R. Sherira,[30] in about[31] 4750 [A.M.],[32] somewhat more or less.

"R. Moses allied himself by marriage with the Ibn Falīja family,[33] which was the greatest of the families of the community of Cordova, and took from them a wife for his son R. Ḥanokh. [Subsequently,] the daughter of R. Ḥanokh was married to one of the Ibn Falīja family. Because of this, they[34] are known by the name of Ibn Falīja to this day.

"R. Moses acquired[35] numerous disciples, one of whom was R. Joseph b. R. Isaac b. Shatnāsh,[36] alias Ibn Abitur. He interpreted the whole of the Talmud in Arabic for the Muslim King al-Ḥakam.[37] Because of his prominence[38] and his learning, he rejected R. Ḥanokh the Rabbi,[39] who had occupied his father's post. Accordingly, after the death of the great Nasi, R. Ḥisdai b. R. Isaac,[40] the community was divided by a bitter dispute. (In the days of R. Ḥisdai there was not a man in the world who could have disputed the authority of R. Ḥanokh.) Every day[41] there used to go out of Cordova to the city of al-Zahrā'[42] seven hundred Jews in seven hundred carriages, each of them attired in royal garb and wearing the headdress of Muslim officials, all of them escorting the Rabbi.[43] A second faction would escort Ibn Shatnāsh. Finally, the party of the Rabbi[44] gained the upper hand, excommunicated Ibn Shatnāsh and banned him. [At that point] the King said to him: 'If the Muslims were to reject me in the way the Jews have done to you, I would go into exile.[45] Now you betake yourself into exile!'

"Ibn Shatnāsh went from Spain to Pechina[46] and encountered there R. Samuel ha-Kohen b. R. Josiah, a member of the community of Fez. The latter was mindful of the ban of the Rabbi, R. Ḥanokh, and refused to converse with Ibn Shatnāsh. Thereupon, Ibn Shatnāsh angrily wrote him a long letter in Aramaic, in which he made a [grammatical] error. R. Samuel ha-Kohen replied to him, pointing out his error to him, but in a mild and tranquil tone. So Ibn Shatnāsh boarded a ship and went to the academy of Rabbenu Hai, being under the impression that Rabbenu Hai would receive him and that the latter was an enemy of R. Ḥanokh. [That impression] derived from the fact that the aforementioned four scholars had cut off the income of the academies, with the result that the academies had been reduced to impoverishment. Nevertheless, Rabbenu Hai let him know that he should not come, for if he should come he would observe the ban declared by the Rabbi. Accordingly, Ibn Shatnāsh went off to Damascus where he died.

"However, prior to that[47] the faction opposing the Rabbi, including those who supported Ibn Shatnāsh, had declined. Among these were two brothers, merchants [and] manufacturers of silk, Jacob ibn Jau and his brother Joseph. They once happened to enter the courtyard of one of the king's eunuchs, who was in charge of the land[48] of Tākurunna,[49] at a time when the Muslim elders of the territory under his charge had come to register a complaint against the officer he had appointed over them. They had also brought him a gift of two thousand Ja'farīya gold pieces.[50] No sooner did they begin to speak than the minister issued an order to humiliate them, beat them with clubs, and have them hustled off to prison. Now in the entrance to the palace there were a number of tortuous recesses into one of which the two thousand gold pieces fell. Although they[51] protested vigorously, no one paid them any attention. However, immediately [afterwards], Jacob ibn Jau and his brother Joseph entered [the palace], found the gold pieces and went off. Once they had arrived home, they took counsel [on the matter], saying: '[Since] we have discovered this money in the royal palace, let us make a solemn agreement[52] to return it there, coupled with gifts and offerings.[53] Perhaps we shall be able in [that way] to rid ourselves of the abuse of our enemies and gain the support of the king.' So they did just that, and they became successful in the silk business, making clothing of high quality and pennants that are placed at the tops of standards[54] of such high quality as was not duplicated in all of Spain. They brought presents to King Hishām and to King al-Manṣūr ibn Abi 'Amir, his guardian,[55] with the result that King al-Manṣūr became very fond of Jacob b. Jau. Accordingly, the former issued him a note[56] placing him in charge of all the Jewish communities from Sijilmasa[57] to the river Duero,[58] which was the border of his realm. [The decree stated] that he is to adjudicate all their litigations,[59] and that he is empowered to appoint over them whomsoever he wishes and to exact from them any tax or payment to which they may be subject. Furthermore, he placed at his disposal eighteen of his eunuchs clad in uniform who conducted him in the carriage of a vicegerent. Then all the members of the community[60] of Cordova assembled and signed an agreement [certifying] his position as Nasi, which stated: 'Rule thou over us, both thou, and thy son, and thy son's son also.'[61] Upon taking office, he despatched a messenger to the Rabbi, R. Ḥanokh, [threatening him] that should he adjudicate [a litigation] between two people he would cast him into the sea in a boat without oars!

"Thereupon, all those who had opposed Ibn Shatnāsh switched to the latter['s side]. All [now] wrote letters to Ibn Shatnāsh [urging him] to return to Cordova and [assuring him] that they would remove the Rabbi, R. Ḥanokh, and appoint him as Rabbi over them. To these he replied sternly, saying of the Rabbi: 'I call upon heaven and earth as my witnesses that there is no one in all of Spain as worthy as he of presiding over the academy.'

"However, at the end of the first year of his rule as Nasi, Ibn Jau was thrown into prison by King al-Manṣūr. The latter had been under the impression that Ibn Jau would produce great profits[62] for him by taking money from Jews in all the communities by hook or by crook and then present it to him. Since [Ibn Jau] failed to do so, [al-Manṣūr] threw him into prison, where he remained for about one year. Finally, on the day of a Muslim festival, King Hishām happened to pass by the prison on his way from the palace to his house of worship, while Ibn Jau was standing in the entrance to the prison directly in the view of King Hishām. When the latter saw him he asked his guardian al-Manṣūr why he had done this to him. He replied: 'Because he does not turn in any tribute from all his domain.' Thereupon, King Hishām ordered that he be released and restored to his office. Although this was done, he did not regain quite the same [powers] which he had previously had.

"Because of this situation and because Ibn Shatnāsh had sent a stern reply to the community of Cordova, the Rabbi was not removed following Ibn Jau's reinstatement in office. Finally, [Ibn Jau] died within the lifetime of the Rabbi. The Rabbi, saint that he was, was extremely grieved at his death [as can be seen from the following.]. [Ibn Jau] died on a Friday evening, and one of the Rabbi's in-laws of the Ibn Falīja family came to him, believing that he would be bearing good tidings with the announcement of Jacob's death. However, the Rabbi burst into loud weeping. Ibn Falīja said to him in amazement: 'I came to bear you the good tidings of the death of your enemy, but you obviously love the man who hated you.'[63] The Rabbi replied to him: 'I am distressed about the poor who ate regularly at his table. What are they to do tomorrow? If you support them, I shall not weep; as for myself, I am unable to give them support.' [This last remark stemmed from the circumstance] that the Rabbi was not a man of means. Because of his saintliness, he had refused to derive any profit from the honor of the Torah and consequently lived a life of austerity.

"The Rabbi, R. Ḥanokh, passed away in 4775, thirteen years before the passing of Rabbenu Hai, of blessed memory.[64] Nevertheless, the communities of West and East did not resume the sending of gifts to the academies,[65] inasmuch as these scholars[66] raised many disciples, and [the knowledge of] the Talmud spread throughout the world.[67]

"Now the custom of the Rabbi, R. Ḥanokh, of blessed memory, was as follows: Every year, on the last day of the Festival,[68] he used to go up [to the pulpit] to complete the reading of the Torah, accompanied by the outstanding men of the generation and the pillars of the congregation. In 4775 he went up in accordance with his custom, accompanied by the others. Since the pulpit[69] was old, it broke and caved in. [In the accident] the Rabbi's neck was broken, and he died a few days later—after having raised up many disciples."

II

Some one hundred thirty years have passed since Solomon Judah Loeb Rapoport first sought to elicit the historical data from this account of the capture and sale of the four captives. Since that time the story has engaged the attention of virtually every Jewish student of the Gaonic period. It suffices to recite the names of some of the major scholars who have tackled the problem of "the four captives" to realize how significant and how elusive it has remained: Rapoport, Lebrecht, Graetz, Halevy, Schechter, Eppenstein, Poznanski, Blau, Aptowitzer, Marx, Assaf, and Mann—to mention only twelve of those who are no longer living—have offered one or more solutions to the problems raised by this simple and yet baffling tale.[70] By and large, the opinions of these scholars are divisible into two groups. The one dismisses the story as pious legend, based perhaps on a grain of truth, and contends, therefore, that students need not trouble themselves about squaring internal contradictions.[71] However, in the absence of conclusive evidence that the story is pure fiction, the other and minority group refuses to discredit the story and accepts it as basically correct. Where there are internal contradictions, the statements are emended; where there are patent misstatements of fact, they alone are summarily rejected.[72] In short, the choice has lain between impugning Ibn Daud's credibility as historian, or doing violence to his text in order to save his reputation. It is the purpose of this paper to demonstrate that, on the one hand, the account is a fiction and was probably not intended by its author to be read as factual history and that, on the other hand, the text and data which have come down to us in *Sefer ha-Qabbalah* are essentially as Ibn Daud wrote them. Ibn Daud, of course, did make use of facts and genuine documents, and his story inevitably sheds light on historical events. However, the facts that do emerge are not necessarily the ones Ibn Daud wished to communicate.

It is perhaps best to begin with a summary of the acknowledged objections to the story as it stands. First, the event could not have occurred in 4790 A.M. (i.e., 990 C.E.), as Ibn Daud says, for 'Abd ar-Raḥmān died in 961. The chronology is further complicated by Ibn Daud's added statement that the events occurred in the days of R. Sherira Gaon, since R. Sherira did not become Gaon until 968, or seven years after the death of 'Abd ar-Raḥmān. It was essentially with these internal contradictions that Jewish scholarship concerned itself until the epoch-making publication in 1899 by Solomon Schechter of a letter from R. Ḥushiel to R. Shemariah b. Elḥanan.[73] That letter demonstrated conclusively that R. Ḥusiel had come to Qairawan quite willingly in connection with a trip that originally was to take him to Cairo. There is not the faintest suggestion in the letter of any mishap, such as capture by pirates or foreign navies. Moreover, R. Ḥushiel prolonged his stay in Qairawan only to await the arrival of his son Elḥanan and in response to the request of the Jewish community there. In other words, Ibn Daud's story with regard to at least one of the principals was patently untrue.

Thanks to the discoveries from the Geniza, the end of the story has not escaped questioning. After his banishment from Spain, Ibn Abitur did not lead as sorry an existence as Ibn Daud would have us believe. Many doors were opened to him, among them that of R. Shemariah b. Elḥanan, that of the Gaon of the Palestinian community, and apparently even that of R. Hai, who corresponded with him and treated him with great courtesy.[74]

In the light of these objections, most modern scholars have agreed that the first portion of this account, the one narrating the story of the capture, redemption, and rise to fame of four captives, is a historical romance in which fact and legend are skillfully interwoven. Ludwig Blau sensed that the story is in reality but a specimen of a legendary genre, but he was unable to point to anything resembling Ibn Daud's story other than the legend about the founding of the medical school of Salerno. According to this legend, the medical school was founded by the Roman Magister Salernitanus, the Jew Elius, the Greek Pontus, and the Saracen Abdallah. However, Blau frankly cautioned that his suggestion was at best a conjecture and hardly a convincing parallel.[75] Nevertheless, Blau did point to a number of internal features of Ibn Daud's story that made it strongly suspect as the product of oral legend, if not of Ibn Daud's own imagination. Since these have occasionally, but by no means universally, been overlooked by other scholars, it would be well to list these also.

It is curious that four great scholars, each of whom was to become the head of a Jewish community, should be assembled on one ship. Ibn Daud tried to account for the problem by saying that they were going to a Kallah assembly. How thin this device was, Ibn Daud himself realized, for in the last analysis he had to admit that the whole affair was part of the divine plan.[76] Incidentally, it should be noted that Ibn Daud does not usually invoke the intervention of God in history except as a pious turn of speech.[77] But in this case he had to begin his story with the statement that what follows can only be explained as a kind of miracle. Indeed, only the Almighty could be called upon to explain why in the second instance the admiral was so kind to Jewish needs as to sell one scholar at a time, precisely in the area where he would be of greatest service.

Thirdly, the story of R. Moses' rise to the *dayyanate* of Cordova is strongly reminiscent of Hillel's rise to power as a result of the failure of the B'nay Bathyra to solve a ritual problem.[78] Moreover, the martyrdom of R. Moses' wife aboard ship is almost a verbatim reproduction of the incident reported in classical Jewish sources of children or adults who, after the destruction of the Temple, resorted to suicide by jumping from aboard ship to avoid compulsory prostitution and pederasty.[79]

As indicated above, despite all these objections and suspicious circumstances, some modern scholars, of whom the most outspoken was Jacob Mann, have resolutely continued to defend the basic authenticity of the story. Now the only way to prove that the story is really a fanciful tale composed from typological themes is to isolate each of the motifs and to indicate exactly from where Ibn Daud or his source may have drawn them. Only in that way can the general impression that the story is not a record of events either be confirmed or, if necessary, be debated. We begin, therefore, with the first suspect circumstance, namely, the presence of four scholars as captives on one ship, each of whom was released on land at a different location.

In the early years of the thirteenth century a number of writers in Provence and Germany explained the origins of the custom of reciting the long *we-hu Raḥum* prayer in the morning service of Mondays and Thursdays. Their explanation was based on a legend recorded in three principal forms, each of them clearly a variation on the same basic theme.[80] One feature common to all of the forms is that the prayer was composed at a time of tribulation by three men, each of whom contributed one section.[81] A second feature common to all of the full accounts is that the authors of the prayer were exiles of Jerusalem who had been cast abroad to foreign parts by Vespasian or Titus.

In several of these legends, there appears an added motif: After the destruction of the Temple, Titus (or Vespasian) cast into the sea three ships filled with men and women, without a helmsman. The Almighty sent a stormy wind which drove the ships to the shores of three different kingdoms. The legends then proceed to tell how following their safe landing the Jews on one of the ships were subjected to terrible persecutions, from which they were miraculously delivered, and in connection with which three wise and pious men of their group composed the *we-hu Raḥum* prayer.

Although some versions of the legend omit the motif of three helmless ships, and, consequently, of their landing in different ports, the theme does appear in at least one form of each of the three principal traditions on the origin of the *we-hu Raḥum* prayer.[82] It makes no difference, as we shall see, whether the theme of three ships driven by divine winds was indigenous to one recension and was later grafted on to the others, or whether the copyists of some of the recensions omitted an original theme of the three ships as irrelevant to the immediate story of the origin of the prayer. Of equally little consequence is the great variation between the different versions on the specific ports at which the ships landed.[83] What is important is that in each version transmitting the theme of the three ships, they were helmless and helpless, and driven to different shores by a miracle.

Here we encounter a motif clearly related to the miraculous landing of the four captives. In both stories helpless captive Jews are placed by divine plan on different and remote spots of the earth. Secondly, in each of the stories, *three* landings are recorded: in the *we-hu Raḥum* story, by means of three separate ships, in the story of the four captives, from one ship. In any event, the landing of the three ships is *typologically equivalent* to the landing of the three captives in Ibn Daud's story.

The late Joshua Starr was the only one, I believe, who noticed the parallelism of motifs between the legend of *we-hu Raḥum* and Ibn Daud's story of the four captives.[84] However, since Starr assumed that the *we-hu Raḥum* legend was first reported in the middle of the thirteenth century by Samuel of Bamberg (died ca. 1250), he cautiously tended to dismiss that legend as late and possibly even as having been formulated under the influence of Ibn Daud's story of the four captives.

This, then, is the crux of the issue. Which version is earlier: Ibn Daud's story or the legend of *we-hu Raḥum*? A closer examination of the origins and transmission of the *we-hu Raḥum* legend will indicate that any question of influence by Ibn Daud is, to say the least, most unlikely.

There is weighty evidence that the Franco-German legend on the three helmless ships antedates Ibn Daud's story by at least a century. As Hans Lewy noted in quite another connection,[85] the motif of Jews put to sea in three ships by Titus (or Vespasian) goes back to early Rabbinic accounts of the destruction of the Temple, specifically to *Abot de R. Nathan*,[86] where it is told that Titus dismantled the sacred vessels of the Temple "and filled three ships with men, women and children[87] in order to boast of his triumph abroad." Hence, the theme of three ships filled with captive Jews is an ancient one, probably of Tannaitic origin.[88]

A second motif in the *we-hu Raḥum* legend is the stress on the tripartite formation of the prayer, and this, too, is traceable to classical Rabbinic legends of the destruction of the Temple. The Midrash on Lamentations states,

Vespasian filled *three ships* with eminent men of Jerusalem to place them in Roman houses of shame. The captives arose and said: "It is not enough that we have provoked Him to anger in His Sanctuary, that we shall now do so also outside the Holy Land [by consenting to such immoral practices]!" They said to the women [who were in the ships], "Do you desire such a fate?" They replied: "No." They then said: "If these women whose [fate is to be used] for normal coition refuse, how much more must we [men refuse to be used for perverted purposes]! Do you think that if we throw ourselves into the sea, we will enter into the life of the age to come [i.e., the Resurrection]?" Thereupon, the Holy One, blessed be He, enlightened their eyes with the verse: "The Lord said: I will bring them back from Bashan, I will bring them back from the depths of the sea (Ps. 68:23)." "I will bring them back from Bashan" [i.e., I will bring them back] from between the teeth of [*bayn shinay*] lions; "I will bring them back from the depths of the sea" is to be understood literally.

The first company [in the first ship] stood up and said: "Surely we have not forgotten the name of our God, or spread forth our hands to a strange god (Ps. 44:21)," and they threw themselves into the sea. The second company [in the second ship] stood up and said: "Nay, but for thy sake are we killed all the day" (*ibid.*, v. 23), and they threw themselves into the sea. The third company stood up and said: "Would not God search this out? For he knoweth the secrets of the heart (*ibid.*, v. 22), and they threw themselves into the sea."[89]

Here we encounter two of the basic motifs present in the *we-hu Raḥum* legend: 1) three ships of exiles put to sea by Vespasian (or Titus) and 2) the recitation of three verses by three groups of martyrs. There is a third motif in this midrash, which is not in the *we-hu Raḥum* tradition, but which is in the story of the four captives—namely, suicide to preserve chastity.[90] But to concentrate for the present on the comparison with the *we-hu Raḥum* tradition, one element is lacking in the Midrash on Lamentations, the motif of helmless ships, which in the *we-hu Raḥum* legends is bound up with the miraculous landing in three different ports. However, this third element is also much older than Ibn Daud and the legendary motifs of the Franco-German school.

Hans Lewy[91] has shown that the story of three helmless ships was known to Christians of France and Spain by 1100, or more than half a century before the writing of *Sefer ha-Qabbalah* in 1161,[92] and at least a century before the recording of the *we-hu Raḥum* legend by its earliest transmitters.[93] Thus, Petrus Alphonsi of Toledo, in his diatribe against the Jews (written ca. 1106–1110), cites in evidence of God's rejection of the Jews the fact that at the time of the Destruction many were cast to sea in helmless ships.[94] Alphonsi, who was trying to convince the Jews of their rejection on their own ground, would hardly cite a legend which the Jews themselves did not know as part of their tradition.[95] In other words, the motif of Jews being cast to sea in helmless or rudderless ships was known in Spain considerably before 1100. Now the motif of the helmless ships is bound up in the *we-hu Raḥum* legend with miraculous landings on three different shores. Since Petrus Alphonsi, and hence, the Jews of Spain knew the legend of the helmless or rudderless ships being cast to sea by Vespasian long before Ibn Daud, it is only logical to assume that they also knew the legend of the ships arriving on different shores, indeed on *three* different ones, as Ibn Daud himself has it in his four captives story.

Lewy has also shown that towards the end of the eleventh century this legend was adapted by the monks of Vézaly, France, to explain the veneration of relics, which the monks claimed were of Mary Magdelene. To be sure, this motif of miraculous conveyance of saints across oceans goes back to pagan myths,[96] but the Christian legend of Vézaly has some of the peculiar earmarks of the Jewish form. Once again, we are driven to the conclusion that the story of the origin of the *we-hu Raḥum* prayer is neither the fabrication of Franco-German Jews of the thirteenth century, nor even the product of reworking by these Jews. It is, rather, an old Jewish motif, which may derive originally from pagan sources, but which by medieval times was part of Jewish tradition the world over.

The antiquity of the *we-hu Raḥum* legend can be further supported by the statements of those reporting the story. A close examination of the names of the transmitters of the *we-hu Raḥum* legend points not to a late German or Spanish source, as was believed, but to an Italian, i.e., a pre–Franco-German, provenance. The story of the three shiploads of exiles is reported in the first instance by R. Eleazar b. Judah of Worms (died 1238), who transmits the story in "the name of the Geonim,"[97] which means that he knew it as a much older tradition, if not indeed as a written one. The fact that in R. Eleazar's version of the legend all three ships land in French ports points to minor reworking of the story, but this is offset by other versions that speak of other countries.[98] On the other hand, these other versions point to the same source of information as R. Eleazar does. The latter, as is well known, reports that he received his copious lore on the origin and significance of the prayers from his father (died in 1199) and from R. Judah he-Ḥasid (died 1217) who, in turn, maintained that his traditions on the liturgy go back to Italy, to which they were brought by Abu Aaron of Bagdad.[99] A second version of the report, the one noted by Starr, is transmitted by R. Samuel b. Barukh of Bamberg (died ca. 1250),[100] whose father and teacher, R. Barukh ben Samuel of Mainz, studied under R. Judah b. Kalonymos, the father of the aforementioned R. Eleazar of Worms.[101] This version points again to the same circle for its transmission, but more interestingly gives two of the three points of debarkation as Italy and Africa.[102] There are two further points about Samuel of Bamberg's version that merit attention. In the first instance, his report ascribes the prayer *we-hu Raḥum* to Amittai, Shefatya, and Yosifya, whose names clearly point to Italian origins.[103] Secondly, even granting that Samuel of Bamberg's version is the product of a grafting of the theme of the three ships on to the story of Amittai,

Shefatya, and Yosifya—with reference to whom, the institution of the *we-hu Raḥum* prayer appears also without the legend of the ships[104]—it is inconceivable that Jews of France and Germany would alter the names of the ports of debarkation from Franco-German ones to totally foreign ones, particularly in the light of the propagandistic overtones which their legend could serve.[105] If names have been altered, it is in the "earlier" version of R. Eleazar of Worms.[106] The reason for this change in R. Eleazar's version is not far to seek, for apart from the claim of antiquity which such changes lent a community, they had eschatological overtones.[107] The internal evidence of the version of Samuel of Bamberg, coupled with the fact that his traditions and those of Eleazar of Worms go back to the first generation of Jewish pietists in Germany, points not only to at least a mid-twelfth-century *terminus a quo* for the legend of the three ships, but more probably to an Italian-Jewish source.[108] This conclusion coincides with everything we know about the sources of Franco-German Jewish lore in halakhah, mysticism, and not least of all, the Italo-Franco-German *payyetanic* tradition and the concern of these communities with the origin of post-Talmudic prayers.[109]

Thus, the evidence from classical Rabbinic tradition, from Petrus Alphonsi, from French-Christian sources, and from the Franco-German Jewish traditions points to a common source much older than the twelfth (and certainly the thirteenth) century for the motifs appropriated independently by Ibn Daud and by the Jews of Northern France and Germany. For his story of the four captives, Ibn Daud drew on an old recension of the legend telling of Vespasian's deportation of Jews by ship.

That the motifs of three ships and helmless ships were in the mind of Ibn Daud will serve to explain two further aspects of the story of the four captives. First, in the account of the Midrash on Lamentations of how Vespasian filled three ships with men and women,[110] the martyrs commit suicide to avoid sexual profanation, and only after hearing the reassurance on resurrection in Psalm 68:23. Here is clear evidence that Ibn Daud had the midrash in mind, for how otherwise shall we explain the curious combination of coincidences—three captives, three ports, and the martyrdom of R. Moses' wife precisely according to a literary pattern?[111] Secondly, the conclusion that Ibn Daud was working from a literary paradigm will illuminate the peculiar threat of Jacob ibn Jau to R. Ḥanokh to cast him into the sea in a boat without oars, i.e., helmless![112] Coming from a Jew, this is a most peculiar threat, for nowhere, to my knowledge, do we find any reference to this form of punishment in Jewish communities. Here the author of the story of the four captives has given himself away, for the imagery that seemed most appropriate to him was one which lay close at hand in the model he had adapted to his immediate use. Moreover, in its context, Ibn Jau's threat is a defiance in kind of the divine plan: R. Ḥanokh had come to Spain through God's design aboard a ship. In retribution for his defiance of R. Ḥanokh, Ibn Abitur had to go into exile across the sea "in a ship."[113] Ibn Daud would, therefore, have Ibn Jau take his revenge against R. Ḥanokh by *lex talionis* and put the Rabbi into a boat, this time, à la Titus or Vespasian.[114] That Ibn Daud is fond of such literary symmetry will be demonstrated even more clearly in the analysis of his story.

Ibn Daud, of course, did not copy the midrashic prototype in its original form. He introduced two basic alterations. First, he rationalized the story by denuding it of miraculous qualities and presented the motif in its simplest classical form, capture by pirates, thereby passing off a likely tale that has troubled scholars down to our own day. The three scholars were placed on one ship, captured and ransomed in forms which were all too common and familiar to everyone in the medieval world,[115] and brought to their respective ports in a most "fortuitous" manner.

Of even greater interest is the second and major innovation of Ibn Daud's account, the change of the number of captives from the paradigmatic number three to four. For the past century, scholars have been at a loss to determine who was this fourth scholar whose name Ibn Daud says he does not know. But in reality, it was not only the name of the fourth scholar that Ibn Daud did not know: of a fourth scholar, who should, by the needs of the story, have been sold in a fourth port of entry, there are only three scholars who landed at three points. Why, then, did Ibn Daud assert and reiterate that there were four?

Here, it must be admitted, we are confronted by two possibilities, but each of them will lead to the same conclusion, one that is already manifest as a result of this discussion. To begin with, Ibn Daud's source on the helmless ships set adrift by Vespasian may have contained a variant tradition stating that there were four ships instead of three. Nor is this mere idle conjecture, for the number four (or its multiples) as a round and formalistic number is frequently encountered in Rabbinic sources[116] and, significantly enough, has even left its traces in the story of Vespasian's ships. In the account of this story in the Babylonian Talmud it is not three shiploads but *four hundred* boys and girls.[117] It is, therefore, quite conceivable that just as there was a variant recension that spoke of three ships and a third variant that spoke of seventy virgins,[118] so there was a fourth form that spoke of four ships, representing the age-old Jewish symbolic number four.[119] I venture to offer this conjecture in view of the many instances in Rabbinic literature where the numbers three and four are variants of each other.[120] Ibn Daud would thus have retained the form of his source, but could not fill in on the details. It surely could not have escaped Ibn Daud that his confession of ignorance with respect to the fourth name would actually serve as an argument in his favor. Having conceded ignorance on one point, no one would be likely to question his air of certainty with respect to the remainder of the story.[121]

The second and by far the more likely possibility is that Ibn Daud himself altered the number three to four. In the first instance, this change would at once disarm any reader who would accuse him of appropriating outright an old form for the events Ibn Daud wants to have his audience believe. More important, the change was to a number that was not a vague, round number in Ibn Daud's mind, but a symbolic figure. In a passage in *Mishnat R. Eliezer* on the symbolic significance of the four species of vegetation employed ritually on Tabernacles, the text states:[122]

> Another interpretation [is that the four species] symbolize the four righteous men whom the Holy One, blessed be He, has placed within each and every empire to bring them [i.e., the Jews] salvation and to spread the Torah among them. They are the following: in the Babylonian empire—Daniel, Hananiah, Mishael, and Azariah; in the Persian empire—Haggai, Zechariah, Malachi, and Nehemiah; in the Greek empire—the four sons of the Hasmonean [of whom there had been five], but of whom Judah the eldest had already been killed;[123] in the Roman empire—Rabban Gamaliel, R. Joshua, R. Eleazar b. Azariah and R. Akiba. *Similarly, after these [empires] the Holy One, blessed be He, will not forget them, as it is written: "For the Lord will not forsake His people. (I Sam. 12:22)."*

This symbolism has made the four righteous in each of the four kingdoms the pivotal point in an old Rabbinic theme on God's eternal covenant with Israel.[124] Furthermore, the general promise in the Talmudic prototype of this midrash, that God's covenant will endure for the age to come, or for the battle of Gog and Magog, is now subtly converted to a promise that the covenant will continue in empires subsequent to the Roman dominion. As is well known, the Jews of Spain regarded Ishmael (Islam) as the small or last born of the fourth kingdom foreseen in the book of Daniel.[125] Hence, in keeping with the symbolism of *Mishnat R. Eliezer,* Ibn Daud could very logically extend the homily by pointing to the *four* scholars who initiated the salvation and spread of Torah among the Jews of the Muslim world after the eclipse of Jewish learning in Babylonia.[126] In other words, four is the number symbolic of divine providence over Israel,[127] and the *four* captives are truly the new dispersion, despatched by God to the four corners of the earth, as it were, to bring the word of the Torah into the new and last stage of the fourth kingdom.[128] Here was a perfect reason for Ibn Daud to seize upon four scholars, for their arrival on the scene of history was a consolation—and consolation, be it remembered, is one of the prime functions of history[129]—and evidence of divine favor to Israel. This is what Ibn Daud means when he begins the story of the four captives with the words that it was the Almighty who brought about the collapse of the academies by His own act of sending "four" scholars to the remote corners of the Jewish world.

The fact that the "four" scholars came to their new homes by divine fiat provides the rationale for the break of Jewish communities throughout the world with the Babylonian academies.[130] Without this rationale, the subsequent behavior of the scholars and the members of their respective bailiwicks would be open to serious question. Not only would they have behaved treacherously to the acknowledged center of Jewish learning, but the four scholars themselves would have assumed their Rabbinic posts without having "received" authorization from a recognized link in the chain of Jewish tradition. Surely the attentive reader of *Sefer ha-Qabbalah* could not have failed to notice that in the whole history of Jewish oral tradition, which is the prime subject of Ibn Daud's tract,[131] these four scholars were the only ones, with the exception of the first Moses, who had not "received" their authority from a recognized predecessor.[132] If the scholars were immune to the charge of behaving like schismatics and rebels against authority, they must have had some special form of authorization.

This explanation helps account for another motif in *Sefer ha-Qabbalah*, to which scholars have pointed as evidence of Ibn Daud's ignorance or of his tendentious motives.[133] Ibn Daud insists that the Babylonian Gaonate came to an end with R. Hai and that the academies closed down completely after the death of Hezekiah the exilarch.[134] Ibn Daud was manifestly aware that this was not quite true, for he himself tells of a Spaniard who presided as Gaon over the academy of R. Hai.[135] Surely, he might have determined that the academies were open and continued to function, even if their influence had been severely curtailed.[136] But Ibn Daud preferred not to know this, for the sake of his subtler arguments. The mantle of Torah was no longer in Babylonia; it had shifted by means of four scholars—who begin a new era—and finally settled upon the shoulders of the Spanish scholars alone.[137]

III

This interpretation of Ibn Daud's use of the number four, I suspect the reader will think, is quite interesting, but what evidence can be offered that this interpretation is not a modern midrash on Ibn Daud rather than Ibn Daud's homily on history? In other words, can it be shown that Ibn Daud takes such liberties with history elsewhere by utilizing moulds into which he casts his facts and thereby alters them? The answer is decidedly yes. It was in the first instance the evidence from Ibn Daud's general method of telling Jewish history that made us suspect that what we are dealing with is not a historical account but a homily, a romance with a moral.

It is a remarkable fact that virtually no modern scholar has taken seriously Ibn Daud's repeated contention that history is not a mere record of past events, but essentially a source of consolation for the Jew.[138] "Behold how trustworthy are the consolations of our God,[139] blessed be His name," he writes, "for [the number of years that transpired in] the redemption of the Jews corresponded exactly to that of their exile. From the beginning of their exile [at the hands of Nebuchadnezzar] until the destruction of the Temple and the cessation of the monarchy [of Zedekiah], twenty-one years passed.[140] Similarly, from the time that the rebuilding of the Temple had been begun until it was completed, twenty-one years passed."[141] Early in the sixteenth century Abraham Zacuto vigorously protested that this effort at a symmetrical reconstruction of Biblical history involved a contradiction of the explicit chronology of the Bible, and he proceeded to "correct" Ibn Daud's errors.[142] But surely Ibn Daud must have known the Bible and understood its plain sense. If, therefore, he departed from it to create a parallelism of twenty-one years for each of the two periods he is describing, the symmetry must have been of crucial importance to him—of such importance, in fact, that he would even emend Scripture![143]

The same symmetrical considerations lie at the bottom of the ostensibly bizarre statement that the first Temple stood for 427 years and was destroyed after a war of seven years.[144] This would give the first Temple a life-span of 434 years, which contradicts Ibn Daud's earlier figure of 433 years,[145] but which corresponds exactly to the number of years that the second Temple stood.[146] Furthermore, although Scripture says the final war in the days of the first Temple lasted only three years (II Ki. 25:1–2), Ibn Daud doubtless felt that the period of its destruction should correspond to the period of building under Solomon (I Ki. 6:38)[147] and to the period of subjection to and war with Vespasian and Titus.[148] Both Temples had to have parallel histories.

Symmetry, too, governs his description of the cycles of Roman and Persian dominion,[149] and finally his problematic dates for the redaction of the Mishna and the beginning of the Gaonic period.[150]

Since he did not hesitate to depart from Scripture, Ibn Daud would obviously not shrink from tailoring Maccabean chronology to fit the frame he had set for it. In his sermon on Zechariah, he writes:[151] "When the prophet said, 'So they weighed for my hire thirty pieces of silver (Zech. 11:12)' he hinted at the thirty years during which the pious rulers reigned. They are: Matthias, surnamed the Hasmonean, one year; his son Judah, six years;[152] his son Jonathan, six years;[152] his son Simon, eighteen years. These are the thirty-one years (!) during which the faithful kings ruled." Note how unembarrassed our author is by the discrepancy between the figures of his own data and the figures of the verse he interprets allegorically. It is enough for him that they should correspond roughly for the homily to be appropriate. In the same vein, he probably tailored chronological data on the basis of Scriptural words which he translated numerically (*gematria*).[153]

Ibn Daud, of course, was not the first to fit chronology into schematized frameworks. He had ample precedent in classical Rabbinic sources for his symmetrical reading of history[154] as well as for his use of *gematriaot* to refer to crucial dates.[155] Moreover, both of these devices were employed independently by many medieval writers,[156] among them Ibn Daud's contemporaries, Judah ha-Levi[157] and Moses Maimonides,[158] as well as by Muslim[159] and Christian[160] theoreticians of history. Ultimately, these devices are all connected with calculations of the date of the Messianic era or of the end of the present world,[161] a concern which Ibn Daud shared profoundly.[162] Ibn Daud merely appropriated a genre of historical writing that was very much in vogue and developed his own system, which he proceeded to conceal.

The significant point about these schematized dates in *Sefer ha-Qabbalah* is that history is always shown to conform to a pattern. It is in this very orderliness of history that Ibn Daud finds a source of consolation,[163] a source of hope that history will yet vindicate the Jewish hope for redemption.[164]

Now the history of the four captives, we have seen, is essentially a composite from old motifs which Ibn Daud refashioned in accordance with a homiletical theme promising regular manifestations of divine consolation for Israel.[165] It is, therefore, a not unreasonable supposition that the puzzling date which Ibn Daud gave for the event was also nothing but a symmetrical figure, i.e., a symbolic one. In the face of modern attempts to correct the date given by Ibn Daud, it should be noted that Ibn Daud knew quite well the names of 'Abd ar-Raḥmān, of his fleet admiral, of his successors on the throne, and the circumstances of their rule.[166] He was, therefore, in a position to determine that the dates of 'Abd ar-Raḥmān's reign did not correspond with those of R. Sherira's gaonate and certainly not with 4750 A.M. Since this date is not the first so-called "error" in Ibn Daud's chronology, which upon closer scrutiny is seen to be quite deliberate, perhaps there is no real date for the story of the four captives. Perhaps this date, like all the other mystifying dates in *Sefer ha-Qabbalah*, is a sermon in itself, a midrash on history. But to validate such a supposition we must first unravel the meaning of this symbolic number.

"This event," Ibn Daud tells us, "occurred in the days of R. Sherira, in approximately 4750 [A.M.] somewhat more or less."[167] The words "somewhat more or less" are all important, for Ibn Daud uses them nowhere else with respect to the several hundred dates in his work.[168] Obviously, then, it means that the figure is not the actual date of the event and that Ibn Daud does not want to be held responsible for it. This is in keeping with the method of a man, who, contrary to the general impression, is extremely careful about the dates he lists for persons and events. Why this sudden vagueness?

Ibn Daud gives the clue to his esoteric meaning by his description of how R. Moses became *dayyan* of Cordova, a description which some scholars have noted is embarrassingly reminiscent of Hillel's rise to the position of Nasi.[169] However, since Ibn Daud did not spell out any clue to the significance of the way in which, or time when, R. Moses achieved recognition, later generations of readers were thrown off the track. To recapture Ibn Daud's symbolism, we must first understand his theory on the status of some of the great luminaries of Jewish history.

As was already noted by Ch. Albeck,[170] Ibn Daud has an amazing theory about the patriarchs of the house of Hillel. Hillel and his successors, he contends, held two separate posts, that of *Nasi* and that of head of the academy (or *Rosh Yeshiba*). However, not always did they hold both positions simultaneously. Thus, when R. Gamliel II was deposed from office in Jamnia, and R. Eleazar b. Azarya elected in his place, the change was made only with respect to the position of *Rosh Yeshiba*. R. Gamliel's authority as *Nasi*, Ibn Daud indicates, was not affected.[171] Upon R. Gamliel's death, his son R. Simeon b. Gamliel took his place as *Nasi*, while R. Akiba became *Rosh Yeshiba*.[172] Only after R. Akiba's death did R. Simeon b. Gamliel become *Rosh Yeshiba*.[173]

To return to our subject, Hillel came to Palestine from Babylonia and became *Nasi* one hundred years before the Destruction of the Temple,[174] i.e., in 3729 A.M.[175] In a later passage, Ibn Daud, quoting a well known Rabbinic statement, tells us that Hillel came from Babylonia at the age of forty, then spent forty years in study and forty years in teaching.[176] Now unless we are to assume that Ibn Daud did not care whether he contradicted himself or not, the two passages taken together can only mean that Hillel came to Palestine one hundred years before the Destruction, functioned simultaneously as *Nasi* and student for forty years and subsequently, for the last forty years of his life, served as *Rosh Yeshiba* as well as *Nasi*. This construction would coincide perfectly with Ibn Daud's theory of the patriarchate in general.[177] In other words, Hillel became *Rosh Yeshiba* in 3769 A.M., or 981 years before R. Moses came to Cordova and became *Rosh Yeshiba* under circumstances similar to those of Hillel's appointment.[178]

We now turn back to Ibn Daud's problematic date for the capture and sale of the four captives: "4750 a bit more or less." Let us take it as "a bit less," or 4749 A.M., and it follows that R. Moses became *Rosh Yeshiba* 980 years after Hillel had attained the same office. Now 980 is twice 490, and is thus a symmetrical figure.[179] However, this figure is all the more significant since 980 is two times 70 weeks of years, a figure which every Jew after Daniel regarded as a revelatory number.[180] Turning now to Ibn Daud's alternative date, "a bit more" than 4750, i.e., 4751, we encounter an even more amazing symmetry. The Talmud, Ibn Daud tells us, was given its final redaction in the days of Rabbah Jose in the year 4260,[181] or 491 years after Hillel became *Rosh Yeshiba* in 3769. R. Moses, on the other hand, became *Rosh Yeshiba* of Cordova in 4751 or 491 years after the redaction of the Talmud. In other words, from Hillel to the redaction of the Talmud the same number of years elapsed as from the redaction of the Talmud to the advent of R. Moses in Spain. Spain, Ibn Daud is guardedly telling his reader, had found a new Hillel. The perceptive reader would now see renewed significance in the statement:[182] "Behold how trustworthy are the consolations of our God, blessed be His name, for [the period of] their redemption corresponded exactly to that of their exile." Every Jew knew, and Ibn Daud had been careful to remind his reader, that490 was originally a number of doom, for that was the number of years which elapsed between the destruction of the first and second Temples.[183] However, the Almighty had manifested crucial signs of His everlasting covenant with Israel by spacing the agents of salvation—Hillel, the Talmud, R. Moses—at corresponding points in time.

There is another curious coincidence about this date as it is reported in the better MSS of *Sefer ha-Qabbalah*. In the superior family of MSS the date is reported not as דתש"ן, as we should expect, and as the poorer MSS have recorded it "correctly," but as בקרוב לשנת דש"ן.[184] Moreover, this curious error occurs in several MSS, none of which copied from the other. Here it is important to note that although the MSS sometimes omit the letter signifying the thousands-cipher, in this case the ד, they never omit the letter representing the figure for a hundreds-cipher, in this case the ת. The error is, of course, easily explicable if we assume that what was originally intended was בקרוב לשנת תדש"ן or even more probably בקרוב לשנ' תדשן. The copyists of the better MSS merely shifted the ת from the date itself to the preceding word. This virtually certain explanation of the queer recording of the date דש"ן is all the more striking, for תדשן is, of course, a Hebrew verb suggesting increase or blessing. Can it be only pure coincidence, therefore, that on the verse in Ps. 23:5, "Thou hast anointed [דשנת] my head with oil, my cup runneth over," the midrash offers the following comment:[185]

On what grounds did the sages institute the four cups of Passover?. . . R. Joshua b. Levi said: "In allusion to the four cups of fury which the Holy One, blessed be He, will make the nations of the world to drink. . . . Corresponding to these the Holy One, blessed be He, will give Israel to drink four cups of salvation in the age to come, as it is written: O Lord, the portion of mine inheritance and of my cup, Thou maintainest my lot (Ps. 16:5); Thou preparest a table before me in the presence of mine enemies. Thou hast anointed [דשנת] my head with oil; my cup runneth over (*ibid.* 23:5); I will lift up the cup of salvations, and call upon the name of the Lord (*ibid.* 116:13). Scripture does not say 'the cup of salvation,' but 'the cup of salvations'—one in the days of the Messaiah and one in the day of Gog and Magog."

If Ibn Daud had this passage in mind, the very form of recording the date would be a hint that R. Moses' arrival was an instance of the divine blessings to Israel.[186] The interesting point about this passage is that the word "salvation" is the same as the one used in the passage cited earlier about the role of scholars in each of the four empires.[187] Once he had arrived at a suitable date based on a symmetrical scheme, Ibn Daud found that the date coincided further with an auspicious mnemonic. He, therefore, recorded the date in a form that would serve as a commentary on the significance of the event: the very year of the event was an illustration of the divine comfort to Israel, a theme to which Ibn Daud devoted his "History of the Kings of Israel in [the days] of the Second Temple."[188] In view of all the other puzzling "coincidences" about the story of the four captives which we have already encountered, I do not think we can dismiss the strange orthography תרש"ן as a mere coincidence. It is probably but one more specimen of mnemonic words (*gematriot*) with which Ibn Daud liked to play on occasion.[189]

Having established the significance of the date and circumstances of R. Moses' rise to authority, we may turn to a further motif that Ibn Daud wove into the story of R. Moses and his companions. While aboard ship, "these sages did not tell a soul about themselves or their wisdom." After arriving in Cordova, R. Moses sat in a corner of the academy like a menial attendant until he was recognized and showered with wealth and honor. What we are encountering in these flourishes is nothing other than a motif well known from classical and medieval literature as well as from the folklore of many nations: the "recognition" motif, whereby the prince or noble is taken for a slave, a menial, or a beggar and finally is recognized by "a sign" (*anagnorisis*) which reveals his true origin and station.[190] Here again we are in a position to point to the Rabbinic source on which Ibn Daud probably drew. In a homily on Prov. 4:2, "For I give you good doctrine," a Rabbinic midrash offers the following illustration:[191]

Once a scholar [חכם] happened to be aboard ship with many merchants, who kept on asking the scholar "Where are your wares?" To this he would reply regularly: "My wares are better than yours." Although the merchants searched through the ship, they were unable to find anything belonging to him, and they began to mock at him. Subsequently, pirates fell upon them and took off with everything that was on board. When the merchants reached port and entered the town, they had nothing to eat or to wear. But what did the scholar do? He went to the house of study and lectured. When the people of the city saw that he was a man of great learning, they got together and began to honor him greatly, by providing him with a worthly stipend ועשו לו ופסיקתו בגדולה ובכבוד]. The pillars of the community began to walk to the right and left of him and to accompany him [wherever he went]. When the merchants [who had been aboard ship] saw what had happened, they came to him and pleaded with him, saying: "We beg of you to do us a kindness and put in a good word for us with the people of the city, since you know who we are and what we lost aboard ship. Please, do us a good turn and ask them for as little as a piece of bread for us, so that we don't die of hunger." He said to them, "Didn't I tell you that my wares are better than yours? Yours are lost, but mine are quite intact." This is what is meant by "For I give you good doctrine."

The first to call attention to this source in connection with the story of the four captives was Z. Jawitz, who felt that the homily was based on Ibn Daud's story.[192] On the other hand, A. Ashtor has recently contended that the likelihood is that Ibn Daud drew on the midrash.[193] In view of all that we have seen of Ibn Daud's method, there can be no doubt that Ashtor is right. The most that may possibly be conceded is that some glossator added a phrase or two to the midrashic homily from *Sefer ha-Qabbalah.*[194] But that the midrashic motif is far older than Ibn Daud is beyond question, for it appears in a somewhat variant form, i.e., with none of the stylistic usages reminiscent of *Sefer ha-Qabbalah,* but with no change in basic motif, in compilations that had no access to Spanish sources.[195] Ibn Daud thus adapted an old sermon on the cash-value of Torah to the needs of his subject. What further proof do we need that it is not history that Ibn Daud has written, but a sermon, an artistic allegory on the special providence reserved for Israel and for the guardians of the Torah!

Ibn Daud does not tell us *how* the other captives became heads of their communities not because he did not know—that would not have stumped an artist like Ibn Daud—but because he did not care. Ibn Daud's real concern is the Jewish community of Spain. To the extent that other Jewish communities illustrated and bore out what Ibn Daud was saying, he invokes them, too. What Ibn Daud wants to tell us is that the arrival of R. Moses in Spain—and of R. Hushiel in Qairawan and of R. Shemariah in Cairo—marks the transition to a new era in Jewish learning, the era of the Rabbinate. The arrival of the "four" captives in their respective new homes spells the end of the Gaonate and the hegemony of Babylonia and, on the other hand, the beginning of learning the world over.

To sum up: Our analysis of the story has shown that each of the motifs and details of "fact" is clearly explicable in terms of sources available to

Ibn Daud and, above all, in terms of Ibn Daud's general method of writing "history." The conclusion is inescapable that the story of the four captives has come down to us as it was written by Abraham ibn Daud. In its present form it is not a legend, but a consciously and brilliantly contrived novella or historical romance. Like many another novella it employs ancient motifs, which its author reworked to provide entertainment, edification, and solace. Moreover, even the belletristic structure conforms to ancient patterns: the tragedy of capture, rape, wandering, reversal of the fortune of the unrecognized hero for good, retribution for the wicked, and ultimate vindication of the righteous.[196] Within the artistic motifs there have been woven subtle Jewish midrashic ideas and chronological devices—such as historical symmetry and *gematriot*. Ibn Daud, we submit, should be read for what he was: not a historian, but an artist, a preacher and a moralist, whose aim was to demonstrate that the Eternal of Israel will not fail or forsake his people.

IV

Even if the story of the four captives must be classified as fiction, nevertheless, its author does hint at certain historical circumstances, which for obvious reasons he was reluctant to spell out. What, then, is the historical substratum of the tale?

First, as has been universally acknowledged by modern scholars, Ibn Daud reflects the sentiment of the leadership of Spanish Jewry that they need not turn to the Babylonian academies for legal advice and religious instruction. There can be little doubt that a positive program to make Spanish Jewry religiously and culturally autonomous was pursued, if not indeed initiated, by the courtier Ḥisdai ibn Shaprut. It was doubtless also under his directive that R. Moses attained the *dayyanate* of Cordova. The appointment was but one of a series in a campaign to attract men of learning and literary talent to the community of Cordova.[197] On occasion, Ibn Shaprut withdrew his support from former favorites and transferred his patronage to more acceptable newcomers. The classic case of such a shift of favor is the transference of support from the native Spaniard, Menaḥem b. Saruq, to an immigrant from Fez and student of the Babylonian academies, Dunash b. Labrat. Moreover, Ibn Shaprut was not above using violence against his former favorite and had Menahem thrown into prison. Significantly, the partisans of both scholars engaged in a bitter factional fight with charges and counter charges of ignorance, ineptitude, and even of religious deviation.[198]

It is inspiring to read in our story of the readiness with which the native R. Nathan the Pious stepped down from his position before the learning of the unknown "captive." A more realistic surmise would be that if there was such a person as R. Nathan, he was removed by Ibn Shaprut, even as R. Ḥanokh was later deposed by Jacob ibn Jau. R. Moses should be regarded as one of the intellectuals who came to Cordova in the wake of the large migration of Jews (and non-Jews) during the reign of 'Abd ar-Raḥmān,[199] or who were invited to Cordova by Ibn Shaprut and provided with a livelihood.[200]

In pursuing this program, Ibn Shaprut was merely applying to the Jewish community what his master, 'Abd ar-Raḥmān III, had done in his break with the Eastern Caliphate and in his proclamation of himself as Guardian of the Faith and Commander of the Faithful.[201] To be sure, Ibn Shaprut did not break openly with the Jews of Babylonia. That was neither necessary nor desirable. With one hand he continued to contribute to the Babylonian institutions,[202] but with the other he set about establishing the Jews of Cordova—and all of Spain—as an autonomous unit.[203] However, in establishing this new autonomy Ibn Shaprut would seem to have structured the community under his power after the pattern of the community of Babylonia. He himself retained civil authority, like the exilarch of Babylonia, while religious authority was relegated to the *Rosh Yeshiba*, the Spanish counterpart of the Babylonian Geonim. This, at least, is how Ibn Daud seems to understand the structure of the Spanish Jewish community.[204]

The Geonim of Babylonia, of course, could not look with equanimity upon these developments. They cajoled, pleaded, and appealed to ancient precedent and sentiments, but they could do nothing.[205] The academies of Babylonia declined steadily, while Spanish Jewry continued progressively to stand on its own feet. But the tension continued for centuries. Shortly after the writing of *Sefer ha-Qabbalah*, Moses Maimonides would unhesitatingly assert to the Gaon of Babylonia that the Rabbis of Spain were Geonim in their own right and need not wait for guidance from Bagdad.[206] Moreover, the evidence suggests that Maimonides had imbibed this sentiment early in life, while yet in Spain, from his own teachers.[207] The last thing Ibn Daud would want to do was to play into the hands of the Karaites, who delighted in internal Rabbanite dissension,[208] by speaking openly of a break with Babylonian Jewry. Accordingly, he wrote in terms that thinly concealed the real issue at hand.

The story, I believe, reveals a second and more immediate purpose, which first emerges from the sequel, namely the account of the vicissitudes of R. Moses' son and successor. Behind the partisan description of R. Ḥanokh's career, there probably lay a bitter feud between the Ibn Falīja–Ibn Shaprut faction, on the one hand, and the Ibn Abitur–Ibn Jau party, on the other. R. Moses and R. Ḥanokh, Ibn Daud makes it clear, were members of the Ibn Shaprut faction, who could not be touched so long as "the great Nasi" was alive.[209] Only after Ibn Shaprut's death, there began a struggle for power in which the Rabbinate took open sides with the contenders for civil leadership over the Jewish community,

R. Ḥanokh siding with the Ibn Falījas,[210] to whom he was related by marriage,[211] and Ibn Abitur with the Ibn Jaus.[212] The real reason for the Caliph's condemnation of Ibn Abitur to exile may well have been not so much his defiance of R. Ḥanokh as an ill-timed espousal of Ibn Jau.[213] One can only hazard the further guess that in his fight against R. Ḥanokh, Ibn Abitur appealed to the Jews of Spain by invoking their tradition of loyalty to the academies of Babylonia, with which R. Ḥanokh had broken quite openly.[214] If he did, he most certainly evoked the suspicion of the Western Caliph, who quickly ordered him out of Spain.[215] In the Orient, Ibn Abitur fought back with all the tools he could muster, and may have attempted to proclaim a counter-excommunication of R. Ḥanokh and his party.[216]

Even after Ibn Abitur and R. Ḥanokh died, their factions doubtless continued to quarrel bitterly for generations. Samuel ibn Nagrela, an arch-disciple of R. Ḥanokh,[217] pursued his master's policy and doubtless continued to buttress it with heated sentiment.[218] As a spiritual descendant of R. Ḥanokh and Ibn Nagrela,[219] Ibn Daud took up his masters' cause.

Accordingly, R. Ḥanokh—as the later Samuel ibn Nagrela[220]—is pictured by Ibn Daud in exclusively laudatory terms. R. Ḥanokh's saintliness is demonstrated by his reaction at the announcement of Ibn Jau's death. However, once again Ibn Daud's credibility is vitiated by the fact that the story is practically a verbatim reproduction of an earlier incident recorded by an Arab chronicler. When in December 897, Sa'id, the Emir of Granada, was murdered, a man who had been unjustly treated by him mourned him in verses which said: "Who will feed and clothe the poor, now that he who was generosity itself lies in the grave!" "What!" cried an Arab who heard these verses, "dost thou sing these verses of him who had thee beaten?" "By Allah!" replied the poet, "even his unjust sentence benefits me. . . ."[221] Ibn Daud need not necessarily have had this incident in mind, but he certainly applied to his subject the sterotype reaction appropriate to the man and the occasion.[222] In the end, even Ibn Abitur is made to acknowledge the superiority of "the Rabbi," thereby vindicating R. Ḥanokh's claims.

R. Ḥanokh's opponents, by contrast, are discredited openly and by subtle digressions. Ibn Abitur's learning is acknowledged but then quickly tarnished by the report of faulty Aramaic in his letter to the Rabbi of Pechina.[223] Such, Ibn Daud seems to say obliquely, was the "great" Talmudist and poet who would set himself up against R. Ḥanokh. Very likely, too, the report that Ibn Abitur interpreted the whole Talmud in Arabic for al-Ḥakam is also inserted to reflect discredit upon him, particularly since the report, at least as Ibn Daud transmits it, can hardly be true.[224] The digression merely indicates that Ibn Abitur had been currying favor with the Muslim ruler even at the price of violating the injunction implied by the Rabbinic homily that God had forbidden Moses to commit the oral tradition to writing lest it fall into the hands of Gentiles.[225] By breaking the tradition associated with Moses, Ibn Abitur showed himself unworthy of succeeding R. Moses b. Ḥanokh.

Ibn Jau is depicted as a scheming and ruthless villain. He gains his power by chicanery,[226] supports a dissident Rabbi and threatens the legitimate one with brutality. Not a hint is dropped of his great popularity among poets and men of learning.[227] Can it be but a coincidence that in transmitting the text of the agreement of the Jews for the appointment of Ibn Jau as Nasi, Ibn Daud cites the text of the proposal made to Gideon?[228] The latter had piously replied, as befits a righteous judge: "I will not rule over you, neither shall my son rule over you; the Lord shall rule over you. (Jud. 8:23)." No so Ibn Jau. His only saving graces were his liberality with the poor, a virtue in which he had achieved renown,[229] and his loyalty to the Jews in refusing to exploit them for al-Manṣūr's coffers. But alas, even the latter virtue was gained only at the cost of failing to live up to the trust he had won after a solemn promise to his Muslim employer, al-Manṣūr.

Viewed in this light, the story of the four captives is not told for the purpose of vindicating R. Moses, so much as to justify R. Ḥanokh and the Ibn Falīja family. It was their cause and their activity which followed in the path laid out by the Author of all history, the path bringing the salvation and consolation of the Torah to Spain.

The modern student will doubtless look askance at the liberties Ibn Daud took with his facts, or, what is worse, dismiss him as a superstitious medieval who could not distinguish between fact and fancy. To anticipate any objections along these lines, it is but necessary to remember that Ibn Daud was a rationalist and critical philosopher and that *Sefer ha-Qabbalah* was written to validate Rabbinic polity.[230] In the tradition of the philosophers of his day, Ibn Daud felt that fables were a means to a higher end—the education of the mases to good conduct. Historical facts as such were probably of little value to him. What mattered most was their effect.[231] However, even in his moralistic tale he left the door open to the initiates of his day to see the fictional character and religio-political significance of a story he attributed to the divine plan.

APPENDIX

Independent Sources on the Four Captives

Obviously, no amount of literary criticism can undo positive testimony. This whole paper is, therefore, subject to the retort that it has not taken account of two pieces of evidence that would seem to confirm the basic veracity of the story. Granted that Ibn Daud "embellished" the story, it may still be contended, he almost certainly did not fabricate the basic fact that R. Moses and R. Hanokh came to Spain as captives and after their release rose to the religious leadership of the community of Cordova. Indeed, one might go even one step further and say with a fair measure of certainty that R. Moses and his son were probably one part of a foursome, who were captured and later ransomed by the Jews of different communities. For these two facts we have independent testimony by men who did not draw from Ibn Daud. If that is the case, Ibn Daud's embroideries appear in a new light. He merely converted a series of *historical* incidents into typological ones and then proceeded to amplify on the facts with motifs taken from archetypal stories that would fit the *dramatis personae* of the tenth century. If that is so, all we can hope to have succeeded in establishing is what most modern scholars had already assumed intuitively: to wit, that the dates, conversations, and other fanciful facts should be ignored, while the events themselves must be accepted as basically credible.

We grant readily that we may have to be content with this possible result. There is always the possibility of new evidence turning up to confirm one or more of the details related by Ibn Daud. On the other hand, it must be insisted that the independent evidence invoked hitherto in support of the story in *SHQ* is not really acceptable and that, in the final analysis, Ibn Daud is still the sole witness to the story.

And now to the independent "confirmations" of the story:

A

Writing probably in Egypt, ca. 1675, R. David Conforte reports the following:[232]

וכתב רבינו שמואל הלוי הנגיד במבוא התלמוד והראב"ד בס' הקבלה כי בימי רב
שרירא גאון ז"ל קרוב לשנת ד' אלפים תש"ן הן פחות הן יתר אירע מעשה שהיו
הולכים בספינה ממדינת בארי למדינת סבסטאן ד' חכמים גדולים וכו'!

Nor is this the only item of importance that Ibn Daud would seem to have drawn from Ibn Nagrela's Introduction to the Talmud. Elsewhere Conforte reports:

[233]I אך הראב"ד ז"ל בס' הקבלה כתב סדר רבנן סבוראי הדור הא' רב יוסי הוא
ראש רבנן סבוראי היה לראש אחר רבינא ל"ד שנה ובשנת כ"ד לגדולתו שהיא ד'
אלפים ור"ס ליצירה נחתם התלמוד וכ"כ במבוא התלמוד לרבינו שמואל הלוי הנגיד
ז"ל שנת דתל"ז ליציר' רבה יוסי הוא ראש רבנן סבוראי בסורא ל"ח [עד] ש' דרע"ד
ובשנת כ"ד לגדולתו נחתם התלמוד חתימת התלמוד דר"ס. ומשם עד שמת רבה
יוסי י"ד שנה שנת דרע"ד.

[234]II ובס' הקבלה כתב בענין זה הדור הב' תלמידי רב סימונא ורב עינא ולא
הוזכרו בשמותיהם כי הישיבות בטלו כמו חמשים שנה אחרי מות ר' סימונא מפני שנאת
מלכי פרס וגזרותיהם ע"כ. וכ"כ במבוא התלמוד לרבינו שמואל הלוי הנגיד ז"ל.

235‏III‏ ואחריהם בסורא היה ר' שישנא ונקרא משרשיא בר תתליפא ורב בוסתנאי
בפומבדיתא וכתב רבינו שמואל הלוי הנגיד במבוא התלמוד כי אלו הם סוף רבנן
סבוראי וכ"כ הראב"ד בס' הקבלה כי אלו הם סוף רבנן סבוראי והם המשה דורות
ושנותיהם קפ"ז.

236‏IV‏ ובמבוא התלמוד לרבינו שמואל הלוי הנגיד ז"ל ובס' הקבלה להראב"ד ז"ל
משמע שהדור הא' מראשי הישיבות של הגאונים מר (בר) רב חיננא גאון מנהר פקוד
היה ראש ישיבה חמש שנים ויש אומרים ח' שנים.

Leaving aside for the moment the passage on the four captives, the
first point to note is that Conforte has cited R. Samuel ha-Nagid in
corroboration of *SHQ* whenever the latter two disagree with the Epistle
of R. Sherira Gaon on an important datum. Three of these passages, indeed, are concerned with the crucial question of the division of eras,
Amoraic, Saboraic, and Gaonic. However, since, as has already been
demonstrated, the division of eras in *SHQ* is predicated on a consistent
use of symmetry,[237] the most that may possibly be argued is that Ibn
Daud appropriated the chronological scheme of R. Samuel ha-Nagid. If
that is the case, the presumption must be made that schematology was
integral to the Nagid's method of writing history and the embroideries
in the story of the four captives, particularly the problematic date 4750,
should be traced back to him. In other words, at worst we have analyzed
R. Samuel ha-Nagid's story and not Ibn Daud's.

But in reality, the likelihood is that the Nagid should not be involved
in this whole enigma at all.[238] In a paper read before the American Academy for Jewish Research on December 30, 1956,[239] Professor Mordecai
Margulies described the method and the style of R. Samuel ibn Nagrela's
Hilkhatha Gabratha, major fragments of which he had discovered among
the remains of the Cairo Geniza.[240] Everything in these fragments and
medieval quotations from the work, he insisted, pointed to strictly
halakhic discourses, with strong emphasis against the interpretations of
R. Hai Gaon, but with nothing of a methodological nature of the kind
preserved in the editions of the *Mebo ha-Talmud* ascribed to R. Samuel
ha-Nagid.[241] Margulies also called attention to the only known MS of
R. Samuel's *Mabo* containing the unpublished chronological portion of
the work, preserved in the Sassoon Library in Letchworth, England.[242]
This portion, too, he contended, had all the earmarks of coming from a
pen other than Ibn Nagrela's. What is more, it contained chronological
data on Ibn Nagrela himself and went way beyond the latter's time. In
fact, it seemed to stop at the very point that *SHQ* does.[243] Accordingly,
Margulies suggested that the enigmatic *Mabo* be ascribed to R. Samuel
ibn Ḥananiah ha-Nagid of Egypt, a (younger?) contemporary of Judah
ha-Levi and Ibn Daud.[244]

Thanks to the kindness of Mr. D. Sassoon, the owner of the only
known complete MS of Samuel ha-Nagid's Introduction to the Talmud, I

have been able to examine from photostats the chronological section of
that work for myself. This examination bore out every one of Prof.
Margulies' contentions on the chronological portion of the *Mabo*. The
latter is nothing more than an abridgement of *SHQ* with occasional
asides to confirm or reject Ibn Daud's data.[245] Secondly, the material on
Ibn Nagrela and the century after him are definitely not a gloss, for the
same anticipatory reference to the death of Joseph ibn Nagrela is included in the Gaonic section at the point parallel to the one in *SHQ*.[246]
Finally, the Nagid's chronicle is by and large a verbatim replica of *SHQ*,
with occasional efforts at paraphrase or even improving on Ibn Daud's
style. This may be illustrated by the Nagid's report of the story of the
four captives:[247]

ואחר חזקיהו ראש גלות וראש ישיבות הגאונים. יקודם (!) לכן היתה סיבה שנפסק
חוק[248] חוק הישיבות שהיה הולך אליהם מספרד וארץ המערב ואפריקה ומצרים וארץ
הצבי וכן היתה הסבה שנשבו ד' חכמים גדולים בספינה הולכת ממדינת בארי לספסטין
הא' ר' חושיאל אביו של ר' חננאל והא' ר' משה אביו של ר' חנוך ור' חנוך בנו
והשלישי ר' שמריה בר' אלחנן הד' לא נודע שמו. והשבאי לא הרגיש בהכמתם כי
נתעלמו ומכר את ר' שמריה באלכסנדריאה של מצרים ומשם עלה למצרים[249] למדינת
אל קורן והיה לראש ושם הוליד את ר' חננאל ז"ל ומכר את ר' משה עם ר' חנוך בנו
בקורדובה והיה לראש והיו לו תלמידים הרבה ומהם ר' יוסף בן אביתר. אז נשמע כל
חכמתו של ר' משה זה בכל ארץ ספרד ומערב ובאו תלמידים הרבה לקראת. ודבר זה
היה בימי רב שרירא בקרוב לשנת דתש"נ ועמד בקורדובה ונפטר שם ר' משה וישב על
כסאו ר' חנוך בנו ורבץ תורה גדולה ונפטר שנת דת"שע"ה קודם פטירת רב האיי
כ"ג שנה. ומפני סבה זו לא השיבו הקהלות חקם לישיבות בבל. ומגדולי תלמידיו של
ר' חנוך היה רב שמואל הנגיד וכו'.

This passage, even allowing for copyist's errors, is patently an abridgement of the one in *SHQ*, rather than the nucleus for Ibn Daud's amplification. Moreover, as already indicated, the chronicle continues with no
alteration of style or sign of hiatus to the next generation.

To conclude, if MS Sassoon is a copy of the chronological section of
R. Samuel ha-Nagid's *Mabo*—and there is no reason to question that it
is—the work drew on *SHQ* rather than vice versa. Accordingly, barring
any new evidence to the contrary, Conforte's statements on Ibn Nagrela
as Ibn Daud's source must be rejected.

B

The second bit of independent testimony on the story of the four captives comes from R. Menahem b. Solomon ha-Meiri's introduction to his
commentary on Pirqay Abot:[250]

ואחריו [= אחרי ר"ש הנגיד] היה ר' חננאל ואביו היה מארץ ספרד ושמו רבי'
חושיאל ונסבה ונתגלגל הדבר שעבר לארץ אפריקא במדינת לקירואן והוליד שם לר'

חננאל הנזכר .. ובאותו פרק נשבה ג״כ רב משה ו׳ חנוך ופדאוהו קהל קרטבא ורב
שלום הכיר הכמתו וסלק עצמו מן השררה ומנוהו לראש. והיה מתלמידיו ר׳ יוסף ז׳
אביותום והיה באותו הזמן ר׳ נסים שקבל מר׳ האיי ז״ל.

Since the Meiri (1) does not know the correct place of R. Ḥushiel's birth, (2) does not know of the capture of four captives, but only of R. Moses, and (3) does not know the name of R. Nathan the Pious,[251] but calls the teacher of Cordova R. Shalom, it follows that his statement on the capture and redemption of R. Moses must have derived from a source independent of *SHQ*. A careful examination of this passage will indicate that this reasoning is untenable.

In the first place, the reading ספרד as the birthplace of R. Ḥushiel is easily accounted for as a corruption of בארי.[252] Secondly, Prof. Alexander Marx long ago suggested that ורב שלום is obviously a corruption ורב שלהם.[253] Thirdly, even if נסבה and not נשבה is the correct reading in this passage,[254] it still does not follow that the Meiri drew on an independent source that told only of the capture of R. Moses and R. Ḥanokh, and not of the others. It is quite out of order to draw a conclusion from an isolated passage in the Meiri's introduction without regard to the whole of his historical essay.[255] Anyone who reads the whole of the Meiri's introduction cannot fail to notice that his most important single source was *SHQ*. As for the section on the later Rabbis, the Meiri may have been writing from memory, or his copy of *SHQ* may have been defective. Finally, the Meiri may not have had any interest in transmitting a full account of a local affair, which after all was not germane to his major purpose. The evidence from the Meiri, even if his own statement has been authentically transmitted, is of the flimsiest nature and cannot be invoked to confirm the historicity of the story in *SHQ*.

NOTES

1. Edited by A. Neubauer, *MJC*, I, 47–82. All references to the text are to this edition and are designated by page and line. The following study was written in connection with a new edition of *SHQ*, which I have been preparing on the basis of all available MSS. Where my text differs with Neubauer's I have indicated this in the notes.
2. The first portion of the story (*MJC*, I, 67:18–69:6) was translated into English by B. Halper, *Post-Biblical Hebrew Literature* (2 vols. Philadelphia, 1921), Translation [vol.], pp. 123–126. A fragment (*MJC*, I, 67:21–68:1) was translated by J. Starr, *The Jews in the Byzantine Empire* (Athens, 1939), p. 165 no. 111. For a German translation (of *MJC*, I, 67:19–69:1), cf. M. Auerbach, "Die Erzaehlung von den vier Gefangenen," *Jahres-Bericht des Rabbiner-Seminars zu Berlin fuer 1925, 1926, 1927 (5686–88)* (Berlin, 1928), pp. 2–6. The story is also to be found in the German translation of the whole of *SHQ* by M. Katz, *Abraham Ibn Daud's Sepher Ha-Kab-bala* (s.1., 1907), pp. 41–46, and in the Spanish translation of *SHQ* by J. Bages Torrida, *Sefer Ha-Kabbalah (El Libro de la Tradición)* (Granada, 1927), pp. 50–55. In the translation, I have annotated only those words and passages re-

quiring clarification for the understanding of the story or for the purposes of this study. A fuller commentary will be supplied in the forthcoming edition and translation.

3. Sc., prior to "the termination" of the Babylonian Gaonate with the death of R. Hai in 1038 and of his successor, Hezekiah the Exilarch in 1040, according to Ibn Daud (*MJC*, I, 66:23–24; 67:10–13, 18–19). The seventh section of *SHQ* follows immediately upon the previous one, which deals with the period of the Geonim, without any indication in the text of a new period. In Ibn Daud's scheme of things, the new period of Jewish history actually begins with Samuel ibn Nagrela and his contemporaries (cf. *MJC*, I, 73:24–25; 78:11). Technically speaking, therefore, the story of the four captives falls within the Gaonic period, while it serves as an introduction to the new and final era.

4. Some MSS: "The Holy One Blessed be He." For the style, cf. I Ki. 12:15.

5. Sc., of Babylonia; cf. n. 3.

6. There can be little doubt that this is the name underlying the various corruptions recorded in the MSS.—The MSS of *SHQ* fall into two classes, one of which is distinctly inferior to the other. The following are the readings of the name in question here and below, p. 157. (The sigla are the ones to be employed in the new edition.): of the superior class of MSS (= שׁ) אבן רחמאץ ק > ה אבן דחמאץ < ה אבן רמחאץ ה אבן דמחאץ > below אבן רמחאץ ה; of the inferior group (= ת) מר > בן דמחאן ל בן דמחאין < דל בן דמחץ < מ בן דמחץ: here only > בן דמאחץ

Disregarding the inconsequential variant of ד for ר at the beginning of the name (these two letters often being indistinguishable from each other in early Hebrew MSS), the admiral's name is recorded in three forms: Ibn Rum(a)ḥāṣ (אפ). Ibn Ruḥ(a)mās (הק), and Ibn Rumāḥiṣ (למר). In ד the final ץ was mistakenly read as ן, an error that is understandable enough in scribal transmission. Thus, there is absolutely no evidence in the MSS to support the emendation of the name to Ibn Riyaḥin (אבן רייאחין), as suggested by Jacob Mann, *Texts and Studies in Jewish History and Literature* (2 vols. Cincinnati and Philadelphia, 1931–35). I, 6, 110, and adopted by V. Aptowitzer, "R. Chuschiel und R. Chananel," *Jahresbericht der Israelitisch Theologischen Lehranstalt in Wien*, XXXVIII-XXXIX (1933), 24 n. 4, and by H. Z. Hirschberg in the Introduction to his edition of Nissim b. Jacob, *Ḥibbur Yafeh me-ha-Yeshu'ah* (Jerusalem, 5714), p. 14 n. 20. Moreover, this emendation requires a further emendation of the dates of these events given by Ibn Daud (cf. p. 159) and a correction of the name of the Muslim ruler in whose reign the events occurred, as fully recognized by Mann, *loc. cit.* and *JQR, NS* (1918), 169. These emendations and corrections are predicated on the assumption that the story before us contains an account of actual events, and that only Ibn Daud and his copyists brought confusion into the data. However, the evidence adduced below will indicate that Ibn Daud's dating of the events is deliberate and "accurate." Furthermore, Ibn Daud's choice of 'Abd ar-Raḥmān's reign for the capture of the four scholars was equally deliberate and "accurate." Since it was in his reign in which the capture was placed, Ibn Daud referred to a distinguished naval commander of the Spanish Caliph's regime. Lebrecht, Graetz and Auerbach, *op. cit.*, pp. 3, 4, 9, 34 (where refs. to earlier discussions are given) recognized full well that the "ben Damāhin" recorded in the editions represents a corruption of the name of the admiral of the fleet ['Abd ar-Raḥmān] ibn Rumāḥiṣ, who served under 'Abd ar-Raḥmān III an-Nāṣir and under al-Hakam; cf. Ibn Khaldun, *The Muqaddimah* (3 vols. Translated by F. Rosenthal. New York, 1958), II, 40; al-Makkari, *The History of the Mohammedan Dynasties in Spain* (2 vols. Translated by P. de Gayanges. London, 1840–43), II, 159; A. Ashtor, *Qorot ha-Yehudim bi-Sefarad ha-Muslimit* (Jerusalem, 1960), p. 289 n. 11. However, in view of the testimony of MSS הק (and the transposition of the long vowel in אפ), there is a second possibility, which I suggest with all diffidence. The reading אבן רחמאץ may represent an abbreviation of the name or *Kunya* of another (?) distinguished admiral of these regimes, [Ghālib] *ibn* ['Abd ar-] *Raḥm*[ān] *aṣ-Ṣ*[iklabī]. If Ibn Daud had any real events in mind when he gave the names of the Caliph and admiral, he may have been referring to the forays of 955–57 conducted by Ghālib under the orders of 'Abd ar-Raḥmān III, when a Spanish vessel captures a Fatimid ship en route from Sicily to Alexandria, an act which precipitated a series of naval conflicts; cf. R. Dozy, *Histoire des Musulmans d'Espagne* (3 vols. Edited by E. Lévi-Provençal. Leiden, 1932), II, 164f. (=R. Dozy, *Spanish Islam*. [Translated by F. G. Stokes. London, 1913], pp. 438f.). If that is the case, Ibn Daud's date for the capture of the four scholars is still "correct"! Cf. p. 165. Ibn Daud, of course, is not to be held responsible for accurate knowledge of the admiral's travel orders ("to capture Christian ships"), which are seemingly contradicted by the conflict with Fatimid vessels; cf. Auerbach, *op. cit.*, p. 34. Ibn Daud had to designate "Christian ships" to explain the capture of scholars traveling on a "Christian" vessel.

7. Reigned 912–961 (proclaimed himself Caliph in 929).

8. No such place is known. For the various conjectures, cf. Auerbach, *op. cit.*, pp. 6 (where it should be added that Rapoport finally suggested Sebaste of Cilicia), 16, 34f. (to which should be added a ref. to N. Bruell, *Jahrbuecher fuer Jeudische Geschichte und Literatur*, IX (1899), 105, who first suggested that the name is a corruption of Siponto). The most likely equivalent of the Hebrew name is something corresponding to Sebastin. To be sure, there was a city of Sebastea in Asia Minor (cf. G. Le Strange, *The Lands of the Eastern Caliphate* [Cambridge, 1905], p. 142 and A. A. Vasiliev, *History of the Byzantine Empire* [Madison, Wis., 1952 (1958)], p. 351), but why should four Jewish scholars have gone there in connection with the purpose given by Ibn Daud?

9. For the various interpretations of this phrase, cf. Auerbach, *op. cit.*, pp. 8ff., 35. To these may be added A. Kohut, *Aruch Completum*, III, 205, s.v. הכנסה, IV, 228 s.v. כלה; B. Halper, *op. cit.*, p. 123; J. Starr, *op. cit.*, pp. 3 and 22f., n. 3, all of whom understand הכנסת כלה as "the collection of money for an academy." Aptowitzer contends that unless this explanation is adopted, Ibn Daud's introductory statement—that as a result of the capture the income of the Babylonian academies was cut off—is left hanging in mid-air. The story can only be understood on the theory that since the income of the academies has been cut off, the four scholars had to be despatched to raise funds. However, Aptowitzer's contention is his own theory, not Ibn Daud's. The latter makes it quite clear that were it not for *the capture* of the four scholars, the income of the academies would probably have continued to flow without interruption; cf. *MJC*, I, 68:23–69:1; 69:18–19. Most scholars have rejected the explanations of Frankel and Halevy, cited by Auerbach, that הכנסת כלה means here what it usually does, attending to and at wedding ceremonies, on the grounds that "the leading of a bride to the bridal chamber" should hardly constitute a suitable motive for four scholars to undertake the kind of trip described by Ibn Daud. Granted! However, this picayune motive has at least idiomatic usage to support it. On the other hand, the loftier motive read into the phrase by the modern scholars listed above rests on a far-fetched meaning of *Kallah*, one which Ibn Daud uses nowhere else. Had Ibn Daud wanted to say academy, he would have employed the term "yeshibah," as he does regularly. Nor it is valid to contend that הכנסת כלה is an idiomatic term for fund-raising activities of the academies, for that remains to be proved. On the other hand, the translation suggested here rests on a well attested usage of the term *Kallah*; cf. Kohut, *op. cit.*, IV, 227–228; JE, VII, 423 s.v. "Kallah"; *MJC*, II, 87–88. The use of הכנסה for "an assemblage" is one of the many Arabisms in which *Sefer ha-Qabba-lah* abounds and represents a Hebrew counterpart to جمع or اجتماع. Moreover, our translation is indirectly supported by the reference to the *Kallah* assemblies in the "editions" of Midrash Tanḥuma Noah, par. 3:

ולפיכך קבע הקב״ה שתי ישיבות לישראל שיהיו הוגין בתורה יומם ולילה ומתקבצין שתי פעמים
בשנה באדר ובאלול מכל המקומות

Note the same usage in the report of Nathan the Babylonian, *MJC*, II, 87:

... לצורך הוצאת התלמידים הבאים מכל המקומות שהם יושבים ומתקבצים ובאין מכל המקומות
בחדש כלה

The Arabic equivalent of מתקבצין would be يجتمعون and the derived substantive would be اجتماع or جمع. This, in turn, could easily become הכנסה in medieval Hebrew. Our translation supplies a worthy motive for the trip of the four scholars and retains the spirit of Ibn Daud's insistence that the trip is a case of God's disposal (dispersion) and man's proposal (an assemblage). Ibn Daud assumes, of course, that his reader will understand how close a connection there was between *Kallah* conventions and the income of the academies; cf. *MJC*, II, 87f.

10. I.e., might she hope for resurrection despite the fact that her body would be consumed by the fish of the sea? On the widespread notion that complete destruction of the body precludes the possibility of resurrection, cf. S. Lieberman, *Shkiin* (Jerusalem, 1939), p. 58; M. Stein, "Mother Earth in Old Hebrew Literature (Hebrew)," *Tarbiz*, IX (1937–38), 257–277, who associates this conception with the widespread fear of lack of burial; cf. esp. p. 273 where our story is cited.

11. Ps. 68:23.

12. As noted by many scholars, this story is virtually a verbatim reproduction of the account in B. Gittin 57b (and parallels) of Jewish martyrs who committed suicide to preserve their chastity. Cf. below, pp. 165–166.

13. Sc., to Jews who ransomed him and set him free, a common phenomenon in the middle ages.

14. Heb., *Miṣrayyim* (Egypt) = Arabic, *Miṣr*; cf. *JE*, V, 60–61; J. Mann, *JQR, NS*, VII (1917), 479f.; M. Auerbach, *op cit.*, p. 4 n. 11.

15. I.e., R. Moses. It goes without saying that the young Ḥanokh was ransomed along with his father.

16. Sc., the Jews.

17. Most MSS and eds. (other than *MJC*) read כנסת המדרש; *midrash* = *bet ha-midrash*, the house of study or college.

18. The Jewish *dayyan* (judge) performed the same functions as the Muslim *qāḍi*; he adjusted litigations and lectured on law and religion.

19. MSS ש read here היה < ה גדול > ר' נתן חסיד וגדול. MSS ת corrected this to ר' נתן וחסיד גדול היה.

20. "Used to preside": lit., there was there.

21. Heb., היו עושין מדרש, which has been translated "they arranged discussions" (Halper), and "stellten sie Untersuchungen an" (Auerbach). Although the phrase is reminiscent of the classical עשה תורה (on which, cf. S. Abramson in *Leshonenu, Qobeṣ Meyuhad* [Jerusalem, 5714], pp. 61–65), the phrase עשה מדרש in that sense would be totally inappropriate here. Moreover, *midrash* does not mean "discussions" or "Untersuchungen." Had Ibn Daud wished to say "they acquired knowledge" or "discussed law," he would have said so much more simply and directly. Here again, I would suggest we have an Arabism, corresponding to مدرسة جعلوا (or مدرسا اسا) "they conducted a school."

22. The Hebrew, ועולין ויורדין, makes no sense if translated literally ("they went up and down"). The translations of Halper ("[conducted] arguments") and of Auerbach ("und disputierten dabei") are manifestly makeshift efforts to read some sense into an impossible phrase. My own translation is also makeshift, but approximates a metaphoric usage of "the sacrifice of greater or lesser value" known as קרבן עולה ויורד. Cf. also the comment of R. Gershom on עולה ויורד, a slaughtering knife that is "uneven" (Hullin 17b), cited by E. Ben Yehuda, *Thesaurus*, IX, 4501 n. 2. Maimonides *Hilkot Sheḥitah* 1:17 interprets the latter phrase to mean a knife that is curved "like a snake." Perhaps Ibn Daud means ועולין ויורדין in the sense of "tortuously, not very smoothly, unevenly."

23. *Tosef. Yoma* 4(3):2, ed. Zuckermandel, p. 187 1. 1. That Ibn Daud does not specify the Tosefta as the source of the statement is not surprising in view of the mass of evidence adduced by Prof. Saul Lieberman showing that many medieval authorities wove quotations from the Tosefta into their discussions of the text of the Talmud quite freely and without specifying their sources; cf. S. Lieberman, *Tosefeth Rishonim* (4 vols. Jerusalem, 1937–39). II, 8–15; *idem, Tosefta Ki-Fshutah, Zeraʿim* (2 vols. New York, 1955), II, 637 n.1.

24. R. Nathan apparently explained the passage to mean that the high priest must immerse himself in the ritual bath before each sprinkling of blood on the altar on the Day of Atonement. To this, R.Moses objected that the number of immersions would be in excess of the five prescribed in *M. Yoma* 3:3. Cf. A. Auerbach, *op cit.*, pp. 5 n. 16, 36f.; S. Assaf, *Meqorot le-Toledot ha-Ḥinukh be-Yisrael* (4 vols. Tel Aviv, 1930–47), II, 16 nn. 3, 5, and esp. Prof. Saul Lieberman's forthcoming commentary on *Tosefta Moʿed*, where R. Nathan's error is discussed fully. I am profoundly indebted to Prof. Lieberman for the source of the quotation and for elucidating this whole passage for me.

25. Heb. פסיקתם. In its original sense פסיקה (Aram. פסיקתא) denotes "a section" or "a chapter"; cf. L. Zunz, *Ha-derashot be-Yisrael* (Edited by C. Albeck. Jerusalem, 5707) pp. 84f., 348 nn. 52–55; H. L. Strack, *Introduction to the Talmud and Midrash* (Philadelphia, 1931 [1945]), p. 211. However, in the present context the word makes far better sense if it is understood as corresponding to the Arabic قضية. The whole clause would thus correspond to an Arabic حتّى يقضوا التلامذة قضيتهم "until the students had completed their case (i.e., the legal problem covered in the lesson of the day)."

26. I.e., instead of waiting for the litigants to enter and present their cases, as was his wont (Auterbach).

27. Lit., guest; i.e., not a regular member of the academy.

28. Sc., inasmuch as he taught R. Nathan the meaning of the law; cf. *Pereq Qinyan Torah* (= *Abot* 6:) 3 and B. M. 33a (view of R. Yose).

29. I.e., directing their legal inquiries abroad; cf. immediately below.

30. Gaon of Pumeditha, 968–1006 (or 1004); cf. J. Mann, *Texts and Studies*, I, 109 n. 2.

31. Reading with MSS ש: בקרוב לשנת < ה משנת > ‏

32. = 989/990 C.E.—Since this date is of crucial importance to our study, we give here the various MS readings. MSS ת read דתש"ן. Of the ש class, the readings are: אבהם דש"ן י דש"ל while פ is corrected on the margin to דתש"ן. Cf. below, pp. 174–175.

33. Both spelling and pronunciation of this name are uncertain. In each instance where the name appears, the MSS vary so widely that any measure of certainty appears beyond reach. I have adopted the form פליגא, which is the one recorded, albeit not consistently, by MSS פק (of the ש class). Professor Shraga Abramson has called my attention to his note in *Sinai*, XXVI (1949–50), 208 on a poem by Isaac b. Khalfon addressed to a Joseph פלגה, who, he suggests, may be a member of this family.

34. Sc., the descendants of R. Moses and R. Ḥanokh.

35. Lit., had.

36. Here again (cf. n. 33), the MSS give no certain evidence on the exact pronunciation of the name. Ibn Abitur himself claimed that the name represented a combination of two words, שוט אנש, "the whip (or scourge) of man" and that it was applied to an ancestor of his because of the latter's powers of capital punishment; cf. Ibn Abitur's letter as edited by J. Mann, "Varia on the Gaonic Period (Hebrew)," *Tarbiz*, VI (1934–35), 87 1. 18–88, 24. Whatever the merits of this etymology, the first and final letters must clearly have been pronounced as "sh." This conclusion seems to be supported by the pejorative interpretations given this name by Ibn Abitur's enemies; cf. J. Mann, *loc. cit.*, and *JQR, NS*, XI (1921), 456 n. 19; S. Assaf. *Meqorot u-Mehqarim* (Jerusalem, 5706), p. 115 n. 4.—In transliterating the name, I have adopted the form suggested by the spelling (שטנאש) in the fragment published by J. Mann, *The Jews in Egypt and in Palestine Under the Fatimid Caliphs* (2 vols. Oxford, 1920–22), II, 59; cf. also, Judah al-Ḥarizi, *Taḥkemoni* (Edited by I. Toporovsky. Tel Aviv, 1952), ch. 3, p. 44.

37. Son and successor of 'Abd ar-Raḥmān III, reigned 961–976.

38. I.e., his lineage, cf. n. 36.

39. Although awkward in English, I have retained the order of the Hebrew to show how he was referred to.

40. Sc., Ibn Shaprut.

41. What follows illustrates the external manifestation of the factional fight.

42. Madīnat al-Zahrā' was the royal city some five miles west of Cordova founded by 'Abd ar-Raḥmān III in November 936; cf. R. Dozy, *op. cit.*, II, 174 (Eng. trans., p. 446). E. Lévi-Provençal, "Madinat al-Zahrā'," *EI*, III, 92–93; *idem, La Péninsule Ibérique Au Moyen-Age* (Leiden, 1938) French trans. p. 117; G. C. Miles, *The Coinage of the Umayyads of Spain* (New York, 1950). pp. 43–46. I have given preference to al-Zahrā', for Ibn Daud seems to hint that the Muslim ruler involved was al-Ḥakam. On the other hand it is conceivable that Ibn Daud had in mind *madīnat al-Zahīra* (cf. *EI, loc. cit.*), the capital established by al-Manṣūr in 978. Whatever the case may be, it is illegitimate to argue in favor of the latter identification from Ibn Daud's statement that Ibn Abitur made off to "the academy of R. Hai," for, as is already fairly obvious, Ibn Daud was not particularly careful about the synchronization of names. R. Hai did not become Gaon until 1003–04 (J. Mann, *Texts and Studies*, I, 109 n. 2), which is far too late a date in which to place Ibn Abitur's expulsion. By 992 Ibn Abitur was already well established as a judge in Egypt; s. Assaf, *Meqorot u-Mehqarim*, p. 116.

43. This entourage (whether factual or not) was patterned after that of the Exilarch in Bagdad; cf. Benjamin of Tudela, *Itinerary* (Edited by M. N. Adler. London, 1907) Hebrew text p. 40, Eng. trans. p. 40. The purpose of these trips to al-Zahrā' was for each side to argue its case before al-Ḥakam, who finally decided the issue in favor of R. Ḥanokh.

44. Cf. n. 39.

45. For ברח in this sense, cf *MJC*, I. 66:9.

46. MSS פק read אי באגנה, which J. Mann, "Varia." *Tarbiz*, V (1933–34), 283 n. 156 suggested emending to עיר, since Pechina was not an island. This emendation is totally

unwarranted, even if אי is not a later gloss, for Pechina was a kind of peninsula and could be referred to as *jezīra* (= אי); cf. E. Lévi-Provençal, *La Péninsule Ibérique*, Translation pp. 47–50.

47. Sc., to the death of Ibn Shatnāsh.

48. I.e., province.

49. MSS ת read here ארץ תרכונה = Tarragona. Of the ש MSS בפק read הארץ an obvious evasion of a misunderstood name. Two remaining MSS give suggestive corruptions: א לארץ תבראנה ה ארץ תאכדנא. As noted by Bages, *op. cit.*, p. 53 n. 2, the reading of ה clearly suggests Takurunna, the province in the southern part of Spain; cf. E. Lévi-Provençal in *EI*, IV, 631; *idem, La Péninsule Ibérique*, Trans. p. 78. Although Tarragona was also the name of a province, it appears to me unlikely that that is what Ibn Daud meant here. The Arabs always spell Tarragona طرکونة for which the Hebrew equivalent would be טרכונה; the distinction between ט and ת was usually carefully maintained in Spanish Hebrew translations. Moreover, the corruption of the relatively unknown תאכרנה to תרכונה is far more easily explained than vice versa. Finally, it should be noted that Takurunna (Ronda) and its mountain range were a fairly recalcitrant area and difficult to control. It is precisely from such an area that one might expect protestations against taxes; cf. R. Dozy, *op. cit.*, II, 3ff. (Eng. trans. pp. 308ff.).

50. These are the *darāhim ja'fariya*, gold dinars minted at Madīnat al-Zahrā' (cf. n. 42) by al-Ḥakam between 967/68 and 969/70; cf. G. C. Miles, *op. cit.*, pp. 323–330.

51. I.e., the humiliated delegation of Takurunna.

52. Lit., let us swear.

53. Viz., of funds and of goods.

54. Apart from eds. and MS י, all other MSS read: ונסים שמעלים על ראשי הדגלים. However, י is obviously corrupt here, for it records the clause as ופסים כמנהג ישמעאלים הלובשים מלבושים. This reading is not attested by any other MS and is consequently of no weight.

55. Heb., אומנו, which *SHQ* probably uses for the Arabic *ḥājib* ("chamberlain"), al-Manṣūr's official title; cf. the legends on coins in G. C. Miles, *op. cit.*, pp. 60f.

56. Lit., wrote him a sheet (=كتب له رقعة).

57. In 976/77 or 979/80, Sijilmasa in Morocco fell to the Umayyad armies; cf G. S. Colin, "Sidjilmasa," *EI*, IV, 404; G. C. Miles, *op. cit.*, pp. 46f.

58. MSS ש spell the name in the following ways: א דיונא ב דויירה ה דנירא פ דאוירנא. MSS ת spell the name דוירנא or דוירנא. The correct spelling is thus preserved only by ב whose orthography corresponds to the Arabic نهر دويرة cf. Ibn Idhārī, *Kitāb al-Bayān al-Mughrib* (2 vols. Edited by G. S. Colin and E. Lévi-Provençal. Leiden, 1951), II. 295; cf. also *ibid.*, p. 178 (very bot.) وادي دوير. MSS א and ה reflect the change of ר and ו respectively into a נ, while פ and MSS ת reflect the corruption of דוירוה to דוירנה.

59. Lit., over all of them. For the rendition of this and other phrases of the document, I have drawn on the translation in Baron, *SRH*, V, 44.

60. "Community" (קהל) signifies here as elsewhere in *SHQ* the Jewish community.

61. This formula is taken verbatim from Jud. 8:22.

62. Lit., gifts.

63. Cf. II Sam. 19:7, from which may be derived the force of Ibn Falija's complaint. The IBN Falijas had probably labored hard and suffered great humiliation for the sake of their kinsman, R. Ḥanokh. The latter now showed less concern for their relief than he did for Ibn Jau's fate.

64. As has been noted by many scholars, there is an obvious error in this statement, for, as Ibn Daud himself states (*MJC*, I, 66:23), R. Hai died in 4798, or twenty-three years after R. Ḥanokh. The reading of Abraham Zacuto, *Yuḥasin ha-Shalem* (Edited by H. Filipowski. London, 1857 [Frankfurt a.M., 1925]), p. 211 placing R. Ḥanokh's death in 4785 is an obvious correction. On the other hand, the reading at this point in the abridgement of *SHQ* by Samuel ha-Nagid (in the chronological section of his *Mebo ha-Talmud*, cf. below, p. 127f.) is כ"ג שנה, which is the way most scholars prefer to emend our text; cf. A. Harkavy, "Le-toledot R. Samuel ha-Nagid," *Meassef* (Edited by L. Rabinowitz. St. Petersberg, 1902), p. 43 n. 3; A. Ashtor, *op. cit.*, p. 308 n. 30.

65. Sc., of Babylonia.

66. The four captives and R. Ḥanokh.

67. Sc., thus making them independent of the academies of Babylonia.

68. Sc., of Tabernacles. The day of R. Ḥanokh's accident was the one now known as *Simhat Torah;* cf. *JE*, XI, 364f. The annual completion in Diaspora communities of the cycle of the reading of the Torah on this day dates back to the Talmudic times; cf. B. Meg. 31a.

69. Lit., the ark.

70. For a survey of opinions and bibliographical references until 1928, cf. M. Auerbach, *op. cit.*, pp. 6ff. For further studies, cf. V. Aptowitzer, *op. cit.*; S. Assaf, "Li-Semiḥat ha-Merkazim ha-Yisraeliyyim bi-Tequfat ha-Geonim," *Ha-Shiloah*, XXXV (1918), 276f., 408f., 506f., *idem,* Review of Aptowitzer's "R. Chuschiel and R. Chananel," *Kirjath Sepher*, X (1933–34), 356; L. Blau, *op. cit.* below, n. 73; H. Z. Hirschberg, *op. cit.*, pp. 14f.; Z. Jawitz, *Toledot Yisrael* (14 vols. Berlin and Tel-Aviv, 5725–5740), X, 122–126, 238–243; J. Mann, *Texts and Studies,* I, 86, 110f., 205; *idem,* "Varia on the Gaonic Period" *Tarbiz*, V (1933–34), 286f.; M. Margulies, ed., *Halachoth Kezuboth* (Jerusalem, 1942), p. 9 n. 68; Baron, *SRH,* V, 46f.; H. H. Ben Sasson, *On Jewish History in the Middle Ages* (Hebrew) (Tel-Aviv, 1958); pp. 107–108; A. Ashtor, *op. cit.*, pp. 155f.

71. The grain of truth would seem to be that only R. Moses and his son suffered the mishap of capture and the subsequent good fortune as recounted by Ibn Daud. Two notable exceptions to this cautious stand are represented by Ludwig Blau (cf. below, n. 75) and Simon Eppenstein, *Beitraege zur Geschichte und Literatur in geonaeischen Zeitalter* (Berlin, 1913), pp. 149ff., and esp. 211ff., who dismiss the whole story outright.

72. The most vigorous defense of the story in recent times has been made by Jacob Mann, who did not hesitate to emend names and dates, and to devise a theory of two Ḥushiels in Qairawan in order to smoothe the embarrassing contradictions to Ibn Daud posed by the letter published by Schechter; cf. next note. For Mann's theory, cf. refs. in M. Auerbach, *op. cit.*, pp. 15f., 19f. and above, n. 70.

73. S. Schechter, "Geniza Specimens. A letter of Chushiel," *JQR*, XI (1899), 643–650.

74. Cf. J. Mann, "Varia," *Tarbiz* V, 283ff., VI, 84ff.; S. Assaf, *Meqorot u-Meḥqarim,* pp. 115–118. On his prolific poetical writing in the Orient, cf. M. Zulay, "Bayn Kotlay ha-Makhon le-Ḥeqer ha-Shirah ha-'Ibrit," *Alei Ayin: The Salman Schocken Jubilee Volume* (Jerusalem, 5708–5712), pp. 91, 100, 110, 114.—In Egypt Ibn Abitur continued to fight against his Spanish opponents, who apparently tried to give him no rest; cf. J. Mann, *The Jews in Egypt,* I, 69f., II, 59f. and the refs. at the beginning of this note; cf. also A. Ashtor, *op. cit.*, pp. 238–242, 246.—Is the vitriolic poem by Joseph b. Isaac Sefaradi published by I. Davidson by him? If so, is R. Ḥanokh its target? Cf. I. Davidson, *Liturgical and Secular Poetry (= Genizah Studies in Memory of Doctor Solomon Schechter,* III. New York, 1928), p. 320. The poem is hardly a satire, but a series of violent oaths!

75. Cf. L. Blau, "Die Vier Gefangenen Talmudlehrer," *Festkrift I. Anlendning af Professor David Simonsens 70-Aarige Foldesdag* (Copenhagen, 1923), pp. 129–133. The legend of the Salerno medical school was taken by Blau from W. v. Brun, "Die Bedeutung Salernos fuer die Medizine," *Neue Jahrbuecher fuer das Klassische Altertum Geschichte und Deutsche Literatur,* XLV (1920), 385. V. Brunn states that in reality nothing is known of the origins of the school of Salerno other than the names of its legendary founders. "Daraus ersehen wir hoechstens, dass die Schule von vornherein auf freiheitslichster Grundlage errichtet war und dass die Zugehoerigkeit zur irgendeiner fremder Nation oder einer andern Konfession kein Hindernis fuer den Eintritt in die Schule gebildet hat." Blau, following v. Brunn, gives no date for this legend. In any event, the motif of this tradition is precisely the opposite of Ibn Daud's. The latter speaks of the dissemination of knowledge from one spot to remote corners of the Mediterranean area. The Salerno legend represents the accumulation of the wisdom of all peoples within the walls of one school.

76. For the significance of "the divine plan," cf. above, p. 170.

77. Cf. *MJC*, I, 56:17; 63:23; 75:3; 80:4, 8f., 23.

78. Cf. Tosefta Pes. 4:1–2 (ed. Zuckermandel, pp. 162f.); B. Pes. 66a; Yer. Pes. 6:1, f. 33a.—Baron, *SRH,* V, 315 n. 65 rightly calls our story "a typical folk-tale about a career from rags to riches"; cf. also the midrashic motif discussed above, p. 176.

79. B. Gittin 57b. For midrashic parallels, cf. below, n. 89. This and other suspicious circumstances were emphasized by S. Eppenstein, *op. cit.*, p. 211.

80. For a full bibliography and classification of the forms of the legend, cf. I. Davidson, *Thesaurus of Mediaeval Hebrew Poetry* (4 vols. New York, 1924–1933), II, 183, No. 152, IV,

301 No. 152. To Davidson's scheme there may be added a possible fourth type, according to which the prayer was explained as a memorial for persons who actually died as martyrs; cf. Asher b. Saul of Lunel, "Sefer ha-Minhagot" in S. Assaf, *Sifran shel Rishonim* (Jerusalem, 1935), pp. 144–145. This "Sefer ha-Minhagot" was composed ca. 1210–1215, according to Assaf, *ibid.*, p. 125. Most recently, versions of types 1 and 3 were reprinted by B. Klar, ed., *Megillat Ahima'as* (Jerusalem, 1944), pp. 55–56. Cf. also next note.

81. To the brief form of the legend cited by Davidson, *loc. cit.*, from *Sedah la-Derek*, may be added the similar statement in Nathan b. Judah, "*Sefer ha-Mahkim*" (Edited by J. Freimann), *Ha-'Eshkol*, VI (1909), 126.

82. 1) The theme is present in the form in which the sages are not named (Davidson's type 1); cf. A. Neubauer, "The Early Settlement of the Jews in Southern Italy," *JQR*, IV (1892), 616–619 (second story beg. with ע״א). In this source the theme of helmless ships may have been grafted on to an original form in which the Jews arrived at one port on one ship. 2) The motif is found in connection with the tradition ascribing the prayer to Joseph, Benjamin, and Samuel (Davidson's type 2). 3) It appears in the form recorded by Samuel of Bamberg, ascribing the prayer to Amittai, Shefatyah, and Yosifyah; cf. J. Perles, "Bibliographische Mittheilungen aus Muenchen," *MGWJ*, XXV (1876), 373.

83. Cf. H. Gross, *Gallia Judaica* (Paris, 1897) pp. 74f.; A. Neubauer, *loc. cit.*, in n. 80; J. Perles, *loc. cit.*

84. J. Starr, *op. cit.*, pp. 115, 165.

85. H. Lewy, "Imaginary Journeys from Palestine to France," *Journal of the Warburg Institute*, I (1937–38), 252 n. 2.—I owe the reference to Lewy's paper to Professor Elias Bickerman.

86. *Abot de R. Nathan* (Edited by S. Schechter. Vienna, 1887. [New York, 1945]), II, 7, p. 20.

87. Note the use of the identical words ספינות נשים אנשים וטף׳ ג׳ ומלא in the *we-hu Raḥum* legends published by Neubauer and Perles; cf. above, n. 82.

88. In the passage in *Abot de R. Nathan* the three ships are an incidental detail representing the round number three; cf. Schechter's note there, p. 20 n. 23.

89. *Midrash Ekhah* 1:45 (to Lam. 1:16); *Midrash Ekhah Rabbah* (Edited by S. Buber. Vilna, 188), pp. 81–82. The two recensions of the Midrash differ here in minor details. The translation is taken with some minor modification, from *Midrash Rabbah*. Lamentations (Translated by A. Cohen. London, Soncino Press, 1939), pp. 124–125.—Other versions of this legend appear in *Midrash Zuta* (Edited by S. Buber, Berlin 1894), p. 64 par. 13 and B. Gittin 57b.—The characteristic common to all of these sources is that they speak in terms of round numbers: B. Gittin 57 mentions 400 children, a stock round number in Rabbinic literature (cf. below, n. 115); *Midrash Zuta* speaks of 70 virgins, while the sources cited in the text speak of 3 shiploads of people.—The motif of punishment by exile in ships goes back, of course, to Deut. 28:68, in explanation of which Midrash Haggadol *ad loc.* cites the passage from *Midrash Ekhah*. Ibn Daud, or his source, may, indeed, have had this verse in mind, for the story of the four captives contains a fulfillment of the second part of the verse, "and there ye shall be sold unto your enemies." That this is not the plain sense of the verse is of no consequence to a homiletician.

90. Cf. above, pp. 168f.—On the other hand, the dependence of the *we-hu Raḥum* tradition upon early Jewish martyrological genres (of which the suicide to preserve chastity is one form), may be indicated further by the presence (in Davidson's type 1) of the motif of the taunt by the captor, "If you are of the seed of Abraham, I shall test you by fire as Abraham was tested," or "I shall test you with the test of fire to which Hananiah, Mishael and Azariah were subjected." On this taunt in early martyrologies, cf. G. D. Cohen, "The Story of Hannah and Her Seven Sons in Hebrew Literature (Hebrew)", *Mordecai M. Kaplan Jubilee Volume* (2 vols. Edited by M. Davis, New York, 1953), Hebrew Vol. p. 116 and n. 38 there. The taunt is thus an alternate form for the martyrology of suicide recorded in Midrash Ekhah. The authors of the *we-hu Raḥum* legend appropriated one form, while the author of "The Four Captives" appropriated the other.

91. H. Lewy, *op. cit.*, pp. 251–253.

92. Cf. *MJC*, I, 61:21.

93. Cf. above, pp. 167f.

94. Petrus Alphonsi, *Dialogi* in J. Migne, ed., *Patrologia Latina*, CLVII, 571c: "In

secunda [sc. captivitate] autem tot et tanta eis opprobria, et tam inaudita intulerunt . . . Occisi quidem sunt, sunt et cremati, et captivorum more venditi, adeoque crevit illa venditio, donec pro uno argenteo triginta darentur captivi, nec tamen inveniebatur qui emeret, sicut promisit Moyses dicens: *Venderis inimicis tuis in servos et ancillas et non erit qui emat* (Deut 28:68); Naves etiam ipsis impletae, sine ullo remige vel gubernaculo vagari per pelagus sunt dimissae, ad ipsorum dedecus et vilitatem. Praeterea postquam in hac captivitate dejecti estis, intolerabilia vobis dabantur mandata etc." The parallelism between the motif of the four captives and the passage in Petrus Alphonsi was first pointed out to me by Professor Saul Lieberman.

95. For Alphonsi's use of Jewish material, cf. S. Lieberman, *Shekiin* (Jerusalem, 1939), pp. 19f., 27f.; A. Lukyn Williams, *Adversus Judaeos* (Cambridge, 1935), pp. 235ff.

96. Cf. H. Usener, *Die Sintfluthsagen* (Bonn. 1889), chs. III–IV, esp. pp. 108, 136; N. Delehaye, *The Legends of the Saints* (New York, 1907), pp. 30f, 52. On myths of exposure and rescue in a boat set adrift, cf. S. Thompson, *Motif-Index of Folk Literature* (6 vols. Bloomington, 1955–58), V, 300 S 141. A closely related motif is one in which the sea (= god) cares for a hero or treasure; cf. B. Nelson and J. Starr, "The Legend of the Divine Surety and the Jewish Moneylender," *Annuaire de l'Institut de Philologie et d'Histoire Orientales et Slaves*, VII (1939–44), 304ff., and esp. 306.

97. A. Neubauer, "The Early Settlement," pp. 619–620.

98. Cf. *ibid.*, pp. 618, 620; J. Perles, *op. cit.*, p. 373.

99. Cf. A. Neubauer and A. E. Cowley, *Catalogue of the Hebrew Manuscripts in the Bodleian Library* (2 vols. Oxford, 1886–1906), I, 418 no. 1204; and cf. the statement of R. Eleazar Roqeah on the tradition of his masters in S. Assaf, "Li-Ṣemiḥat ha-Merkazim," pp. 282f.; B. Klar, *op. cit.*, p 57 and notes *ad loc.*, p. 128.

100. J. Perles, *op. cit.* On Samuel of Bamberg, cf. M. Brann, A. Freimann et al., *Germania Judaica* (Frankfurt a.M. and Breslau, 1917–1934), p. 18; V. Aptowitzer, *Mabo le-Sefer Rabiah* (Jerusalem, 1938), p. 408; E. E. Urbach, *The Tosaphists* (Hebrew) (Jerusalem, 1955), pp. 354ff.

101. Cf. E. E. Urbach, *op. cit.*, p. 352.

102. Cf. H. Gross, *op. cit.*, p. 75; A. Neubauer, "The Early Settlement," p. 618 n. 1. Whatever the second point of debarkation was in this version, it manifestly was not a French or German one!

103. Cf. I. Elbogen, *Der Juedische Gottesdienst in seiner geschichtlichen Entwicklung* (Leipzig, 1913), p. 77; J. Starr, *op. cit.*, pp. 70ff.; B. Klar, *op. cit.*, p. 58.

104. A. Neuebauer, "The Early Settlement," p. 616; M. Grosberg, ed., *Sefer Hoazmim* (London, 1901), pp. 51f.

105. Cf. H. Lewy, *op. cit.*

106. It should be noted that the version transmitted by R. Isaac b. Joseph (of Corbeil?), published by Grosberg *loc. cit.*, which is the same as that published by Neubauer in *JQR*, IV, 616, also goes back to R. Judah he-Ḥasid. This may well apply also to the second report on the three ships, in which the men who instituted the prayer are unnamed. In any case, the observations on the names of the ports of debarkation hold for this version, too. Finally, the version transmitted in the name of R. Judah b. Eliezer Zevi in I. Baer, *Seder 'Abodat Israel* (Roedelheim, 5628), p. 112 is a verbatim reproduction of the version of R. Eleazar of Worms.

107. Cf. S. Klein, "Mi-Saviv le-Milḥamot Bethar," *Horeb*, III no. 1–2 (April-Sept., 1936), 54–55.

108. B. Z. Benedict, "On the History of the Torah Centre in Provence (Hebrew)," *Tarbiz*, XXII (1950–51), 86 has contended that "the Geonim" in whose name R. Eleazar of Worms cites his tradition must have been the scholars of Narbonne. In support of his view, he cites the fact that the scholars of Narbonne were called "Geonim" (p. 86) and notes the great esteem in which the scholars of Northern France-Germany held the scholars of Narbonne (pp. 91, 94). Accordingly, he urges (p. 95) that many of the influences on Franco-German Jewry hitherto traced to Italy now be retraced to Provence. Whatever the merits of this contention in general, it certainly has not been argued convincingly with regard to the *we-hu Raḥum* tradition. In the first case, "Geonim" in the usage of R. Eleazar of Worms did not refer exclusively to Narbonnese scholars. Secondly, Benedict himself has pointed to the early close contact between Italian and Provençal Jewry (pp. 90f., 95), and

by his own canons it is possible to conjecture that the *we-hu Raḥum* tradition came to Northern France from Italy by way of Provence. However, even this explanation is not quite acceptable, in view of the fact that the Provençal scholars do not have the identical traditions on the subject as the Jews of the north. The Provençal codes record either a story of a single ship (Davidson's type 1), or refer to persecutions in a vague sort of way (the fourth type; cf above, n. 80). In other words, the motif of the three ships must have come from a non-Provençal source. It is at least this part of the tradition which, I contend, must have come from Italy.

109. For characterizations of the Franco-German pietists, cf. M. Guedemann, *Geschichte des Ereziehungswesens und der Kultur der abendlaendischen Juden waehrend des Mittelalters und der neueren Zeit* (3 vols. Vienna, 1880–81), I, chs. IV–VII; G. Scholem, *Major Trends in Jewish Mysticism* (New York, 1941), ch. III; Baron, *SRH*, VIII, 42. It should be noted, too, that the *we-hu Raḥum* tradition coincides in spirit with the general tendency of the Franco-German pietists and esp. of R. Judah he-Hasid to account for post-Talmudic rituals and prayers on mystical and homiletical grounds; cf. Guedemann, I, 93f., 158f.; Judah b. Kalonymos, *Sefer Yiḥusay Tannaim wa-Amoraim* (Edited by J. L. Fishman. Jerusalem, 5702), pp. 13f. That the *we-hu-Raḥum* prayer also had mystical (or, at least, symbolic) significance may be seen from the statement of R. Aaron ha-Kohen of Lunel, *Orḥot Ḥayyim* (Jerusalem, 5717), I, 47a:

ויש בפסוק [„והוא רחום"] י"ג תיבות כנגד י"ג מדות וכנגד שמות האבות שהם י"ג.

In the light of all that has been said on the probable Italian provenance of the *we-hu-Raḥum* LEGEND, a word of caution is in place lest this be interpreted to mean that the prayer itself is of Italian origin. If it is, it certainly was a local rite that later spread far and wide. The Italian *Seder Hibbur Berakhot* (MS JTSA, acc. no. 48003; cf. A. Schechter, *Studies in Jewish Liturgy* [Philadelphia, 1930]) p. 79 states:

ויש קהילות שנוהגין בשיני בשבת ובחמישי בשבת ליפול על פניהם אחר שמתפללין שמונה עשרה בתפילת הרבים ומבקשין רחמים מלפני הקב"ה לאחר עושה השלום.

This may be an oblique reference to the prayer in question, but there is no mention of the *we-hu-Raḥum* prayer as such.

110. Cf. above, n. 89.

111. Cf. above, n. 90.

112. Cf. above, p. 161.

113. Cf. above, p. 159.

114. It goes without saying that Ibn Daud had no way of knowing, except from possible unreliable hearsay, how Ibn Jau had threatened R. Ḥanokh, or whether he had merely deposed him without any threat whatever. As a medieval historian, Ibn Daud would supply the words appropriate to the occasion; cf. the observations of S. W. Baron, "Saadia's Communal Activities," *American Academy for Jewish Research, Texts and Studies II, Saadia Anniversary Volume* (New York, 1943), p. 64 n. 123.

115. Cf. the letter published by J. Mann, "The Responsa of the Babylonian Geonim as a Source of Jewish History," *JQR, NS*, XI (1922), 454f., in which a communal representative on the way from Rome to Bari (! cf. above p. 58) announces that he has been robbed of his funds by pirates. Piracy and kidnapping were, of course, semi-official occupations during the reign of 'Abd ar-Raḥmān; cf. R. Dozy, *op cit.*, II, 154 (Eng. trans., p. 430); E. Lévi-Provençal, *Histoire de l'Espagne Musulmane* (3 vols. Paris, 1950–53), II, 154ff. On the regular redemption of captives by the Jewish communities, cf. Baron, *SRH*, IV, 177f., 326 n. 34, and Index, s.v. "Captives," and "Ransom of Captives." Cf. also S. D. Goitein, "Autographs of Yehuda Halevi (Hebrew)," *Tarbiz*, XXV (1955–56), 397–401, 403–407.

116. In Rabbinic usage, "four" has several connotations: 1) It reflects the ancient concept of encirclement, "four" representing all directions (cf. below, n. 116), as in *Pirqay R. Eliezer* 4, לפני הקב"ה; שבעה ימים וארבעה נהרות (end) B.B.B. 74 b; ד' כתות של מלאכי השרת מקלסין, שמקיפין את י"י (On the relationship between four and seven, cf. below, n. 116.) 2) "Four" figures prominently in ritual and legal contexts and thus reflects an ancient usage of "four" as a "sacred" number; cf. *JE*, XII, 117f.; *Encyclopaedia Talmudit*, II, 153ff. G. Scholem, *Jewish Gnosticism, Merkabah Mysticism, and Talmudic Tradition* (New York, 1960), p. 27 n. 17. 3) "Four" served frequently as a stock or formulistic number of schematization; cf. L. Finkelstein, "The Sources of the Tannaitic Midrashim," *JQR, NS*, XXI (1941), 225; *idem*, *Mabo le'Massektot Abot ve-Abot d'Rabbi Natan* (New York, 1950), pp. 83f., 97f.; and the

collections in *Pirqay Rabbenu ha-Qadosh* in S. Schoenblum, *Shelosha Sefarim Niftahim* (Lemberg, 1877), f. 21aff., L. Gruenhut, *Sefer ha-Liqqutim*, III (1899), 64ff., and M. Higger in *Horeb*, VI (1941), 128f., and 118 where other such collections are listed. Cf. also the modern collections of Z. Lerinman, *Osar Imray Abot* (Jerusalem, 1959), I, 372ff.; I. Zeligman, *The Treasury of Numbers* (Hebrew), (New York, 1942), pp. 135ff., which includes Biblical refs.—All this evidence, we believe, makes the conjecture on a possible variant of the story of Vespasian's ships with four as its schematic number all the more plausible. In the context of *SHQ*, the number clearly signifies the four ends of the earth.— "Four" as a formulary and sacred number is, of course, not an exclusively Jewish phenomenon; cf. S. Thompson, *op. cit.*, A 1029.2, Z 71.2; W. Wundt, *Mythus und Religion, III* (= *Voelkerpsychologie*. ed. 2. 6 vols. Leipzig, 1904–1915, VI), 388f., 354f.; M. Plessner in *Sefer Yohanan Lewy* (Edited by M. Schwabe and J. Gutman. Jerusalem, 1949), p. 134; F. M. Cornford, *From Religion to Philosophy* (New York, 1957), pp. 204ff. The same observation holds true for many of the other motifs incorporated in our story. However, our purpose here is not to trace the general dissemination of these motifs but to show their accessibility to, and possible influence on, Ibn Daud.

117. Cf. above, n. 79.—"Four hundred" represents a magnification of the symbolism represented by the number "four." On multipes (or fractions) of a number signifying ideas closely related to the primal number, cf. R. Gordis, "The Heptad as an Element of Biblical and Rabbnic Style," *Journal of Biblical Literature*, LXII (1943), 17ff.—Multiples of four by ten, one hundred, etc. are frequently encountered: 1) For "forty," cf. Z. Lerinman, *op. cit.*, pp. 35ff. and I. Zeligman, *op. cit.*, pp. 273ff.; W. H. Roscher, "Die Zahl 40 im Glauben, Brauch und Schriftum der Semiten." *Abhandlungen der philologisch-historische Klasse der koenigl. Saechsischen Gessellschaft der Wissenschaften*, XXVII (1909), 100–116. Roscher has shown that in Jewish as well as in other Semitic cultures, "forty" itself became a primal symbolic number. Thus, the frequently encountered expressions of forty days and years represent Rabbinic continuations of the Biblical usage of "forty" as a cultic unity of time or as a generation. Similarly, the usage of "forty" in B. Gittin 57b (end)–58a is a metaphorical extension of the levitical usage of "forty *se'ah*' (cf. M. Miqwa'ot 1:7; 2:1), which Roscher, p. 102 n. 14, connects with "forty" as a cultic symbol of purification and atonement. Roscher's contention for the independent significance of "forty" is strengthened by the wide prevalence of this number as a significant one in Semitic and classical antiquity; cf. *ibid.*, pp. 93–138 and R. Hirzel, "Ueber Rundzahlen," *Berichte Ueber die Verhandlungen der koeniglich-Saechsischen Gesellschaft der Wissenschaften zu Leipzig Philologisch-Historische Classe*, XXXVII (1885), 6ff. Consequently, it may be contended, "forty" cannot always be traced directly to the symbolism of "four." On the other hand, there can be little doubt that the number "four" and its symbolism lie at the root of the Biblical legal and schematic usages of "forty" and can, therefore, never really be dissociated from the number "forty" even in later Rabbinic usage; cf. Hirzel, *op. cit.*, pp. 62f. and below, n. 116 for a fuller explanation. This assumption will explain the usage of "forty" as a round number in M. R. H. 1:6 and in the expression of B. Ber. 28a. תני מינה ארבעין זמנין. "Forty" and the four directions are explicitly connected by R. Simai in his homily on the tablets of the Decalogue, which he describes as "tetragons" in Yer. Sheq. 6:1, f. 49d (ed. A. Schreiber, p. 71); 2) for "four hundred," cf. *Zion* (Hebrew), I (1840), 30. I. Zeligman, *op. cit.*, pp. 355ff.; Z. Lerinman, *op. cit.*, pp. 373f. In this connection it may be observed that even an "erroneous" figure may serve as partial confirmation of the frequency with which stock figures were used and, consequently, accepted. For examples, cf. L. Ginzberg, *A Commentary on the Palestinian Talmud* (3 vols. New York, 1941), III, 39f.; R. Margaliot, "Le Heqer ha-Misparim ba-Talmud," *Sinai*, XLIV (1958–1959), 31ff., and esp. 35ff. Cf. also B. Gittin 57b where the victims of Bethar are said to have numbered four hundred myriads or four thousand myriads. To sum up, however the numbers are interpreted, "four" and its extensions are frequently encountered in Rabbinic literature, and we should not eliminate the possibility of another version of the Midrash on the shiploads of exiles containing the number "four."

118. Cf. above, n. 89.

119. On the "four" winds, directions and ends of the earth, cf., e.g., Is. 11:12; Ezek., 7:2; Zech. 2:1–4. 6:1 (and cf. Y. Kaufmann, *Toledot ha-'Emunah ha-Yisraelit* [8 vols. Tel Aviv, 1936–1956] VIII, 235, 258ff.). The same symbolism underlies the four-sided crea-

tures of Ezek. 1; cf. G. A. Cooke, *A Critical and Exegetical Commentary on the Book of Ezekiel* (= *I.C.C.* New York, 1937), p. 11. In the book of Daniel, of course, "four" attains a new significance representing "kingdoms" or stages in history; cf. Dan. 2:38–39; 7:1f.—As a symbol of the four winds and hence of the four corners of the earth, "four" has pre-Israelite roots; cf. J. and H. Lewy, "The Origins of the Week and the Oldest Asiatic Calendar," *HUCA*, XVII (1942–43), 8f., 18f. The evidence adduced there shows that "four" is an ancient variant of "seven." This would explain the frequent connection between multiples of four and seven. Thus, forty *and* seventy years signify stock events of time in the Bible, as in other literatures; cf. W. H. Roscher, *loc. cit.* Note, also, the relationship of "seven" to "forty" in the chronology of the Flood (Gen. 7:4, 10, 12) and in the theophany at Sinai (Ex. 24:16, 18). The reason that "four" itself is less prominent in the Bible than "forty" is because "four" as a cultically significant number was totally displaced by "seven," which was sanctified by the Creation. Hence, the "four"-scheme remained prominent and obvious only in larger units of time, i.e. forty days or years. In any event, I see no reason to explain the origin of "forty" in any way other than one would explain that of "seventy," namely as a multiple of the primal number; cf. above, n. 117.

120. Cf. *Pirqay Rabbenu ha-Qadosh*, ed. Schoenblum, f. 21b, no. 5, f. 22a nos. 6, 7, 10, f. 23a nos. 20, 24, 26, f. 26b no. 4, f. 28a no. 24; S. Lieberman, "Ḥazanut Yannai." *Sinai*, IV (1938–39), 22f. Further examples may be found in Z. Lerinman, *op. cit.*, pp. 372ff. In the same vein, cf. the three-fold injunction in Abot 3:1 with the four-fold parallel in Abot de R. Nathan, I, 19 p. 69, II, 35; M. Sanhed. 10:2 שלשה מלכים and Tosef. Sanhed. 12:11 (ed. Zuckermandel, p. 433) ארבעה מלכים. (As in nn. 116–119, these are random examples, and no pretense is made here at full and systematic recording.)—An interesting variant of this sort is the discrepancy about the number of followers assembled by the Egyptian prophet: Josephus, *Wars*, II § 261 refer to 30,000 while Acts. 21:38 reports 4,000 ! —Two possible objections need to be anticipated. First, the fact that other numbers have variants, or that three or four have other variants, does not gainsay our observation that four as a variant of three is a discernible phenomenon. Secondly, the fact that the variant statements have corresponding differences in the number of details explanatory of the numbers also does not gainsay our contention. All we need establish is that in oral traditions three and four often interchange. Obviously, when the tradition is spelled out an effort will be made to supply a corresponding number of details.

121. On the confession of ignorance as a mark of critical scholarship in Ibn Daud's milieu, cf. G. E. von Grunebaum, *Medieval Islam* (Chicago, 1946), pp. 242f.

122. *The Mishnah of Rabbi Eliezer* (Edited by H. G. Enelow. New York, 1933), pp. 103–104.

123. Lit., since Judah the eldest had already been killed. The tradition is based on *Megillat Antiochus;* cf. S. A. Wertheimer, *Bate/Midrashot* (2 vols. Edited by A. J. Wertheimer. Jerusalem, 1950–1953), I, 327 n. 51. Note that in n. 53 there, Judah himself is reckoned as the equivalent of his four brothers.

124. Cf. B. Meg. 11a (and R. N. Rabbinowicz, *Variae lectiones*, p. 41 *ad loc.*); E. Z. Melamed, *Halachic Midrashim of the Tannaim in the Talmud Babli* (Hebrew), (Jerusalem, 1943), p. 323.

125. Cf. Moses Maimonides, *Epistle to Yemen* (Edited by A. S. Halkin. New York, 1952), pp. 18f., and esp. Halkin's note there, p. 21 n. 21.

126. It is pointless to object that there would be a hiatus of some nine centuries between the last link of four mentioned in the passage of *Mishnat R. Eliezer* and the one which we are suggesting as Ibn Daud's extension of the chain. In the first place, homiletical constructions are absolved of conforming to logical canons (אין מקשין על האגדות). Secondly, the passage in *Mishnat R. Eliezer* does not claim that four scholars arise in every generation or even century, but only in every "kingdom."—Professor Moshe Zucker, who is currently preparing for publication the portions of R. Saadia Gaon's commentary on the *Pentateuch*, which he has rescued from Geniza MSS, kindly informs me that in the Gaon's comments on Lev. 23:40 many homilectical interpretations of the four species of vegetation are given but not the one we have cited from *Mishnat R. Eliezer*. Nevertheless, I cannot help feeling that the passage derives from one who was at least an admirer of Saadyanic homily, even as Zucker has shown that a great part of *Mishnat R. Eliezer* itself is derived from actual Saadyanic material; cf. M. Zucker, "Le-Pitron Ba'yat Lamed-Bet Middot u-Mishnat

R. Eliezer," *PAAJR*, XXIII (1954), Hebrew section pp. 1–39. To begin with, the enumeration of the Hasmonean sons can hardly be an early Rabbinic one, the remonstrances of G. Alon to the contrary notwithstanding; cf. G. Alon, *Studies in Jewish History* (Hebrew) (2 vols. Tel-Aviv, 1957–58), I, 24. As indicated above, n. 123, the passage clearly postdates *Megillat Antiochus*. The interest of R. Saadiah Gaon in *Megillat Antiochus* and in the Maccabean warriors is well known; cf. H. Malter, *Saadia Gaon, His Life and Works* (Philadelphia, 1921), pp. 173, 355; S. A. Wertheimer, *op. cit.*, I. p. 312; S. Atlas and M. Perlmann, "Saadia on the Scroll of the Hasmoneans, *PAAJR*, XIV (1944), 1–21. Secondly, the passage in *Mishnat R. Eliezer* has shifted the burden of the homily in B. Meg. 11a from the promise inherent in the covenant between God and Israel, where the saviors of Israel are mentioned by way of example, to the *four righteous* men of each empire. In the homily of *Mishnat R. Eliezer* the central role is assigned to the teachers of Israel (להושיען ולרבץ תורה). This new emphasis coincides strikingly with the one expressed by R. Saadia in his introduction to the *Sefer ha-Galuy:* "The fourth chapter will show that God does not leave his nation at any period without a scholar whom He inspires and enlightens, so that he [in turn] may instruct and teach her [i.e. the nation], whereby her conditions may be improved. The cause for this discussion was what I have witnessed [of His bounty] towards me and towards the people through me." (This translation is by H. Malter, "Saadia Studies," *JQR*, NS, III [1912–13], 492; for the Arabic, *ibid.*, p. 497 11. 14–18, and A. Harkavy, *Zikron la-Rishonim* [6 vols. St. Petersburg and Berlin, 1879–1903], V, 155, Heb. trans. p. 154). Here, the righteous man, in this case the Gaon himself, is the divine instrument for bringing salvation to the people. This conception is a Jewish expression of feelings that gained wide currency in Muslim circles; cf. M. Zucker, *Rav Saadya Gaon's Translation of the Torah* (Hebrew) (New York, 1959), p. 8 n. 19. Whether or not the passage in *Mishnat R. Eliezer* was composed under Saadyanic influence, direct or indirect, it certainly coincided with ideals that Ibn Daud had absorbed from classical Jewish and from Judeo-Arabic sources, not the least of these being the works of the Gaon. Ibn Daud, accordingly, felt perfectly justified in carrying the homily further. In this connection it is worth noting the symbolic importance of the number four in Saadiah's exegesis of verses; cf. Atlas and Perlmann, *op. cit.*, pp. 2f., 14f. (Is it mere coincidence that Saadia chose to speak of his own destiny in the fourth chapter of *Sefer ha-Galuy?*)

127. Incidentally, the literary symmetry of which Ibn Daud is so fond is already inherent in the passage in *Mishnat R. Eliezer*, where each of the *four periods* is granted *four righteous men*.

128. That Ibn Daud shared the view, widely held by Jews in the twelfth century, that the Jews (and for that matter, the world at large) were rapidly approaching the fulfillment of messianic prophecies, specifically those of the Book of Daniel, will be shown in a separate study on the chronological scheme of *SHQ*.

129. Cf. below, n. 138.

130. Cf. above, pp. 161–162.

131. *MJC*, I, 47:1ff.; 78:15ff.; 81:10.

132. Note how careful Ibn Daud is to repair the breach in the chain of transmission when he comes to the first generation of the new period of Jewish history, the era of the Rabbinate. The disciples of the "four" scholars, who had "received" their authority from the original "four," are reauthorized by R. Hai himself; *MJC*, I, 73:12–16.—There is, of course, no way of questioning the coincidence that the name of the scholar who comes to Spain without "authority" was Moses. For the present, therefore, there is no alternative but to assume that the wording in a responsum of Maimonides listing some outstanding authorities of Spain, (!) רבנו חנוך ור' משה בנו is a *lapsus calami* either of Maimonides or of a copyist; cf. Moses Maimonides, *Responsa* (Edited by A. Freimann, Jerusalem, 1934), p. 364. The slip is, of course, explicable in the light of the fact that the name of R. Moses' father was indeed Hanokh; cf. J. Mueller, *Die Responsen der spanischen Lehrer des 10. Jahrhunderts* (Berlin, 1889), pp. 26ff. and sources cited there; B. M. Lewin, *Otzar ha-Geonim* (11 vols. Haifa and Jerusalem, 1928–43), VIII, 163 no. 411, X. 151 (end). That the name of Hanokh's father was Moses is, of course, also independently attested; cf. Mueller, pp. 30ff.

133. Cf. S. Eppenstein, *op. cit.*, pp. 211f.

134. Cf. above, n. 3.

135. Cf. *MJC*, I, 75:14–17. Note Ibn Daud's conclusion there that the Torah now had to be imported to Babylonia from Spain!

136. On the Gaonate after R. Hai cf. S. Poznansky, *Babylonische Geonim im nachgaonaeischen Zeitalter* (Berlin, 1914); J. Mann, *Texts and Studies*, I, 202ff.; S. Assaf, *Tequfat ha-Geonim we-Sifrutah* (Edited by M. Margulies. Jerusalem, 5715), pp. 125ff.

137. Note the outspoken statement in *MJC*, I, 73:25: וחזר כח התלמוד בארץ ספרד. The subject of Egypt has been quietly dropped, either for lack of information, which is highly doubtful, or because Ibn Daud is concerned with demonstrating the supremacy of the Maghreb.

138. Cf. *MJC*, I, 49:17 (the source of the quotation that follows); 53:7; 81:3–4; 82–1; Abraham Ibn Daud, *Dibray Malkhay Yisrael be-Bayyit Sheni* (Mantua, 1514; Amsterdam, 1711), ed. Amsterdam f. 50a-b, 79a-b. The view that the record of history can afford consolation, i.e. can help to uphold the Jew in times of stress and persecution, is also expressed by Maimonides, *Epistle to Yemen*, pp. 8–26. The bleak past foretold by the prophets, he indicates, can serve as assurance that their predictions of comfort will also be realized; cf. *ibid.*, pp. 78 and XV; *idem, The Guide of the Perplexed*, II, ch. 29. For the Talmudic roots of this view, popularized by Augustine and Orosius, cf. B. Mak. 24a-b. On the motif of consolation in Jewish literature, cf. A. S. Halkin, "Le-Toledot ha-Shemad Bihay ha-Almu'aḥiddin," *Joshua Starr Memorial Volume* (New York, 1953), p. 101.

139. The consolations alluded to by Ibn Daud are of the type expressed in Jer. 31:27 (28), 32:42; Zech. 8:13, all of which prophecy a national restoration in a manner (which to Ibn Daud meant the extent of time) corresponding to the downfall of the people.

140. The following is Ibn Daud's explanation of the first half of this statement; *MJC*, I, 49:19–50:2. "This follows, since the year which was partly the third and partly the fourth of Jehoiakim's reign [cf. Jer. 25:1 and Dan 1:1], Nebuchadnezzar began to reign and went up against Jerusalem. The Lord gave Jehoiakim, king of Judah, into his hand, as well as Daniel, Hananiah, Mishael and Azariah in the third year of Jehoiakim's reign. This was the first year of the reign of Nebuchadnezzar king of Babylon. Seven years later, Jehoiakim died and Jechoiachin began to reign [cf. II Ki. 23:36; 24:12]. Then Nebuchadnezzar came up and carried away Jehoiachin king of Judah and . . . a total of seventeen thousand persons [cf. *ibid.*, 24:10–16]. However, in the book of Jeremiah [only] three thousand and twenty-three are recorded [cf. Jer. 52:28], for Jeremiah merely recorded [the number of] heads of families. . . . Nebuchadnezzar came up again in the sixth year of Zedekiah's reign, which was the eighteenth year of Nebuchadnezzar's reign, and carried away eight hundred and twenty-two men of Israel [sic! cf. Jer. 52:29]. Again in the twenty-third year of Nebuchadnezzar, he carried Zedekiah away and destroyed the Temple [cf. Jer. 52:30]. Because of the incomplete years among these [twenty-three of Nebuchadnezzar], only twenty-one complete years elapsed between the captivity of Daniel and the captivity of Zedekiah." That Ibn Daud is certain that Scripture reckoned twenty-three regnal years to Nebuchadnezzar from the third-fourth of Jehoiakim until the eleventh of Zedekiah follows also from the statement in *MJC*, I, 48:4–5. Why, it will be asked, does Ibn Daud insist on so untenable a chronology, one which contradicts Scripture (cf. II Ki. 25:8 and Jer. 32:1!) and defies simple arithmetic? Underlying this seemingly bizarre arithmetic is the embarrassing Rabbinic tradition that the first Temple stood 410 years; cf. *Midrash Wayyikra Rabbah* 21:9, ed. M. Margulies, pp. 487f., and parallels listed there. However, any actual computation of the reigns of the kings from Solomon onward belies this figure. Accordingly, Ibn Daud adopted the following solution. In any reckoning of *dates*, the figure 410 is the correct one and hence the real working figure. Thus *MJC*, I, 48:3–5 gives the data of the Exodus as 2449 A.M. (so MSS פ except for א) and the date of the construction as 2929 (so also *MJC*, I, 49:11) corresponding to the statement in I Ki. 6:1. Since the Seleucid era began in 3449 (cf. below, n. 140 b), there elapsed 520 years from the date of the construction of the first Temple until the Seleucid era: X of the Temple + 70 of exile + 40 of the second Temple, where X must = 410. However, since the total number of years of the kings during the first Temple did not coincide with 410, Ibn Daud said that with regard to that period of history the 410 referred only to the period when the Jewish kingdom had been free; *MJC*, I, 48:4–5. From the point of subjection, i.e., the third-fourth year of Jehoiakim, a new era begins and corresponds to the chronology of Nebuchadnezzar's reign recorded in Jer. 52:29–30. Unaware of, or having rejected, the classical interpretation of the chronology of

the invasions listed in these verses (*Seder 'Olam* 26: cf. *MJC*, II, 61 or *Seder Olam Rabbah*, ed. B. Ratner [Vilna, 1897], pp. 119f.), Ibn Daud concluded that the invasion of Palestine in the twenty-third year of Nebuchadnezzar's reign (Jer. 52:30) must be identical with one in which the Temple was destroyed. From this point Ibn Daud worked backwards in his synchronization of the earlier invasions of Nebuchadnezzar with the data given elsewhere in Scripture. The invasion listed in Jer. 52:29 as having occurred in the eighteenth year of Nebuchadnezzar must have been synchronous with the sixth year of Zedekiah's reign (against Jer. 32:1). On the other hand, since the date in Jer. 52:28 obviously could not fit this scheme, Ibn Daud interpreted it as recording the lapse of time following the first invasion in the third-fourth year of Jehoiakim (and not as the regnal year of Nebuchadnezzar). Finally, Dan. 1:1 enabled Ibn Daud to date the actual beginning of Nebuchadnezzar's reign in the third year of Jehoiakim. This gave Ibn Daud the advantage of reckoning nine years of Jehoiakim's reign in the category of subjection to Babylon, thus enabling him to arrive at a figure of twenty-one years "from the beginning of the exile until the destruction": 9 of Jehoiakim + 1 of Jehoiachin + 11 of Zedekiah. The only problem that remained for Ibn Daud was to resolve the contradiction between his own total of twenty-one years and the twenty-three which Jeremiah records. This he did by stating that Jeremiah records the offical number of regnal years claimed by Nebuchadnezzar, while Ibn Daud's own figure represented the actual lapse of time. Those two figures do not tally, for between the terminal points of Nebuchadnezzar's first and last invasions, some of the regnal years of Nebuchadnezzar were "incomplete years." Thus, the first chronological year of Nebuchadnezzar's began at the end of Jehoiakim's third year (Dan. 1:1), let us say in the eleventh month of the year. In Nisan, Jehoiakim began to reckon the fourth year of his reign and Nebuchadnezzar his second regnal year. However, Jer. 25:1 still regarded this as the first actual year of Nebuchadnezzar's rule. In other words, Nebuchadnezzar's rule was credited with at least ten months more than actually belonged to it. In the course of the twenty-one years between the first invasion and the final one, the Jews intercalated their calendar regularly, i.e., seven times in the course of a nineteen-year cycle, while the Babylonians did not. (Let it not be wondered that Ibn Daud might entertain the notion that the Jews employed a nineteen-year intercalatory cycle in the days of the first Temple. Had not R. Saadiah Gaon stated that the cycles were instituted by Moses! Cf. M. Zucker, "Shnay Qeta'im Neged Qara'iyyim," *PAAJR*, XVIII [1948–49], Hebrew sect. 16 n. 66; S. W. Baron, "Saadia's Communal Activities," pp. 36f.). This would require a subtraction of another seven months from Nebuchadnezzar's twenty-three years. Finally, the Temple was destroyed in the fifth month of the year, requiring a subtraction of another seven months from Nebuchadnezzar's twenty-third year, giving a total of twenty-four months to be subtracted from Nebuchadnezzar's reign. To this explanation there are the serious objections that Ibn Daud is tailoring his figures to meet his preconceived needs, for the actual computation of years requires crediting to the chronology of Israel the very months he is denying to Babylon. Furthermore, I am at a loss to see at what point a sufficient number of "incomplete years" accumulated to allow for Nebuchadnezzar's regnal years to jump so far ahead after suffering a handicap of two years of Jehoiakim. It was certainly not at the end of the twenty-third year, for according to Ibn Daud's own explanation (cited at the beginning of this note), by Zedekiah's sixth year Nebuchadnezzar was already reckoning his own eighteenth. In other words, by Zedekiah's sixth year, which would normally correspond to Nebuchadnezzar's sixteenth (at most, seventeenth, according to our explanation), Nebuchadnezzar's official chronology had caught up with the total represented in Jer. 52:30. Indeed, this is not the only or even the most serious objection to his statements, as can be seen from Zacuto's protestations (cf. nn. 142–143). On the other hand, it must be borne in mind that Ibn Daud has an axe to grind and is therefore not overly concerned with details that contradict his theory. The juggling of figures gave Ibn Daud the results he wanted: a "harmonization" of Biblican and Rabbinic data; a total of twenty-one years from the beginning of the Destruction until its consummation, thereby giving a period corresponding to the period of rebuilding (cf. next note); a total of 433, which provided him with a symbolic mnemonic (cf. n. 146), but which he never intended to be used as a basis for the computation of dates. It is this last point that Ibn Daud's critics ignored causing them to reject his calculations or to emend his figures.

141. This figure is explained in *SHQ* (*MJC*, I, 51:5–10) as follows: The rebuilding of

the Temple was begun in the first year of the reign of Cyrus (Ezra 1:1f.), and final clearance to complete it was secured in the second year of Darius (*ibid.* 4:24). The interval between Cyrus' edict and the second year of Darius was of twenty-one years; 3 of Cyrus (cf. Dan 10:1) + 16 of Ahasureus (which is arrived at by the difference required to make up the 70 years of exile; cf. below) + 2 of Darius = 21. Ibn Daud takes as his terminal date that of Ezra 4:24 (rather than that of Ezra 6:15), because the second year of Darius completed the seventieth year from the Destruction (cf. Dan. 10:2) in the following way: the year of the Destruction (cf. *MJC*, I, 50:21) + 22 of Nebuchadnezzar after the Destruction (since Nebuchadnezzar reigned 45 years [cf. B. Meg. 11b] and 23 before the destruction [n. 136]) + 22 of Evil Merodach (arrived at by reduction for the 70 years of *Babylon itself*; cf. Jer. 25:11–12, 29:10) + 3 of Belshazzar (Dan. 8:1) + 1 of Darius the Mede (Dan. 6:19, 9:1) + 21 of rebuilding = 70 years of destruction. (I have deviated in one detail from Ibn Daud's own explanation in *MJC*, I, 50:23–25, by including the year of the Destruction. Ibn Daud himself gives the impression there that the first year of Cyrus should be reckoned both to the first 49 years and to the last 21. In *MJC*, 50:25 the erroneous כ״ח of MS ק should be corrected to כ״א of all other MSS; cf. *MJC*, II, 252 *ad loc.*)

142. A Zacuto, *op. cit.*, pp. 81bf. Zacuto took vigorous exception to the chronology explained in n. 136, for Ibn Daud's scheme had compelled him to date the destruction of the Temple in the twenty-third year of Nebuchadnezzar's reign contrary to II Ki. 25:8 and Jer. 52:8. This premise involves further deviations from the Scriptural account such as the statement that there were two captivities within the reign of Zedekiah; cf. *MJC*, I, 49:25–50:1.

143. Viz., in the case of Jer. 34:1, which Ibn Daud corrects to the sixth year of Zedekiah's reign in accordance with the premise explained in the previous note. It should be mentioned in passing that the liberties which Ibn Daud took were not entirely without precedent, cf. the statement of R. Tanḥum b. Hanilai in Yer. Ta'an. 4:8f. 68c, "The chronology of Scripture is in error" (קלקול חשבונות יש כאן) with regard to Jer. 39:2; cf. also Tosafot to B. R. H. 18 b, s.v. זה תשעה בתמוז.

144. *MJC*, I, 49:11–12. Azariah da Rossi, *Me'or 'Enayyim* (Edited by D. Cassel. Vilna, 1864–66), ch. 35, p. 392 noted the strange figure here and proposed emending it to three. Ibn Daud's statement may go back ultimately to *Seder 'Olam Zuta* (*MJC*, II, 70) which states that Nebuchadnezzar put the Temple under siege in the fifth year of Zedekiah's reign.

145. Cf. nn. 140 and 153. Of course, the two figures can be harmonized no matter how one interprets Ibn Daud's statement. If the statement means that the seven-year war followed the period of 427 years, then it could be reasoned that the last of the 427 years and the first year of the war overlapped. If on the other hand, the war period is included in the 427 years, one could say that the last of the seven years of the construction of the Temple overlapped with the first of the 427 years. In any event, had Ibn Daud really wanted to remain consistent he could easily have done so by stating that the Temple stood for 426 years. That he did not indicates that his scheme was of far greater importance than chronological consistency. In this statement Ibn Daud tells us that the first Temple stood for sixty-two weeks of years (62 × 7 = 434) precisely as the second Temple did; cf. next note.

146. In the case of the chronology of the second Temple, Ibn Daud's figures are so contradictory and puzzling as to have evoked the same type of proposal made with reference to his figures on the first Temple, viz., to emend his text. In reality, the contradictions dissolve once we unravel Ibn Daud's schematology. As in the case of the first Temple, Ibn Daud gives three chronological totals for the duration of the second Temple: an official-traditional one, a "real" one, which in turn, is derived from an exegetical one, at which he only hints. We take up each one in turn: 1) According to Rabbinic tradition the second Temple stood 420 years; cf. B. Yoma 9a. Ibn Daud not only cites this figure in *MJC*, I, 50:13 but uses it throughout *SHQ* as his actual working figure; cf. *MJC*, I, 51:16, 21–22 with the date on 54:21–22. (Incidentally, the statement in 51:22 והיא שנת ג' אלפים ות"ן ליצירה is lacking in MSS ש and should be deleted.) According to *SHQ*, the second Temple was built, and its chronology begins, in 3409 and was destroyed in 3829. 2) However, Ibn Daud felt required to harmonize the traditional figure of 420 with the divisions of history spelled out in Dan. 9:25–27. In accordance with these verses he allowed 441 years, or 63 weeks, from the beginning of the construction of the Temple until its destruction. This tallied perfectly

with the requirements of Scripture and tradition, for it included the 21 years of construction and the 420 of the actual lifespan of the Temple; cf. *MJC*, I, 49:13–16, 50:25–27. The difficulty begins when one tries to fit the traditional figure of 420 years into the scheme described by Daniel. Accordingly, Ibn Daud concocted a new category which would combine both sets of data, "the years that the kingdom stood" or "the years of habitation" (*MJC*, I, 50:26, 27), which numbered 420 years. These were followed by a war of seven years giving the following totals: a) 427 years from the beginning of this era until the destruction of the Temple; *MJC*, I, 50:13, 26–27, 51:1–4; b) 434 years from the beginning of the construction until the war began; c) 441 years from the construction to the destruction. However, in pointing to the era of 434 years corresponding to the 62 weeks of Dan. 9:25, Ibn Daud does not give the correct figure but says instead that 62 weeks of years equal 420 (*MJC*, I, 50:26, 51:1), which I. Loeb charitably corrected to 434; cf. I. Loeb, *Joseph Haccohen et les Chroniqueurs Juifs* (Paris, 1888), p. 90. Now, we submit that Ibn Daud knew that 62 × 7 = 434, but that he felt he should not say so, for he would quickly expose and undo his reckoning of an era from 427 years before the Destruction. To retain the scheme of 420 in the face of the divisions of Daniel, the beginning of an era would have to be placed fourteen years after the beginning of the 434, or seven years before the end of the twenty-one year period of construction. For this Ibn Daud could produce no Scriptural evidence. Accordingly, he insisted that he was working with the traditional figure of 420 and fitting it in with the divisions of history described in Dan. 9. Thus, according to Ibn Daud, there is a difference between the chronology of the Jewish state and that of the Temple, precisely as there was in the case of the first Temple; cf. n. 136. Finally, he hints, only the real chronologies of the two Temples and kingdoms differed; the first Temple stood 410 or 433 years, while the second stood 420 or 441 years. However, the symbolic figures were very much the same: 427 and 434 and a war of seven years in the case of both.

147. Incidentally, it may be noted that even on so indisputable a matter, Ibn Daud contradicted Scripture, for he repeats himself that the construction of Solomon's Temple began in the *third* year of his reign; cf. *MJC*, I, 48:8, 11–12. Since he needed to arrive at a total of 433, the statement of I Ki. 6:1 and II Chr. 3:2 could be ignored. This point was already noted by A. A. Akavia, *Sidray Zemanim Le-fi ha-Masoret* (Tel-Aviv, 1943), p. 287.

148. Cf. above n. 140 b and cf. also Ibn Ezra to Dan. 9:24.

149. *MJC*, I, 59:18f. For the Arabic source of Ibn Daud's division of the cycles of Persian and Roman domination, cf. G. Levi della Vida, "La Traduzione Araba della Storia di Orosio," *Al-Andalus*, XIX (1954), 286.

150. The redaction of the Mishna is dated 500 years after the termination of prophecy; (*MJC*, I, 51:22–23, 57:2, where all MSS, with the exception of הֹ אַ, read correctly וֹשְׁנַת קַ"ך לחורבן). The Saboraic period is closed 500 years later; *MJC*, I, 62:17. The fact that these are symmetrical figures, and not based on faulty sources emanating from the academy of Sura, at once disqualifies the theory proposed by A. Epstein, "Meqorot le-Qorot ha-Geonim vi-Yeshibot Babel," *Festschrift zu Ehren des Dr. A. Harkavy* (Edited by D. v. Guenzberg and I. Markon. St. Petersburg, 1903), Hebrew section pp. 164–174 (= *Kitbay R. Abraham Epstein.* 2 vols. Edited by A. M. Habermann, Jerusalem 5710–17, II, pp. 410ff.). This will be elucidated fully in a paper on the chronological scheme of *SHQ*.

151. Abraham ibn Daud, *Dibray Malkhay Yisrael*, ed. Amsterdam, f. 79b.

152. This is the correct reading, recorded in ed. Mantua, 1514; the Amsterdam ed., *loc. cit.*, reads erroneously "seven"; cf. *MJC*, I, 52:18; *Dibray Malkhay Yisrael* f. 53a.

153. In *MJC*, I, 48:3, 11 (cf. also 49:11–12), the Temple is said to have stood 433 years, which da Rossi, *op. cit.*, ch. 35 pp. 292f. suggested emending to 430. However, cf. above, n. 140. Accordingly, I believe that the figure 433 derives from a mnemonic גלת which may derive from the defective spelling in Obad. 20. Ibn Ezra *ad loc.* quotes R. Moses Gikatilla for the interpretation of גלת החל as signifying the first exile. Ibn Daud defends the figure 433 by reckoning 38 years to the Temple in Solomon's reign (cf. *MJC*, I, 48:8, which contradicts I Ki. 6:1, II Chr. 3:2).—In *MJC*, I, 52:14 the Antiochene persecutions are dated in the year 212 of the second Temple, contrary to the 213 of *Megillat Antiochus;* cf. S. A. Wertheimer, *op. cit.*, I, 319. Ibn Daud may have derived his date from a recension of *Seder 'Olam Zuta;* cf. *MJC*, II, 74:28 (= A. Zacuto, *op. cit.*, p. 92 col. b.). On the other hand, the agreement of *SHQ* with one datum of one recension of *Seder 'Olam Zuta* requires explanation, since Ibn Daud usually draws his information from *Josippon.* I submit that 212 is a

mnemonic (ריב) going back to Is. 34:8: "For the Lord hath a day of vengeances, a *year* of recompense for the *controversy* (לריב) of Zion." Matthais, the emissary of God's vengeance, reigned for one year; *MJC*, I, 52:17. In the absence of early evidence for such an interpretation, this is admittedly only a guess, but one which accounts for the peculiar datum.— The suggestion that Ibn Daud was fond of symbolic mnemonics, particularly at crucial points of chronology, will explain the peculiar feature in the dates of death of R. Ashi and R. Hai Gaon. Normally, dates of death are given in terms of *anno mundi*, but in the case of these two men the equivalent date of the Seleucid era is supplied *in addition to* the one regularly given; *MJC*, I, 59:4–5; 66:22–23. Why the sudden pleonasms? In the case of R. Ashi, Abraham Zacuto, *op. cit.*, p. 201 col. b, understood the Seleucid date תשל"ח as a mnemonic reference to Ps. 80:12, and his suggestion is most plausible. In the case of R. Hai, the mnemonic שמ"ט (as in MSS טש) is suggestive of the withdrawal of Babylonian hegemony from the Jewish world and the end of the Gaonate, points which Ibn Daud belabors in *SHQ*. Thus the date of R. Hai Gaon's death stands in blatant contrast to the mnemonic date recorded by the MSS for the time of the arrival of R. Moses in Cordova; cf. above, pp. 174f.—Taken *individually* each of these suggestions may strike the skeptical reader as fanciful. However, viewed as a *group*, and coupled with all the other puzzling phenomena in *SHQ*, these *gematriot* are by no means bizarre.

154. Ibn Daud's scheme of periods of joy compensating for periods of sadness is an extension of the ancient interpretation of Ps. 90:15, "Make us glad according to the days wherein thou hast afflicted us, according to the years wherein we have seen evil"; cf. B. Sanhed. 99a; *Pesikta Rabbati*, ed. M. Friedmann, 1, f. 4a–b; and esp. the statement of R. Yose b. Halafta in Midrash Ekhah, Petihta, par. 21 (ed. Vilna, f. 4d), explained further by Resh Laqish and R. Yohanan in Midrash Ekhah, ed. Buber, p. 16 (I am indebted to Professor Judah Goldin for calling my attention to the passage in Mid. Ekhah). The symmetrical interpretations in these passages are eschatological; cf. below n. 161. Ibn Daud's statement, cited above pp. 174–175, and his symmetrical examples are strikingly reminiscent of the statement in Pesikta Rabatti. 8, f. 24 a הקב"ה נפלאותיו של הקב"ה, which is illustrated by examples from the symmetrical design of the universe, and then by R. Ḥanina by examples from *history*. References to passages of this type of interpretation of history as well as of nature could easily be multiplied from classical Hebrew sources and are an outstanding feature of Jewish midrashic genres; cf. I. Heinemann, *The Methods of the Aggadah* (Hebrew) (Jerusalem, 1949), pp. 64ff. and esp. A. Mirsky, "The Origins of the Forms of Liturgical Poetry" (Hebrew), *Studies of the Research Institute for Hebrew Poetry in Jerusalem*, VII (1958), 11–127.

155. Cf. S. Lieberman, *Hellenism in Jewish Palestine* (New York, 1950), p. 69; *JE*, V, 589f.; *Ozar Yisrael* (10 vols. Edited by J. D. Eisenstein. New York, 1951), III, 208f.; *Encyclopaedia Hebraica*, X, 683f.; A. H. Silver, *A History of Messianic Speculaton in Israel* (New York, 1927; Boston, 1959), pp. 244f. For use of *gematria* in legal exegesis, cf. also *Encyclopedia Talmudit*, V, 32f.

156. For symmetry, cf. A. H. Silver, *op. cit.*, pp. 71, 85f., 87, 244 type C; for *gematria*, pp. 58f., 66f., 85, 210f.

157. Judah ha-Levi, *Diwan* (6 vols. Edited by H. Brody. Berlin, 1899–1930), Texts II. 302. Two points about ha-Levi's use of the mnemonic תת"ץ (= 890) should be noted. First, the mnemonic is an old one, as shown by the independent use of it by Franco-German Jews; cf. A. Marx, "Studies in Gaonic History and Literature," *JQR, NS*, I (1910–11). 76. Secondly, the mnemonic itself is based on a symmetrical calculation. The messianic era is dated in a year 890 corresponding to the period that elapsed from the Exodus until the destruction of the first Temple (cf. *Seder 'Olam* 11, ed. Ratner, p. 48; B. Gittin 22a [bot.]: 480 from the Exodus until the construction of the Temple (I Ki. 6:1) + 410 of the Temple (cf. above, n. 140).

158. For Maimonides' use of symmetry, cf. S. W. Baron, "The Historical Outlook of Maimonides," *PAAJR*, VI (1935), 100f. and esp. 101 n. 192; Maimonides, *Epistle to Yemen*, p. 82, where a mnemonic is also invoked. To be sure, Maimonides is citing old traditions (cf. Prof. Halkin's notes there and p. xii), but the point is that this type of tradition was quite in vogue and palatable even to a "philosopher." Note, too, the playful *gematria* possibly employed by Joseph b. Judah in a letter to Maimonides; Moses Maimonides, *Epistulae* (Edited by D. H. Baneth. Jerusalem, 1946), I, 19.—On Maimonides' use of schematic

numbers, cf. L. Strauss, "Maimonides' Statement on Political Science," *PAAJR*, XXII (1953), 125ff., 129.

159. Cf. Ibn Khaldun, *op. cit.*, I, 235f., 238f.; II, 190ff., 204ff. Note the symmetrical eschatology on p. 188.

160. Cf. H. Gelzer, *Sextus Julius Africanus und die Byzantinische Chronographie* (2 vols. Leipzig, 1898), I, 24f., 54, 66; Paulus Orosius, *Seven Books of History Against the Pagans* (Translated by I. W. Raymond. New York 1936), II:2–3, pp. 73ff.: VII:2, pp. 320f.; VII:27, pp. 360f. Symmetry plays a basic role in the scheme of Ibn Daud's younger Italian contemporary Joachim of Floris; cf. K. Löwith, *Meaning In History* (Chicago, 1949), p. 149; E. Benz, *Ecclesia Spiritualis* (Stuttgart. 1934), pp. 4ff.

161. Cf. the brilliant analysis of G. Scholem, *Sabbatai Zevi* (2 vols. Tel-Aviv, 5717), I, 7ff. and esp. 75–78. Calculation of "the end" by these methods falls in the category of what Prof. Scholem calls (*ibid.*, p. 57) philosophic messianic speculation, for the calculator arrives at his date by application of the laws operating in the universe (= history). Messianic dates that are based on Scripture seek to derive from the revelations of the prophets the date of the fulness of time. In other words, the date of "the end" is not a break in the process of history but a preordained aspect of Creation and thus falls in the category of natural law. That is why "rationalist" philosophers like Ibn Daud and Maimonides, who shied away from what Scholem calls messianic fantasy, i.e., detailed descriptions of the wonders of the messianic age, could nevertheless entertain traditions or even speculate on the date of the end of the present age.

162. This will be shown in a separate paper on the chronological scheme of *SHQ*.

163. Cf. above, n. 138.

164. Cf. esp. *MJC*, I, 82:1f.; Ibn Daud, *Dibray Malkhay Yisrael*, p. 50 a.

165. Cf. above, pp. 170f.

166. Cf. above, nn. 6, 7, 42, 49, 50, 55.

167. Cf. above, p. 159.

168. Ibn Daud regularly uses כמו, "approximately," to indicate approximate intervals of time or durations of reigns. However, he does not use this word with reference to actual dates. Thus in *MJC*, I, 62:4 כמו חמישים = forty-nine, for the resultant date is given without qualification.

169. Cf. above, nn. 75, 78.

170. Ch. Albeck, "Ha-Sanhedrin U-Nesiah," *Zion*, VIII (1942–43), 166 n. 3.

171. *MJC*, I, 54:27, 55:12. This theory was taken up independently by modern scholars; cf. Albeck, *loc. cit.*, and L. Ginzberg, *A Commentary on the Palestinian Talmud*, III, 193f.

172. *MJC*, I, 55:15, 17.

173. *Ibid.*, 56:12; cf. also the meticulously careful wording in 54:11, 22; 56:17.

174. *Ibid.*, 48:15 (cf. also 54:2, paraphrasing B. Shab. 15a).

175. Sc., since the Temple was destroyed in 3829; *ibid.*, 54:22.

176. *Ibid.*, 53:24–25, based on *Sifre Deut.*, par. 357 (ed. L. Finkelstein, p. 429).

177. Cf. above, nn. 170–173. Incidentally, this explanation accounts for the puzzling statement in *Dibray Malkhay Yisrael*, f. 54b that John Hyrcanus served as high priest for forty years but *ruled* (= served as Nasi or king) for but thirty-one. (In *MJC*, I, 52:25, only ק reads שמונים; all other MSS, except for פל which give no figure at all read 'מ or ארבעים).

178. Ibn Daud is thus giving a tacit commentary on the tradition in B. Pes. 66a, which reports that after Hillel vanquished the B'nay Bathyra הושיבוהו בראש ומינוהו נשיא עליהם. To Ibn Daud, the important datum here is הושיבוהו בראש, i.e., appointed him Rosh Yeshiba, while the phrase ומינוהו נשיא עליהם, which also appears in the parallel accounts (cf. n. 78) is disregarded. In the light of the contradictions of classic sources encountered elsewhere in *SHQ*, the present divergence from an explicit Rabbinic tradition should occasion no surprise.

179. I.e., it represents the end of two periods of equal length; cf. above, p. 172.

180. For Ibn Daud himself, cf. *MJC*, I, 50:7ff.

181. *Ibid.*, 61:18.

182. Cf. above, p. 230.

183. *MJC*, I, 50:13.

184. Cf. above, n. 32.

185. Gen. R. 88:5 (ed. Theodor Albeck, pp. 1081–83). The translation, with minor modifications, is taken from *Midrash Rabbah, Genesis* (2 vols. Translated by H. Freedman. London, Soncino Press, 1939), II, 816–17.

186. It should be noted that the Midrash does not state that all "the cups" will be given to Israel in the Messianic age. In fact, in view of the end of the passage, the לעתיד לבוא might easily be construed by Ibn Daud to mean the future in general.

187. Cf. above, n. 122.

188. Cf. above, n. 138.

189. Cf. above, nn. 153f.

190. For a summary of these motifs and their dissemination in classical and European literature, cf. S. Trenkner, *The Greek Novella in the Classical Period* (Cambridge U., 1958), pp. 31ff., 60ff., 91ff.—As Prof. A. S. Halkin observed in a discussion of this point, the "recognition motif" was very much in vogue in Ibn Daud's day, as evidenced by the essential role it plays in the *maqama* form; cf. S. M. Stern, "The Arabic Original of the Maqam of 'The Cock' of al-Harizi (Hebrew)," *Tarbiz*, XVII (1945–46), 98. Significantly enough, the *maqama* form occasionally contains the theme of a man who claims that he has fled from a Christian country and appeals on that ground to his sympathetic (Muslim) audience; *ibid.*, p. 89 and n. 8a there. The story of R. Moses is thus a variation of a stereotype much in vogue at the time. Cf. below, n. 196.

191. *Mid. Tanḥuma*, Terumah, par. 2 (end); cf. also below, n. 195.

192. Z. Jawitz, *op. cit.*, X, 238ff.—Besides the obvious parallelism of capture by pirates, "recognition" and change of fortune as the consequence of a public lecture, Jawitz made much of the expression in the Tanhuma, ועשו לו פסיקתו וכו', cf. *MJC*, I, 68:22.

193. A. Ashtor, *op. cit.*, p. 290 n. 14.

194. Sc., the phrase referred to in n. 192.

195. *Midrash Tanḥuma* (2 vols. Edited by S. Buber), P. Terumah, par. 1, p. 89, which is the source of this passage in *Yalqut Shim'oni*, Exodus, par. 363, and *idem* Prov. 4:2, par. 936. The homily also appears in this form, with minor verbal changes, in *Sefer we-Hizhir le-Seder Shemot* (Edited by I. M. Freimann. Leipzig, 5633), p. 153. Those sources lack the phrase cited in n. 182 but have an interesting variant that bears mention. In this version, when the men aboard ship ask the *haber* what his wares are, he replies: "My merchandise is concealed" (מוצנעת היא). *Sefer we-Hizhir* says that while all the others boasted of their merchandise, the scholar sat in quiet seclusion (וזה היה מוצנע יושב ושותק). Cf. Ibn Daud's words (*MJC*, I, 68:6) "These sages did not tell a soul about themselves or their wisdom." The motif of *concealment* of the merchandise is not expressed quite so clearly in the Tanḥuma "edition" (cf. n. 191).

196. Although each of the elements in the novella can be traced to Rabbinic sources earlier than Ibn Daud, the *combination* of elements is strongly reminiscent of the *form* of the Greek novella; cf. ref. in n. 180. It is quite possible that Ibn Daud had a novella paradigm in mind, which he filled in with details adapted from older Jewish sources. The novella form was certainly available to him from Arabic literature, which gave the old Hellenistic motifs new life from the ninth century onward; cf. G. E. von Grunebaum, *op. cit.*, ch. IX and esp. pp. 298ff.

197. On Ibn Shaprut's cultural policies, cf. A. Ashtor, *op. cit.*, pp. 152ff.

198. Cf. Baron, *SRH*, VII, 20f.; A. Ashtor, *op. cit.*, pp. 160–170.

199. Cf. A. Ashtor, *op. cit.*, pp. 146ff.

200. Cf. *ibid.*, p. 160 and the remarks of Baron, *SRH*, VII, 22 (text to n. 21).

201. Ibn Daud makes this quite clear by his statement that the King was delighted by R. Moses' arrival in Cordova. Ibn Daud's testimony is confirmed by Ibn Juljul *apud* Ibn Abi 'Usaibia; cf. P. Luzzatto, *Notice sur Abou-Ioussouf Hasdai Ibn-Shaprout* (Paris, 1852), p. 8; J. Mann, "The Responsa of the Babylonian Geonim," *JQR*, NS, IX (1918), 169 n. 163. The fact that Ibn Abi 'Usaibia places the break with Babylonia in the reign of al-Ḥakam in no way conflicts with our thesis. Ibn Abi 'Usaibia may have slipped or he may have attributed the open break to Ibn Shaprut, although the policies first became apparent in the days of al-Ḥakam with the complete triumph of the anti-Babylonian faction. On 'Abd ar-Raḥmān's policies, cf. R. Dozy, *op. cit.*, II, 146f., 173f. (Eng. trans., pp. 423f., 445f.). That the Jewish break with Babylonian hegemony occurred at the time, and as a consequence, of the Muslim break with the Eastern Caliphate was noted by J. Mann, *Texts and Studies* I, 111f.; cf.

also E. Rivkin, "Some Historical Aspects of Authority in Judaism," *Central Conference of American Rabbis, Yearbook,* LXI (1951), 373.

202. Cf. Dunash b. Labrat, *Shirim* (Edited by N. Allony. Jerusalem, 1947), p. 70 l. 35–36, and esp. S. Abramson's note *ad. loc.,* p. 134.

203. How far the break with Babylonia went may be gathered from the report of Ibn Juljul (cf. above, n. 190) that under Ibn Shaprut the Jews of Spain began to regulate the calendar without recourse to the academies of Babylonia; cf. H. J. Bornstein, "Dibray Yemay ha-'Ibbur ha-Aharonim," *ha-Tequfa* XVI (1922–23), 286f.

204. Cf. below, nn. 206, 228.

205. Cf. J. Mann, *Texts and Studies,* I, 87, 111f.; A. Ashtor, *op. cit.,* pp. 157ff.

206. Cf. Maimonides, *Responsa,* pp. 364–365; cf. also *ibid.,* pp. 43f., 80 l. 2. Maimonides' statements, of course, reflect not only the break with Babylonian hegemony but also the extended application of the term "Gaon" that began with the rise of autonomous academies in Palestine, Egypt, and the West; cf. S. Poznanski, *Babylonische Geonim im nachgaonaeischen Zeitalter,* pp. 79ff. and esp. 104ff. Indeed, Maimonides categorically defines "Geonim" as the scholars of note who flourished after the redaction of the Babylonian Talmud and elucidated it; cf. Maimonides, *Epistulae,* I, 58 n. to 1. 4, where refs. are given.—As observed by B. Z. Benedict, *op. cit.,* p. 86, the addition of the title "Gaon" in the West indicates that at least some of these communities tried to set themselves up as a neo- or quasi-Babylonia. It is, therefore, no coincidence that the office of "Nasi" or "Nagid" begins to appear locally at about the very time that the title "Gaon" is appropriated outside Babylonia; cf. H. Z. Hirschberg, "The Salars and Negidim of Kairawan (Hebrew)," *Zion,* XXIII-XXIV (1958–59), 166ff.

207. The late Professor Saul Lieberman kindly called my attention to Maimonides' Commentary on M. Bekhorot 4:4, where Maimonides distinguishes sarcastically between the bearers of titles and the bearers of valid authority. Cf. further, Maimonides, *Epistulae,* I, 54ff.

208. Cf. the Prologue to *SHQ. MJC,* I, 47:1f. and esp. 1. 6f. For the Karaite charge on this ground, cf. S. Pinsker, *Lickute Kadmoniot* (Vienna. 1860), Appendix, pp. 24, 26f.; J. Mann, *Texts and Studies,* I, 558f., and esp. L. Nemoy "Al-Qirqisani's Account of the Jewish Sects and Christianity," *HUCA,* VII (1930), 377f., 396. Cf. also Z. Ankori, *Karaites in Byzantium* (New York, 1959), pp. 269, 357f.; M. Sultanski, *Zeker Saddiqim* (Edited by S. Poznanski. Warsaw, 1920), Introduction p. 15 n. 2; M. Margulies, *The Difference Between Babylonian and Palestinian Jews* (Hebrew) (Jerusalem, 1938), pp. 20–23, 52–56; Baron, *SRH,* V, 22, 282.

209. Cf. above, p. 66; *MJC,* I, 69:8–9.

210. It is worthy of note that in a poem addressed by Isaac b. Khalfon to Joseph Falija (?) (cf. above n. 33), the poet omits the name of the addressee because of the fear of enemies; cf. A. Scheiber, 'Qeta 'Hadash mi-Diwan ha-Meshorer R. Isaac b. Khalfon," *Sinai,* XXVII (1950), 219, no. 5, and S. Abramson's notes thereto, *ibid.,* XXVIII (1950–51), 125. If the poet is serious about his fears, and the addressee is indeed a member of the Ibn Falija family, we have an additional sidelight thrown on the intrigues that were carried on between the contending parties. Ibn Khalfon wrote at the very time that the Ibn Falijas and the Ibn Jaus would have been in the thick of their battle; cf. H. Schirmann, "Isaac ibn Halfon (Hebrew)," *Tarbiz,* VII (1935–36), 294ff.

211. Cf. above, p. 159.

212. Baron, *SRH,* V, 45 suggests that Ibn Abitur lost face with the Jewish community by betting on Ibn Jau, who could not retain his hold on the position of Nasi for more than a year.

213. Ibn Daud appears to hint that prior to its rise to power the Ibn Jau family had been suffering serious disability owing to the activity of their enemies; cf. above. p. 160, "Perhaps we shall be able *to rid ourselves of the abuse of our enemies.*"

214. Ibn Abitur, who claimed an exalted genealogy (cf. above, n. 36), doubtless appealed to nativist sentiment among Spanish Jewry in his battle against R. Hanokh, the foreign interloper. Paradoxically, but quite understandably, this conservative nativism would appeal to the tradition of loyalty to Babylonia, while the foreigner, R. Hanokh, would not feel bound by such sentiments. This nativist sentiment is reflected particularly in the defense of Menahem b. Saruq by his disciples against the foreign school headed by Dunash;

cf. above, n. 200 and esp. A. Harkavy, "Le-Toledot R. Samuel ha-Nagid," p. 38 n. 3. Note, too, the formulation of the fifth question in Moses ibn Ezra's work on Hebrew prosody: "Why are children of the Spanish exile [i.e. the Jews of Spain] *superior* to those of other exiles in their composition of Hebrew poetry, rhymed prose and letters" [italics mine]," Moses b. Ezra, *Shirat Yisrael* (trans. by B. Z. Halper. Leipzig, 5624), p. 62. On nativism in medieval Jewish and Arab society, cf. S. W. Baron, "Saadia's Communal Activities," p. 51 n. 93.

215. It cannot be over-emphasized that the intervention of the king in the Jewish dispute is not an extraordinary event that resulted merely from the Jews washing their linen in public. The fact is that the case *had* to come before the Caliph, for all appointments to major religious offices within his domain had to be approved by him, particularly if they involved a public dispute; cf. N. Edelby, "L'autonomie législative des chrétiens en terre de l'Islam," *Archives d'Histoire du Droit Oriental*, V (1950–51), 320, 325. Note also the incident recorded by R. Dozy, *op. cit.*, I, 340 (Eng. trans. p. 289). Although the refs. cited deal with Christians, Prof. S. W. Baron (to whom I owe the ref. to Edelby) quite properly observes that the same conditions must have obtained with respect to the Jews; cf. Baron, *SRH*, V, 294 n. 2.

216. Cf. above, n. 74. I hope to deal with Ibn Abitur's propaganda against R. Ḥanokh in a separate paper.

217. Cf. *MJC*, I, 7:16 and A. Harkavy, "Le-Toledot R. Samuel ha-Nagid," pp. 3, 43 n. 2.

218. The evidence for this statement is collected in Prof. Mordecai Margulies' forthcoming edition of Samuel ibn Nagrela's *Hilkhatha Gabratha*. I am profoundly indebted to Prof. Margulies for having permitted me to read the manuscript of his introduction in 1957. Cf. also above, Appendix.

219. Ibn Daud himself was trained by his maternal uncle, R. Baruk Albalia (*MJC*, I, 77:13), the son and pupil of R. Isaac Albalia of Cordova (*ibid.*, 77:1–2). As a young man, the elder Albalia has been the recipient of Ibn Nagrela's favor, and he later maintained close relations with, and received material support from, the Nagid's son Joseph (*ibid.*, 74:12ff.).

220. *MJC*, I, 71:16–73:4. Moreover, even Ibn Nagrela's relations with R. Hai Gaon are referred to as quite favorable; *ibid.*, 73:15. On the other hand, it should be emphasized that Ibn Daud's description of Samuel's rise to power is but one more instance of a "rags to riches" tale (cf. above, n. 76). In this instance the literary paradigm for the story in *SHQ* was discovered fairly recently by S. M. Stern, "Life of Shmuel Ha-Nagid (Hebrew)," *Zion*, XV (1950). 135–138. As Stern observes, the story is told originally of al-Manṣūr and is as untenable for him as the one told of Ibn Nagrela. Moreover, J. Schirmann, "Isaac ibn Halfon," p. 300 noted much earlier that Ibn Daud's dates on Ibn Nagrela's early life are unacceptable in the face of manuscript evidence to the contrary; cf. also *idem*, "The Wars of Samuel Ha-Nagid," *Zion*, I (1935–36), 266–67 and *ibid.*, II (1936–37), 185–6. In the case of Samuel ibn Nagrela, as in that of the two captives, Ibn Daud wrote history with his own criteria of what the public ought to believe. He did not hesitate to adopt a stock tale that sounded plausible and to improvise dates.

221. R. Dozy, *op. cit.*, II, 79 (Eng. trans. p. 370).

222. Cf. above, n. 114.

223. For a much more impartial, and apparently widely entertained, evaluation of Ibn Abitur's style, cf. al-Harizi, *op. cit.*, pp. 41, 44. This is not to say that Ibn Abitur could not have slipped grammatically. However, Ibn Daud has given the error a prominence it could hardly have deserved. (One need but recall the importance attached to such errors in other disputes among Spanish Jewish men of letters to realize how exaggerated an importance was attributed to linguistic imperfection.) More than likely, the "error" was a neologism of which Ibn Abitur was fond. For the probable style, cf. J. Mann, "Varia," *Tarbiz* V, 23 n. 157.

224. Cf. J. Mueller, pp. 5, 22 n. k; A. Marx's note in *Orientalistische Litteraturzeitung*, III (1900), 134 n.; S. P. Rabbinowitz's note in H. Graetz, *Dibray Yemay Yisrael* (10 vols. Warsaw, 1916), III, 365 n. 2; Baron, *SRH*, VI, 264.

225. Cf. Midrash Tanḥuma, ed. Buber, II, 116 and n. 120 there.

226. The story of Ibn Jau's rise to power through bribery is not transmitted merely as a fact but has invidious overtones. Ibn Daud's opinion of *nesiim* who buy their way into office may be seen from *MJC*, I, 65:16–17; 67:1–3. To be sure, these statements are based on

Iggeret R. Sherira Gaon 92:13ff., but they are much more poignantly worded than the latter.

227. Cf. J. Schirmann, "Isaac ibn Halfon," p. 296; Dunash b. Labrat, *Shirim*, pp. 92, 162; A. Ashtor, *op. cit.*, p. 245.

228. Cf. above, n. 61. It is hardly likely that Ibn Daud has transmitted the text of the Jewish agreement verbatim. In the first place no Jewish community could commit itself to a dynasty of its own choice, for its Nagid had to be appointed by the Caliph; cf. above, n. 215 and esp. H. Z. Hirschberg, "The Salars and Negidim of Kairawan," p. 166. Ibn Daud makes no such claim for Ibn Nagrela or for his son Joseph, for he knew the real basis of their claim to power. Secondly, if the community did indeed present Ibn Jau with some testimonial expressing the hope that he and his family would rule forever, it would have been worded much more circumspectly, and probably in Arabic. This testimonial corresponds to the Arabic *bay'a* or agreement of investiture ideally required by Muslim tradition for the legitimization of a Caliph; cf. E. I. J. Rosenthal, *Political Thought in Medieval Islam* (Cambridge, 1958), pp. 31f., 44f. Note, too, that Ibn Daud says that the Jews agreed to his appointment to civil authority (*nesi'ut*), thus implying that Ibn Jau had no moral right to impose his will on R. Ḥanokh, the head of the academy; cf. above, p. 161. At best, therefore, one may suggest that Ibn Daud translated or paraphrased, but, alas, how cleverly he did it.—Character assassination, of which Ibn Daud's treatment of Ibn Abitur and Ibn Jau is a specimen, is a well known motif in medieval Hebrew poetry; cf. Baron, *SRH*, VII, 149.

229. Cf. above, p. 161 and refs in n. 227.

230. Cf. *MJC*, I, 47:1ff.; 78:9ff.; 81:3ff.

231. Cf. L. Strauss, *Persecution and the Art of Writing* (Glencoe, 1952), pp. 10, 34f., 65 and esp. pp. 16, 30, 61f. on the literary devices used by philosophers to hint at esoteric significance, among them "errors" and self contradiction. The purpose of stories and history was the consolation of the community and the furtherance of public morale; cf. above, n. 134 and esp. L. Strauss, "Farabi's Plato," *Louis Ginzberg Jubilee Volume* (2 vols. New York, 1945) English Section pp. 377ff., 382ff.; *Averroes' Commentary on Plato's Republic* (Edited and translated by E. I. J. Rosenthal. Cambridge, 1956), I:11:1f. pp. 30, 125f., II:16:6f. pp. 77, 202f. That Ibn Daud stands in the medieval philosophic tradition of al-Farabi, Maimonides and the younger Averroes is today a truism; cf. J. Guttmann, *Die Religionsphilosophie des Abraham ibn Daud aus Toledo* (Goettingen, 1879), *passim*, esp. pp. 14f. J. Guttmann, *Ha-Filosofia shel ha-Yahadut* (Jerusalem, 1951), pp. 134ff., M. Arfa, *Abraham Ibn Daud and the Beginnings of Medieval Jewish Aristotelianism* (Unpublished doctoral dissertation. Columbia University, 1954).

232. Cf. D. Conforte. *Qoray ha-Dorot* (Edited by D. Cassel. Berlin, 1846; New York, 1944), f. 5a. For the date of Conforte's work, cf. *ibid.*, p. iv.

233. *Ibid.* f. 2b = *MJC*, I, 61:17f. The following is the text of R.Samuel ha-Nagid's report, MS Sassoon (for full ref., cf. below n. 225). p. 58:

רבנן סבוראי דרל״ז. רב יוסף הוא ראש רבנן סבוראי בסוריא ל״ח שנה סימן דרע״ר. ובשנת כ״ד לגדולתו נחתם התלמוד. חתימה [!] התלמוד רד״ס. ומשם ועד שמת רבה יוסי י״ד שנה שנת דרע״ר.

234. Conforte, *loc. cit.* = *MJC*, I, 62:3f. MS Sassoon, pp. 58–59 reads:

הדור השני תלמידי דרב סמא ורב עינא ולא הוזכרו בשמותיהם כי הישיבות בטלו כמו נ׳ שנה אחרי מות רב סמא עד שנת דשמ״ט מפני שנאת מלכי פרס ושמדותיהם.

235. Conforte, *op. cit.*, f. 3a = *MJC*, I, 62:16f. MS Sassoon, p. 59 reads:

ואחריו רב ששנא ורב בוסנאי רב ששנא נקרא רב משרשיא בר תחליפא בשנת דתמ״ט. סוף רבנן סבוראי דתמ״ט.

236. Conforte, *loc. cit.*, = *MJC*, I, 62:19f. MS Sassoon, p. 59 reads:

סדר גאונים דתמ״ט רב חיננא מנהר פקוד תחלת הגאונים בפום בדיתא ח׳ שנים

Actually, Conforte is citing R. Samuel Ha-Nagid and *SHQ* only for the point at which the Gaonic period begins. The remaining data in his statement are drawn from *Iggeret R. Sherira Gaon* (Edited by B. M. Lewin. Haifa, 1921), 106:4–6; this accounts for the מר before the Gaon's name and for the duration of his term. The alternate term is the one given by the Nagid and *SHQ*.

237. Cf. above, pp. 172f. and esp. n. 150. The same observation holds true for the citation from the *Mabo* in Estori ha-Parḥi's *Kaftor wa-Peraḥ*; cf. A. Epstein, *loc cit.* On the other hand, the statement cited by R. Estori is not recorded in MS Sassoon, and Filipowsky's conjecture, cited by Epstein, is as good as any.

238. Sc., beyond the partisan attitude for R. Ḥanokh and against Ibn Abitur discussed above, p. 180.

239. Cf. *PAAJR*, XXVI (1957), viii.

240. As of the present writing, Prof. Margulies kindly informs me, the introduction and texts are in galley proof and will be published shortly.

241. Cf. M. Steinschneider, *Catalogus librorum Hebraeorum in Bibliotheca Bodleiana* (3 vols. Berlin, 1852–1860), II, 2471–2472; *idem, Die Arabische Literatur der Juden* (Frankfurt a.M.,1902), pp. 109, 130; A. Epstein, "Meqorot le-Qorot ha-Geonim," pp. 167–169, (= *Kitbay R. Abraham Epstein*, II, 413–415).

242. Cf. S. D. Sassoon, *Ohel David* (2 vols. Oxford, 1932), II, 1066–1068. Incidentally, the MSS listed by A. Epstein, *loc. cit.*, n. 8 do not contain the chronological portion of the work.

243. To be sure, the material on Ibn Nagrela and the century after his death could be dismissed as a later gloss. However, in view of Sambari's testimony on the identity of a man who had been the Nagid of his own community (cf. next note), Margulies felt that this would be a cavalier dismissal of written evidence. There can be no question that Margulies is correct; cf. below.

244. Such a work, Margulies pointed out, is indeed ascribed to him by Joseph Sambari of Egypt, who completed his chronicle in 1672; *MJC*, I, 156 (end). On Samuel ibn Hananiah ha-Nagid, cf. also S. Abramson, "R. Judah ha-Levi's Letter on his Emigration to the Land of Israel (Hebrew)," *Kirjath Sepher*, XXIX (1953–54), 133–144.

245. Cf. the citation in S. D. Sassoon, *op. cit.*, II, 1068 col. a in support of *MJC*, I, 54:1–2. Note, too, the citation of Maimonides in confirmation of the identification of R. Judah the Prince (cf. B. Hamburger, *Maimonides' Einleitung in die Misna*. [Frankfurt a.M., 1902,] pp. 19f., 65, 67). The words במסכת אבות in the citation from MS Sassoon begin a new clause.—In this connection, MS Sassoon may be cited to illuminate the citation by A. Zacuto, *op. cit.*, p. 146 col. a (bot.). The MS reads, p. 59:

סדר גאונים דתמ"ט. עיקר ישיבה היתה בפום בדיתא ולפיכך נגמנה סדר הגאונים שבפום בדיתא תחלה
ואחר כך נגמנה שבסוריא ושאר מקומות כמו שעשינו בשאר.

246. *MJC*, I, 67:13–17. MS Sassoon p. 64 reads:

וברחו ב' בניו אל רב שמואל הנגיד לגרנטה והיה שם עד השמד וברח האחד לסרקסתה ונשא אשה
והוליד בנים ומהם ר' חייא בן אל דוארי (!) ונפטר בשנת דתתקי"ד בארץ קשטיליאה ואחריו לא נשאר
בארץ ספרד אדם מפרסם שהוא מבית דוד לבד לבד יאשיהו בנו.

(The last three words are found in no MS of *SHQ* except for MS Epstein-Halberstamm, which I have not seen, but the collations of which were made by N. Bruell and presented to me by my late teacher, Professor Alexander Marx. Bruell's note reads: נגיד בנו יאשיהו. The word נגיד is obviously a corruption of לבד.

247. MS Sassoon, pp. 64f. The statement follows immediately upon the one cited in n. 242.

248. Perhaps חלוק or חוק with deletion over it.

249. A sentence has been omitted by homoioteleuton.

250. Menahem B. Solomon ha-Meiri, *Bet ha-Behirah, Perush 'al Pirqay Abot* (Edited by S. Stern, Vienna, 1854) p. 16b; *MJC*, II, 225; copied by Isaac Lattes, *ibid.*, p. 234.—For the evaluation of the evidence presented in the text, cf. M. Auerbach, *op. cit.*, pp. 17, 35.

251. Cf. above, n. 19.

252. For an alternate conjecture, cf. V. Aptowitzer, *op. cit.*, pp. 24f., n. 11.

253. A. Marx. Review of Poznanski's *Anshay Kairawan* in *Zeitschrift fuer Hebraeische Bibliographie*, XIII (1909), 74.

254. Cf. *MJC*, II, 234.

255. The same point is made in a different way by V. Aptowitzer, *loc. cit.* in n. 252.—The section of the Meiri reprinted in *MJC* is only a fragment of the Meiri's historical introduction.

The Soteriology of
R. Abraham Maimuni[*]

I

However else R. Abraham Maimuni's *Kifāyat al-ʿAbidīn* or "Compendium for Devotees"[1] may be characterized—as a handbook of *halakhah*, a treatise on moral theology, and a philosophic-mystical interpretation of Judaism—it was, in the first instance, an apologia for the Sufi-like Jewish pietism of which the author had become an adherent and indeed an ardent champion.[2] From the documents published recently by Professor Goitein it has become quite clear that neither Abraham Maimuni nor his colleague and close associate in pietism, R. Abraham ibn Abu'l-Rabiʿa the Ḥasid, began the pietist movement in Egypt.[3] While they were responsible for introducing into Egyptian synagogues the liturgical reforms that were inspired by pietist motives,[4] they had both aligned themselves with an existing group of *ḥasidim* whose devotional practices no less than their mystical doctrines had much earlier identified them to the community at large as a formal or semi-formal fraternity.[5] However, as Nagid of Egyptian Jewry, and hence *ex officio* as the most distinguished member of this circle in the first quarter of the thirteenth century, Abraham Maimuni felt required to defend this apparently novel form of Jewish devotionalism against the charge of *bidʿa* or innovation.[6]

As the studies of Wieder and Goitein have made quite clear, this defense was not necessitated merely by idle tongue-wagging of community gossips and malcontents, who reveled in the opportunity to find some

[*]The research for this paper, part of a larger study on the history of medieval Jewish messianism and messianic doctrines, was assisted by a grant awarded by the Committee on Faculty Research Grants of the Social Science Research Council.

fault with their *rayyis*. The enforcement of the reforms and the high inroads which the new tendency succeeded in making in some of the most
fashionable Jewish circles of Egypt evoked the organized opposition of
men who combined attachment to the more accepted forms of tradition-
alism with their own political aspirations. Some of the opponents of
Maimuni and his circle included men who were determined to wrest the
Nagidate from the Maimuni family, and to restore it to aristocratic Jewish families which had been native to the Middle East for centuries. In
their view the new tendency could be construed as but one more innovation that a family of Andalusian interlopers had brought to, and forced
upon, an old and proud Jewish community. In the days of Abraham
Maimuni they once again resorted to the extreme measures they had
employed against his father by going to the Muslim authorities for help,
knowing full well that the charge of *bid'a* even within the Jewish community was not one that the Muslims would dismiss lightly.[7] Temporal and
theological interests thus dovetailed neatly on both sides of the fence.
Hence, at the very height of his career, Abraham Maimuni postponed his
work on literary projects that were close to his heart and took up the
cudgels in defense of his view of the Jewish "way" and "goal."[8]

Since the immediate model of inspiration for this brand of pietism
was apparently the Sufi way of life as it had crystallized in North Africa
and Egypt in the twelfth and thirteenth centuries, Abraham Maimuni appropriated not only whole chunks of characteristically Sufi vocabulary,
but also some of the principal forms of apologia and argument that had
been adopted by leading orthodox Muslim expositors of this trend.[9] Like
al-Qushayri and al-Ghazzali, Maimuni acknowledged only one way to the
mystical life, namely the one embodied in the laws and doctrines of traditional religion, which to him, of course, meant rabbinic Judaism.[10] Accordingly, in the first instance he summoned the lax and the impious to
religious observance and sincerity. The transgressors of his day,
Maimuni's work made it apparent, were not all of a piece. Some were the
weak and the hypocritical of every age, who conformed only to the extent that they had to, that is, to the extent that the threat of force or some
similar pressure compelled them to, or out of some positive ulterior motive.[11] Considerably less reprehensible morally, but no less of a threat to
genuine religion, in his view, were the mechanically pious, who performed by rote or out of fear of God in the crassest sense of the term.
Within this category, as we shall see, he included even religious functio-
naries of his community, the general run of halakhists and *dayyanim*,
who were, to a large extent, unconscious of the true meaning and purpose of religion.[12]

A far more serious challenge to Judaism in Maimuni's eyes was represented by those who neglected one or more of their religious duties deliberately, and ostensibly out of sincere motives: namely, out of the

feeling that *tefillin*, *ṣiṣith*, and *mezuzah*, or even the normal requirements of interpersonal relations, were basically irrelevant to true religion. To men of this school of thought, contemplation of God in solitude and the religious rapture of one hour were of far greater merit than the scrupulous fulfillment of a hundred religious prescriptions. After all, rites and social law were but a means to an end, and it was precisely the ultimate goal of religion of which the common run of devout most frequently lost sight. If one had finally found his own way to the *wuṣūl* or goal, what need did he have to perform acts that were intrinsically meaningless or expendable?[13] Muslim Sufism of the anti-nomian, no less than of the orthodox, brand had gained an audience within the Jewish community, as shown by the specimens of Muslim Sufi writings that were transcribed into Hebrew characters for the sake of Jewish readers.[14] Accordingly, Maimuni addressed himself to Jewish Sufis as much as to Jewish cynics, for they neglected their duties to their fellow Jews and to the Jewish community even as much as they did to God Himself. However genuine their motives, they, too, were on the wrong track. Access to the elevated way of life, and especially to ultimate religious knowledge, he contended, lay exclusively within the paths fixed by traditional Judaism. "The way" could only be reached and traversed through the most scrupulous fulfillment of the Law, ritual as well as moral, prescribed by God through His prophets. Moreover, one could hope to arrive at the special road only after having successfully, i.e., properly, traversed the common one. In evidence, he constantly cited examples from the *sira* or lives of the prophets and of the pious men of earlier generations as well as texts from Scripture and rabbinic literature showing how modern and pietistically oriented their teachings and way of life had been.[15]

The whole burden of his argument was, therefore, that the sincerely motivated Jew need no longer repair to a Sufi retreat. He had but to comport himself at home, in the synagogue, or in the marketplace in accordance with the letter and spirit of the Torah to attain the heights that had been vouchsafed the pious of Israel.[16] Indeed, his claim went further than that. If it was love of God, religious knowledge, and the assurance of immortality of which one was in search, it was only in traditional Judaism that he would find it. This Judaism had long since described all the rungs of the ladder of religious virtue[17] that the Sufis were proclaiming and publicizing: abstinence, liberality, sincerity, mercy, gentleness, withdrawal, all of which led to the final goal of knowledge and love.[18]

While all of these religious types were the objects of his concern, his immediate tactical problem, as we indicated, was with the pillars of the community. Some of these men opposed him with no ulterior motive, but only out of a sincere suspicion that the supererogatory liturgical practices of the pietists—purifications, genuflexion, prostrations, weeping, abstinence, withdrawal—were Muslim-inspired and quite contrary to the established practices and the spirit of the Jewish religion.[19] To these Maimuni appealed in the way that many a great reformer has invoked in support of his program. He was not reforming at all, he contended, but merely restoring. In proof, he cited ancient sources attesting the antiquity, and hence the religious validity, of *ḥasidic* practices. The fact that these practices had been neglected, forgotten, and but recently rediscovered and revived, in a milieu where, to be sure, they had become characteristic of Gentile devotees, did not detract from their merit. The practices of the *ḥasidim* could not be legitimately condemned as "ways of the Gentiles" or as "imitations of the heretics."[20]

As has often been the wont of mystics and religious reformers, he carefully (re)defined classical as well as later terms denoting religious and moral qualities, thereby providing linguistic "attestation" to his ideological program. Needless to say, his linguistic distinctions and redefinitions were at least as much an effort to read his own convictions into classical categories as they were to recover the original meanings of the postures and practices of the true devotee.[21]

Since these apologetic techniques, not to speak of terminology and concepts, reflect the deep inspiration of Sufi literature and practice, it was natural for modern scholars to suggest that even the structure of Maimuni's *magnum opus* must have been composed on a plan suggested to him by one or more Sufi manuals such as al-Ghazzali's *Iḥya 'ulūm al-dīn*. After all, was not Maimuni's book, like al-Ghazzali's, constructed as a tetralogy?[22] Did both not defend the mystical way of life in their respective religions in much the same way, i.e., as authentic fulfillments of their respective Scriptures and with examples from the *sīra* of the prophets and *awliyā'*? Did not the Muslim manuals also spell out the stages and the states through which the devotee had to pass and in which he had to perfect himself before attaining the ultimate goal? Maimuni's heart obviously lay with the Sufis, for he openly conceded that their way of life was more creditable than the mechanical and frequently disingenuous type of practice that he encountered within the confines of his own community. If any further proof was required by modern scholarship for Maimuni's infatuation with Muslim pietism, it could be found in the fact that though he opposed the imitation by Jews of a Muslim practice of purification, he no less vigorously refused to condemn it as a "way of the Gentiles," inasmuch as the Muslims were monotheists.[23]

Now while I have no desire to question the profound impact that Sufism had on Maimuni and the members of his circle, that is by no means the only crucial factor in his thought or in the style of his argument. To mention but the affinity of vocabulary, it is interesting that while Maimuni does use many terms in common with the Sufi thinkers he was also, apparently, careful to avoid others.[24] Certainly, there is no evidence that in his conception of the religious experience to which he aspired, and to which he hoped to guide his disciples, he in any way went beyond the limits which his father had indicated constituted the ultimate in religious bliss. To put the matter bluntly, Maimuni in no way gives even the remotest hint that man's soul can become one with God. The transcendence and otherness of God are never even remotely questioned in *Kifāyat al-ʿAbidīn*, for Maimuni's type of religious experience apparently could not exceed the limits of vision and knowledge.[25] As for the specific instance of ritual in which Maimuni seemed to show his prejudice in favor of Sufi usage, careful consideration of the details of the case will show the very opposite of what it has been said to show. Maimuni had refused to condemn as *"ḥuqqot ha-goyim"* (usages of the Gentiles) a practice that some Jews had adopted of washing the limbs, Muslim fashion, before prayer. On the other hand, let it not be overlooked that he condemned the practice in no uncertain terms. The practice, he claimed, was strictly Gentile usage and having no basis in classical Jewish sources should be avoided. However, he could not categorize it as one of *ḥuqqot ha-goyim*, since that was a technical category which was inapplicable in this case.[26] Both sides of his argument were thus predicated on the same criteria, objective halakhic canons. By these standards of measurement he could not characterize as idolatrous a practice which his understanding of the law gave him no right to condemn as such.[27] Whether his halakhic judgment in this instance was one on which all jurists would have agreed is quite another matter[28] and totally irrelevant to our evaluation of Maimuni himself. In prayer, as in morals and faith, he advocated restoring only what could be attested as authentically Jewish, i.e., halakhically verifiable.[29] Indeed, the instance in question is an excellent case in point. *Ḥasidut*, or piety, he contended repeatedly, was ancient, indeed the most ancient form of Jewish devotion. He advocated following only those ways that could be verified as authentically ancient Jewish forms of worship, but not practices that could not be described in those terms, no matter how pietistically motivated they were. To have argued in any other way would have defeated the very purpose of his book and played right into the hands of his opponents.

Despite his admiration for the sincerity of Muslim ascetics and pietists, he made every effort to show that not only were the details of his program attested by Jewish sources but that the spirit of his program, to the extent that it was Sufi, derived originally from Judaism. The Sufis had taken from the Jews, not the Jews from Sufis.[30] In the considerable portions of his work that are available for examination either in print or in manuscript, not a single Gentile author, Greek or Muslim, is cited by name, except for an aphorism by Galen.[31] This is all the more remarkable in view of the fact that *ḥasidim* like Maimuni were by no means averse to the study of secular literature, particularly scientific tracts.[32] Clearly, this was no accident. Abraham Maimuni was no less of an Aristotelian than his father,[33] and yet unlike his father or Baḥya, who influenced him profoundly, he did not invoke Gentile authorities even obliquely in support of his scientific theories.[34] Finally, there is absolutely no evidence, although it is not unlikely, that Maimuni studied Sufi literature. There is also no evidence, and it is most unlikely, that Maimuni came to espouse *ḥasidut* and Sufi-like attitudes and practices primarily as a consequence of conversations with, or observation of, Muslim pietists. Doubtless, the spirit of his time and of his environment influenced him, even to the extent of trying to adjust Judaism to some of the ideas and goals popularized by the Sufi movement of his day. Most notable in this regard, as Wieder's studies have shown, were his concern with prayer as a basic vehicle for the life of piety and his reformation of certain synagogue practices toward that end. However, it should not be overlooked that despite the importance of these stresses and activities to his program; they were *but a part* of a much more inclusive religious regimen.[35] In his most Sufi-like moments, he exercised a critical selectivity that derived from his primary thesis: *ḥasidut*, like philosophy—and like his father, he believed that the two were very much in harmony with each other—was not basically Gentile; it was Jewish. In other words, he would evaluate every idea and practice by the one source that he acknowledged as legitimate in the area of religion, and that was the Torah as rabbinic Judaism understood it. Perhaps he himself was unaware of how deeply Sufism had affected him. But unless we are to dismiss Maimuni as a major dupe or charlatan, we must reconsider his infatuation with Sufism that is generally invoked as the sole explanation for his work. Perhaps more weight should be accorded to his claim that sources closer to home determined the content and structure of his thinking and of his major literary enterprises.

Indeed, it stands to reason that, inasmuch as his work sought to demonstrate to his opponents the basically Jewish character of his program, he would even structure his work along Jewish lines rather than after some alien pattern that might expose him to renewed charges of attempting to import religious notions from the outside. In view of the fact that only a small portion of the work has survived even in manuscript, the structural plan of the work has so far remained a puzzle. However, I believe that enough information is at hand, both from what Maimuni himself has divulged as well as from what is reported by others who saw portions of the work now lost, to reconstruct the external plan of the book. The results will be most significant for a new evaluation of his teachings.

The *Kifāyat al-'Ābidīn* consisted of four books, which were, in turn, subdivided into ten parts. The first seven of these parts were included in the first three books, while the remaining three parts were made subdivisions of the fourth and final book. Significantly, Book I was preceded by seven introductory sections (*muqaddimāt*), and Book IV by three such "preambles."[36] For the present, we cannot say with certainty whether each *muqaddima* was meant to correspond with the respective part of the book. What is apparent is that as a medieval author who was trained in the techniques of literary exposition, Maimuni took pains with form no less than with content and gave his work a symmetrical structure.[37] More important, the provision of separate groups of introductions to Books I and IV demonstrated graphically what Maimuni had repeatedly emphasized in his book, namely that *Kifāyat al-ʿAbidīn* consisted of two discrete expositions of religion. The first, contained in Books I–III, represented the "common path," that is, the one that is equally obligatory for all men. The second, contained in Book IV, set forth the "special" or "elevated path" open to the relatively few but true devotees of God.[38] In a renowned letter on his literary activity, Maimuni indicated that the *Kifāya* was constructed on the two pillars (lit., roots, basic principles) of fear and love of God.[39] Since even a glance at the preserved portion of the work on the "special path" will suffice to indicate that the elevated way of devotion was predicated on the love of God,[40] it is clear that in Maimuni's view the common path was basically one deriving from, and expressing, fear of God.[41] Put differently, fear of God was a stage in man's religious development, through which the true devotee had to pass. Fear, then, was represented in the first instance by absolute compliance with the legal obligations of Judaism. Love, on the other hand, consisted in infusing this compliance with a certain attitude, a state of mind and type of concentration that led to special knowledge.

While both these categories are to be found in the works of Muslim theologians and are singled out as aspects of devotion by Sufi thinkers,[42] whatever the ultimate source of Maimuni's inspiration, he doubtless knew that these two religious stages had been described in much the same way by his father. Maimonides not only asserted that fear is but a stage on the road to the ultimate goal, namely, the love of God;[43] he also indicated that while fear of God is inculcated by actions, the love of God is achieved through opinions inculcated by the Torah.[44] Now if there is any author whom Maimuni cites constantly, it is his father.[45] Indeed, he frequently glides over a discussion with a statement that he has no need to expatiate on the point in view of the fact that it has already been treated at length by his father in the commentary on the Mishna, in the *Mishneh Torah,* or in the *Dalāla.*[46] If we would, therefore, look for a source from which Maimuni could have drawn this neat classification, the most likely one is the work of his father. If it will further be borne in mind that Maimonides' distinction between fear and love was closely connected with his explanation of the term *ḥasid* as applying to one who fulfills the Torah beyond the mere requirements of the Law, and that both of these discussions—namely, the distinction between fear and love and the definition of the *ḥasid*—come near the very end and climax of the *Guide of the Perplexed*,[47] it becomes even clearer that Maimuni, whose work was predicated on fear and love with a view to showing the way to live the life of the *ḥasid*,[48] was essentially extrapolating from, and building his own system around, what his father had indicated were the foundations of Jewish piety.

Given Maimuni's source of inspiration, and especially the Maimonidean definition of fear-actions, love-opinions, it can be no coincidence that the strictly halakhic portions of Maimuni's work (actions) were confined to the first three books of the *Kifāya*, while the fourth dealt exclusively with opinions and states of mind or with actions expressing such states.[49] Indeed, the opening verse in the prolegomena to his book may now be understood to have been cited as the theme of the work *in accordance with the pietist Hebrew jargon which Maimuni would employ throughout his book:* מי בכם ירא ה' שמע בקול עבדו אשר הלך חשכים ואין נגה לו יכטח בשם ה' וישען באלהיו. "Whoever among you *fears the Lord* and heeds the voice of his devotee, though he walks in darkness and has no light, let him trust in the name of the Lord and rely upon his God (Isa. 50.10)."[50] That is to say: Abraham Maimuni, the servant and devotee of the Lord, summons the masses of men who as yet only fear the Lord[51]—i.e., observe the legal requirements of the Torah only exoterically and in the common way—and, therefore, necessarily still walk in darkness, to show them the path to real trust (*beṭiḥah*) in God,[52] in order that they may gain some of the light reserved for the authentic devotee. Once again, the reader cannot fail to notice that this opening summons merely expressed in somewhat different words the very same figure of speech that had been employed by Maimonides in the prolegomenon to his *Guide*; for Maimonides, too, had stated that he was showing the perplexed how to enable the light to permeate the darkness in which the habit of life had enveloped them.[53] To be sure, Maimonides' "perplexed" were apparently far more sophisticated than Maimuni's "fearers of the Lord." However, that is only another way of saying that the son was not merely rehashing the father, but adapting his concepts and even figures of speech for a new and wider audience. The basic aim and approach were the same.

Having opened with a thematic statement, the remaining "preambles" touched on some of the sensitive points over which Maimuni had been drawn into conflict with some of the pillars of his community,[54] and which reflect the apologetic motives of the book.[55] While in the body of the work itself, the author turned to a straightforward exposition of Judaism, he took occasion to expatiate on those aspects of law to which he and the members of his circle attributed special importance.[56] However, it was not a detailed manual of Jewish law that "is now in force," but rather an exposition of the principal aspects of law that were obligatory to all.[57] On the basis of Maimuni's own comments on this portion of the work, Rosenblatt has characterized Book I as Maimuni's counterpart to the first book of his father's *Mishneh Torah*, the *Sefer ha-Mada'*.[58] This may well be the case, for in addition to the information assembled by Rosenblatt, we may now add that the first book also probably included a section on laws of idolatry.[59] However, the burden of the first section, according to the testimony of Maimuni himself, was the study of the Torah and the way of acquiring Torah (*qinyan Torah* and *darkah shel Torah*, in classical Hebrew).[60] In short, Book I set forth the foundations of the life of Torah in the way of basic opinions and in the habits necessary for acquiring knowledge of the Torah. The subject of Book I, therefore, was Torah.

While the first of the three parts of Book II has also not survived even in manuscript form, we can be even more certain of the contents of this section from details provided by Maimuni himself as well as from a brief but valuable quotation from it in a work by a later author. From the section of Book II part 2 that has been published[61] we learn that Maimuni had devoted special chapters in the preceding section to concentration in worship (*kawwanah*) and to the laws of the recitation of the *Shema'*.[62] From a meager quotation in a medieval work on ethics, we learn further that the second chapter of Book II was entitled "On the Unity [of God] and [His] Freedom from Imperfection."[63] While the connection between this title and the laws of liturgy is not immediately apparent, its inclusion in the context of the laws of prayer makes it likely that the chapter treated the attributes that one may employ in worship and was thus connected with the theme of the unity of God proclaimed in the *Shema'*.[64] Maimuni himself reports that Book II also included a section on the laws of fasting.[65] Hence, it is quite evident that while Book I dealt with the relationship of man to the Torah, Book II turned to man's relationship to God himself.

This was clearly the theme of part 2 of Book II, the contents of which have long been known. Treating all aspects of ritual worship that were not confined to specific days of the year, prayer, *tefillin, ṣiṣith, mezuzah,* circumcision, its overall subject was obviously *'abodah* or worship.[66] Maimuni extended this concept to include not only formal acts of liturgy, but other acts relating to man's service to God. Hence, he included in this section the laws of vows and oaths, as well as a section on sincerity and duplicity. While the latter theme obviously also dealt with relations between man and his fellow, Maimuni's primary emphasis in this chapter was on the lie that was not socially provable (*genebat da'at*). Significantly enough, in this chapter he treated all those incidents in Scripture that would appear to sanction occasional lying.[67]

From Maimuni, too, we know that Book II contained a section on the obligation to procreate children.[68] This chapter, incorporated in part 3, was doubtless part of a much broader section dealing with 'arayot, a fragment of which has been preserved in a MS in Columbia University.[69] Now while strictly speaking these laws do not come under the laws of 'abodah as the term is generally understood, it will soon become evident that Maimuni treated these matters in this part of his work inasmuch as he classified them in the light of his father's earlier classification of these laws.[70]

Book III treated the laws of interpersonal relatonships—business, torts, criminal assault, charity, and friendship.[71]

With these laws, Maimuni's handbook of *law* came to an end. Since, as we have indicated, Book IV was intended by its author to be read as a work unto itself, whatever overall plan the work did have should become manifest from Books I–III, which were dedicated to perfection in the service of God through *acts*.

Now a quick glance at the unifying theme of each of the books and of their sequence will suffice to indicate that *Kifāyat al-'Abidīn* was constructed on the pattern formulated by Simeon the Righteous as the foundation of the world: the Torah, worship, and acts of kindness.[72] Since Books I–III had been defined as the *sulūk al-'āmm*, the popular and universally obligatory way of life, they came to teach that the world—that is Jewish mankind at large—must base its life on three pillars: first, on the Torah, under which Maimuni, like his father, included not only the study of the Torah but also the foundations or basic opinions of the Torah; second, on liturgical service, under which, as we have seen, Maimuni included more than mere devotional exercises; and, finally, on a just and charitable society.

This division is of interest on two accounts. In the first place, it shows that however Sufistically oriented Maimuni was, the technique he employed in the exposition of his synthesis of Judaism was deliberately structured in terms of classical categories. No less important, it reveals that in his overall plan he divided his work in accordance with his father's explanation of the three-fold purpose of the revelation at Sinai. In the *Guide of the Perplexed*, Maimonides explained that every one of the six hundred thirteen commandments has been enjoined with a view to one of three purposes: "either with a view to communicating a correct opinion, or to putting an end to an unhealthy opinion; or to communicating a rule of justice, or to warding off an injustice; or to endowing men with a noble moral quality, or to warning them against an evil moral quality. *Thus all [the commandments] are bound up with three things: opinions, moral qualities, and political civic actions.*"[73] That by Torah Maimonides understood correct opinions there can be no doubt, for in his commentary on the dictum of Simeon the Righteous he translates that term by *'ilm*.[74] From his *Guide*, we are able to see why Maimuni included the laws of sex under the category of *'abodah*. Maimonides, it will be recalled, had explained the purpose of many of the ritual laws as being the control of the appetites and the training of man for the proper posture in his approach to God.[75] Furthermore, in his explanation of his division of Jewish law into fourteen categories, he indicates explicitly that the laws of family life are regulations that come under the general rubric of affairs between man and God.[76] It was for this very reason that in the *Mishneh Torah*, the section on sexual prohibitions (*'issuray bi'ah*) was incorporated into the Book of Holiness.[77] In other words, positive law was propaedeutic and aimed at purification of the moral qualities so that man may proceed to religious contemplation and correct knowledge.[78] Maimuni fully accepted this view of the Torah and its laws. He, too, regarded the essence of Torah as knowledge,[79] and the positive law as a vehicle for the ennobling of man.[80] His *opus* was structured in accordance with his father's division of the contents and purposes of the Torah, i.e., of religious virtues, into intellectual, moral, and practical,[81] and simultaneously in accordance with the ancient scheme of Simeon the Righteous.

II

A consideration of the three parts of Book IV will reveal that the same basic plan determined their contents and sequence. The burden of this fourth book was to indicate the way in which a man who had perfected himself in the fear of God, i.e. in the fulfillment of *actions* prescribed by the Torah, could proceed to achieve knowledge and love of God. That the reader of *Kifāyat al-'Abidīn* had, in beginning his study of the fourth book, now entered an entirely new and higher plane of religious devotion is indicated by Maimuni graphically, it will be recalled, by a new set of *muqaddimāt* that preceded, and corresponded to the number of parts of, Book IV.[82] However, Maimuni was even more explicit about the matter. He emphasized that the true devotee is one who studies not only the injunctions and exoteric meaning of the Torah but also their esoteric implications. Words and concepts in Scripture are possessed of more than one meaning. While they mean one thing to the average student of the Torah, they have many more and profounder meanings to the pietist.[83] Accordingly, Book IV had to recapitulate, albeit on a different plane and in an entirely different fashion, the areas taken up in the first three books of the *Kifāya*.

Although no fragment of part 1 of Book IV is known to have survived, on the basis of indications in the available portions of the work Rosenblatt has plausibly suggested that this section contained, among other matters, a discussion of the qualities necessary for, and conducive to, prophecy.[84] As was the case with the virtues advocated by Maimuni generally, examples of these qualities were located in the lives of the patriarchs, who to Maimuni, as to other Judeo-Arabic philosophers, represented the exemplars of perfect religion.[85] Prophecy, in the view of these philosophers, was basically a state of spiritual perfection, a stage of knowledge, or, to paraphrase the philosophers themselves, a state of illumination through and with perfect and complete opinions. In this conception of prophecy, which was shared by Maimonides and his son Abraham,[86] the most direct and complete stage of religious knowledge was represented by the revelation of God to Moses.[87] Men of post-Scriptural times who would aspire to a high stage of illumination that would be prophetic or akin to it could do so, in the first instance, only by the mastery of the opinions embedded in the prescriptions and teachings of the prophetic books and most notably of the Torah. This was a most appropriate theme with which to begin the portion of the *Kifāya* dedicated to the special way, for to Maimuni, as to his father, knowledge of God was a consequence of, indeed another way of designating, the love of God; and the opening discussion on prophecy was thus an immediate introduction to the aim and essence of true love of God.[88] It is almost certain, therefore, that that part of Book IV that dealt with prophecy was dedicated to the exposition of the esoteric or special opinions and knowledge concealed in the text and commandments of the Torah. Indeed, Maimuni indicated in no uncertain terms that the commandments, properly fulfilled and *considered,* would lead to the knowledge that corresponded to what his father had indicated was the true aim of philosophy, the understanding of the acts of creation and metaphysics (*ma'asay bereshit* and *ma'asay merkabah*).[89] In short, the esoteric section of the *Kifāya* opened with a theme parallel to the one in the corresponding part of the first section of the work, the acquisition of Torah.

In all likelihood, a chapter of this first part of Book IV is to be identified with an essay by Maimuni that has circulated as a separate tract known as *Ma'amar 'al ha-Derashot.*[90] Although in its present form this little treatise is somewhat suspect, having come down to us only in a few manuscripts of late Ashkenazic provenance,[91] we have the reliable attestation of Maimuni and of the sixteenth-century scholar Abraham ibn Megash that such a section did indeed constitute a portion of the *Kifāyat al-'Abidin.*[92] Our reasons for suggesting that this treatise constituted a part of Book IV is that it dealt with the figurative meaning of rabbinic homily, and thus constituted a commentary on Torah in the wider sense of the term, while neighboring chapters treated mistaken notions about immortality and the real nature of the ultimate reward.[93] Thus, the contents of the essay and of chapters next to it pointed to the ultimate goal (*wuṣūl*) of religion with which the work came to a final climax.

Part II of Book IV has been published in full by Rosenblatt, and its contents are, therefore, not a matter of conjecture at all. This section spelled out the qualities of mind and heart that must be brought by the devotee to his performance of the way of life enjoined by the Torah: sincerity, mercy, generosity, gentleness, humility, faith, contentedness, abstinence, war against the appetites, government of the faculties, solitude.[94] Just as in the part of the work which exposed the exoteric way of Judaism, Maimuni often took occasion to show how specific commandments were conducive to the attainment of these qualities,[95] here, in the avowedly esoteric division of the book, the aim was to require the infusion of the observances with these virtues.[96] In a word, this part of Book IV spelled out the proper stance in worship and all ritual performance, i.e., the correct mental and emotional attitude in the course of one's daily service to God, or his ‘abodah. Once again, the identification of these rungs in the ladder of virtues with moral qualities demonstrates how in his view the ultimate function of ‘abodah was to train man to nobility of character, which, along with correct opinions, were indispensable to the good life.[97]

The last and third part of Book IV spelled out the goal which the pietist must strive to attain.[98] Consisting in love and knowledge of God that approached, if it did not indeed achieve, the state of prophecy,[99] this state was a foretaste of the bliss vouchsafed the righteous in their final state of immortality and in the messianic era.[100] Designated in Arabic as *wuṣūl* or the goal,[101] it was this way of life and its fulfillment that were embedded in the Hebrew term *ḥasidut*.[102]

Although our definite knowledge of the contents of this third part is confined to the indications made by Maimuni himself at the end of the second part of Book IV, a specimen of the actual text of this final part of the work is, I believe, contained in a Bodleian manuscript of some eleven leaves.[103] Badly damaged and faded in many spots beyond readability,[104] this fragment from the Geniza contains a sizeable portion of a chapter on the eternity of the Torah and its immutability.[105] Among other things, it discourses on prophecies that were fulfilled in the days of the Second Temple and on the obligatory nature of the Torah in the days of the future Third Temple in the face of passages from Scripture that would seem to suggest that the Almighty may retract His original commandments. These themes are well known from the works of other Judeo-Arabic thinkers,[106] and there is nothing odd about the fact that Maimuni should have seen fit to make reference to them in his work. What is of interest is that he saw fit to reserve a discussion or recapitulation of some of them for the final sections of his work. Clearly they were appropriate here not only because they treated a "pillar" of Judaism, but more especially because they were particularly germane to one of the audiences of special concern to the author.[107] To the ingenuous Jewish Sufi, to the man of good faith and perfect sincerity, who assumed that a particular confession and ritual way of life were irrelevant to true piety, since they were essentially tools for the vulgar masses that would in the fulness of time pass out of existence, the author reaffirmed the eternity of the Torah and its unchanging primacy in religion. The Torah would stand as part of God's covenant with heaven and earth as the way ordained for service to Him even after the advent of the redemption of Israel and the reconstruction of the Temple. In other words, Maimuni implied that the way of *ḥasidut*, which, as we have seen, was the subject of this section, was not merely a temporary device for piety in the present age, but would endure, indeed would become the normal way of life even after the redemption of Israel, even as it had been followed in antiquity by the patriarchs and the prophets. *Ḥasidut* was, therefore, not merely the end to which the Jew must strive at present; it was the *telos* of religion from ancient times to the end of the world.

To recapitulate, our examination of the structure of Maimuni's work has revealed that the three parts of Book IV of the *Kifāyat al-'Ābidīn* treated the subject matter of Books I–III of the work with the difference that in the final Book the themes of Torah, *'abodah* and *ḥasidut* were elucidated in terms of their special, esoteric (*khāṣṣ, bāṭin*) implications. Now if the maxim of Simeon the Righteous underlay the structure of Maimuni's work, it is apparent that the term *gemilut ḥasadim* in that classic maxim had now been invested with a new meaning, one quite different from what it had had in the first three books and one quite different from what had generally been understood by that term. In Maimuni's new usage, *gemilut ḥasadim* had little connection with civic action or even with acts of kindness; rather, it represented a state of moral and spiritual perfection. *Gemilut ḥasadim* in this context and usage clearly means a life of *ḥasidut*[108] in the sense that Maimonides had explained the words *ḥesed* and *ḥasid* in his commentary on the Ethics of the Fathers and in *The Guide of the Perplexed*.[109] In the introduction to his commentary on Abot, Maimonides had also indicated the importance of this quality: "There is no higher virtue than *ḥasidut*, except for prophecy, to which indeed *ḥadisut* leads, as the Sages said: '*Ḥasidut* leads to the Holy Spirit [= prophecy].'"[110] We shall soon see that Maimuni concurred fully with his father not only in his estimate of *ḥasidut*, but also in his definition of the ultimate goal to which it leads.

For the moment, however, we must examine further the implications of Maimuni's tacit use of the maxim of Simeon the Righteous as a blueprint for the structure of his work. In view of the new and esoteric meanings with which the three pillars of Judaism had now been invested, the key word in that classic maxim, *ha-'olam*, now also took on a new significance. If *ha-'olam*, as Simeon the Righteous taught, stands on knowledge, moral virtues, and the supererogatory way of life known as *ḥasidut*, clearly *ha-'olam* designated not only this world—which it assuredly did[111]—but also, and no less, a spiritual state to which only the pietist could gain access. It was a world to be attained, a final reward to be reached only after successfully mastering the three pillars,[112] a world for which life in this world was only preparatory.[113]

Now, in the course of his work Maimuni frequently took occasion to indicate what the ultimate goal and fruit of a life of *hasidut* were. Consisting essentially in prophetic knowledge and spiritual bliss, these states were associated by Maimuni, as they had been by his father, with the world to come (*ha-'olam ha-ba*).[114] In other words, the goal or *wuṣūl* that the pietist might attain at the present time was but a foretaste of the enduring state that would encompass the earth with the advent of "the world to come."[115] In any event, the word *ha-'olam*, in the maxim of Simeon the Righteous, was obviously now interpreted esoterically as synonymous with *ha-'olam ha-ba*, which Maimuni is quoted as having defined as "the final reward."[116]

Obviously, the first question that comes to mind is whether our reading of Maimuni's tacit interpretation of the term *ha-'olam*, in contrast with the fuller expression *ha-'olam ha-ba*, can be supported by cogent evidence from other sources. Here, once again, we are drawn back to Maimuni's principal and immediate source of inspiration, namely the teachings of his father, Moses Maimonides.

As is well known, one of the pivotal points in the controversy in Europe over the works of Maimonides centered around Maimonides' seemingly novel reading of the eschatological rewards mentioned in rabbinic literature. In the view of Maimonides, the *ultimate* reward of the righteous was not the messianic redemption and the resurrection connected with it, but the incorporeal state of the soul in the world to come.[117] In attempting to understand Maimonides' reading of classical texts, Nahmanides noted that Maimonides' view of the sequence of eschatological rewards derived from the latter's understanding of the term *ha-'olam ha-ba*. According to Nahmanides, Maimonides could say that *ha-'olam ha-ba* was not a world to be created in the future but one that is already in existence, one into which the souls of the righteous enter immediately after death,[118] because Maimonides understood this Hebrew expression as it was used by Andalusians. Only among the latter, Nahmanides claimed, would one find the usage of the expression *ha-'olam ha-ba* as the state of immortality enjoyed by the soul at the present time immediately after the death of the body.[119] Not only was Nahmanides right that Andalusians used the words *ha-'olam ha-ba* in that sense, but evidence can also be adduced that they even used the single word *'olam* and its inflections in that sense.[120] Abraham Maimuni, brought up under an Andalusian curriculum, absorbed such usage as a matter of course, and he understood the word *ha-'olam* in the maxim of Simeon the Righteous to mean *ha-'olam ha-ba* even as the same word was used in that sense elsewhere in the Ethics of the Fathers.[121] Thus, in his

Milḥamot ha-Shem, composed in defense of his father's eschatology, he cited in proof that the state of incorporeal bliss is one reached by the great sages even in the present world the Talmudic blessing:

עולמך תראה בחייך
ואחריתך לחיי עולם.[122]

In other words, the attainment of *ha-'olam ha-ba* was, in Maimuni's view, dependent very much on man's behavior and opinions and, what is even more important, reserved for the select few who had achieved the heights of special religious knowledge.[123] Once again, we see how much akin his views on religion were to those of his father.

III

Now, if all that the structure of *Kifāyat al-'Abidīn* had revealed to us was an implicit new exegesis or homiletical interpretation of Abraham Maimuni on the maxim of Simeon the Righteous, the point would be of interest enough. However, further reflection on the implications of structuring a compendium on Jewish devotion on the model of this classic dictum throws a number of isolated but by no means insignificant phenomena into focus. In the first place, it shows that the plenitude of quotations from Pirqay Abot in *Kifāyat al-'Abidīn* is not a coincidence. This tractate is quoted more than any other post-Biblical book, and in a sense Maimuni's work may be construed as a commentary on the Ethics of the Fathers.[124] Clearly, this tractate was not only sacred to him; it held a special place in his library of classical religious texts. The most obvious explanation for this in the light of his overall view of life was the remark from the Talmud cited by his father at the very beginning of his renowned introduction to Abot: ראי מאן רבעי למיהוי חסידא, ליקיים מילי ראבות. "Whosoever would become a *ḥasid* (!) should fulfill the stipulations of [the tractate] of Abot."[125] Now the becoming of a *ḥasid,* it will be recalled, was precisely the burden of Maimuni's major work. That the fulfillment of Abot with this aim in mind was Maimuni's underlying purpose is further borne out by the explicit importance he attached to his father's introduction to that work in a statement in the very chapter which serves as the climax to the moralistic section of the *Kifāya.*[126]

Here again, our attention is drawn to the special place that this tractate held in the Andalusian-rabbinic curriculum. Baḥya ibn Paquda, whose thought has universally been acknowledged to be very much akin to that of Abraham Maimuni, singles out this tractate from the rest of Hebrew literature as being the most lucid guide to the piety enjoined by the Rabbis.[127] When Abraham ibn Daud wishes to praise or condemn the religious heroes or villains of Jewish history of the Gaonic period and after, he does so in terms clearly inspired by the virtues enumerated in Pirqay Abot.[128] Of the esteem of Maimonides for Abot we need say little, except to point to the fact that it was the only tractate of the whole of the Mishna to which he provided a special introduction. Why? "For," Maimonides explained in his introduction, "this tract over and above its other virtues shows the way to perfection and to true happiness [sa'āda]. ... Now the sages of blessed memory have long since taught: "Whoever wishes to become a pious man [ḥasida] let him fulfill the teachings of Abot. Now there is nothing higher than piety [ḥasidut] except for prophecy itself; indeed, the former leads to prophecy. ... Hence, it becomes clear from their statements that conformity to the disciplines enumerated in this tractate is conducive to prophecy."[129] This evaluation of the tractate as a compendium for the therapy of the soul[130] became a characteristic feature of the disciples of Maimonides. Joseph b. Judah ibn Aqnin and David Maimuni both composed commentaries of their own on the tractate.[131] Isaac Abravanel informs us that this tractate was held in special esteem in Spanish circles, some of whom saw in its maxims a reflection of Greek philosophy, and some of whom, in reaction, saw in it a kind of appendix to Biblical wisdom literature.[132] While the work was by no means neglected in Ashkenazic Jewry, in Sefardic circles it remained the subject of a steady stream of commentaries from the eleventh to the seventeenth centuries, serving as a vehicle for the advocacy of the ideal Jewish type—rationalist, halakhist, mystic—favored by the authors of these commentaries.[133] Indeed, the striking thing about the place of Abot in the medieval Jewish curriculum is that it held a quite different place of honor in the academies of Ashkenazim and Sefardim. Whereas in France, Pirqay Abot was recited liturgically and elucidated, we are expressly told, in such a way as to attract and influence the 'ammay ha-areṣ,[134] in Spain the work was studied as a part of rabbinic literature and did not apparently make its way into the liturgy until about the fourteenth century, and even then probably only as a consequence of the pressures of the Ashkenazic scholars who had come to Spain after the expulsion from France and as a consequence of worsening conditions in Germany.[135] However, irrespective of when the recitation of that tract was finally introduced into the synagogue in Spain, the Sefardim certainly did not think of the book as a popular treatise, as one intended primarily for the ignorant. To the Spaniards and those under their influence, the book encased profound truths of moral discipline, the mastery of which was indispensable for the intellectual and spiritual perfection that culminated in prophetic bliss.[136]

Now there was a profound reason for the special attraction that the tractate of Pirqay Abot exercised over Moses Maimonides and his son. Both of these men, it will be recalled, had tried desperately to restructure the tenets and prescriptions of Judaism into a coherent and rational system of life as well as of education. More than any other classical Jewish work, Abot doubtless seemed to them to be the great manual of Jewish paideia reflecting their scale of values. Dedicated principally to the advocacy of a life of Torah, which was easily reinterpreted to mean religious contemplation, Pirqay Abot more than any other classical work was addressed to the individual man in the second person singular, exhorting him to attain religious perfection. Unlike so much of the Talmud, which prescribed law in the third person as it was commonly enjoined upon all men, whatever their station and whatever their individual gifts, Pirqay Abot quite plainly addressed itself to a special class of men, to men of superior endowments in Torah or in moral capacities. Moreover, the injunctions and exhortations of the tractate left room for constant improvement, for the ascent of greater and greater heights intellectually, morally, religiously. In a sense while all the rest of the Mishna was a program for *darkan shel benay adam*, this tractate was quite plainly dedicated to *darkan shel talmiday ḥakhamim*. What is more, the work fitted in perfectly with their views on the ultimate rewards in store for the righteous man, for unlike so much of the remainder of the Mishna this tractate stressed the reward in store for the righteous and it did so almost exclusively in terms of *ʿolam ha-ba*.[137] However, in Andalus, and especially in philosophic circles, *ʿolam ha-ba* was a state of bliss and knowledge, and, above all else a state of ultimate freedom that was impossible of realization in the mortal state.[138] Hence, in keeping with the Andalusian view, Maimonides and his son saw in this tractate not only a guide to the good life, but a very special guide that led to the attainment of the ultimate goal in store for the noble in soul, i.e., perfect freedom for the truly pious. Thus, Abraham Maimuni's structuring of his work on a pattern suggested to him in a dictum in the Ethics of the Fathers was not a mere device or fancy. It was intimately connected with his view of the ultimate goal of man, namely, the attainment of the Holy Spirit and of the world to come.

No one of his audience, who was learned enough to understand *Kifāyat al-ʿĀbidīn*, could fail to notice that the road advocated by Maimuni was but a latter day reformulation of the ladder of soteriology portrayed in classical days by R. Phinehas b. Jair: "Diligence leads to cleanliness, cleanliness to purity, purity to abstinence, abstinence to holiness, holiness to humility, humility to fear of sin, fear of sin to *ḥasidut*, *ḥasidut* to prophecy, prophecy to the resurrection, the resurrection coming through the agency of Elijah, may he be remembered for good."[139] The same reader could also not fail to notice that in Maimuni's scheme, no less than in that of R. Phinehas, *ḥasidut*, which came about through the fulfillment of the teachings of Abot, represented the ultimate rung in a scale dependent on man's will and acts, before he entered upon the stages that were dependent exclusively on the grace of God.

There were, of course, two important and manifest respects in which Maimuni departed from his father's approach to the religious life, and both of them were related to matters of technique rather than of content or ideology. The first was his espousal of a Sufi-type asceticism and devotion. Although Maimonides advocated extreme moderation in the enjoyment of material goods, and indeed saw great merit in the extreme asceticism and withdrawal of some of the great men of times past, he regarded the extreme measures of Sufis of his own day, with their disciplines of extreme self-mortification, the way of fools.[140] While a careful examination of the *Kifāya* will show that Maimuni also cautioned against going to extremes,[141] there can be no doubt that he was much less sparing in his unequivocal admiration for extremes of asceticism and solitude.[142] Why, then, did Maimuni adopt so much of the Sufi-like behavior and ideology? To reply that he had become converted to this point of view will not suffice. He may well have become an adherent of pietism and kept the matter to himself. Why did he try to impress some of his Sufi-like reforms on the synagogal ritual? The problem is not why he joined the way of *ḥasidut,* but why he espoused it *publicly.* Let us not forget that as a Nagid and as a son of Maimonides, Abraham had been schooled in the political arts. He was presumably an astute leader no less than a responsible one.

The second respect in which the *Kifāya* reflects a departure from the father's technique was in its public appeal for a special way avowedly reserved for the few.[143] Whatever one may believe Maimonides' real view on the question to have been, the fact of the matter is that he stated and reiterated that his *Guide* was not meant for the reading public at large but only for those who had had the necessary propaedeutic training and were in need of his exposition. He enjoined the addressee of the book not to reveal it to others. Maimonides thus remained at least formally consistent: the work was an introduction to *maʿasay bereshit* and *maʿasay merkabah* and, therefore, had to be treated in accordance with the halakhic limitations imposed on those subjects.[144] But no such circumspection, or even better, limitation of appeal is implied in *Kifāyat al-ʿAbidin.* Although much of the work is not available for perusal, it is quite evident from the parts that have survived that Abraham Maimuni was deliberately aiming at a much wider audience than his father admitted that he was. The popular style, the plenitude of anecdotes, and the many illustrations taken from the *realia* of daily life, all testify to the wide appeal that the work was intended to have.[145] Why did he appeal to masses to follow a special way? Is such a quest not almost a contradiction in terms by his own very canons of thought?

I have put both of these questions together, for I believe that the answer to both is very much the same. Times had changed somewhat from the days when Maimonides had first decided to expose his synthesis of Torah and metaphysics to a few perplexed souls. While disdain for Jewish observance and confusion over the basic theoretical tenets of religion was an old story—remember the complaints of Baḥya, the protests of Judah ha-Levi, the apologia of Abraham ibn Daud—these backslidings or even occasional defections had never become serious enough to merit real alarm or an outright attack on the problem by the heads of the community. To be sure, they would protest; they would explain and exhort; Maimonides could even construct a whole system for the sincerely perplexed. But, at least officially, the problem could have been said to be one with regard only to the few.

However, by the first quarter of the thirteenth century, conditions had worsened considerably, and the sensitivity of the leaders of the community to new problems within the Jewish community had doubtless become markedly sharper. In the first place, there was deep anguish over the suppression of Judaism in Andalus, the Maghreb and Ifriqiya by the Almohade regimes. While the program of physical extermination that had characterized the first years of the Almohade conquest seemed to have abated considerably, the humiliation of the Jews, many of whom by now were formally Muslims, continued. The Jew who remained steadfast in those areas were in a state of continual anxiety and anguish. The number of converts who were permanently lost to the Jewish community continued to mount steadily under such conditions, thereby adding to the general agony and despair.[146]

But this was by no means all. From all corners of the Muslim world, and particularly from the Middle East and Egypt, news came of conversions to Islam on the part of learned Jews, whose defection could by no means be attributed to venal motives. To mention but three men whose names are on record, Abu'l-Barakat, Samau'al al-Maghribi and Isaac b. Abraham ibn Ezra had left Judaism and become devotees of Muslim philosophy. While the motives of Abu'l-Barakat are not known and Ibn Ezra soon repented, Samau'al's explanation of his apostasy is a matter of record: he had had a vision, a religious experience.[147] Reading his account of his conversion—and even after allowances are made for his pathological and vituperative egotism—it is difficult to overcome the feeling that Abu'l Barakat the Jew had been overcome with the kind of despair of the redemption that overtook many a distinguished Jew in Egypt in Mameluke times and in Spain in the following century.[148] Almohades in Spain and the Maghreb, Zaydis in Yemen, Crusaders in Palestine—all seemed to point to the validity of the argument of Christian and Muslim alike that the Jewish hope for redemption was vain and chimerical. While many were reluctant to betray their ancestral heritage in so extreme a form, they were attracted to a seemingly more innocuous form of union with the majority by way of Sufism. This form of mysticism often prided itself on its religious neutrality and on its openness to people of any confession.[149] It was an easy avenue of escape, for it did not require active renunciation. A Jew might easily pretend to have his cake and eat it at the same time. However, from the point of view of a traditionalist this was religious nihilism.

To a communal leader like Abraham Maimuni, and to his highly placed associates, the potential dangers of the new tendency were terribly grave and had to be checked. Doubtless, they were ingenuously convinced of the rectitude of the mystical form they had come to espouse. But there can be little doubt that the actual conditions in the community gave added substance and force to their convictions.

This was no time for mere pious rebuttal of skepticism or of heretical views. Even a full exposition of the theory of Judaism along the lines of Bahya's *al-Hidāya 'ila fara'id al-qulūb* (*Hobot ha-Lebabot*) or Maimonides' *Guide* was not enough. Nothing short of a full and specific compendium spelling out the way of the religious life in all of its details was what was required. Like the works of al-Qushayri and the guides of al-Ghazzali to the mystical life along strictly legalist lines, Maimuni's work was very much of a reaction to, and of an attack upon, the mystical nihilism that had made deep inroads into all religious communities of the Mediterranean world. Moreover, the searing impact of the defection and backsliding of some highly placed persons necessitated broadening the base of appeal and the mending of fences on a wide scale. The special way had now to be opened to many more than in the past, for many of the intelligent and of the semi-intelligent were seeking new means of salvation for their souls and for the amelioration of their Jewish lot. As a responsible communal leader, Abraham Maimuni did what leaders in many another challenging situation had done and would continue to do. If he could not "lick 'em" he would seem to "join 'em." *'Et la'asot la-shem heferu torateha* (Ps. 119.126).[150] How much more necessary was it to join a way that was a means to the most authentic translation of the life of Torah as set forth in Pirqay Abot.

Indeed, even his contention that the special way was reserved for the very few, coupled with his exposition of this way in a popular and highly accessible style, was probably a device to make it more attractive to people who aspired to intellectual respectability.

In this connection, we may note that despite Maimuni's reiterated contention that the ultimate reward of man was a purely spiritual one, and despite his ridicule of popular messianic hopes in terms that were no less sharp than those employed by his father,[151] he nevertheless hinted—by way of concession to the masses—that the way of piety would also make life in this world far more physically comfortable than the mere pursuit of daily needs and pleasures.[152] While, like his father,[153] he insisted that a measure of true freedom and deliverance could be attained in his day and in the very heart of the exile through contemplation, he reaffirmed his faith in the traditional messianic redemption and in the deliverance of the people of Israel.[154]

However, it may well be that even in his espousal of asceticism and self-mortification he had taken a cue from his father. While Maimonides had denounced excessive mortification and abandonment of social life, he had also indicated that in an age of degeneration, "*such as obtains in our times,*" when there is no place to which the good man may repair with the hope of finding a decent society, withdrawal was meritorious, "As it is written: 'Let him sit alone and keep silence (Lam. 3.28).'"[155] What is more, Maimonides had also indicated that he who mortifies himself for the Torah is indeed living in the one way that is certain to achieve the realization of the Torah in his life.[156] There can be little doubt that Maimuni was aware of these doctrines and that he had weighed the factors of his society in coming to the conclusions that he did.

There is one further element to which students of Maimuni have not given any consideration and which I believe merits it. In his *Epistle to Yemen,* Maimonides had indicated that according to a tradition transmitted in his family for generations, prophecy would be restored to the people of Israel in the year 1210 or 1216.[157] Moreover, the restoration of prophecy was, in his view, one of the signs indicating the approach of the messianic age, as it is said: "And your sons and your daughters shall prophecy."[158] Now, if this proof text means anything, it means that the sign of the imminence of the messianic age will be the widespread manifestation of the prophetic spirit. This would be the remarkable thing about that period, for prophecy as such was available, in Maimonides' view, to the elect even before that time. However, in the light of Maimonides' general theory of prophecy, he doubtless meant that even after the advent of the promised year, prophecy would be granted only to the deserving pious and those with deserving intellects.

Since this tradition was one of the Maimuni family, one which Maimonides considered the most trustworthy of all traditions on the promise of the redemption, it is almost unthinkable that Abraham Maimuni should not have known it. Whether he accepted it or not we, of course, have no way of knowing with certitude. However, it is a reasonable assumption that he did in view of his acceptance of his father's theories in this area generally. Assuming that he did accept this tradition, his publication ca. 1225 of a popular manual on the way to achieve the state of prophecy becomes doubly significant. *Ruah ha-qodesh,* while still the perquisite of the elect and the select, would, nevertheless, now be open to many more than it had been in the period of his father's prime. If that were so, what would be holding back the full manifestation of the glorious period vouchsafed the people of Israel was not the fact that the appointed time had not yet arrived, but that the people were not meriting what was potentially available to them. In a word, what had, half a century earlier, been accessible only to those who had mastered physics and metaphysics, was now accessible to all who were truly pious.[159] If that was the case, the need for *Kifāyat al-'Abidīn* was indeed one of great urgency. In a sense, such a work was even more urgent than *Dalālat al-Hā'irīn*, for the age that would require a *Dalālat al-Hā'irīn* to guide it to prophecy had passed. *Dor dor ve-dorshav.* What his father had done for his own age by means of tools appropriate to his own day, Abraham was now doing for a subsequent age by means of new techniques that had now become relevant and necessary.

NOTES

1. References to published portions of the work are given by page and line number of the following works: Simon Eppenstein, פרק כ"ד וחלק מפרק כ"ה מכתאב כפאיה אלעאבדין לר' אברהם ב"ר משה ב"ר מיימון *Festschrift zu Israel Lewy's siebzigstem Geburtstag* (Breslau, 1911), Hebrew section, pp. 33–59; Samuel Rosenblatt, *The High Ways to Perfection of Abraham Maimonides* (2 vols. New York and Baltimore, 1927–38); Naphtali Wieder, *Islamic Influences on the Jewish Worship* [in Hebrew] (Oxford, 1947).—For the Arabic title of the work, cf. Rosenblatt, I, 130.1; MS Oxford Poc. 135 (Uri 316) (= Cat. Neubauer-Cowley, no. 1274), f. 1b; and the references listed in the index to פירוש רבינו אברהם בן הרמב"ם ז"ל על בראשית ושמות [henceforth referred to as *Payrush*] edited by S. D. Sassoon and trans. into Hebrew by E. J. Wiesenberg (London, 1959), p. 539. For my translation of the title, cf. below, nn. 21, 51. In his review of the first volume of Rosenblatt's edition, D. S. Baneth took exception to Rosenblatt's free translation of the title of the work; *Kirjath Sepher*, VIII (1931–32), 52.

2. On the Sufi orientation of Abraham Maimuni's *magnum opus*, cf. Rosenblatt, I, 48ff.; Wieder, pp. 7ff.; S. D. Goitein, "Abraham Maimonides and his Pietist Circle," *Jewish Medieval and Renaissance Studies*, edited by Alexander Altmann (= Philip W. Lown Institute of Advanced Judaic Studies, Brandeis University. *Studies and Texts*, IV. Cambridge, Mass., 1967), pp. 146ff. (hereafter referred to as Goitein, "A.M. (Eng.)").

3. S. D. Goitein, "Documents on Abraham Maimonides and his Pietist Circle" [in Hebrew], *Tarbiz*, XXXIII (1963–64), 181ff.; *idem*, "A.M. (Eng.)," pp. 150f.; Wieder, pp. 32ff.

4. Wieder, pp. 31ff.

5. Wieder, pp. 33f., 38; Goitein, "A.M. (Eng.)," p. 152.

6. Wieder, pp. 54f., 9 sec. 4, lines 1ff.

7. On the communal frictions that erupted almost immediately after R. Abraham's accession to the Nagidate, cf. S. D. Goitein, התחדשותה של המחלוקת בענין „הרשות" אחר עליתו של רבנו אברהם בן הרמב"ם *Ignace Goldziher Memorial Volume* (2 vols. Budapest and Jerusalem, 1948–58), II, Hebrew section, pp. 49ff. On the efforts to involve the government in the internal religious dispute, cf. *idem*, "New Documents from the Cairo Geniza," *Homenaje a Millas-Vallicrosa* (2 vols. Barcelona, 1954–56), I, 707ff. and *idem*, "Documents on Abraham Maimonides," p. 184. Our contention that *Kifāyat al-'Abidīn* was motivated largely by apologetic-defensive considerations is supported by the chronology of the events. As Goitein has shown, the appeal to the government was made no later than 1218, while the *Kifāya* was composed only after that time (cf. Rosenblatt, I, 3). Cf. further in n. 8. That the controversy had derived also from nativist sentiment is clearly indicated in the inquiry of R. Joseph b. R. Gershom to R. Abraham and in the latter's reply; Abraham Maimuni, *Responsa* (Edited by A. H. Freimann. Jerusalem, 1937), pp. 13ff. (reprinted in Abraham Maimuni, *Milḥamot ha-Shem* [Edited by Reuben Margalioth. Jerusalem, 1952–53], pp. 101ff.). R. Joseph writes that Hodaya the Nasi, one of the leaders of the opposition to Maimuni's religious reforms, "called me a bastard, reviled my late and learned ancestors with the epithet 'accursed son of accursed' [=excommunicated] and categorized all *[Jewish] Frenchmen* as sectarians and heretics who worship God anthropomorphically [lit., attribute, body, form and shape to the Creator]. Moreover, he bears tales about sages who are no longer alive and declared a ban *against anyone who would contribute to the support of a Byzantine or French [Jew].*" See also R. Abraham's reply and his reference to the campaign

against his religious practices, pp. 17f. Cf. also Jacob Mann, *Texts and Studies in Jewish History and Literature* (2 vols. Cincinnati and Philadelphia, 1931–35), I, 399 and especially n. 13 there; Wieder, p. 57. For the statement that these tensions were in large measure a continuation of the internal struggles for power that had begun with the arrival of Maimonides in Egypt, cf. S. D. Goitein, "Maimonides' Life in the Light of New Discoveries from the Cairo Geniza" [in Hebrew], *Perakim*, IV (1966), 30ff.; *idem*, "A Treatise in Defense of the Pietists by Abraham Maimonides," *JJS*, XVI (1965), 108. What is more, this factional tension probably continued into the lifetime of Abraham's son and successor, David, whose career as Nagid was even interrupted for a while by suspension from office; *idem*, "A Letter to Maimonides and New Sources Regarding the *Negidim* of this Family" [in Hebrew], *Tarbiz*, XXXIV (1964–65), 236f.; note that during the period of his removal from office, his place was taken by a Babylonian of the exilarchic family, *ibid.*, p. 243. To be sure, in the course of time, some of the oldtimers of the Near East joined the supporters of the Maimonides family (*ibid.*, p. 238).

8. Cf. Abraham Maimuni's own statement in the (fragmentary?) letter on his literary projects in *Israelitische Letterbode*, III (1877), 53 (reprinted and translated in Rosenblatt, I, 124ff.; reprinted in Abraham Maimuni, *Milḥamot ha-Shem*, p. 129). For the authenticity of this letter, cf. Jacob Mann, *The Jews in Egypt and in Palestine Under the Fatimid Caliphs* (2 vols. Oxford, 1920–22), II, 332 no. 4.—Although an apologetic purpose underlay his *magnum opus, Kifāyat al-'Abidin*, this motivation was only made explicit in a minuscule treatise dedicated to a defense of the brand of pietism advocated by Maimuni; cf. Goitein, "Documents on Abraham Maimuni," pp. 196f.; *idem*, "A. M. (Eng.)," pp. 149f.; and especially *idem*, "A Treatise in Defence of the Pietists," pp. 108f.

9. On the trends of Sufism in this period, see A. J. Arberry, *Sufism: An Account of the Mystics of Islam* (London, 1950), pp. 75ff., and especially pp. 84ff.; see also I. Goldziher, *Vorlesungen ueber den Islam* (Heidelberg, 1963), pp. 175f. (Heb. trans. *Harṣaot 'al ha-Islam* [Jerusalěm, 1951]), pp. 128f.

10. Rosenblatt, I, 132/3ff. and especially 136/7f. Note his repeated contention that it is impossible to be pious without fulfilling the commandments enjoined upon all: *ibid.* 144/5.18ff.; II, 64/5.10ff., 140/1.19ff., 420/1f.

11. *Ibid.*, I, 152/3.8f.; II, 106/7.18ff., and note the characterization of them as "inward unbelievers" (*ibid.*, 108/9.14). That there were even pseudo-pietists with ulterior motives, Maimuni knew from experience. Cf. Goitein, "Documents on Abraham Maimuni," pp. 187f.

12. *Ibid.*, I, 156/7.10f.; II, 174/5.4ff., 176/7.13f. There can be little doubt that it was this type of religiosity that Maimuni derided in his description of the faith of ignoramuses and of rabbinically oriented Jews who despised philosophical reflection; *ibid.*, II, 128/9.8f., 130/1.5f. Needless to say, Maimuni was resigned to the inevitability, indeed even social necessity, of this type of religion, for the masses of men could not be kept in line without crass threats and promises of punishment and reward: *ibid.*, II, 196/7, 272/3.8f. For better or for worse, the masses of men are feeble minded, and to think of them otherwise is a sheer pipe-dream; *ibid.*, II, 244/5.3. Note also his derisive remark about those who are scrupulous about the external mechanics of prayer without grasping their meaning and, therefore, behave ridiculously; Eppenstein, פרק כ"ד וכ"ה, p. 50 (on Responses in the Kaddish). His disdain for the purely Talmudically trained was a feature characteristic of philosophically oriented Jews of Andalus; cf. Bahya ibn Paquda, *Al-Hidāja 'ila Fara'id al-Qulūb* (Ed. by A. S. Yahuda, Leiden, 1912), p. 15, line 1 (=Heb. trans., ed. Zifroni, p. 79) and G. Vajda, *La Théologie Ascétique de Bahya ibn Paquda* (Paris, 1947), pp. 18 n. 1, 45. Maimonides, *Commentary to the Mishna* [Arabic and Hebrew, ed. Kafiḥ], IV, 200f. (introduction to "Heleq"): *idem, Treatise on Resurrection* (Ed. by J. Finkel. New York, 1939), p. 3. (However, cf. I. Twersky "Some Non-Halakic Aspects of the *Mishneh Torah*," in *Jewish Medieval and Renaissance Studies*, ed. Altmann, p. 111, n. 70).

13. Maimuni opens and closes Book IV, part 2 of the *Kifāya* with a warning against pietism that contravenes normal observance of the Torah and with an affirmation that perfection in the "common way" must antecede and then continue simultaneously with devotion according to the "special way": Rosenblatt, I, 144/5.18f. (and note his pointed example in I, 147/7.20f.); II, 64/5.10f., 420/1.2f. The observance of the Law is a debt to the Almighty, the pursuit of piety a gift. The Creditor will not forego His debts for mere gifts; I, 146/7.8–

10. His insistence on compliance with the Law was not confined to ritual but included social requirements as well; *ibid.*, II, 118/19.19f. Indeed, the true pietist did not defy even mere convention; II, 74/5.19f., 78/9.8f. Maimuni was sensitive to the charge that some of his disciples gave offense precisely in such ways; see Goitein, "A Treatise in Defence of the Pietists," pp. 110f., especially sections E and seq., and note Maimuni's admonition in Rosenblatt, I, 154/5.17f. Thus, while he himself tried to reform certain practices in the synagogue and derided those who opposed his reasoning, he cautioned against lending any support to those who mock scrupulous observance of the laws of worship; Eppenstein, p. 53 (near end).

14. On Muslim suspicions of Sufi heterodoxy and attempts to overcome them, cf. Goldziher, pp. 173f. (Heb. trans., pp. 127f.); Arberry, pp. 66f. On the influence of Sufi anti-nomianism on Jews, cf. S. D. Goitein, "A Jewish Addict to Sufism," *JQR*, NS, XLIV (1954–55), 38f. Cf. also Wieder, pp. 40f. For Sufi literature in Hebrew characters, cf. Hartwig Hirschfeld, "A Hebraeo-Sufic Poem," *JAOS*, XLIX (1929), 168–73 and the important notes thereto by A. R. Nykl and M. Sprengling in *AJSL*, XLVI (1930), 203–4. While there is no way of dating the Sufic fragments from the Geniza with certainty, the admonitions of Maimuni, cited in the previous note, coupled with the Muslim testimony assembled by Goitein, lend high probability to our conclusion that Jewish Sufism, or Sufi-like posture, that was relativist, anti-nomian, and interconfessional was quite noticeable by the time of Abraham Maimuni's Nagidate.

15. Cf. Rosenblatt, I, 134/5.15 and his repeated emphasis that the purpose of the stories in the Bible is to teach moral qualities by example (*ta'addub li-l'mutasharri'in*); cf. introduction to *Payrush*, p. 64, n. 410. To these could be added many more examples where the principle is applied without any explicit statement; cf. *ibid.*, pp. 92/3 to Gen. 29.25, 224/5 to Ex. 2.20. In the *Kifāya*, models for imitation are presented in the lives of Biblical as well as rabbinic personages: Abraham, the "father of generosity" (Rosenblatt, I, 176/7.1f.; cf. especially 180/1.5–6: "So know that [about Abraham] and imitate it and do the same in whatever way that you can."); Lot (*ibid.*, I, 176/7.21f.); Joseph for his mercy (I, 160/1.20) and so on. The general burden of these examples was to show that the elevated way of life enjoined by the Scriptures and rabbinic literature, and pursued by the prophets and pious of all ages, was identical with the ascetic-contemplative program of the *hasidim*; *ibid.*, II, 232/3.20f., 248/9.10f.—To be sure, the invocation of the *sira* of the prophets and the Rabbis as models of religious behavior (*exempla*) is well nigh universal among Jewish teachers and has many precedents in classical rabbinic literature; cf., e.g., *Abot de Rabbi Nathan, passim,* and M. Gaster's introduction to his translation of the *Ma'aseh Book* (2 vols. Philadelphia, 1934), I, xviif. However, the use of the *exemplum* as a vehicle for advanced religious instruction attained renewed vogue in Sufi circles, where the *sirah* of Muhammad and of early *awliyā'* (saints, beloved of God) were made part of the regular religious curriculum and were invoked as proof that the Sufi way of life was the original and most authentic form of Islam; cf. Arberry, pp. 13, 32f., 66f.—For the extent of Maimuni's quotations from Scripture and rabbinic literature, see the Index in Rosenblatt, II, 427f.

16. Cf. Rosenblatt, II, 296/7.2 on the Torah and the implications of his explanation of the oracle of Balaam, *ibid.*, 292/3.15f.

17. For this simile, cf. *ibid.*, 382/3.18.

18. Cf. Rosenblatt, I, 51f.

19. Orthodox Jewish suspicious of pietism, doubtless because of its potentially anti-nomian character, were encountered already by Bahya ibn Paquda; cf. Franz Rosenthal, "A Judaeo-Arabic Work Under Sufi Influence," *HUCA*, XV (1940), 439f.

20. Wieder, pp. 21f., 49f. Wieder notes with amazement that Maimuni drew support for his view of genuflexion from a statement of Rashi rather than from Gaonic precedent. However, this was probably a tactical device, for by citing the confirming opinion of a Jew living in the land of Edom, the non-Muslim provenance of the usage was demonstrated.

21. Cf. Rosenblatt, I, 134/5.1f. I hope to deal with the special vocabulary of Maimuni and his circle, its sources and its influence, in a separate paper.

22. Cf. Baneth, *loc. cit.*, p. 52.

23. Wieder, pp. 8f., 31f.; Rosenblatt, I, 48f., 95f.

24. Thus, Rosenblatt, I, 50f., could adduce no instance of Maimuni's use of some characteristically Sufi terms for states or stations, and could only point to terms resembling

them. However, Maimuni's avoidance of such terms can hardly be an accident. (According to Maimuni, the virtues are paths that must all be traversed simultaneously, if religious perfection is to be attained; Rosenblatt, II, 418/19.20f. They could, therefore, not be characterized as states or stages at all.) Wieder's assumption, *op. cit.*, p. 33, that the term דרך ה' was appropriated from the Sufis is unwarranted. It was all the more probably inspired by Maimonidean usage, if not by Scripture itself; cf., e.g., the opening Hebrew poem to the *Guide of the Perplexed*, where the way of piety is called דרך קדש (after Isa. 35.8), which is synonymous with דרך ה'. (On the authenticity of this poem, which plays on the concept of walking in the proper path in every one of its stichs, cf. W. Bacher, "Hebraeische Verse von Maimuni," *MGWJ*, LIII (1909), 581f.) In the same vein, the source of the word *Kifâya* in the title of Maimuni's work is probably to be located in the statement in *Mishneh Torah*, Shemittah, 13.13 where the righteous man is one who finds dedication to God as דבר המספיק לו. (In our paper on Maimonidean vocabulary, we shall try to show that this passage in the *Mishneh Torah*, which is quoted verbatim by Maimuni in Rosenblatt, II, 280/81, is of crucial importance for locating the source of some basic vocabulary of the *ḥasidim.*).

25. While Rosenblatt, I, 28f., 52, 95f., properly indicates that in Maimuni's view "the goal," whenever it is described, is intellectual, even in its ecstatic states, in the text of the *Kifâya*, he regularly, and in our view unfortunately, translated the term *wuṣûl* as "mystic union;" cf., e.g., II, 418/9.17f. This choice of words obscures the careful and innocuous term employed by Maimuni himself. For a clear and unequivocal statement by Maimuni, cf. *Milḥamot ha-Shem*, p. 64.

26. For the passage, see S. Eppenstein, *Abraham Maimuni, Sein Leben und Seine Schriften* (Berlin, 1914), p. 17, n. 1. In view of the fact that the passage may not be readily accessible to all scholars, I offer a translation of his remarks: "Now with regard to this matter [washing of the orifices of the body before prayer], let it be clear that whoever has bathed at home or washed his hands and feet for the sake of prayer has fulfilled his duty, for having immersed himself voluntarily he is on the verge of fulfilling his obligation. Whoever washes his forearm and imposes upon himself the obligation of washing behind his ears, combing the tangled hair of his head and washing his orifices before prayer after the fashion of the Gentiles, let him refrain and desist, since that is not Jewish practice and is not warranted either by written or by oral tradition. However, I cannot say unequivocally that this practice is in the category of Gentile religious practices (*huqqot ha-goyim*), inasmuch as those who practice these rites, namely the Muslims, are monotheists who abhor idolatry. Nevertheless, there is certainly no compelling need for aping them in this way, for our law and usage are quite sufficient, by God . . ."—For a Muslim tract on purification for worship, which illuminates the milieu and motivations of the objects of Maimuni's remarks, cf. al-Ghazzali, *The Mysteries of Purity* (Trans. by N. A. Faris. Lahore [Pakistan], 1966).

27. Underlying Maimuni's decision, of course, was his father's legal opinion that Islam was not in the category of idolatry; cf. Moses b. Maimon, *Responsa* (3 vols. edited by Jehoshua Blau. Jerusalem, 1957–61), II, 725f. and literature cited there. Maimuni's limitation of "usages of the Gentiles" to "idolatrous usage" may well have derived from the Talmudic discussion of royal funeral pyres (*B. Abodah Zarah* 11a), where the term "*huqqah*" is understood as a practice *for the sake of*, or inherently connected with, idolatry. This was clearly how the term was understood by many medieval commentators; cf. Tosafot to *Sanhed.* 52b, *s. v.* אלא; R. Hananel to *B. Abodah Zarah* 11a; Rashi, *ibid.*, *s. v.* אלמא; Tosafot, *ibid.*, *s. v.* ואי; Menahem b. Solomon Meiri, *Bet ha-Behirah 'al Massekhet 'Abodah Zarah* (Ed. by Abraham Schreiber. Jerusalem, 1944), p. 20. The latter commentator has conflated this interpretation with that of Abraham b. David of Posquières, which explained "*huqqah*" as "standard usage;" cf. Abraham b. David, *Commentary on the Treatise of Abodah Zarah* (Ed. by Abraham Schreiber. New York, 1960), pp. 22f.

28. Those who favored outright condemnation could well have pointed to the much more general definition of "*huqqot ha-goyim*" in Moses Maimonides, *Sefer ha-Misvoth* (Ed. by Ch. Heller. Jerusalem and New York, 1946), p. 106, prohibition no. 30, and *Mishneh Torah*, 'Abodah Zarah, 11.1.

29. Cf. Eppenstein, פרק כ"ד וכ"ה, pp. 45, 47 (end of first parag.).

30. Rosenblatt, II, 252/3.7, 266/7.5f., 318/9.5f., 16f., 320/1.7f., 322/3.6f., 382/3f.

31. Cf. Rosenblatt, I, 57f.; *Payrush*, introduction, p. 54. The reference to Aristotle in II, 134/5.14 is not to a work at all.

32. Cf. Wieder, p. 36.

33. Rosenblatt, I, 58f.; J. Guttmann, *Philosophies of Judaism* (Trans. by D. W. Silverman. Philadelphia, 1964), pp. 192f. Maimuni makes his position on this subject quite clear in ch. 22 of the section published by Rosenblatt. In setting forth his views on psychology he refers the reader to his father's commentary on Abot (II, 328/9), which is explicitly grounded in philosophy. However, Maimuni demonstrates his own method by grounding these theories in verses from the wisdom of Solomon in Scripture (II, 332/3). The distinctions between Abraham Maimuni and his father which Guttmann discerns are differences of emphasis explicable in the light of the different audiences to which the two authors were directing their respective works.

34. Maimuni's references to Greek philosophy, cf. Rosenblatt, I, 57, are more often than not pejorative. The difference between Bahya and Maimuni in their orientation to Jewish precedent has been well summarized by Vajda, *Théologie Ascétique*, p. 133; see also *ibid.*, p. 78. While Bahya did not mention his Muslim sources by name, modern scholarship has confirmed his debt to Muslim thought; *ibid.*, *passim*, and especially pp. 17f., 23, 25, n. 4, 41, n. 1, 44, n. 1, 57f., 83f.—For Bahya's influence on him, cf. Rosenblatt,, I, 54, 58f. However, Rosenblatt's many and apposite references to parallels between Bahya and Maimuni do not convey the basic affinity that Maimuni felt for Bahya's system more than for that of any other Jewish thinker save that of his father. These affinities range all the way from the basic approach to religion—exoteric versus esoteric, faith, asceticism, love of God, the meaning of ultimate religious bliss—and the use of common vocabulary to concern with literary symmetry in the presentation of the materials. A reading of the masterly analysis of Bahya by Vajda alongside the *Kifāya* will illustrate the point conclusively.

35. Cf. especially, Wieder, pp. 41f. However, Wieder glosses over the fact that in Maimuni's view not only prayer but many rituals lead to higher states of piety; cf., e.g., Rosenblatt, II, 88/9 on commandments leading to *ittikāl* (faith, surrender to God). In claiming that Maimuni failed to live up to his own preachments, Wieder, p. 41, seems to have judged Maimuni by the evaluations he has set up for Maimuni's program. A more judicious evaluation would perhaps have led to the conclusion that Maimuni was trying to show how piety could be achieved within the framework of traditional Jewish categories, among which life in society ranked very high.

36. Rosenblatt, I, 30–35.

37. Cf. Vajda, *Théologie Ascétique*, pp. 22f., 35, 42, 47, 85; Abraham ibn Daud, *Sefer ha-Qabbalah* (Ed. and trans. by G. D. Cohen. Philadelphia, 1967), pp. 189f.; *idem*, "The Story of the Four Captives," *PAAJR*, XXIX (1960–61), 95f., 104f.

38. Rosenblatt, I, 30 (end), 134/5.11f., 21f. The respective terms in Arabic, '*āmm* and *khāṣṣ*, mean not only popular and special but also connote mass, common and vulgar as opposed to elitist and aristocratic. Thus *khāṣṣat Baghdad* means the aristocracy of the city.

39. Cf. above, n. 8; *Payrush*, p. 120/1 to Gen. 35.4.

40. Rosenblatt, I, 156/7.4f., and note especially lines 15–16; II, 238/9.1f. Even in the love of God there are degrees, for in the *hasidic* terminology not אהבה was the ultimate but חשיקה; I, 142/3.11. Baneth, *loc. cit.*, has noted that in comparison with other mystical writers, Maimuni was sparing in his discussion of the love of God. In part, this was doubtless owing to the ineffable character of this stage of faith; cf. in a related connection, II, 140/1.1f. But in part it derived from the fact that in Maimuni's view formal love of God is also enjoined upon the common path, I, 140/1.1f., while true and elevated love of God may never be sundered from exalted fear of God, I, 142/3.1f., II, 158/9.4f. Obviously, Maimuni could never make the distinction between the obligations of love and fear as neat as we have, for both terms are enjoined in Scripture. However, the general burden of these terms in his work is clear throughout.

41. Note his emphasis on the fear of punishment in his description of the common path; I, 136/7.14f., 138/9.4f. The interior forms of trust in God are characterized by compulsion, fear, and hope; II, 174/5.2f., 200/1.13f.

42. Cf. Arberry, pp. 37, 42f. On Muslim precedents for the division of the religious life into exoteric and esoteric, cf. Vajda, *Théologie Ascétique*, pp. 16, 35f. On the definition of *tawakkul* (faith, trust, surrender), which is the subject of a whole chapter in Maimuni (Rosenblatt, II, 88f.), cf. Vajda, pp. 66f., 74f., 77f. Many of Maimuni's examples and

expressions are paralleled in the literature assembled by Vajda.—For Maimuni's reassertion of general predestination very much in the way that Baḥya and many Muslim theologians did, cf. Rosenblatt, II, 88/9.16f. On the rectitude of pursuing a livelihood, or reliance on physicians, *ibid.*, II, 90/1.16, 20f. On the impiety of relying on contingent or proximate causes (*asbāb*), cf. *ibid.* and 106/7.19f.

43. The Maimonidean texts dealing with fear and love of God have been assembled, translated, and analyzed by G. Vajda, *L'Amour de Dieu dans la Théologie Juive du Moyen Age* (Paris, 1957), pp. 118f. For a summary of Maimonides' view, cf. *Mishneh Torah, Teshuba*, ch. 10, which to a considerable degree recapitulates Maimonides' discussion in his introduction to M. Sanhed. ch. 10; cf. *Mishnah 'im Payrush R. Moses b. Maimon* (ed. Kafiḥ), IV, 197f. Cf. also the progression in *Mishneh Torah*, Melakim, 12.2 (near end).

44. Moses Maimonides, *Guide of the Perplexed* (Trans. by S. Pines. Chicago, 1963), III, 52 (end), p. 630.

45. Cf. Rosenblatt, II, 441; *Payrush*, p. 539; Wieder, p. 85.58.

46. Cf., e.g., Rosenblatt, II, 284/5.6f., 328/9, 354/5.20f.

47. Moses Maimonides, *Guide* III.52–3, pp. 630f., cf. also *idem, Mishneh Torah* (Ed. by S. Lieberman. Vol. I, Jerusalem, 1964), De'ot 1.5, p. 140 and parallels listed there. Since at the beginning of the *Guide*, III.53, Maimonides refers to his commentary on Abot, he clearly meant to have his remarks in the *Guide* amplified by what he had said in his earlier work. Accordingly, the *ḥasid* must be defined as one who meets the requirements of religion in terms of correct opinions (=Torah) and goes beyond the requirements of the Law in terms of moral acts; see *Mishnah 'im Payrush* (ed. Kafiḥ) to Abot 2.10 and 5.5, pp. 425, 458. The importance of these stipulations for understanding Maimuni's system will be seen below.

48. Rosenblatt, I, 134/5.15f.; cf. also below, n. 102.

49. Cf. *ibid.*, 30f.

50. Rosenblatt, I, 31; II, 418/9.10f. That Maimuni employed verses to summarize the theme of his work is clear from his explicit statement, *ibid.*, 424/5.18–20. As far as I can determine the use of verses at the beginning of the work was begun by Maimonides; in any case, it was certainly the latter's regular practice; cf. *Mishnah 'im Payrush* (ed. Kafiḥ), I, 1; *Mishneh Torah* (ed. Lieberman), I, 1, 93; *Guide*, pp. 5, 21; *Maimonides' Treatise on Resurrection* (Ed. by J. Finkel [=*PAAJR*, IX (1939)]) Hebrew text, p. 1; the opening and closing line of each of the 14 books of *Mishneh Torah*. Professor Isadore Twersky kindly calls my attention to the fact that this was noted by David Feuchtwang in *Haaretz*, 14 Nisan 1935. These verses were in addition to the introductory verse of Gen. 21.33, on which cf. Professor Lieberman's remarks in Moses b. Maimon, *Hilkhoth ha-Yerushalmi* (Ed. by S. Lieberman. New York, 1947), p. 5 and n. 7 there.—Whether such practice became common among Maimonides' disciples, I cannot say. Cf., however, Goitein, "Documents on Abraham Maimuni," p. 185 and the introductory verses to the sermons of Jacob Anatoli, *Malmad ha-Talmidim* (Lyck, 1866).

51. For this translation, cf. Rosenblatt, I, 132/3.19; II, 258/9.8, 280/1.5, and above, nn. 39–41.

52. Cf. Rosenblatt, I, 18; II, 204.6, 208.4, 214.2.

53. *Guide*, trans. Pines, pp. 6f.

54. Rosenblatt, I, 31.

55. Cf. above, pp. 75f.

56. Cf. the sections published by Eppenstein, פרק כ״ד וכ״ה and Wieder, pp. 83f.

57. Rosenblatt, I, 134/5.12. Maimuni's occasional references to Temple practice in connection with prayer were to emphasize that prayer is a surrogate for sacrifice; Eppenstein, פרק כ״ד וכ״ה, pp. 38, 43f. Cf. also Wieder, pp. 13f.

58. Rosenblatt,, I, 31.

59. *Payrush*, p. 54/5 to Gen. 24.12, where the chapter is entitled "Chapter on the Prohibitions Connected with the Usages of Idolators."

60. Cf. Rosenblatt,, II, 36/7 (beg.).

61. These are the fragments edited by Eppenstein and Wieder; cf. above, n. 1. That Book II consisted of at least three parts is indicated by the title-page of the MS coupled with information supplied by Maimuni on chapters following this part; cf. Rosenblatt, I, 32.

62. Eppenstein, פרק כ״ד וכ״ה, pp. 34, 36.

63. A. Harkavy, "Ḥadashim gam Yeshanim," pt. 10, p. 7, section 3 (at the end of vol. V of the Hebrew translation of Graetz's *History of the Jews*).

64. Cf. the remainder of the quotation in Harkavy, *ibid.*: "The Creator of all existence, God of the world, blessed be His name, the Unique with whose existence nothing has anything in common." In view of Maimonides' strong objections to the recitation of *piyyutim* in which the absolute unity or transcendence of God seemed to be compromised (*Guide*, I, 59, tr. Pines, pp. 140f.), this chapter may have stressed the limitations on independent formulation in prayer.

65. Rosenblatt, I, 32, text to n. 31.

66. *Ibid.*

67. The relationship of vows to sincerity is clear from Scripture; Deut. 23.22–24. The relationship of the laws of vows to worship is clarified by Maimonides, *Guide*, III.35 class no. 13 (laws of temperance), and at the end of the chapter, where these laws are all classified as prescribing the obligations of man to God. In addition to Rosenblatt's summary, I have consulted a microfilm of the MS in the Library of the Jewish Theological Seminary of America.

68. Rosenblatt, I, 32.

69. MS Columbia, X893.15, M28.

70. *Payrush*, p. 368/9 to Ex. 23.25; cf. also above, n. 67 and below to nn. 74–76.

71. Harkavy, pp. 3f.; Rosenblatt, I, 32.

72. Abot 1.2.

73. *Guide*, III.31 (end), trans. p. 524.

74. Maimonides' commentary on Abot 1.2 = *Mishnah 'im Payrush etc.* (ed. Kafiḥ), IV, 408; *Guide*, III.52 (end). Cf. further, Twersky, "Some non-Halakic Aspects," pp. 113f.

75. *Guide*, III.33, 35 (classes 13 and 14), 48–49; cf. also "Shemonah Peraqim," chap. 4 = *Mishnah 'im Payrush* (ed. Kafih), IV, 384f. Note that in chapter 6, *ibid.*, Maimonides deliberately omitted sexual law from the category of purely rational. Kafiḥ's remark in n. 14 misses the point. Cf. further in Twersky, pp. 104f.

76. *Guide*, III.35 (end), Eng. trans., p. 358.

77. Professor Saul Lieberman kindly called my attention to the statement of R. Judah b. Pazi in Wayyikra Rabbah 24.6 (ed. Margulies, p. 559) and parallels that provides the classical source for this classification.

78. Cf. Twersky, pp. 104f.

79. Cf. part 2 of this paper, esp. nn. 123, 138.

80. Cf. Rosenblatt, I, 33 to n. 40; *ibid.*, 198/9.7f.; II, 38/9.9–44/5 (on commandments leading to humility); 270/1.9f. (abstinence); 314/5.7f. (on the appetites); cf. also II, 236/ 7.11f., 250/1.2f. Maimuni's classification of ritual law as *adab* coincided with the views of al-Chazzali, who devoted a special treatise to the subject, *al-Adab fi-'l-Dīn.* (I am grateful to Professor John Badeau for calling this treatise and its contents to my attention.)

81. Twersky, p. 104; Rosenblatt, II, 12/3, bottom. While I do not wish to press the point, it may be that the division of Book II of the *Kifāya* into three parts was also motivated by this general scheme. The first part treated the laws of concentration and the recitation of the Scripture (corresponding to Torah and *'ilm*), the second with prayer (*adab*) and the third with family life (or interpersonal relations on the ritual level).

82. Cf. Rosenblatt, I, 33f. and *PAAJR*, XXXV 89 and above, pp. 214–215.

83. Cf. his exoteric and esoteric interpretations of Psalm 84 in Rosenblatt, II, 400/1f.; cf. also 418/9.6–11. Note also his elucidation of the many possible levels of interpretation open to persons following the "special path"; *ibid.*, I, 140/1.7f. Note also that while there is a common way of zealousness enjoined upon all observers of the Torah, there is an elevated kind of zealousness to be pursued by *hasidim*; *ibid.*, II, 316/7.13f.

84. *Ibid.*, I, 33, and cf. I, 182/3.11–12. Note also the subject-matter of the preambles to this book.

85. Cf. above, n. 15 and *Payrush*, p. 120/1 to Gen. 35.4.

86. Cf. H. A. Wolfson, "Hallevi and Maimonides on Prophecy," *JQR*, NS, XXXII (1941–42), 347f., XXXIII (1942–43), 70f.; Guttmann, *Philosophies of Judaism*, pp. 79f.; A. J. Heschel, "Did Maimonides Strive for Prophetic Inspiration?" [in Hebrew], *Louis Ginzberg Jubilee Volume* (2 vols. New York, 1945), Hebrew vol., pp. 159f. For the views of Maimuni, cf. Rosenblatt, I, 64f.; below, n. 100.—On medieval views of prophecy, cf.

Wolfson, *Philo,* II, 62f.; S. H. Wilensky, *The Philosophy of Isaac Arama* [in Hebrew] (Jerusalem, 1956), pp. 166f.; M. Mahdi, *Ibn Khaldun's Philosophy of History* (London, 1957), pp. 84f.

87. Cf. Maimonides, *Guide,* II.32, 35 (beg.) and Rosenblatt, I. 65.

88. Cf. Maimonides, *Sefer ha-Misvoth,* positive commandments no. 3; *idem, Mishneh Torah,* Yesoday ha-Torah 2.2 (and see Professor Lieberman's note thereto, in his edition, p. 100), Teshubah 10.6; *idem, Guide,* III.28, Eng. trans., pp. 512f. Cf. also above, n. 40 and below, nn. 99–100.

89. Cf. Rosenblatt, I, 140/1f.; II, 56/7.21f.; and the introductory essay to the Eng. trans. of the *Guide* by Leo Strauss.

90. Printed in *Qobes Teshubot ha-Rambam* (Ed. by Abraham Lichtenstein. Leipzig, 1859), part III, pp. 40f., and reprinted in Abraham Maimuni, *Milhamot ha-Shem* (ed. Margalioth), pp. 81f.

91. The printed version (cf. previous note) is a copy of MS Oxford, Neubauer-Cowley, *Catalogue,* no. 1649, 4; cf. Steinschneider, *Die Arabische Literatur der Juden,* pp. 231f. MS Jewish Theological Seminary 891 (=MS Schwager, no. 39–40, described in the typescript catalogue of MSS JTSA, section on "Liturgy, Poetry, Cabbala," pp. 29f.) f. 5a–10, contains a copy of the *Ma'amar 'al ha-Derashot.* This manuscript, copied along with other texts by Eliezer b. Abraham Eilenburg of Brunswick from a manuscript of Joseph b. Levi of פאראע, is a poorly transcribed version of MS Oxford, with a rewording of the introduction to make the work appear as that of the copyist! However, by the time the text had reached the copyist it had already been amplified with a passage from *Ma'amar ha-Dorban* (f. 10a).

92. *Payrush,* pp. 264/5 to Ex. 12.40; Abraham ibn Megash, *Kebod Elohim* (Constantinople, 1585), f. 104a–106a, and quoted by Harkavy, pp. 7f. That the tract was part of the *Kifaya* is also indicated by the copyist of the *Ma'amar 'al ha-Derashot,* ed. Leipzig, f. 40c (=ed. Margalioth, p. 82).

93. Cf. Ibn Megash, f. 105a, bottom and seq.; Samuel b. Sorsah ibn Sana, *Meqor Hayyim* (Mantua, 1588/9), f. 123c. Since Ibn Megash includes all of these subjects in the portion of the treatise that he claimed to have translated into Hebrew, they must have been fairly near each other in the original work.—Admittedly, our suggestion is at best a guess. However, the general burden of our argument would not be weakened at all, even if our conjecture on the original setting of these chapters should prove to be wrong.

94. Rosenblatt, I, 130/1f.; cf. also Harkavy, p. 6, section 2.

95. Cf. Rosenblatt, II, 38/9–44/5, 88/9, 270/1, 314/5.7f.

96. Cf. *ibid.,* I, 136/7f.; II, 306/7f., 328/9f.

97. Cf. nn. 95–96; *Payrush,* pp. 302/3 to Ex. 19.6, 368/9 to Ex. 23.25.

98. Rosenblatt, I, 34f.

99. *Ibid.,* II, 52/3.4, 194/5.1f., 282/3.19f., 380/1.9f. and especially 422/3.7f. with its repeated reference to the prophets as models.

100. *Ibid.,* II, 58/9.3f. (Note the reference by Maimuni to a later section, line 7); 294/ 5.14f.; *Milhamot ha-Shem,* pp. 61f.; below, n. 115.

101. Cf., above, n. 25.

102. Rosenblatt, I, 146.21 (where the noun is used adverbially!); II, 298.17. Note that in the latter passage the highest stages of *hasidut* are declared to be close to prophecy; cf. below, n. 110. Cf. also I, 146/7.16 where the *hasidim* of Israel are placed next to "the disciples of the prophets." That *hesed* and *hasidut* bespeak the way of life advocated by Maimuni is explicitly stated in I, 134/5.16f. The group was called "al-hasidim" by Maimuni and his contemporaries (Goitein, "Documents," pp. 182f.; *idem,* "Treatise," p. 114 recto, line 21, margin line 1) and their meeting-place מקום החסידים; Rosenblatt, II, 364.21. On דרך החסידות as the expression that became accepted in these circles, cf. Rosenthal, p. 435.

103. Bodleian Library, MS. Heb. d 23; Neubauer-Cowley; *Catalogue,* no. 2752. Cf. also Rosenblatt, I, 35. That the place of this fragment was in the third part of Book IV emerges from Maimuni's statement in the fragment (f. 3b): וקד דכרנא דלך פי פצל אלחלם, referring to the passage in Rosenblatt, I, 212/3. In referring to other parts of his own work, Maimuni was always careful in his use of perfect and imperfect verbs to distinguish parts that had preceded from those that were to follow; cf., by way of contrast, Rosenblatt, I, 150.14, II, 204.18 with II, 220.2, 418.11.

104. Besides using the microfilm of this MS housed in the Library of the Jewish Theological Seminary of America, I was able to examine the MS at first hand at the Bodleian Library. I must register my thanks to the Keeper and Assistant Keeper of the Oriental Division for their gracious efforts on my behalf.

105. The beginning of the fragment contains the last portion of a chapter preceding this one and seems to have aimed at proving that nothing in the Torah was stated by Moses without explicit divine mandate. All statements, even the negotiations with the two and a half tribes that settled east of the Jordan, were made in accordance with instructions from God. On fol. 1b there follows "A Chapter Concerning the Immutability of the Torah," which begins with the statement: "Among the indubitable foundations of the Torah . . . is that this Torah which has come to us [through the agency of] Moses Our Master will not be altered in whole or in part."

106. Cf. D. Kaufmann, *Geschichte der Attributenlehre in der juedischen Religionsphilosophie des Mittelalters* (Gotha, 1877), p. 49, n. 92 and p. 502 *ad loc.*; Saadiah Gaon, *The Book of Doctrines and Beliefs* (Abridged and trans. by A. Altmann. Oxford, 1946), pp. 111f. and notes thereto; M. Zucker, *Rav Saadya Gaon's Translation of the Torah* [in Hebrew] (New York, 1959), pp. 29, 247. Cf. also Wolfson, *Philo,* I, 188, II, 378f., 427f.

107. Cf. above, to nn. 13–15.

108. A play on words may well have been intended, for *gemilat* (or *gemilut*) is similar to the Arabic *'amaliyya,* which signified the practical arts, and of which political science is a part; cf. H. A. Wolfson, "The Classification of the Sciences in Mediaeval Jewish Philosophy," *Hebrew Union College Jubilee Volume* (Cincinnati, 1925), pp. 265f., 281. *Hasadim* could, of course, be used as a synonym for *hasidut,* for the former form in ancient Hebrew signifies abstraction very much like other masculine plurals—e.g., *pesahim, 'arakhin, sheqalim,* etc. That *gemilut hasadim* represented an esoteric way of life is also indicated by Bahya ibn Paquda, *al-Hidaja 'ila Fara'id al-Qulub* (Ed. by A. S. Yahuda. Leiden, 1912) Arabic text 19.10–13 where *gemilut hasadim* as used in *B.* Abodah Zarah 17b is interpreted as خلوص القلوب (= בר הלב in Heb. trans., *Hobot ha-Lebabot,* ed. Zifroni, p. 84).

109. Cf. above, n. 47.

110. *Mishnah 'im Payrush* etc., (ed. Kafih), IV, 372.

111. Note Maimuni's interpretation of Eccl. 3.11 in Rosenblatt, II, 242/3.5f.

112. Cf. J. Goldin, "The Three Pillars of Simeon the Righteous," *PAAJR,* XXVII (1958), 54.

113. *Abot* 4.16.

114. From Maimuni's *Responsa* (ed. Freimann) no. 94, p. 136 and especially from his *Milhamot ha-Shem,* pp. 61f., 64, it is clear that Maimuni accepted his father's soteriology and eschatology *in toto.* On Maimonides' theory of the nature and purpose of the world to come, cf. Maimonides, *Mishneh Torah,* Teshubah, chs. 8–10 and notes thereto in ed. Lieberman, pp. 325f.; *idem, Treatise on Resurrection* (ed. Finkel), pp. 4f. On the reward of the world to come as one for those who perform the commandments with knowledge (*'ilm*), cf. Twersky, p. 101, n. 26. On Maimuni's views of the world to come, cf. Rosenblatt, II, 124/5.21f., 224/5f. and especially 272/3.8f. On the reason for the incorporeal nature of this reward, cf. *ibid.* 242/3.3f.

115. Cf. above, n. 100. On this state as a foretaste of the world to come, cf. Rosenblatt, II, 52/3.1f., 56/7.19f., 194/5.1f., 230/1.17f. That the yearning for incorporeality is the natural proclivity of the soul, cf. *ibid.,* 306/7 (beg. of chap. 21). Cf. also 196/7f. on the hope for material rewards.

116. Cf. Harkavy, p. 8 end of sec. 4, which is to be understood in the light of *Milhamot ha-Shem,* pp. 61f.

117. Cf. Maimonides, *Treatise on Resurrection*; Meir ha-Levi Abulafia, *Kitab al-Rasa'il* (Ed. by Y. Bruell. Paris, 1871), pp. 1f., 13f. For modern treatments, cf. J. Sarachek, *Faith and Reason* (Williamsport, Pa., 1935), pp. 14f.; D. J. Silver, *Maimonidean Criticism and the Maimonidean Controversy* 1180–1240 (Leiden, 1965), pp. 64f., 109f.

118. *Mishneh Torah,* Teshubah, 8.8. Cf. also Maimonides on Abot 4.16–17 (in ed. Kafih, IV, 448 to Abot 4.21–22) and note the correspondence with the parable in the *Guide,* III, 51. For similar conceptions among Sufis, cf. Arberry, p. 37.

119. Moses Nahmanides, *Torat ha-Adam,* pt. III (=*Sha'ar ha-Gemul*) (=*Kitbay Ramban,* ed. Chavel, II, 291f., 311).

120. In addition to the examples cited by Naḥmanides from Ibn Gabirol, "Keter Malkhut," strophes 27 and 40, cf. Abraham ibn Daud, *Sefer ha-Qabbalah* (ed. Cohen), Hebrew text 64.290–91: לך לרב יצחק אלפאסי ואמור לו שהריני יוצא מן העולם הזה ונכנס לעולם הבא. Cf. also *idem, Emunah Ramah,* pp. 39–41. For the use of *'olam* alone to designate *'olam ha-ba,* cf. ibn Daud, *Sefer ha-Qabbalah.* Hebrew text 5.44: יהושע מסרה לזקנים ונפטר לחיי עולם and see variant readings there.—For one's *'olam* as one's share in the world to come, cf. *B.* Abodah Zarah 10b: יש קונה עולמו בשעה אחת; Ibn Gabirol's line לעולמך פני לילך ויומך in Solomon ibn Gabirol, *Poems* (Ed. by I. Davidson. Philadelphia, 1923), p. 69 and see Davidson's note thereto on p. 165 1.3 (=H. Schirmann, *ha-Shirah ha-Ibrit bi Sefarad u-bi-Provence,* I, 237, no. 3 strophe 2). Interestingly enough, Isaac Albalag, the thirteenth-century Spanish Jewish Averroist, seems to have equated *ha-'olam* in Abot 1.2 and 18 with the divine will; cf. G. Vajda, *Isaac Albalag (=Etudes de Philosophie Médiévale,* XLIX [1960]), 16.

121. Cf. Maimonides' comment on Abot 4.5 (in *Mishnah 'im Payrush* etc., (ed. Kafiḥ), IV, 441 to 4.7); cf. also his remarks on 4.21 (Kafiḥ, 4.27, p. 450) and note the similarity of the style to his comment on 3.10 (Kafiḥ, 3.13, p. 433) as contrasted with 2.11 (Kafiḥ, 2.14, p. 428). Maimuni's preserved works contain no quotations from these passages, except for Abot 4.21 in Goitein, "Treatise," p. 113, where the passage is adduced without comment.—It is quite possible that Maimonides understood the expression מוציאין ... מן העולם as the causative form of the expression יצא ... מעולמו, which, as Professor Lieberman has shown, was used in the sense of to die to the Jewish community through apostasy and, of course, to lose thereby one's share in the "world to come"; cf. S. Lieberman, "Yaṣa le'olamo," *Ginze Kedem,* V (1934), 177f. Interestingly enough, David Maimuni, in his commentary on Abot, straddles the fence with respect to this phrase and tries to include both worlds within the same expression; cf. David ha-Nagid, *Sefer Pirqay Abot* (Alexandria, 1900/01), 2.11 (16) f. 37a (Heb. trans. *Midrash David,* Jerusalem, 1943/44, p. 49, top) where מוציאין את האדם מן העולם is explained as causing אלמות, ואלהלאך ואלאוקטאע, i.e. death, damnation, and eternal removal. (אלאנקטאע = כרת; cf. *Mishnah 'im Payrush,* (ed. Kafiḥ), IV, 205.) Cf. also David ha-Nagid to Abot 3.10 (14), f. 51a (Heb. trans., p. 67).

122. *Milḥamot ha-Shem* (ed. Margalioth), p. 61 (citing *B.* Ber. 17a). See also R. N. N. Rabbiniovicz, *Variae Lectiones,* I, 80, no. 7, where Maimuni's reading is attested. The crucial phrase here is obviously the first one. While Rashi explains *'olamkha* to be "fulfillment of your needs," and Solomon Edels explains it as referring to this world, Maimuni understood it to mean the bliss that scholars attain in this world, thereby attaining a state resembling that of the angels, as indicated by Zech. 3.7b.

123. See the very revealing discussion and citation of Rabbinic statements in Rosenblatt, II, 274/5.15f. The passage must be understood in the light of *Milḥamot ha-Shem,* p. 63, where the Garden of Eden is interpreted as a state of bliss.

124. To the list collected by Rosenblatt, II, 437, the following passages may be added: Abot 1.1 and 4.21 in Goitein, "Treatise," p. 133 II. 18–19; Abot 2.13, 5.5, 5.7 in Eppenstein, פרק כ"ד וכ"ה, pp. 37, 44, 47; Abot 5.5 in Wieder, p. 89.—To put the matter statistically, in the section edited by Rosenblatt, Maimuni quotes 20 passages from the works of his father 23 times; 17 passages from *B.* Berakot 22 times; 11 citations from *B.* Ta'anit 30 times; 29 passages from Abot 34 times!

125. *B.* Baba Kamma 30a, cited in the introduction to "Shemonah Peraqim," *Mishnah 'im Payrush* (ed. Kafiḥ), IV, 372.

126. Rosenblatt, II, 328/9.

127. Cf. Baḥya, *Fara'id,* pp. 10, 19 (Heb. trans., ed. Zifroni, pp. 74, 84).

128. Cf. Abraham ibn Daud, *Sefer ha-Qabbalah* (ed. Cohen), p. 128, n. 52 and pp. 265f.

129. *Mishnah 'im Payrush* (ed. Kafiḥ), IV, 372.

130. For the latest discussion, cf. H. Davidson, "Maimonides' *Shemonah Peraqim* and Alfarabi's *Fuṣul al-Madani,*" *PAAJR,* XXXI (1963), 33f.

131. Joseph b. Judah ibn Aknin, *Sepher Musar* (Ed. by W. Bacher. Berlin, 1910). Note that on p. 1 he calls it a work of *musar,* i.e. *adab.* For David Maimuni's work, cf. above, n. 121.

132. Isaac Abravanel, *Naḥalat Abot* (New York, 1953), pp. 32f. Of the second type,

the commentary of Ibn Aknin is an excellent example. On the significance of these types of exegesis of Abot, cf. below, n. 136.

133. This may easily be verified by a glance at the names of commentaries on Pirqay Abot in I. A. Benjacob, *Ozar ha-Sepharim* (Vienna, 1880), pp. 458f.; C. Taylor, *An Appendix to the Sayings of the Jewish Fathers* (Cambridge, 1900); P. Jacob Kohn, *Osar ha-Beurim we-ha-Perushim* (London, 1952), pp. 96f.; M. M. Kasher and J. B. Mandelbaum, *Sarei ha-Elef* (New York, 1959), pp. 217f.; A. Freimann, *Union Catalogue of Hebrew Manuscripts and Their Location,* II (New York, 1964), pp. 294–96, nos. 7571f. For commentaries known only by name, cf. Joseph b. Judah, *Sepher Musar,* p. xvi; Samuel da Uzeda, *Midrash Shemuel* (Jerusalem, 1959/60), p. 1.

134. Cf. *Mahzor Vitry* (Ed. by S. Hurwitz. Nuernberg, 1923), p. 461.

135. Cf. L. Finkelstein, *Ha-Perushim ve-Anshe Keneset ha-Gedolah* (New York, 1950), p. 24, n. 105. Cf. also Abraham Yarhi b. Nathan, *Sefer ha-Manhig,* Laws of Sabbath, no. 63. Needless to add, once the Sefardic synagogues had introduced the liturgical recitation of the tractate, even Maimonides' commentary made its way into prayer books; cf. Taylor, p. 5, no. 5; p. 9, no. 14; p. 10, no. 16.

136. The differences between the two approaches to, and methods of interpretation of, Abot parallel the differences in approach to the interpretation of the sapiential books of the Bible in Christian circles of the twelfth and thirteenth centuries. With the advent of Aristotelian philosophy to Latin Europe, the Christian commentators veered from moralizing to greater textual literalism in their interpretation of Scripture and to new efforts at squaring their theories of natural and political science with the teachings of the sapiential books; B. Smalley, "Some Thirteenth-Century Commentators on the Sapiential Books," *Dominican Studies,* II (1949), 318f., II (1950), 41f., 236f. In many ways, the old and new exegetical tendencies reflect the different approaches of the classical Ashkenazic and Sefardic schools in their approaches to Scripture and rabbinic homily; cf. provisionally, H. J. Zimmels, *Ashkenazim and Sephardim* (London, 1958), pp. 142f., 152f. Along with the new philosophy, which in large measure came to northern Europe by way of Spain, the Christian commentators may have absorbed some basic Sefardic approaches to the exegesis of sapiential literature, of which Abot must be reckoned an outstanding specimen. The greater philosophical weight which the Sefardim placed on works like Abot corresponds, of course, to the greater weight which people trained in the medieval Hellenistic, i.e. Arabic, tradition placed on the proverb generally.

137. Cf. Abot 2.7, 14–16; 3.11; 4.1, 16–17; 5.19, 20; 6.4, 7. The one exception is 3.5, where rewards of this world are stressed.

138. Cf. Maimonides, *Mishneh Torah,* Teshubah, ch. 8; Rosenblatt, II, 52/3.1f., 54/5.9f., 56/7.2f., 62/3.16f.; 224/5.6f., and see especially 230/1.17f., 232/3.12f.

139. M. Sotah 9.15 (in Mishna texts). For the various recensions of this dictum, cf. S. Lieberman, *Hayerushalmi Kiphshuto* (Jerusalem, 1934), pp. 35f. The probable reasons for Maimuni's divergence from this scheme will be discussed in the paper referred to in n. 21. For a later presentation of the scale of Jewish pietistic grades according to the progression of R. Phinehas' maxim, cf. Rosenthal, *op. cit.*

140. Maimonides, Introduction to Abot (*Mishnah 'im Payrush* (ed. Kafih), IV, 379f., 382f., 384f.)

141. Cf. Rosenblatt, II, 238/9f., 264/5 and cf. above, n. 13; Rosenblatt, I, 148/9 on Abba Hilkiah.

142. See ch. XX in Rosenblatt, II, 224/5f. Note that in 266/7.9–10 he indicates that he wears Sufi undergarments. See also his praise of celibacy in 264/5, 278/9 and his efforts to rationalize the marriages of the ancient prophets, 320/1. Solitude is not only an ideal in his view but a goal; *ibid.,* 260/1, 382/3.18f. Note especially his invocation of his father's authority for the meritoriousness of renunciation as the highest form of devotion; *ibid.,* II, 280/1.11 and cf. below, nn. 155–56. On the other hand, Maimuni conceded that the ability to dispense with making a living was only an *ideal,* and he cautioned that the attainment of such a stage was a pure gift of God; Rosenblatt, II, 124/5.13f.

143. Cf. *ibid.,* I, 138/9.4f. Note also the clear statement on the concessions made by the promises of the Torah to the needs of the masses of men; *ibid.,* II, 272/3f., 296/7.17f.

144. Cf. Maimonides, *Guide,* Epistle Dedicatory, Introductions 1 and 3, and *ibid.,* I. 33–34; cf. also L. Strauss' introductory essay to the Eng. trans., *ibid.,* pp. xivf.

145. Rosenblatt, I, 35f. Maimuni was well aware of his prolixity and repetitiveness. However, his expository technique was deliberate; cf. *ibid.*, I, 184/5.19f. Note, too, his eagerness to explain laws and stories that would seem to contradict his theories; *ibid.*, I, 148/9.9f.; II, 194/5.21f., 290/1.15f., 296/7.17f.

146. On the gloom over conditions in the Maghreb, cf. Abraham ibn Daud, *Sefer ha-Qabbalah* (ed. Cohen), pp. 87f., 294f.; A. S. Halkin, "Le-Toledot ha-Shemad bi-may ha-al-Muwaḥiddin," *The Joshua Starr Memorial Volume* (New York, 1953), pp. 101f.; Moses Maimonides, *Epistulae* (Ed. by D. H. Baneth. Jerusalem, 1946), p. 1, lines 7f.

147. Samau'al al-Maghribi, "Ifḥam al-Yahud," (Ed. and trans. by M. Perlmann) *PAAJR*, XXXII (1964), 16f., 81f.

148. Cf. Samau'al's ridicule of the messianic aspirations of the Jews in his account of the pseudo-messiah, Menaḥem ar Ruḥi, pp. 72f. The resurgence of messianic literature and of messianic reaffirmations on the part of the Jewish leadership in the twelfth century points to the fact that the faith in the redemption had been seriously challenged. For the responses of the Jewish leadership, cf. Abraham ibn Daud, *Sefer ha-Qabbalah* (ed. Cohen), pp. 212f.; G. D. Cohen, "Messianic Postures of Ashkenazim and Sephardim," *Studies of the Leo Baeck Institute* (Ed. by M. Kreutzberger. New York, 1967), pp. 133f. (=Leo Baeck Memorial Lecture, no. 9, pp. 19f.) On the wave of conversions in Mameluke Egypt, cf. E. Strauss, *Toledot ha-Yehudim be-Miṣrayyim we-Suria* (2 vols., Jerusalem, 1944–51), I, 279f.

149. Cf. Goitein, "A Jewish Addict to Sufism," pp. 38f.

150. That this was Maimonides' explicit principle in rationalizing his own reforms has been shown by Wieder, pp. 27f.

151. *Milḥamot ha-Shem*, pp. 61f.

152. Rosenblatt, II, 270/1f.

153. The "way of holiness" in Maimonides' prefatory poem to the *Guide* (Eng. trans., p. 2) is the way of redemption, as indicated by the context from which the phrase is drawn; cf. Isa. 35.8, 10.

154. Cf. above, text to n. 106; *Milḥamot ha-Shem*, p. 64; Rosenblatt, II, 208/9.

155. Maimonides, *Mishneh Torah*, De'ot, 6.1.

156. *Ibid.*, *Talmud Torah*, 3.12; and cf. Twersky, p. 99.

157. Moses Maimonides, *Epistle to Yemen* (Ed. by A. S. Halkin, New York, 1952), pp. xii, 80f. Cf. also Abraham ibn Daud, *Sefer ha-Qabbalah* (Ed. Cohen), p. 220, n. 158.

158. Joel 3.1, cited by Maimonides, *Epistle*, pp. 84/85, line 1. Although Maimonides was later to qualify the implications of this verse in *Guide*, II.32, Eng. trans. p. 363, the popular-exoteric understanding of the verse probably remained the same in most circles.

159. Cf. above, pp. 219–220.

Esau as Symbol in Early Medieval Thought

I. EDOM—ROME

The affirmation of the sovereignty of God in the Rosh ha-Shanah liturgy comes to a climax with a series of verses from Scripture which makes the credo as much a view of history as a declaration of first principles, a pre-amble to eschatology no less than to theology:

> Thus saith the Lord, the King of Israel,
> And his Redeemer the Lord of hosts:
> I am the first, and I am the last,
> and beside Me there is no God (Isaiah 44:6).
>
> And saviours shall come up on mount Zion
> to judge the mount of Esau;
> and the kingdom shall be the Lord's (Obadiah 1:21).
>
> And the Lord shall be King over all the earth;
> In that day shall the Lord be One, and His name one (Zechariah 14:9).
>
> Hear O Israel, the Lord is our God, the Lord alone! (Deuteronomy 6:4).[1]

That the most diverse Jewish rites concur in the inclusion of the verse from Obadiah can hardly be a coincidence.[2] Hallowed throughout Jewry by the authority of Amoraic and perhaps even late Tannaitic usage,[3] they bespeak the antiquity of the Rabbinic view of universal monotheism as inseparably bound up with a conflict to the finish between the kingdom of God and the pretensions of human rulers.[4] In this liturgical passage and in the Rabbinic frame of reference as a whole, the war against the idols is synonymous with the conflict of Jacob with Esau, archetypal symbols of Jewry and Rome.

Ever since the destruction of the Temple, the Jews were obsessed with the blatant contrast between their election in Heaven and their subjection on earth. Since the rationale for collective survival precluded the possibility that God had rejected His people, the present state was inevitably construed as temporary. Indeed, Rome, the "wicked kingdom," would yet pay dearly, irrevocably, for its *hybris* and cruelty, for having afflicted Israel far beyond what God had decreed. Given such assumptions, sad reality generated comforting fantasy, and the despair of history was overcome by apocalyptic.[5]

Apocalyptic fantasy and literature is but one form of that genre of midrash characterized by Professor Wolfson as historical and eschatological predictive interpretations of Scripture. The historical interpretation attempts "to find in scriptural texts predictions of future events already known . . . to have taken place"; the eschatological interpretation attempts to "find in Scripture non-literal meanings referring to the events which are to take place in the end of days, such as the advent of the Messiah."[6] By such midrashic equation, Rome was identified with the Biblical Edom, and every name connected in Scripture with Esau was applied to the city of Romulus and the empire of the Caesars.

Although the Rabbinic identification of Rome with Esau and Edom is commonplace and often cited, the exact origins of this identification have not yet been satisfactorily ascertained, and the question merits a fresh examination. The earliest known source often thought to make this identification dates from the latter part of the first or early part of the second century.[7] In an obscure passage in the Apocalypse of Ezra, the visionary implores God to reveal to him a sign by which the end of time will be recognizable. Although the heavenly response is both opaque and textually suspicious, the figures by which the present age and the one to come are characterized are quite clear: "From him sprang Jacob and Esau, but Jacob's hand held the heel of Esau from the beginning. The heel of the first age is Esau; the hand of the second is Jacob." Latin and Arabic versions of the book render the answer even more pointedly: "For Esau is the end of this world, and Jacob is the beginning of the one which follows."[8] Since the Apocalypse of Ezra is one of the products of the despair and new eschatology born of the destruction of the Second Temple, the equation of the rulers of the present age with Esau, some scholars have felt, leaves no doubt as to the meaning of the reference.

Nevertheless, the passage in no way warrants the conclusion that the designation of Rome by Esau or Edom had been consciously made. In IV Ezra, Jacob and Esau clearly represent cycles of history as much as they do specific empires. They are archetypal symbols of the objects of God's love and God's hate and derive from the same bedrock of associations from which Paul of Tarsus had drawn his figures for "children of the promise" and children of rejection.[9]

Actually, it is only from the middle of the second century that we can discern the conversion of what may have been but one midrash among many—in any event, of a restricted apocalyptic circle—into a popular and explicit symbolism.

As far as I can determine, the first Rabbi to have clearly identified Rome with Esau and Edom was none other than Rabbi Akiba ben Joseph. He, it would appear, was the one who explained that the verse "The voice is the voice of Jacob, but the hands are the hands of Esau" (Genesis 27:22) was illustrated by the *anguished cry* of Jacob because of what the hands of Esau had done to him.[10] The meaning of Esau is here clear and unequivocal.

Moreover, as is a matter of common knowledge, at the time of the last great revolt against Rome, Rabbi Akiba pointed to Simeon bar Koseba and said: "This is the messianic king," and maintained that the verse "A star rises from Jacob" applied to the leader of the revolt.[11] The application of the verse to Bar Koseba clearly points to the bloody conflict that would usher in the end of days (compare Numbers 24:14, 19) and culminate with the defeat of Edom by Israel: "A star rises from Jacob; a meteor comes forth from Israel. It smashes the brow of Moab, the foundation of all children of Seth. *Edom becomes a possession, yea, Se'ir a possession of its enemies; but Israel is triumphant. A victor issues from Jacob to wipe out what is left of 'Ir"* (Numbers 24, 17–19.) 'Ir to the Rabbis was clearly "urbs," the city of Edom and the capital of the empire. Bar Koseba became Bar Kokhba (The Star), for he was locked in battle with the very nation whom Rabbi Akiba had identified with Edom.[12]

Once Rabbi Akiba had made the identification, his disciples could easily read Rome into other Scriptural passages where Edom was named. In a prophecy on the vengeance of the Lord against Edom, Isaiah says: "And the wild oxen (*re'emim*) shall come down with them" (34:7). Rabbi Meir punned on the word *re'emim* and read *Romiyyim*.[13] Furthermore, Isaiah's oracle on Dumah (21:11) was recorded in the scroll of the same Rabbi Meir as the oracle on *Rumi*.[14] This is a piquant play on words, since *Dumi* and *Romi* were written virtually identically in Hebrew script at that time, as noted already by Jerome.[15] Rabbi Simeon ben Yohai could speak of the exile of Edom as the last in the series of exiles endured by Israel.[16] Henceforth, the meaning of Edom would be well known, as attested by the countless passages in Rabbinic literature, where the name is clearly invoked with respect to the Roman empire and its way in the world.[17]

The real question that faces the student is why Edom of all Biblical figures should have become the stock one for Rome; or better still, given the homilies of apocalyptic writers and Rabbinic preachers, why should this one have seized the popular imagination and become part of the regular medieval vocabulary? That the identification is not an obvious one may be seen from the fact that the author of the Christian Apocalypse, who was no less midrashically oriented than any Rabbi of his day, invoked the more obvious figure of Babylon as a more appropriate designation, and from the fact that even Jews employed this figure for Rome.[18] Moreover, ancient Jewish exegetes had understood the Bible to have referred to the Romans by the name of *Kittim*,[19] whom the Bible had classified as the offspring of Japheth (Genesis 10:4), whereas Edom clearly was Semitic. Finally, of all the exiles described in Scripture, that of Edom was surely the least obvious, and it is odd that of all the dispersions and calamities suffered by Israel that of Edom should have been characterized as the most enduring and the most painful.

However, given the period in which the identification was made, it does not, after some reflection, appear strange at all. From the Rabbinic point of view, the situation of Palestinian Jewry and especially of Jerusalem in the years immediately following 70 C.E. corresponded perfectly to the state of affairs reflected in the Book of Lamentations: "How doth the city sit solitary, that was full of people! How is she become as a widow! . . . The ways of Zion do mourn, because none come to the solemn assembly. . . . Her adversaries are become the head; her enemies are at ease. . . . The adversary hath spread out his hand upon all her treasures; for she hath seen that the heathen are entered into her sanctuary" (1:4, 5, 10).[20] The accusing finger soon points at the guilty agent: "Rejoice and be glad, O daughter of Edom, that dwellest in the land of Uz; the cup shall pass over unto thee, also, thou shalt be drunken, and shalt make thyself naked. . . . He will punish thine iniquity, O daughter of Edom; he will uncover thy sins" (4:21–22). Since it was Rome who had brought about the state of affairs reflected in Lamentations, was not Edom patently its Biblical name? Conversely, the book made no reference to Babylon or to the Chaldeans. Clearly, though Jeremiah had composed the work as a reaction to the calamities he had witnessed, he prophetically phrased the work in such a way that it would apply no less appropriately to the tragedy of the future.

There were other Scriptural considerations in support of this identification. The whole oracle of Obadiah is directed exclusively against Edom, and his characterization seemed to fit Rome to the last detail: "The pride of my heart beguiled thee, thou that dwellest in the clefts of the rocks, thy habitation on high; that sayest in thy heart: 'Who shall bring me down to the ground?' Though thou makest thy nest as high as the eagle, and though thou set it among the stars, I will bring thee down from thence, saith the Lord." Most important, it was with the downfall of Edom that Obadiah foresaw the final judgment, the restoration of dominion to God Himself. Who but a cosmocrator could have destroyed the

Temple?[21] Who but a cosmocrator would serve as a fitting adversary to usher in the day of fulfillment, the era of the Messiah? Scripture named Edom, and history pointed at Rome. By the most elementary syllogism, the two became one.

The facts of life made this midrashic identification far more apt than could be attributed by a Jew of the second century to mere coincidence. After all, there was a basic similarity between Rome and Judea in patterns of thought and expression. Neither of them could accept their existence as a mere fact. Each considered itself divinely chosen and destined for a unique history. Each was obsessed with its glorious antiquity. Each was convinced that heaven had selected it to rule the world. Neither could accept with equanimity any challenge to its claims.

This collective self-consciousness and obsession with past and future, with duty and destiny, came to its greatest expression in Rome in the Augustan age and most notably in the works of Livy and Virgil. Though shaken by civil wars and the decline of ideal Roman society, the average learned Roman echoed of his people what the Jew said of his own: "Thou didst choose us from among all peoples; thou didst love and favor us; thou didst exalt us above all tongues and sanctify us with thy commandments. Thou, our King, didst draw us nearer to Thy service and call us by Thy great and holy name."[22] As the Jews spoke of an eternal covenant between Israel and God, the Roman could quote the promise of Jove to Rome: "Imperium sine fine dedi."[23]

Although the Jewish feelings of election are clearly enunciated in, and derived from, Scripture, the doctrine of the election of Israel was accorded renewed emphasis in the generation following the Destruction. It was that generation which promulgated the allegorical interpretation of the Song of Songs as a record of the marital covenant between God and Israel at Sinai. It was the same Rabbi Akiba who approved of the revolt against Edom and who emphasized, "Beloved are Israel, for they were called children of God. Extraordinary is the love made known to them that they were called children of God. . . . Beloved are Israel, for to them was given a precious implement with which the world was created, as it is said 'For I give you good doctrine, forsake ye not My Torah' (Prov. 4:2)."[24] The witty conversations between Rabbis and "philosophers" and between Rabbi Akiba and Tineius Rufus on the subject of Jewish faith and way of life are but homespun formulations of the conflict of two peoples (and their gods) wrestling for absolute dominion. Little wonder, therefore, that Jewish realists of the generation could lose heart and echo the Roman line by admitting that "this empire has been established by Heaven."[25] In that generation, the doctrine of election was no longer mere dogma. It had become a rallying cry.

Given two such mutually exclusive self-appraisals, and given the confrontation on the fields of battle, it was simple to make of Rome the archfoe of all times, far worse than Nebuchadnezzar. What more appropriate picture could come to mind than Jacob and Esau contending for the same blessing?

Such a conflict would inevitably be expressed by the Jews midrashically, by reading Rome into appropriate Scriptural passages. It cannot be overemphasized that verses were not just pulled out of the Scriptural hat and promiscuously associated with Rome. There is a method to this kind of homily that must be understood if we are to understand the Jewish—and for that matter, Christian—mentality. When the Aramaic Jewish translator of Isaiah 34:9 renders the verse: "And the streams of *Rome* shall be turned into pitch," and a midrash on the same verse identifies these streams with the Tiber and Mare Tyrrhenum,[26] they were merely spelling out what is clearly implied by that section, given the Jewish definition of Edom.

Once this identification had been made and accepted, all the classical associations, Biblical as well as Rabbinic, connected with the name of Esau and his descendants could come into play in connection with Rome. The dominant feeling in all of Hebrew literature is summed up in Rabbi Simeon ben Yohai's comment: "It is an axiom: Esau hates Jacob."[27] It was the same sentiment which provoked plays on words by later homilists on the name Edom as "bloodthirsty" and on the word "senator" as an abbreviation for three Hebrew words meaning hostile, vindictive, vengeful.[28]

To be sure, one can point to any number of counter-sentiments in Rabbinic literature expressing even appreciation, let alone acceptance of the positive values of the Roman imperial machine and of its contribution to civilization.[29] But at best these were *ad hoc* concessions made perforce. In the main, the more passive the Jews had become, the more graphic and extended became their exegetical fantasies on the prophetic oracles of doom for the enemy and of comfort and restoration for Israel. No possible hint in Scripture with reference to the contemporary situation was left uninterpreted. The succession of empires enumerated by Daniel was now readjusted to reality and "Rome condemned" became the fourth kingdom.[30]

Thus it came about that more often than not Rome was referred to in medieval Hebrew literature not directly but by symbolic names and terms which had been drawn from the Bible and which carried with them a whole train of historic associations and emotional overtones. "Esau," "Edom," and "Se'ir"—these are but the most common of a whole series of classical appellatives universally and unequivocally employed for imperial as well as medieval Rome, and in consequence for all of medieval Christendom.[31] The father of Spanish Hebrew poetry, Dunash ben Labrat (*circa* 950), was playing on time-worn motifs and allusions when he versified in his hymns:

The press of Bozrah do thou treat,
The vat in Edom of arrogant head.

Destroy Alvan and Manahath . . .
Humble Shepho and seed of Nahath.
Restore the mount and Lebanon
Crush hastily the house of Pinon.

Uproot Edom for having sought
God's shoots to cut and turn to naught.[32]

We have here the old pleas for the destruction of Rome and medieval Christendom and for the redemption and restoration of Israel. Such hopes and prayers are a stock motif repeated in various forms by virtually all Hebrew poets of the Middle Ages in symbols and allusions which were perfectly clear to both Jew and Christian of the medieval world.

To the Jew of the high Middle Ages, even more than to his Christian contemporary, Rome was very much alive. If anything, the Jew required even less persuasion than his Christian neighbor that the ancient imperium had never disappeared but rather enjoyed an uninterrupted translation from one Caesar to another. Unlike Christian apologists, the Jews had to undergo no change of heart about Rome.[33] The Jew entered the medieval world with a fully developed view of Rome—and of her spiritual and political heirs—that had been crystalized in the course of five centuries when Roman rule over the Mediterranean world had altered the course of Jewish life forever. The official establishment of the Christian Church as the religion of the empire made no discernible impression on the Jews of the fourth century, for by that time the chasm between Judaism and Christianity had grown so deep and wide that the alignment of the machinery of state with the Church was of no greater moment than the succession of one emperor by another. To the Jew, it was a shift from one idolatry to another, one more aggressive and openly hostile, but not a change in kind.[34] Thus, it required no effort on the part of Jewish homilists to extend the name of Edom to Christendom. Esau might exchange his eagle for a cross, but he was Esau nonetheless.[35]

Such are the foundations of Jewish feelings and symbolism for Rome and its successor nations. Medieval commentators and anthologists drew constantly on the rich fund of ancient exegesis on "the wicked empire" and unquestioningly applied it to the kingdoms and empires of their own later days. Nor was this merely idle rehashing of ancient dreams. It was the substance of the Jewish *raison d'être* in a hostile atmosphere in which they constantly heard the taunt that they had been rejected of God and displaced forever. To this the Jew had only one possible reply: If Scripture is revealed, then either God's prophecies had already been fulfilled, or they were as yet in the category of unfulfilled promise. If the latter, there was room for hope; indeed, the hope was a certainty. Accordingly, considerable energy was spent to prove by detailed references to historical facts that the prophecies of consolation had in no wise yet been fulfilled, that, in other words, the Christian claim was void and the Jewish hope well grounded.

The argument from history was of no little moment in the world of medieval polemic. Evidence is not lacking that Jews in alarming numbers on occasion did despair of a divine vindication of their people and even rationalized their despondency with the observation that the prophecies of consolation had long since been fulfilled. The Jews had been restored from Babylon; the Temple had been rebuilt, and the house of David restored in the person of Zerubbabel; a Jewish monarchy under the Hasmoneans had endured for a century and more. Clearly, the prophets had foretold correctly, but their predictions had already come to pass. Now that God had clearly rejected His people a second time, what hope was left? In reply Jewish theoreticians pointed out that the basic features of the prophecies had not been realized. In the first place, the truly cataclysmic changes forseen by Isaiah, Micah, Ezekiel, and Zechariah had manifestly not yet come to pass. Not only was Israel physically dispersed but the miraculous changes in natural phenomena proclaimed by Scripture for the messianic age had not yet been witnessed. Moreover, even the history of the Jews proved that the prophecies of redemption could not possibly have been fulfilled in the days of the Second Temple. Zerubbabel had had no royal powers (*melukhah*) but merely *ad hoc* and interim authority (*serarah*); the Hasmonean dynasty was of no consequence in this respect, for it lacked the indispensable quality of Davidic lineage.[36]

Nevertheless, the increasing worldly success of Christendom ultimately did begin to have an effect. In the first place, Christians could point to the futility of Jewish tenacity to the ancient symbols of comfort in the face of divine rejection. Where was there a Jewish king or ruler anywhere on the face of the earth?[37] Was it not madness to equate the successful dominion of Christendom, the steady augmentation of which constituted proof of divine favor, with Edom? Nor did Christians remain silent about the Jewish symbols of hope. Christian typology had appropriated the very symbols that provided the substance of Jewish eschatological theory and had turned them against the Jews. If the character of Rome had not changed, as far as the Jew was concerned, the Jewish symbolism soon had to be defended, validated in ways that would seem cogent to a dispassionate observer. By the tenth century, no Jew could ignore the fact that Christian theory had clashed head-on with the Jewish view of Isaac's first-born son.

II. ESAU THE JEW

In his commentary on Isaiah, written toward the close of the fifteenth century, Don Isaac Abravanel included a long excursus in refutation of the "distortions" and "calumnies" spread by Paul of Burgos in identifying the Biblical Edom with the Jews.[38] The Christian typology, the bishop had argued, was appropriate inasmuch as the Jews live by the precepts of the Mishna, the present form of which derives from a recension redacted by Rabbi Meir, who, the Talmud proclaimed, was an Idumean convert.[39] What doubtless hurt Abravanel even more than the learned chicanery of Paul of Burgos was that an apostate quite well versed in Hebrew literature should have subscribed and lent his "Jewish" prestige to anti-Jewish homiletics. Paul's exegesis appeared like a gratuitous stab in the back, all the more unpardonable in that it seemed deliberately to turn Jewish exegesis on its head. Abravanel may well have judged Paul's motives correctly. What he did not appreciate or admit was that Paul of Burgos had turned up with nothing strikingly new, but had merely revived a classical Christian typology which had long since forced Jews to reappraise their own symbolic name for Rome.

Had the Romans of the second century known or cared about the stigma of Esau which the Jews had pinned on them, they might have been amused to learn that almost simultaneously the Gentile Christians of Egypt, Palestine, and Asia Minor had turned the very same epithet against the Jews. However, the new Christian usage of Esau did not originate as a retort to the Jews, but rather as a taunt inspired by the apostle Paul's Epistle to the Romans (9:6–13), quite without regard to—or, probably, even the vaguest knowledge of—what the Rabbis were saying about their pagan Roman overlords.

In arguing that not all born Jews were God's elect, Paul cited as evidence that only one of Abraham's sons was a child of God's promise. Moreover, of Isaac's two sons, Esau was hated by God and Jacob beloved; indeed, the former was doomed by divine decree to serve the younger. In other words, natural birth has nothing to do with whom God elects and whom He rejects. God had elected Israel. However, Jew and Israelite were not necessarily synonymous. The Jew who did not align himself with Paul's Israel[40] was as rejected as Paul himself conceded the seed of Esau to be.[41]

There is not the remotest suggestion in this argument that Paul considered the Jews to be the incarnation of Esau. However, it did not take too much effort for Gentile Christian typologists to convince themselves that that was precisely what he had meant. Paul had elsewhere explicitly designated Ishmael as a symbol of the covenant of Sinai, and Isaac as a symbol of the covenant of the Christ (Galatians 4:24–25). Clearly, these two sons must have represented the same values in the passage in

Romans. Now, since Paul had there proceeded to give a second example of a disparate Biblical pair, the beloved and rejected of each pair clearly represented the same things. Ergo: Isaac = Jacob = the Church; Ishmael = Esau = the Jews.[42]

The steps by which this indigenous Christian exegesis came to full flower are fairly clear. First faintly echoed in the Epistle of Barnabas and in the Dialogue of Justin Martyr, the new midrash bears the stamp of the intensified allegorization of the Hebrew Bible of which pagan converts to Christianity were especially fond.[43] In expressing the encouragement derived by second-century Christians from the catastrophic blows suffered by the Jews between 67 and 136, this new typology reflects the ever-widening chasm between Jewish and Gentile Christians, as the number of the latter increased and their animus to Jews of any ilk attained greater intensity. Both circumstances provided the Gentile (= anti-Judaistic) wings of young Christendom with renewed vigor in their claim that the true Israel was destined to be essentially of Gentile stock.[44] It is no coincidence that the unsuccessful Jewish wars for liberation from the Romans, culminating with the revolt of Bar Koseba, coincided with the emergence from within the Christian community of a series of homilies which invoked the very terms which Jewish preachers had employed for different purposes. Jewish defeat on earth, to the Christians, was clear evidence of their rejection in heaven,[45] and many a Christian theoretician, in ancient times as well as modern, would claim that the downfall of Jewish self-government in the second century marks the end of the people of Israel; henceforth, Judaism would be carried by the Jews, who are to be distinguished from the true Israel. It is interesting to follow the steps by which the homilies become more explicit and increasingly pretentious. Thus, Barnabas invokes the promise of Genesis 25:23 that the older shall serve the younger fleetingly, and quickly passes to the case of Manasseh and Ephraim in support of the contention that the younger (the Church) is the favored one.[46] Justin harps on the new typology of Leah (the Synagogue) and Rachel (the Church), closing this particular homily, "Jacob was hated for all time by his brother; and we now, and our Lord himself, are hated by you and by all men. . . . Jacob was called Israel; and Israel has been demonstrated to be the Christ."[47] If the Jews are Esau, they are still Esau only by implication, and only because they are now to be reckoned with mankind at large.

However, even this sufficed for Irenaeus in the latter part of the second century to take but one step further and spell out the implication that Jacob-Israel-Christendom had supplanted Esau-Jewry in birthright and blessing, the "younger" destined to freedom and victory, the "older" to eternal rejection and servitude.[48] Paul's example for the sake of argument had now become a *typos*, a theological term of reference. In the Pseudo-Cyprian polemic (*circa* 210–240), *De montibus Sina et Sion,*

Esau and Jacob parallel Sinai (the Synagogue) and Zion (the Church) respectively.[49] In an allegorical interpretation (*mystica interpretatio*) of Hippolytus of Rome, cited by Jerome, Esau is represented as the incarnation of the devil, successor to Cain and prefigurative image of the Jews, Jacob as successor to Abel and anticipatory of Christ and the Church.[50] Hence, Origen could speak of this exegesis as "common knowledge"—when he claims that "even the unbelieving Jews know [scilicet, that Christians say:] that one people has taken the place of another, i.e., that the Church has taken the place of the Synagogue, and that the elder is now the servant of the younger."[51] Indeed, the claim must have reached at least some Jewish ears, for it was being shouted far and wide, and in virtually identical terms, by these men as well as by their contemporaries Tertullian and Commodian, all of whom clearly drew on earlier funds for such interpretations.[52]

However, at this early stage of Christian history, the Christian midrash on Esau and Jacob bore no particular sting. After all, the Christians were at this point politically no better off—in many cases, far worse off—than the Jews. The Christian claim that the Synagogue was destined to serve the Church must have struck many Jews as downright ludicrous, particularly since the very same exegetes were shouting that the Jews were in league with Rome against the Church.[53] As for the specific midrash on Genesis 25:23, it was only one among many allegorical figures drawn from the Bible and applied to the Christian claim against the Jews. Cain and Abel, Hagar and Sarah, Ishmael and Isaac, Leah and Rachel, Manasseh and Ephraim, Eli and Samuel, Saul and David—all of these pairs, among many other figures, were regularly invoked as clear symbols of the old and the new covenants.[54] Even Christians were only too well aware that these typologies—like midrashic etymologies[55]—were but allegorical interpretations, and Christians themselves laid greater stress on the new emotional overtones they sought to infuse into the distinction between "Jews" and "Israel."[56] To Christians as well as Jews, the latter were real and "objective" terms that had to be coped with, whereas Esau was a quasi-mythical figure, whose servitude to Jacob was as yet a dream, a wish by no means fulfilled. How could the oracles of the prophets on high-and-mighty Edom be applied to the lonely and defeated Jewry of the third century by a Church which, although on the increase, had as yet hardly achieved perfect security?

However, the events of the fourth century provided the Christian apologists with the necessary fuel with which to give their typology a grounding in real events. With the imperial enactments curbing former Jewish liberties and then increasingly imposing restrictions on the Jews, the allegory of the oracle of Genesis 25:23 suddenly became a fact.

The shift from theoretical exegesis to political theory is most dramatically represented in legislation outlawing Jewish ownership of Christian slaves, explained by Constantine's early biographer as having been enacted "in order that those who tormented the prophets and crucified the Christ may not have possession of those who were saved by the Christ."[57] Although neither the Constantinian legislation nor the theological rationale of "Eusebius" makes reference to any specific Christian Scriptural foundation for the new restriction, the patristic exegesis of Genesis 25:23 clearly underlies the spirit and substance of the new enactments. If in the long and variegated history of Christian legislation with regard to Jewish ownership of Christian slaves, clear reference to the exegesis of Genesis 25:23 is not made explicit until much later, that is only because laws and legal decision were constantly harking back to the precedent of earlier formulations[58]—and in the earliest instance no reason had been inserted into the law itself—and because the impropriety of Christian subjection to the Jew, singly and collectively, had become accepted as basic. However, the underlying motive of separation from the Jews on the grounds of Christian superiority was soon made explicit. Repeated conciliar pronouncements, beginning with the Council of Vannes in 465, forbade Christian clerics to accept invitations to Jewish meals lest their acceptance be construed as a mark of Christian inferiority. Some forty years later the prohibition was extended to the laity. By 581 the prohibition against Jews' holding any public office was rationalized on the same grounds: "lest, Heaven forbid, Christians seem to be subject to the Jews."[59]

Once the Roman state itself had become officially Christian, it no longer could be the whore of Babylon; the Jewish identification of Rome with Edom could be dismissed as idle fantasy; the fate of the Jew vindicated the accuracy of Scripture: "The elder shall serve the younger." In the writings of Jerome[60] and more especially of Ambrose and Augustine,[61] of Gregory the Great,[62] and Isidore of Seville,[63] the classical typology had become *political* theory.[64] Superficially one author parrots his predecessors, and there is little difference between the expositions of Genesis 25:23 by Tertullian and Isidore. However, what in the third century had been but an allegorical midrash provided the theory for the legal disabilities imposed on the Jews, which would later be justified by the theological doctrine aptly summarizing the situation: "servitudo Judaeorum." The oracle on Jacob and Esau now had to be and was increasingly implemented by law.[65] It was not any lack of tenderness that impelled Ambrose, for example, to protest against compelling Christians to restore a synagogue they had deliberately destroyed,[66] nor were the restrictions against Jewish rights to acquire slaves, the right to build new synagogues, or hold public office arbitrary harassments. They grew out of the pious desire to translate a doctrine into a reality. This is particularly apparent in the case of ecclesiastical authorities, who refrained from, and even denounced, fanatical and arbitrary measures against the

Jews. To moderates no less than to extremists it did not seem proper for the slave to exercise authority over the freeman, "Ne igitur per eos nomen Domini blasphemetur, *nec deterior sit Christianorum libertas, quam servitus Judaeorum.*"[67] As a finishing touch, learned churchmen occasionally invoked the Philonic etymology which explained "Jacob" as meaning "the one who supplants" and Edom as mere "terrestrial" to further rationalize the pattern of thought permeating all Jewish–Christian relations in the Middle Ages. Jacob the spiritual Christian had supplanted and displaced Esau the carnal Jew.[68]

III. THE RESTORATION OF EDOM

Christian exegetes were not content with advancing their own interpretation of the types of Esau and Jacob. By the fourth century, they had become aware of the Jewish translation of Edom and vigorously denied it.[69] This was one among the many Jewish interpretations of Scripture which ecclesiastical authorities denounced again and again.[70] Two circumstances which had become closely intertwined were at work. In the first place, the Jewish typology was an open challenge to the Church, which in the eighth century increasingly identified itself with the name and glory of ancient Rome.[71] With the growing influence of the Papacy, coupled with the fact that the never-ending conflicts over authority in the West always seemed to hinge on the question of authority over the city that had been mistress of the world, Jews had a new and added confirmation that Edom had never died. Accordingly, Christian exegetes had to prove that not their empire, but corporate Jewry was the Antichrist. Coupled with this was the desire to undermine Jewish exegesis wherever possible, and here Christian interpreters knew they were on surer footing. Christian apologists struck home when they pointed out that official Jewish sources themselves had identified the Romans with the Kittim of Scripture, and the Kittim were sons of Tubal the son of Japheth, not children of Esau the son of Isaac.[72] Here were "facts" that could not be dismissed.

From the Jewish point of view, once Jewish servitude had become an undeniable fact, the Christian exegesis of servitude could not long be ignored. Put otherwise, if Jewish exegesis was to be saved, the problems raised by the enemy camp could not be sidestepped.

It should, therefore, occasion no surprise that considerable Jewish effort was expended in the Middle Ages to vindicate the Rabbinic symbol without contradicting ethnological "facts." These solutions were not mere exegetical exercises. They sought to restore the bedrock of Jewish eschatology, the rationale for hope and survival.

As in so many other areas of medieval Jewish literature and tradition, two different sets of answers gained wide currency in the medieval world. The one was an Italian solution and the other a Babylonian-Spanish theory.[73]

The first medieval apologia for the Rabbinic theory of Edom-Rome comes from the work known as *Josippon,* a Hebrew abridgement and adaptation of Josephus composed by a Jew of southern Italy probably in 953.[74] Although the principal theme of this work is the history of the Jews from the rebuilding of the Second Temple until its destruction, after the fashion of many medieval chronicles the book opens with a brief introduction identifying the various nations of its own day with the peoples listed in the Noachian genealogy of Genesis 10. Having presented his classification of the nations at large, the author pauses to dwell in considerable detail on the origins of Rome and other Italian cities. This introduction on Italian antiquities is an interesting little document on several counts. In the first place, the essentials of Livy and Virgil are set forth in Hebrew for the first time from a Jewish point of view. Supernatural-mythological tales have been scrupulously omitted, while a number of details have been reworked so completely as almost to obscure their connections with well known stories of classical antiquity. Nor can Josippon's bizzare departure from standard mythology be dismissed as sheer ignorance. His accuracy in the genealogy of early Italic kings and his familiarity with the legends associated with local antiquities clearly indicate that he had access to good sources of information from which he departed on occasion quite deliberately.[75] Secondly, the excursus on Italy clearly shows Rome to be the real center of the author's interest. Josippon's concern with Rome and its antiquities reflects not only an interest in the power which more than any other affected Jewish destiny but also a sensitivity to the medieval ideal of *Renovatio* which was always focused on the eternal city and which took on new life after the ninth century.[76]

To let Josippon speak for himself:[77] after the Lord dispersed the nations of the world, the Kittim settled in the plains of Campania on the banks of the Tiber, from which point they expanded and established a number of Italian cities. However, their way of life was destined to be radically reshaped from another quarter. According to a Talmudic legend, when Joseph and his brothers were conveying the remains of their father to Palestine for burial, the inhabitants of the country, the descendants of Esau, Ishmael and Qetura, attempted to block his entry.[78] At this point Josippon amplifies on his source and relates that in the course of the skirmish, Esau's grandson, Zepho, was taken captive by Joseph, and brought back to Egypt. Zepho managed to escape and make his way to Carthage, where he entered the service of Aeneas, who was ruler of that land.[79] Since Aeneas was engaged in constant war with the peoples of Italy, Zepho accompanied him on these expeditions until he finally defected and settled down to live with the natve Kittim of Italy. Because of a heroic feat which he performed for the natives, Zepho was made king of the Kittim and his name was changed to Janus-Saturnus, after the name of the beast he had killed and after the star worshiped by the natives. Janus-Saturnus was succeeded by many kings of his line until finally one of his descendants, a certain Romulus, founded the city of Rome. (*Romulus was thus a direct descendant of Esau.*) During the reign of Romulus, some Arameans and Idumeans sought asylum in Rome, having fled from the arm of David, King of Judah and Israel. Although Romulus was most cordial to the newcomers, he fortified Rome heavily for fear of King David and even signed a nonaggression pact with him.

Obviously, the long introduction is intended to alert the reader to the centrality of Rome in the story which follows. On the other hand, this is not its only aim, for it has gratuitously introduced a number of mythological elements that might easily have been omitted. Furthermore, this account of Roman origins is interesting not only for what it says but also for what it does not say. Not only does the author distort Roman mythology, but he also shuns some Jewish mythology as well. According to a story found in several versions in classical Rabbinic sources, Rome indeed had a supernatural origin. On the day that King Solomon wedded the daughter of Pharaoh, Michael or Gabriel descended from heaven, plunged a reed into the sea and there emerged an island which became a forest, which, in turn, later became the great city of Rome.[80] On the day that Jeroboam the son of Nebat set up the two calves in Bethel and in Dan, Romulus and Remus built two huts in Rome, thus initiating their dominion.[81] The Rabbinic story, adapted from ancient "foundation" motifs,[82] sets forth in legendary terms the view that the very existence of Rome was a divine punishment for Israel's sins. The rulers of Israel themselves sowed the seed of the destruction of their people, and the conflict between Rome and Judea is rooted in the decree of Heaven.

The author of *Josippon* is concerned no less than the Talmud to explain the enduring conflict between Rome and Israel. Although he will not break with basic religious vocabulary—Rome is to him "the fourth empire"[83]—he will have nothing to do with supernatural explanations, even Jewish ones, or with purely homiletical plays on words, which one must take or leave by faith alone. He prefers an ethnological explanation, by going, after the fashion of the ancients, to a people's origins. In Josippon's view the Romans are indeed identical with the Biblical Kittim, but they became Edomites as well, once Zepho the Idumean and his lineal descendants had established their rule over them.[84] It was Zepho's grandson Latinus who gave the Kittim their language and their alphabet. Thus, their very culture is an Edomite one. Since Zepho came to the West hostile to the descendants of Jacob, he doubtless imparted some of the hostility to his lineal and cultural heirs. This fear of and hostility to Israel was reinforced during the reign of David when Edomite refugees conveyed their enmity across the Mediterranean to the city of Romulus. Henceforth, the Romans would always keep a watchful eye on the deeds of their ancestral enemies.

The author of *Josippon*, a south-Italian who was much enamored of his country and its lore, had highly ambivalent feelings about the Roman–Jewish conflict. But his first loyalties were to his own ethnic group, and his ethnographic introduction was a tacit reply to the Christian polemic he heard round about him. Later readers, such as Abravanel,[85] understood his motives very well, and they gratefully invoked his evidence as proof of the authenticity of the Jewish identification of Edom.

It may be objected that Josippon merely replaced a beautiful Rabbinic allegory with a highly drab fabrication of his own or of some earlier source. Even more to the point, no polemical antagonist would readily accept this new explanation as more trustworthy than the Christian denial of the Jewish claim of the Edomite origins of Rome. To this the author would have replied that in reality he was merely providing the historical background for a "fact" accepted by *consensus omnium*. As already indicated, the author came from southern Italy, where Arabic and Byzantine influences were strongly felt. Now in Arabic, Greeks, Christians, and by extension the peoples of Europe generally, were called *Banu Asfar*, which means literally "yellow, or light colored, people," but which learned medieval Arabs claimed means "sons of the red one": that is, Edom or Esau. In modern days, Ignaz Goldziher showed that the latter explanation is indeed the correct one, although *asfar* does not mean "red" at all. Actually, the word in this connection is merely an Arabization of the Septuagintal rendition of Zepho, the grandson of Esau. *Banu Asfar* is thus a synonym for *Ahl al-Rum* ("the people of Rome").[86] In telling the story of Zepho's escape to the West, Josippon had merely invoked and doctored somewhat an old midrash that explained quite plausibly an accepted linguistic usage, which he, like everyone else, regarded as quite valid.

Since Josippon soon gained a wide circulation and appeal, his theory made its way into a popular anthology of apocryphal stories on the Biblical period, *Sefer ha-Yashar*,[87] and in a somewhat "improved" form into exegetical works of a more traditional and respectable genre. This tailored version merits special notice in view of its potential consequences.

According to Scripture, after Jacob returned to Canaan from the home of Laban, Esau took his family "and went to another land because of his brother Jacob" (Genesis 36:6). Though earlier exegetes were at a loss to identify the place to which he repaired, those who had access to *Josippon* now knew very well. They explained that Esau went to Rome, for he had heard that his grandson Zepho, the founder of Rome, had been killed in battle with Turnus, King of Elishah. Accordingly, the old man came to avenge his grandson's death and remained there.[88] Later exegetes could not be satisfied with the flimsy explanations of *Josippon* invoking descendants of Esau but insisted that Rome had been taken over by Esau himself. Rome was New Edom, the second home of the father of all Edomites.

Once such theories became generally known, there was always the danger of their being taken seriously and made the basis of practical policy in the realm of *halakhah*. "You shall not abhor an Edomite," Deuteronomy enjoins, "for he is your brother" (Deuteronomy 24:8). The same collection of laws enjoins: "You shall not deduct interest from loans to your brother . . . you may deduct interest from loans to foreigners, but not from loans to your countryman" (Deuteronomy 24:20). Now, if Rome is the progeny of Esau, may one take interest from Christians or even more specifically from *an Italian of the vicinity of Rome*? Were they not brothers? Obviously, what was at stake here was the harmonization of law with the exigencies of life. It was at this point that jurists turned skeptics and categorically denied that the interdiction against usury applied to Christians. The latter were Edomites only theologically, not historically.[89] This was not a meretricious evasion. It was commonsense refusal to build law on polemical fantasy. Even Abraham ibn Ezra, who, as we shall see, vehemently denied the Edomite origin of Rome, had referred to Christendom in his poetry as Israel's "brother."[90] Poetry and myth were one matter, exegesis and law quite another.

To some, the issue was not so clear in matters of conversion, since the Bible by implication forbids marriage with Edomites until the third generation. Most authorities sanely followed Tannaitic precedent in regarding Biblical ethnic tabus void in this case as well as in those specifically nullified by the Talmud.[91] Abraham Maimuni insisted that the marital interdictions on Edomites applied only to those whose genealogy could be attested, and that, he stressed, was not the case with Italians of his day.[92] However, as late as the eighteenth century some jurists still felt that Roman stock had not been as tainted as that of other nations—since they had never been exiled by Sennacherib—and that since Romans may, therefore, be of pure stock the course of stringency should be followed.[93] The issue, to be sure, was raised only at rare intervals, and even then only in circles where *Josippon* had been taken seriously.

An entirely different approach to the problem of Edom-Rome was taken by Babylonian, Spanish, and Provençal Jewish scholars. Under the influence of Muslim genealogical science, they rejected out of hand the identification of Rome with Edom on the grounds that the Romans were clearly the Biblical Kittim, who, in turn, were of Ionian origin.[94] In the view of this school of thought, the name of Edom thus applied to Rome only secondarily. In the first instance the name Edom applied to the Christian Church, which became identified with the Roman empire in the days of Constantine. According to this view, Jesus was not the father of Christianity at all. Jesus had been just one more false Jewish prophet, who had come to an ignominious end. Long after his death, the pagan priests of Edom associated his name with their idolatrous religion, which they persuaded Constantine to adopt and impose on his empire. The books of the New Testament and the Christian claim to uninterrupted apostolic succession were among the fabrications of these Idumean priests or of Constantine himself.[95]

This solution actually reversed the process by which Rome and Edom had originally been made identical. In the Talmudic scheme—and for that matter, in Josippon's as well—the name of Edom had applied originally to Rome and by extension to Christendom. Now the situation was quite the reverse. In any event, the theory removed Christendom from an ethnic-political level to a strictly theological plane, for one obvious implication was that Edom was not a contemporary *empire* and could, therefore, not be identified with the fourth monarchy of Daniel's visions. Clearly this theory reflects the Judeo-Arabic milieu in which it originated, for to Jews of Muslim lands, especially of Muslim Spain, the fourth kingdom had to be that of Ishmael, and it was with the collapse of the Muslim empire that the messianic era would be inaugurated.[96]

The motives for this new classification of empires are quite obvious, but the exegetes of the Judeo-Arabic milieu were not unanimous in the way they squared the Rabbinic traditions on Edom-Rome with the new needs of eschatological theory. Saadia and Ibn Aqnin maintained that the fourth kingdom consisted of a dominion shared by Edom and Ishmael—a common designation of Islam in Judeo-Arabic sources is "the partner"— while Ibn Ezra, adjusting exegesis to the facts of life, eliminated Rome completely from the fourth dominion and designated the latter as the exclusive legacy of Ishmael.[97] Rome, in Ibn Ezra's scheme, was identical with the Biblical Kittim and was but an offshoot of the third empire, which, he contended, was clearly that of Greece. Maintaining a rigid consistency, Ibn Ezra denied emphatically that Edom should in any way be implicated in the destruction of the Temple. That calamity was the work of the wicked Greek empire, which exists to this very day.[98] The subordination of Rome to Greece and its reclassification in the third empire did not necessarily lessen the role of Rome in the eschaton, for, Ibn Ezra noted, the third empire was destined to play a crucial role in ushering in the end of days. That end would be heralded by the mortal combat between the third and fourth empires: that is, between Rome, the Christian standard-bearer of Greece, and the eleven horns or petty kingdoms of Ishmael-Islam. Moreover, he pointed out, Daniel had not claimed that any but the fourth empire would be utterly destroyed. The others would survive, albiet denuded of their power.[99] Ibn Ezra's Spanish-Jewish orientation did not require that the Christian nations should be destroyed.

It was enough that their power should be shattered in the fullness of time, and that Israel would then be redeemed. Now by making the Roman Kittim a subcategory of the Greeks, Ibn Ezra had by implication clearly distinguished between the empire (*imperium*) and the specific monarchy (*regnum*) in control of it at any given moment. The Greek empire remained Greek whether its ruler was a Greek or a Roman.[100]

Ibn Ezra's solution represented the ultimate refinement of Danielian exegetes in accordance with the requirements of ethnology, exegesis, eschatology, and the facts of history, all of which had now been brought into perfect accord. To be sure, Israel was still at war with Edom, but that was a religious conflict. However, the Danielian eschatology foresaw a conflict of nations and empires, and in that regard Edom had no special function. Ibn Ezra's Edom was only a secondary characteristic of the essential enemies, Roman Greece and Ishmael.

When later, under the impact of the Reconquista, Ishmael's identity as the fourth monarchy had to be rejected, Edom regained its political connotation. Rome, the Jewish theoreticians explained, would suffer the fate of Edom, for the prophet had clearly foretold that Christianity and the Roman empire would become one. Ethnologically, the Romans might be Kittim. Religiously and eschatologically they were the seed of Esau.[101]

The Jewish–Christian polemic on Esau persisted to the end of the Middle Ages. However, the arguments that came from either side were essentially those formulated in the period we have surveyed. Speculation would continue on the date of the end and the identity of the actors in the final drama. But underlying the pursuit of that elusive day was the necessary theoretical foundation substantiating the reality of ancient Esau.

NOTES

1. On the *malkhuyot,* or proclamation of the sovereignty of God, see I. Elbogen, *Der jüdische Gottesdienst in seiner geschichtlichen Entwicklung* (Leipzig, 1913), pp. 141ff. On the date of the earliest form see L. Finkelstein, *Akiba* (New York, 1936), p. 312. For a representative text and translation, see *High Holyday Prayer Book,* trans. by P. Birnbaum (New York, 1951), pp. 377–384.

2. On the earlier variations in the structure of the *malkhuyot* see Elbogen, *Der jüdische Gottesdienst,* pp. 141ff., and especially S. Lieberman, *Tosefta Ki-Fshutah* (New York, 1955–62), V, 1053f.

3. The verse appears in the *malkhuyot* of Yose b. Yose (6th century) אהללה אלהי; see *Siddur R. Saadja Gaon,* ed. by I. Davidson *et al.* (Jerusalem, 1941), pp. 226f.

4. On the multifaceted character of the concept of the kingship of God in Rabbinic literature, see M. Kadushin, *The Rabbinic Mind* (New York, 1952), pp. 18f. On the insertion of passages bespeaking retribution against the Gentiles, see *Tos. R.H.* 2:12, p. 311 (ed. Lieberman) and Lieberman, *Tosefta Ki-Fshutah,* V, 1054. A specific example of such a

verse, cited in *B.R.H.* 32 b, is Ps. 137:7: "Remember, O Lord, against the children of Edom the day of Jerusalem," etc.

5. Cf. G. D. Cohen, "Zion in Rabbinic Literature," *Zion in Jewish Literature*, ed. by A. S. Halkin (New York, 1961), pp. 56f.; A. Marmorstein, *Studies in Jewish Theology*, ed. by J. Rabbinowitz and M. S. Lew (Oxford, 1950), Hebrew section, pp. 1f.; J. Neusner, *A Life of Rabban Yohanan ben Zakkai* (Leiden, 1962), pp. 129f.; H. J. Schoeps, *Aus frühchristlicher Zeit* (Tübingen, 1950), pp. 144f.

6. H. A. Wolfson, *The Philosophy of the Church Fathers*, I (Cambridge, 1956), 27. See also I. Heinemann, *The Methods of the Aggadah* (in Hebrew; Jerusalem, 1949), chaps. iii–v.

7. The widely entertained view that the name Edom was projected onto Rome from the Idumean origin of Herod was first suggested, I believe, by L. Zunz, *Zur Geschichte und Literatur* (Berlin, 1845), p. 483. However, as far as I can determine, this conjecture cannot be substantiated by any literary evidence, quite apart from the fact that the identification of Rome *through* Herod appears to be putting the cart before the horse. A. Schlatter, *The Church in the New Testament Period*, trans. by P. Levertoff (London, 1955), pp. 255f., subscribes to this view and adds an original twist. Recognizing that the identification of Edom with Rome is not discernible in the earliest strata of Rabbinic literature or in the Pauline epistles, he suggests that the midrash emerged as an anti-Herodian barb of the Zealots and was appropriated by the Rabbis only much later. There is no more evidence for this view than for the more popular version of the Herodian *Sitz im Leben* of the equation. Even more farfetched is the suggestion that the name Edom derives from the Hebrew name for Mars; see A. Epstein, *Mi-Qadmoniot ha-Yehudim* (Jerusalem, 5717), p. 33.

8. IV Ezra 6:7–10 (trans. G. H. Box).

9. G. H. Box, *The Ezra Apocalypse* (London, 1912), p. 68. Cf. also Rom. 9:6–13 with IV Ezra 3:13–16. The use in Josephus, *Antiquitates*, I, 275, of IV Ezra 6:7–10 as proof that Esau represents Rome is unwarranted, particularly since Josephus merely paraphrases Gen. 27:39–40; see I. Heinemann, "Josephus' Method in the Presentation of Jewish Antiquities" (in Hebrew). *Zion*, 5:193 (1940).

10. *Ber. R.* 65:21, p. 740 (ed. Theodor-Albeck). Cf. also W. Bacher, *Die Agada der Tannaiten*, 2nd ed. (Strassburg, 1903), I, 21, n. 2.

11. *Yer. Taʿan.* 4:8, f. 68d; *Ekha R.* to 2:2 (and in ed. Buber, p. 101).

12. G. F. Moore, *Judaism* (Cambridge, Mass., 1927–30), II, 116. In Targum Pseudo-Jonathan to Num. 24:19, ʿIr is rendered by Constantinople (i.e., Nova Roma), while Rashi and other medieval commentators identify ʿIr with Rome itself.

13. *Pesiqta de Rav Kahana*, p. 134 (ed. Mandelbaum) and parallels.

14. *Yer. Taʿan.* 1:1, f. 64a. On orthographic changes in R. Meir's texts, see Bacher, *Agada der Tannaiten*, II (1890), 10; S. Lieberman, *Hellenism in Jewish Palestine*, 2nd ed. (New York, 1962), pp. 24f.

15. *Comment. in Isa.*, V, to Isa. 21:11 (Migne, *PL*, XXIV, 199), cited in part by N. Brüll, *Jahrbücher für jüdische Geschichte und Literatur*, 1:236 (1874); cf. L. Ginzberg, "Die Haggada bei den Kirchenvätern, VI," *Jewish Studies in Memory of George A. Kohut*, ed. by S. W. Baron and A. Marx (New York, 1935), p. 299, who cites Jerome and adduces further material on scribal changes in Rabbinic sources.

16. *Yer. Taʿan.* 1:1. f. 64a; *B. Meg.* 29a. As to whether the citation in *Mekhilta de R. Ishmael*, Pisha 14 (ed. Lauterbach, I, 114), is to be credited to R. Akiba, see Bacher, *Agada der Tannaiten*, I, 281, n. 2; E. Z. Melamed, *Halachic Midrashim of the Tannaim in the Talmud Babli* (in Hebrew; Jerusalem, 1943), p. 102, notes to par. 50; A. J. Heschel, *Theology of Ancient Judaism*, I (in Hebrew; New York, 1962), 68, n. 1.

17. On Rabbinic attitudes toward Rome, see S.J.L. Rapoport, ʿErek Millin (Prague, 5612), s.v. אדום and אדריינוס; M. Sachs, *Beiträge zur Sprach-undAlterthumsforschung* (Berlin, 1852–54), II, 134f.; M. Grünbaum, "Beiträge zur vergleichenden Mythologie aus der Hagada," *ZDMG*, 31:305–309 (1877); S. Krauss, "Griechen und Römer," *Monumenta Hebraica: Monumenta Talmudica*, V, part 1 (Vienna, 1914); idem, *Paras ve-Romi ba-Talmud u-ba-Midrashim* (Jerusalem, 5708); I. Heinemann, *The Methods of the Aggadah*, pp. 32f.; N. N. Glatzer, "The Attitude Toward Rome in Third-Century Judaism," *Politische Ordnung und menschliche Existenz: Festgabe für Eric Vögelin* (Munich, 1962), pp. 243–267.

18. H. L. Strack and P. Billerbeck, *Kommentar zum Neuen Testament*, 3rd ed. (Munich, 1961), III, 816, to Rev. 14:8 (cf. also I Peter 5:13); *Tanhuma*, Tazriʿa (ed. Buber), par. 16,

II, 42; L. Ginzberg, *Geonica* (New York, 1909), I, 29; Y. Baer, *A History of the Jews in Christian Spain*, I (Philadelphia, 1961), 392, n. 49.

19. H. L. Ginsberg, *Studies in Daniel* (New York, 1948), p. 78, n. 21; Y. Yadin, *The Scroll of the War of the Sons of Light Against the Sons of Darkness* (in Hebrew; Jerusalem, 1955), pp. 22f.

20. That the Book of Lamentations was regarded even by the Tannaim as a prophetic description of the destruction of the Second Temple (and later of the fall of Bethar) is a commonplace. Cf. the revealing incident in *Sifre Deut.*, par. 43, pp. 94f. (ed. Finkelstein), where phrases from Lam. 2:1 and 5:17–18, among others, are quoted.

21. Ginsberg, *Studies in Daniel*, p. 5; *idem*, "Daniel" in *Encyclopedia Biblica* (in Hebrew), II, 689f. Cf. also *Mekhilta de R. Ishmael*, Beshallah 2 (ed. Lauterbach, I, 196f.); *B. Git.* 56b (beginning).

22. *Daily Prayer Book*, trans. by P. Birnbaum (New York, 1949), p. 589.

23. C. N. Cochrane, *Christianity and Classical Culture* (New York, 1957), pp. 16f., 63f.; R. Koebner, *Empire* (Cambridge, 1961), pp. 7f.; P. E. Schramm, *Kaiser, Rom und Renovatio* (Leipzig, 1929; I², Darmstadt, 1957), I², 29f., 340, where much further literature is cited.

24. *Abot* 3:14; the translation is by J. Goldin in *The Living Talmud* (New York, 1957), p. 140. That the sentiment expresses the mood of the generation may be seen from the fact that the leader of the opposing school, R. Ishmael, uses a similar expression; noted by Bacher, *Agada der Tannaiten*, I, 280, n. 2.

25. Bacher, *Agada der Tannaiten*, I, 78f., 165f., 280f.

26. *The Bible in Aramaic*, ed. by A. Sperber (Leiden, 1959–62), III, 68; text and English translation in *The Targum of Isaiah*, ed. by J. F. Stenning (Oxford, 1949), pp. 112f.; M. Grünbaum, "Beiträge," p. 305.

27. *Sifre Num.* 69, p. 65 (ed. Horovitz); on the passage see Lieberman, *Hellenism in Jewish Palestine*, p. 45.

28. *Piyyute Yannai*, ed. by M. Zullay (Berlin, 1938), p. 45, line 13 (based on *Ber. R.* 63:8, p. 688); *Ber. R.* 67:8, p. 763 (ed. Theodor-Albeck).

29. See N. N. Glatzer, "The Attitude Toward Rome."

30. *Mekhilta de R. Ishmael*, Baḥodesh 9 (ed. Lauterbach, II, 268).

31. For lists of these usages see M. Steinschneider, *Polemische und apologetische Literatur* (Leipzig, 1877), pp. 266f., 278f.; L. Zunz, *Die Synagogale Poesie des Mittelalters*, ed. by A. Freimann (Frankfurt am Main, 1920), pp. 453f.; S. Krauss, "Die Hebräischen Benennungen moderner Völker," *Jewish Studies in Memory of George A. Kohut*, pp. 380f. Edom and Rome were so clearly synonymous in the Middle Ages that in a not uncommon error scribes substituted the name Rome for Palestinian Idumea! See F. Baer, "Eine jüdische Messiasprophetie," *MGWJ*, 70:16 (1926); Abraham ibn Daud, "Dibre Malkhe Yisrael be-Bayyit Sheni," *Seder 'Olam Rabbah* (Amsterdam, 5471), f. 52a (*bis!*), 54a, 57a. Cf. also Y. M. Grintz, *Sefer Yehudith* (Jerusalem, 1957), p. 14, where, however, the translation and emendations of "de Romanis" are by no means certain.

32. Dunash b. Labrat, *Shirim*, ed. by N. Allony (Jerusalem, 1947), p. 58, verse 5 (and see notes *ad hoc.*, p. 117); pp. 56–57, verses 2 and 5; p. 59, verse 1. Even if, in the first citation, וגת באדום is not the original reading, the fact that it should have been substituted for וגם בבל is illuminating.

33. On Christian ambivalence toward Rome in the fifth century see T. H. Mommsen, *Medieval and Renaissance Studies*, ed. by E. F. Rice, Jr. (Ithaca, 1959), pp. 266f., 302f., 336f.

34. For a modern view that the early Christianized Roman aristocracy itself felt this way, see F. Schneider, *Rom und Romgedanke im Mittelalter* (Munich, 1926), pp. 17f., 21f.; Schramm, *Kaiser, Rom und Renovatio*, I, 30f. I do not mean to deny that much of Rabbinic polemic was anti-Christian, or that this polemic did not increase in volume as Christianity grew stronger. However, I am not aware that the official establishment of Christianity caused any basic reorientation on the part of the Rabbis either to Rome or to Christianity.

35. On the identification of the Church with Rome, see R. Folz, *L'Idée de l'empire en Occident* (Paris, 1953), pp. 12f., 190f., and especially W. Ullmann, *The Growth of Papal Government in the Middle Ages*, 2nd ed. (London, 1962). See also the sources cited below,

note 71. Although the Church did not identify with "Romanitas" until the eighth century (Ullmann, pp. 61f, 120f.), the fact that imperial legislation against the Jews emanated from Nova Roma (Constantinople) was doubtless sufficient for the Jews to equate the two.

On medieval Jewish theory and practice with regard to Christians, see J. Katz, *Exclusiveness and Tolerance* (Oxford, 1961).

36. On Jews who felt that prophetic capital had run out, see A. H. Silver, *A History of Messianic Speculation in Israel* (Boston, 1959), pp. 209, 215ff.; B. M. Lewin, "Pirqe Peraqim mi-Milḥamot R. Saadiah Gaon," *Ginze Kedem*, 6:3–14 (1944). For the Jewish replies summarized here, see Saadiah, *The Book of Beliefs and Opinions*, trans. by S. Rosenblatt (New Haven, 1948), pp. 312ff.; Abraham ibn Daud, "Dibre Malkhe Yisrael," f. 50a, 79a–b; Judah Hadassi, *Eshkol ha-Kofer* (Eupatoria, 1836), Alphabet 377, f. 153c, and Z. Ankori, "Studies in the Messianic Doctrine of Yehuda Hadassi the Karaite," *Tarbiz*, 30:194 (1960–61); Moses Maimonides, *Mishneh Torah*, Melakhim 11:4 (ed. Rubinstein; Jerusalem, 1962), p. 415; *idem, Epistle to Yemen*, ed. by A. S. Halkin (New York, 1962), p. xv; *idem, Guide of the Perplexed* II:29; Abraham b. Moses Maimonides, *Perush ha-Torah*, ed. by S. D. Sassoon (London, 1959), p. 204. Moses Nachmanides, *Sefer ha-Geʾulah*, ed. by I. M. Aronson (Jerusalem, 1959), pp. 12, 21f., 51; O. L. Rankin, *Jewish Religious Polemic* (Edinburgh, 1956), pp. 178ff., 200; Jacob b. Reuben, *Milhamot ha-Shem*, ed. by J. Rosenthal (Jerusalem, 1963), pp. 157ff.; J. Rosenthal, "From 'Sefer Alfonso' [in Hebrew]," *Studies and Essays in Honor of Abraham A. Neuman*, ed. by M. Ben Horin *et al.* (Leiden, 1962), p. 589; Joseph Albo, *Sefer ha-ʿIkkarim*, ed. by I. Husik (Philadelphia, 1929–30), IV, 424ff.; Isaac Abravanel, *Comment. on Isa.* 35 (end).

37. See A. Poznánski, *Schiloh* (Leipzig, 1904), pp. 55f. (Origen), 61f. (Jerome), 71f. (Augustine), 206f., 288f.; for medieval Christian writers see also B. Blumenkranz, "Les Auteurs chrétiens latins du moyen âge sur les juifs et le judaisme," *REJ*, 111:12, 19, 38.

38. Abravanel, *Comment. on Isa.*, 35; *idem, Mashmiʿa Yeshuʿah* III:7. On Paul of Burgos, see A. Lukyn Williams, *Adversus Judaeos* (Cambridge, 1935), pp. 267f.

39. *B. Erub.* 96b (and parallels). Cf. H. L. Strack, *Introduction to the Literature of the Talmud and Midrash* (Philadelphia, 1945), p. 22. According to *B. Git.* 56a it was Nero who was coverted to Judaism and then begot R. Meir!

40. Cf. Gal. 3:7f.; 6:16.

41. C. H. Dodd in *Moffatt Commentary* to Rom. 9:6f.

42. See below, Note 54.

43. See H. Wolfson, *The Philosophy of the Church Fathers*, chap. ii and especially pp. 43f. For this whole section I am particularly indebted to N. Bonwetsch, "Der Schriftbeweis für die Kirche aus den Heiden als das wahre Israel bis auf Hippolyt," *Theologische Studien: Theodor Zahn zum 10 Oktober 1908 dargebracht* (Leipzig, 1908), pp. 3–22, and to the superb study of B. Blumenkranz, *Die Judenpredigt Augustins* (Basel, 1946).

As examples of typology derived from etymology (a method employed by Philo as well as the Rabbis; see above, Note 28), note the Pseudo-Cyprian midrash on Sinai as signifying hate, and the explanation of Melito of Sardis that the Jews were called Edom, because they were red with the blood of Christ; Blumenkranz, p. 14; S. W. Baron, *A Social and Religious History of the Jews*, 2nd ed. (Philadelphia, 1952–58), V, 126.

44. Cf. Schlatter, *Church in the New Testament Period*, pp. 310f. For the most recent discussion see I. Baer, "Israel, the Christian Church, and the Roman Empire from the Days of Septimus Severus to the 'Edict of Toleration'" [in Hebrew], *Zion*, 21:3f. (1956).

45. The argument goes back to Cicero, *Pro Flacco* xxviii:69 (Loeb Classics; trans. by L. E. Lord, p. 440/441; cf. J. H. Lewy, *ʿOlamot Nifgashim* (Jerusalem, 1960), pp. 86f.

46. *Epistle of Barnabas*, 13. For the dating of the Epistle of Barnabas around the time of the Bar Koseba revolt, see J. Quasten, *Patrology* (Utrecht, 1950–60), I, 90.

47. Justin, *Dialogue*, 134 (trans. by G. Reith in *The Ante-Nicene Fathers*, I, 267).

48. Irenaeus, *Against Heresies*, IV:21, 2–3.

49. Blumenkranz, *Judenpredigt*, p. 14; cf. also Williams, *Adversus Judaeos*, p. 14.

50. Quoted by Jerome, Epist. 36, Migne, *PL*, 22:460 (Eng. trans., *Ante-Nicene Christian Library*, VI, 421f.); cf. Bonwetsch, *Theologische Studien*, p. 16.

51. Hom. in Gen. 12:3, cited by J. Daniélou, *Origen*, trans. by W. Mitchell (New York, 1955), p. 164. The theme occurs in Origen's commentaries repeatedly; see Baer, "Israel, the Christian Church . . . ," pp. 18f.

52. Tertullian, *Adversus Judaeos*, I, Migne, *PL* 2:597f. (Eng. trans., *Ante-Nicene Christian Library*, XVIII, 202); Blumenkranz, *Judenpredigt*, pp. 9f., 23f.; Bonwetsch, *Theologische Studien*, p. 15.

53. Blumenkranz, *Judenpredigt*, p. 25; Baer, "Israel, the Christian Church . . . ," p. 19, n. 83.

54. Blumenkranz, *Judenpredigt*, p. 170, n. 26. See also H. J. Schoeps, *Paul*, trans. by H. Knight (Philadelphia, 1961), pp. 141f., 229; J. Daniélou, *From Shadows to Reality* (London, 1960); *idem*, "La Typologie d'Isaac dans le christianisme primitive," *Biblica*, 28:363–393 (1947); E. E. Urbach, "Homilies of the Rabbis on the Prophets of the Nations and the Balaam Stories" (in Hebrew), *Tarbiz*, 25:276 (1955–56). Ironically enough, even the typology of antithetical pairs is probably a Christian midrash on a Jewish homily. The panegyric on Wisdom in Wisd. of Sol. 10 lists seven contrasts of righteous versus wicked who followed the Torah or spurned it, to their salvation and destruction respectively: Adam and Cain (verses 1, 3); Noah and the generation of the Flood (4); Abraham and the generation of dissension (5); Lot and the people of the Pentapolis as well as Lot's wife (6, 7); Jacob versus Esau and Laban (8–12); Joseph and Potiphar's wife (13); Moses and Israel versus Pharaoh and Egypt (15–21). This list could easily have been construed as one of contrasting pairs. Furthermore, to philosophically oriented Christians, who in the wake of Philo would see in Biblical personalities ideal types, the pairing of Biblical personalities blended perfectly with the philosophical dualism which was so much a part of the Hellenic mode of thought; see F. M. Cornford, *From Religion to Philosophy* (New York, 1957), pp. 62f., 218f.

55. Cf. the difference between the allegorical meaning of Ishmael (= the Jews) and the literal meaning (= Saracens) in Bede, summarized by Southern, *Western Views of Islam in the Middle Ages*, pp. 16f.

56. On Christian claims to the title of "Israel" and the opprobrium attached to the word "Jew," see Blumenkranz, *Judenpredigt*, pp. 116f., 171f., 181f. On "Jews" as an epithet for a Christian heretic, see James Parkes, *The Conflict of the Church and the Synagogue* (London, 1934), pp. 300f.; H. A. Wolfson, *Religious Philosophy* (Cambridge, Mass., 1961), p. 169. Cf. also B. Blumenkranz, *Juifs et Chrétiens dans le monde occidental* (Paris, 1960), p. xvi. The conflict over the term *Israel* and its theological implications has been treated extensively; cf. W. D. Davies, *Paul and Rabbinic Judaism*, 2nd ed. (London, 1955), pp. 58f., Schoeps, *Aus Frühchristlicher Zeit*, pp. 153f.; M. Simon, *Verus Israel* (Paris, 1948). Although beginning with Cassiodorus (d. ca. 580) Christian writers would often claim even the title "Judei" for Christendom (cf. Romans 2:25f.), the term never lost its basically pejorative connotation; see Blumenkranz, "Les Auteurs chrétiens," *REJ*, 109:45f. (1948–49); 111:47, 58 (1951–52); 113:31 (1954); 114:56, 70, n. 1 (1955); 117:26 (1958).

57. J. Juster, *Les Juifs dans l'empire romain* (Paris, 1914), II, 72. While it may be conceded to Simon, *Verus Israel*, p. 340, and Parkes, *Conflict of the Church and the Synagogue*, pp. 202f., that the limitations on Jewish rights in the slave market were partially motivated by the desire to prevent Jews from Judaizing, this will not explain the special formulation given to Jewish-Christian relations generally and specifically to Jewish disabilities in the case of Christian slaves, which were clearly in a *special* category; see Juster, II, 71, n. 3. On the doctrinal problem generated by Jewish ownership of Christian slaves, see also Blumenkranz, "Les Auteurs chrétiens," *REJ*, 109:60, n. 30 (1948–49).

58. Juster, *Les Juifs*, II, 72f.; Baron, *Social and Religious History*, III, 14, 30f.

59. J. Aronius, *Regesten zur Geschichte der Juden* (Berlin, 1902), pp. 5, no. 10; 7, no. 17; 15, no. 40. The papal chancellery represented these enactments of total separation from the Jews as part of a consistent policy inaugurated in the days of Constantine; see A. Erhardt, "Constantine, Rome and the Rabbis," *Bulletin of the John Rylands Library*, 42:288f., and especially 296f. (1960). I owe this reference to Professor E. J. Bickerman.

60. Jerome, *Comment. in Obad.*, Migne, *PL*, 25:1101f. For Jerome's heretical contemporaries, see *Pelagius' Exposition of Thirteen Epistles of St. Paul*, II (ed. by A. Souter; Cambridge, 1926 [= *Texts and Studies*, IX]), p. 74; Blumenkranz, "Les Auteurs," *REJ*, 109:9 (Maximian the Arian).

61. Blumenkranz, *Judenpredigt*, pp. 42, 95f., 100f., 169f.; see also Augustine, *City of God* XVI, 35. On Eugarius (fifth century) see Blumenkranz, "Les Auteurs," *REJ*, 109:20, n. 17; on Pseudo-Augustine, *ibid.*, p. 31 and *passim*.

62. Baron, *Social and Religious History*, III, 29; see further, S. Katz, "Pope Gregory the Great and the Jews," *JQR*, N.S., 24:119 (1933–34).

63. *Allegoriae quaedam sacrae scripturae*, 25–26, Migne, *PL*, 83:105.

64. By the tenth century Remigius could argue that the prophecy of Gen. 25:23 had been fulfilled through the destruction of the House of David and through the dispersion of the Jews; Migne, *PL*, 131:101. Somewhat later, a bishop of Verceil contended that the fulfillment of this prophecy was so obvious as to require no explanation; Blumenkranz, "Les Auteurs," *REJ*, 114:79f. (1955). Thus, the interpretation of Gen. 25:23 was now brought into conjunction with medieval Christian exegesis of Gen. 49:10; see above, note 37.

65. See Juster, *Les Juifs*, I, 226f., who stresses the theological motivation behind legislation against the Jews; Blumenkranz, *Judenpredigt*, pp. 66f.; Baron, *Social and Religious History*, III, 43; IV, chap. xx; V, 125f.; Parkes, *Conflict of the Church and the Synagogue*, pp. 179f., 326f.; S. Katz, *The Jews in the Visigothic and Frankish Kingdoms of Spain and Gaul* (Cambridge, 1937), chaps. vii–x. For the theory and practice in medieval times, see G. Kisch, *The Jews in Medieval Germany* (Chicago, 1949), pp. 145f.; S. W. Baron, "Plenitude of Apostolic Powers and Medieval 'Jewish Serfdom'" [in Hebrew], *Yizhak F. Baer Jubilee Volume*, ed. by S. W. Baron et al. (Jerusalem, 1960), pp. 102–124; S. Grayzel, *The Church and the Jews in the XIIIth Century* (Philadelphia, 1933).

66. Cf. Baron, *Social and Religious History*, II, 189; Blumenkranz, *Judenpredigt*, pp. 37f.; Parkes, *Conflict of the Church and the Synagogue*, pp. 166f.

67. Innocent III in Grayzel, *The Church and the Jews*, p. 108; see also *ibid.*, pp. 25f., 41f.

68. Blumenkranz, "Les Auteurs," *REJ*, 111:43 (1951–52); Migne, *PL*, 123:39; 131:102. For the pejorative overtones of "terrestrial" Edom, see H. A. Deane, *The Political and Social Ideas of St. Augustine* (New York, 1963), pp. 28f. As evidence of the great currency which the homily on Gen. 25:23 had gained we may note that early in the twelfth century Honorius of Canterbury invoked it, in connection with the struggle between royal and papal authority, as evidence of the superiority of the *sacerdotium* to *regnum*. Esau the elder son, he observed, typifies the king and the lay population, while Jacob the younger son typifies the Church. Honorius also traces the history of the relationship between Jacob and Esau back to Adam, Cain and Abel, etc., thus drawing a direct line from carnal Cain to Esau and from spiritual Abel to Jacob; cited by Ullmann, *Growth of Papal Government in the Middle Ages*, p. 415, n. 3. Needless to say, a homily with so long and venerable a history would make its way into the popular theater, where it would take on the rich and clear overtones of medieval symbolism. Thus Esau can symbolize not only the Jews and the synagogue but the Old Testament and the Law; cf. K. Young, *The Drama of the Medieval Church* (Oxford, 1954), II, 258f., 264f., 484f. (I owe this reference to Professor Norman Cantor.) Cf. also H. O. Taylor, *The Mediaeval Mind* (Cambridge, Mass., 1962), II, 67f.

69. While a number of modern scholars noted that Jerome was aware of the Jewish interpretation of Edom (see above, note 15; M. Rahmer, *Hieronymus' Commentar zu den zwölf kleinen Propheten* [Berlin, 1902], I, 14; II, 4f.), it is no less important to indicate that each time Jerome cites this Jewish interpretation, he dubs it an *idle fantasy.* In this connection, note must be made of the effort by R. Duval, "Notes sur la Peschitto, I. Edom et Rome," *REJ*, 14:49–51 (1887), to interpret the Peschitta translation of Ps. 12:9 as "Like obscene Rome of the seed of Edom," a conjecture that has since made its way into other works as an established fact. Actually, the fact is far from established. A glance at R. Payne Smith, *Thesaurus Syriacus*, I, 34, s.v. ܢܘܥܐ; 1123, s.v. ܐܝܨܐ, and II, 3860, s.v. ܐܡܘܨ will establish that Duval's suggestion is clever but fanciful. Duval himself had to emend the Peschitta reading from ܐܝܨܐ to ܐܝܨܢܐ. His contention that this interpretation was suppressed and accordingly not incorporated in the *Targum* because of fear is even more difficult. A more plausible explanation of the Peschitta rendering can be found in the similarity of the Syriac to the Hebrew. Not knowing what to make of the Hebrew of Ps. 9:12 b, the Syriac translator(s) took similar Syriac words, which were only a little less opaque than the original. The Peschitta passage in question is decidely *not* proof of Christian acceptance of the Jewish interpretation of Edom. In conclusion, the early Christians are consistent: those who mention the Jewish interpretation do so out of a desire to be thorough and to refute it. Thus, the medieval Syriac lexicographers mention the Jewish interpretation of Edom as

"some say"; see Smith, *Thesaurus Syriacus*, I, 34. For further Christian denials, see Rosenthal, "From 'Sefer Alfonso'" (cited above, note 36).

70. Blumenkranz, *Judenpredigt*, pp. 162f.; *idem.*, "Les Auteurs," *REJ*, 109:22 (1948–49); 113:6 (1954).

71. Cf. D. Comparetti, *Vergil in the Middle Ages*, trans. by E.F.M. Benecke (New York, 1929), pp. 176f.; J. Bryce, *The Holy Roman Empire* (New York, 1961), *passim*, and especially pp. 8f., 13f.; Schramm, *Kaiser, Rom und Renovatio*, I, 31f., 46f., 225, who traces the coalescence of two originally discrete concepts, *Roma aeterna caput mundi* and *urbs sacra*; see also above, note 35.

72. See above, notes 19, 69.

73. Cf. Baron, *Social and Religious History*, IV, 3; V, 61; H. J. Zimmels, *Ashkenazim and Sephardim* (London, 1958).

74. For the date see D. Flusser, "The Author of the Book of Josiphon: His Personality and his Age" (in Hebrew), *Zion*, 18:108 (1953).

75. See the useful Latin translation and commentary in the edition of J. F. Breithaupt, *Josephus Gorionides* (Gotha, 1707); Breithaupt gives full references to the classical sources underlying Josippon's mythology. For further observations on this section see Flusser, pp. 112f.; Y. Baer, "Sefer Yosifon ha-Ivri," *Sefer Dinaburg* (Jerusalem, 1949), pp. 180f.; Baron, *Social and Religious History*, VI, 188f.

76. On the resurgence of the ideal of Roman *Renovatio* in this period, which explains the *Sitz im Leben* of Josippon's Kittim theory, see Schramm, *Kaiser, Rom und Renovatio*, I, 44f. I owe the recognition of the connection between the ideal of *Renovatio* and Josippon's point of view to the study of Y. Baer, mentioned in the previous note. However, the analysis offered here is in no way contingent on the date of the coronation scene, which, Flusser has shown, is a later interpolation found only in the recast of *Josippon* known from Spanish authors. On the two recensions of *Josippon* see Flusser, pp. 110f., 114, n. 24, 119; *idem.*, "An 'Alexander Geste' in a Parma MS," *Tarbiz*, 26:166 (1956–57); G. D. Cohen, "The Story of Hannah and Her Seven Sons in Hebrew Literature" (in Hebrew), *Mordecai M. Kaplan Jubilee Volume* (New York, 1953), Hebrew vol. pp. 118f. In presenting Josippon's views on Rome, I have deliberately referred to both recensions to indicate that which clearly represents the point of view of the original.

77. *Josippon* (ed. Hominer) chaps. i–iii, pp. 2f. (ed. Breithaupt, p. 9; ed. Mantua-Günzburg, col. 4f.).

78. B. *Sota* 13a. Cf. also Ginzberg, *Legends*, II, 153f., who has combined all of the legends into a running narrative; M. M. Kasher, *Torah Shelemah* VII, 1869f. (to Gen. 50:9), nos. 24, 28, 30.

79. "Agnios" of the Hebrew sources, as Breithaupt recognized, is clearly Aeneas. The enthronement of Aeneas over Carthage rather than Rome is part of Josippon's distortion (based on the stay of Aeneas with Dido) designed to make the foundation of Rome an Edomite achievement. The Arabic Pseudo-Orosius and, later on, Ibn Khaldun also regarded Dido as a lineal descendant of Esau; see G. Levi della Vida, "La Traduzione araba della storie di Orosio," *Al-Andalus*, 19:264f. (1954).

80. On the reed and forest, see Grünbaum, *Beiträge*, p. 305.

81. Krauss, "Griechen und Römer," p. 9, n. 16; *idem.*, *Paras ve-Romi*, pp. 14f.

82. See R. Rieger, "The Foundation of Rome in the Talmud," *JQR*, N.S., 16: 227f. (1925–26).

83. *Josippon*, chap. xxiii (ed. Hominer, p. 90; ed. Breithaupt, p. 221; ed. Mantua-Günzburg, col. 148); see also Baer, "Sefer Yosifon," pp. 180f.

84. Ginzberg, *Legends* V, 372, n. 425.

85. See above, note 38.

86. I. Goldziher, "Asfar," *Encyclopedia of Islam*, I, 477 (rev. ed., I, 687); see also G. Levi della Vida, "The 'Bronze Era' in Moslem Spain," *JAOS*, 63:190 (1943).

87. *Sefer Ha-Yashar*, ed. by L. Goldschmidt (Berlin, 1923), pp. 202f. (The genealogical opening of *Josippon* is reproduced by *Sefer ha-Yashar*, pp. 31f.) On the work see L. Zunz, *Ha-Derashot be-Yisrael*, ed. by H. Albeck (Jerusalem, 5707), pp. 69f.

88. S. A. Wertheimer, *Bate Midrashot*, ed. by A. J. Wertheimer (Jerusalem, 1950–53), I, 160, par. 72; J. Mann, *The Bible as Read and Preached in the Old Synagogue* (Cincinnati, 1940), Hebrew section, p. 327; Samuel b. Nissim Masnuth, *Bereshit Zuta* (Jerusalem,

1962), p. 281—No one of these texts is quite correct. Thus in Masnuth, read רבתא for ובתה; in the other texts, read לנקמו for לנחמו. Mann's dating of this version in n. 412 is unacceptable, since תורגוש מארץ אלישע obviously derives from *Josippon*, except that *Josippon's* details have been garbled somewhat. Moreover, the lateness of this version is evidenced by the fact that Rashi, Nachmanides, Kimhi, and other medieval collections know nothing of it. Cf. further Ginzberg, *Legends*, V, 372, n. 424. Turnus, as noted by Breithaupt, p. 11, n. 10, is clearly Turnus, King of the Rutuli, of the *Aeneid* 7:56.

89. J. Rosenthal, "The Law of Usury Relating to Non-Jews" (in Hebrew), *Talpioth* 6, 1–2:143, 149 (1953); L. Stein, "The Development of the Jewish Law on Interest from the Biblical Period to the Expulsion of the Jews from England," *Historia Judaica*, 17:30f. (1955).

90. For reference to Christendom as "the brother" (i.e., Esau), see Zunz, *Synagogale Poesie*, p. 464.

91. *M. Yad.* 4:4. Cf. Jacob b. Asher, *Arbaʿah Turim*, Eben ha-ʿEzer, 4.

92. Abraham Maimuni, *Perush*, p. 126.

93. Rosenthal, "The Law of Usury," pp. 139, n. 11; 152; *Encyclopedia Talmudit*, I, 71a.

94. See the material collected by Rosenthal, "The Law of Usury," pp. 141f. That the denial of the Edomite origin of Rome represented an effort to meet the challenge of Christian exegesis of Gen. 25:23 was noted by S. A. Wertheimer, *Geon ha-Geonim* (Jerusalem, 5685), pp. 56, n. 1; 57, n. 1.

95. See the copious references collected by A. S. Halkin in his edition of Maimonides, *Epistle to Yemen* (New York, 1952), p. 14, n. 15. Cf. also Abraham Maimuni, *Perush*, p. 64; Rosenthal, "From 'Sefer Alfonso,'" pp. 593, 611. So ingrained did this view become that some Jews credited Constantine with instituting the practice of having Christian males worship bareheaded; Leon Modena, *She'elot u-Teshuvot Zikne Yehudah* (Jerusalem, 5716), p. 34.

The theory that Constantine composed the New Testament is the Jewish counterpart of the medieval Christian theory (voiced by the Spaniard Petrus Alfonsi) that the Quran was composed after the death of Muhammad; N. Daniel, *Islam and the West* (Edinburgh, 1960), pp. 34f. On the other hand, it echoes the comparison of Constantine to Moses made in Christian circles; Schramm, *Kaiser, Rom und Renovatio*, I, 142f. Jews thus regarded him as the *nomothetes* of Christendom in every respect.

96. Ibn Ezra to Dan. 2:39 and especially "Abraham Ibn Ezra's Short Commentary on Daniel," ed. by H. J. Mathews, *Miscellany of Hebrew Literature*, 2:3 (1877), where Ishmael is explicitly called "the fourth kingdom." (Thus, the strictures of Steinschneider, *Polemische und apologetische Literatur*, p. 269, must be rejected.) Cf. further *Pirqe R. Eliezer* (ed. Higger) 27, *Horeb*, 10:187 (1948); *Midrash ha-Gadol*, Genesis (ed. Margulies) to Gen. 15:9, p. 254; *Maʾor ha-ʾafelah* (ed. Kafih), p. 87. These Yemenite anthologies also contain the Saadyanic tradition that Edom and Ishmael are "partners" in the fourth kingdom; however, the presence of traditions crediting Ishmael with exclusive dominion is undeniable. For parallel views of Christians living under Muslim domain, see R. W. Southern, *Western Views of Islam in the Middle Ages* (Cambridge, Mass., 1962), pp. 23f.

97. Ibn Ezra's *Shorter Commentary to Daniel*, pp. 3, 7; Joseph b. Judah ibn Aqnin, *Divulgatio mysteriorum luminumque apparenta, commentarius in Canticum Canticorum*, ed. by A. S. Halkin (Jerusalem, 1964), pp. 414–415. I am indebted to Professor Halkin for making this information available to me prior to the appearance of his edition.

98. See Ibn Ezra to Gen. 27:40; Zech. 11:15, where the edition of Venice of 1524 and manuscripts of Ibn Ezra read:

כי יון הגלה ירושלם לא אדום

(courtesy of the collation of Mr. Melvin Libman).

99. Ibn Ezra to Dan. 7:14, *idem, Shorter Commentary*, p. 4. Exegetically, Ibn Ezra was on solid ground; see H. L. Ginsberg, *Studies in Daniel*, pp. 6f. The fact that Rome was really part of the Greek empire was information that was received with enthusiasm in Byzantium; see Z. Ankori, "Studies in the Messianic Doctrines of Yehuda Hadassi the Karaite," *Tarbiz*, 30:203, n. 51 (1960–61); *idem*, "The Correspondence of Tobias ben Moses, the Karaite, of Constantinople," *Essays on Jewish Life and Thought Presented in Honor of Salo Wittmayer Baron*, ed. by J. L. Blau *et al.* (New York, 1959), p. 5, n. 13.

100. The same view underlies the fanciful account of the Sassanid call to arms in Abraham ibn Daud, *Sefer ha-Qabbalah* (ed. Neubauer, p. 60, lines 17f.; trans. G. D. Cohen, chap. iv, lines 131f.). The identity of the Greeks and Romans was a Sassanid conception, which probably came to Ibn Ezra and Ibn Daud by way of Arabic historiography; cf. T. Noeldeke, "Geschichte des Artaschir i Papakan," *Beiträge zur Kunde der indogermanischen Sprachen*, 4:36, n. 1; 54 (1878).

101. See Moses Nachmanides, *Commentary on the Torah* (in Hebrew), ed. by C. B. Chavel (Jerusalem, 1959–60), II, 302; *idem, Sefer ha-Ge'ulah*, pp. 51f.

Messianic Postures of Ashkenazim and Sephardim

(Prior to Sabbethai Zevi)[*]

Although the subject of my paper is temporally—and to some extent even spatially—far removed from the themes usually discussed under the auspices of this Institute, it will, I trust, not be devoid of interest to students of modern Jewish history and particularly to the broader concerns of the Leo Baeck Institute. As heirs to a long tradition, Jews of our own day consciously and unconsciously give expression to ideas, and reflect patterns of behavior, the roots of which are enmeshed in the depths of the remote past. No better or more obvious example is afforded than by modern Zionism, which through its political, social, and cultural achievements has set Jewish history on an entirely new course. Yet Zionism drew much of its substance and momentum from the traditional Jewish messianic faith, a faith which has been transmitted through the ages.

In examining some of the roots of pre-modern messianism, we must inevitably touch on a second subject, which also is not without interest to us: that is, the Jewish response to pressure and persecution, to alternatives of life through compromise or of death through steadfastness and martyrdom. For messianism provided the energy and ideological substance for Jewish resistance in a world in which the Jews were always outnumbered and in which they frequently had to contend with unbridled animosity. In scrutinizing some of the forms and circumstances in which

[*]Leo Baeck Memorial Lecture 9—The Leo Baeck Institute was founded by representative organizations of Jews from Germany for the purpose of collecting material on and sponsoring research into the history of the Jewish community in Germany and in other German-speaking countries from the Emancipation to its dispersion. The Institute is named in honor of the man who was the last representative figure of German Jewry in Germany during the Nazi period.

Jewish ultimate hope was persistently maintained, we offer some humble tribute to the name of the man who for our age was the symbol *par excellence* of Jewish faith in vindication and of steadfast hope while in the very bowels of darkness. To Leo Baeck the *Essence of Judaism* and *This People Israel* meant eternity and ultimate redemption; and to countless of his people Israel, Leo Baeck spelled a hold on faith, hope, justification.

While the Jewish hope for "our Messia that is yet to come"[1] is so well known as to be a virtual commonplace, close examination of the way this hope was expressed will reveal considerable differences among various Jewish groups. Like any other cultural phenomenon, this religious national dream underwent a certain amount of development and took on many different forms not only in ancient times but throughout the medieval period as well.

To make but brief reference to the earliest messianic movements of the Middle Ages, Near Eastern Jewish messianism found expression in three distinct, and frequently mutually exclusive, types of behavior. The first may be categorized as an elitist-rabbinic-quietist millenarism, which was expressed in the Hebrew apocalyptic tracts that were compiled in Palestine in the first two centuries of the Muslim conquest.[2] Although quite violent in *tone*, these documents paradoxically became vehicles of emotional release for a Jewish ruling class whose interests and program of life led them to renounce all millenarist activity which might upset the smooth and steady functioning of their community. Rabbinism in the Near East realistically channeled messianism into commemorative ritual and into visionary fantasy.[3] At best, the rabbis tolerated the yen of some Jews to settle in the Holy Land, but the extremely restricted extent of such settlement betrays the true nature of the elitist-rabbinic messianic posture. Israel was to hope and to be ready for the end, but it was not to anticipate it. We shall see that while later rabbinic authorities of Europe played several variations on this theme, their policy and programs were basically identical with those of the elitist elements of Palestine and Babylonia.

The second type of messianic expression in the Near East consisted of popular uprisings under leaders, who, on occasion, combined aggressive military action with extreme pietism or sectarian innovation.[4] While the military programs of each of these visionaries were nipped in the bud, the leaders of these uprisings were able to begin their movements by generating local popular sentiment to white heat, thereby inducing many to follow them into battle, flee to the desert, dispose of their possessions and subsequently, even after defeat, to organize themselves into loyal fellowships that became known as distinct sects. What is revealing about their respective fates is not that they encountered the quick and determined opposition of the Muslim government, but that the gentile overlords found willing allies in the rabbinic authorities themselves, who helped eliminate these dissidents as active threats to the peace and well-being of the Jewish community.

The third type of messianic expression can be conveniently subsumed under the rubric of mature Karaism. While the extent of the messianic orientation of Ananism and early Karaism is a matter of considerable scholarly dispute, the Palestinocentricism of later Qumisian Karaism is not subject to question.[5] Indeed, it has been recently, and I believe plausibly, argued that the renowned mourners of Zion, far from having been one of the elements which Karaism drew upon, were actually an outgrowth of the new schism, which incorporated settlement in the Holy Land, and/or extreme mourning for its desolation and subjection, into its ideology as one of the pivots of its anti-Rabbanite orientation.[6] Be that as it may, the messianic posture of Karaism is best understood not as pure messianic activism but as a compromise between the extreme quietism of the Rabbanite elite and the explosive activism of fringe groups in the Iraquian and Persian Jewish community. Daniel al-Qumisi's brand of messianism—settling in Palestine and hastening the end of time by wailing and weeping over the destruction and the Dispersion—was a new form of nomian quietism, a carefully harnessed pre-millenarism, which gratified and yet controlled the hopes of restive and disaffected masses.

These salient types of messianic posture in the Near East afford us considerable insight into the variety of forms of Jewish messianism on the Continent of Europe. As is well known, the two branches of medieval Jewish culture—namely the Andalusian-Spanish, or Sephardic, and the Franco-German, or Ashkenazic—trace their cultural parentage to Babylonia and Palestine, the early Sephardic drawing almost exclusively on Babylonian books and teachings, the Ashkenazic deriving much of its heritage from Palestine. What was true of *halakah,* philosophy, liturgy, poetry, and Hebrew style had its counterpart in messianic posture and expression as well.

If we survey the history of messianic activity and speculation in Europe, we are immediately confronted with several striking differences in the manifestation of this faith between Andalusian and Spanish Jewry, on the one hand, and Franco-German or Ashkenazic Jewry on the other. In the first place, we must note the remarkable phenomenon that while between c. 1065–1492 there were close to a dozen messianic pretenders—and I include under that category men who claimed only to herald the Messiah—in Andalus, Christian Spain, and North Africa, there is not a single unequivocal instance of such activity among Franco-German Jewry.[7] The only apparent exception was a messianic movement, which Maimonides reported to have taken place c. 1065 in the city of Linon in

Ifranja, or the land of the Franks.[8] While most scholars have identified this place as Lyon, France, I believe there are cogent reasons to locate the incident in Leon of Christian Spain, which Arab geographers also called the Land of the Franks, and with which the Jews of Andalus did have relatively easy and indeed direct contact.

It may not be inappropriate to mention here that just shortly before this messianic incident, the descendants of the Babylonian exilarch, Hezekiah, had moved from Andalus to Christian Spain, while one of them, the renowned Hiyya al-Daudi, was buried in the land of Leon c. 1150.[9] Whether there was any connection between the appearance of these Davidides in the north and the messianic incident reported by Maimonides, we, of course, have no way of knowing. But the fact that all of our information on this family comes from Andalusian sources strengthens our feeling that the Linon mentioned in Maimonides' *Epistle to Yemen* is to be identified with the Leon of Spain. While from the point of view of an Andalusian like Maimonides, the Jews living there were dwelling among Franks, the contiguity of the northern Spanish community to Andalusian culture makes it highly likely that the incident was fomented by a Jew or Jews very much under the influence of Judeo-Arabic culture. The incident is probably a case of Sephardic messianism, not French.

The location of other instances of messianic activity in Spain is far less equivocal.[10] Some forty years after the incident in Linon-Leon (i.e., c. 1105), a certain Ibn Aryeh in Cordova was designated as the Messiah after astrological signs were interpreted to point to the year, the place, and the man. Some fifteen to twenty years after that, a Moroccan Jew, who had been educated in Lucena under Rabbi Joseph ibn Megash, stirred up a messianic affair in Fez. The incident had repercussions in Spain, of which Morocco was culturally a branch, for the father of Maimonides tried desperately to stop people from following his lead. Why there should have been three such incidents in relatively rapid succession, I shall try to explain later on.

The rabbinic authorities of Spain rebuffed Abraham Abulafia, a prophet of Avila, a pretender of Ayllon, and perhaps one or two other would-be messiahs in the latter part of the thirteenth century. Whatever the extent of their adherents, these messiahs and their followers were all Spaniards.

Throughout this period, no segment of Ashkenazic Jewry is known to have risen in messianic revolt. Indeed, we may go even further and say that there is not a single case of a messianic movement or of a pseudomessiah known from Ashkenazic Jewry until the beginning of the sixteenth century, and even that one instance, namely the call of Asher Laemmlein, is an obscure and short-lived affair, which shows traces of Sephardic influence on the mind of an Ashkenazic Jew.[11]

On the other hand, again, the great messianic ferment after the expulsion from Spain, which was expressed in a variety of ways—in Abravanel's tracts, in the great attempts of David Reubeni and Solomon Molko, in the millenarian activity of the kabbalists of Safed, and finally in the first real *mass* messianic movement that swept all strata of the Jewish population off their feet, that of Sabbetai Zevi—emanated from and found greatest support in the Sephardic elements of Jewry.[12] To be sure, even the Sephardic messianic attempts were few and far removed from each other, but surely it is a matter of no mean interest that whatever messianic activity occurred in Western Europe almost entirely emanated from one corner of occidental Jewry.

I trust that my remarks will not be misconstrued to mean that there were never any messianic movements elsewhere. The surprises held in store for us moderns in the arcana of the Cairo Geniza have been too rich and revolutionary in their revelations to deny that new instances will not yet turn up. Indeed, from the Geniza, we have learned of two messianic incidents in Byzantium, c. 1096, and in Sicily, at a time which has not yet been definitely determined.[13] But in the first place, each of these two communities had cultural affinities with the East and Spain respectively. Moreover, they seem to have been isolated incidents of hysteria that left no impression in Jewish literature. The basic classification we have laid down, that messianic activity in Europe was essentially of Babylonian-Spanish vintage, still holds true.

In this connection we must repeat the findings of sober scholarly analysis that another seeming exception to our generalization is reflected by the migration of several hundred rabbis from France and Germany to the Holy Land in 1210 and 1211. That event, however, does not constitute an exception at all, for the migrants betrayed little, if any, messianic activity. Certainly they made no move to carry masses of Jews along with them. The migration, which probably did not number the hundreds of whom later chroniclers wrote, seems to have been motivated by general considerations of piety rather than by millenarist anticipations.[14]

This is as we should expect, for messianic acts in Europe no less than in Asia were usually undertaken without rabbinic sanction. Those rabbis of Spain from whom we do have opinions, like the Geonim before them, in their charitable moments looked on messiahs as sadly deluded men, or more probably, downright impostors. There is no reason to believe that in this regard at least, the rabbis of France and Germany were any different from those of Babylonia, Spain, and North Africa. In other words, messianic activity in Europe was, as it had been in the East, a manifestation of popular revolt against what the millenarists considered "the establishment."[15]

Although, as far as we can determine, the attitudes of the Sephardic and Ashkenazic rabbinates to popular messianic uprisings were basically identical, there were some notable differences in the way the two Jewish elites gave expression to the traditional messianic hope. Among the many differences in the type of literary productivity which emanated from Sephardic and Ashkenazic circles, and these embrace differences in approach to, and expression of, the Hebrew language, exegesis, halakhic codification, writing in the vernacular, belles-lettres, science, and philosophy, we must also include the genre of messianic speculation. While in Spain messianism appears constantly to have been on the agenda of scholarly exchange and to have evoked a whole string of messianic tracts, such discussion was extremely limited in medieval France and Germany and has left only the faintest traces in literature.

By way of documentation, perhaps it is best to begin this aspect of our survey with Ashkenaz, which until the sixteenth century produced no original messianic literature whatever. This startling phenomenon stands out in much bolder relief if we examine closely the nature of those literary traces of early messianic speculation in France and Germany that have come down to us. Actually, they amount in sum total to three fragmentary statements and one exegetical work. The first consists of an early tenth-century (906) query from the sages of the Rhineland to the academy of the Holy Land concerning the expected date of the messianic redemption. The inquiry, Professor Marx has suggested, was evoked not by any spontaneous messianic ferment but by the text of the "Apocalypse of Zerubbabel" which had by that time gained a quasi-official status and which seemed to point to a date close at hand.[16] In other words, the logic of a text, not the independent research of a learned group, stimulated curiosity. No less significant is the fact that the inquiry seems to have been a brief one and was appended to a second question concerning the criteria for disqualifying ritually slaughtered meat. The text gives not the faintest trace of any real messianic awakening.

The second Ashkenazic literary manifestation of any overt interest in messianism is Rashi's commentaries to the Book of Daniel and the Talmud, in which he indicated that the Messiah was to be expected in 1352 or in 1478.[17] However, Rashi's conclusions, far from betraying an avid expectation of the messianic redemption, actually lend support to our contention. Rashi's dates were nothing more than an exegete's elucidation of texts, which he interpreted with no greater emphasis than he had the rest of the vast corpus of Scripture and the Talmud. He could not very well have skipped over these particular passages in Daniel and the Talmud. But there is a far more revealing point about Rashi's interpretations, which excludes them from the genre of genuine messianic speculation. If there is one characteristic that underlies the two thousand years of messianic literature from the Book of Daniel in the second century B.C.E. to the commentary of Rabbi Meir Leibush Malbim in the nineteenth century C.E., it is the relative imminence of the messianic denouement. The function of messianic tracts is to alert and console the audience in the context of contemporary events, not by postponing comfort to the remote future, which the author's audience could not have the faintest hope of living to see and enjoy. Far from being messianically oriented, Rashi's commentary, by postponing the end some three or four centuries, was the very antithesis of millenarist excitation.

How quiescent Franco-German Jewry really was may be seen from the reports of several authors that the Messiah was expected to come sometime between Tishri of 1084 and Tishri of 1103, or in the 256th cycle of creation. The date was derived from a word in Jeremiah 31:6: "For thus saith the Lord: Sing with gladness for Jacob רנו ליעקב שמחה, and shout at the head of the nations; announce ye, praise ye, and say: 'O Lord, save thy people, the remnant of Israel.'" However, this calculation did not make its way into Ashkenazic *literature* until considerably after it had failed to materialize. What is more, even this messianic symbol seems to have come to Ashkenazic circles from the outside, for the Jews of France and Germany apparently first became aware of it through the *Leqah Tob,* in which Rabbi Tobiah ben Eliezer of Castoria had recorded this date as his own discovery.[18] Now, Rabbi Tobiah was a Byzantine, not an Ashkenazi. Moreover, as we have already indicated, the messianic ferment in Salonica and its environs at the time of the First Crusade, with which this messianic date was connected, was a local and ephemeral affair which was confined to visions and miraculous manifestations that had no repercussions, and the stimulus for which is to be sought outside the Jewish community itself. But whatever the case, the event betrays no sign of having been connected with a general messianic ferment in the Jewish communities of the world or of having been inspired by other Jewish messianic incidents.

A rash of messianic predictions did begin to crop up, almost dramatically, in France and Germany in the twelfth and thirteenth centuries in the circles of the Tosafists and German mystical pietists. However, what is revealing about this wave of speculation is the nature of the predictions and the extent to which they were communicated. Interestingly enough, much of the Tosafistic-pietistic messianic speculation is communicated to us second-hand, that is to say, not by the speculators themselves but by reporters who heard of their statements. Thus, Rabbi Joseph Bekhor Shor cites the Spaniard Abraham bar Hiyya for his computation, while Rabbi Isaac ben Judah ha-Levi invokes the authority of Rabbi Joseph and of the biblical commentary known as *Sefer ha-Gan.*[19] The derivative character of the messianic communications of the pietists is even more apparent in a little messianic excursus inserted into a thirteenth-century commentary on the *Ethics of the Fathers* by an as yet not fully identified member of the German pietist school.[20] What this little parenthesis affords us is a report of messianic computations made by the author's father, a certain Rabbi Solomon, and the latter's teachers and colleagues. Most prominent among the latter are the renowned Rabbi Judah of Paris, Rabbi Samuel he-Ḥasid and his son Rabbi Judah he-Ḥasid, Rabbi Isaac of Dampierre, Rabbi Ezra the prophet of Montcontour, and Rabbi Troestlin the prophet. Mention is also made of a certain book of visions or visionaries, *Sefer ha-Ḥozim,* from which the astrological signs associated with the advent of the messianic era are cited.[21] Apart from these few instances, and they are decidedly not evidence of a messianic literature of the kind we encounter from Spain, there has come down no real messianic literary genre from France and Germany. To the contrary, the few fragments that have survived from Ashkenaz testify to speculation that was conducted esoterically, in the confines of a very restricted circle. Most important, we have no evidence of any communal reverberations of messianic speculation in France or Germany. The only trace of some wider echo of these computations is from a letter written in Arabic—in other words from an oriental or Andalusian area—to the community of Alexandria. This letter tells of reports, arriving from Marseille and from France generally to Qabes in Tunis, of the arrival of Elijah sometime after 1225/6 and of the coming of the Messiah in 1232/ 33. Among those reported to have verified the prophecies, which the late Professor Assaf conjectured were uttered by Rabbi Ezra of Montcontour, was the renowned Rabbi Eleazar Rokeaḥ.[22] At best, then, we have in this letter the echo of an isolated incident. Nevertheless, careful analysis of some of the circumstances surrounding these prophecies of the Franco-German pietists will once again serve to place the nature of the far different Spanish messianic activity in bolder relief.

The most salient characteristic of the messianic predictions of the Franco-German rabbis is the prophetic character of the informants and of their information. Thus, two of the pietists mentioned in the little German appendix, Rabbi Ezra and Rabbi Troestlin, are specifically called prophets.[23] Rabbi Ezra of Montcontour was reported to have ascended to Heaven and determined the date of the end by consulting with Haggai, Zechariah, and Malachi. Rabbi Samuel and Rabbi Judah, the pietists, and Rabbi Meir ben Baruk of Rothenberg ascertained the date of the end through information imparted in dreams.[24] It hardly needs belaboring that such messianic calculation as well as the title of prophet were distinctly alien to the Sephardic rabbinic temper. Indeed, the only upper-class Spaniard who was openly recognized as a prophet, Rabbi Sheshet Benveniste of Barcelona, was a product of the French academy of Narbonne.[25] One need but recall the reception that Abraham Abulafia reports he received and Rabbi Solomon Ibn Adret's fulminations against would-be prophets to appreciate the vast difference between the Sephardic and Ashkenazic ways of eschatological speculation.

To be sure, there are points in common in the detailed explanation of messianic dates of the Sephardim and Ashkenazim. Both groups, for example, worked with *gematriaot* (cryptographs) and with symmetrical periodizations of Jewish history. However, here again there is a thin, but quite palpable, line that divides them. Whereas in Sephardic calculations the *gematriaot* play an ancillary role, and are usually invoked as vital only for points in the remote past, in Franco-German calculations the *gematriaot* are central to the calculation and as often as not point to the future, to the denouement of history. For example, the Sephardim frequently cited the Talmudic mnemonics of תת״ץ, ונושת״ם, בתמ״ח but these were always invoked as classically attested dates or hints, and only as *part* of a much wider exposition on messianic calculation.[26]

In the case of the Ashkenazic computations, the *gematriaot* are often quite novel and point to the exact date of the end of the present stage of history: for example, רנו ליעקב שמחה ("Sing with gladness for Jacob"— Jeremiah 31:6), as pointing to the 256th cycle of creation (1084–1103); or דודי צח ואדום ("My beloved is white and ruddy"—Song of Songs 5:10), as referring to the year 1238 C.E.; or הסתר אסתיר ("I will keep . . . hidden"—Deuteronomy 31:18), as being equal to 1235 years in Daniel 12:12; and so on.[27]

Now the modern student, to whom *gematria*-style thinking is so basically alien, may easily be tempted to lump Spanish and Franco-German *gematriaot* into one medieval bag. But in reality, there is a chasm dividing them. As traditional Jews, the Spaniards invoked *gematriaot* that had been formulated by their rabbinic forebears. However, the German mystics took the ancient *gematriaot* as a hint that all of classical Jewish literature—the Bible as well as the liturgy—was worded in accordance with the principles of *gematria*. Accordingly, they were forever coming up with new *gematriaot*, thus extending to messianic calculation the methods they employed in their liturgical devotions.

To a certain extent, it is true, the new tendencies in Ashkenazic messianic calculation may also be discerned in thirteenth-century Spanish kabbalistic circles, notably in the writings of Naḥmanides and especially in the works of Abraham Abulafia and the Zohar. These Spanish circles are notorious for the new techniques of substitutions of letters and words of equal numerical values which they employed for mystical theosophy and messianic calculation.[28] However, it is hardly an accident that the first Sephardim to employ these characteristically Ashkenazic techniques were those dwelling in Christian Spain at the very time when the influence of Ashkenazic literature and orientations had made significant inroads into Spain. The men of Spain who indulged in these typically Franco-German interpretations of texts were people who had been subjected to much influence from areas beyond the Pyrenees and who attempted to integrate the wisdom of Ashkenaz with the legacy of Andalus. These were the very times and the very same areas in which the controversy over the works of Maimonides was inflaming Jewish passions as a consequence of the Ashkenazic challenge from Provence and France. Ashkenazic fundamentalism had gained ground in many respectable areas in Spain, and even some fine Sephardim had more or less absorbed the northern temper.

But the new cross-influences were by no means unilateral, for the men, academies, and literature of Spain had a deep impact on Ashkenazic leadership. Whatever the source of Provençal and Franco-German mysticism, it is significant that this speculation north of the Pyrenees was undertaken largely by men who had either studied in Spain or had access to Sephardic literature and especially to the works of Saadiah and Maimonides. I am not suggesting that Franco-German pietism drew its inspiration from Spain; what I do contend is that these circles did have access to Andalusian literature and reflected the effects of some of its seminal ideas. And among the Sephardic preoccupations which could easily have excited the pietists of Ashkenaz and stimulated them to further speculation was the authentically Jewish concern with the date of the messianic redemption. In other words, even the brief messianic ferment among the pietists of Ashkenaz probably drew much of its inspiration from Sepharad. How crucial the influence of the Andalusian Maimonides was on the messianic computations of the Ashkenazim may be seen from the way the French pietists cited legends about Maimonides and Arabs in support of their calculations.[29] Maimonides' *Epistle to Yemen* came to Provence no later than 1215, and though the work was not translated into Hebrew until at least a decade later,[30] it may well be that its messianic calculation had made its way northward even before Ibn Tibbon released a Hebrew version. In short, France and Germany had little by way of an indigenous tradition of messianic speculation, and this tradition, to the extent that it did exist, had few literary or public reverberations.

By way of contrast, Andalus had a long, continuous, and, what is most important, public tradition of messianic calculation. Beginning with Abraham bar Ḥiyya's *Megillat ha-Megalleh* down to Isaac Abravanel's *Mashmi'a Yeshu'ah*, *Ma'ayenay ha-Yeshu'oh*, and *Yeshu'at Meshiḥo*, the date of the Messiah was forever being discussed publicly and with an originality of approach in each new work that puts this whole body of literature on an entirely different plane from the fragments deriving from Franco-German circles. Circa 1125, Abraham bar Ḥiyya calculated the advent of the messianic age from several points of view: from the account of creation in Genesis, from the Torah as a whole, from astrological signs, and from an exegetical analysis of Daniel. In other words, he used what a medieval man recognized as strictly empirical data. Now, although Abraham bar Ḥiyya's tract is the first full-scale discussion in Spain of the date of the Messiah, there is ample evidence that his was not the first public conjecture on the messianic end in the rabbinic circles of Andalus. Abraham ibn Ezra reports that Solomon ibn Gabirol early in the eleventh century had also invoked astrological data to predict the end, while not much earlier Samuel ibn Nagrela had infuriated the Muslim Ibn Ḥazm by contending that he was himself a fulfillment of the messianic promise "until Shiloh come." If we recall that not much earlier (c. 950) Ḥisdai ibn Shaprut was said to have written to Joseph, King of the Khazars, and to have inquired, among other things, whether the Khazar monarch had any trustworthy information on the date of the messianic end, we begin to realize that Abraham bar Ḥiyya's work was perhaps the first systematic treatise and the climax of several generations of speculation, but by no means the inauguration of a totally new genre.

Indeed, five of Abraham bar Ḥiyya's contemporaries, some of them far removed from one another, testify to the extent of the elitist but open discussion in Andalus of the probable date of the fulfillment of the messianic promise. Judah ben Barzillay of Barcelona, though he was opposed to astrological calculation, reaffirmed the tenability of other methods of calculation based on older rabbinic schemes of discerning the fulfillment of history.[31] At approximately the same time Judah ha-Levi expressed in poetry the general grief that the Messiah had not come at the date popularly believed to be the time of the end (1069), and then proceeded to recount his own vision of the imminent fulfillment of another classically attested rabbinic promise.[32] A Jewish prophecy of the age, predicting on astrological grounds the beginning of the messianic era for 1186–87, made its way into Christian circles and has been preserved in Latin.[33] At about the same time, Maimon the Dayyan imparted to his children a tradition which he had received from his father—that the messianic age would be initiated with the reinstitution of prophecy around 1210 or 1216. Although his son Moses Maimonides, in his renowned *Epistle to Yemen*, protested vigorously against public speculation on the date of the end and obliquely criticized others for doing so, he himself proceeded in good Andalusian fashion to report and explain the tradition he had received from his father.[34] Shortly after Maimonides had written his *Epistle*, Abraham ibn Daud of Toledo wrote a series of works in each of which he vigorously reaffirmed the traditional messianic faith. My own investigation into Ibn Daud's work has led me to the conclusion that his historiography was in reality a thinly disguised trilogy, the real purpose of which was to reassure the learned classes that the messianic age would soon be inaugurated by great upheavals in Spain in 1188–89. In other words, far from being objective historiography, Ibn Daud's works deserve to be reckoned among the Sephardic works dealing at least in part with eschatology.[35]

Before going any further with examples of Spanish literature in this vein, it would be well to pause and recapitulate some of the features of this learned Sephardic messianology. Apart from the fact that this speculation was conducted quite out in the open with little practical regard for the rabbinic injunction against messianic speculation, the conjectured dates are reported to us at firsthand—that is, by the speculators themselves. What is more, without indulging in apocalyptic fantasy, the Sephardim created or revived eschatology as a Jewish literary genre. Far more important, Spanish calculations were derived not by mystical techniques but by means of rationalist exegesis either of Scripture or of rabbinic traditions. This point must be underscored, for just as Franco-German speculation constituted an extension of the literary canons of German pietism to messianology, so, too, the Spanish calculations were made in consonance with the general *weltanschauung* of the Andalusian elite.

It is noteworthy that every one of the names I have mentioned in connection with Sephardic messianic calculation is known to us as a protagonist of the distinctly Andalusian Jewish way of life, and is associated with the golden age of Spanish Jewish creativity. Rationalism, science, philosophy, and Hebrew classicism were the hallmarks of this group. Superstition and non-rational exegesis were anathema to them all. Indeed, much of their intellectual energy was expended in reinterpreting into rational categories what they regarded as the embarrassing legacy of miracles, anthropomorphisms, and trivial stories of their classical literature. Hence, they would have little truck with apocalyptic fantasy. Accordingly, it is not surprising to discern in their writings an effort to calculate the end by the movements of the stars or by rhythmic periodizations of history. Having been trained in philosophy, they regarded the universe and human history as mechanisms or organisms, the functioning of which had been committed by the Creator to immutable laws. Built into these mechanisms as part of the law of their operation they postulated laws of time which would—in the fullness of time—catapult the elect segment of the cosmos—indeed, the world at large—into a happier and more harmonious course. Since it was all a question of a particular manifestation of the laws of nature, fixed by God, to be sure, but capable of rational analysis nonetheless, if one could but permeate the complex secrets of the essential part of the machine or organism, one could determine when its course would change.

Accordingly, in the view of the Sephardim, the key to the secret of the destiny of Israel lay not in ecstatic ascents to Heaven for revelations by angelic powers, who would inform men whether the Almighty had decided that the Jews had had enough; rather, it lay in a study and proper understanding of God's books of laws—the Bible and the Talmud—and of their prerequisites, logic, mathematics, physics, astronomy, metaphysics, and history. Sephardic messianology was harmoniously blended with philosophy and a rationalist approach to life.

While eschatology obviously bespeaks an intense yearning for national redemption and rebirth—and the predominance of this longing in Andalusian Hebrew poetry is too well known to be belabored here—the two, the prayer for redemption and messianic speculation, were by no means synonymous. Jews have prayed for the sound of the horn of redemption since ancient times, but relatively few gave way to the temptation to permeate the heavenly veil concealing the secret of the time appointed for the end. Indeed, there were strong religious injunctions inhibiting the Jews against giving vent to their impatience or against revealing what they believed to be the appointed time. The open speculation of the philosophers of Spain, however well intentioned and however well precedented by earlier generations, was not likely to appeal to meticulous adherents of classical rabbinic teachings. Even Maimonides had qualms about divulging the tradition he had inherited on this score. And if a philosopher felt squeamish about such speculation, how much more so would a penitent like Judah ha-Levi have felt about men who enter areas strictly forbidden to them![36]

Viewed from this perspective, Judah ha-Levi's apparently messianic act of leaving Spain for Palestine was not a logical conclusion of Andalusian messianism but a total rejection of it. His decision, it will be recalled, was taken only after the rationalist system in which he had been reared had, in his estimation, broken down. The rabbi in ha-Levi's *Kuzari* and Judah ha-Levi in his later poems rejected, bag and baggage, the whole mechanistic view of the universe which had become the regnant view of life in the circles of the Spanish-Jewish upper classes. It is no coincidence that the very work of medieval Jewish philosophy that reaffirmed in unequivocal terms the traditional forms of Jewish faith—the superiority of Israel, the uniqueness of the Holy Land, the mystery of prophecy—offered no solace in the form of a messianic prediction. The *Kuzari* suggested no date for the Messiah, for such speculation had become alien to a man who had reappropriated Talmudic faith in God's Providence. The Almighty would act in His good time; man's task was but to try to earn His mercy. Judah ha-Levi's departure for Palestine was an act in that direction and nothing more. Far from attempting to anticipate the Messiah, ha-Levi's move was a rejection of the Sephardic culture of his day; it was a Franco-German-type act of piety that committed all into the hands of a free and inscrutable God.

One of the factors that doubtless helped ha-Levi rationalize his latter-day negative evaluation of Andalusian Jewish culture was the wide currency which a second type of Sephardic messianic speculation, totally at variance with the predominant Sephardic eschatological schools, had gained in his environment. Grounding its views in a scientific study of Scripture, this school of exegesis denied whole blocs of biblical messianic lore as valid sources of hope or prediction for the future. The three names associated with this type of exegesis are Moses ha-Kohen ibn Gikatilla and Judah ibn Balaʿam, of the eleventh century, and Ḥayyim Galipapa of the fourteenth. From Naḥmanides and Abravanel's reports, it would seem that a fourth name is to be added to this list, namely that of Abraham ibn Ezra of the twelfth century. In reality, they were by no means the only skeptics of Spain.

The view shared by all these exegetes was that the messianic prophecies in the Bible could not be interpreted eschatologically. Rather, these visions were to be understood as exhortations and predictions that the prophets had intended for immediate fulfillment. Indeed, study of history convinced these rationalists that these prophecies had been fulfilled in the days of Hezekiah and especially in the early days of the Second Temple. Whether the prophecies were *ad hoc* predictions or merely sermons *ex eventu*, they could not serve as sources of hope to the Jews of the Middle Ages, for their capital had run out long since. These men, it should be emphasized, did not deny the validity of the messianic dogma; they affirmed it as a rabbinic tradition only, not as a legacy of Scripture. However, there can be little doubt that many in Spain regarded the messianic reaffirmation of these exegetes as mere lip service, as formal concessions to the requirements of official piety. With the undermining of the Scriptural foundations for faith in the messianic redemption, to many a thinking person the messianic dogma seemed to rest on thin air.

To Judah ha-Levi the skepticism engendered by this school of thought was only one or two steps removed from the rationalism that saw in Scripture the clues to the mathematics of the Divine economy. Nor was he wrong, for, in its own way, the more tradition-oriented rationalism had also conceded its embarrassment with some of the graphic promises of miraculous upheaval and had thereby added fuel to the fire of doubt and even despair. The outstanding literary expression to the watered-down traditionalist view, the writings of Moses Maimonides, appeared long after ha-Levi's death, but the views Maimonides expressed on the subject were well known in Spain much earlier. Far from innovating in this respect, Maimonides' attenuation of certain traditional messianic hopes betrays how widespread the skepticism had become, had indeed permeated even the highest rabbinic circles.[37] Thus, whether Maimonides had really meant originally to eliminate the doctrine of the resurrection—one of the cardinal promises vouchsafed for the messianic era—from his creed of Judaism, and substitute for it the more philosophically fashionable doctrine of immortality, is a matter on which latter-day Maimunists and anti-Maimunists are still divided. What is beyond question is that Maimonides and many of his disciples considered the promises of resurrection and even of the messianic deliverance far less important than the more rationally acceptable assurance of immortality. Moreover, in his *Guide of the Perplexed,* Maimonides made it very clear that he considered many of the miraculous portents foretold by the prophets for the messianic age mere figures of speech that had not been meant literally. From this last position he never retreated, and even in his legal magnum opus, he indicated that he was not committed to belief in their literal fulfillment.[38]

Maimonides, of course, was in the first instance the great spokesman of an intelligentsia that was bent on restructuring all of Jewish education and indeed even community life on rationalist principles. While the Maimunist controversy in the thirteenth century was soon focused on the question of allegorical interpretations of the ritual commandments and the study of philosophy as the source of all evil within the Jewish community, it should not be forgotten that the first signs of protest against the *Guide* were evinced by Arabically cultured Jews who were astounded at the flippancy with which Maimonides had treated the promise of resurrection.[39] And the promise of resurrection, be it not overlooked, is the central rabbinic motif in its representation of the messianic promise. These protesters sensed, quite rightly, that an authoritative rabbinic license to gloss over the resurrection struck at the root and the heart of the Jewish messianic faith.

While Maimonides' orthodoxy was vindicated, the continued extreme skepticism in the camp of the Andalusian intelligentsia on the meaning of messianic doctrines gave renewed stimulus to the traditionalists to add to the corpus of Spanish eschatological literature. In the thirteenth century, Moses Naḥmanides defended the integrity of the traditional messianic faith not only in his commentary on the Pentateuch, but in a special treatise on the messianic redemption, as well as in his Hebrew summary of the disputation of Barcelona in 1263. While recapitulating many of the older arguments, Naḥmanides' treatise on redemption reflects the newer emphasis of the rabbinic circles of which he was a member, on *gematriaot,* thereby providing a bridge between the Franco-German computations and the indigenously Andalusian literary genre. In the middle of the fourteenth century, when Abner of Burgos shook the Jewish community of Spain by his apostasy, and then proceeded to rationalize his defection by eschatological arguments, his Porphyrian-like exegesis of Daniel evoked a vigorous denunciation coupled with a defense of traditional messianism on exegetical grounds by Rabbi Joseph Shalom.[40] That the eschatological debate, provoked by continued skepticism in upper-class circles, remained alive, may be seen in the vigorous reaffirmation of Hasdai Crescas, the equivocal acceptance of Joseph Albo, and the compendious recapitulations of the whole question by Dov Isaac Abravanel. Thus, a second source of Spanish eschatology was a widespread skepticism over messianic articles of faith, of which we have no evidence from Ashkenazic circles, and which prompted Sephardic traditionalists to speculate on the end of history in much the same way that rationalist Andalusians had done much earlier.

Having seen that underneath the consistent rabbinic opposition to messianic movements there was a vast difference between the rabbis of the Sephardim and of the Ashkenazim in their treatment of the traditional messianic dogma, the question that commands our attention is whether there is any discernible relationship between elitist expression and the behavior of the laity. Given the rabbinic renunciation of any precipitous messianic behavior, is it nevertheless possible to correlate Spanish intellectual expression with the messianic behavior of occasionally rebellious Spanish laity and the French rabbinic posture with the behavior of French-Jewish masses?

It will be noted that in posing the question this way, we have quite deliberately sought to account for particular messianic postures in the psyche of the Jews themselves rather than in any external or objective set of circumstances. For, if there is any one conclusion that the data force upon us, it is that, contrary to the popular impression, there is no discernible connection between persecution and messianic movements. Jewish messianic movements were not "the religion of the oppressed."[41] The Crusades, the Almohade invasion, the expulsions from England and France, the blood libels, the Pastoureaux onslaughts, and the persecutions at the time of the Black Death, indeed, even the expulsion from Spain and the Chmelnitzki massacres did not generate a single messianic movement. Conversely, all the messianic efforts made in Iraq and Persia, and above all in Spain and North Africa, were undertaken in areas and periods of relative stability. Active messianism or quiescence must have derived from sources other than politics or economics. If Franco-German Jewry produced neither a messianic pretender nor a messianic literature, it must be because quiescence and passivity had somehow so permeated the whole mentality of that community as virtually to eliminate such aggressive behavior. Doubtless fear of failure and reprisal played a major role; but hysteria is often strong enough to overcome realistic considerations and we must, accordingly, seek other explanations.

Perhaps the explanations I shall suggest will be a bit more cogent if we revert to the contrast afforded by the data from Spain. Intellectual activism in the form of open speculation on the date of the end by the intellectual elite was paralleled by occasional unbridled eruptions of Jews who could not wait. Activism of two kinds, literary and physical, seems to have permeated Spain much more than France and Germany. But it was a peculiar form of activism, quite unlike the military-sectarian ventures known from Babylonia. In Spain this activism consisted in reading the signs of the times independently of rabbinic authorities and then proceeding to announce miraculous portents and the advent of the redemption. It was, paradoxically enough, Spanish traditionalist rationalism carried to its logical end by the acting out of what Spanish rabbis had merely contemplated. Put differently, it was the translation of the theory of the elite into acts of popular piety. The announcement of a miracle or portent could induce credulous groups of ingenuous believers to divest themselves of their wealth and assemble in readiness for the great deliverance. Conversely, the intellectual quietism of the rabbis of Ashkenaz, motivated in the first instance by religious injunctions against calculating the date of the Messiah, doubtless percolated outward and downward to the laity and lower strata of society and inhibited them from attempting to alter their destiny.

However, in reality, this explanation only pushes the problem back a step. The fact is that the rabbis of Spain, no less than those of France and Germany, advocated political quietism, and both groups of leaders grounded their stance in very much the same classical rabbinic sources. Given the basic uniformity of the classical rabbinic tradition in Spain and France and Germany, what in Jewish culture oriented the one group to intellectual or physical activism and the other to a basic passivity? In the first instance, it seems to me, we must go back to the particular cultural roots of each of the two branches. Ever since the downfall of Bar Kokhba, Palestinian Jewry had politically been fairly quiescent. Its leadership released deep emotions of hostility and hope in prayer, poetry, and apocalyptic literature. But as custodians of the *Pax Romana* in Palestine, the patriarchate and the rabbinate taught submissiveness and acceptance of the Divine decree until the Almighty should intervene in history and restore His people. This basic attitude of submission permeated even the ostensibly explosive literature of Palestinian mysticism and apocalypticism. As in the case of Daniel of old, so, too, in later apocalyptic literature, while the visionary is reassured of Divine vengeance against the Gentiles, he is no less emphatically enjoined to wait for the deliverance of God. In the meantime, he may take comfort in violent and bloody fantasies that will one day become a reality. In other words, far from inciting to riot, apocalyptic literature actually tranquilized and served as a release, a channel by means of which excess emotions were syphoned off. So it was in the case of the Dead Sea sect and the early Christians; so it was in Roman and medieval Palestine.

This attitude and posture were doubtless conveyed to all parts of the Diaspora over which the academies of the Holy Land exercised influence. It is not surprising, therefore, that when in 960 the elders of the Rhineland sent their two inquiries to the Holy Land—on the date of the Messiah and the laws of *terefot*—they were roundly rebuffed on the first question: "You are unworthy of a reply concerning the advent of the Messiah. Do you not trust the words of the sages and the signs which they provided? These have not yet been fulfilled." The mere question was an affront, a violation of religious propriety.

How much the Franco-German spirit owed to its Palestinian progenitor is also reflected in some of the forms surrounding Ashkenazic messianic speculation. Like its Palestinian apocalyptic models, which circulated in France and Germany as early as the tenth century, Ashkenazic calculation depended largely on information gleaned in the course of mystical ascents to the heavens, where a prophet or angel disclosed the secret.

The quietism of the Palestinian-Ashkenazic branch was given its endorsement by the tenth-century Italian paraphrase of Josephus in Hebrew, *Sefer Yosifon.* The major burden of the work was to demonstrate that the Zealots, the lawless ones of Israel who had tried to defy the Divine decree which had installed the fourth empire as mistress of the world, had brought incalculable misery and suffering on their people. Conversely, the righteous of old willingly accepted their fate of martyrdom, confident in the fulfillment of the promises of the great illumination and the resurrection which were vouchsafed for them. What Josephus had failed to convey to his people in Aramaic and Greek, a pseudepigrapher now avidly embraced in Hebrew, and his authority as an authentic interpreter of Jewish history was widely acknowledged.[42]

Spain, on the other hand, modeled itself largely on Babylonian paradigms. From Baghdad it had received not only Gaonic responsa, a translation of and commentaries on the Bible in Arabic and legal codes, but also the guidelines for a Jewish philosophy, and to a large extent the foundations of their own *weltanschauung* and *paideia.* Like the Babylonians in Babylonia, the Sephardim in Andalus became extremely nativist, proud of their genealogy, sensitive to the challenges of Arabic poetry, science, and philosophy, and speculative on the secrets of the universe and of Jewish history. And as in Babylonia, the Jews of Spain witnessed two types of political posture: elitist cooperation with the government, and dissident revolt on the part of disaffected groups. Hence, even though Abraham ibn Daud gave his full approbation to the political stance of *Yosifon,* his endorsement could not dissipate the basic restlessness in the Sephardic temper. Indeed, the very same Ibn Daud had preached quietism out of one side of his mouth and theorized on the end of history out of the other.

However, there were other factors as well. To a certain extent, the political successes of Jews in Spain must have whetted the appetites of the elite for even further conquests. The rise of Jews to heights of power unknown since ancient times was accompanied by a neo-classicism that revived biblical Hebrew and biblical imagery in "secular" as well as religious poetry. It was a Jewish vizier of Granada who defiantly proclaimed: "I am the David of my generation."[43] To a potential David, relative deprivation is much more irritating than absolute deprivation. To a would-be king, as the same Ibn Nagrela confessed, nothing short of conquest of the heavens and the heights of the moon would satisfy. The elite of Spain were restive and eager; and lesser pretenders caught the bug and from time to time announced their messiahship.

Moreover, political success underscored the new confidence in the powers of human understanding that was born of the scientific and philosophic studies cultivated in Spain. While the elite would forever be prudent and judicious, the more deprived and the less stable would lose their inhibitions and jump to messianic action.

But in the final analysis the two different messianic postures of medieval European Jewry betray two different approaches to the same religious faith. Quiescence, passive resistance, is symptomatic of absolute faith in the total transcendence of God, in His unbounded liberty and power, and of perfect certainty that the Divine promise will be fulfilled. It was no coincidence that Ashkenazic Jewry was always basically fundamentalist, unabashed by anthropomorphism or outlandish legends. Who was man to sit in judgment on God or His word?

Activism of the Andalusian type, on the other hand, emanated from a society, which, although formally proclaiming its faith in the classical God of Israel, had in reality appropriated much of the Hellenic scientific spirit; it was largely fatalist-predestinarian and committed to a belief in the inexorable law of nature and, we may add, of history. When the time came for the end to unfold, if indeed it ever would, nothing could stop it.

This difference in underlying faith, of which the form of messianism is but one significant symptom, is far more important than what appears on the surface, for I believe that it provides a clue to understanding the Jewish posture in the face of pressure and dire persecution. While, as I have already affirmed, there is no demonstrable connection in Jewish history between periods of extreme persecution and messianic uprisings, the record of history does entitle us to establish a close connection between a particular type of faith generally, and of messianic faith in particular, and the Jewish response to the challenging alternative of conversion or death. That is because messianism is the substance on which all Jewish tenacity was predicated. God's elect would be vindicated, and on the basis of that promise alone Jews would endure not only persecution but interminable alienation and humiliation. It is a reasonable assumption, then, that the form of a Jew's ideology of resistance will be reflected in the nature of his response to physical threats.

During the Middle Ages, there were four instances, of which we have some rather full accounts, in which scores of Jewish communities and thousands of Jews were confronted by the alternative of apostasy or death, two of them affecting Ashkenazic Jewry and two of them

Sephardic. I make reference, of course, to the First Crusade of 1096, to the Almohade persecutions in North Africa and Spain beginning in 1147, to the riots of 1391 in Spain and the persecutions that followed, and to the Cossack uprisings in Poland and Russia in 1648 and after. Now in each of these instances, many Jews were killed outright. Of those who remained, some fought back; some preferred martyrdom to apostasy; and some converted as a means of saving their lives. Of the last, while some attempted to return to Judaism, others found the final solution to their Jewish problem and remained Christians or Muslims. However, if no one description will suffice to describe the behavior of all the Jews involved in any one of these upheavals, it is nevertheless fair to say that in each of these instances there was a dominant behavioral pattern, one that was so pronounced as to make an indelible impression on eyewitnesses and chroniclers.

In each of the two cases involving Ashkenazic Jewry, those of 1096 and 1648 and after, the outstanding feature of the Jewish response was *kiddush ha-shem*—martyrdom. In both of the persecutions endured by Sephardim, although *kiddush ha-shem* was by no means lacking, the dominant behavioral pattern, the one that left the greatest impression on witnesses and future generations, was apostasy and marranism.

There were, of course, basic differences between each of the two experiences affecting Ashkenazic Jewry, even with respect to the martyrdom accepted by the Jews involved. In the later Chmelnitzki onslaught, it would seem that far fewer Jews had any choice in the matter than in the other three cases. The Cossacks often seemed to have been bent on outright murder, rapine, and pillage. But even in those cases where Jews were in a position to choose between alternatives, they elected to die fighting or to die *passively at the hands of their attackers*.[44] That had not been quite the case in 1096. Then, while many Jews died fighting or even passively, many of them took an active hand in their martyrdom by committing a kind of ritual suicide. The ritual slaughter-knife was used, a blessing was pronounced, and blood of the human sacrifice was even smeared on the pillar of the ark in the synagogue.[45] Martyrdom was not mere sanctification of the Name through faith; it was an atonement sacrifice, an *aqedah*. That is important to bear in mind, for the commemorative chronicles, dirges, and penitential prayers that subsequently emerged from Ashkenaz frequently construed martyrdom as an *aqedah* sacrifice, the highest act of worship, the martyr being referred to as *ha-Qadosh*, the saint.[46] Hence, despite the different circumstances surrounding the voluntary death of thousands of Jews in the two great massacres of Ashkenazic Jewry, the ideal of service to God through martyrdom, in whatever form, had become for Ashkenazic Jewry the only legitimate choice in times of persecution. This is not to say that Ashkenazim did not sympathize with those who could not stand up to the ultimate test. What it does mean is that, under such circumstances, death on behalf of God was the only admissible solution in theory. Consequently, every martyr, willing or unwilling, would attain the rank of the saint, of the one who had willingly, indeed gladly, offered up his life as a sacrifice.

Now the obvious feature of voluntary martyrdom is its stance of profound trust, its unflagging certainty of vindication and ultimate triumph. In Jewish literature, the souls of the righteous were described as stored under the Throne of Glory, accepted into the great light vouchsafed for the world to come, and held in readiness for the resurrection and redemption.[47] Quiescence, passivity, resignation were possible for thousands of Ashkenazic Jews, for to them the age of the Messiah was not a concept, or a vision of bliss, or even primarily an age when the Holy Spirit would be restored to Israel. The day of messianic redemption was the one when "eye to eye they would see the Lord restoring Zion" (Isaiah 52:8), that is, themselves, their loved ones, their people, their Temple, their king, their home. Quiescence and martyrdom sprang from a classical faith untroubled by rationalist doubts or scholastic distinctions between the intentions of the heart and the utterances of the lips.

That this was the case may be seen by a closer examination of the circumstances under which Ashkenazim preferred to undergo martyrdom. At the time of the First Crusade, many of the leadership and learned preferred suicide to death at the hands of their tormentors, despite the formal prohibition in Judaism against suicide; for they construed the Talmudic injunctions against suicide in the context of Talmudic literature as a whole. Now, while rabbinic law formally prohibits suicide, there are a considerable number of cases in the Talmud recording suicide as a religiously praiseworthy act not only to avoid apostasy or forced immorality, but even as a form of voluntary atonement. The penitent, in popular views, could justifiably impose the death penalty on himself as a form of expiation.[48] To many, the willingness of Isaac to be sacrificed by his father Abraham, in proof of which there was an amplitude of rabbinic legend, was construed as a form of voluntary religious martyrdom.[49]

Please do not misunderstand me as arguing the halakhic rectitude of their acts. That is a matter for jurists to decide, though I may add that I have support for my understanding of their behavior in the juridic defenses of these acts by outstanding halakhists of the Middle Ages.[50] What I am trying to do is to understand their religious temper. The Ashkenazim were not at all *emotionally* passive in their martyrdom. To the extent that their religious sentiments would allow the chroniclers and poets to admit, many of the martyrs and their contemporaries expressed great resentment over the fate that God had meted out to them. While some piously rehashed the ancient platitudes of Job's friends and claimed that it was because of their sins that they were suffering, others protested that it was not because of their shortcomings that they were dying but, rather, because of their perfection. As a generation unmatched in piety since the days of Rabbi Akiba and the ten martyrs, they had been elected to serve as the sacrifice of atonement for all others.[51]

It may well be that the Christian environment had stimulated them to think along these particular rabbinic lines rather than along others, which I will suggest influenced many Sephardim. But the crucifixion motif as a vicarious atonement had ample parallels in authentically Jewish sources to allow them to construe their choice as a totally Jewish one.[52] In a word, they treated *aggadah* and *halakhah* as a unit and behaved accordingly.

In the case of the dominant Sephardic responses to persecution through marranism and even unqualified apostasy, the situation is far more complex. Many doubtless elected to live out of sheer instinct. But why assume that Ashkenazic instincts are weaker than Sephardic ones? Obviously other factors came into play, and it is these that interest us in the present context.

In his famed *Treatise on the Sanctification of the Name*, Maimonides informs us that some Jews, although they had the opportunity to escape to safer pastures, elected to remain under Almohade rule as marranos, for they were sure the Messiah would soon be at hand in any case.[53] This is a most revealing statement, for the same messianic faith that prompted Ashkenazim to elect death at their own hands prompted some Sephardim—of whom the North Africans were a part—to try to have their cake and eat it too. What better evidence do we need of the messianic predestinarianism that had circulated in Sephardic circles? Nor can this be dismissed as the quirk of a few Jewish crackpots, for Maimonides regarded the notion as sufficiently serious to treat it as a problem. The fact of the matter is that this point of view became one of the dominant characteristics of marranist thinking in the second great period of persecution confronting Sephardic Jewry, that is, in the persecutions of 1391 and after. What Professor Baer has regarded as evidence of a messianic movement on the part of many marranos shortly before the expulsion from Spain, will, upon more dispassionate examination, be seen to be not so much a movement as expressions of hysterical guilt, of hope, and of reaffirmation of faith in the *inevitability* of the imminent messianic deliverance.[54] In other words, whereas Ashkenazic political quiescence could generate mass emotional religious activism in the form of martyrdom, the open speculation and even occasional active outbursts of the Sephardic milieu would, in times of severe stress, produce extreme religious passivity.

In the case of the marranos of the Almohade period, we are beset by a lack of copious source materials. There are only two circumstances that do appear worthy of mention in the present context. While Maimonides unequivocally recognized the martyrs of the Almohade persecutions as sacrifices in sanctification of the Name, he nevertheless urged Jews to avoid martyrdom if they could. He, of course, justified his directive on strictly halakhic grounds. But I wonder if it is not more than a coincidence that a representative of those circles of Judaism that had reservations, at least with regard to the primacy of the resurrection in the messianic fulfillment, should be more reluctant to put his stamp of approval on wholesale martyrdom? As is widely known, even after all the apparent halakhic differences on martyrdom between Maimonides and the Franco-German codifiers have been leveled and harmonized, there exists a hard core of dispute between them which cannot be resolved and of which many Jewish jurists have taken note. That is the question of the option open to a person to undergo martyrdom in certain situations when the law does not prescribe it. Maimonides in his *Mishneh Torah* absolutely forbade it, while the Franco-Germans proclaimed almost to a man that it is a matter for the individual himself to decide.[55] Although what was formally at issue was the interpretation of classical texts, I cannot help but feel that in borderline cases the spokesman of each branch of Judaism read the texts in accordance with the overall pattern of his thinking. The hesitancy that attended such reservations on the ultimate reward and on the right of a man to decide his own destiny through martyrdom doubtless percolated down to the laity and influenced their behavior. Add to this the widespread skepticism of the extreme type that we discussed earlier and you have the seedbed on which marranism could sprout and ultimately become a phenomenon of major proportions.

If that is a matter of conjecture in the case of the Almohade persecutions, in the case of the riots of 1391, and the environment of the fifteenth century, the pattern is much clearer. Indeed, a whole complex of Jewish factors was available to rationalize sympathy for the "forced converts." Whatever rationalizations were invoked after the fact, Baer has argued convincingly that the deep religious skepticism that had spread in the economically higher classes of Sephardic Jewish society was one of the chief factors in bringing about wholesale Spanish apostasy. Christian polemicists and missionaries made capital of the widespread doubts in the messianic fulfillment that had become part of many a Jewish man's spiritual baggage. Despair of the messianic promise to Israel was doubtless a major factor in swaying many to make the decision they did between 1391 and 1492.[56]

Coupled with skepticism there was yet another product of the Andalusian golden age that colored the Spanish temper. That was the posture of the Arab-type philosopher, whose conclusion was that true salvation was being held in store only for the worthy individual rather than for the group as a whole. Moreover, what counted ultimately was not what one did so much as what one believed. If one's heart remained steadfast, then formal defection was of secondary importance. Add to this the ever-growing conviction in respectable Jewish circles that Christianity was not really an idolatry[57] and you have fertile soil for the rationalization of those marranos who remained secretly loyal, and above all for the indubitable and widespread rabbinic sympathy for them. They knew that the Messiah must come and soon, and they were sure that those who could justify their innermost intentions would also be redeemed. Spanish activism coupled with Spanish sophistication and skepticism helped to produce the characteristic Sephardic response to the Messiah and His challengers.

To sum up, two traditions, two distinct medieval approaches to the Messiah gained strong footholds in medieval society. Although the times and circumstances that generated them have changed radically, the traces of these two approaches, and variations on them, have remained down to modern times.

NOTES

1. Christopher Marlowe, *The Jew of Malta*, Act II, ed. by R. W. Van Fossen (Lincoln, Neb., 1964), pp. 52, 1. 305.

2. These have been collected, edited, and annotated by J. Even-Shmuel in *Midreshay Geulah* (2nd ed., Jerusalem, 1954).

3. Cf. further A. S. Halkin, ed., *Zion in Jewish Literature* (New York, 1961), pp. 38ff., 65ff., 83ff.

4. For a convenient collection of the relevant texts, see A. Z. Aescoly, *Jewish Messianic Movements* [in Hebrew] (Jerusalem, 1956), pp. 117ff. Cf. further, S. W. Baron, *A Social and Religious History of the Jews*, V (2nd ed., Philadelphia, 1952–65), 182, 191ff.

5. For the latest discussions of the stages in the development of Karaism, cf. M. Zucker, *Rav Saadya Gaon's Translation of the Torah* [in Hebrew] (New York, 1959), pp. 145ff.; Baron, *op. cit.*, V, chap. XXVI.

6. M. Zucker, "Tegubot li-Tenu'at Abaylay Zion ha-Qarraiyyim ba-Sifrut ha-Rabbanit," *Sefer ha-Yobel le-R. Hanokh Albeck* (Jerusalem, 1963), pp. 378ff.

7. For surveys of medieval Jewish messianic efforts, see Aescoly, *op. cit.*, chaps. IV–VI; A. H. Silver, *A History of Messianic Speculation in Israel* (Boston, 1959), chaps. III–V.

8. Moses Maimonides, *Epistle to Yemen*, ed. by A. S. Halkin (New York, 1952), pp. 102/103; Eng. trans. *ibid.* (by B. Cohen), p. xx.

9. Abraham ibn Daud, *Sefer ha-Qabbalah*, ed. and trans. by G. D. Cohen (Philadelphia, 1967), Hebrew text, p. 45 1. 148 and variants; Eng. trans., VI. 217; *idem* in *Medieval Jewish Chronicles*, I (ed. by A. Neubauer), 67.

10. On the following incidents see Moses Maimonides, *op. cit.*, pp. 100/101ff.; Eng. trans., pp. xixff.; Aescoly, *op. cit.*, pp. 194ff.; Silver, *op. cit.*, pp. 87ff.

11. Cf. Silver, *op. cit.*, pp. 143ff. For reasons which will be fully spelled out elsewhere, I have not reckoned either reports about Jewish messianic movements that are not attested by Jews or obscure incidents that cannot as yet be dated with certainty.

12. To be sure, a number of Jews of Ashkenazic descent were prominent in the messianic "ferment" in the century and a half following the Spanish expulsion, but the dominant Jewish temper in the Ottoman Empire, where this speculation took place, was clearly Sephardic.

13. Aescoly, *op. cit.*, pp. 154ff., 286ff.

14. J. Prawer, "The Jews in the Latin Kingdom of Jerusalem" [in Hebrew], *Zion*, XI (1945–46), 50ff.; *idem, A History of the Latin Kingdom of Jerusalem*, II [in Hebrew] (2 vols., Jerusalem, 1963), 387ff.; *idem*, "Hobebay Zion bi-May ha-Baynayyim," in *Ma'arabo shel Galil we-Hof ha-Galil* (Jerusalem, 1965), pp. 129ff. Certainly the considerations of piety motivating settlement of the Holy Land were messianically oriented, but they were "pre-millenarist" in character, very similar to those motivating the move of Judah ha-Levi; cf. below. On Ashkenazic realism and coolness to migration to Palestine at that time, cf. E. E. Urbach, *The Tosaphists* [in Hebrew] (Jerusalem, 1955), pp. 108ff., 231.

15. On Maimonides' views, cf. Halkin's introduction to *Epistle to Yemen*, pp. xxviff. On Abulafia's conflict with traditionalists, cf. Aescoly, *op. cit.*, pp. 198ff.; G. Scholem, *Major Trends in Jewish Mysticism* (3rd ed., New York, 1961), pp. 128ff. On the "anti-establishmentarian" character of messianism, cf. *idem, Sabbethai Zevi*, I (2 vols., Tel-Aviv, 1957), 9ff., 74ff.

16. For the text and bibliography, see *Sefer ha-Yishub*, II, ed. by S. Assaf and L. A. Mayer (Jerusalem, 1944), pp. 22 no. 30, 113 no. 20; Aescoly, *op. cit.*, pp. 133ff. Aescoly recounts all the scholarly conjectures on the fragment with the exception of the one which, it seems to me, best explains the motivation of the query, namely that of A. Marx, "Studies in Gaonic History and Literature," *JQS*, NS, I (1910–11), 75ff. Aescoly's efforts to connect the question of the rabbis of the Rhineland with the "mourners of Zion," described in a gloss to Benjamin of Tudela's *Itinerary*, is unconvincing. Whatever the historical value of that gloss, it does not reflect messianic activity or ferment, but only messianic faith, which all Jews shared and which some expressed a bit more conspicuously than others; cf. Aescoly, pp. 152ff.

17. J. Sarachek, *The Doctrine of the Messiah in Medieval Jewish Literature* (New York, 1932), p. 59; Silver, *op. cit.*, p. 66.

18. *Ibid.*, pp. 58ff.; A. M. Habermann, ed., *Sefer Gezerot Ashkenaz we-Sarfat* (Jerusalem, 1945), pp. 24, 83; Tobiah ben Eliezer, *Leqah Tob*, ed. by S. Buber (Vilna, 1880), part 2, p. 20.

19. Rabbi Joseph Bekhor Shor, *Payrush 'al ha-Torah*, III (Jerusalem, 5719), p. 65; Silver, *op. cit.*, pp. 85ff.

20. A. Marx, "Ma'amar 'al Shenat ha-Geulah," *Hazofeh le-Hokmat Israel*, V (1921), 194ff.

21. On the eschatological interests of that circle, cf. Scholem, *Major Trends*, pp. 88ff.

22. Aescoly, *op. cit.*, p. 188; S. Assaf, *Meqorot u-Mehqarim* (Jerusalem, 1946), pp. 146ff.

23. A. J. Heschel, "'Al Ruah ha-Qodesh bi-May ha-Baynayyim," *Alexander Marx Jubilee Volume* (New York, 1950), Hebrew vol., p. 184; and cf. Scholem, *Major Trends*, p. 85.

24. Marx, *op. cit.*, pp. 195ff.; Heschel, *op. cit.*, p. 184; and cf. L. Zunz, *Gesammelte Schriften*, III (3 vols., Berlin, 1875–76), 227. On knowledge acquired in dreams in Ashkenazic rabbinic circles, cf. Heschel, *op. cit.*, pp. 195ff.; R.J.Z. Werblowsky, *Joseph Karo* (Oxford, 1962), pp. 42ff. On an inquiry on the date of the Messiah in a dream, cf. *ibid.*, p. 43, n. 1.

25. Heschel, *op. cit.*, pp. 185ff. Significantly, Sephardim occasionally used the term "prophet" to designate a poet; cf. D. Yellin, *Torat ha-Shirah ha-Sefaradit* (Jerusalem, 1940), p. 3 n. 1.

26. Cf. Abraham b. Hiyya, *Megillat ha-Megalleh*, ed. by A. Poznanski (Berlin, 1924), pp. 36ff.; Maimonides, *Epistle to Yemen*, pp. 82/83; and cf. G. D. Cohen, "The Story of the Four Captives," *Proceedings of the American Academy for Jewish Research*, XXIX (1960–61), 102 n. 146, 104 nn. 148, 150. For an Andalusian view of *gematriaot*, cf. Abraham ibn Ezra to Gen. 14:14. That Ibn Ezra's skepticism was not peculiar to him may be seen from Nahmanides' impassioned defense of *gematriaot* in his treatise on redemption; *Kitbay Ramban*, I, ed. by D. Chavel (2 vols., Jerusalem, 1963), 262. The freest use of *gematria* by a Sephardic Jew known to me is in the third chapter of Abraham b. Hiyya's *op. cit.*; cf. pp. 67, 79ff. However, even he uses *gematriaot* only as supporting evidence and not as the sources of his findings. Moreover, as a Jew of Barcelona, Abraham b. Hiyya may well have been inspired in this regard by northern scholars, who were closer to the Ashkenazic spheres of

influence and to the emphasis on the power of letters propounded in *Sefer Yeṣira*, which strongly influenced Ashkenazic circles.

27. Cf. Silver, *op. cit.*, pp. 59ff., 85ff. On the importance attached to *gematriaot* in Ashkenazic circles, cf. *Encyclopaedia Judaica*, VII, 178; Scholem, *Major Trends*, p. 100.

28. Cf. *ibid.*, pp. 127, 135; Aescoly, *op. cit.*, pp. 196ff. Cf. also n. 26.

29. Marx, *op. cit.*, p. 195.

30. Halkin's introduction to *Epistle to Yemen*, p. xxxii.

31. Judah ben Barzillay, *Commentar zum Sepher Jezira*, ed. by J. Halberstamm (Berlin, 1885), pp. 237ff.

32. Silver, *op. cit.*, pp. 67ff.; Cohen, *op. cit.*, p. 104, n. 150.

33. Y. Baer, "Eine jüdische Messiasprophetie auf das Jahr 1186 und der dritte Kreuzzug," *MGWJ*, LXX (1926), 113ff.; *idem*, *A History of the Jews in Christian Spain* (2 vols., Philadelphia, 1961–66) I, 66.

34. Moses Maimonides, *Epistle to Yemen*, pp. 58ff., 80ff.

35. Cf. the Analysis in my ed. of *Sefer ha-Qabbalah*, chaps. III–V, where this interpretation is documented in detail.

36. Judah ha-Levi's famous suggestion of a date for the fall of the Muslim Empire, which ha-Levi credited to a dream, could easily be dismissed by his contemporaries as poetic fancy; cf. Judah ha-Levi, *Diwan* (ed. Brody), II, 302.

37. In support of his views Maimonides refers to Ibn Bala'am and Ibn Gikatilla approvingly; cf. "Maimonides' Treatise on Resurrection," ed. by J. Finkel, *PAAJR*, IX (1938–39), Hebrew section, p. 21, par. 31.

38. Cf. Maimonides, *Guide of the Perplexed*, II, 29, trans. by S. Pines (Chicago, 1963), 337ff.; *idem*, *Mishneh Torah*, Melakhim, 12.1ff.; cf. also J. Levinger, *Maimonides' Techniques of Codification* [in Hebrew] (Jerusalem, 1965), p. 163. On the curious silence of Joseph ibn Aqnin on messianic dogmas, see A. S. Halkin, "Li-Demuto shel R. Joseph b. Judah ibn Aqnin," *Harry Austryn Wolfson Jubilee Volume* (Jerusalem, 1965), Hebrew vol., p. 111.

39. Cf. "Maimonides' Treatise on Resurrection," pp. 10ff.; Meir ben Todros ha-Levi Abulafia, *Kitab al-Rasail*, ed. by J. Brill (Paris, 1871), p. 1.

40. J. Rosenthal, "From 'Sefer Alfonso'" [in Hebrew], in *Studies and Essays in Honor of Abraham A. Neuman* (Leiden, 1963), pp. 621ff.

41. See the observations of G. Scholem, *Sabbethai Zevi*, I, 1ff.

42. Baer, "Sefer Yosifon ha-'Ibri," *Sefer Dinaburg* (Jerusalem, 1949), pp. 178ff.

43. Samuel ibn Nagrela, *Diwan*, ed. by D. S. Sassoon (Oxford, 1934), p. 41, line 38 (= ed. A. M. Habermann and S. Abramson, I, part 1, p. 37); J. Schirmann, *Ha-Shirah ha-'Ibrit bi-Sefarad u-bi-Provence*, I, 111. For the ascent to the heights of the moon, cf. *ibid.*, p. 83 (ed. Habermann, I, part 3, p. 5).

44. While there were, of course, instances of suicide even in the Chmelnitzki onslaughts, the contrast with the widespread and organized suicides of 1096 is quite evident. For sources on the events of 1648, *see Gezeros Tah* [in Yiddish] (Vilna, 1938); M. Hendel, *Gezerot Taḥ-Tat* (Jerusalem, 1950); S. Bernfeld, *Sefer ha-Dema'ot*, III, 109ff.; H. J. Gurland, *Le-Qorot ha-Gezerot 'al Israel* (Odessa, 1892).

45. See the account of Solomon ben Simeon in Habermann, *Sefer Gezerot Ashkenaz we-Ṣarfat*, pp. 24ff. For the sprinkling of the ark, cf. p. 37.

46. See the classic study of S. Spiegel, "The Legend of Isaac's Slaying and Resurrection" [in Hebrew], *Alexander Marx Jubilee Volume*, Hebrew vol., pp. 471ff. and especially pp. 477ff., 534ff., where the connection of the *aqedah* with sacrifice and resurrection is documented; cf. also *idem*, "Payrur me-Aggadot ha-Aqedah," *The Abraham Weiss Jubilee Volume* (New York, 1964), pp. 553ff.; H. J. Zimmels, *Ashkenazim and Sephardim* (London, 1958), pp. 263ff.

47. On the rewards vouchsafed the martyrs, cf., in addition to the works listed in n. 46, Y. Baer's paper referred to in n. 42; *idem*, "Geserot Tatnaw," *Sefer Assaf* (Jerusalem, 1953), pp. 126ff. For the sources of these expressions cf. V. Aptowitzer, "Bet ha-Miqdash shel ma'alah 'al Pi ha-Aggadah," *Tarbiz*, II (1930–31), 264, n. 8; S. Lieberman, "The Martyrs of Caesarea," *Annuaire de l'Institut de Philologie et d'Histoire Orientales et Slaves*, VII (1939–44), 443ff.

48. On the meritoriousness of martyr-suicide in earlier literature, cf. *Mishnah of*

R. *Eliezer* (ed. Enelow), p. 169; H. Fischel, "Martyr and Prophet," *JQR*, NS, XXVII (1946–47), 275; Cohen, *The Story of the Four Captives*, pp. 59, 74. On meritorious suicides of remorse and repentance, cf. *Bereshit Rabba* 65:22 (ed. Theodor-Albeck), pp. 742ff.; B.A.Z. 18a (the latter is told of a Gentile executioner). I hope to deal with the subject at greater length in another paper. On the sentiment in Ashkenaz, cf. J. Katz, *Exclusiveness and Tolerance* (Oxford, 1961), pp. 90ff.; N. Guedemann, *Geschichte des Erziehungswesens und der Cultur der Juden*, I (Vienna, 1880), 150 n. 5. The sacrificial and expiatory quality of physical suffering, especially of death, although quite evident in rabbinic literature, is given renewed emphasis by the German pietists; cf. Eleazar of Worms, *Rokeah* (Jerusalem, 1960), p. 3.

49. Cf. n. 46.

50. Menahem ben Solomon ha-Meiri, *Magen Abot* (Jerusalem and New York, 1958), p. 89; cf. also Zimmels, *op. cit.*, p. 263 n. 4; cf. also n. 55.

51. Cf. Solomon ben Simeon, *op. cit.* (ed. Habermann), *passim* and especially pp. 25, 27, 46.

52. Cf. G. F. Moore, *Judaism*, I, 546ff.; S. Schechter, *Some Aspects of Rabbinic Theology*, pp. 310ff. On the souls of the righteous—who have already died—as the materials of sacrifice in the heavenly Temple, cf. Aptowitzer, *op. cit.*, pp. 257ff.

53. Moses Maimonides, "Iggeret ha-Shemad," *Hemdah Genuzah*, ed. by Z. H. Edelmann (Königsberg, 1856), p. 12 a-b; = *Rambam La'am* (Mosad ha-Rav Kuk), XX, 66.

54. Y. Baer, "Ha-Tenu'ah ha Meshihit bi Sefarad bi-Tequfat ha-Gerush," *Zion*, V (1932–33), 61ff. Cf. also Aescoly, *op. cit.*, p. 295. Needless to say, inquisitors would inflate such local manifestations into major movements.

55. For a full discussion and references to earlier literature, see M. Krakovsky, *Abodat ha-Melek* (Vilna, 1931), f. 6a and seq. to Maimonides, *Mishneh Torah*, Yesoday ha-Torah, 5. 1,2,4; cf. also Jacob ben Asher, *Tur*, Yoreh Deah, par. 157 and Joseph Caro's notes thereto.

56. Y. Baer, *History of the Jews in Christian Spain*, II, 253ff., 273ff.

57. Katz, *op. cit.*, pp. 115ff.

German Jewry as Mirror of Modernity[*]

I

The culmination of two decades of fruitful activity constitutes an achievement worthy of celebration in the lifetime of any young institution, but also a fitting occasion to appraise the impact of its original goals and purposes. The "Annual Collection of Essays on the History and Activity of Jews in Germany During the Past Century"—the subtitle of the volumes of *The Leo Baeck Institute Year Book* characterizes the series in which the present collection is the twentieth—has provided significant contributions to the history and, above all, the memory of a great segment of the Jewish people which, along with several others, met its end in the catastrophe that overcame the overwhelming portion of European Jewry during the Second World War. To the scholar and the student of history, as to the survivors and descendants of that particular segment of modern Jewry, indeed to anyone concerned with understanding the story of that tragedy and with the preservation of the deposit of the rich and multifaceted experience of that body of Jews, the activities of The Leo Baeck Institute, especially its scientific publications, provide sufficient justification of the enterprise. The *Year Book*, the *Bulletin*, the annual memorial lectures, the many scholarly volumes issued by the institute on a host of subjects provide the most scintillating possible tribute to the vision and determination of the founders of the institute, the planners of its activities, and the persons responsible for the implementation of its programs.

[*]Year Book XX of the Leo Baeck Institute, London, 1975.

To confine ourselves for the moment to the *Year Book*, a mere glance at the table of contents of each volume should dispel the need for any further rationale for such collections or for any hermeneutical statement that will link this already vast collection of researches, documents, photographs, and bibliographies with any wider, more encompassing frame of reference. The time has long passed when historians should feel required to demonstrate the legitimacy of their pursuit by explicating the relevance or utility of their findings and interpretations. But, in reality, for all their scholarly character, the publications generally and the *Year Books* especially are of great moment to a much wider group than the professional or the specialist. To anyone for whom German-Jewish history has any special significance—and the volumes of *The Leo Baeck Institute Year Book* prove beyond need for further argument that German-Jewish history is of significance not only to anyone concerned with any aspect of modern Jewish history but to everyone concerned with German history and with the history of modern Europe generally—the materials of the twenty volumes are a virtually inexhaustible treasure trove of information and interpretation that has earned for the series an everlasting place in the annals of scholarship.

If any evidence is required for the impact of the aims and activities of The Leo Baeck Institute—as described in the *verso* of the title page of the *Year Book*—it may be quickly encountered in the vast bibliographies that have been a regular feature of each of the volumes in this series. But the point is now demonstrated graphically and quite immediately to readers of the present volume in the papers incorporated in it from two sessions in conferences of general historical scholarship held since the nineteenth volume was compiled: one at the *Braunschweig Historikertag* of 1974 and the other at the 1974 annual meeting of the American Historical Association in Chicago, both of which were cosponsored by the institute and both of which testified, through the authorship of the papers as well as their contents, that German-Jewish history was a vital key to major aspects of German history in the last one hundred and seventy-five years. There may be a bitter irony in the fact that it took the tragedy of the Holocaust to gain for German Jewry even *recognition* as not only a legitimate, but indeed as a vital subject for study for anyone who would understand the course of modern German history. Moreover, it may be idle to speculate whether German-Jewish history would have aroused such widespread and diversified study had the institute not existed or gained the record of achievement that it has, but the fact is that German-Jewish history has now become a subject of wider and more intensive study than that of any other European Jewish community. And however this phenomenon is to be explained, the impact of the institute, its library, its conferences, and its publications has quite patently enriched and set the tone for much of the research conducted throughout the world.

The study of history, it is universally acknowledged today, cannot be divorced from its *Sitz im Leben*. The fact that German-Jewish history remains a subject of living interest that is gaining ever wider recognition is testimony to the moral fibre of men and women who, having survived the Nazi horror, in 1955 organized "for the purpose of collecting material and sponsoring research into the history of the Jewish Community in Germany and in other German-speaking countries from the emancipation to its decline and new dispersion." Given the patently delicate and volatile nature of the subject of these volumes, one cannot but take note of the dispassionate tone that pervades them. After all, the fact underlying them all is tragedy, calamity, catastrophe. Such a series would have required no apology had it comprised one extended dirge and indictment of Germany, of Europe, of Christendom, of modern civilisation. To some, indeed, the volumes bespeak an eerie quality of unreality in their depiction of "the past in a detached, impartial spirit, *sine ira et studio*,"[1] for even a twenty-volume jeremiad could hardly have sufficed to give adequate expression to the pain—and, yes, let us confess, to the condemnation of humanity—that anyone even thinking about the subject must of necessity feel. But, on second thought, the atmosphere of elegant decorum and self-restraint that one encounters on every page, the triumph bespoken by this posture over the forces of brilliantly orchestrated hate and brutality, is in itself a deposit of the Jewish experience generally and most notably of the German-Jewish experience. Sheer sentimentality, however genuine and merited, is, in the final analysis, of limited durability and communicability. The bald truth, however difficult to absorb, is, if properly recorded and preserved, ineluctable, even if only a few will agree to confront it. But, in the final analysis, it is on such that the preservation, cultivation, and transmission of civilization depends, and it is they that volumes such as these reflect and address.

The achievement is all the more notable in view of the bad press that German Jewry has had in recent literature. Eastern Europe has had great spokesmen who have taken upon themselves to be affectionate memorialisers: S. J. Agnon, Lucy Davidowicz, Hayyim Grade, Abraham Joshua Heschel, Jacob Shatzky, Mark Zborowski, to mention only a half dozen of the legion who have attempted to preserve the warm flavour of a great Jewish civilisation that was totally wiped off the map of the earth. The memory of Germany, by contrast, has generated no wistful literature of nostalgia. To be sure, certain aspects of German-Jewish life have evoked fond and inspiring memorials. The moving papers on the typology of German Jewry in volume XIX of the *Year Book*, not to mention the tributes and profiles of many charismatic persons and institutions, prove that Germany was not merely the home of a community careening to destruction. However, it remains true that invidious evaluations of the two great segments of European Jewry have been perceived in the terms made renowned by such great scholars as Jacob Katz and Gershom Scholem, to wit, as a society that lived on internal contradictions that could not possibly be resolved. As we shall attempt to emphasise, the record articulated in these volumes can and should generate not only a more complex and balanced perception, but a new respect for German Jewry coupled with sympathy and even empathy.

It is relatively easy to point to the shortcomings and shortsightedness—perhaps even blindness—of much of German Jewry and its leadership to the realities that should have been apparent to them in every quarter of their lives. On the other hand, it was German Jewry that provided Jews everywhere with mature alternative models of Jewish response to modernity, from radical assimilation to militant Zionism and neo-Orthodoxy, as well as a fresh rediscovery of the Jewish past and reinterpretation and reformulation of the foundations of Jewish identity and commitment. It is to the everlasting credit of the Leo Baeck Institute that it has enabled those who would seek to understand this portion of the Jewish past, without prejudgment or the bitterness generated by the hindsight elicited by catastrophe, to do so.

In this connection, a very special salute must be accorded to the original editor of this series, Robert Weltsch, who provided the introductory essays to all of the volumes prior to this one. Dr. Weltsch's essays are a unit unto themselves, which, read consecutively, provide not only a fine entree to each of the volumes but a penetrating commentary on many aspects of modern Jewish history and, above all, of the inner cultural, institutional, and spiritual life of German Jewry. Many of the major spiritual and ideological issues that confronted modern European Jewry—East and West European Jewry, but most of all those Jewish communities living within the orbit of German culture—are raised and analysed in these essays.

However, *au fond,* what stands out most poignantly in Dr. Weltsch's essays and pours into the body of the volumes is what many have come to identify as a classical Weltschian posture of unshakeable pride coupled with unflagging dignity and self-control. Weltsch's essays articulate some of the great expressions of synthesis of Judaism, Jewish nationalism, German culture, and universalism that were bespoken in the lives and works of the aristocrats of the Jewish spirit in German-Jewish life— men such as Franz Rosenzweig, Martin Buber, and Leo Baeck, to mention only a few.

The indomitable Jewish dignity and determination that Dr. Weltsch maintained in the *Judische Rundschau,*[2] over which he presided as editor from 1919 to 1938, and that sustained untold thousands by his controlled but unmistakable defiance of the monster, have never failed him. To him all students of Jewish history will forever be indebted, if only for his unflagging activity during and after the calamity to preserve and to penetrate the legacy of the great German-Jewish community, to which he migrated from Prague, and to the shaping of which he himself contributed so much. His perception of the goals of the Arden House Conference conducted by the Institute in 1973[3] reflect his profound understanding of the enduring challenge embedded in the German-Jewish experience to all Jews even long after the eclipse of any real German-Jewish community or German-Jewish history. He has understood that the calamity that befell German Jewry, and indeed all of European Jewry, has not really terminated the historical chapter and process of which German Jewry was a pivotal part. Robert Weltsch awaits the encompassing—and I am sure he would insist, dispassionate—study of his long and fruitful career which has stimulated so many other persons, movements, and institutions. Anyone even remotely familiar with his activity knows that a study of Dr. Weltsch must inevitably not only examine his own life and work, but also provide a major commentary on Jewish history in the twentieth century. Can any man ask for more?

As Weltsch approaches his eighty-fifth birthday, it is only fitting that world Jewry take note of this pillar of strength, wisdom, and dignity, and say to him, in the words of the poet Bialik to Ahad Ha-am (1903): *Sa' berakhah ha-moreh, sa' berakhah.* "Great and many are your rewards," not the least of which is this monument of continuity—yes, of enduring vitality—to a culture and history of which you were one of the most responsible fashioners and spokesmen. May those who continue your labours be worthy of the standards you have set.

II

The history of German Jewry during the last two centuries provides not only a fascinating story of one segment of modern European Jewry, but a luminous cross-sectional specimen of the Jewish encounter with the forces of modernity generally in modern Europe. Put differently, the history of the Jews of Germany and of German-speaking areas is significant not only for an understanding of the Jews (and, to be sure, of the general population) of those areas, but also because it provides an excellent introduction to, and point of focus on, all modern Jewish history. Virtually every characteristic associated with the Jews of Germany has its analogue and parallel in the history of the Jews of Central and Eastern Europe: enlightenment, assimilation, conversion, religious reform, nationalism, social mobility, rediscovery of the Jewish past, articulation of Jewish culture in modern terms, and so on endlessly.

To be sure, analogue and parallels in no way mitigate the enormous differences that one encounters between different groups of Jews. No aggregate of parallel phenomena can blur the vast differences in lifestyle and in Jewish expression between the Jews of Galicia, for example, and the Jews of Germany, despite the close contacts between many

Jewish intellectuals of those two areas. Markus Jost and Leopold Zunz could have close ties with Nachman Krochmal and Salomon Judah Loeb Rapoport, but the disparities in their concerns and goals, let alone in the external circumstances that governed their lives, were at least as great as those that drew them together. Accordingly, it would be a gross distortion of history to study all of European Jewry together, or even to stress the common elements in their various confrontations with the forces of modernity at the expense of the specific and singular characteristics and events within the Jewish as well as the gentile communities that are strikingly reminiscent of parallel phenomena in the Austro-Hungarian empire and in Polish-Russian domains. The similarities were consequences of the two sets of factors that combine to the making of a genuine Jewish history: The first, gentile policies with respect to, and attitudes towards, the Jews, which for all their variations from one locale to another had common foundations and many common forms; and second, Jewish responses to the fact of their Jewishness, which for all their varieties both within one community and in different areas, drew their energies from common foundations and from sources of inspiration that transcended geographic and linguistic boundaries. Jewish responses must, of course, be subdivided into the category of Jewish flight from active Jewish identification—and beyond a certain point such a response ceases to be the concern of the student of Jewish history as an effective element in collective Jewish behaviour—and responses in Jewish terms, i.e., responses made to assert and assist in the preservation and cultivation of a distinctive Jewish group.

Clearly, then, Jewish history cannot be reduced to any single set of factors, whether it be Jewish faith and the internal Jewish drive for survival, on the one hand, or antisemitism or Jew-hatred, on the other. This is as true for Germany as for Eastern Europe. Indeed, not even the combination of these two sets of factors, I believe, really exhausts the sources of energy that have combined to give the Jews everywhere a sense of corporate destiny and relationship. Now, if there have always been forces sufficiently strong to enable Jews far removed from each other in experience, collective memory, language, area of habitat, economy, and social class to identify, in however attenuated a fashion, with all other Jews as members of one people distinct from all others—in a word, to feel that for all the disparate elements in their regional experiences and responses, they are justified in claiming a Jewish history common to them all—how much more is this true of Jews, even those of different social class and educational attainment, of one political, geographical, and linguistic orbit. In our case there is a discrete unit of study that we must classify as "German-Jewish" history that is important for itself and important for Jewish history generally. Platitudinous this may be, but how often it has been ignored every student of Jewish history knows only too well. In sum, the drives, both external and internal, making for a sense of Jewish destiny—and that, after all, is predicated in large measure on a sense of common history—were largely the same everywhere. Inevitably, the responses by Jews in one area, such as Germany, will often appear to have striking resemblances to the responses of Jews in others, but they can never serve as a surrogate for the intensive study and analysis of Jewish responses to the environment and to internal drives in any other specific, clearly delineated area where Jews constituted a self-conscious group.

History remains the story of change and of specificity. But for a people whose history is fragmented by many factors far beyond the "normal" state of affairs obtaining with other historically related groups, to wit, by diverse geographic, linguistic, social, political, and economic factors, the common assumes a degree of importance even beyond those which are seen by historians of large political-linguistic units, in which the local dialectical, religious, and economic interests are also at least as centrifugal as they are centripetal. It is in this sense that I have stressed that German Jewry provides an illuminating specimen of, and point of perspective on, the general European Jewish confrontation with, and response to, the forces of modernity—to nationalism, industrialisation, urbanization, social stratification and upheaval, secularisation, religious reform, and so on. On the other hand, these remarks are also meant to be a flat repudiation of those who would seek to describe modern Jewish history without analysis in depth of the *two* sides in the life of so crucial a Jewish group as German Jewry. To the Jew of German origin, this may appear all too obvious, but much modern Jewish historiography has not yet, I believe, come to genuine grips with these principles.

Accordingly, whether the reader approaches the vast collection of materials contained in the twenty volumes of the *Year Book* out of an interest in German-Jewish history or in modern Jewish history generally, he must come prepared with a contextual framework in which to absorb the rich materials. The latter may well, indeed hopefully will, compel the student to amplify, modify, or discard much of the intellectual baggage with which he approaches these materials. That indeed is one of the measures of worth of any new publication. But the material is enriching in direct proportion to the propaedeutic bedrock with which the student will have come to the new materials. What will be suggested here is one possible approach to these materials.

III

A coherent frame of reference is clearly provided by the terminal points of modern German-Jewish history—the beginning, expressed in the quest for emancipation, and the end, or final liquidation. However, both beginning and end, as well as the fifteen decades of intervening history, must be seen from two separate aspects, neither of which in and of itself suffices to give a coherent picture of German-Jewish history. Nevertheless, of the two, it is the environmental framework—the political, economic, linguistic, and social—that underlies all further study.

It was in Germany that the vision of total equality and the accordance of full civil rights to the Jews was first articulated some one hundred and ninety-five years ago; and it was in Germany exactly one hundred and sixty years later that the total liquidation of the Jews through physical decimation was openly and unequivocally expressed and adopted as a policy of state. Our terminal points are, accordingly, Christian Wilhelm von Dohm's *Uber Die Burgerliche Verbesserung Der Juden*[4] and the Wannsee Conference of January 1942.[5] Ironically and tragically, both visions, the one of complete freedom and the other of total annihilation, were motivated by one underlying and indeed common goal, and that was the elimination of the Jews as a discernible and effective corporate entity on German soil.

Obviously, there is qualitative difference between Dohm's vision of the ultimate elimination of a significant Jewish presence in Germany through *burgerliche verbesserung* and the Nazi programme of a total and final "solution." However, it is, I believe, possible to understand much of modern German-Jewish activity and of modern German history generally only by keeping in mind the underlying and enduring common purpose and drive both of advocates of Jewish rights and of antisemitic ideologies during the last one hundred and seventy-five years of German-Jewish history. Both groups drew their inspiration from common assumptions, which, when stripped of all circumlocutions and methodological qualifications, proclaimed that residual loyalties to Judaism constituted an insuperable obstacle to the incorporation of the Jews into German society on an equal footing with gentiles. Conceptually, racial antisemitism merely added a demonic dimension by contending that residual loyalties, since they were biologically rooted, were fundamentally ineradicable. But that Jewishness in any form was an insidious element hostile to the modern nation and to the progress of humanity became part of German *volkisch* axiology. Jewishness by definition was sinister, and to many Germans, the more masked and externally attenuated the Jewishness, the more insidious the threat of corruption to Germany and its civilisation.[6]

For a moment, indeed, during the riotous upheavals of 1848, it appeared to many German Jews that the liberal wagon to which they had hitched their cause would steer them into an age of total equality, when the whole ugly record of the past would be relegated to the realm of memory. Indeed, the sporadic attacks against them by reactionary mobsters only fired their faith and determination further. But the political reversal that quickly surfaced the following year can be seen today for what it really was. External progress and legislative concession merely disguised and deluded many about the impassable divide separating German and Jew.

If, accordingly, it is evaluation from a Jewish perspective that the student of history seeks, he is driven, it seems to me, to the conclusion that ultimately the most implacable enemies of a genuine and dignified Jewish presence in Germany were the German "liberals," who no less than conservatives and populists were simply incapable of shedding the widespread German postulate that Jews as Jews were ultimately unassimilable, if not legally, at least socially.[7] Werner Sombart, for example, could shamelessly disavow any fundamental hostility to the Jews; his "findings" and conclusions were, in his view, both objective and diagnostic. In short, modern German-Jewish history, by which I mean Jewish response to social forces, corporately and individually, was largely determined, and accordingly structured, by the need (or desire) to cope with the reality of Jewish alienation.

The Jews never ceased to be a "problem" or a "question" to the Germans, and Jewishness, accordingly, soon became an obsessive problem to the Jews themselves. "Wie es sich Christelt, so Judelt sich es" inevitably became true to some degree for every Jew of German society and drove Jews to a variety of courses that have become the subject of study of scholars of diverse areas—from theology to politics and art. (To annotate these statements would require classification of much of the material comprising the twenty volumes of the *Year Book*, not to mention the countless studies of every aspect of Jewish life in Germany and German-speaking lands in the last one hundred and seventy-five years and more.) It is this underlying motif in modern German history that provides the most significant and most encompassing element for the construction of a frame of reference by which to study German-Jewish history.

Such a perspective, it seems to me, provides a valid and utile taxonomic handle with which to approach and absorb many of the diverse studies incorporated in these volumes. Obviously this perspective cannot overlook the history of political, economic, and social change that determined the life of all Jews in Germany and enabled a not insignificant number of Jews to attain not only general culture but wealth and political influence. But one distorts Jewish history as well as German history if one does not take account of the pervasive atmosphere in explaining the behavior of, and German attitudes towards, the Jews who rose to great public heights, such as the Bleichroders, the Rathenaus, the Cassels, *et al.*

To understand the last mentioned phenomenon one must describe the specific characteristics of the contemporary German environment. But to comprehend the roots of the prevailing German mentality with respect to the Jews in depth, one must go back not only to the Enlightenment, to Romanticism and to Idealism, but to the Middle Ages, for major residual elements of Christian ideology with respect to the Jews survived and exercised influence down to Weimar days and beyond.[8] Thus The Leo Baeck Institute's publications, while focusing on the fate of modern German Jewry, must of necessity allow—indeed, encourage—scholars to probe into layers of history that antecede and transcend the purview of the institute's specific purposes.

There is no end to the uncovering of antecedents. For all the premodern roots of latter-day movements and ideologies that scholarship may quite properly detect, there is no gainsaying the reality of major new developments in the life of the Jews of Germany in the last one hundred and seventy-five years. If one is to begin with a major development in the atmosphere of Europe and in Jewish status and behavior, the most reasonable is, of course, the Enlightenment.

Confining ourselves to its implications for Jewish history, the significance of enlightenment and nineteenth-century German thought about the Jews and Judaism was two-fold. In the first place, it sounded the death knell for the medieval framework of Jewish life, internal as well as external in Germany, and opened the possibilities of a new horizon of freedom and advance for the Jews. It also, of course, surrounded the Jews with an atmosphere with which they never learned to cope. Thus, the Enlightenment provided along with the hope of emancipation a theoretical underpinning for vast anti-Jewish literature and for persistent resistance to total acceptance of the Jews. In this respect, the studies of Reinhard Rurup,[9] two of which are included in the present volume, and the struggle for Jewish emancipation in Baden are particularly illuminating and illustrative, for they demonstrate the moral-political bankruptcy of German liberalism in the face of the dominant prejudices.

Given this frame of reference, one appreciates the significance for German-Jewish history of the vast amount of nineteenth-century gentile scholarship and reflection on Judaism. Much of this expression was part of the renewed interest in the origins of Christianity and of the relatively new quest for the origins of religion and the dynamics of culture generally. Inevitably, the Jew found his tradition being evaluated (under the guise of description) and, more often than not, invidiously compared with other cultures and religions. In this connection as in so many others a key figure was the arch-philosopher Hegel. In view of the authoritative impact that Hegel's reflections on history and theology had on virtually all subsequent German thought in the nineteenth and twentieth centuries, however removed Hegel himself may have been from any direct involvement with the Jewish struggle for acceptance—indeed, however repelled he may have been by German political behavior with respect to the Jews—his thought must be studied as part of modern Jewish history, for it reflected as well as shaped the dominant mood and ultimately pervaded every treatment of the Jews and Judaism.[10] Hegel is particularly significant and characteristic, for his civilised attitude towards Jews and his simultaneous disdain for Judaism were pregnant with significance for German attitudes and for Jewish responses to the prevailing mood. It may be idle and demagogic journalism to implicate Hegel, Mommsen, Burckhardt, and Meinecke with direct responsibility for the catastrophe of modern Jewry, but the historian cannot overlook the role that their ideas played, irrespective of the intentions of their authors. Not all expressions were quite as rancorous as the Von Treitschke-Graetz controversy,[11] but the underlying soil was the same: a stone wall of fundamental disdain and hostility summed up in a phrase that became a catchword epitomizing fundamental alienation and incompatibility— *Judenfrage.*[12]

However, this is only one aspect of the overall frame of reference suggested here. Far more tragic and pathetic is the record of Jewish efforts to respond to this challenge, to overcome what amounted to a demonic miasma that had been cast over them. In retrospect one sees that the despair that engulfed educated Jews who aspired to creative careers turned into an epidemic of obsessiveness. The wave of conversion and intermarriage that began early in the nineteenth century and never came to an effective end until the collapse of the Weimar republic is a story that is too well known to require documentation here. Two particularly pathetic case studies of extreme Jewish response are provided in papers of this series. The one is a study by H. G. Reissner of early Jewish attempts to eradicate the "deep seated malignancy" of Jew-hatred. The terse catalogue of names of the participants in the effort and of their fates is electrifying,[13] for clearly the situation confronting many Jews demanded nothing short of suicide, either physical or symbolic. No less pathetic is the study of Lamar Cecil in this volume[14] on Jewish efforts at the end of the nineteenth century and early parts of the twentieth to gain *de facto* acceptance of what they had achieved *de jure,* only to encounter a loneliness far more frustrating than their pre-emancipated ancestors had ever had to endure.[15]

IV

From the perspective of Jewish history, all that we have established thus far—assuming, of course, that our perception is a valid one—is but the outer framework of German-Jewish history. Under the heading of *outer framework* we include all legislation pertaining to Jews, gentile-German attitudes and activities with respect to Jews, and, finally, the discernible reactions of Jews to these phenomena, whether these reactions were expressed in migration, social mobility, political organisation, polemic and self-defence, or flight from Judaism and Jewish identification.

However, from the perspective of Jewish history itself, there is a second current which, while to some extent a derivative of the outer framework and one that was forever shaped by it, was made up of an entirely different and quite discrete body of data that was generated by purely Jewish considerations. In other words, although this current can neither be critically recounted nor understood without reference to that part of German-Jewish history which we have insisted is really part of German history, it is quite a separate history, even a more genuinely Jewish history, for its bearers and fashioners were conscious of their activity as Jews and motivated by Jewish considerations. Albeit its history is that of a sub-culture in the midst of the general German culture, it had its own wellsprings of energy and was shaped as well as motivated in no small measure by internal and autonomous drives and purposes.

It is especially in this respect that this "inner" German-Jewish activity provides a window onto—as well as a mirror of—the Jewish encounter with modernity. The frame of reference that we are now attempting to identify represented part of the age-old process of Jewish exegesis and internal communal adjustment to new eras and new circumstances. What we have termed "inner" German-Jewish history was but part of the continuing process of midrash and development, and applied to communal institutions no less than to texts and ideas.

In a discussion of this point my colleague Ismar Schorsch has graciously pointed out that for all the changes that the German-Jewish communities sustained in the century and a quarter before their decimation, they remained to the very end and quite formally continuations of the medieval pre-emancipation *Gemeinde*. Thus, since German Jewry never became an amorphous group and continued to retain a hold on its constituency,[16] even, from this aspect, the changes within it are also part of this midrashic development. Clearly, the German environment would constitute a crucial element in the response, but the Jewish heritage was at least an equally important factor.

Obviously, it is quite impossible to determine with any measure of precision exactly how much of any German-Jewish activity was governed by inner Jewish drives and aspirations; the responses of any group, even of any mature individual, are too complex to be totally and neatly unravelled. Nevertheless, we must insist on the reality of a German-Jewish internal life and on the legitimacy of its claim to its own corporate history and to its share as a component in modern Jewish history generally. I belabor the point a bit over-strongly perhaps, for owing to a variety of reasons, it is this part of German-Jewish history that, I believe it is fair to say, has not yet won the place it deserves in contemporary Jewish historiography and has accordingly not yet been absorbed by Jews who are not of German origin or who lack some special interest in German-Jewish history. To put it bluntly, German-Jewish culture and communal life have not yet attained the place in the collective Jewish memory that East European Jewish history has. (To be sure, even that history is still orientated by considerations that validate the neglect of whole areas of Jewish activity, but that is a story unto itself.)

Such neglect is regrettable not only because of the injustice to German-Jewish history, but also because it obscures the enormous impact that German-Jewish cultural activity had not only on Jewish life in America and in Israel, but also on modern thought generally. One need but mention Franz Rosenzweig, Martin Buber, and Gershom Scholem to realise how important German-Jewish history is for an understanding of modern culture generally, let alone Jewish culture. And these men, even to the extent that they were rebellious against established institutions and modes of thought, were part of a long and colorful history. They were, in a profound sense, its products as well as its final architects.

As in the case of the broad historical framework which the studies of the *Year Books* have greatly illuminated, so it is in the case of the inner history of German Jewry. The Leo Baeck Institute's publications must be approached from a new perspective into which to fit the many fragmentary materials of which any view of history is ultimately composed.

Here, again, it seems to me, the logical point of departure is the Enlightenment, but in this instance it should be viewed as an intellectual current that swept through great segments of European Jewry irrespective of what was transpiring in the world at large. In Italy, Galicia, France, and Germany, Jews in the eighteenth and nineteenth centuries were examining their tradition with new critical methods and evaluating it by new criteria. To be sure, many of these new techniques and evaluations had been derived from the outside, but once appropriated they became the vehicles and substance of purely internal Jewish concern. Wherever this new current made inroads into the Jewish community there was a discernible change in the expression of Jewish yearnings, and often also of Jewish behavior. Most palpably there was a restiveness against the restrictions that were imposed on Jews by society at large as well as a desire for a new freedom, which, in the first instance, meant release from the rabbinic form of self-rule that governed Jewish life. The challenge to Jewish tradition and traditional modes was everywhere very much the same. It was the Jewish responses that differed so markedly in the different areas of Jewish concentration.

To elucidate some of the contrasting reactions, perhaps it is best to begin with a general description of the metamorphosis that overcame European Jewry and brought about the dissolution of the medieval framework of Jewish life generally. Then, in order to put our thesis about German-Jewish development into bolder relief, we will describe first the general outlines of the East European Jewish response to the new universe of discourse that was rapidly altering the perspective and life-style of an ever mounting number of Jews.

It was not political emancipaton or the quest for it that set in motion the great wave of Jewish revolt against rabbinism and the religious framework of life within which it determined the life-style of European Jewry. Rather, it was the other way around.[17] It was the mounting renunciation of rabbinic values and authority in the seventeenth and eighteenth centuries that impelled Jews in ever growing numbers to seek some escape from, and alternative to, traditional Judaism as they knew it. Put in a nutshell, secularisation and assimilation preceded emancipation; it was secularisation and antinomianism, at least in rabbinic terms, that first impelled Jews even to seek political emancipation.

One need no greater proof of the disintegration of Jewish life than the manifestation of demoralisation and antinomianism which historical scholarship has established as major waves in Eastern Europe: crypto-Sabbatianism, Frankism, early Ḥasidism, Haskalah. Indeed, Professor Scholem has cogently argued that there was a progressive connection between the first two and the latter two. The denominator common to all of them was a despair with, and renunciation of, the halakhic framework that had previously determined every aspect of Jewish life. Krochmal, Chajes, Erter, and Rapoport were the final products of a process of change, not its heralds or progenitors. Large numbers of Jews, of whom only a tiny fraction were intellectuals in any sense of the word, had decided to seek new avenues of fulfillment and gratification outside the pale of what rabbinic authority had regarded as legitimate.

Very much the same process, to be sure with some local variations in detail, was simultaneously taking place in Western Europe. Here, too, widespread defiance of rabbinic authority and open violation of accepted Jewish norms, including conversion to Christianity, became increasingly noticeable. The quest for general culture and for new social, religious, economic, and political freedom pervaded Jewish communities, and the remonstrations of rabbis and traditionalists against these trends were futile. In a word, Mendelssohn, even under the most extreme evaluation, must be considered a very conservative Jew. He, too, was but a mild symptom of a process, not its architect or advocate.

In short, the forces of modernity—secularisation, spiritual autarchy, the quest for economic advancement along with political equality—had breached the walls of the ghetto and stimulated considerable numbers of Jews to strive to eliminate completely all barriers impeding their advancement. The early German-Jewish religious reformers merely reflected the spiritual metamorphosis that the Enlightenment had wrought in them and an effort to find some Jewish alternative to the vacuum that they encountered in their own lives. In Eastern Europe, too, Jews like Krochmal were seeking Jewish alternatives to paralysis and dissolution. Indeed, the inner history of all European Jewry in the nineteenth and twentieth centuries can be summed up as a series of efforts to find a substitute for the Jewish communal framework which had first dis-integrated in consequence of internal Jewish revolt and which then had to contend with mounting physical attack from the outside and progressive spiritual defection from within.

In the nineteenth century European-Jewish intellectuals who sought some form of Jewish regeneration all advocated modernization of Jewish life. Modernization meant changes in modes of speech and dress, change in economic pursuit, change in orientation to world culture. The quest, then, cut across borders, but the form that the Jewish quest took differed with locale, and in large measure because of the divergent Jewish perception of the gentile world with which the Jews came into direct contact.

In Eastern Europe the Jews were confronted by a new Russian nationalist policy which made any and every effort at modernization of Jewish life politically and culturally irrelevant. Nothing that the Jews would do short of ceasing to exist would ameliorate their collective condition. Moreover, East European Jewry found the world surrounding it not only hopelessly closed to it but fundamentally inferior. There was no Russian middle class to speak of to which the Jew could look as a model and yardstick by which to measure attainment. The Russian aristocracy was beyond contact, the masses (and the clergy) fanatical, repulsive, and ignorant. Russification was not an ideal with which the average Jew could ever really sympathize. (While in Poland, to be sure, the picture was considerably different—and Jewish assimilation in Poland especially between the two wars is a story that remains to be told—the fundamental hatred of the Polish masses and later of the Polish government for the Jews made Poland and its culture objects with which relatively few Jews could identify.) It is, I believe, fair to say that the overwhelming number of Jews perceived the East European environment as one of implacable hostility. In a society where pogrom and wanton oppression had become policies of state, socio-political meliorism was a pipe dream. In Eastern Europe there were but three realistic alternatives open to the Jews: Orthodox intransigence, which for all its fanaticism had a dignity, learning, and faith that, during the First World War and later, shook a few German Jews to the foundations; revolution, in which Jewish identity attained a new messianic, ethical, quasi-prophetic dimension; and emigration. Zionism was basically a secular solution born of despair with Europe that combined some elements of social revolution with emigration. Its special emotional appeal lay in its reappropriation and infusion of renewed dignity into classical elements of Judaism that were now perceived and identified as the hallmarks of a normal nation and that, in consequence, lent the movement a sense of Jewish pride and confidence. To be sure, the possibility of attaining recognition as a Russian or Polish Jew, in which the Jewish component of one's life—as formulated

by the Jews themselves—would serve as a base for ethnic-cultural autonomy, as well as a legitimate anchor for citizenship and civil equality was
advocated by some and, as is well known, was even endorsed by the Mi-
norities Treaty of 1919. The hope went up in smoke not only in Poland,
but in Soviet Russia as well. In any event, to the East European Jew the
only real alternative to the extremes of Orthodoxy or apostasy was some
form of secular messianism or nationalism—socialist, communist, Zionist, or Yiddishist. Religious reform as a response to modernity was irrelevant, for there was no East European Christian parallel to speak of,
certainly none that would really tolerate Judaism in any form. What is
more, religion in all its manifestations had become synonymous with
political stagnation and cultural paralysis.

Paradoxically, it was only in America, where some of the German-
Jewish responses to modernity were striking new roots, that Jews of East
European extraction would find religious ethnicism—largely in the form
of Conservative Judaism—an attractive and viable form of Jewish
identification.

A sufficiently different set of circumstances confronted the German
Jew to generate different types of response to the inroads of secularisation. The forces of internal disintegration and the spirit of hostility to
Jews and Judaism may have been much the same, but there were
countervailing factors that stimulated quite different Jewish forms of expression. In Germany the Jews encountered a gentile group that aspired
to culture and sought to get the Jews to absorb that culture. As the Jew
changed, that is to the degree that he absorbed German culture, so
would doors open to him. At least so Germans professed. *Burgerliche
verbesserung*, it should never be forgotten, was understood by enlightened Christians as well as Jews as a two-way street. German society
would have to change for the better, too. While Jews in Germany were
seeking to restore the vitality of their tradition by reform and reformulation, by the reconquest of a healthy past that would sustain a pride in a
present and future open with potential, at that very time Germans—
Deists, Christians, Romantics, Idealists—were engaged in the very same
quest for Germany. It was not only Judaism that was invited and challenged to improve itself. Germany as a whole was in quest of "regeneration." In hindsight it is easy to detect and to identify insurmountable
blocks that militated against the absorption of Jews on an equal footing
with Germans. Many Jews perhaps intuited this early in the nineteenth
century and took the "logical" course of abandonment of Judaism. But
most German Jews did not despair of social and political progress, by
which they would finally overcome the alienation of centuries, until
much later. Until the days of the Nazi regime most German Jews had reason for hope that liberalism would triumph over bigotry and irration-
alism. What better proof did German Jews need than what they had

achieved within their own community and the palpable change for the better in the physical conditions of life.

All shades of German Jewry, to the extent that they affirmed their Jewishness—not merely refrained from renouncing it or denying it, but affirmed it—insisted on affirming it in terms that articulated Jewish commitments in ways and in terms that did not require abdication of intelligence or radical separation between the Jew and humanity at large. Whatever else German Jews sought to be as Jews, they passionately sought to be urbane Jews and urbane Germans, loyal and dignified *citizens* with a distinct identity as Jews.

This passionate quest frequently rubbed Central and East European Jews the wrong way—and not without cause. *OstJuden* and German Jews irritated each other for reasons that are today quite intelligible. East European Jews often found the inner life of German Jewry impenetrable and irrelevant, although it was from the orbit of German culture that many of their own leaders drew much of their training and inspiration. East European Jews often perceived the acculturation of German Jews as evidence of a progressive program of total assimilation and German-Jewish articulation of their Judaism as governed primarily, if not exclusively, by apologetic considerations.

To be sure, there were real irritants that inhibited many *OstJuden* from trying to penetrate the all too frequently encountered surface of German-Jewish stiffness, downright arrogance, particularly towards East European Jews, and above all, totally different style of life. German Jews, for their part, had their own bill of grievances against East European Jews, whom they often found to be uncouth, uncultured, and offensive. Clearly, these stumbling blocks were not all pure fantasy on either side of the fence. But, in reality, they were but the superficial manifestations of far more profound—and far more meaningful—differences in perception of the gentile milieu and consequently in approach to the task of shaping a politically viable and intellectually acceptable approach to Jewish life in the modern world.

It is noteworthy that of the many responses to modernity expressed by German Jewry, and these were many and quite different in form and content, Orthodox withdrawal to a totally insulated world was not one of them. In this respect Isaac Bernays had set the tone, and Samson Raphael Hirsch was no different from Abraham Geiger. The machinery of state and ideologues of society held out hope for some genuine negotiation and compromise, if not too often for genuine dialogue. The German university may not have provided the most welcoming atmosphere to the Jew, but it did provide him with a *kultur* which he found ennobling, with which he could identify, and which left room—at least in the view of many—for the retention of the Jewish name, identity, and sense of Jewish purpose. What the Jew had to provide was an acceptable form and formulation for his own tradition. This the Jew found necessary for *himself* at least as much as for his gentile neighbors and it is this that the preponderant portion of German-Jewish internal activity in the nineteenth century was about. The cue and guidance were provided by Moses Mendelssohn, or at least it was thus that his strictly Jewish writings—his translation of the Bible, his *Biur,* his *Jerusalem*—were perceived and utilised.

Critical scholarship became the first significant effort at a meaningful Jewish response to a wave of Jewish defection early in the nineteenth century and to the intellectual climate that had made traditional form and theory obsolete. This effort at regeneration and reaffirmation of the Jewish legacy became the outstanding and characteristic feature of German-Jewish leadership of every hue and cast.

The first aspect of German-Jewish scholarship that strikes the observer is the methodological maturity of its practitioners from the very moment of their adoption of the technique. Leopold Zunz became the paradigmatic model of the craft and his technique and posture are evident in the works of such disparate giants as Moritz Steinschneider, Julius Aronius, Moritz Stern, Yitzhak Baer, and Gershom Scholem, to mention but a few. Bibliographical thoroughness, tireless efforts towards the recovery of lost documents, meticulous dating of the materials, publication of carefully edited texts, philological exactitude in interpretation—all these and more became the hallmarks of German-Jewish scholarship.

No area of the Jewish past was immune to fresh examination, interpretation, and reevaluation. But since for all its pretension to objectivity, no great scholarship is really totally free of some *tendenz*—even granting its unconscious role in the mind of the scholar—the real question is what German-Jewish scholarship hoped to achieve by its research and publication. Fortunately, we do not have to speculate too much, for one of the singular features of German-Jewish scholarship was its ingenuousness; if anyone pretended about his real motives, it was not Zunz, Geiger, Frankel, Graetz, or David Hoffman—indeed, to name some of their contemporary heirs, not Albeck, Baer, Scholem, or Salo Baron—but Moritz Steinschneider, the would-be mortician of Jewish learning and literature. If Steinschneider deserves any reproach, I submit, it is for his *dissimulating* contention that his work aimed at giving Judaism a decent burial. But Steinschneider was a maverick in many ways, not the least of which was his compulsive scholarly fecundity. And why should a culture be evaluated by its eccentrics? To cite another example, the pessimism and Jewish ambivalence of such men as Markus Jost are today not intelligible, but have their counterparts in some members of every great scholarly tradition.

The roots of German-Jewish scholarship were, to be sure, not really indigenous. It had great antecedents in sixteenth-century Italy and a more immediate source of direct inspiration in the pioneering scholarship of the Jewish intellectuals of Galicia, but German-Jewish scholarship rapidly outgrew its models and attained a self-sustaining independence and continuity that were unmatched anywhere until the Jewish resettlement of Palestine and the birth of the State of Israel. Moreover, it set the style—even linguistically!—for Jewish scholarship in the Austro-Hungarian empire and became the training ground for many East European *Yeshiva Baḥurim* who sought to substitute critical scholarship for mere learning, even of the secular kind.

In short, if one wishes to understand the history, techniques, and quests of modern Jewish critical scholarship anywhere, including the United States and Israel, one must look to Germany.

While German-Jewish scholarship covered the whole field of Jewish activity and thought, some of its most impressive and enduring contributions were in areas of classical rabbinics and of medieval Jewish literature. All German-Jewish scholars—even those who proclaimed loudest that Judaism was the most authentic representation of the biblical faith and ethic—understood full well that it was not in Scripture itself so much as in its exegesis that the message of the Bible achieved any real impact on society. In the exegetical process, in other words, in rabbinism, they rightly discerned the repository of the dynamics of Jewish religious history. Accordingly, if Judaism was to develop and gain a fresh relevance for contemporary Jewry, it could do so only by developing in the spirit and by the laws of its own inner history. Hence, each school of scholar-theologians—Reform, historical, Orthodox—sought to pinpoint and describe the structure of rabbinic faith and literature, and thereby to gain not only new insight into the sources themselves, but the foundations for legitimatizing their respective religious responses to the contemporary world. No one school attained a monopoly on excellence in this area of research. The study of postbiblical literature and religion was illuminated by brilliant fruits of research from the pens of leaders of all three tendencies in German Jewry. Indeed, even today no student of rabbinic culture can consider himself initiated into the techniques and problems of rabbinic research in all its aspects and ramifications without having studied the works of Frankel, Geiger, Hoffman, N. Brull, Bacher, Isaac Hirsch Weiss, Ludwig Blau, and, of course, the architectonic genius of all areas of Jewish history, Heinrich Graetz. Any rabbinic scholarship of consequence in our own age builds on the foundations of these probers into "The Sea of the Talmud."

From one perspective these men were but continuing and refining the techniques of rabbinic study that had been pursued by scholars from the Middle Ages down to those of their own day, the disciples of Elijah of Vilna and the new critical scholars of Galicia. Hence, the rabbinic scholarship of the nineteenth century was aeons ahead of the pioneering scholarship then being cultivated in Germany into other ancient civilisations. The Jewish scholarship may not have attained some of the polish and refinement of technique that was being applied in the study of Greek and Roman classics, but, on the other hand, it was hardly as immature as students who even today come to the field from the outside seem to think. It had its own tools and techniques that were often inaccessible to the tyros with Ph.Ds. who presumed to pass judgment on the form and substance of Judaism on the basis of the New Testament, church fathers, and the principles of comparative religion. On the other hand, it cannot be denied that even the most penetrating Jewish critical scholarship in this area was in part polemically motivated. It admittedly hoped to provide massive refutations of the Christian versions of the history of Judaism and simultaneously a rationale for the various Jewish versions of rabbinic development. What should never be overlooked is that for all their break with traditional methods and perspectives, each of the great scholars was simultaneously representing his school as the most authentic link in the chain of rabbinic tradition. They are remained to the last proud *rabbis.*

The study of medieval literature and thought had a somewhat different overtone. Doubtless the emphasis here, too, was in no small measure motivated by apologetic and political considerations. After all, it was the medieval experience to which German Romantics turned to discover the authentic expression of the German *volk,* and since Jews were trying to gain recognition and legitimacy for their tradition—as is Zunz's *Etwas Zur Rabbinischen Litteratur*—it was only natural for German-Jewish scholars to seek creativity and cultural variety in the works of their own medieval ancestors—poets, philosophers, mathematicians, and exegetes. However, even had they not been quite openly motivated by ideological stimuli of their cultural *umwelt,* and even without conscious effort at Jewish "me-too-ism," the inspiration and stimulation of the scintillating models of German scholarship into medieval history would inevitably have alerted Jewish scholars to the potential riches hidden in the deposit of medieval Jewish religions and cultural activity.

But, in truth, German-Jewish scholarship was at least as inwardly oriented—indeed, I believe it can be argued, far more so—as outwardly. German-Jewish scholarship sought to provide a new spiritual framework for German Jewry by rediscovering a colorful, variegated, and coherent Jewish past that would also provide the rationale for variety, orderly change, and development within the modern Jewish community. German-Jewish scholarship was a massive effort at reinfusing vitality into what many Jews had understandably come to regard as a fossil that was totally irrelevant to contemporary spiritual life. In the reconquest of the past and in the mastery of the dynamics of history—of law, liturgy, philosophy—the scholars hoped to provide the rationale and motivation for adherence and guidelines for a spiritual rebirth and future creativity. Zunz never pretended otherwise, nor did Geiger or David Hoffman or Martin Buber or Franz Rosenzweig, or Harry Torcxyner. *Literaturgeschichte, Ritusgeschichte, Religionsgeschichte* were all oriented towards parallel goals.

Despite all the ulterior motives of this scholarship, and in the face of all the modern criticism that has been directed at it, one can only stand in awe before the effort at objectivity and critical analysis of areas that were so precious to the scholar. That their objectivity fell short of perfection is well known. That it, nevertheless, succeeded in attaining the levels that it did should never be overlooked, for this too was, in part, a consequence of the German *Sitz im Leben* of their work.

Jewish scholarship in Germany—and one, alas, must add: for all intents and purposes in Germany alone—was intimately connected with theology and philosophy. In this respect, the model of the German university, where the dividing line between scholarship and creative thought was often a very thin one—and this was true not only of theological faculties but of law, history, art, sociology, and political theory—dovetailed remarkably with the history of Jewish tradition. The great Jewish spokesmen of the Middle Ages—Saadia, Rashi, Abraham ibn Ezra, Maimonides, Don Isaac Abravanel—often functioned simultaneously as communal leaders, scholars, philosophers, and creative liturgical authors. German-Jewish religious spokesmen now sought to provide the new synthesis that would make Judaism a legitimate component of the contemporary Germany as well as the historic Jewish tradition.

Much has been said in derision of the efforts of some German-Jewish theologians to mute and even eliminate the national elements in Jewish liturgy and ritual and to substitute, especially for traditional Jewish messianism, an abstract concept of Jewish mission and a universalist prophetic ethic. This ideology is widely pilloried for having sapped Jewish community life of its vital marrow and of an underlying commitment to the unity and continuity of the Jewish people. However, it is too often overlooked that this was but one of several ideologies of Jewish life in modern Germany; and that the fundamental weakness, even sterility, of this posture not only became evident to many German Jews by the beginning of the twentieth century, but was actually repudiated from the outset by those scholars who formed the first rabbinical seminary in Breslau under the leadership of Zacharias Frankel. As a case in point, Von Treitschke may have been a Jew-hater, but he knew how to read a history book; he understood very well what Graetz's gut conception of Jewish history and the Jewish people was. Graetz could not sunder Judaism from the Jewish people, and his monumental *Geschichte* will forever remain not only one of the classic expositions of Jewish history, but one of the great nineteenth-century affirmations of the national and religious integrity of world Jewry. However alone he had to stand in a public po- lemic that all German Jews, Graetz included, would have preferred to avoid, he had the courage to stand up to his opponent without flinching or cringing. When the chips were down, the enduring reality and legiti- macy of the Jewish people would be affirmed by many German-Jewish spokesmen long before the birth of political Zionism.

On the other hand, if the goal of the study of history is to understand as well as to know, the time has come for us—who live in an age when classical reform theology has become a historic memory—to attempt to appreciate the role it sought to play in all sincerity in the context of German-Jewish life in the nineteenth century (and in the context of its American offshoots as well).

It is, I submit, a partisan and myopic perception of classical reform theology and eschatology that evaluates it as basically and essentially apologetic and gentile-oriented. Certainly such considerations were in the minds of reform spokesmen, for they passionately sought to put an end to their alienation from society at large. On the other hand, it was not this motivation alone that impelled them to call Berlin or New York their new Jerusalem. The fact is that they and their constituencies had despaired of, and ceased to believe in, the possibility of a physical ingathering of the Jewish exiles with a return to an earthly Jerusalem. Given this new vacuum in belief, some other rationale had to be found for Jewish steadfastness and separation from the majority. Mendelssohn himself had had to face up to the issue: Given the "universal" acceptance of biblical monotheism and its prophetic ethic, why preserve cleavages that were not only divisive but invidious? Once Christianity had been shorn of its medieval Christology and magical sacramentalism, and per- ceived afresh as the supreme expression of *humanitas* or total submis- siveness to a transcendent master, what need was there to keep mankind divided? How cogent and effective the argument was should be evident to any dispassionate observer of Jewish mass behavior in the last two cen- turies. Classical Reform sought an answer, one that would provide not only a Jewish *raison d'être*, but a sense of proud service to mankind at large. In one form or another it was this that all German-Jewish theology sought to do. Neither Abraham Geiger nor Samson Raphael Hirsch would flee from the challenge. They sought to speak to Jewry in contem- porary form and with cogent arguments that could simultaneously be proclaimed to the world at large.

German Jewry at its best was not apologetic Jewry. Leo Baeck took on Adolf von Harnack in a public forum with vigour and dignity that gained him eternal renown, without the remotest hope of convincing a single Christian. But he did assume the obligations of *philanthropia* by provid- ing *consolatio* (in the classical philosophical sense of these terms) to his own community. This is the import of the history of more recent German-Jewish theology, from Hermann Cohen to Martin Buber and then later Leo Baeck himself. Ultimately, the only tenable posture for a minority people such as the Jews—even of the state of Israel—to adopt in a world that sees no room for them (and often convinces Jews to that effect) is to try afresh in every age to formulate in transcendent terms the reason for its continuity.

Nor can the efforts, however unacceptable they may seem to us, in any way be dismissed as futile. Whatever actually triggered Rosenzweig's own affirmation of Judaism, he, too, had to take a stand on the place of the Jews and Judaism in the context of a world with an enduring Christian majority. The German Jew could not ignore the world, and he would, accordingly, not pretend to his fellow Jews that they could afford to ignore it. The ethics and theology of each age may soon become part of the soil of the past, but, like the Torah itself, the teachers of every age must speak in terms apposite to their present, or, as the medieval philosophers interpreted a classical rabbinic phrase, in the language of men.

In this context, the great rabbinical schools of Germany, of Breslau, the *Hochschule*, and the Hildensheimer Seminary of Berlin, were not only or even primarily professional schools. They were the seedbeds of scholarship and of learning, which in Germany achieved a harmony that is so often missed in contemporary universities. These seminaries were classical Jewish universities, for they bridged between the Torah of Shem and the Wisdom of Japheth. Moreover, they provided the link between critical scholarship and faith. Ultimately, even they became too stolid and remote to satisfy the needs of thinkers such as Rosenzweig and Buber. Hence, the latter and others devised new educational modes and institutions that produced many a creative disciple. To them even philological criticism had arrived at a dead end. What emerges in sum is a pulsating quest for new forms to conquer of the essence and the essential of the old. It may have been but a handful who were directly involved in these enterprises, but their impact was enormous.

There is an irony in the later phases of this Jewish activity, for ultimately German-Jewish intellectuals who had staked so much in rationalism and liberalism were progressively impelled to affirm a Jewish romantic approach in which the authentic spirit of the Jewish people (read: *volk*) would be upheld against the nomian disciplines of rational philosophy, orderly Halakhah, and critical exegesis. Germany became the breeding ground for sympathetic reevaluation of all that Graetz had condemned—mysticism, Ḥasidism, messianism, the Jewish "free spirit." In consequence, a new sympathy for the native genius of the Jewish people as an enduring force was proclaimed to Jews who had long sought to sweep these populist "aberrations" under the rug. While loudly protesting a greater objectivity in the study of the Jewish past than displayed by classical *Judische Wissenschaft,* even these later scholars could hardly conceal their goal of providing educated Jews with a new source of hope for totally new dimensions of creativity. For those who cared to read the record of Jewish religious expression afresh the continuity of Jewish history became not an accident or the tool of a dominant rabbinic class but a repository of vast resources of energy and imaginative powers that belied everything that Hegel and his disciples had said in their characterizations of Judaism.

V

The threads of German-Jewish history are by no means exhausted by the external and internal frameworks, the outlines of which we have sought to sketch. There was a second Jewish community that may have no real place in Jewish history except as a vital statistic. That group was made up of the *religionslos* and *konfessionslos,* the Jew whom everyone knew was Jewish but who, for his part, refrained from identifying himself as a Jew but simultaneously scorned the invitation to join the camp of Christendom. It was a group of Jewish universalists—neither Jewish nor Christian, but a modern *ethnos triton* that was a people unto itself. Often, but by no means always, politically radical, this group has become renowned as having contributed so much to art, even more to art history and to criticism, literature, journalism, science, jurisprudence, sociology, and philosophy. So neutral was this group ethnically and religiously that its origins were of consequence only to antisemites and psychoanalysts. These men, it may properly be said, found in the Weimar Republic the soil and climate most conducive to their burgeoning. Thus, it came about that Peter Gay could write an engaging work entitled *Weimar Culture*[18] without mentioning Jews, although it is "Jews" who make up much of the fabric of his story and analysis.

The story of Weimar, I suppose, can be read in a number of ways. It can be evaluated as the story of what, from a classical Zionist perspective, or from a socio-economic perspective articulated by Hannah Arendt, or from an Orthodox Jewish theological perspective, can properly be called a Jewish *danse macabre.* It can also be read simply as the tragedy, or indictment, of Western secularism. Clearly, even this series of alternatives does not begin to exhaust the list. Whatever the vantage point from which the record is read—and who can possibly read it without confronting the challenge of its failures?—ultimately the story must be classified as one of the tributaries of that endless river called Jewish history. Accordingly, however removed its Jewish expatriates were from the mainstream of Jewish history, until Nazism forced many of them back, their story is really very much part of Jewish history—of the Jewish effort to break what many regarded as a demonic fate that could be overcome, and to fashion a world where the exalted visions of Isaiah 2:4,

11:1–9 and Micah 4:3–5 (in a secularised form, of course) could be turned into realities.

For some for a while, they indeed were realities or at least the heralds of them. And now that Freud has made us aware of the driving power of people's origins, even when the participants themselves are unaware of them, who can today sunder these free-floating artists, intellectuals, businessmen, and politicians from the intricate web of Jewish history? They are part of the story, and they are, accordingly, also within the legitimate purview of the studies of The Leo Baeck Institute.

These are some of the reactions that a renewed encounter with two decades of research and expression in the *Year Book* and other publications of The Leo Baeck Institute have evoked in one reader. The renewed encounter and fresh reflection have compelled him—and will, perhaps, stimulate others—to try to identify the threads connecting the hundreds of disconnected studies in the *Year Books* to each other, to German-Jewish history, to Jewish history as a whole, more especially. If these reflections are valid, I hope they will provide a point of departure for fresh reexamination of Jewish history in other areas and other periods.

History does not repeat itself, nor does it provide any sure guide to the present or the future, but the history of a people is forever operating within and upon the group. The raising of that history to a conscious collective memory is in itself a reflection of the vitality of the people and of its collective will and dream. If The Leo Baeck Institute has in any way contributed to making German-Jewish history part of the kinetic collective memory of the Jewish people, and of others interested in its history—and I am one of the many for whom it has clearly done so—it has done supreme honour not only to the man for whom the institute is named, but to all those who conceived it and made its work possible. May we hope that the twentieth year is but the end of the introduction and the transition to a new chapter of study, memory, and vitality.

NOTES

1. The quotation is taken from the opening passage in the first essay of these volumes: Selmar Speir, "Jewish History As We See It," in *LBI Year Book* 1 (1956), p. 3.

2. See *Encyclopedia of Zionism and Israel*, ed. Raphael Patai, 2 vols. (New York, 1971), s.v. *Judische Rundschau*, and Weltsch, Robert. Cf. also the passing reference in Lucy Davidowicz, op. cit., *infra*, n. 5, pp. 176f. How vital and illuminating a thorough study of Dr. Weltsch's life and work would be, may be gleaned from the brief references and remarks by Walter Laqueur, *A History of Zionism* (New York, 1974), cf. Index, s.v.

3. See Fritz Bamberger, "The Arden House Conference: Exploring a Typology of German Jewry," in *LBI Year Book* 19 (1974), pp. 9f.

4. Two vols. (Berlin, 1781–1783). For the latest discussions of Dohm, see A. Altmann, *Moses Mendelssohn: A Biographic Study* (Philadelphia, 1973), pp. 449f.; Jacob Katz, *Out of*

The Ghetto: The Social Background of Jewish Emancipation, 1770–1879 (Cambridge, Mass., 1973), ch. 5; idem, *Emancipation and Assimilation: Studies in Modern Jewish History* (Gregg International Publishers, 1972), pp. 21ff.

5. For the latest treatment, superseding all others, see Lucy Davidowicz, *The War Against the Jews 1933–1945* (New York, 1975), ch. 7. Clearly, even these are but approximate terminal points. Mendelssohn's vision of, and plea for, civil equality antedated the work by Dohm, but with the latter's work the drive enters the arena of general history. As for the end, Mrs. Davidowicz makes it clear that the final solution had been put into action before January 1942. *Wannsee* is now merely a symbolic catchword.

6. For a brief but lucid treatment, see George L. Mosse, *Germans and Jews. The Right and the Left, and the Search for a "Third Force" in Pre-Nazi Germany* (New York, 1970), esp. chs. 2, 3, and 4. Cf. also idem, *The Crisis of German Ideology. Intellectual Origins of the Third Reich* (New York, 1964).

7. On the whole question, see the penetrating study by Uriel Tal, *Christians and Jews in Germany. Religion, Politics, and Ideology in the Second Reich 1870–1914*, trans. Noah Jonathan Jacobs (Ithaca, London, 1975).

8. Cf. Hans Liebeschutz, "The Relevance of the Middle Ages for the Understanding of Contemporary Jewish History," in *LBI Year Book* 18 (1973), pp. 3ff.

9. Cf. also Reinhold Rurup, "Die Judenemanzipation in Baden," *Zeitschrift fur Die Geschichte des Oberrheins* 114 (1966): 241f.

10. Nathan Rotenstreich, "Hegel's Image of Judaism," *Jewish Social Studies* 15 (1953): 33f.; Shlomo Avineri, *Hegel's Theory of the Modern State* (Cambridge University Press, 1972), ch. 2. On Hegel's own posture toward Jews see ibid., p. 120 n. 12 and esp. p. 170; Hans Liebeschutz, *Das Judentum im Deutschen Geschichtsbild Von Hegel Bis Max Weber* (Tubingen, 1967) (Schriftenreihe Wissenschaftlicher Abhandlungen Des Leo Baeck Instituts 17).

11. Cf. Michael A. Meyer, "The Great Debate on Antisemitism," *LBI Year Book* 11 (1966), pp. 143f.

12. See Jacob Toury, "The Jewish Question"—A Semantic Approach," *LBI Year Book* 11 (1966), pp. 85f. and esp. 95f.

13. H. G. Reissner, "Rebellious Dilemma: The Case Histories of Edward Gans and Some of His Partisans," in *LBI Year Book* 2 (1957), pp. 170–193.

14. "Jew and Junker in Imperial Berlin," pp. 47–58.

15. For a fine study of the Jewish attempts to cope with this framework, see Ismar Schorsch, *Jewish Reactions to German Anti-Semitism, 1870–1914* (New York–Philadelphia, 1972).

16. Cf. Kurt Wilhelm, "The Jewish Community in the Post-Emancipation Period," *LBI Year Book* 2 (1957), pp. 47f.

17. Students of Jewish history will easily detect the deep indebtedness of these observations to Yehezkel Kaufmann, *Golah ve-Nekhar*, 2 vols. (Tel Aviv, 1929–1932), 2, chs. 1–2; Azriel Shohet, *Beginnings of the Haskalah Among German Jewry* (in Hebrew) (Jerusalem, 1960); Gershom Scholem, *Major Trends in Jewish Mysticism*, 3rd ed. (New York, 1961), pp. 299f.; idem, *The Messianic Ideal in Judaism* (New York, 1971), pp. 78f.; idem, *Kabbalah* (New York, 1974), pp. 287f.

18. *Weimar Culture. The Outsider as Insider* (New York, London, 1968).

Afterword

Professor Gerson D. Cohen is obviously one of the foremost Jewish scholars in our time. His writings reflect the class of three strong passions—his love for the Jewish people, his love for the land of Israel, and his love for historical research. Out of these classes emerges the remarkable book you have just read. It brings to the reader a deep insight into the facts of Jewish history. He understands very clearly why the *Song of Solomon* could not be regarded by rabbinic readers as a secular song. It had to be interpreted as a dialogue portraying the love of the Deity for Israel and Israel's turning away from Him as disloyalty by the wife for a husband. The outraged Husband thunders:

> They incensed Me with no-gods,
> Vexed me with their futilities;
> I'll incense them with a no-folk,
> Vex them with a nation of fools.

Professor Cohen shows that this interpretation of the *Song of Solomon* is a natural one. He deals with equal clarity and insight with all his subjects and thus enriches our understanding of Jewish history and Jewish literature. He has placed us all in his debt.

Louis Finkelstein
September 1990

Index